EMU
and the
International Monetary System

EMU
and the
International Monetary System

Proceedings of a conference held in Washington DC on March 17–18, 1997, cosponsored by the Fondation Camille Gutt and the IMF

Editors
Paul R. Masson
Thomas H. Krueger
and Bart G. Turtelboom

International Monetary Fund

Cover and Design by IMF Graphics Section

Library of Congress Cataloging-in-Publication Data

EMU and the international monetary system : proceedings of a conference held in Washington DC on March 17–18, 1997, cosponsored by the Fondation Camille Gutt and the IMF / Editors, Paul R. Masson, Thomas H. Krueger, and Bart G. Turtelboom.

p. cm.
Includes bibliographical references.
ISBN 1-55775-664-3
1. Monetary unions—European Union countries—Congresses. 2. Foreign exchange—Congresses. 3. Foreign exchange—European Union countries—Congresses. 4. European currency unit—Congresses. 5. International finance—Congresses. I. Masson, Paul R. II. Krueger, Thomas H., 1956– III. Turtelboom, Bart G. IV. Fondation Camille Gutt. V. International Monetary Fund.
HG3942.8.E64 1997
332.4959096—DC21 97-25671
CIP

Price: US$35.00

Please send orders to:
International Monetary Fund, Publication Services
700 19th Street, N.W., Washington D.C. 20431, U.S.A
Telephone: (202) 623-7430 Telefax: (202) 623-7201
E-mail: publications@imf.org
Internet: http://www.imf.org

Preface

This volume is the record of a conference on EMU and the International Monetary System that was held at the International Monetary Fund in Washington, D.C., on March 17–18, 1997, cosponsored by the Fondation Camille Gutt and the IMF. The papers included in the volume were the basis for the presentations by the authors at the conference, though they include some subsequent revisions. Comments of discussants and, in some cases, of the general discussion accompany the papers. Speeches by the IMF's Managing Director Michel Camdessus, Minister Philippe Maystadt, and Banker's Trust Director Paul Volcker, as well as contributions by the participants of two roundtable discussions have also been included. The book's introductory chapter by the editors presents an overview and summary of the main themes that emerged at the conference.

We were particularly honored that the Fondation Camille Gutt agreed to be a cosponsor for this conference. The Fondation Camille Gutt, a nonprofit organization located in Brussels, is devoted to the encouragement of teaching and research in economics, in particular in the areas of public and private finance. The Fondation is named after the first Managing Director of the International Monetary Fund in recognition of his many contributions during a multifaceted career as a journalist, cabinet member in Belgium, and international civil servant.

The views expressed in this volume are those of the individual authors and participants—subject to any misinterpretation that might have crept in through the editorial process, for which we alone are responsible—and should not be attributed to the International Monetary Fund or any institution with which an individual author is affiliated.

We are grateful to a number of people for helping us with the organization of the conference and the editing of this volume, and we appreciate that the contributors kept to tight deadlines to ensure a speedy publication of the volume. Many colleagues helped us in formulating themes and in attracting participants, especially Michel Camdessus, Michael Mussa, and Massimo Russo. We are grateful to Carol Ball and Pat Davies for their expert and tireless help with the organizational details, to Marina Primorac for the long hours she spent editing the text and overseeing the production of the book, and to Jeffery Gable, Kellett Hannah, and Pamela Sak for help during the editorial process.

Many assistants spent countless hours helping with various phases of the conference and the preparation of the book; we would like to thank Katia Berruetta, Celia Burns, Maria Orihuela, Julie Reiter, and, most important, Norma Alvarado and Rosalind Oliver. We would also like to express our appreciation to Baron Godeaux and Michel Vanden Abeele of the Fondation Camille Gutt.

Paul R. Masson
Thomas H. Krueger
Bart G. Turtelboom

Contents

Session IV
Euro Financial Markets and the International Financial System
Chair: Daniel Kaeser

Session V
The External Dimension of the European Policy Mix
Chair: Michael Mussa

SESSION VI
RELATIONS AMONG THE IMF, THE ECB, AND FUND/EMU MEMBERS
Chair: Jean-Jacques Rey

The following symbols have been used throughout this volume:

. . . to indicate that data are not available;

0.0 to indicate that the figure is zero or less than half the final digit shown;

n.a. to indicate that the item does not exist;

– between years or months (e.g., 1994–1995 or January–June) to indicate the years or months covered, including the beginning and ending years or months;

/ between years (e.g., 1994/95) to indicate a crop or fiscal (financial) year.

"Billion" means a thousand million.

Minor discrepancies between constituent figures and totals are due to rounding.

The term "country," as used in this volume, does not in all cases refer to a territorial entity that is a state as understood by international law and practice; the term also covers some territorial entities that are not states, but for which statistical data are maintained and provided internationally on a separate and independent basis.

List of Abbreviations

APEC	Asia-Pacific Economic Cooperation Council
BCEAO	Banque Centrale des États de l'Afrique de l'Ouest
BEAC	Banque des États de l'Afrique Centrale
BIS	Bank for International Settlements
BONY	Bank of New York
CEMAC	Central African Economic and Monetary Community
CSD	central securities depository
DTB	Deutsche Terminbörse
EBRD	European Bank for Reconstruction and Development
EC	European Community
ECB	European Central Bank
ECOFIN	Council of European Union Economies and Finance Ministers
ECU	European currency unit
EFC	Economic and Financial Committee
EMF	European Monetary Fund
EMI	European Monetary Institute
EMS	European Monetary System
EMU	Economic and Monetary Union
ERM	exchange rate mechanism
ESCB	European System of Central Banks
EU	European Union
FEER	fundamental equilibrium exchange rates
FRA	forward rate agreements
FTAA	Free Trade Area of the Americas
IMF	International Monetary Fund
ISD	Investment Services Directive
LIFFE	London International Financial Futures Exchange
LOLR	lender of last resort
MATIF	Marché à Terme International de France
NCB	national central banks
OCA	optimum currency area
REER	real effective exchange rate
ROW	rest of the world
RTGS	real-time gross settlement

SDR	special drawing right
TARGET	Trans-European Automated Real-Time Gross Settlement Express Transfer
UDEAC	Union Douanière des États d'Afrique Centrale
UMOA	Union Monétaire Ouest Africaine

1

Introduction

Paul R. Masson, Thomas H. Krueger, and Bart G. Turtelboom

Economic and monetary union in Europe (EMU) will produce profound changes in exchange and financial markets, and these are likely to affect in a fundamental way the activities of a broad range of market participants and private and official institutions. As part of an ongoing effort at the International Monetary Fund to understand the broader, systemic implications of EMU, a conference was held in Washington, D.C., on March 17–18, 1997, which brought together a distinguished group of several hundred academics, officials, and policymakers. The conference, cosponsored by the Fondation Camille Gutt and the International Monetary Fund, was on the subject of EMU and the international monetary system, and it generated many insights into the effects of the introduction of the euro.

Given the widespread interest in this topic, it was felt useful to disseminate this work to a wider audience, and the present book, reporting on the papers and proceedings of the conference, is the result. This introduction gives a short summary of the papers, three speeches, and two roundtable discussions, organized along five main themes: the characteristics of the euro and its potential role as an international currency; EMU and international policy coordination; EMU and the relationship between the Fund and its EMU members; lessons of European monetary integration for the international monetary system; and the transition to EMU. The papers, which appear in the chapters that follow in the order in which they were presented at the conference, are accompanied by discussants' comments, and in some cases by a summary of the general discussion. Written versions of the presentations at the roundtables and of the speeches are also included in the book.

Characteristics of the Euro and Its Potential Role as an International Currency

The attractiveness of the euro is likely to be determined mainly by the macroeconomic policy stance in Europe, and, in particular, by the success of the European Central Bank (ECB) in achieving low inflation. On the latter issue, there was general agreement that the ECB would follow in the steps of the Bundesbank in its dedication to price stability, and be independent of political interference as provided in its statutes. Other factors are also likely to be important in affecting the international use of the euro, including the development of integrated, liquid, and efficient European financial markets. Reserve currency use is likely to evolve slowly, but the euro would start as the second most important reserve currency and could, over time, rival the dollar.

Will the Euro Be a Strong Currency?

Several chapters in this book deal with the potential strength of the euro, focusing in some cases on portfolio diversification as the primary factor influencing the initial strength or weakness of the euro.

Fred Bergsten, in Chapter 2, addresses the issue of the potential strength of the euro by first reviewing the criteria determining the global role of a currency. The euro zone will be bigger than the United States, both in terms of the size of the underlying economy and the extent of its external trade. In the absence of exchange controls, European capital markets, presently small by U.S. standards, should expand strongly in the medium term. Given the strong anti-inflationary mandate of the ECB, the European economy should be stable and perform well, though Bergsten acknowledges the resistance in Europe to much-needed structural reforms. Taken together, he posits, the euro has all characteristics to become a strong currency in the international monetary system. He takes a more nuanced view of the prospects for an immediate appreciation of the euro, though in his view European currencies are now overdepreciated (perhaps deliberately) against the dollar, making an appreciation appropriate. Bergsten also stresses that despite his general preference for target zones for the major currencies to facilitate policy coordination, uncertainty surrounding the implementation of EMU would make target zones undesirable initially.

Chapter 3, by *George Alogoskoufis and Richard Portes*, analyzes the impact of EMU on the euro-dollar exchange rate and the external position of the European Union (EU). They argue that there will be excess demand for the euro, which will lead it to appreciate. Their argument for the enhanced international prominence of the euro compared with the deutsche mark is based on the existence of network externalities for a currency: when more people use a particular currency as a means of payment, transaction costs decrease, which induces even more people to use that currency. The need to use the U.S. dollar for intervention purposes within the euro region will disappear with the arrival of the euro, and in foreign exchange markets the position of the euro will be enhanced and the currency will be cheaper to use. Many foreign exchange transactions are now intermediated through the dollar because a "dollar round-trip" is often cheaper than directly trading two other currencies, but this will tend to change with the introduction of the euro.

With regard to the unit of account function, the euro is also likely to hasten the decline of the dollar as the denomination of international trade. All intra-European trade will be invoiced in euros and those countries pegging their currency to the euro are likely to see a growing fraction of their trade invoiced in euros rather than dollars. Finally, the euro will reinforce the declining trend of the dollar for the denomination of financial assets.

Paul De Grauwe, in Chapter 4, is more agnostic about the potential strength of the euro. His analysis of the "ins" and "outs" of EMU underscores that the early behavior of the euro could be affected by the specific countries participating in EMU. Notably, some of the candidates like Italy and Spain have currencies that, he argues, are presently undervalued; should these countries not participate in EMU from the outset, the euro might initially depreciate.

Robert McCauley and William White, in Chapter 12, point to the possibility that the supply of assets in euros might eventually increase more than the demand for those assets, leading to depreciation, not appreciation, of the euro. This view contrasts with both the analysis in Alogoskoufis and Portes, and Bergsten's expectation. Indeed, because of relatively underdeveloped European financial markets, the share of the world supply of assets in EU currencies falls at present well short of Europe's economic importance. This might well change with EMU, when in addition to the redenomination of existing liabilities in EU currencies into euros, foreign issuers might want to do a larger share of their borrowing in euros than in existing EU currencies, provided integrated European financial markets meant efficiency gains and hence lower borrowing costs.

Volatility

Even a strong euro might be subject to considerable volatility—a subject discussed in several chapters.

Chapter 7, by *Agnès Bénassy-Quéré, Benoît Mojon, and Jean Pisani-Ferry*, sets out to address the question of how economic and monetary union will affect exchange rate volatility between the euro and the dollar. In answering this question, the paper focuses on the preferences of the ECB in the steady state and does not address credibility issues during the transition.

To study the volatility issue, these authors develop a small three-country model with short-run nominal rigidity but long-run flexibility. Their results suggest that monetary union of two countries ("EMU") increases the volatility of the real effective exchange rate of the currency of the third country ("United States") to U.S. shocks or symmetric European shocks. This is so because the ECB can internalize the externality coming from macroeconomic interdependence; the ECB would adjust interest rates more than individual European countries and the dollar exchange rate would move more. Asymmetric shocks in Europe do not affect the dollar exchange rate since they are automatically offset in Europe. The authors use this model to present quantitative evidence on the question of euro-dollar rate volatility and conclude that EMU is likely to lead to moderately higher volatility of the real effective exchange rate if the central bank targets the exchange rate in addition to inflation.

Daniel Cohen shares the conclusion that exchange rate volatility is likely to increase. Indeed, he presents a numerical example in Chapter 13 that suggests that the increase in volatility could be substantial relative to the present monetary and exchange rate regime. His model allows for both price and demand shocks. The policymaker's objective function takes into account inflation and aggregate demand, as well as a fiscal variable, while allowing for different degrees of policy coordination. While the author's overall assessment is that EMU would raise exchange rate volatility, his analysis also indicates that the result depends critically on the dominance of price shocks. By contrast, if demand shocks dominate, Cohen's model suggests that exchange rate volatility might even decline under monetary union.

Paul Masson and Bart Turtelboom (Chapter 8) argue that, given the paucity of reliable EMU-wide economic indicators at the start of EMU and the practical challenges involved in devising new monetary policy operating procedures, the ECB may have little choice but to place considerable weight on the exchange rate in the early stages of EMU. This may indeed result in a relatively stable euro exchange rate.

De Grauwe identifies another potential aspect of exchange rate volatility: the relationship between the countries adopting the euro and those EU countries that do not join EMU. A successor to the exchange rate arrangements under the ERM has been designed to link the "ins" and the "outs"—termed the ERM II. This mechanism would involve wide bands and the proviso that exchange market intervention should not endanger the price stability objective of the ECB. It is envisaged that realignments be jointly decided, done in time to prevent "one-way bets" from developing, and small enough so that new central rates would be within the old bands of fluctuation.

De Grauwe argues that though the above features, and the achievement of a considerable amount of economic convergence, would deter speculation and make less likely the type of crisis that occurred within the ERM in 1992–93, other features might make the ERM II vulnerable. In particular, the crucial nature of the Maastricht fiscal criteria might make countries vulnerable to shifts in market sentiment, especially if they have high debt levels. For instance, a country whose commitment to entering EMU was thought to be flagging might pay higher interest rates on its debt, widening the budget deficit and setting in motion a self-fulfilling spiral. De Grauwe presents a model of self-fulfilling speculative attacks that illustrates these potential risks—risks that rise as the level of government debt increases. Another problem facing the ERM II, as De Grauwe argues, is the present overvaluation of the core currencies relative to the peripheral ones, so that the latter might therefore need to appreciate over time.

Use of the Euro as Official Reserve Currency

Several chapters discuss the potentially attractive features of the euro as a reserve currency, though its use for that purpose may only develop gradually. In Chapter 8, *Masson and Turtelboom* use stochastic simulations to analyze the effects of replacing European currencies by the euro, including the impact on official reserve holdings. The simulations are performed for two monetary policy scenarios, allowing for the ECB to be guided by either a monetary or an inflation target; the authors also analyze a variant of inflation targeting whereby the ECB places some weight on output conditions. The simulation results suggest, for given structural relationships, that macroeconomic variables for the EU should be at least as stable after EMU as at present.

Masson and Turtelboom then analyze the potential demand for reserves after EMU in the light of the results from the stochastic simulations. Simulation results suggest that the incentives to hold foreign exchange reserves in euros for store of value purposes should be somewhat greater than for the deutsche mark at present, and hence that there should be incentives to diversify away from the dollar. However, they argue that holdings of dollar reserves by EU central banks, though they appear to be too large in the light of EMU, are unlikely to be a major influence on the exchange rate between the euro and the dollar. Masson and Turtelboom argue that more important than these factors will be the relative stance of monetary policies and economic conditions. They also point out that the bulk of reserves outside the EU are held by East Asian countries, which are unlikely to want to use the euro as an exchange rate anchor, so substitution of dollars by euros would likely result from gradual portfolio diversification.

Bergsten and *Alogoskoufis and Portes* concur with the view that the euro will have attractive features and that, after some transition period, the euro should constitute a rival to the dollar as a reserve currency: it would be based on a wide economic area and would develop as a vehicle for invoicing trade and for effecting foreign exchange transactions. Nevertheless, the potential for a shift out of dollar reserves is generally not viewed as a major issue for exchange rates.

The Euro and Financial Markets

Two chapters—Chapter 11 by *Alessandro Prati and Garry Schinasi* and Chapter 12 by *McCauley and White*—see the introduction of the euro as a catalyst for the development of integrated money and bond markets in Europe. Even without EMU, technological progress and regulatory changes are already forcing a rationalization of European banking systems. The arrival of the euro will further increase competition among banks and between banks and alternative sources of funds. While this should eventually lead to a further consolidation of the sector, McCauley and White suggest that slow regulatory progress and the value of local expertise will retard this process.

Prati and Schinasi focus on prospective developments for European and international capital markets, including the impact of EMU on banking institutions and capital flows. They argue that the introduction of the euro will likely reinforce existing trends toward more liquid and integrated capital markets, which could rival U.S. markets in size. The paper sees scope for further securitization of European finance, the development of more precise measures of credit and liquidity risk, regulatory initiatives to reduce or eliminate existing cross-border restrictions on investment, and increased opportunities for portfolio diversification. All these trends will be reinforced by technological advances in derivatives and securities markets. Over time, they argue, this will lead to a harmonization of trading practices and, ultimately, fully integrated markets.

The development of EMU-wide repo and interbank markets will depend importantly on the legal and tax system and on the instruments employed by the monetary authorities, including the extent to which reserve requirements will be imposed on repo operations. The disappearance of foreign exchange risk will refocus the pricing of government bonds on credit risk and the related ratings; in this regard, they expect a narrowing of yields but remain agnostic as to its effect on market liquidity. Prati and Schinasi also argue that further disintermediation and increased competition for investable funds will lead to mergers and acquisitions among banks and between banks and specialized firms and institutional investors. At the retail level, it is argued that the introduction of the euro would further stimulate cross-border mergers and alliances but regulatory reform would be essential to support the needed, and more far-reaching, consolidation in this sector.

The chapter by *McCauley and White* addresses similar issues, though focusing more narrowly on bond markets and banking developments. The paper first sets out the background for the banking system in which the introduction of the euro will take place. Many banks in continental Europe, though experiencing rising profitability, are still substantially less profitable than their Anglo-Saxon and Scandinavian counterparts. Hence, even in the absence of the euro, restructuring will likely be the order of the day. As for the competition from nonbank sources of capital, the paper puts the advantage squarely on the side of direct market access. Although inertia on the part of market participants, legal, regulatory, and supervisory differences, and continuing political sensitivities to takeovers and mergers, especially with foreign firms, are likely to check the pace of increasing competition, it will still be important to ensure that banks and their personnel face the right incentives to avoid excessive risk-taking when coping with the additional competition. It is thus not unlikely that national regulators will increasingly have to cooperate or at least make sure that the home rule principle is working effectively. For world financial markets, it seems likely in the longer term that supervisory and regulatory structures will become more harmonized.

In bond markets, McCauley and White see the arrival of the euro as a potential driving force toward an integrated market, although some of the changes may take time to manifest themselves given very different market structures. In government bond markets, the disappearance of national currencies will likely increase the focus of market makers on creditworthiness and its measurement, leading to very small pricing differences between high-quality borrowers but larger ones among countries with different debt-to-GDP ratios. Overall, the euro bond market is likely to be a growing, highly liquid place. Disintermediation will stimulate the growth of securities markets and the depth, breadth, and liquidity of the market could attract net portfolio flows into the euro zone.

EMU and International Economic Policy Coordination

A number of conference participants, including *Bergsten* and *Alogoskoufis and Portes*, expressed concern that EMU would lead to Europe having less interest in international policy coordination. In addition, the Maastricht Treaty raises complicated issues of responsibility for international economic policy and of representation of the EU in international forums. The ECB has clear responsibility for monetary policy, and the Council for formal exchange rate agreements, in addition to providing general orientations for exchange rate policy. There is a gray area between them, which might make the ECB reluctant to venture into agreements where jurisdiction is unclear. In practice, international monetary cooperation might not be facilitated by the concentration of monetary powers in the ECB, since coordination might need to involve fiscal authorities as well; but here, there will be no clear, single interlocutor.

While the problem of representation is also acknowledged in the chapter by *Masson and Turtelboom*, they argue that in a situation of considerable uncertainty concerning the economic structure—knowledge of which was essential to carrying out an intermediate targeting framework, whether for money or inflation—the ECB might be receptive to international coordination initiatives.

Bergsten argues that EMU should in effect lead to a replacement of the Group of Seven industrial countries by a Group of Three for economic and monetary issues. However, for that to occur, it would be necessary for Europe to have a clear counterpart to the ECB when it came to fiscal policy and exchange rates. Until this occurs, he is concerned that a situation of "benign neglect" will prevail; this would be dangerous as it would slow the responses of Europe to potential crises.

Alogoskoufis and Portes also discuss the implications for international monetary policy coordination. In order to avoid an appreciation of the euro, the ECB could loosen monetary policy or other central banks could tighten monetary policy. The authors prefer the latter since this would be the more appropriate stance from the perspective of monetary conditions in the international monetary system.

John Berrigan and Hervé Carré, in Chapter 5, discuss the implications of EMU for neighboring non-EU countries and the CFA franc zone. A central theme of the paper is that EMU does not entail a radical change of the present system that would call for altering existing agreements or concluding new exchange rate arrangements between the euro bloc and these regions. With respect to the CFA franc zone countries, the authors argue that the special historical relationship with the French treasury has had clear advantages for these countries in the past and that its continuation should be in their best interest, even as the French franc is replaced by the euro. For the countries in Central and Eastern Europe, some may eventually enter into euro-based exchange rate arrangements with the EU. However, Berrigan and Carré suggest that these countries should not prematurely adopt a pegged exchange rate before convergence is achieved, and points out that the ERM II was designed for existing EU countries, which in most cases are close to qualifying for EMU. For the Mediterranean countries, it is argued that the euro may become an anchor currency over time, but not in the immediate future.

Fabio Ghironi and Francesco Giavazzi investigate the implications of various degrees of policy coordination among regions (Chapter 14). Their model highlights the incentives and potential conflicts for various policymakers in deciding on the initial size of EMU. The analysis is based on a three-region model with each region having two policymakers—a fiscal and a monetary authority.

Ghironi and Giavazzi show that the incentives for the specific size of EMU may be different not only for the different regional groups, but also for the two policymakers within the same region. Their results depend importantly on the degree of policy coordination among the regions and on the fiscal activism allowed in the EMU area, with the authors arguing that the most likely scenario is one where the Stability and Growth Pact will severely limit active fiscal policy, at least initially. Under these circumstances, and assuming that the relationship between the ins and outs of EMU is one in which there is no active coordination of policies, the ECB would prefer that only a relatively small group of countries participate in EMU while the fiscal authorities would prefer a larger union. Thus, a potential conflict between fiscal and monetary authorities over the number of EMU participants may emerge when the decisions are taken in 1998.

EMU and the Relationship Between the Fund and Its EMU Members

Both papers on this topic, by *Jacques Polak* and *Niels Thygesen* (Chapters 16 and 17, respectively) concur that EMU will not affect the rights and obligations of members under the IMF's Articles of Agreement. However, they argue that the transfer of monetary policy responsibilities to the ECB and the replacement of existing European currencies by the euro raise a number of important issues for the IMF. These include how surveillance is to be carried out, whether and how Fund resources should be made available to EMU members, how Fund quotas might be affected, whether the special drawing right (SDR) needs to be redefined, and how the euro would be used in Fund operations. It is clear, also from the discussion at the conference, that no simple answers are yet available, but that work on these questions is urgently needed.

Polak and Thygesen stress the importance of a continuation of Fund surveillance; indeed, it may be more relevant in the context of a complicated transition to EMU of a subset of EU countries and of the establishment of the ERM II arrangement. Clearly, Fund surveillance should involve the ECB; modalities for consultations with it as well as the national authorities, which will retain responsibilities for other macroeconomic policies, need to be worked out. This also includes the possible representation of the ECB at the IMF Executive Board, which *Thygesen* argues would be helpful when macroeconomic policies in the EU are discussed within the context of multilateral surveillance.

On the issue of possible use of Fund resources, *Polak* argues that, though they were unlikely to draw on them, individual EU countries might nevertheless be somewhat more likely to come to the Fund after EMU, since monetary bailouts and EU balance of payments assistance would not be forthcoming. He also suggests that a member country would still have a balance of payments, and hence the criterion of "balance of payments need" would still be relevant under EMU, a point challenged by some other conference participants.

In his lunchtime speech reported in Chapter 6, *Philippe Maystadt* also discusses the implications of EMU for the IMF and concurs with Polak and

Thygesen that EMU members, at least for the time being, will remain individual members of the Fund. But he also sees EMU as having profound external ramifications, of which many have not yet been fully addressed. Among these issues are the principles governing the SDR, including whether the SDR should be a country- or a currency-based basket. Also to be investigated is the scope of Fund surveillance of EMU members; while Maystadt agrees with Polak and Thygesen that the Fund would have an important surveillance role, many aspects still remain to be specified, including its appropriate counterparts (other than the ECB) at the EMU-wide level. Maystadt also argues that individual EMU members should continue to have access to Fund resources; however, the concept of balance of payments need as it would apply to individual countries participating in EMU should be reexamined.

Lessons of European Monetary Integration for the International Monetary System

Chapter 9 presents the interventions of five participants in a lively roundtable discussion of whether EMU provided general lessons for the future development of the international monetary system. Several participants in this roundtable are skeptical that EMU will be a stepping stone to a similar arrangement on a broader scale. Some also point to the uniqueness of the historic experiment that will leave the ECB without a direct counterpart responsible for European-wide fiscal and structural policies.

Jacob Frenkel sees the international monetary system as being characterized by an enhanced role for financial markets and capital movements and a reduced role for policy instruments. Fiscal policy is guided by medium-term considerations, protectionist commercial policies have been discredited, monetary policy surprises are not a useful policy instrument, expected monetary changes are ineffective in influencing output, and exchange rate policies must be consistent with other macroeconomic policies. In sum, there is a new world in which policymakers need to engage in a dialogue with markets. This requires transparency and better-defined policy objectives. As for the lessons of European monetary integration for the international monetary system, Frenkel believes the world will remain a multipolar place in which the debate over the relative merits of fixed and flexible exchange rates will continue.

Takatoshi Kato provides a Japanese perspective on EMU. First, he sees long-term benefits from EMU resulting from expanded trade flows and increased capital flows. Japanese banks and investors are taking a wait-and-see approach, but Kato expects increased investment in euro-denominated assets if European markets become more liquid after the introduction of the euro. Second, he notes that the transition toward EMU will coincide with implementation of the financial sector reforms that the Japanese government has recently announced. These reforms will boost the role of the yen and it is therefore not clear that the introduction of the euro will lead to a reduced role of the yen in international capital markets and as a reserve currency.

Mervyn King points out that monetary history associates one currency with one country. The Maastricht Treaty has turned the "one country, one currency" principle into "one market, one money." Hence, he argues that the single most important implication of EMU is that a broad set of decisions will now need to be taken jointly. In his opinion, the success of EMU will depend on the degree of sustainable convergence among its participants.

André Szász poses the goal of European monetary integration as a solution to France's desire to have a European rather than German monetary policy and Germany's desire for tighter European integration. In the German view, monetary union is a way toward political union, provided it is underpinned by stable macroeconomic policies.

Edmund Truman sees European monetary integration more as a natural outgrowth of postwar integration efforts in Europe than as a mechanical reply to the demise of the Bretton Woods system. He is not convinced that EMU will lead to something bigger on a world scale. As for EMU's practical implications, he raises the issue of political accountability of the ECB. He also does not see the arrival of the euro as a threat to the dollar; the advantages from international use of a currency are in any case often overstated.

Paul Volcker, in his dinner remarks collected in Chapter 10, also considers the lessons and challenges of EMU for the international monetary system. He terms EMU a crowning development for the EU. The ECB is a "unique enterprise" since it will operate without a parallel government agency. Though some may applaud this extreme form of central bank independence, he does not believe that a central bank can operate in a political vacuum and is in favor of the establishment of an intergovernmental council for the ECB to interact with.

As for the long-term implications of EMU, Volcker stresses that the ultimate role of the euro in the international monetary system is uncertain and warns of the danger of neglecting exchange rates by the three major central banks. If financial markets sense this, large amounts of capital will ride currency trends and any attempt at international policy coordination would face a difficult task. Although he suggests that the size of the three main currency blocs could weaken the influence of the IMF, he argues that it is in the interest of all concerned—central banks and the IMF alike—to determine and defend ranges of equilibrium exchange rates.

Transition to EMU

Though the conference primarily dealt with the international monetary system after EMU, the issue of the transition to EMU was discussed at a final roundtable (Chapter 18), as well as during a good part of a lunchtime speech by the IMF's Managing Director, *Michel Camdessus*. The roundtable participants had differing views of the extent that transition was likely to proceed smoothly, and of the possible pitfalls in the early years after the start of EMU. Also raised was the issue of a possible delay of the start of EMU. Several participants as well as the Managing Director stressed that progress in this historic enterprise should not be jeopardized by a postponement.

Lars Heikensten highlights some dangers associated with the transition. He is skeptical that EMU would operate smoothly with rigid labor markets, and is concerned that EMU might not be a good thing for Sweden if it faced asymmetric shocks. Nevertheless, staying out has disadvantages since, in any case, the Swedish financial sector would begin adopting the euro, and volatility of the exchange rate against the euro might pose significant problems.

Paul Jenkins argues that increased confidence in financial markets is needed to ensure a successful transition to EMU. In his view, sound economic performance, sustained by transparent and clearly articulated procedures governing the transition, are prerequisites for a stable financial market environment. In this regard, *Xavier Larnaudie-Eiffel* stresses the progress made in ensuring a smooth transition and in giving legal certainty to the euro when it is created, including outside the EU. In addition, he emphasizes that the selection of qualifying countries will be part of a transparent process and subject to clear criteria.

Klaus Regling reiterates the German position that the criteria should be applied strictly, pointing to the need to satisfy German public opinion that monetary union would ensure stability. Since many countries are still above the deficit criterion, more fiscal measures are needed. Given the use of "creative accounting," in his view there is no more room for interpretation in meeting the criteria. He does not exclude the possibility that Germany might not qualify, which might therefore lead to postponement of EMU. However, the German government intends to take the necessary measures to avoid this possibility.

In a luncheon speech, *Michel Camdessus* suggests that EMU is one of the most important and promising developments in the international monetary system in recent decades and, indeed, a historic enterprise (Chapter 15). He argues that the benefits from EMU will be substantial and that the conditions for EMU's successful start are largely in place, including a broad consensus in Europe on the approach to macroeconomic management. In these circumstances, much would be lost from a delay of EMU, and he emphasizes that it is now time to put to rest any lingering doubts about the future of EMU and its timely implementation. This would require also addressing squarely the remaining tasks, including those specified in the Maastricht Treaty and the Stability and Growth Pact, as well as moving ahead with structural reform—tasks that are not only necessary for EMU, but also constitute good policies from the perspective of each country. Among the remaining tasks is a need to devote more attention to the external dimensions of EMU. In this context, EU countries not participating in EMU from the start will have an important self-interest in seeing a successful launch of the euro. However, these countries would need to be given a clear framework for joining EMU as soon as possible thereafter. Camdessus also discusses some aspects of the potential role for the Fund under EMU, emphasizing that the Fund's expertise could be usefully employed, in particular in assessing, and addressing, exchange rate misalignments in the future international monetary system.

Session I
Policy Coordination and a Tripolar International Monetary System

2

The Impact of the Euro on Exchange Rates and International Policy Cooperation

C. Fred Bergsten

The creation of the euro will be the most important development in the evolution of the international monetary system since the widespread adoption of flexible exchange rates in the early 1970s. It will almost certainly be the most important development for the monetary (as opposed to adjustment) dimension of the system since the dollar succeeded sterling as the world's top currency during the interwar period.

These historic results occur because a successful euro based on a consolidated European capital market is virtually certain to become the first real competitor to the dollar since it surpassed sterling as the dominant currency about 65 years ago. At a minimum, the euro will become the world's second key currency with a role far greater than that of the deutsche mark. A bipolar currency regime, with Japan as an important but far less significant player, will replace the dollar-dominated system that has prevailed for over half a century.

The EU as a group accounts for about 31 percent of world output and 20 percent of world trade (excluding intra-EU transactions). The United States provides about 27 percent of global production and 18 percent of world trade (Table 1). Yet the dollar maintains a share of global financial transactions (40 to 60 percent, depending on the category of transactions and whether intra-EU holdings are excluded; see section on key currency criteria and Table 2) that is considerably larger than the combined total of the European national currencies (about 10 to 40 percent) and three to four times that of the only European currency (the deutsche mark, about 10 to 20 percent) that

The author gratefully acknowledges the extremely helpful commments of his colleagues Morris Goldstein and C. Randall Henning in the preparation of this paper. Research assistance was provided by Francesca Balcells and Neal Luna.

Table 1. Share of World Output and Trade, 1995
(In percent)

	Output	Trade[1,2]
United States	26.7	18.3
EU	30.8	20.4
"Core" EU[3]	18.4	18.9
Germany	8.9	12.4
Japan	21.0	10.3

Sources: UNCTAD; World Bank; WTO.
[1] Goods and services.
[2] Excluding intra-EU trade.
[3] Austria, Benelux, France, and Germany.

is now used globally. Incumbency advantages and inertia are powerful forces in international finance, and sterling preserved a global role far in excess of the strength of the British economy for half a century. A sharp reduction, and perhaps eventual elimination, of this gap is nevertheless highly likely—perhaps to a position of about 40 percent each for the dollar and the euro, with about 20 percent remaining for the yen, the Swiss franc, and a few minor currencies.

Even an initial EMU comprising only the half-dozen assured "core countries"[1] would constitute an economy about two-thirds the size of the United States and almost as large as Japan, and with global trade exceeding that of the United States. Even a closure of only half the gap between the current market share of the dollar and the individual European currencies would produce a huge swing in global financial holdings and power relationships among the major countries.

Substantial implications emerge for the functioning and management of the international monetary system. Absent a new EU–U.S. agreement to limit volatility, the dollar-euro exchange rate is likely to fluctuate considerably more than have the rates between the dollar and individual European currencies in recent years—replicating or even exceeding the sharp dollar-yen fluctuations that have marked the entire era of floating rates. There will probably be a huge portfolio diversification of $500 billion–$1 trillion into euros, mainly out of the dollar, which will have a significant impact on exchange rates throughout a longish transition period. European positioning in the pretransition period, to prepare for the subsequent appreciation of the euro without undermining their competitive positions, could produce a further substantial weakening of European currencies over the next year or so, which will raise major problems for the United States and perhaps others. Creation of the euro will thus raise

[1]Austria, Belgium, France, Germany, Luxembourg, and the Netherlands. As of this writing, there is an increased prospect that the initial EMU could be considerably larger and include most of the "Club Med" (Italy, Portugal, and Spain). Such a result would tend to accelerate the realization of all the effects cited in this paper.

Table 2. Currency Shares in Global Finance, 1995
(In percent)

	Dollar	Deutsche mark	All EU[1]	Yen
Official foreign exchange reserves	64.1	15.9	21.2	7.5
Of which:				
Developing countries	(63.5)	(15.6)	(21.9)	(8.3)
Foreign holdings of bank deposits	47.5	18.4	42.5	4.2
International security issues (1990–95)	38.8	. . .	40.6	20.6
Developing countries' debt	50.0	. . .	16.1	18.0
Denomination of world exports (1992)	47.6	15.3	33.5	4.8
Foreign exchange market turnover	42.0	19.0	28.0[2]	12.0
All international private assets[3]	37.9	15.5	32.0	12.4
(excluding intra-EU holdings)	(50)	. . .	(10)	(18)

Sources: BIS; IMF.

[1] Includes intra-EU holdings so considerably overstates consolidated EU position (and hence understates dollar and yen positions), except in final line.

[2] Includes only deutsche mark, sterling, and French franc.

[3] Includes international bonds, cross-border bank liabilities to nonbanks, euro currency liabilities to domestic nonbanks, and euronotes.

a series of key policy issues for the IMF, Group of Seven industrial countries, and other international financial bodies over both the short and longer run that will require intensive consultation and resolution.

On the institutional side, the new ECB should increasingly represent Europe in international monetary discussions and negotiations. This will pave the way for converting the Group of Seven/Group of Ten into a Group of Three, initially in the Bank for International Settlements (BIS) and other central banking forums but, as fiscal and other policies become Europeanized, in the meetings of finance ministers as well. A similar consolidation should take place in European representation at the IMF and other multilateral financial institutions.

This paper will attempt to analyze the implications of EMU for the world economy. It first covers the state of the international discussion on this issue. Then it presents criteria for key currency status and applies the model to the euro in an effort to forecast its global role in the eventual steady state, and subsequently addresses the longish transition period to that steady state. The paper next draws a number of implications for the pretransition period, namely, the next couple of years. After a short comment on the yen, the paper lays out a series of questions for international policy cooperation that derive from the analysis and suggests responses to them.[2]

[2]This paper will divide the analysis into three distinct time periods: the long-run *steady state*, when the euro is fully established as both the currency of Europe and a major international money; the *transition period* between the creation of the euro (presumably 1999) and its reaching that steady state; and the *pretransition period* between now and the euro's start-up. These distinctions are clear conceptually, though one cannot of course date them—particularly the intermediate transition period—precisely.

Benign Neglect of the Global Impact of EMU

In sharp contrast to the extensive analyses of EMU itself, there has been surprisingly little official or even private discussion of its international implications. The initial blueprints, the reports of the Delors Committee (1989) and the Committee of European Central Banks (the Pöhl report), totally ignored the topic. The European Commission belatedly produced a chapter on the subject in *One Market, One Money* (Emerson and others, 1992) but there has been little subsequent discussion even within Europe itself except for a very general view that EMU will enhance Europe's global influence. The work program of the European Monetary Institute (EMI) to plan the EMU, which will eventually mobilize more than a hundred task forces, reportedly has not yet taken up its external dimension. Some outside observers have interpreted this *European* neglect of the topic as further evidence of Europe's inward looking, and even "fortress Europe," mentality.

Non-European governments, however, have been equally casual about the issue. The United States, Japan, and others outside Europe apparently believe either that EMU will never happen (or will happen beyond the watch of current officials) or that it will be of little international consequence, so that discussing it is a waste of time; or that it is bound to be good for the world as well as for the Europeans so there is no need to worry about the results; or that it is a purely "internal" European matter and thus solely up to the Europeans themselves (or that they will reject any outside involvement anyway). This paper will argue that all these views are incorrect.

This *international* neglect of EMU continues the neglect of European developments that has characterized the Group of Seven industrial countries and the IMF in recent years. Developments in the EMS, ranging from German unification through the currency crises of 1992–93 and the conversion of the narrow-band system into a regime of very wide target zones in response to the latter, have had major global consequences. The Group of Seven industrial countries' failure even to discuss them is one striking indicator of its sharp decline. It is a telling example of the "nonaggression pact" that has emerged within the Group of Seven, under which each participant largely eschews criticism of its peers in order to forestall criticism of its own policies—even when events emanating elsewhere have substantial impact on the "silent partners" and the global system, for which the Group of Seven is supposed to provide leadership.[3]

The result of this prolonged and universal neglect is that there has been relatively little consideration of (1) how EMU will affect the international monetary system; (2) the policy issues that will be raised as a result, and (3)

[3]As elaborated and analyzed in Bergsten and Henning (1996).

how the international community, particularly through the IMF and the Group of Seven, should respond. The Fund is therefore to be congratulated for convening this conference to foster serious consideration of the topic. It is to be hoped that the relevant officials will promptly follow suit.[4]

Key Currency Criteria and the Euro

The central systemic issue is the global role that the euro will play, most importantly in private global financial markets but also as an official reserve asset. There are nuanced differences between the criteria for the two (transactions currency and reserve currency) roles but there are five central considerations for both (Bergsten, 1996a, especially Chapters 4–6 as summarized on pp. 197–202):[5] (1) the size of the underlying economy and its global trade; (2) the economy's independence from external constraints; (3) avoidance of exchange controls; (4) the breadth, depth and liquidity of its capital markets; and (5) the strength and stability of the economy and its external position.

The unified Europe is slightly superior to the United States on the first two structural criteria. The *gross domestic product* of the EU was $8.4 trillion in 1996, slightly above the $7.2 trillion of the United States. The United States has been growing more rapidly for several years and may continue to do so in the period immediately ahead (Table 3). For the longer run, however, growth of potential output in the two regions is similar, so their rough parity in terms of economic weight is likely to continue.

The EU also has a modestly larger volume of *global trade flows*. Excluding intra-EU trade, the volume of total EU trade (exports plus imports) totaled $1.9 trillion in 1996. The comparable total for the United States was $1.7 trillion.

In terms of *openness*, the share of exports plus imports of goods and services is now about 23 percent in both the EU and the United States (Table 4). This ratio has doubled for the United States over the past 25 years, while rising only modestly in Europe.[6] Both ratios are likely to continue growing slowly

[4]Academic analysis of the international implications of EMU has also been sparse. Exceptions include Alogoskoufis and Portes (1992), Cooper (1992), Gros and Thygesen (1992, Chapter 9), Henning (1996 and 1997), and Kenen (1995, Chapter 5, and 1997).

[5]A slightly different, four-way breakdown is presented by Eichengreen and Frankel (1996). Their criteria include patterns of output and trade, history, the country's financial markets, and confidence in the value of the currency. Frenkel and Goldstein (1997) use a sevenfold categorization that largely covers the same topics.

[6]The EU ratio jumped after both oil shocks but dropped back to "normal" levels after the oil price receded in the mid-1980s.

Table 3. Economic Growth in the EU and United States

(In percent)

	EU-15	United States
1986	2.8	2.9
1987	2.9	3.1
1988	4.1	3.9
1989	3.5	2.5
1990	3.0	0.8
1991	3.4	−1.2
1992	1.0	3.3
1993	−0.8	2.4
1994	2.5	3.3
1995	2.3	2.0
1996	1.6	2.4

Source: IMF, International Financial Statistics.

as globalization proceeds, but they too are likely to remain broadly similar. Both regions are thus fairly independent of external constraints and can manage their policies without being thrown off course by any but the most severe exogenous shocks.

It is virtually inconceivable that either the EU or the United States would unilaterally resort to *exchange or capital controls*. Globalization of capital mar-

Table 4. Economic Openness Ratios in the EU and United States

(In percent)

	EU	United States		EU	United States
1971	18.4	10.7	1984	27.4	18.3
1972	17.9	11.2	1985	27.2	17.3
1973	19.2	13.2	1986	21.9	17.8
1974	24.8	16.8	1987	20.7	18.7
1975	23.3	15.8	1988	20.6	19.9
1976	24.5	16.5	1989	21.3	20.4
1977	24.8	16.8	1990	20.5	20.9
1978	23.5	17.3	1991	19.6	20.8
1979	23.8	18.9	1992	18.9	20.4
1980	25.9	20.8	1993	21.1	20.7
1981	27.7	19.9	1994	22.3	21.6
1982	26.7	18.2	1995	22.5	23.1
1983	25.8	17.3			

Sources: IMF, International Financial Statistics and Direction of Trade Statistics; OECD, National Accounts.

Notes: "Economic openness" is defined as exports plus imports of goods and services divided by GDP. The share of intra-EU trade in services is assumed to be the same as for goods.

Table 5. Capital Market Indicators in the EU, Japan, and United States, 1995

(In billions of dollars)

	EU	Japan	United States
Total equity capitalization	2,828	3,000	5,136
Domestic debt capitalization	5,314[1]	4,958	10,725
Domestic equity issues	49[2]	5	73
Domestic debt issues	329[1]	393	763
International debt outstanding	799[1]	368	273
International debt issues	105[1]	7	61
International equity placements	11[2]	. . .	6

Sources: BIS; IFC; IMF; and OECD.

[1] Includes only France, Germany, Italy, and the United Kingdom.

[2] Includes only France, Germany, and the United Kingdom.

kets has reached the point where all major financial centers, including Japan and many in the developing world, would have to act together to alter international capital flows with any degree of effectiveness. The traditional option of using such controls to protect national reserve or balance of payments positions no longer exists for the money centers. Such actions are thus highly improbable in any context short of global military conflict, and perhaps not even then in light of the nature of modern warfare. In any event, they could only be sensibly pursued by the United States and the EU together. Hence the two regions will remain parallel on this key currency criterion as well.

It is less clear when, or even if, Europe will reach full parity with the United States in terms of the breadth, depth, and liquidity of its *capital markets*. The American market for domestic securities is about twice as large as the combined European markets (Table 5). The European financial markets are highly decentralized at present—both across countries and, for Germany, within as well. There will be no central governmental borrower like the U.S. Treasury to provide a fulcrum for the market. It may take some time to align the relevant standards and practices across the EU, especially if London is included—and the results will be much weaker if it is not. Germany may oppose wholesale liberalization, as the Bundesbank has traditionally done within Germany, on the grounds that doing so would weaken the ability of the ECB to conduct an effective monetary policy.[7]

On the other hand, the total value of government bond markets in the EU is 2.1 trillion ECUs as compared with 1.6 trillion ECUs in the United States

[7]More broadly, Germany (especially the Bundesbank) may be no more enthusiastic about a global role for the euro than it has traditionally been for the deutsche mark. By contrast, leading Frenchmen have spoken often of wanting to use EMU to enhance Europe's global status. This issue of fundamental policy orientation appears to be unresolved at this point in time.

(Henning, 1997, citing an estimate by Salomon Brothers). The issuance of international bonds and equities is already considerably higher in the current European markets, taken together, than in the United States (Table 5). Futures trading in German and French government bonds, taken together, exceeded that in U.S. notes and bonds in 1995 (McCauley, 1997). Expectations of the launch of EMU have already provided a substantial convergence in the yields of government bonds throughout Europe, including for countries (such as Italy and Spain) outside the "core group." There are already clear signs of the development of an integrated European capital market for private bonds. So European parity on this key criterion is likely eventually, though it could take a while to achieve.

The final criterion is the *strength and stability of the European economy*. There is obviously no risk of hyperinflation or any of the other extreme instabilities that could disqualify the euro from international status. To the contrary, the ECB is virtually certain to run an extremely responsible monetary policy and rapidly achieve a reputation for credibility (see the next section). It is true that Europe, even when united on a common currency, may not carry out the structural reforms needed to restore dynamic economic growth on a continued basis. Markets prize stability more than growth, however, as indicated by the continued dominance of the dollar through extended periods of sluggish American economic performance. Hence, the euro is sure to qualify on these grounds as well.

In addition, America's *external economic position* will continue to pose doubts about the future stability and value of the dollar. The United States has run current account deficits for the last 15 years (Table 6). It now has a net foreign debt of about $1 trillion (Table 7), by far the largest in the world and rising by 15 to 20 percent annually. That debt is still modest as a share of U.S. GDP or exports and is not climbing at the explosive level of the mid-1980s, which prompted the sharp dollar depreciation of 1985–87 (Marris, 1987), but Amer-

Table 6. U.S. Current Account Balance

(In billions of dollars)

1980	2.2	1989	−104.3
1981	4.8	1990	−94.3
1982	−11.6	1991	−9.3
1983	−44.2	1992	−61.4
1984	−99.0	1993	−99.7
1985	−124.5	1994	−147.8
1986	−150.5	1995	−148.2
1987	−166.5	1996	−165.0
1988	−127.7		

Source: IMF, International Financial Statistics.

Table 7. Net International Investment Position of the United States
(In billions of dollars)

	At Current Cost	At Market Value
1982	379	265
1983	363	292
1984	231	173
1985	133	136
1986	45	136
1987	−11	71
1988	−135	15
1989	−250	−77
1990	−251	−212
1991	−355	−349
1992	−513	−568
1993	−504	−413
1994	−580	−492
1995	−814	−774
1996[1]	−999	−959

Source: U.S. Department of Commerce, Survey of Current Business.
[1]Estimated by the author, based on U.S. current account deficit in 1996.

ica's external position will remain a source of doubt in the minds of both markets and officials. The EU, by contrast, has a roughly balanced international creditor position and has run modest surpluses in its international accounts in recent years (Table 8). On this important criterion, the EU position is decidedly superior to that of the United States.

These five criteria qualify a currency for international status. If the specification is accepted, a prognosis for the relative shares of different currencies then depends on two variables: the relative position of the different currencies on the criteria, as already discussed, and the relative importance of the criteria.

Severe data limitations have precluded persuasive econometric tests of the latter. There is good reason, however, to believe that the relative size of key currency countries' economies and trade flows is of central salience. A large economy has a naturally large base for its currency and thus possesses important scale and scope benefits. A large volume of trade gives a country's firms

Table 8. Current Account Position of the EU
(In billions of dollars)

1990	−81.9	1993	6.6
1991	−81.9	1994	21.2
1992	−6.6	1995	53.8

Source: IMF, International Financial Statistics.

considerable leverage to finance in the country's own currency. Large economies are less vulnerable to external shocks than smaller ones and thus a "safe haven" for investors. They are more likely to have the large capital markets that are also required for key currency status.[8]

There is a clear historical correlation between size and key currency status. Sterling and the dollar became dominant currencies during the periods when the United Kingdom and the United States, respectively, were the world's dominant economies and, especially, traders. The only significant key currencies today are those of the world's three largest economies and traders: the United States, Japan, and Germany. Japan's economy is considerably larger than Germany's (Table 1) so the yen should have a larger role than the deutsche mark on that criterion, but Germany's trade (including with the rest of the EU) is larger than Japan's and its exports even exceeded those of the United States in some fairly recent years.

Crude statistical analysis by Eichengreen and Frankel (1996, pp. 363–66) buttresses these conclusions and suggests that the size of the currencies' constituent economies may play a central role. They find that "one can explain much of the downward trend in the dollar's share of world reserves over the last 25 years, and the upward trends in the yen and deutsche mark shares, by the falling share of U.S. GDP in the world economy and the rising share of the Japanese and German GDPs." They estimate econometrically that every rise of 1 percentage point in a key currency country's share of world product is associated with a rise of 0.5–1.33 percentage points (depending on whether GDPs are calculated at market or PPP exchange rates) in its currency's share of central bank reserve holdings.[9] Not even crude estimates are available for private markets, so we will simply assume that the same relationships apply to them as for central bank holdings.[10] We will apply the Eichengreen-Frankel ratios to countries' shares of world trade as well as of world output (as Eichengreen himself does in his comments on this paper).

The relevant comparison for present purposes is between the full (initially core) EU and the euro, on the one hand, and Germany and the deutsche mark,

[8]Kenen (1995, pp. 111–12) cites several other technical size advantages that will accrue to the euro.

[9]See Eichengreen's comments on this paper, which slightly modify this relationship and include a trade as well as GDP variable.

[10]Table 2 suggests that European national currencies account for a substantially larger share of private international transactions than they do in official reserves. However, these totals are substantially made up of intra-EU holdings that will disappear as "international" assets when EMU commences. Excluding such holdings, McCauley (1997) has estimated that the dollar's share of "all international private assets" jumps to about 50 percent and the share for all European currencies drops to about 10 percent, as indicated in the last line of Table 2. This is about the same gap (40 percentage points) as revealed by the standard IMF data for official reserve holdings.

on the other. It would be improper to compare the euro, which will meet all of the key currency criteria, with the sum of all (or even a few) of the individual European currencies, most of which do not.[11]

Hence, there will be a quantum jump in the size of the economy and trading unit in question: from Germany's 9 percent of world output and 12 percent of world trade to the EMU's 31 and 20 percent, respectively (or the core group's 18 and 19 percent) (Table 1).[12] This jump of about 50–100 percent in the early part of the transition period even with involvement of only a small core group should, according to the Eichengreen-Frankel estimates, produce a rise of about 25–133 percent in the role of the euro compared with the deutsche mark. In the eventual steady state, a rise of 65–250 percent in the size of the relevant economic base could be expected, which would expand the potential size of the currency's role by 30–335 percent.

The deutsche mark, on most calculations, accounts for about 15 percent of global financial assets in both private and official markets (Table 2). Hence, the postulated expansion of the economy underlying the key currency, from Germany to the EU, could produce a rise in the euro's role to 20–30 percent even if EMU included only the core countries. The share could rise as high as 65 percent if the entire EU were eventually involved. The midpoints of these ranges, 25 and 42½ percent, may provide rough indicators of the likely future global role of the euro in the initial and eventual steady states. Such shifts would, respectively, eliminate half and more than all of the present gap between the dollar and the deutsche mark.

As Eichengreen and Frankel themselves stress, their coefficients cannot be taken too seriously. The numbers do suggest, however, that the sharp increase in the size of the economy and trading unit underlying the European key currency could produce a quantum leap in the international role of that asset. Assuming that most of the increase in the euro's role came "at the expense" of the dollar, the euro could eventually achieve parity with the dollar.[13]

---

[11]Failure to recognize this is a common error in numerous analyses of the issue. Kenen (1995, p. 118), for example, criticizes Gros and Thygesen (1992) for hypothesizing that private investors will want to equalize their holdings of dollars and euros on the grounds that such investors do not do so now—failing to recognize the systemic change that will occur with the creation of a new currency based on an economy that is four times as large.

[12]Germany's "share of world trade" *includes* its trade with the rest of the EU. The EU's "share of world trade" *excludes* intra-EU trade. This conceptual distinction is consistent with the comparison between the *national* role of the deutsche mark and the group role of the euro. Empirically, it means that the difference between German and EU trade is considerably less than the difference between German and EU GDP.

[13]Eichengreen and Frankel agree that "a single currency coming into use throughout Europe . . . would indeed pose a challenge to the supremacy of the dollar" (p. 366) and that "the creation of the euro would mean a new and increasingly powerful rival for the dollar as the international monetary system's leading reserve currency" (p. 372).

It is worth reiterating that the GDPs and trade volumes of the United States and a united Europe will be quite similar. Ceteris paribus, one might therefore expect their currencies to play roughly similar roles in the world economy. Ceteris are of course not paribus, however, and it was suggested above that it may be some time before the pan-European capital market equals that of the United States. For the remainder of this paper, I will therefore postulate that the euro's role will eventually increase over the present role of the deutsche mark by between one-half the current gap between the deutsche mark and dollar—which, as just indicated, could occur even when the euro rested only on an initial core group—and by enough to achieve full parity. This would leave their relative shares at about 30:50 or 40:40 percent, respectively, with about 20 percent remaining for the yen, the Swiss franc, and a few minor currencies in either case.[14]

The structural features of a united Europe are thus likely to produce a euro that will ultimately challenge the dollar as the world's key currency. The extent and timing of this challenge will depend largely on the ability of Europe to forge a single capital and financial market,[15] and thus in part on whether the United Kingdom will integrate with the Continent; on whether Europe can nurture and sustain a policy environment for steady and sustained economic growth; on the continuing advantages of incumbency and inertia that favor the dollar; and on whether the United States itself falters in ways that accelerate the decline of its currency. The timing questions are addressed in the next section.

From a systemic perspective, it is not very important whether the euro comes to equal the dollar, slightly exceed it, or slightly trail it. The achievement of rough parity, whatever the precise relationship, would convert an international monetary system that has been dominated by the dollar throughout the postwar period into a bipolar regime. Several very important policy consequences of that evolution are addressed in the section on the implications for policy coordination.

It is worth noting here, however, that such a transformation on the financial side would replicate developments on the trade side at a much earlier time. As noted above, the external trade of the combined EU roughly equals that of the United States. A united Europe has in fact always had a market position on trade comparable to that of the United States. In addition, Europe has had a common trade *policy* and spoken with a single voice on these issues from the very outset of the European integration process. Hence, the policy regime in that area has already been bipolar for over three decades, as indicated by the necessity of agreement between Europe and the United States to bring all of

---

[14]A similar calculation is presented by Gros and Thygesen (1992, pp. 297–301).

[15]EMI President Alexandre Lamfalussy (1997) concurs that the euro "won't supplant the dollar, but it will compete with it. To have a genuine competition with the dollar, we have to have the development of a Europe-wide financial market."

the major multilateral rounds in the GATT (and recent sectoral agreements in the World Trade Organization) to a successful conclusion. The prospective developments on the monetary side would repeat that evolution, both equating Europe's market position and generating institutional consolidation—the common currency and ECB—to produce a similarly bipolar regime.

Transition Period

The evolution suggested above could produce a very large diversification of portfolios into euros, mainly out of dollars, as the new key currency increases its global role. The timing issues then become paramount. How rapidly will the shift occur? How long will the transition take? The following guesstimates are again intended solely to provide ballpark orders of magnitude for the transition period.

Global *official* holdings of foreign exchange total about $1.4 trillion, divided roughly in half between industrial and developing countries (including Brazil, China, Taiwan Province of China, and several of the other largest holders). The developing countries hold about 60 percent of their reserves in dollars and 15–20 percent in European currencies[16] (Table 2). Equalization of these ratios would require a shift of $100–150 billion. Cutting the difference roughly in half, with a resultant portfolio composition of 50:30 instead of the present 60:20, would produce a diversification of $50–75 billion.

Shifts in industrial countries could be of similar magnitude. Japan alone holds over $200 billion, virtually all of it in dollars, and could shift at least $50 billion into euros to position itself to intervene effectively in the euro market. Depending on the nature of any systemic arrangements that it might work out with Europe, the United States might want to build a reserve of euros that substantially exceeded its periodic holdings of deutsche mark (recently about $20 billion; see Table 9) and other national currencies (including $15 billion in yen).

The reshuffling of European portfolios will turn largely on the EMU arrangements themselves but could roughly net out. The "ins" will need fewer reserves in total and will of course no longer hold deutsche mark (as they will not exist). There have in fact been estimates that the EMU, by the time it includes all EU countries, could have "excess reserves" of $50–200 billion (Emerson and others, 1992; Gros and Thygesen 1992; Leahy, 1996) that it might want to dispose of—but the entire EU held only $171.3 billion in dollars at the end of 1995 (see Masson and Turtelboom's paper in this volume) so any conversions would have to be toward the lower end of that range and it is

[16]The smaller number includes only the currencies of the "core countries," while the larger includes other EU currencies, notably sterling.

Table 9. Foreign Currency Holdings of U.S. Monetary Authorities
(In millions of dollars, December 1996)

	Federal Reserve	U.S. Treasury Exchange Stabilization Fund	Total
Deutsche mark	13,030	6,595	19,625
Japanese yen	6,153	9,024	15,176
Mexican pesos	0	3,500	3,500
Total	19,183	19,118	38,301

Source: New York Federal Reserve Bank, *Quarterly Report.*

doubtful that the Europeans would push up the euro by "dumping" dollars. Moreover, the "outs" will need a substantial reserve of euros if they aspire to eventual membership in EMU and thus need to pursue stable exchange rate relationships with the "ins." The reserve pooling envisioned for the ECB is too small to have any significant effect (McCauley, 1997).

Official reserve shifts into euros, largely though not wholly out of dollars, could thus range between 100 and 300 billion dollars.[17] Sales of official dollars could be larger if the EMU members themselves decided to liquidate their "excess reserves."

Private portfolio diversification could be much larger. Global holdings of international financial assets, including bank deposits and bonds, total about $3.5 trillion (excluding intra-EU holdings). About 50 percent are in dollars and only about 10 percent in European currencies (Table 2, last line). A complete balancing of portfolios between dollars and euros would thus require a shift of about $700 billion (McCauley, 1997, pp. 8–9) while a halfway move (to 40:20) would reallocate about $350 billion. Combining the official and private guesstimates produces *a potential diversification range of between $500 billion and $1 trillion.*[18]

Such a shift, even spread over a number of years, could have substantial effects on exchange rates. Assuming no responses through interest rates, McCauley (1997) has estimated that a fall of 1 percent in the exchange rate of the dollar against the euro would be required to achieve a portfolio shift of about $15 billion from dollars into euros. A cumulative portfolio diversification of $500–1,000 billion would thus require a currency adjustment of 35–70 percent.

[17]Kenen (1995, p. 116) agrees that the euro "will be widely held as a reserve asset" but believes that holdings of it "will grow gradually via accumulation, not rapidly via asset switching." Some of the shift could come from the minor non-EU key currencies, such as the Swiss franc and perhaps the yen; see the discussion of the yen below.

[18]Some earlier estimates also fall into this range, for example, Gros and Thygesen (1992) foresaw a shift of $400–600 billion (at 1992 levels) and Thygesen (1995) projected a shift of about $600 billion.

Again, none of the specific numbers should be taken seriously. For one thing, interest rates would undoubtedly respond to such large portfolio shifts and temper the impact on exchange rates. Moreover, official holders—at least in the major industrial countries—would surely recognize the need to avoid destabilizing markets with their own diversifications and would presumably take collective actions to do so (see the section on implications for policy coordination).

In addition, international borrowers as well as asset holders would increase their use of the euro and thus generate an increase in its supply that could partially (or even wholly) offset the increase in demand for it (as stressed by McCauley, 1997, and addressed further by McCauley and White in their paper in this volume). The chief key currency countries have in fact traditionally run overall balance of payments deficits that added to world liquidity and frequently placed *downward* pressure on their currencies.

The actual magnitude of the net exchange rate impact of the rise of the euro could thus be considerably less than 35–70 percent. However, it will probably still be quite substantial.[19] In light of the anticipatory nature of most markets at most times, it could also occur much more quickly than is now anticipated. Given the bandwagon effects that frequently characterize those markets, an overshoot that magnifies the impact for a time is also quite plausible.

The closest parallel in modern history was the international diversification of portfolios of large Japanese financial institutions after Japan lifted its exchange controls at the end of 1980. Prior to that time, the huge volume of Japanese investments generated by the country's rapid economic growth and high saving rate had been held almost wholly in yen assets. Attracted by the high real interest rates in the United States that accompanied the sharp increases in American budget deficits in the early 1980s, Japanese investors placed about $230 billion in foreign (mainly dollar) assets from 1980 to 1985. The dollar appreciated by about 25 percent against the yen (and 75 percent against all Group of Ten currencies) during this period, due importantly to this Japanese portfolio shift.

The timing, extent, and even direction of the shift between dollars and euros in the transition period will be critically affected by the conduct of monetary policy by the new ECB. Many Europeans believe that the euro will be relatively weak at the outset, at least until the ECB has time to develop a credible reputation and especially if the initial membership in EMU extends beyond the core countries as defined above. (Some also *hope* that the euro will be weak, in order to improve Europe's trade competitiveness and thus help res-

[19]Gros and Thygesen (1992) agree that there will be very large portfolio shifts into the euro but believe "they should not have any disruptive effects on exchange rates or capital flows because they will be distributed over time and because financial markets have become so sophisticated . . ." (p. 292).

cue it from its continuing economic doldrums. See the section on the pretransition period.) Uncertainty alone is viewed as likely to push the euro downward. And even if the euro rapidly attains credibility, borrowing in euros and other "supply side" effects as noted above could equal or even outweigh the demand for euro assets and thus push its exchange rate down rather than up.

Part of the answer of course depends on the relationship between the dollar and the European national currencies at the creation of the euro, and thus the initial exchange rate between the two. If the European currencies had appreciated substantially in the pretransition period, and moved well above their "fundamental equilibrium exchange rates" (FEERs), the euro would be likely to depreciate. It will be argued in the next section, however, that the opposite is much more likely: that the European currencies will lodge at levels below, perhaps considerably below, their individual FEERs between now and 1999. Hence the more likely direction of change for the euro, based solely on its starting point, will be upward.[20]

Even without the "advantage" of an undervalued initial rate, my own judgment is that the euro will be quite strong from its inception (which, for overriding European political reasons, is likely to occur as scheduled).[21] The Maastricht Treaty gives the ECB a mandate to emphasize price stability. The management of the new ECB will clearly make every effort to establish its credibility as promptly as possible. There will be no government to pressure the ECB to pursue an easier course,[22] and EU unanimity would be required to alter that condition. The ECB will be especially chary of any depreciation of the exchange rate of the euro. To the contrary, it is likely to view euro appreciation as an early sign of success.

Moreover, Germany will simply not let EMU happen unless it is assured of a strong euro. The Bundesbank can file a dissent to the EMI's report on launching the plan, and its doing so would almost certainly lead the Bundestag or the German courts to veto German participation. Moreover, the Social Democratic Party would probably seize on any prospect for a weak euro by opposing EMU, and thereby catering to a majority of German public opinion, in its effort to unseat Chancellor Kohl in the election in 1998.[23] The effective

[20]The initial exchange rate is thus an important topic for *international* consideration. See the section on policy cooperation.

[21]Kenen (1995, p. 116) agrees that the euro "is more likely to be strong than weak" and that it "is likely to appreciate after Stage Three begins." See also Cooper (1992).

[22]Although France has recently proposed a "Stability Council," presumably largely for this reason.

[23]SPD leader Oskar LaFontaine floated several anti-EMU trial balloons in late 1995 and deputy party leader Gerhard Schröder, who is currently the only SPD candidate given a chance by the polls to defeat Chancellor Kohl, has raised doubts about the idea. German opinion polls continue to show substantial opposition to EMU.

Bundesbank veto over the entire arrangement is another reason to believe that the euro will be strong from the outset.

Comparisons with the Bundesbank are both inevitable and instructive. The ECB charter is much more single minded in emphasizing the goal of price stability. The ECB will be the first central bank in history without a government looking over its shoulder and possessing at least some powers over it. Because it lacks the 50-year history of the Bundesbank, the ECB will have to be especially tough in pursuing a responsible monetary policy.[24] This will be especially true if, as seems likely, the Maastricht Treaty criteria are interpreted flexibly to permit the startup to proceed on schedule and/or if the initial membership extends beyond the core group.

Fiscal policy developments are likely to reinforce this outcome. The Maastricht fiscal criteria will probably be fudged to at least a modest extent to enable EMU to start on time (and, largely for political reasons, to include countries beyond the core group). The Stability and Growth Pact seems likely to have substantial loopholes. If unemployment remains high and pervasive at the startup point, the national governments are likely to deploy their only remaining macroeconomic tool—fiscal policy—in an expansionary direction.[25] This would intensify the pressure on the ECB to pursue a restrictive monetary policy.

The result could be a (hopefully mild) European version of Reaganomics two decades later. Many Europeans seem to believe that expansionary fiscal policies after 1999 would produce a weak euro. To the contrary, combining such fiscal policies with a resolute ECB will strengthen the euro further. The proper analogies are with the Federal Reserve in the early 1980s, in the face of rapidly growing U.S. budget deficits, and with the Bundesbank in response to growing German budget deficits brought on by unification in the early 1990s: both produced very strong currencies. There are legitimate reasons for concern about this policy mix but a weakening of the euro is not one of them.

If this set of assessments is correct, even without the additional impetus from expansionary national fiscal policies, it sharply enhances the possibility that the euro will quickly become the world's second key currency. The addition of a credible monetary policy to the structural attributes listed above would accelerate the postulated portfolio diversification.

---

[24]Cooper (1992, p. 521) argues that "the new 'Eurofed' thus will be tempted to pursue a monetary policy that is tighter than required, and than would be pursued by a monetary authority whose reputation was secure."

[25]This is a conceptually correct outcome. The Treaty's numerical limits on budget deficits and, especially, public debt positions are totally arbitrary and ignore such fundamentals as the state of the economy and the overall saving rates of the potential members. The theory of optimum currency areas stresses the need for budgetary flexibility in the constituent states rather than adherence to strict limits on budget deficits (Bayoumi and Masson, 1994).

This effect could be intensified by contemporary events in the United States. It now appears possible that the Administration and Congress will reach a fairly credible agreement to eliminate the remaining deficit in the U.S. federal budget by 2002. Every dollar decline in the budget deficit is associated with a decline of one-third to one-half of that amount in the current account deficit. That correction is achieved through a depreciation of the real exchange rate of the dollar, prompted by the decline in interest rates fostered by the reduced credit demand of the federal government.[26]

Exchange market developments of the late 1990s and early twenty-first century could thus represent a reversal of their evolution in the first half of the 1980s. During 1980–85, U.S. budget deficits soared. The elimination of Japanese exchange controls triggered large investments in the dollar. Fiscal tightening in Europe and Japan further enhanced the dollar's appreciation. In the period ahead, to the contrary, further reduction of the U.S. budget deficit could coincide with European fiscal expansion and a large diversification out of the dollar triggered by creation of the euro. Substantial dollar depreciation could thus occur in the transition to EMU.

This discussion highlights the importance of the policy mix, especially in Europe but also in the United States, in determining the exchange rate impact of the euro. A tough and effective Stability and Growth Pact in Europe, contrary to my expectations as noted above, would enable the ECB to pursue a less restrictive monetary policy and thus reduce the speed at which it is likely to assume a prominent global role. A reversion to growing budget deficits in the United States could push U.S. interest rates upward and "defend" the dollar against loss of its international role in the short run (while eroding it in the longer run by promoting further increases in U.S. current account deficits). The structural characteristics outlined in the previous section would inevitably propel the euro into international prominence but such circumstances would slow, and perhaps for some time limit the extent of, that evolution.

An "effective" Stability and Growth Pact could, however, produce much more severe international risks than a more permissive variety as postulated here. If the EU truly abandoned all flexibility in the conduct of fiscal as well as monetary policy, the resulting absence of macroeconomic instruments could portend the use of other, far less desirable, tools to counter the region's severe unemployment and growth problems. One would be competitive depreciation—but, as noted, this would run counter to the desire for a strong euro. An-

[26]The Administration's models suggest that about one-third of the cut in the budget deficit will be reflected in a cut in the current account deficit; other models suggest a ratio of about one-half. The baseline budget deficit for 2001–2002 is about $200 billion so the external deficit should decline by $65–100 billion if zero balance is achieved domestically. Each 1 percent depreciation of the trade-weighted dollar produces an improvement of about $10 billion in the current account after a lag of two years. Hence, the implied decline of the dollar is 6½–10 percent.

other would be trade protection, for which there are already substantial pressures in Europe, which would be devastating to the global trading system in light of its bipolar structure as noted above. The possibility of such outcomes underlies the imperative of discussing EMU and its potential global effects in the Group of Seven and other multilateral forums, as proposed in the section on implications for policy coordination.

Many analysts share the view that the euro will eventually rival the dollar as the world's key currency (e.g., Kenen, 1995). The conventional wisdom, however, is that such a shift will take considerable time to eventuate (an exception is Alogoskoufis and Portes, 1992). None of the authors has hazarded a specific guess but they imply that the transition will be measured in decades rather than years.

Such analysis implicitly assumes that the redistribution of private and official international portfolios is a linear function that occurs incrementally over time. There is evidence from the history of key currencies, however, that major shocks can produce rapid changes in portfolio composition. The devaluation of sterling in 1931, for example, dramatically reduced the international role of that currency and propelled the dollar unambiguously into the dominant spot that it has held ever since. The onset of double-digit inflation in the United States in the late 1970s produced a sharp drop in the reserve currency share of the dollar in only a few years.[27]

These examples reveal, however, that the major nonlinear shocks have derived more from poor performance and policy on the part of the incumbent than from the improved position of a new rival. Continued good performance by the United States could thus delay, or even limit permanently, the rise of the euro. The euro's achievement of the criteria for key currency status, as outlined here, is a necessary condition for its moving up alongside the dollar, but its actually doing so may have to await a serious policy relapse by the United States—or enough erosion of the U.S. external debt and deficit position to again raise severe concerns around the world, even if its internal economy is in relatively good shape, as in the mid-1980s.

The issue is thus whether the combination of (1) the creation of a new economic and trading unit roughly equal in size to the United States and (2) the rapid establishment of the credibility of its currency could overcome (3) the incumbency advantages and inertia that favor the dollar. I believe there is a significant possibility that it might do so, and that any serious consideration of the international policy implications of the euro must take that possibility into account.

[27]Cooper (1992, p. 519) refers to a "tipping point" as the development of the euro market accelerates and hits a level "at which international asset holders may wish to switch their assets into (euros) in large volume."

Pretransition Period

As noted, plans and expectations for the euro will increasingly affect the exchange markets during the pretransition period between now and the startup, presumably at the outset of 1999. I will not discuss the implications for exchange rates among the potential members, or between the "ins" and "outs," or vis-à-vis non-EU European countries (Norway and Switzerland), but rather concentrate on the likely implications for the dollar and the global system.

The chief consideration is the desire of the putative EMU membership to avoid a dilemma. On the one hand, most of them—certainly Germany—want a strong euro. On the other hand, at least some of them—including France—have argued (at least until very recently) that their currencies are overvalued against the dollar.[28] Some members of the latter group may even want a weak euro, as noted above. At a minimum, they would not want it to appreciate to any significant extent.

The only way to avoid the dilemma is to achieve a competitive depreciation of the European national currencies in the pretransition period. This would enable the EU, if permitted by the United States, to engineer an initial exchange rate below—well below?—the FEER for the euro. (It would also provide some immediate support for the Continental European economies, all of which are struggling with high unemployment and sluggish growth especially as they tighten fiscal policy in pursuit of the Maastricht criteria.) The euro could then appreciate in its early years without undermining the long-run competitive position of the European economy.[29]

The continued impressive growth of the American economy and the continued sluggishness of the Continent have provided persuasive, market-based reasons for dollar strength in the recent past. So has uncertainty about the start-up of the euro itself, with every new doubt about the fiscal rectitude and membership of EMU suggesting unfavorable comparisons with the deutsche mark. The European desire for depreciation of their currencies could be explained simply by a desire to help extricate themselves from their current economic woes by improved trade performance. And the Europeans could have driven their currencies down farther by more aggressive relaxation of monetary policy, which could have easily been justified in purely domestic terms.

[28]This view is extremely hard to square with the fact that the United States is running an external deficit of about $200 billion and is by far the world's largest debtor country. It is much more defensible with respect to the yen, since Japan is still running by far the world's largest surpluses and is by far the largest creditor country. See the section below on "Initial Exchange Rate."

[29]I assume that the initial external exchange rate of the euro will reflect a weighted average of the market exchange rates of the national currencies that participate at the outset just before the new currency is launched. The burgeoning literature on the *internal* conversion rates is reviewed and expanded in De Grauwe and Spaventa (1997).

Nevertheless, there is considerable evidence that prepositioning to avoid the euro dilemma has already been affecting the posture of European officials toward the exchange markets. The Bundesbank, despite its traditional support for a strong deutsche mark, has periodically joined the call for a "stronger dollar" despite the absence of any evidence (or even argument) that the dollar is undervalued. This jawboning, especially prior to the Group of Seven meeting in Berlin on February 8, helped propel the dollar in early 1997 to its highest levels against the deutsche mark and other European currencies since 1994.

In the two years remaining before the start-up of the euro, numerous changes in the economies and policies on both sides of the Atlantic will of course affect the exchange markets. It was suggested above that a new budget agreement in the United States could place significant downward pressure on the dollar (although it must be noted that the largest part of the actual budget correction is likely to be programmed toward the end of the adjustment period, around 2001–2002). A slowdown (or especially recession) in the U.S. economy could also lead to reduced U.S. interest rates and intensify that effect. Some pickup in Europe is likely and could produce upward pressure on its currencies before the initial exchange rate is established. The probability of some or all of these developments has intensified the desire of the European authorities to take advantage of the current environment, which has been bullish for the dollar and bearish for almost all their currencies, to promote a depreciation that will be sufficient to permit the euro to commence at an undervalued level even if some reversal occurs before its start-up.

A Note on the Yen

This analysis has so far largely ignored the yen. The reason is that we do not now have, nor are we ever likely to have under foreseeable developments, a tripolar monetary system in any meaningful sense of the term.

Japan's economy is about twice the size of Germany's and its trade is only slightly smaller, and it has an even better record of price stability over the past 15 years. Its currency plays a much smaller role than the deutsche mark (Table 2), however, suggesting a significant deficiency in its meeting the other key currency criteria—notably, the capabilities of its financial markets (Garber, 1996). Indeed, the role of the yen in denominating Japan's own export contracts has recently dropped to a 7-year low, from its peak of 43 percent in March 1993 to 35 percent in September 1996. As noted in the *Nihon Keizei Shinbun* of January 27, 1997, the Japanese Ministry of International Trade and Industry's (MITI) latest report on the topic concludes that "the yen is nowhere near achieving the status of a truly international currency."

In a world of two economic superpowers, a unified Europe along with the United States, Japan's weight relative to the other two will decline. Japan's continued failure to deregulate and modernize its capital and financial markets, despite the recent proposals of the Hashimoto government, is likely to remain a major barrier to such a role for the yen. Indeed, the continued fragility of Japan's financial sector—and the inability of its leadership to acknowledge, let alone resolve, that problem—is more likely to repel than attract international interest.

Japan is also still engulfed in a prolonged period of stagnation. Despite living in the world's fastest growing region, and despite a series of fiscal stimulus programs totaling $500 billion and near-zero interest rates, it has experienced very little growth for five years. Deep structural problems, focused on but going well beyond the financial system, are clearly involved.

Indeed, Japan may have missed the moment when it—and its currency—could play a substantial international role. Its leadership even within Asia is being challenged, most notably by China. Hong Kong and Singapore threaten to bypass it as a financial center. Serious deregulation and a revitalization of the Japanese economy cannot be ruled out but, on present readings, there is little reason to believe that the yen will play in the same league with the dollar and the euro.

Analogies with trade policy are again instructive. Many analysts, particularly in the 1980s and early 1990s but some still today, have hypothesized the emergence of a tripolar world economy with a triad of north-south regional groupings centered around Europe, Japan, and the United States. The logic has been much more compelling regarding trade than finance because Japan's status as a premier exporter and large surplus country has been far more extensive than its prowess on monetary matters.

It has turned out at least so far, however, that major trade groupings have developed around Europe (the EU itself, EuroMed, and the other association agreements) and the United States (NAFTA and the planned Free Trade Area of the Americas) but not around Japan. The only regional trading arrangements within Asia are the minor Australia–New Zealand and ASEAN free trade areas. The big regional arrangement in the area is the Asia-Pacific Economic Cooperation Council (APEC), which links Japan (and China, Korea and the rest of East Asia) across the Pacific with North America. A two-bloc world, within the global context of the World Trade Organization, may in fact be evolving in the trade area (Bergsten, 1996b) along the lines projected in this paper for the monetary arena.[30]

At the same time, the yen obviously cannot be ignored. It will probably continue to play a minor key currency role, perhaps maintaining (or even modestly increasing) its 10–15 percent market share. Japan may yield to China as

[30]Such a two-bloc outcome is far more desirable than a three-bloc world (Bergsten, 1990, and Krugman, 1991).

the world's third largest economy (behind the EU and United States) within the next decade or so but China will still be a poor nation without many of the other attributes of a key currency country. Moreover, Japan is likely to continue to be extremely competitive in world trade and to bolster its position as the world's largest creditor country. Japan will thus remain a junior partner in the management of the international monetary system that will need to be included in any new EU–U.S. arrangements.[31]

Implications for Policy Cooperation

The achievement of rough parity by the euro would convert an international monetary system that has been dominated by the dollar throughout the postwar period into a bipolar regime. Hence, the entire structure of international financial cooperation will change dramatically. This analysis suggests four major policy issues that should be addressed in this new context, in the Group of Seven and/or the IMF:

- the initial exchange rate between the euro and outside currencies, especially the dollar;
- the portfolio diversification into euros that could have major exchange rate consequences during the (possibly longish) transition period;
- management of exchange rates between the euro and the dollar (and the yen) in the eventual steady state, when fluctuations could be considerably greater than in the past due to the altered economic structure of Europe; and
- the international representation of Europe with the centralization of its monetary policy in the ECB.

Initial Exchange Rate

I have argued above that Europe has already been seeking, and will probably continue to seek, sufficient depreciation of its national currencies to justify a substantially undervalued start-up rate for the euro (relative to its FEER). The United States and the rest of the world should reject this strategy. It represents a blatant effort to achieve competitive depreciation, both to

[31]Ilzkovitz (1996) of the European Commission has made the novel argument that the euro is more likely to rival the dollar if the yen also asserts a larger role, on the grounds that the dollar would then be more likely to lose its scale and inertial advantages. The opposite is much more likely to be true: continued stagnation of the yen's international role will enable the euro to compete across a wider range of the globe, notably in the rapidly growing markets of Asia, than if the yen were more effectively involved as well.

help rescue Europe from its high unemployment and to enable the euro to become a "strong currency" without any substantial costs to the competitive position of the European countries.

France is running sizable trade and current account surpluses, even adjusting for its high level of unemployment. Germany is running the world's second largest trade surplus and is the world's second largest creditor country. The EU as a group has been in surplus for the past few years. By contrast, the United States is the world's largest debtor nation, with a net foreign debt in excess of $1 trillion that is rising annually by 15–20 percent. Its trade and current account deficits each approximated $185 billion in 1996 and will soar well above $200 billion in 1997. On these long-term fundamentals, it would be extremely difficult to make a case that the European currencies are overvalued and the dollar is undervalued.

Hence, the Group of Seven should, at a minimum, actively resist further dollar appreciation. Its statement at Berlin on February 8 endorsed such a view. The difficulty of course is that the short-run fundamentals strongly favor the dollar, and it would be highly undesirable to pursue the proposed currency strategy through higher interest rates in Europe or lower interest rates in the United States at this time. But the Group of Seven should "put its money where its mouth is," if and when tested by the markets, to demonstrate its seriousness in avoiding further deviation from the long-run fundamentals and thus major problems over the longer term.

Transition Period

The postulated portfolio diversification from (mainly) the dollar into the euro could have substantial effects on the exchange rate between the two. I have made ballpark guesstimates on the magnitude and timing of that impact but there is simply no way to predict either with any degree of confidence.

Moreover, other events during the (presumably longish—five to ten years?) transition period may substantially affect the outcome. For example, EMU enthusiasts believe that the forging of the monetary union will itself induce—perhaps force—European governments to seriously address their structural rigidities and thus enable them to restore more rapid and sustainable growth rates. By contrast, strict adherence to the Maastricht fiscal criteria and a tough follow-on stability pact could prolong Europe's current economic malaise.

Hence, it would be impossible to calculate FEERs for the euro, and perforce the other major currencies, that would emerge at the outset of the new steady state. It would therefore be a mistake to deploy target zones or any other predetermined mechanisms to attempt to limit dollar-euro fluctuations during the transition period (as proposed by Henning, 1997), extensive and volatile though those fluctuations may be. There would simply be no sound basis on which to base such ranges.[32]

On the other hand, markets could become extremely unstable because of the uncertainties surrounding the transition. It will thus be important for the Fund and the Group of Seven to monitor events closely, to attempt to form judgments as to the likely outcome as the process evolves, and to intervene to limit unnecessary volatility. In light of the uncertain level of rates in the eventual steady state, however, such intervention would have to be mainly of the traditional smoothing variety, rather than aimed at correcting disequilibria as under target zones or other more defined regimes.

It could also become desirable at some point, presumably during the transition period though perhaps even later, to negotiate off-market transactions, perhaps through a Substitution Account, to limit the market impact of central bank conversions of dollars if such conversions appeared likely to be large enough to destabilize markets (Kenen, 1995). If world reserves were to fall sharply as a result of rapid dollar depreciation, triggered by switches into euros, a new issuance of SDRs might be needed to fill the gap (Eichengreen and Frankel, 1996). Such devices should be considered if the hypothesized events were to eventuate.

Steady State

The more difficult, and ultimately much more important, question is whether a more structured exchange rate regime should be envisaged to manage the steady-state relationship that will eventually emerge between the dollar and the euro (and the yen). There is obviously no need to answer the question now. Nevertheless, it is instructive to begin thinking about it as the implied bipolar regime will suggest to many observers—including businesses planning their long-term investment strategies—that a sea change may occur in international monetary and thus economic relationships.

Theoretically, the availability of a more attractive alternative to the dollar could reduce the ability of the United States to finance its large external deficits and thereby force it either to adopt more internationally consistent policies or to accept greater dollar depreciation. The huge level of U.S. gross external liabilities (more than $4 trillion) and the array of alternative assets available to international investors are already sufficient today, however, to

[32]Target zone advocates such as myself and John Williamson have always acknowledged that the zones might need to be rebased, perhaps substantially, to accommodate major systemic shocks that had large and unpredictable effects on the underlying FEERs. As examples, we have cited the two oil shocks of the 1970s and German unification. The creation of the euro would clearly represent another such event, which would call for reassessing any target zones that already existed or for deferring their installation if—as is the case—they do not.

place considerable limits on the policy autonomy of the United States. Indeed, such constraints were already felt in Washington in the late 1970s—when it was still the world's largest creditor country—when a free fall of the dollar signaled the need to tighten monetary policy sharply and triggered the $30 billion "dollar support package" of October 1978. Similar pressures emerged in 1987, when the dollar began to fall too rapidly after the Plaza adjustment effort, forcing the United States to call a halt to its depreciation strategy and negotiate the Louvre Accord in an effort to stabilize rates. They were felt again in early 1995 when the dollar fell to record lows against the deutsche mark and the yen. The international adjustment process may not be too different for the United States in the new bipolar world from the way it is today.

The change is likely to be greater in the European case. The individual European countries already pay relatively little attention, at least in terms of policy reaction, to fluctuations in their currencies vis-à-vis the dollar and yen.[33] But external events will play a much smaller role in the larger, unified European economy. Hence, even larger and more frequent exchange rate changes can be accepted with equanimity.

From the European standpoint, the key implication is its enhanced ability—for better or worse—to resist external pressures to change internal economic policies and thus a reduced interest in international policy cooperation (Cooper, 1992, and Kenen, 1995). One result will be larger fluctuations and probably greater volatility between the two lead currencies. The EU may indeed promote greater currency movements to achieve external adjustment, as the United States has done on occasion in the past.

One of Europe's few motivations to take an interest in external monetary developments has been the problem caused for intra-European currency relationships by a weakening dollar: dollar depreciation strains the EMS by pushing the deutsche mark up against the weaker European currencies as well as itself.[34] This effect will of course disappear when the euro comes to encompass all EU currencies. Hence, creation of the euro will eliminate one of the EU's chief interests in international cooperation in managing exchange rates.

Nevertheless, there will be strong systemic reasons for the installation of new currency management arrangements between the EU and the United

[33]There has been little enthusiasm from most Europeans for any of the major currency initiatives adopted by the Group of Five or the Group of Seven in the past 12 years, including the Plaza and Louvre agreements as well as the more recent yen support program in 1995 and "dollar capping" statement of February 1997. France is a partial exception to this generalization, but even then primarily in the earlier 1985–87 episodes.

[34]Henning (1997) in fact hypothesizes that renewed dollar weakening in 1997–98 could jeopardize the startup of EMU. This adds to the European interest in keeping the dollar strong until EMU starts as developed in the text.

States (and Japan) once the euro has moved up alongside the dollar. The euro and the dollar will dominate world finance, but both Europe and the United States will be constantly tempted to practice "benign neglect." The likely result will be sharply increased volatility between their currencies and the omnipresent possibility of prolonged misalignments if the outcome is left solely to market forces. Both outcomes could be extremely destabilizing for other countries and the world economy as a whole.

Prolonged misalignment would also be costly for the EU and the United States themselves. The United States learned this lesson in the 1980s, when much of its manufacturing and agricultural sectors was severely victimized by acute dollar overvaluation. Though both Europe and the United States are less open to external events than most other economies, the share of international transactions in each is sufficiently large to provoke major distortions if sizable currency disequilibria are permitted to persist.

Such misalignments would also inevitably generate strong trade protectionism, as in the United States in the early 1980s when the "free trade" Reagan Administration was forced to impose import quotas on automobiles, machine tools, steel, and other sectors because of the dollar overvaluation generated by its own macroeconomic policies and its benign neglect of the currency. Given the pivotal responsibility of the EU and the United States for global trade policy, as noted above, any such relapses would be extremely harmful to the world economy. The case for a new currency stabilization arrangement will be very strong.

We cannot now calculate a credible FEER for the euro when it reaches its eventual steady state. There is good reason to believe, however, that we will be able to do so when that time arrives. Given the likely volatility that will otherwise ensue, and the prolonged misalignments that can result, there will be a strong case for negotiating and installing a target zone system at that time among the Group of Three: the EU, Japan, and the United States.[35]

The history of the yen-dollar exchange rate since the onset of floating in the early 1970s is instructive in this context. The United States and Japan have been the two largest economies and two of the three largest trading countries throughout this period, just as the United States and the EU will be the two largest economies and traders once European unification is completed. There are of course important structural differences between U.S.-Japan and U.S.-Europe trade and economic relations, such as the absence of huge imbalances and the much greater role of U.S. direct investment in Europe, which will probably persist in the future. There are also obvious political, security, and cultural differences between the two relationships.

[35]The details are presented most recently in Bergsten and Henning (1996).

It is nevertheless important to recall that the Japan–United States economic relationship has been plagued by large and volatile currency swings that have produced sustained misalignments. We are now in the fifth such cycle since the late 1960s. During each cycle, the dollar becomes substantially overvalued and the yen substantially undervalued. Large increases in both countries' external imbalances result. Protectionist pressures emerge in the United States (and in some other countries) that undermine the relationships between the countries and threaten the global trading system. The yen then appreciates precipitously, generating international financial instability and substantial adverse effects on the Japanese economy itself (as most recently in 1993 and 1995). Such results from these cycles occurred in 1971–73, 1978–79, 1985–87, and 1993–95.[36] The current depreciation of the yen to a level (125:1 at this writing) far below its FEER indicates that another such cycle is well under way.

It would have been highly desirable for the United States and Japan to have limited the extent of these problems by installing a target zone for their currencies, as they in fact did for a short time in late 1986 (as the precursor to the Louvre Accord that subsequently extended the arrangement to Europe).[37] Such a regime may commend itself to the two economic superpowers of the future as a means of avoiding prolonged misalignments that could otherwise disrupt their trade, monetary, and overall economic relations—with extremely adverse effects on world trade and finance as well.

Many Europeans believe that international policy cooperation and even coordination will be facilitated by EMU. Europe will then speak with a single voice, enabling it to interact more confidently with the United States and perhaps forcing the United States to adopt a more consistently cooperative stance. Indeed, some Europeans view this outcome as an important goal of EMU.[38]

The analogy with trade policy cited at the outset provides some support for this concept. The "multilateral trading system" has been essentially bipolar since the creation of the original Common Market, which has always spoken with a single voice on most trade matters. Most observers believe that this

---

[36]This history is traced in Bergsten and Noland (1993).

[37]These initiatives were short lived because they were undertaken before the dollar had completed its necessary depreciation after the massive overvaluation of the early and mid-1980s (Funabashi, 1988).

[38]Cooper (1992, p. 524) raises the intriguing possibility that the EMU could assume the "nth country role," played by the United States throughout the period of dollar dominance, and thus become the pivot currency for the entire system. This would be consistent with the sharp increase in Europe's ability to ignore external events, a key currency criterion as noted earlier, but could run counter to its resulting disinterest in international monetary cooperation as postulated here (and also by Cooper).

negotiating structure, despite producing prolonged stalemates, played an instrumental role in facilitating the eventual success of the three large postwar liberalization negotiations (the Kennedy Round in the 1960s, the Tokyo Round in the 1970s, and the Uruguay Round in the late 1980s–early 1990s). It has been on display again recently in forging the two most important liberalizing steps since the end of the Uruguay Round, the agreement in early 1997 on trade in telecommunications services, and the Information Technology Agreement on trade in high-technology goods.

The contrary view is that the most successful periods of international monetary history have been those of "hegemonic stability," dominated by a single power—the United Kingdom in the late nineteenth century and the United States in the first postwar generation. We have never experienced a successful monetary regime managed by a committee of (even two) relatively equal powers. Most historical efforts to achieve such cooperative leadership have in fact failed.

Several scenarios can be envisaged. The United States could react defensively to its loss of monetary dominance, seeking to create a formalized dollar area—perhaps based on the APEC (Asia-Pacific Economic Cooperation Forum) and FTAA (Free Trade Area of the Americas) that it has been promoting in the trade arena—as the United Kingdom created the sterling area in the 1930s. The EU could adopt a strategy of "benign neglect," arguing that the United States has done so repeatedly in the past and that its turn had now come. Conflict between the two poles could easily arise.

As with the economics, there is no a priori answer. It will be a major task of policy in both regions, however, to realize the promise of potential cooperation rather than falling into new patterns of conflict. The underlying strength and history of the North Atlantic relationship should bode well for a successful outcome but achieving it will clearly be a major policy challenge in the early twenty-first century.

Institutional Implications

The final question concerns the institutional implications of EMU and the ECB. Some are obvious but others are more complex. It seems axiomatic that the ECB will replace the individual European central banks in all forums where the latter are now represented. The Group of Ten in the BIS (which is really a Group of Eleven), for example, will become a Group of Five (the EU, United States, Japan, Canada, and Switzerland) if it continues to exist. The Governor of the ECB will be the counterpart of the Chairman of the Federal Reserve and of the Governor of the Bank of Japan in the meetings of Group of Seven finance ministers and central bank governors.

The more complex issues relate to those forums where the representatives of Europe must discuss, and even negotiate, issues that range beyond monetary policy. These include the Group of Seven, where finance ministers represent their governments, and the IMF, where Executive Directors are appointed by governments (and come from central banks in only a few cases).

The answer is presumably that the national European governments will continue to play their current roles until fiscal and other economic policies are consolidated à la monetary policy with the ECB. National and ECB representatives will thus participate together in forums that link monetary and broader economic policy, like the Group of Seven. There is an analogy with the current Group of Seven summits, where the President of the European Commission attends, along with the heads of state of four EU member governments, because of the Commission's competence for EU trade policy and some other issues. The arrangement is untidy but workable.

Conclusion

Whatever one thinks of the specific proposals made here, the major message is that all of the issues cited need to be thoroughly and consistently addressed by the leadership of the international economic and financial community as well as by the EU itself. The evolution of all these developments will have major impact on the United States, Japan, and the rest of the world. The benign neglect of the topics described in the second section is anomalous and needs to be promptly rectified. This conference should help point the way to such consultations in the near future, and thus enhances the prospects for managing the international implications of EMU in a constructive and cooperative manner.

When Giscard d'Estaing and Helmut Schmidt decided to create the EMS in 1978, one of their goals was to avoid the instabilities being generated at that time by the United States and the dollar—and thereby to foster a more effective international monetary system. The evolution of the EMS into EMU could bring that vision closer to reality, in large part because Europe has already demonstrated the feasibility and benefits of intensive international policy coordination.

In the absence of effective cooperation between the EU and the United States, however, the creation of the euro could create greater international instability. This would be a deeply ironic outcome in light of the goals of the original Giscard-Schmidt initiative and its contemporary successor. It is up to the governments of the two regions to achieve a smooth transition from the sterling- and dollar-dominated monetary regimes of the nineteenth and twentieth centuries to a stable bipolar system in the early twenty-first century, thereby strengthening rather than jeopardizing the foundations for global economic cooperation.

References

Alogoskoufis, George, and Richard Portes, 1992, "European Monetary Union and International Currencies in a Tripolar World," in *Establishing a Central Bank: Issues in Europe and Lessons from the U.S.*, ed. by Matthew B. Canzoneri, Vittorio Grilli, and Paul R. Masson (New York: Cambridge University Press), pp. 273–300.

Bayoumi, Tamim A., and Paul R. Masson, 1994, *Fiscal Flows in the United States and Canada: Lessons for Monetary Union in Europe,* CEPR Discussion Paper No. 1057 (London: Center for Economic Policy Research, November); also published in *European Economic Review*, Vol. 39 (February 1995), pp. 253–74.

Bergsten, C. Fred, 1996a, *Dilemmas of the Dollar: The Economics and Politics of United States International Monetary Policy*, (New York: M.E. Sharpe, 2nd ed.).

———, 1996b, "Globalizing Free Trade," *Foreign Affairs*, Vol. 75 (May–June), pp. 105–20.

———, 1990, "The World Economy After the Cold War," *Foreign Affairs*, Vol. 69 (Summer), pp. 96–112.

———, and C. Randall Henning, 1996, *Global Economic Leadership and the Group of Seven* (Washington: Institute for International Economics).

Bergsten, C. Fred, and Marcus Noland, 1993, *Reconcilable Differences? United States–Japan Economic Conflict* (Washington: Institute for International Economics).

Cooper, Richard N., 1992, "Will an EC Currency Harm Outsiders?" *Orbis*, Vol. 36 (Fall), pp. 517–31.

De Grauwe, Paul, and Luigi Spaventa, 1997, "Setting Conversion Rates for the Third Stage of EMU" (unpublished; Leuven: University of Leuven; London: CEPR; and Rome: University of Rome).

Delors Committee for the Study of Economic and Monetary Union, 1989, *Report* (Luxembourg: Office for Official Publications of the European Communities).

Eichengreen, Barry, and Jeffrey A. Frankel, 1996, "The SDR, Reserve Currencies, and the Future of the International Monetary System," in *The Future of the SDR in Light of Changes in the International Financial System*, ed. by Michael Mussa, James M. Boughton, and Peter Isard (Washington: International Monetary Fund), pp. 337–78.

Emerson, Michael, and others, 1992, *One Market, One Money: An Evaluation of the Potential Benefits and Costs of Forming an Economic and Monetary Union* (Oxford: Oxford University Press).

Frenkel, Jacob A., and Morris Goldstein, 1997, "The International Role of the Deutsche Mark" (unpublished; Washington: Institute for International Economics).

Funabashi, Yoichi, 1988, *Managing the Dollar: From the Plaza to the Louvre* (Washington: Institute for International Economics).

Garber, Peter M., 1996, "The Use of the Yen as a Reserve Currency," *Monetary and Economic Studies*, Vol. 14, pp. 1–21.

Gros, Daniel, and Niels Thygesen, 1992, *European Monetary Integration* (New York: St. Martin's Press).

Henning, C. Randall, 1997, *Cooperating with Europe's Monetary Union* (Washington: Institute for International Economics).

———, 1996, "Europe's Monetary Union and the United States," *Foreign Policy*, Vol. 102 (Spring), pp. 83–100.

Ilzkovitz, Fabienne, 1996, *Prospects for the Internationalization of the Euro*, DG-II doc. II/362/96-EN (Brussels: European Commission, June).

Kenen, Peter B., 1995, *Economic and Monetary Union in Europe: Moving Beyond Maastricht* (New York: Cambridge University Press).

———, 1997, "The Outlook for a Tripolar Monetary System," speech delivered at the Annual Convention of the Italian Forex Club, January.

Krugman, Paul, 1991, "The Move Toward Free Trade Zones," in *Policy Implications of Trade and Currency Zones: A Symposium Sponsored by the Federal Reserve Bank of Kansas City, Jackson Hole, Wyoming, August 22–24, 1991* (Kansas City, Missouri: Federal Reserve Bank of Kansas City).

Lamfalussy, Alexandre, "The Market Needs a Single Currency," *Newsweek* (European edition), February 3, 1997, p. 19.

Leahy, Michael P., 1996, "The Dollar as an Official Reserve Currency under EMU," *Open Economies Review*, Vol. 7 (October), pp. 371–90.

Marris, Stephen, 1987, *Deficits and the Dollar: The World Economy at Risk* (Washington: Institute for International Economics, 2nd ed.).

McCauley, Robert, 1997, "The Euro and the Dollar," BIS Working Paper (Basel: BIS).

Thygesen, Niels, 1995, *International Currency Composition and the Future Role of the European Currency, Final Report of the Working Group: European Monetary Union—International Monetary System* (London: Kluwer Law International).

Comments on Bergsten

Barry Eichengreen

This paper is vintage Bergsten. It tackles an important issue in a clear and reasoned way. It reaches striking and provocative conclusions. It drives home the implications for policy. On the vast majority of issues I am in agreement with the author. In the long run, there is at least the possibility that the euro may rival the U.S. dollar as an international currency. In the short run, however, EMU may diminish the scope for the international coordination of policies. And it will pose a challenge to the institutions of international monetary cooperation, including the IMF.

Since Bergsten has ably summarized his paper, I will focus on our relatively few areas of disagreement. These are two.

- First, I think Bergsten overstates the threat the euro poses to the dollar's reserve-currency role. To the extent that the euro gains importance as a reserve currency, those gains will come mainly at the expense of "subsidiary" reserve currencies like the French franc and the Swiss franc, and not the U.S. dollar, except in the unlikely event that the U.S. authorities seriously mismanage their currency and their economy.
- Second, Bergsten if anything understates the threat that EMU poses for international monetary cooperation. Cooperation requires surmounting serious coordination and collective-action problems, something that can be done by constructing institutions to monitor the adherence of the participants to the terms of their agreement to cooperate. EMU will necessarily disrupt the operation of those institutions, and too little has been done to date to adapt them to the coming of a single European currency.

The Euro and the Dollar as International Currencies

Bergsten argues, you will recall, that the euro is likely to rival the dollar as a reserve currency relatively soon after the beginning of Stage III. In the introduction to his paper, Bergsten asserts that the gap between the shares of inter-

For help with data and advice the author thanks Benjamin Cohen and María Soledad Martínez Peria.

national financial assets accounted for by the dollar and European countries could disappear after five or ten years, the end point being "perhaps . . . a position of about 40 percent each for the dollar and the euro, with about 20 percent remaining for the yen and a few minor currencies." This contrasts with the current situation, in which the deutsche mark only accounts for perhaps 15 percent of international financial assets and 16 percent of official foreign exchange reserves, and the U.S. dollar accounts for 38 and 56 percent, repectively.[1]

The basis for Bergsten's argument is that the more dominant a country is economically, the greater the utility of its currency in international transactions. The EU accounts for larger shares of world trade and output than the United States; from this it follows that the euro will ultimately play at least as large a role as the dollar in international reserves and international financial transactions.

This argument allows no role for other determinants—notably history—of reserve-currency status. Bergsten acknowledges that history is an important determinant of reserve-currency status, citing the pound sterling, whose position as the world's second leading reserve currency after World War II can only be understood as a legacy of its prior reserve currency status, acquired in the age when Britain was the world's leading industrial power, financial center, and trading nation. If history is important, Bergsten's rule of thumb may hold only in the very, very long run.[2] And the historical relationship between key country size and reserve-currency status, based on the modest trends of the last three decades, may not be an accurate guide to the consequences of a radical, discontinuous event like EMU.

In advancing these criticisms I am in a peculiar position, of course, since Bergsten bases his forecasts on some back-of-the-envelope calculations Jeffrey Frankel and I did for an IMF conference on the future of the international monetary system a year ago (see Eichengreen and Frankel, 1996). Using time series for the dollar's share of global reserves over the last 25 years, we estimated that a 1 percentage point rise in a key country's share of world product (measured at purchasing power parities) was associated with a 1.33 percentage point rise in its currency's share of central bank reserve holdings. Besides the fact that we constructed these estimates only for official holdings, not private markets (as acknowledged in Bergsten's paper), there is the problem that we constructed them for an environment characterized by small changes in key countries' respective shares of global GDP and did not intend them to apply to a radical, discontinuous change like EMU.[3]

[1]The 38 percent figure comes from Bergsten's Table 2. The 56 percent comes from the IMF's *Annual Report;* the Fund's figures seem to differ significantly from those reported by Bergsten in his table.

[2]Much longer than what he refers to on p. 40 as a 5- to 10-year transitional period.

[3]As Henning (1997) puts it, "models of past behavior are not good models of future behavior because the formation of EMU represents a quantum change." See also Leahy (1996).

To get at this question, one would want a model with roles for both economic size and historical inertia. I have therefore reestimated the Eichengreen-Frankel model adding lagged reserve shares as a measure of historical inheritance.[4] I included the shares of the key currency countries in both global GDP and global exports. I think of the export variable as capturing the incentive to hold the currency of a trading partner, and the GDP variable as capturing the residual effects of having large financial markets.[5]

While the new results are consistent with the earlier ones, the impact effects are smaller: the impact effect of raising a key-currency country's share of global GDP is two-thirds as large as before.[6] For the yen, the long-run effect is the same as the short-run effect; there is no evidence of network externalities or, in other words, that the currency's history gives it a key-currency advantage. There is modest evidence to this effect for Germany.[7] For the dollar, the evidence of historical inertia is striking: the short-run effect of changes in U.S. GDP is only one-tenth as large as the long-run effect.[8]

This means that whether or not the euro comes to rival the dollar depends on whether the proper way of thinking about EMU is as simply replacing Germany and the deutsche mark with a larger European trade and monetary bloc (say, as the sum of the 15 EU member states), with no necessary decline in U.S. shares of world trade and GDP. If so, the share of international reserves denominated in dollars will remain above 50 percent for a very long time to come, the hold of network externalities and historical inertia being strong.

---

[4]Data on reserves are taken from the IMF's *Annual Reports* and, prior to 1978, from Heller and Knight (1978). Data on GDP are from the Penn World Tables, those on trade from the World Bank's World Tables. I estimated the model using Liviatan's method, instrumenting the lagged dependent variable. Intuitively, instrumenting leaves only the predicted, or systematic, component of lagged reserves and lends plausibility to the assumption that the lagged value is capturing historical inertia and not simply persistent random effects. Since the instrumental variables are uncorrelated in the probability limit with the disturbance, substituting the instrumented value will yield consistent estimates. The obvious instruments, given the model, are lagged trade and output shares.

[5]I estimate the equations for the United States, Germany, and Japan simultaneously, constraining the GDP and export share elasticities to be identical across countries. This constraint is not rejected by the data at the 95 percent confidence level.

[6]Increasing a key-currency country's share of global GDP (measured at purchasing power parities) by 1 percentage point immediately raises the share of its currency in global reserves by $\frac{9}{10}$ of a percentage point, not by $1\frac{1}{3}$ of a percentage point, as before.

[7]Where the long-run effect is half again as large as the short-run effect.

[8]The same multiplier applies, of course, to changes in U.S. trade shares.

The increase in euro-denominated reserves relative to deutsche mark–denominated reserves will come mainly at the expense of other EU currencies like the French franc and so-called minor currencies like the Swiss franc.[9]

This is my best guess of what will happen: if the euro's share of international reserves is half as large again as the deutsche mark's present share (Bergsten's lower-bound estimate), then that increase will come almost entirely at the expense of EU currencies; if it rises by 100 percent (Bergsten's upper-bound estimate), then that increase will also come at the expense of the Swiss franc and other minor reserve currencies. And whether the euro's share rises to 24 or 30 percent, depending on which of these scenarios one prefers, it will continue to be dwarfed by the dollar, which will still account for the majority of global reserves.[10]

If Europe's growth is greatly stimulated by EMU, as anticipated in the Emerson Report, and the increase in Europe's shares of global trade and GDP comes at the expense of U.S. shares, then the network externalities to which the dollar owes its dominance will be eroded. The long-run effect would be more like Bergsten forecasts. Conversely, if EMU inaugurates a period of stagnation in Europe, as EMU's critics fear, Bergsten will have greatly overestimated the impact of the euro on the international role of the dollar. My point is that one cannot forecast the international role of the euro simply by replacing a Germany that accounts for 9 percent of world output with an EU that accounts for 31 percent. The international role of the euro will hinge critically

[9]This appears to be the case that is relevant to competition between the dollar, deutsche mark, and yen over the last decades. For example, there is no evidence that the increasing shares of Japan and Germany in global GDP have had a negative impact on the share of international reserves denominated in dollars; when added to the equation for the share of dollar-denominated reserves, both German and Japanese GDP shares enter with coefficients of essentially zero. Citing Kenen (1995), Bergsten warns that it is inappropriate to compare the EU and the euro in Stage III with the EU and its 14 central banks in Stage II, since not all 14 of those currencies satisfy the conditions for key-currency status. My point is that this comparison may in fact be relevant when the question posed is whether the tendency of extra-European central banks to expand their holdings of euros relative to their present holdings of deutsche marks will come at the expense of the dollar or not.

[10]Bénassy-Quéré, Italianer, and Pisani-Ferry (1994) reach similar conclusions. Unlike in this comment, they also consider the international demand for currencies arising from sources other than central banks. But their conclusions for private transactions run along similar lines: they argue that private transactions-derived demands for euros may well be smaller than existing demands for European currencies on the basis of Bourguinat's square-root law—that transactions balances in a currency are proportional to the square root of transactions carried out with the issuing jurisdiction. See Bourguinat (1992).

on the economic vitality, or lack thereof, of the euro zone, and the economic vitality of the United States.[11]

The historical process by which the dollar acquired its reserve currency status in the first place is consistent with this view. By World War I, the United States had significantly surpassed the United Kingdom in terms of sheer economic size. But sterling, the beneficiary of historically conferred network externalities, continued to dominate it as a reserve currency. Only the major shock of World War I (during which British trade and lending were disrupted and the country was forced to sell off many of its foreign assets) and economic mismanagement in the 1920s (a persistent macroeconomic slump caused by currency overvaluation, creeping protectionism, and the imposition of a variety of open and covert capital controls) allowed it to be surpassed by the dollar. Similarly, the most dramatic decline to date in the dollar's share of international currency reserves took place in the second half of the 1970s, a period of inflation and unemployment when the U.S. economy was on the ropes. Thus, for the euro to come to rival or surpass the dollar, not just healthy growth in Europe but economic mismanagement by an erratic Federal Reserve and a protectionist U.S. president would be required—something that hardly seems likely.

Let me suggest two more reasons why the transition to a world in which the euro rivals the dollar as a reserve currency will be slow (if we get there at all). First, the starting point will be less favorable for the euro than suggested by current statistics. With monetary unification, those who hold currencies for trade- and balance-of-payments-related reasons will no longer have a reason to regard trade and payments within the euro zone as relevant to their calculations. The share of the dollar in world trade and payments will rise automatically from 48 percent to 55–60 percent.[12] The share of euros in international reserves will decline with the advent of Stage III. The Bundesbank's French franc reserves and the Bank of France's deutsche marks will no longer

[11]It will also hinge on the monetary policies pursued by the ECB. I am in full agreement with Bergsten's conclusion that it will pursue policies consistent with price stability. While heavily indebted countries might press for it to keep interest rates down in order to limit their debt-servicing costs, I believe that the statutory independence of the members of its Governing Board, the priority its statute attaches to price stability, and the fact that Germany still possesses an exit option (however costly the latter would be to exercise) will all be conducive to price stability. Low inflation will be consistent with a strong euro. This is in contrast to the present Stage II situation, in which European central banks are happy to see their currencies decline against the dollar. Here again I am in full agreement with Bergsten (see Eichengreen, 1996). But I am not as convinced as Bergsten that this strategy is ill advised, given the relative macroeconomic condition of the U.S. and European economies.

[12]Depending on precisely what transactions are counted and what one assumes about the composition of the monetary union. See Hartmann (1996).

count as reserves. The European System of Central Banks (ESCB) will find itself holding proportionately more dollars at the start of Stage III than it did at the end of Stage II. It will not be unhappy about this, since there will be no intra-euro-zone foreign exchange market intervention.[13] While the author acknowledges this in a footnote to Table 2, this point becomes critical once one recognizes the importance of historical inertia.

Second, the prospects for the reserve currencies will depend on where economic growth (and the demand for reserves) is concentrated, leaving aside the key-currency countries themselves. One view is that Asia will continue to grow exceptionally fast. China and the South Asian countries are not only fast growers but also have voracious appetites for reserves. Their demands will grow even more quickly if they seek to operate some kind of joint basket peg, as one influential economist has recently proposed.[14] But they trade much more extensively with the United States and Japan than with the EU, which is less open to imports from the newly industrialized countries. If output, trade, and the demand for reserves keep growing fastest in Asia—a forecast that has of course been disputed—this bodes well for the reserve-currency status of the dollar and the yen and poorly for the euro.[15] Rapid growth in Eastern Europe works in the opposite direction, of course, but only so long as the countries of that region remain outside the EU and its monetary union.[16]

---

[13]The extent of the change is hard to forecast. Estimates by Bénassy-Quéré, Italianer, and Pisani-Ferry (1994) for 1992 run as follows. If the EU wishes to maintain its traditional ratio of reserves to imports, it would be able to liquidate about one-third of its reserves when Stage III begins. The vast majority of this liquidation (say, 80 percent) would occur automatically, as reserves denominated in the currencies of EMU members were converted into internal credits of the ESCB. Thus, the initial decline in reserves held in European currencies *in Europe* would far outstrip any reduction in the ECB's holdings of extra-European currencies. If the ECB further reduced its reserves to the lower level in relation to trade that is typical in the United States (European central banks having traditionally held higher levels of reserves to finance EMS interventions), then the differential would shrink but not be eliminated. (Bénassy-Quéré, Italianer, and Pisani-Ferry estimate that more than two-thirds of the consequent liquidation of reserves would take the form of the conversion of reserves of European currencies into internal credits.) A more recent study by Goldman Sachs (1996) assumes that only the so-called BAFFLING countries (Belgium, Austria, Finland, France, Luxembourg, Ireland, the Netherlands, and Germany) are founding members of the monetary union, and reaches broadly similar conclusions.

[14]Williamson, 1996.

[15]In fact, the Asian economies have been gradually diversifying the currency composition of their reserve portfolios. But there is still good reason to think that so long as they continue to trade disproportionately with the United States they will be inclined to hold disproportionate shares of dollar reserves. See also Bénassy-Quéré (1996).

[16]And at the 1994 Copenhagen Summit, the members of the EU of course committed to admit the more advanced Eastern European countries in the early twenty-first century.

International Monetary Cooperation, Target Zones, and the IMF

Here I again find myself in broad agreement with Bergsten. While I obviously think that there is less need for a Substitution Account to mop up excess dollar reserves, setting one up could not hurt. I am even less optimistic than Bergsten about the prospects for transatlantic monetary cooperation in the early years of Stage III. The ECB will have to prove that it is credibly committed to the pursuit of price stability; it will be reluctant to give primacy to other objectives like exchange rate stabilization for fear that this will be interpreted as taking its eye off the ball.[17] The EU will become more of a large, closed monetary area like the United States; the theory of optimum currency areas suggests that it will be precisely the kind of economy inclined to follow policies of benign neglect toward its exchange rate.[18]

I share Bergsten's skepticism that the early years of Stage III are a good time to set up a global system of target zones. The structure of the European economy—both real and financial—will be transformed. This will make fundamental real exchange rates exceptionally difficult to estimate and exchange rate flexibility especially valuable.[19]

I do not share Bergsten's optimism that with the advent of Stage III the Group of Seven will collapse into a Group of Three.[20] In my estimation, the ECB will not represent Britain and Italy at the outset, but it will represent Finland, Austria, Ireland, and the Benelux countries, none of which are Group of

[17]The counterargument is that its constituencies will regard the exchange rate as a leading indicator of inflationary trends and that this will give it an incentive to target the currency. Insofar as the future euro zone resembles the United States in terms of economic size and degree of openness, I think that this is no more likely to be true of Europe in Stage III than it presently is of the United States.

[18]There is an additional concern. Traditionally, agreements for concerted intervention, like the Plaza Agreement and Louvre Accord, have required not just monetary but also fiscal adjustments (or at least promises of fiscal adjustments); these may be harder for European countries to offer if they are bound by the straitjacket of the Maastricht Treaty and the Stability and Growth Pact. On balance I do not find this worry compelling, because I doubt that these agreements will be strictly enforced, for what are ultimately political reasons.

[19]This appears to be something of a shift, which I find congenial, from the position in Bergsten (1994), where the author called for the establishment of target zones as soon as possible. I would go further, on the basis of arguments that space prevents me from elaborating on here, and argue that the inevitability of high capital mobility, in conjunction with the inevitable politicization of monetary policy, makes target zones unlikely to be feasible in the long run as well. The only feasible options will be relatively freely floating exchange rates between the euro and the dollar and a transatlantic monetary union. And for obvious political reasons the latter is pie in the sky. See Eichengreen (1994) for an extended version of this argument.

[20]An argument made previously in Bergsten and Henning (1996).

Seven members.[21] While countries outside the monetary union will be subject to the Maastricht Treaty's Excessive Deficit Procedure and the Mutual Surveillance Procedure (under which EU macroeconomic policies are to be coordinated), it is too strong to assume that the EU will control their fiscal policies; it is worth observing that the Mutual Surveillance Procedure is already operating in Stage II, and policy coordination is hardly close. For all these reasons, Group of Seven consultations will become more complicated, not less.

So will Article IV consultations by the IMF, since responsibility for monetary policy will not lie with EMU member states, but responsibility for fiscal policy still will. Consultations with individual member states will have to be harmonized and coordinated with Article IV consultations with the EU itself. The Fund passes judgment on the policy mix in the CFA countries of West and Central Africa even though they share common central banks and do not control their own monetary policies. While it consults periodically with the two regional central banks, these discussions are not reflected in reports to the IMF Executive Board, according to Polak (this volume). While the CFA franc zone does not loom large relative to the international system, the euro zone will. More systematic arrangements are therefore called for.

Now that the topic of the Fund has come up, it is worth noting that Stage III is a good opportunity to revise IMF quotas and voting rights. These are loosely based, as you know, on the magnitude of countries' international trade and financial transactions. In Stage III, intra-EU trade and payments (precisely, trade and payment among members of the monetary union) should not count any more than trade and payments among the 50 U.S. states.[22] This provides a welcome and overdue occasion to increase the voting rights of Japan and other countries whose reserves and international transactions have grown rapidly.

Conclusion

In summary, I cannot do better than to echo Bergsten's conclusion, "Whatever one thinks of the specific proposals made here, the major message is that

[21]While the President of the European Commission and the head of government or finance minister of the country holding the presidency of the Council of Ministers regularly attend Group of Seven summits, they do not yet play the formal role required of full participants in coordination exercises. And in the case of exchange rate policy, both the Council of Ministers and the ECB will want a voice, and the weights attached to their opinions will vary (according to the Maastricht Treaty) depending on whether the issue is concerted intervention (in which case the Council proposes but the ECB disposes) or a formal target zone system (in which case the Council ostensibly has the last word).

[22]The reason being that the member states of a European monetary union cannot experience balance of payments problems vis-à-vis one another any more than can the 50 states that comprise the U.S. monetary union.

all of the issues cited need to be thoroughly and consistently addressed by the leadership of the international economic and financial community as well as by the EU itself."

References

Bénassy-Quéré, Agnès, 1996, "Potentialities and Opportunities of the Euro as an International Currency," CEPII Working Paper No. 96-09 (Paris: Centre d'Etudes Prospectives et d'Informations Internationales, August).

———, Alexander Italianer, and Jean Pisani-Ferry, 1994, "The External Implications of the Single Currency," *Économie et Statistique* (special issue), pp. 9–22.

Bergsten, C. Fred, 1994, "Managing the World Economy of the Future," in *Managing the World Economy: Fifty Years After Bretton Woods*, ed. by Peter B. Kenen (Washington: Institute for International Economics), pp. 341–74.

———, and C. Randall Henning, 1996, *Global Economic Leadership and the Group of Seven* (Washington: Institute for International Economics).

Bourguinat, Henri, 1992, *Finance Internationale* (Paris: Presses Universitaires de France).

Eichengreen, Barry, 1994, *International Monetary Arrangements for the 21st Century* (Washington: Brookings Institution).

———, 1996, "Sensible EMU: How to Avoid a Maastricht Catastrophe," *International Economy*, Vol. 10 (May/June), pp. 16–19.

———, and Jeffrey A. Frankel, 1996, "The SDR, Reserve Currencies, and the Future of the International Monetary System," in *The Future of the SDR in Light of Changes in the International Financial System*, ed. by Michael Mussa, James M. Boughton, and Peter Isard (Washington: International Monetary Fund), pp. 337–78.

Goldman Sachs, 1996, "EMU's Excess Foreign Reserves," *EMU Briefing*, 6 (London: Goldman Sachs).

Hartmann, Philipp, 1996, "The Future of the Euro as an International Currency: A Transactions Perspective," LSE Financial Markets Group Special Paper No. 91 (London: London School of Economics, November).

Heller, H. Robert, and Malcolm D. Knight, 1978, *Reserve-Currency Preferences of Central Banks*, Princeton Essays in International Finance, No. 131 (Princeton, New Jersey: Princeton University, Department of Economics, International Finance Section, December).

Henning, C. Randall, 1997, "The Global Impact of Economic and Monetary Union" (unpublished; Washington: American University).

Kenen, Peter B., 1995, *Economic and Monetary Union in Europe: Moving Beyond Maastricht* (Cambridge: Cambridge University Press).

Leahy, Michael P., 1996, "The Dollar as an Official Reserve Currency Under EMU," *Open Economies Review*, Vol. 7 (October), pp. 371–90.

Williamson, John, 1996, "The Case for a Common Basket Peg for East Asian Countries" (unpublished; Washington: Institute for International Economics).

3

The Euro, the Dollar, and the International Monetary System

George Alogoskoufis and Richard Portes

The Maastricht Treaty seems to have locked the EU countries into a process that is likely to lead their economies to full monetary unification by the year 2002. Following the decisions taken at the Madrid European Council in December 1995, the main uncertainties have now been dispelled. An agreement was reached then on the name of the single currency, to be called the euro, and the timetable for its introduction was set.

In spring 1998, the European Council will name the first group of EU countries to take part in EMU, that is, those member countries that meet the convergence criteria laid down in the treaty. The ECB will be established no later than July 1, 1998. On January 1, 1999, EMU will effectively start, with the rates of conversion between the euro and the participating currencies being fixed irrevocably. The ECB, in conjunction with the participating national central banks, will start using euros for its monetary policy operations, and new issues of tradable public debt will be denominated in euros. Most participating countries are likely to redenominate outstanding stocks of public debt from January 1, 1999. Banks and firms in the EU will have the option of operating in euros. In the first half of 2002, the national currencies of participating countries will be substituted by new notes and coins denominated in euros. The final changeover to the single currency will thus be completed by July 1, 2002, at the latest. All EU countries appear committed to the final goal, with the possible exception of Britain, although some of them may take longer to fulfill the criteria laid out in the Maastricht Treaty.

Many operational uncertainties remain (Portes, 1996), and there are still potential blocks—more political than economic—associated with the "con-

The authors are grateful to Hélène Rey, our discussants Barry Eichengreen and Masahiro Kawai, as well as Tom Krueger and Bart Turtelboom for helpful comments. The comments of participants in the seminar were also useful.

vergence criteria." Nevertheless, it is reasonable to assume that a major new international currency will emerge from January 1, 1999. We shall go even further and assume that not too long after that, the euro area will cover the entire existing EU, although it will take longer to bring in the countries expected to join the EU from 2002–2003 onward. We assume also that the ECB will quickly establish its credibility and reputation, and our arguments are based on the presumption of a "neutral" monetary policy relative to the initial (pre-euro) position.

EMU and the introduction of the euro are bound to have important international implications. The new currency will be issued on behalf of a large economic area, by a new central bank that will be responsible for the joint monetary policy of the EU. International institutions such as the Group of Seven industrial countries, the IMF, and the OECD will have to adapt (see Alogoskoufis and Portes, 1991), but, most important, there will be a major shock to the existing international monetary and exchange rate system. Within a time frame that is difficult to specify, the euro will emerge as a serious challenger for the role of the U.S. dollar as the dominant international means of payment, unit of account, and store of value. The monetary policies of the new ECB will have far more important international spillovers than those of any of the existing central banks of the EU countries. The extent of these spillovers is likely to affect the process of international policy coordination and the exchange rate regime of all the main industrial economies.

In this paper we examine the prospective implications of the creation of the euro for the international monetary system. We confine our attention to the implications after the year 1999, when, according to the timetable agreed upon in the 1995 Madrid summit of the EU, the euro will be introduced in asset markets. Part of our discussion is more relevant for the period after 2002, when the existing EU currencies will have been replaced by the single currency.

We concentrate on two main issues: first, on the prospective role of the euro as an international means of payment, unit of account, and store of value, and the process through which these roles develop; and second, on the prospective changes that EMU will imply for the exchange rate between the dollar and the euro, both in the short and in the long run.

We suggest that the introduction of the euro in financial markets in 1999 is likely to upset the role of the dollar as the major international currency. Following an initial period of consolidation after the introduction of the euro in financial markets, we anticipate strong demand to use the euro as an international store of value, unit of account, and means of payment. Thickness externalities in the use of the euro as a means of payment, together with integration of the East European countries into the EU, as well as the development of euro financial markets, will be major medium- to long-term influences. Because of inertia and hysteresis, however, the dollar will remain quantitatively dominant for some time. With the possibility of multiple equilibria and threshold effects, we would not expect a quick transition to a new equilibrium. But the early period could see considerable instability associated with the emergence of the euro.

Early on, the main effect of the introduction of the euro will come through portfolio shifts that are likely to favor a sharp appreciation of the new currency vis-à-vis the dollar (and the yen). As euro securities markets become deeper and more liquid, and transactions costs fall, euro assets will become more attractive and the use of the euro as a vehicle currency will expand.

Because of the sluggish response of trade flows, the current account surplus of the EU will widen, and the initial appreciation will overshoot the long-run equilibrium exchange rate of the euro. This will be followed by a gradual depreciation, with interest rates falling. After the initial J-curve effects have worked through, the current account of the EU will worsen. The EU will become a net capital importer. This process of importing capital will help expand the international use of the euro as an international means of payment and as a store of value. The synergy between these two roles will further enhance the international significance of the euro. Finally, if the euro does challenge the dollar's hegemony, this is likely to be a cause of instability in the international monetary system, which appropriate policy coordination could mitigate.

International Role of the Euro

Like national currencies, international currencies have three major roles. They serve as means of international payment, as units of account, and as stores of value. There is one major difference between national and international currencies. Within national borders, the sole use of one currency is usually imposed by government fiat. Thus, the question of which characteristics make one currency more in demand than another does not usually arise, since normally market participants have little option but to use the currency designated by the government and supplied by an agency such as the national central bank. It is only in exceptional circumstances, such as very rapid inflation, that national currencies are replaced in one or more of their functions by other currencies or commodities.

In the international economy, demand factors play a much more important role in the determination of which currencies are being used. Since there is no supranational authority that can impose the use of a single currency, these issues are decided in the marketplace, by the behavior of public and private agents of all countries. Because of economies of scale in the use of currencies, the externalities involved, and the considerable degree of uncertainty and asymmetric information, there is no guarantee that the world will end up with the best monetary system, let alone a single international currency. In addition, there is the possibility of ***multiple equilibria*** and hence considerable *instability*, as the expectations and beliefs of agents are among the major factors that will determine which equilibrium will prevail.[1]

History teaches us that many of the institutions and modes of behavior from previous regimes do not change overnight, or do not change at all. There has been considerable continuity in the international monetary system, even after the breakdown of coordination and major changes in regime, following shocks to the fundamentals or the preferences of governments.[2] And in a world with many equilibria, history and institutions also play a key role in determining which equilibrium will prevail or in determining the transition path from one equilibrium to another.

EMU can be seen as an important change in the fundamentals of the international monetary system. A subset of countries have decided to coordinate on the use of a single currency. The remainder of this section is concerned with the implications of this decision for the currencies that are used as international means of payment, units of account, and stores of value.

Means of Payment Function

Let us start with the means of payment function of international currencies. Many seem to think that this function is the most important. For example, according to Cohen (1971, 25–6):

> An international economy with only national moneys is like a barter economy. . . . Transactions costs are high because of the practical problem of achieving the required double coincidence of wants in the foreign-exchange market. However, as in a barter economy, transactions costs can be substantially diminished for an individual if he adapts his own currency mix to that of other individuals, holding for specific use as international exchange intermediaries inventories of the most widely demanded foreign currencies. These are of course the currencies of the countries that

[1]There is a theoretical literature investigating the emergence of media of exchange when there are more than two traders, such as Jones (1976) and Kiyotaki and Wright (1989). The "random matching" models typically assume the indivisibility of money and have no real supply side, so it is hard to use them for open economies and a world of more than one money. Matsuyama, Kiyotaki, and Matsui (1993) do so, but focusing only on currency substitution and with only two countries, so there can be no indirect exchange, nor any vehicle currency. Recently, however, Rey (1997) has modeled the emergence of vehicle currencies in relation to the pattern of trade in goods and financial assets, with a central role for the "thick market externalities" that we believe underlie the evolution of international money. In her model as well as in the earlier literature, multiple equilibria are an essential feature.

[2]See Yeager (1976) for a comprehensive history of the international monetary system since the nineteenth century. Kindleberger (1984) provides a history focused on Western Europe.

are predominant in world trade—the countries that account for the largest proportion of international transactions (pp. 25–26).

To assess the potential role of the euro we must look to demand for means of international payment by official bodies and by the private sector.

We begin with the demand by official bodies. As Krugman (1984) among others suggests, "Probably the most important reason for holding reserves in dollars is that the dollar is an intervention currency" (p. 273). Data on the composition of official international reserves suggest that the share of the U.S. dollar in official reserves, although declining, is overwhelmingly higher than the share of any other single currency.[3] In fact it is still higher than the combined share of all the other currencies taken together. From 76.1 percent of total official currency reserves in 1973, the share of the U.S. dollar fell to 63.3 percent in 1994. The share of major European currencies shows a steady increase, and has risen from 14.3 percent in 1973 to 21.9 percent in 1994. The share of the deutsche mark has risen from 7.1 percent in 1973 to 15.5 percent in 1994. The most impressive rise has been that of the Japanese yen, which rose from almost zero in 1973 to 8.5 percent of the total in 1994. Despite significant efforts (e.g., Dooley, Lizondo, and Mathieson, 1989), we do not have a satisfactory empirical account of the determinants of reserve-holding behavior and these observed trends.

The trend decline in the share of dollar reserves in the portfolios of central banks is likely to be reinforced as a result of the process of EMU. The reduced need for exchange market intervention in dollars by EU central banks that will follow establishment of EMU will entail a significant decline in the use of the dollar as an international means of payment by official bodies (see the evidence in Frenkel and Sondergaard, 1996). But this will not necessarily make the euro a major reserve currency outside the EU, unless foreign exchange intervention by non-EC countries is also in euros. The euro will substitute for the dollar in the portfolios of EU central banks that do not participate in the final stage of EMU, or in the portfolios of non-EU central banks that decide to peg their exchange rate to the euro. These may in due course include, for example, the central banks of the economies of Central and Eastern Europe. On the other hand, there will be a one-off, "arithmetic" reduction in nondollar reserve holdings when European currencies going into the euro that are held by European central banks become converted into euros—and hence are no longer international reserves.

Additional demand could arise if the European Bank for Reconstruction and Development (EBRD) were to conduct a large part of its borrowing and

[3]See Alogoskoufis and Portes (1991, 1992), Bénassy-Quéré (1996), Frenkel and Sondergaard (1996), Ilzkovitz (1996), and Tavlas (1991).

lending in euros rather than dollars or yen. Such a preference toward the euro on the part of the EBRD would of course cause an even higher increase in the demand for euro reserves by the central banks of the Central and Eastern European economies.[4]

We next turn to the means of payment function of international money as it applies to the private sector. Note that whereas international transactions in goods markets are arranged between importers and exporters, eventual payment is intermediated through commercial banks. Thus, what one should look for are the "thickness" externalities that cause dealers to prefer indirect exchange, through a vehicle currency, over direct exchange of one currency for another. These externalities have to do with transactions costs that become lower as the users of currencies increase. Such network externalities are very important in monetary transactions. If there are many dealers prepared to exchange dollars (the dollar market is "thick"), then a dealer wishing to exchange pesetas for drachmas finds it less costly to go through two exchanges, one of pesetas for dollars and one of dollars for drachmas, than to go through a direct exchange of drachmas for pesetas. However, even when this is not the case, a vehicle currency is still often used to finance bilateral trade imbalances (Krugman, 1980).

The market for euros will be thicker than the market for any of the existing EU currencies. This will make it more likely that the euro will emerge as a medium of exchange more on par with the dollar in foreign exchange markets. The dollar is currently used in 83 percent of two-way transactions in foreign exchange markets, while the deutsche mark is used in only 37 percent; other EMS currencies in 21 percent of transactions; sterling in 10 percent; and the yen in 24 percent (BIS, 1996, and Ilzkovitz, 1996). The euro is bound to occupy a larger share because of thickness externalities. Thus the fundamentals point toward a potentially large shift in favor of the euro. Note that if the world consisted of only the United States and the EU, the establishment of the euro would eliminate all interbank markets for foreign exchange, except for one—that between the dollar and the euro. Thus, the dollar would immediately lose its importance as a vehicle currency and it would be as widely used as the euro.

Of course, the dollar's role is important because it also intermediates in the financing of trade between the EU and third countries, as well as trade of third countries among themselves. One of the reasons is again lower transaction costs in the interbank market. The euro will not necessarily substitute for the dollar in these other markets. But the reduction in transaction costs in all

[4]Note that the capital of the EBRD is denominated in ECUs. There are signs that the central banks of Central and Eastern European economies will be using the euro, as many are already using the ECU as a unit of account and currencies such as the deutsche mark as intervention currencies.

markets involving the euro, vis-à-vis the markets involving the existing EU currencies, will make some substitution likely.

The EU accounts for a higher percentage of world exports and imports than the United States, even when intra-EU trade is netted out. The average share of the EU in world exports in the 1970s was on the order of 14 percent, as opposed to about 12 percent for the United States and 7 percent for Japan. In the 1980s the EU share rose to about 16 percent and Japan's rose to 9.5 percent, as opposed to a stagnant share for the United States. In 1992, the U.S. share of world exports was 12.3 percent, versus 9.3 percent for Japan and 16.9 percent for the EU when intra-EU trade is netted out.

These facts point toward a significant potential for the euro as a means of payments in international markets. The dollar will be displaced significantly as an intervention, reserve, and vehicle currency. The trade fundamentals are favorable to the euro. In all this, however, it is worth keeping in mind an important lesson from the models of international money, stressed by Rey (1997). This is that "history will matter: once an exchange structure is established, it will persist unless the structure of payments shifts enough to make it untenable or unless the system experiences a shock large enough to shift it from one equilibrium to another" (Krugman, 1980, p. 523).

EMU will be a large enough shock that it will significantly affect the current position of the dollar and is likely to upset the foreign exchange market. Even the experience with the replacement of the pound sterling by the U.S. dollar in the interwar period may not have involved as large and as abrupt a change in the fundamentals of the international monetary system as EMU is likely to bring (see Brown, 1940, for a classic treatment of this episode).

The precise nature of the new equilibrium is difficult to predict, however, especially as even the simplest triangular exchange models have multiple equilibria, and beliefs may play an important role in determining which equilibrium prevails. To paraphrase Newlyn (1962, p. 2), international money "falls within that perplexing but fascinating group of phenomena . . . affected by self-justifying beliefs. If the members of a community think that money will be generally acceptable, then it will be; otherwise not."

It is also worth noting that for both the interbank market and the nonbank private sector the euro will not be adopted unless transaction costs are low and banking in it is as cheap as the alternatives. The extent to which this will be the case will also depend on the success of financial deregulation in bringing down the cost of banking in the EU (Giovannini and Mayer, 1991). It will also depend on central bank and regulatory policies determining the costs of using the euro payments mechanism (Folkerts-Landau and Garber, 1992).

Unit of Account Function

We next turn to the unit of account role of international money. This is closely linked to the means of payments role for national economies, although less so in the international monetary system. The unit of account role for an international currency depends first on whether importers and exporters invoice in that particular currency. Black (1985) presents evidence that whereas European firms invoice a very large proportion of their exports in their own currencies, the proportion of their imports that is invoiced in other currencies, and especially dollars, is quite significant. On the other hand, Japanese firms invoice mainly in dollars, while developing countries invoice overwhelmingly in dollars. In an update, Black (1990) found that the share of Japanese exports invoiced in dollars has been falling over time, while the share denominated in yen has been rising. He also reports some indirect evidence that the share of U.S. trade denominated in foreign currencies is rising. Recently Hartmann (1996) reported that 48 percent of world exports are invoiced in dollars, 15 percent in deutsche mark, 18 percent in other major European currencies, and still only 5 percent in yen. At the same time, the Japanese and European shares of world exports have also been rising, while the share of U.S. exports seems to have been stagnant.[5]

The consequence seems to be a trend decline in the share of dollar-denominated world trade. In all probability EMU will result in the almost exclusive invoicing in euros by EU firms. The only likely exceptions are imports from the United States and Japan and some primary commodities, if invoicing by commodity producers were to continue to be in U.S. dollars. It is also quite possible that the economies of scale created by the substitution of a number of European currencies by a single one will induce firms from other areas that trade mainly with the EU to start invoicing in euros. This may include the Central and Eastern European economies and many Middle Eastern Mediterranean economies. It may also induce many multinational Japanese and U.S. firms to follow suit, as they will also benefit from such economies of scale. Again, however, there will be an initial one-off "arithmetic" effect raising the share of dollar-denominated trade, when intra-EU trade becomes "domestic"—but this will not change the trends.

To the extent that trade relations become concentrated in regional blocks (e.g., Europe-Africa-Middle East, Japan-Southeast Asia, United States-Latin America), we might end up with, at least three vehicle cum unit-of-account currencies. But insofar as trade is multilateral and more uniformly distributed geographically, there will still be powerful forces behind the use of a single dominant currency for these roles. In the latter case the change in the funda-

[5]These trends have also been examined by Tavlas (1991) and Tavlas and Ozeki (1992).

mentals will favor the euro, but history (inertia) will favor the dollar. For example, it seems unlikely (although not unthinkable) that the OPEC countries and producers of other internationally traded commodities would switch from dollar to euro invoicing soon after the establishment of EMU. Again, any change will depend on the extent and the speed with which the euro displaces the dollar as a means of payments in international trade. As we suggested above, the fundamentals point toward a large displacement of the dollar as a means of international payments. Displacement of the dollar as an international unit of account is bound to follow at least partially, and possibly at a later stage.

The second aspect of the unit-of-account role of an international currency is related to whether there are countries that peg their own currency against it. This is also a reflection of the importance of a currency as an international unit of account. Of the 47 countries that either pegged their currency or maintained limited flexibility against a single other currency in March 1994, 25 did so against the U.S. dollar and 14 against the French franc. All these economies are small, however, and even jointly they do not amount to a significant share of the world economy. Although the euro will have a long way to go in order to become a major international unit of account, a number of factors will favor such a development. One is the growing integration of the Central and Eastern European economies with the EU. This makes it far more likely that both their firms and their central banks will use the euro as a unit of account. Bénassy-Quéré (1996) stresses the potential "anchor" role for the euro (which goes beyond pegging strictly defined) at the regional level.[6]

Traditionally, the means of payment and unit-of-account functions of money go hand in hand. This was the case with sterling during the gold standard, and with the dollar during the Bretton Woods system and beyond. It is very likely that the euro will eventually become the dominant unit of account and means of payment in Europe and its immediate vicinity (like North Africa and the Middle East). But it is more uncertain whether it will replace the dollar elsewhere. Much will depend on whether the dollar displays weakness because of the persistence of global imbalances, on the relative stability (inflation performance) of the two currencies, and on the attitudes of traders in the interbank market.

Store of Value Function

The final issue related to the fundamentals of whether the euro will become an important international currency has to do with the desire of private

[6]The process will also depend on the stability of exchange rates between the dollar, the yen, and the euro. If the U.S. dollar were to display high volatility against the yen and the euro, while their bilateral exchange rate was relatively stable, it would boost the chances of the euro (and the yen) to substitute for the dollar as an international unit of account.

investors to hold assets denominated in euros. Some of the factors that affect international investors also affect central banks. However, central banks have an additional transactions motive, as they have to intervene in support of their home currencies.

As in the case of central bank reserves, U.S. dollar bonds make up a significant proportion of the international bond market. The data suggest a substantial decline of the role of the U.S. dollar since the early 1980s: from 62 percent of the stock of bonds outstanding in 1985 to only 38 percent at end-1996 (of a total stock amounting to $3,200 billion), with a corresponding sharp rise in the share of yen-denominated bonds to 16 percent (BIS, 1997, p. 11). Normally stocks change slowly, so this is a significant movement. The shares in new issues fluctuate substantially from year to year—for example, dollar-denominated bonds accounted for 24 percent of total issues in 1995 and 43 percent in 1996 (some of this reflects the appreciation of the dollar in 1996). Clearly, the fundamentals are related to risk and return, and there are considerable uncertainties both about the fundamentals and about the appropriate model for analyzing international financial investments.

The "domestic" market in Europe for private bonds is already fairly unified, and with outstanding stocks of $2,948 billion, it is two-thirds of the U.S. market. The segmentation that one observes in this market appears to derive primarily from the existence of separate currencies. According to McCauley and White's paper in this volume, "In the pricing of government debt, prospects for integration in the trading of the bonds of the most creditworthy governments look brighter than is generally acknowledged" (p. 331). Total public sector domestic debt in the EU-15 amounts to $4,618 billion, two-thirds of that in the United States (BIS, 1997, p. 47).

The initial share of international assets denominated in euros will be much lower than the size of the EMU bloc in world GDP and trade. And as the euro financial markets integrate further, they will become more liquid and deeper, transactions costs will fall, and they will therefore be more attractive to external investors. A private sector portfolio shift to bring the share of euro asset holdings close to parity with the economic size of the EMU bloc might involve increasing euro asset stocks by $700 billion (McCauley and White, pp. 358), that is, 15–20 percent of the total outstanding stock of international assets. We analyze the potential exchange rate consequences of such a shift in the next section.

Supply will of course respond endogenously to the increase in demand—that is, debt issuers will be inclined to increase their offerings denominated in euros. This will tend to moderate the appreciation of the euro. But changing debt issue denominations will, we believe, be a much slower process than the portfolio shifts. To illustrate this point, note that total new dollar issues of international bonds in 1990–95 were $828 billion, that is, slightly under $140 billion annually. If *all* were in euros, it would take *five years* to absorb a stock increase in demand of $700 billion. It is also true that European institutional investors are currently very little diversified into foreign assets, except those in the United Kingdom (see Artus, 1996). But they may initially prefer to diversify across countries, in the newly integrated European capital markets, without incurring exchange risks. Meanwhile, U.S. institutional investors—who also show very high home preference currently—are likely to find the new euro financial market attractive as they diversify, especially if euro bond interest rates are less correlated with U.S. bond yields than are current European government bond rates. This is to be expected. The ECB is likely to be a more independent actor in monetary policy, if only because of the size of the monetary area it covers, than were the individual central banks relative to the United States.

A number of developments may work in the euro's favor in the longer term. First, we may witness a diminution of the so-called "safe haven" motive for dollar holdings. If the liberalization of the Central and East European economies proves durable and not a forerunner of political instability, and if the EU is successful in "widening" as well as "deepening," then Europe may eventually seem a much safer haven than previously. This, together with the liberalization of financial markets in the EU, could increase the attractiveness of euro-denominated assets. The second factor at work may be the anti-inflationary reputation of the Bundesbank, if it can credibly be transferred to the ECB. Conversely, if liberalization in Central and Eastern Europe were to stall and Balkan instability were to deepen and spread (or, *a fortiori*, if there were serious instability east of Poland), it would be that much more difficult for euro assets to displace dollar assets in international portfolios.

In the presence of "thickness externalities" on foreign exchange and financial markets, there are interactions between the medium of exchange and the store of value function of currencies (see Algoskoufis, Portes, and Rey, 1997). According to McCauley and White (p. 333), "the euro money market is likely to prove a very liquid market from its inception." This will increase the potential of the euro to become a vehicle currency and will strengthen its international role.

However, the substantial inertia and history dependence that characterizes the international monetary system should not be discounted. After all, many models with multiple equilibria suggest that big shocks to the fundamentals are required to effect a shift from one steady state to another. The introduction of the euro is likely to be a big shock. The resistance of the dollar in its position as an international currency will also be strong, however, and it will slow down the process of the internationalization of the euro.

The Euro and the Dollar

We now consider the exchange rate implication of the process through which the creation of the euro would affect international markets for foreign exchange, as well as the dynamic process that is likely to be initiated by the tendency to substitute euros for dollars in international portfolios. Here, it is important to recognize that the analysis abstracts from both cyclical and trend developments. We take current cyclical positions as the baseline and assume that the trends of the past decade or so will continue.

From our examination of the demand-side fundamentals in the previous section it appears that the creation of the euro will cause a potentially large substitution of euros for dollars by both central banks and private asset holders. The question that arises is how this higher demand will be translated into a higher supply of euros in international portfolios.

Euro-denominated assets will be supplied even before the year 2002, as banks and financial intermediaries will be allowed to issue liabilities denominated in euros. In the first half of 2002, the stock of financial assets denominated in the existing EU currencies will be denominated in euros. This will of course include assets held by the rest of the world. Since one also expects a substitution of euros for dollar holdings, however, additional euro-denominated assets will need to be created. What will be the impli-cations of this process for the exchange rate between the euro and the dollar?

To examine this issue we need to look at the interaction between the current and the capital account of the EU. The shift in favor of the euro in international financial markets cannot cause a matching supply of euros immediately, since there would be nobody on the other side to provide the quantities of euro-denominated assets. The result will be a rise in the price of the euro against the dollar, that is, a real euro revaluation.

If the euro revaluation caused an increase in the current account deficit of the EU, then the EU would be able to start correcting the excess demand for euros through the capital account. By supplying additional euros or disposing of dollar holdings through the capital account, the EU would support the process of establishing the euro as an international currency.

This process will not start immediately, however, because of the J-curve. The immediate reaction of the current account to a revaluation is sluggish and even perverse. Thus, in the short term we may see a narrowing rather than a widening of the current account of the EU following a revaluation of the euro. This possibility suggests that the euro will have to overshoot its long-run revaluation in the short run, causing expectations of a future devaluation that will cause European real interest rates to rise temporarily. That rise in interest rates raises net domestic private sector savings, as is necessary to accompany a current account improvement.[7]

Over time, the revaluation of the euro will cause a current account deficit, and an increased inflow of capital into the EU, causing higher euro holdings internationally. European real interest rates will fall, as the euro will weaken toward long-run equilibrium.

The outcome in steady state is a euro appreciation relative to the initial position vis-à-vis the U.S. dollar. How much might we expect? Just for illustration, note that the $700 billion stock shift suggested above would convert about 20 percent of existing dollar assets into euro assets. If the initial levels of the two are about the same, and if the values of the two debt stocks and of interest rates were held constant, the dollar would have to depreciate by 40 percent. Note that in 1996, capital flows into the United States were $395 billion ($123 billion official and $272 billion private), and the dollar appreciated by 30 percent with respect to the deutsche mark.

This scenario of major change must be evaluated in the light of the likely willingness of the ECB to allow the euro to become an international currency. The ECB may resist the widespread international use of the euro because of the perceived burden of acting as an international lender of last resort.

There are two recent historical examples: the postwar prohibition on the part of the United Kingdom of the use of sterling balances for third-country credits, which may have been a stimulus to the growth of the Euromarkets; and the reluctance of the Bundesbank to allow the deutsche mark to be used as an intervention currency in the EMS, because this would have brought greater external influences on domestic monetary policy. Nevertheless, even if the ECB were to take a similar attitude, this would merely slow down the emergence of the euro as an international currency, not stop it.

On the other hand, if the ECB pursues the opposite route, actively promoting the international use of the euro, one cannot discount the possibility of an overt tug of war between the euro, the incumbent (the dollar), and the major other contender (the yen) for international monetary supremacy. Some of the recent language of European political leaders suggests that they look forward to this prospect and that they believe the United States—despite its official pro-EMU position—in fact opposes the single European currency because it regards the euro as a threat, in this sense. We regard such attitudes themselves as a threat and such a prospect as a potentially dangerous development. One might draw this lesson from the interwar experience of the rivalry between sterling and the dollar, with the French franc on the sidelines (Eichengreen, 1987). Even without such a potential rivalry, if EMU were to result in large-scale substitution of euros for dollar balances and a quick ap-

[7]The model we are using to analyze the shifts involved is due to Krugman (1989); it is a variant of a portfolio balance model of the exchange rate.

preciation of the euro against the dollar (and the yen), along the lines we have analyzed, this may be a cause for concern. There may well be an increased need for better monetary policy coordination at the international level to cope with such an eventuality.

Policy Implications

We now turn to the assessment of the likely implications of EMU for the process of international policy coordination and the determination of the exchange rate regime between the dollar, the euro, and the yen. Let us start by briefly discussing the rationale for international policy coordination and cooperative exchange rate management.

International Macroeconomic Policy Coordination

The main argument in favor of international macroeconomic policy coordination is that, in its absence, macroeconomic policies may result in inefficient global outcomes. Inefficiency is defined here in terms of the well-known Pareto criterion that some countries can be made better off without any country being made worse off. Because the policies of large economies have international "spillovers," the perceived outcomes of particular policy actions for any one country depend on the actions of other countries. In such cases, as in classical oligopoly, the nationalistic pursuit of economic policy by all countries is unlikely to be optimal. World macroeconomic policy may well end up being too expansionary or too contractionary, because individual countries cannot properly account for international spillovers in a regime without coordination.

A well-known example from flexible exchange rate regimes leads to deflationary bias. Suppose that each country tries to reduce inflation through restrictive policies that operate through a nominal appreciation of its currency. Because the exchange rate cannot appreciate for everyone, the efforts of at least some of them, if not all, will be frustrated. Meanwhile, the attempt to achieve exchange rate appreciations in a noncoordinated fashion leads to an overrestrictive monetary policy for everyone, which in the short run would result in too much unemployment. Everybody could be made better off by a coordinated monetary contraction that would achieve a better balance between the reduction of inflation and the increase in unemployment. This example has often been invoked to explain the worldwide rise in unemployment in the early 1980s.

An unwarranted increase in inflation could equally well occur if countries are concerned not with inflation, but with domestic unemployment and balance of payments deficits. An attempt to achieve depreciations of the nominal and real exchange rate in a noncoordinated fashion would result in over-expansionary monetary policy, as the exchange rate depreciations cannot occur for everybody. Since the world is a closed economy, world inflation would rise, and the effects on average unemployment and trade imbalances would be minimal. A coordinated monetary expansion could result in a better balance between inflation, unemployment, and trade imbalances. This example has equally often been invoked to explain the worldwide rise in inflation in the aftermath of the first oil shock.

If coordination is beneficial, why is it not more prevalent? Some coordination in the monetary sphere undoubtedly characterizes fixed exchange rate regimes. In fact, all such regimes have been asymmetric, in the sense that in some form or another one country or central bank has acted as a (Stackelberg) leader. World outcomes are not Pareto-efficient under this type of coordination, but in many circumstances they can be shown to be better than uncoordinated monetary policies (see Canzoneri and Henderson, 1991). Yet coordination of fiscal policies has not occurred, even in fixed exchange rate regimes, and fixed exchange rate regimes often face tremendous pressures and eventually break down. Thus, one is still left with the puzzle of why, despite the presumed benefits of coordination, very little coordination exists.[8]

To begin with, continuous coordination, in the sense that countries negotiate and agree on their reactions in each instant, may be extremely costly, because of the negotiation, implementation, and monitoring costs that would be involved. Such costs explain not the lack of coordination, however, but the prevalence of coordination in setting the "rules of the game" over coordination of "how to play" at each instant. It is thus widely agreed that any coordination ought to take the form of agreements on relatively simple rules that would focus on a selected range of intermediate targets, such as exchange rates and nominal income growth, together with some arrangements for crisis management and avoidance of conflicts over shared targets such as bilateral exchange rates or current accounts. The objective of continuous full coordination of all policy actions appears unattainable because of the costs involved. In any case, the potential benefits from full coordination have been estimated to be modest and skewed in favor of the EU and against the United States; moreover, most of the benefits accrue even in moderately cooperative regimes in

[8]The macroeconomic literature on policy coordination started with the pioneering work of Hamada (1976). It took a major step forward with the empirical investigation of Oudiz and Sachs (1984) and the conference volumes edited by Buiter and Marston (1985) and Bryant and Portes (1988). Nontechnical assessments of the record can be found in Artis and Ostry (1986) and Dobson (1991), and a rigorous analysis of monetary policy coordination can be found in Canzoneri and Henderson (1991), who also discuss instances in which macroeconomic policy coordination can be counterproductive (see Rogoff, 1985). Obstacles to macroeconomic policy coordination are discussed in Frankel (1988) and the survey of Currie, Holtham, and Hughes Hallett (1989). More recently, see the major work of Bryant, Hooper, and Mann (1993).

which there is some joint targeting of intermediate targets such as nominal exchange rates or nominal GDPs.

But there are several obstacles to agreeing and sustaining the "rules of the game" even in moderately cooperative regimes. One problem is uncertainty about the objectives and priorities of foreign countries, although empirical research based on simulations of macroeconometric models has not shown the benefits from coordination to be particularly sensitive to this source of uncertainty. Another problem lies in disagreements about how the international and national economies function. This has been shown to affect the estimation of benefits from coordination significantly and is a major source of disagreements in international policy discussions. It affects the choice of intermediate targets (e.g., nominal exchange rates versus nominal income or money growth) and the drafting of the rules of how to respond to particular developments. Eichengreen and Ghironi (1997), for example, in an initial effort to model policy coordination between an "EMU bloc" and the United States, find that the incentives to coordinate differ greatly according to how they specify the consequences of fiscal contraction or expansion.

In conclusion, although in principle the coordination of macroeconomic policies can be shown to lead to better macroeconomic outcomes at the world level, it is realistic to expect that the international monetary system will not change to one of full coordination of policies in the aftermath of EMU. The costs of negotiating, sustaining, and monitoring coordinated policies, the vexed question of the distribution of the benefits, uncertainty about the objectives of foreign authorities, and disagreements about how the macroeconomy functions preclude not only the full coordination of policies, but even coordination in the form of agreeing on simple rules for the cooperative conduct of monetary and fiscal policy. In the few instances when coordination has succeeded it seems to have focused around the management of exchange rates (monetary policy coordination), and it is to this question that we now turn.

EMU and International Exchange Rate Management

The cooperative management of exchange rates through monetary policies has been the major focus of most attempts at coordination and of much of the analytical literature (e.g., Kenen, 1988, and Miller, Eichengreen, and Portes, 1989) since the collapse of the Bretton Woods system of fixed exchange rates. Exchange rate management is no longer seen as anathema, as the experience with floating rates in the 1970s and the first part of the 1980s is not viewed as particularly successful (empirical evidence suggests, for example, that inflation persistence is greater in flexible exchange rate regimes; see Alogoskoufis, 1992). In addition, since the exchange rate is a variable shared by at least two countries, it is a natural focus for coordination.

Coordinated exchange rate management had a high point in the late 1970s: in November 1978 the Group of Three industrial countries intervened heavily to halt the depreciation of the dollar, while in 1979 and early 1980 the United States intervened to halt the dollar's appreciation, by selling dollars and acquiring substantial exchange rate reserves. The Reagan administration then adopted a policy of "benign neglect" toward the dollar, and cooperative exchange rate management (and macroeconomic policy coordination) was avoided until September 1985. The Plaza Agreement then marked the beginning of another period of active exchange rate management that culminated in the Louvre Accord of February 22, 1987, to "foster stability of exchange rates around current levels" (Funabashi, 1988). Since then, the resolve of the Group of Three industrial countries to stabilize exchange rates has been diluted. The consequences of events in Eastern Europe and the run-up to the 1992 U.S. presidential election brought some of the worst failures in the coordination of monetary and exchange rate policies of recent years.

Will European monetary union and the creation of the euro create more pressure for exchange rate management, or will it allow the maintenance of "benign neglect" about exchange rates? Analytical models (e.g., Giavazzi and Giovannini, 1989) suggest that more symmetry may generate instability in the international monetary system. If one economy is much larger and more closed than the others, it will be quite happy to act as a (Stackelberg) leader, using the money supply as its monetary policy instrument, without regard for its nominal exchange rate. We may then have an equilibrium in which the large economy sets its money supply while the small economies intervene to affect their nominal exchange rates. If another major player were to emerge, however, in the absence of full cooperation, the greater symmetry could lead to instability. Both economies will have an incentive to try to use exchange rate policy, as their bilateral exchange rate vis-à-vis the other large country matters more, and in such a case instability will arise. Thus, in the presence of large shocks we may see both economies trying to manipulate their exchange rates, that is, use beggar-thy-neighbor monetary policies, in which case there is a reversion to flexible exchange rates. As Giavazzi and Giovannini (1989) put it, "when the size of the *N*th country is much larger than that of the other country (or countries), so that bilateral exchange-rate fluctuations do not significantly affect the *N*th country's output and real income, a regime of managed rates does not display the instability that characterizes the symmetric case" (p. 208). The results suggest that the greater symmetry that EMU will imply for the international monetary system may result in greater difficulty in managing exchange rates internationally.

It may well be that it is not practical in today's circumstances to move away from fully flexible exchange rates. This has less to do with asymmetries and more with the technological and communications advances that have speeded up capital mobility and created global financial markets.

What scope is there for monetary policy coordination then? If our analysis in the previous sections is broadly accepted, there should be scope for monetary policy interventions that would help avoid the overshooting of the exchange rate of the euro, after the third stage of EMU starts. This could be achieved through either monetary relaxation in Europe, following the start of the third stage, or monetary tightening in the United States. Such actions would slow down the appreciation of the euro vis-à-vis the dollar and could help avoid turbulence in the exchange markets. But such a policy would be a difficult task for the newly established ECB to execute. If it went wrong it would risk its anti-inflationary credibility exactly at the time when there would be need to build it up. On the other hand, the U.S. Federal Reserve would have less to fear in tightening monetary policy to avoid a sharp dollar depreciation.

In any case, it is difficult to envisage major monetary policy switches in response to the appreciation of the euro after the start of EMU. Such a response would come only if Europe were to face a worsening unemployment problem that would deepen still further following the appreciation of the euro, or if the U.S. economy were expanding too vigorously. In all probability, the appreciation and subsequent depreciation of the euro vis-à-vis the dollar remains the most likely scenario after the start of the final stage of EMU.

Conclusions

In this paper we have analyzed the changes in the fundamentals of the international monetary system following the introduction of the euro after the year 1999, as well as the likely transition scenario to the new world monetary equilibrium. We suggested that the introduction of the euro will bring about potentially important changes in the international monetary scene, as the euro will substitute to a large extent for the dollar as an international means of payment, unit of account, and store of value. Such changes in the fundamentals will bring about an increased demand for euros shortly after the introduction of the new currency in international markets.

The first manifestation of the increased demand for euros will be an appreciation of the new currency against the U.S. dollar (and the yen). Although this may initially cause a narrowing of the EU current account deficit, due to the J-curve, eventually the EU current account deficit will get larger, allowing the substitution of euros for U.S. dollars through the capital account. The overreaction of the exchange rate will gradually be corrected, through a process of expected depreciations of the euro. Finally, if the euro does challenge the dollar's hegemony, this is likely to be a cause of instability in the international monetary system, which appropriate policy coordination could mitigate.

References

Alogoskoufis, George S., 1992, "Monetary Accommodation, Exchange Rate Regimes and Inflation Persistence," *Economic Journal*, Vol. 102 (May), pp. 461–80.

Alogoskoufis, George S., and Richard Portes, 1991, "International Costs and Benefits of EMU," in "The Economics of EMU," *European Economy*, Special Edition No. 1, pp. 231–45.

———, 1992, "European Monetary Union and International Currencies in a Tripolar World," in *Establishing a Central Bank: Issues in Europe and Lessons from the US*, ed. by Matthew Canzoneri, Vittorio Grilli, and Paul Masson (Cambridge: Cambridge University Press and CEPR), pp. 273–300.

———, and Hélène Rey, 1997, "The Emergence of the Euro as an International Currency" (unpublished; London: CEPR).

Artis, Michael, and Sylvia Ostry, 1986, *International Economic Policy Coordination* (London: Royal Institute for International Affairs).

Artus, Patrick, 1996, "A Strong Euro or a Weak Euro?" Document de Travail No. 1996-02/EI (Paris: Caisse des Dépôts et Consignations).

Bank for International Settlements, 1997, *International Banking and Financial Market Developments* (Basle: BIS, February).

______, 1996, *Central Bank Survey of Foreign Exchange Market Activity* (Basle: BIS).

Bénassy-Quéré, Agnès, 1996, "Potentialities and Opportunities of the Euro as an International Currency," Centre d'Etudes Prospectives et d'Informations Internationales, Working Paper No. 96–09 (Paris: CEPII, August).

______, and Pierre Deusy-Fournier, 1994, "La concurrence pour le statut de monnaie internationale depuis 1973," *Economie Internationale*, Vol. 59, pp. 107–144.

Black, Stanley W., 1985, "International Money and International Monetary Arrangements," in *Handbook of International Economics*, Volume 2, ed. by Peter B. Kenen and Ronald W. Jones (Amsterdam: North-Holland).

______, 1990, "The International Use of Currencies," in *The Evolution of the International Monetary System: How Can Stability and Efficiency be Attained?* ed. by Yoshio Suzuki, Junichi Miyake, and Mitsuaki Okabe (Tokyo: University of Tokyo Press), pp. 175–94.

Brown, W.A., Jr., 1940, *The International Gold Standard Reinterpreted, 1914–1934* (New York: AMS Press and NBER).

Bryant, Ralph C., and Richard Portes, 1988, *Global Macroeconomics: Policy Conflict and Cooperation* (New York: St. Martin's Press in association with International Economic Association and CEPR).

______, Peter Hooper, and Catherine L. Mann, eds., 1993, *Evaluating Policy Regimes: New Research in Empirical Macroeconomics* (Washington: Brookings Institution).

Buiter, Willem H., and Richard C. Marston, 1985, *International Economic Policy Coordination* (Cambridge: Cambridge University Press).

Canzoneri, Matthew B., and Dale W. Henderson, 1991, *Monetary Policy in Interdependent Economies* (Cambridge, Massachusetts: MIT Press).

Cohen, Benjamin J., 1971, *The Future of Sterling as an International Currency* (London: Macmillan).

Currie, David A., Gerald Holtham, and Andrew Hughes Hallett, 1989, "The Theory and Practice of International Policy Coordination: Does Coordination Pay?" in *Macroeconomic Policies in an Interdependent World*, ed. by Ralph C. Bryant and others (Washington: International Monetary Fund), pp. 14–46.

Dobson, Wendy, 1991, *Economic Policy Coordination: Requiem or Prologue?* (Washington: Institute for International Economics).

Dooley, Michael P., J. Saúl Lizondo, and Donald J. Mathieson, 1989, "The Currency Composition of Foreign Exchange Reserves," *Staff Papers*, International Monetary Fund, Vol. 36 (June), pp. 385–434.

Eichengreen, Barry, 1987, "Conducting the International Orchestra: Bank of England Leadership Under the Classical Gold Standard," *Journal of International Money and Finance*, Vol. 6 (March), pp. 5–29.

______, and Fabio Ghironi, 1997, "How Will Transatlantic Policy Interactions Change with the Advent of EMU?" paper prepared for CEPR Workshop, Brussels.

Folkerts-Landau, David, and Peter Garber, 1992, "The ECB: A Bank or a Monetary Policy Rule?" in *Establishing a Central Bank: Issues in Europe and Lessons from the US*, ed. by Matthew Canzoneri, Vittorio Grilli, and Paul Masson (Cambridge: Cambridge University Press and CEPR).

Frankel, Jeffrey A., 1988, *Obstacles to International Macroeconomic Policy Coordination*, Princeton Studies in International Finance, No. 64 (Princeton, New Jersey: Princeton University, Department of Economics, International Finance Section).

Frenkel, M., and J. Sondergaard, 1996, "The Effects of EMU on International Reserves" (unpublished; Washington: Georgetown University).

Funabashi, Yoichi, 1988, *Managing the Dollar: From the Plaza to the Louvre* (Washington: Institute for International Economics).

Giavazzi, Francesco, and Alberto Giovannini, 1989, "Monetary Policy Interactions Under Managed Exchange Rates," *Economica*, Vol. 56 (May), pp. 199–213.

Giovannini, Alberto, and Colin Mayer, eds., 1991, *European Financial Integration* (Cambridge: Cambridge University Press and CEPR).

Hamada, Koichi, 1976, "A Strategic Analysis of Monetary Interdependence," *Journal of Political Economy*, Vol. 83 (August), pp. 677–700.

Hartmann, Philipp, 1996, "The Future of the Euro as an International Currency: A Transactions Perspective," LSE Financial Markets Group Special Paper No. 91 (London: London School of Economics, November).

Ilzkovitz, Fabienne, 1996, "Prospects for the Internationalization of the Euro," DG-II, docII/362/96-EN (Brussels: European Commission, June).

Jones, Robert A., 1976, "The Origin and Development of Media of Exchange," *Journal of Political Economy*, Vol. 84 (August), pp. 757–75.

Kenen, Peter B., 1988, *Managing Exchange Rates* (London: Royal Institute of International Affairs).

Kindleberger, Charles P., 1984, *A Financial History of Western Europe* (London: Allen and Unwin).

Kiyotaki, Nobuhiro, and Randall Wright, 1989, "On Money as a Medium of Exchange," *Journal of Political Economy*, Vol. 97 (August), pp. 927–54.

Krugman, Paul R., 1980, "Vehicle Currencies and the Structure of International Exchange," *Journal of Money, Credit and Banking*, Vol. 12 (August), pp. 513–26.

______, 1984, "The International Role of the Dollar: Theory and Prospect," in *Exchange Rate Theory and Practice*, ed. by John F.O. Bilson and Richard C. Marston (Chicago: University of Chicago Press for NBER).

______, 1989, "The J-Curve, the Fire Sale and the Hard Landing," *American Economic Review, Papers and Proceedings*, Vol. 79 (May), pp. 31–35.

Matsuyama, Kiminori, Nobuhiro Kiyotaki, and Akihiko Matsui, 1993, "Towards a Theory of International Currency," *Review of Economic Studies*, Vol. 60 (April), pp. 283–320.

Miller, Marcus, Barry Eichengreen, and Richard Portes, 1989, *Blueprints for Exchange Rate Management* (London: Academic Press and CEPR).

Newlyn, Walter T., 1962, *Theory of Money* (Oxford: Oxford University Press).

Oudiz, Gilles, and Jeffrey Sachs, 1984, "Macroeconomic Policy Coordination Among the Industrial Economies," *Brookings Papers on Economic Activity: 1*, Brookings Institution, pp. 1–75.

Portes, Richard, 1996, "Implementing EMU," *American Economic Review, Papers and Proceedings*, Vol. 86 (May), pp. 139–42.

Rey, H., 1997, "International Trade and Currency Exchange," CEPR Discussion Paper No. 322 (London: Centre for Economic Performance, February).

Rogoff, Kenneth, 1985, "Can International Monetary Policy Cooperation Be Counterproductive?" *Journal of International Economics*, Vol. 18 (May), pp. 199–217.

Tavlas, George S., 1991, *On the International Use of Currencies: The Case of the Deutsche Mark*, Princeton Essays in International Finance, No. 181 (Princeton, New Jersey: Princeton University, Department of Economics, International Finance Section, March).

______, and Yuzuro Ozeki, 1992, *The Internationalization of Currencies: An Appraisal of the Japanese Yen*, IMF Occasional Paper No. 90 (Washington: International Monetary Fund, January).

Yeager, Leland B., 1976, *International Monetary Relations: Theory, History, and Policy* (New York: Harper and Row).

Comments on Bergsten and on Alogoskoufis and Portes

Masahiro Kawai

This discussion has two objectives. One is to make comments on the papers by Alogoskoufis and Portes and by Bergsten, which examine the prospective implications of the creation of the EMU and the introduction of a single currency, the euro, for the international monetary system. Another objective is to reexamine this issue from Asian perspectives.

General Comments on the Papers

The creation of EMU and the introduction of the euro will fundamentally alter the international monetary system. Both papers argue that economic and monetary unification of some of the EU countries will produce a euro capable of challenging the U.S. dollar dominance and converting the international monetary system into a bipolar regime centered on both the U.S. dollar and the euro. The Japanese yen, while still important, would play a far less significant role.

Lingering Questions

There are, however, some questions to be answered before we can conclude that the euro will indeed become a real competitor currency for the dollar.

1. Is the Bundesbank anti-inflationary credibility easily transferrable to the newly established ECB? Any central bank would have to deliver price stability before it can convince the public that it is indeed pursuing an anti-inflationary policy. It usually takes a long time to build such credibility.
2. How many countries will join EMU? If the de facto deutsche mark–area countries—Austria, Belgium, France, Luxembourg, the Netherlands, and Germany—become the only members of EMU, the Bundesbank credibility would be easily transmitted to the ECB. However, if a wider array of countries, particularly the so-called Club Med (Italy, Spain, and

Portugal), were to be included in EMU, it would be harder for the ECB to establish its reputation as an anti-inflation central bank.

3. If the ECB is successful in pursuing a credible anti-inflationary policy, will countries in Central and Eastern Europe, the Mediterranean, and North Africa be able to peg (or stabilize) their exchange rates to the euro? To the extent that exchange rate pegging (or stabilization) is considered too costly because the ECB's restrictive monetary policy is detrimental to their growth and employment, these countries will choose not to join the euro area and the role of the euro will be limited.
4. Is the ECB willing to promote the euro as an international currency, while the Bundesbank has not promoted the deutsche mark for fear of losing the ability to conduct an effective monetary policy? If the ECB wishes to retain effective monetary control mechanisms for price stability, it may not want to promote the euro as an international currency, thereby limiting the global role of the euro.
5. Will EMU countries maintain tight fiscal policy in accordance with the Stability and Growth Pact? If fiscal policy is too tight, adhering to a strict interpretation of the Pact, it may continue to depress the European economy. If fiscal policy is too expansionary, assuming a more flexible interpretation of the Pact, monetary policy credibility may be adversely affected and a weak euro may emerge.
6. Can Europe establish a full-fledged money and capital market that is comparable to that of the United States in terms of breadth, depth, and liquidity? The euro is unlikely to evolve into a currency capable of rivaling the U.S. dollar without such a market.
7. Fundamentally, can a unified Europe exhibit dynamic economic performance, despite the well-known rigidities in the labor market that have kept the rates of unemployment high? EMU would simply become another huge welfare state with an unattractive currency, if major structural reform were not undertaken.

These are some of the important questions to consider before predicting a bright future for EMU and the euro during the transition period.

Fundamentals Versus Inertia (or History)

Both the Alogoskoufis and Portes paper and the one by Bergsten discuss the presence of two opposing forces—changes in fundamentals versus inertia or history—affecting the global roles of the euro and the dollar. Bergsten reports that the trade flow of the EU's Core-Six members (Austria, Belgium, France, Germany, Netherlands, and Luxembourg) is already larger than that of the United States. The relative weight, measured by GDP, of the EU-15 is greater than that of the United States. In addition, Central and Eastern European countries have increasingly been integrated with the EU and are expected to be EU members in the twenty-first century. Given the contention that large relative size is an important criterion for a key currency, the creation of EMU itself constitutes a fundamental change, pointing to the eventual emergence of the euro as a competitor for the U.S. dollar. However, the force of inertia and history of the U.S. dollar as the world's only key currency, enjoying incumbency advantages, will continue to work in the opposing direction. The U.S. economy's relative weight in the world has declined over time and the United States has run persistent current account deficits since the first half of the 1980s, with a consequent, long-term decline in the value of the U.S. dollar relative to the deutsche mark and the yen since 1985. Despite all this, the U.S. dollar continues to play a dominant international currency role for reasons of economies of scale, network externalities, hysteresis, and its public goods nature. Many traders and investors still rely heavily on the U.S. dollar, despite the less favorable conditions that have generated the strength of the dollar.[1] The incumbency advantage suggests that it requires a great deal for a newly emerging currency to seriously challenge the dominant one. This includes, for example, a dynamic, sustained economic growth of the EU relative to the United States, an issue I would like to come back to below; critical, discontinuous disruptions in the world economy; and a set of fundamental economic difficulties in the United States such as rampant inflation, large-scale dollar depreciation, and severe capital controls. Without such fundamental breaks, it would be hard for the euro to seriously challenge the dollar's global key-currency role.

Structural Rigidities

I would like to close this part of my discussion by pointing out that both papers significantly underestimate the implications of structural rigidities in Europe's labor market for the external value of the euro. It is quite possible that such structural rigidities will be a severe impediment to the rapid emergence of the euro as the world's major international currency, and as a serious competitor currency for the U.S. dollar. This is because the euro, which must

[1]The U.S. share in world output, though declining over time, remains larger than the share of the EU-12, so a noticeable decline in the international role of the U.S. dollar is not to be expected, at least in the foreseeable future. The output level of the United Kingdom was overtaken by the United States in the 1880s and the gap continued to widen after that. Despite this, the pound sterling remained the most dominant international currency until the 1930s, when the role of the U.S. dollar became equally important. The dollar became the most dominant currency only in the 1950s and 1960s. Bergsten, however, argues that trade flows would be a more appropriate measure of economic size.

challenge the incumbency advantage of the U.S. dollar, will be severely handicapped as a serious contender if structural rigidities are not addressed. Without structural reform, the EU's dynamic growth prospect would be limited. The euro would not be as attractive an international currency as the incumbent U.S. dollar, and relative parity between the euro and the dollar would never be achieved. Bergsten's claim that markets prize stability more than growth may apply to the incumbent, but not necessarily to a newly emerging challenger, which would place a higher weight on growth.

Nominal Anchor Currency Role of the Dollar, Euro, and Yen

Although Bergsten uses the term key currency, he does not clearly define what it is. He appears to be using the term interchangeably with "dominant international currency," particularly for transactions and reserve purposes. The term key currency was used 50 years ago by John Williams (1947) more narrowly to mean a target or nominal-anchor currency to which other countries attempt to peg their exchange rates. In this part of my discussion, I would like to focus on the nominal anchor currency role of the U.S. dollar, the prospective euro, and the Japanese yen and to report the measured size of the respective currency areas.[2]

First of all, we identify what currency or currency basket each country has so far chosen as a nominal anchor, that is, as a target currency or currency basket for exchange rate stabilization. To do this, we extend work by Jeffrey Frankel and his coauthor (Frankel and Wei, 1993 and 1994) and attempt to find whether each country's exchange rate is affected by the currencies of major industrialized countries, such as the U.S. dollar, deutsche mark, French franc, pound sterling, Japanese yen, and SDR, and several other regional currencies depending on colonial, historical, geographical, and other relevant considerations.[3] Specifically, we regress the log first difference in a country's exchange rate (measured in terms of the Swiss franc) on a constant term and the log first differences in the exchange rates of the major and other relevant minor currencies (all measured vis-à-vis the Swiss franc).[4] The coefficients

[2]Statistics cited here draw on Kawai and Akiyama (1997).

[3]Since some countries are known to stabilize their exchange rates against currencies other than major industrialized countries' currencies (i.e., the South African rand in Africa, and the Australian dollar, the Singapore dollar, and the Indian rupee in Asia), we include in the regression equation the exchange rates of such relatively minor or regional currencies for certain groups of countries.

[4]In carrying out econometric exercises, we have deleted data observations with values of log first differences greater than 0.1 to eliminate the effects of discrete currency revaluations or devaluations.

that are estimated to be statistically significant are interpreted as the weights assigned by the authorities to the corresponding currencies in their exchange rate stabilization policies.

Next, GDP is used to measure the economic size of the currency areas for the euro, the U.S. dollar, and the yen. For a country pegging its exchange rate to a particular currency, its entire GDP is classified as belonging to the currency area formed by this particular currency. If a country does not peg the exchange rate to a single currency but instead assigns several different weights to a basket of major or regional currencies, its GDP is divided according to these weights and distributed to the corresponding currency areas. See Table 1 for a summary.

Bergsten's Table 1 considers the case of the Core-Six forming EMU, the case of the EU-12, which includes all countries currently in the ERM, forming EMU, and the case of the EU-15 forming EMU. The last scenario, while highly unlikely in the near future, is presented for reference purposes. The intermediate case indicates that about 45 percent of the world economy is covered by the U.S. dollar area, 30 percent by the euro area, and less than 20 percent by the Japanese yen area. The dollar area is large because many developing countries regard the dollar as the most important global anchor. The Japanese yen area occupies 19.4 percent, which is slightly larger than the weight of the Japanese economy in the world. The yen area outside Japan is less than 0.3 percent of the world economy and, hence, the yen cannot be said to be a full-fledged, global nominal anchor currency.

Limits to the Yen's International Currency Role

The weight of the Japanese yen as an international currency has been limited both in comparison to the U.S. dollar and the deutsche mark and relative to the size of the Japanese economy. The yen has not been playing a major role as international money or as a nominal anchor to which other countries may peg, or stabilize the value of, their own currencies. Several explanations can be given for the limited use of the yen as an international currency.

First, use of the Japanese yen in invoicing Japan's trade has been limited due to the country's specific trade structure. Japan has been dependent on the United States as its major export market and on imports of large quantities of minerals, fuels, raw materials, and basic commodities for its industrial production. Trade with the United States and trade in primary commodities tend to be dollar denominated, further reducing the use of the yen.

Second, Japanese money and capital markets, particularly for treasury bills and other private short-term instruments, have not been as well developed as markets in New York or London. Functional and institutional limitations, the lack of a market infrastructure with a global standard, and overregulation in Tokyo money and capital markets have been pointed to as severe impediments to an expanded use of the yen by many authors (see Hamada and Horiuchi, 1987; Kawai, 1996; and Garber, 1996). As a result of these impediments in the Tokyo markets, foreign monetary authorities and private investors have been reluctant to use yen instruments to carry out international trade and capital transactions.

The third explanation concerns the historical context of Japan's postwar economic development. The post–World War II reconstruction and growth of the Japanese economy were made possible by financial aid and trade opportunities provided by the United States. Japan received U.S. aid during the reconstruction period, depended on the open U.S. market for its subsequent exports, and relied on the U.S. dollar money markets to finance its trade and balance of payments. Essentially, Japan commenced its postwar growth as a dollar-area country, just as many other East Asian economies and, to some extent, Western European countries did. Western European countries were at a similar stage of economic development, and their economic interdependence, particularly through foreign direct investment and intra-industry trade, deepened naturally and rapidly after the postwar reconstruction. Therefore, given the high degree of regional trade and investment interdependence, it is not surprising to see a high proportion of intra-European trade being invoiced in these countries' own national currencies. In contrast, Japan's postwar development far outpaced other East Asian economies and its trade with developing East Asia tended to be an interindustry, rather than intra-industry, type. Most of Japan's trade with other East Asian economies, which were basically dollar-area economies, was invoiced primarily in the U.S. dollar. This is the historical context of Japan's rapid economic growth and trade expansion, which has not been matched by a commensurate increase in the use of the yen as an international currency.

Fourth and finally, the developing East Asian economies have had little incentive to stabilize their currencies against the Japanese yen. The rapid economic development and growth in East Asia in the last 10 years have been made possible partly by the steep appreciation of the Japanese yen vis-à-vis the U.S. dollar that started in 1985. The steep yen appreciation has forced Japanese manufacturing firms to cope with the reduced international price competitiveness and generated foreign direct investment in the manufacturing sectors in the developing East Asian economies, particularly Asian newly industrializing economies and ASEAN, which have been transformed into a cost-competitive industrial base. (Since the late 1980s, ASEAN countries have received foreign direct investment inflows from the Asian newly industrializing economics, which have experienced currency appreciation and wage-cost increases.) The foreign direct investment inflow into East Asia has expanded exports of industrial products and contributed to dynamic economic growth. To summarize, the East Asian economies would not have enjoyed an explosive economic performance if they had stabilized their exchange rates against the Japanese yen. They have maintained stable exchange rates vis-à-vis the U.S. dollar, thereby importing monetary discipline from the United States and taking advantage of the yen rate appreciation to accomplish substantial restructuring of the economy.

Possibilities for an Increased Role of the Yen

Bergsten argues that the international role of the yen will continue to be limited owing to Japan's continued failure to deregulate and modernize its money and capital markets, the continued fragility of its financial sector, and a prolonged period of stagnation. One of the possible implications of the limited role of the yen would be a larger role of the euro in East Asia. However, one can make a case for a growing role of the yen, since the above-mentioned factors limiting the international use of the yen are gradually disappearing.

First, Japan's trade structure has been changing in the last 10 years. With diversified trade partners and increased intra-industry trade, Japan has been importing increasing amounts of manufactured products, particularly from East Asia. These changes are expected to increase the international use of the Japanese yen as a trade-invoicing currency.

Second, serious deregulation and liberalization of Japanese money and capital markets may proceed over time. This can be brought about partly by the U.S. pressure (*gaiatsu*, or external pressure) to further liberalize and to open the Japanese financial markets, and partly by the Japanese government's reaction to the "hollowing out" of the Tokyo money and capital markets. The latter example includes Prime Minister Ryutaro Hashimoto's November 1996 announcement of Japanese-style "big bang," overhauling and liberalizing the Japanese financial sector by the year 2001.

Third, Japan's economic interdependence with East Asia will increase over time, aided by previous substantial yen appreciation and the rising trends of intra-industry trade in machinery and equipment, direct investments, and various types of financial flows.[5] This points to a possibility of a rising international role of the yen in East Asia. This process will be hastened as the East Asian economies grow further, raise their per capita income, and become sim-

[5]See Kawai (1997) for the interactions between Japan's trade and foreign direct investment particularly vis-à-vis developing East Asia. One must note that, even though new foreign direct investment flows have been declining in volume, reinvestment of retained profits has been rising and is now an important part of Japan's foreign direct investment in East Asia.

ilar to Japan in their economic and industrial structure and in the composition of output and trade. In addition, there is evidence that the yen is being used widely to denominate long-term debts in East Asia; the East Asian economies have shifted the currency composition of external debts away from the dollar toward the yen since the 1980s (Tavlas and Ozeki, 1992, and Kawai, 1996).

Fourth, Japan's low, stable inflation together with the continuous current account surpluses will enhance the attractiveness of the Japanese yen as an international currency.[6] In contrast, the continuous current account deficits posted by the United States and the precipitous decline in the value of the dollar may reduce its international role. If the international use of the dollar declines relatively in East Asia, it is likely to be accompanied by a rise in the use of the yen in East Asia.

Thus, one cannot deny a distinct possibility that the East Asian economies will start regarding the yen as one of the important nominal-anchor currencies, while the role of the U.S. dollar will continue to be significant because of the effects of inertia and history. The yen may come to share the nominal anchor-currency role with the dollar in East Asia, in the sense of receiving greater weights assigned by the East Asian authorities in their currency basket policies.[7]

Broader East Asian Perspectives

How will the developing East Asian economies be affected by the creation of EMU? What benefits and costs will it bring to East Asia? Will the euro become an important key currency in the region? It is important to examine the impact that the creation of EMU and the introduction of the euro might have on East Asia, because East Asia is relatively large in economic size, it is a dynamically growing part of the world economy, and it holds large quantities of foreign exchange reserves.

There are three positive effects on East Asia. First, the emergence of the euro will give private traders and investors a wider menu of dominant international currencies to choose from. They will be able to reduce exchange risks

[6]Current account surpluses, other things being equal, are expected to increase the use of the yen in Japan's international trade and finance for two reasons (see Kawai, 1994). Since exports exceed imports, the weight of the yen used to denominate trade becomes higher than otherwise, given that the proportion of exports denominated in yen is generally bigger than that of imports. Japanese investors, to the extent they care about exchange risk, are likely to demand increasingly that their foreign investments be denominated in yen.

[7]Hence, the yen's role will not be as distinct as the one played by the deutsche mark in the EMS. Even in Western Europe, however, the nominal anchor-currency role of the deutsche mark appears to have been shared by the French franc in recent years (see Kawai and Akiyama, 1997).

by diversifying the currencies used in international transactions. Second, investors will have greater access to a larger, and more efficient, financial market in a unified Europe, which does a great service to everyone in the world. East Asian investors will be able to diversify their portfolios across international financial instruments in a broad, deep, liquid market. Third, as Fred Bergsten suggests, the emergence of the euro will place considerable limits on the policy autonomy of the United States. The United States will be forced to pursue macroeconomic policies conducive to maintaining sustainable current accounts and avoiding rapid dollar depreciation. This is a welcome consequence because it ensures a stable purchasing power and increased attractiveness of the U.S. dollar, the dominant international currency in East Asia.

Despite its predicted increased role in East Asia, the euro is unlikely to rise to the status of a major key currency, because this region is less integrated in trade and foreign direct investment with Europe than with Japan and the United States. The continued structural rigidity of the EU economy is another reason why the euro may not serve as an important key currency in East Asia where economic growth will be much higher than in Europe. The EU is expected to continue to face aggressive trade behavior by East Asian firms, and this trend would be strengthened if East Asia chose to stabilize its exchange rates to the euro. The Asian economies in the euro area, therefore, would be forced to realign exchange rates frequently. This suggests that, while its international role may rise in East Asia, the euro is not a realistic candidate for East Asia's nominal anchor currency.

One must point out some possible costs of EMU to East Asia. First, to the extent that the emergence of the euro increases currency substitution, greater fluctuations of the exchange rates among the euro, the U.S. dollar, and the Japanese yen are expected. Given that the East Asian economies trade with the United States, Japan, and to a lesser extent Europe, exchange rate fluctuations among the three major currencies can pose a large strain on many economies. Second, a unified, larger Europe tends to exert a greater financial and macroeconomic influence on the East Asian economies, which have so far been affected largely by U.S. and Japanese economic conditions. They increasingly will have to take into account shocks emanating from Europe in their macroeconomic management. In addition, greater financial interdependence with Europe implies that there will be a greater risk of sudden capital inflows and outflows, increased pressure on the exchange rate, and undesirable effects on financial institutions in East Asia.

The East Asian economies have developed several forums for financial cooperation by finance ministers and central bankers, such as EMEAP (Executives Meeting of East Asia and Pacific Central Banks), the Six Markets Meeting, and the APEC Finance Ministers Meeting. One of their objectives is to establish a cooperative framework to cope with possible currency and financial crisis of a Mexican type through frequent exchanges of information and bilateral repurchase agreements involving U.S. dollar–denominated foreign exchange reserves. There is even a talk of establishing an Asian BIS. A possible rise in the international use of the euro in East Asia would eventually require closer coordination of financial and exchange rate policies between East Asia and Europe. In addition to the existing arrangements, a framework for geographically wider cooperative mechanisms would have to be developed to ensure exchange rate, financial, and macroeconomic stability.

International Policy Coordination in a Tripolar World Economy

The creation of the euro is highly desirable from a global perspective. It is important, however, to emphasize that the transition process should be orderly, without causing large disturbances to the rest of the world. Both Alogoskoufis and Portes and Bergsten correctly point out that the emergence of the euro as a major international currency is likely to be a cause of instability in the international monetary system and, therefore, requires effective monetary cooperation between the EU and the United States. Regardless whether the forthcoming international monetary system is bipolar or tripolar, Japan must be part of such cooperative arrangements given its large economic size and influence over East Asian economies. In the steady state, avoiding wild exchange rate fluctuations among the major currencies will continue to be an important policy objective not only for Europe, the United States, and Japan, but also for the rest of the world, particularly developing economies that need stable exchange rates among the major currencies. Greater effort is needed to develop a framework for international monetary coordination to maintain stable exchange rates among the euro, the dollar, and the yen.

References

Frankel, Jeffrey A., and Shang-Jin Wei, 1993, "Is There a Currency Bloc in the Pacific?" *The Exchange Rate, International Trade and Monetary Policy*, ed. by Adrian Blundell-Wingnall and Stephen Grenville (Sydney: Reserve Bank of Australia), pp. 275–307.

———, 1994, "Yen Bloc or Dollar Bloc?: Exchange Rate Policies of the East Asian Economies," *Macroeconomic Linkage: Savings, Exchange Rates, and Capital Flows*, ed. by Takatoshi Ito and Anne Krueger (Chicago: University of Chicago Press), pp. 295–329.

Garber, Peter M., 1996, "The Use of the Yen as a Reserve Currency," *Monetary and Economic Studies*, Bank of Japan, Vol. 14 (December), pp. 1–21.

Hamada, Koichi, and Akiyoshi Horiuchi, 1987, "Monetary, Financial, and Real Effects of Yen Internationalization," in *Real-Financial Linkages among Open Economies*, ed. by Sven W. Arndt and J. David Richardson (Cambridge: MIT Press), pp. 167–91.

Kawai, Masahiro, 1994, "Accumulation of Net External Assets in Japan, 1994," *Japan, Europe and International Financial Markets: Analytical and Empirical Perspectives*, ed. by Ryuzo Sato, Richard M. Levich, and Rama V. Ramachandran (Cambridge: Cambridge University Press), pp. 73–123.

———, 1996, "The Japanese Yen as an International Currency: Performance and Prospects," *Organization, Performance and Equity: Perspectives on the Japanese Economy*, ed. by Ryuzo Sato, Rama V. Ramachandran, and Hajime Hori (Boston: Kluwer Academic), pp. 305–55.

———, 1997, "Interactions of Japan's Trade and Investment: A Special Emphasis on East Asia," *East Asian Trade after the Uruguay Round* (tentative title), ed. by David Robertson (Cambridge: Cambridge University Press, forthcoming).

———, and Shigeru Akiyama, 1997, "An Empirical Analysis of Exchange Rate Arrangements: Changing Influences of the World's Major Currencies" (unpublished; Tokyo: Institute of Social Science, University of Tokyo, May).

Tavlas, George S., and Yuzuru Ozeki, 1992, *The Internationalization of Currencies: An Appraisal of the Japanese Yen*, IMF Occasional Paper No. 90 (Washington: International Monetary Fund, January).

Williams, John H., 1947, *Postwar Monetary Plans, and Other Essays* (New York: Alfred A. Knopf, 3rd ed.).

Jean-Pierre Patat

These two papers have addressed the main issues of the future international monetary system. They have provided us with insightful ideas about the consequences of the creation of the euro. I will briefly add a few points. First, I will focus on the cooperation that could occur in such a world. Second, I will make some comments about the likely evolution of the euro rate, as it is described in these two papers.

Obviously, the international monetary system will be progressively completely transformed by the introduction of the euro, for the euro is likely to become a major international reserve currency.

International monetary cooperation would be strengthened because of EMU. The euro will rapidly become a major currency in the world for settlements and transactions, whatever the size of the monetary union at the outset.

Things could be much more progressive as far as the status of the major reserve currency is concerned. A reserve currency needs a large, safe, and liquid financial market. It is precisely one of the objectives of the Stability and Growth Pact in assessing financial convergence to promote a situation of total substitutability of public debt bonds issued by the European countries and thus to create the conditions for a large and unified financial market. That is a first reason why I do not share the view that the European decision makers will be inclined toward a benign neglect: vigilance will prevail over carelessness in the transition period as well as in the steady state.

Furthermore, from a central bank point of view, benign neglect is impossible because the ECB objective will be to deserve the highest confidence of national and international savers with a view to securing the best possible financial conditions for the development of our economies and the limitation of social imbalance. The stability of the internal value of the euro will be the primary objective of the ECB. Therefore, obviously, ensuring the external value of the euro will also be a key issue. It is misleading to believe that the management of a currency can be divided into two separate purposes, one being to maintain the internal value of the currency, and the other concerning its external value. The primary objective of the ECB will clearly be price stability. And this is entirely consistent with exchange rate stability. This is why Europe will make its best efforts to avoid and, if needed, correct the misalignments that might endanger the world economy (trade difficulties) and world finance. In this context, the United States will surely be prepared to make similar efforts.

For all these reasons, the scope of international monetary cooperation is likely to be broadened by EMU. The international monetary system will most likely be a tripolar one, before perhaps becoming multipolar later on; I therefore do not concur with Fred Bergsten's expectations that the system will be a bipolar one.

The system will be tripolar insofar as it would not make sense to exchange views and, if needed, take any decision to maintain an orderly exchange rate environment without the active participation of the world's largest creditor country, namely, Japan. I see no reason why the creation of a unified European area would oust Japan from the cooperation forums (with an acceptable stake in the debate).

Therefore, I do not think that Japan will just play a "minor key currency role." No other country in Asia is likely to outweigh Japan from a monetary point of view in the near future. From a global perspective, a bipolar system is indeed preferable to a "hegemonic system," and a tripolar system is certainly preferable to a bipolar one.

Therefore, in such a tripolar system, Europe is unlikely to adopt a "benign neglect" behavior concerning its exchange rate. The two papers provide most of the reasons why there is a solid common interest in international cooperation, and why carelessness would be collectively dangerous.

These two papers already anticipate the future changes of the euro exchange rate. However, their scenarios are questionable. According to Bergsten, the European countries would try to reach a deliberate depreciation of their currencies (competitive depreciation, as he terms it) in the pretransition period because they know that in the transition period, the euro has to be appreciated to gain credibility. Such a scenario draws too much on an alleged capacity and deliberate willingness of European decision makers to "tailor" the process. Moreover, two elements are missing: first, the rest of the world, and more precisely, the United States. There is no reason why the U.S. authorities would agree to play such a game; and second, more fundamentally, the market itself: such a scenario gives too much weight to the opinion that governments can lead the exchange market wherever they judge it useful. This opinion is obviously untrue.

The recent fluctuations in the dollar have just helped to smooth out the cyclical divergences of the world's three main economies, which is the desirable role of the exchange rate in a flexible system, provided that these movements remain orderly.

Both papers foresee an appreciation of the euro during the "transition period" that will follow its creation. They argue that portfolio adjustments will make the euro appreciate because of an increasing demand for assets in euros. I am very skeptical about this because the supply of euros will also increase, as there will be more borrowers in euros. Therefore, the portfolio effects on the exchange rate are likely to be mixed between demand and supply effects.

This supply effect is mentioned in the Alogoskoufis and Portes paper, but the authors consider it will be very slow. It is questionable that this will be so.

I am also doubtful about this appreciation due to portfolio effects for another reason. Even if investors' demand for euro-denominated assets increases more than the supply of liabilities in euros, the balance will not necessarily be restored by an appreciation of the euro. It could also be achieved by a decrease in interest rates in Europe, which would be more profitable for the European economies.

Fiscal consolidation is a necessary condition for economic stability. Its impact on the exchange rate as presented in Bergsten's paper is questionable. The connection between fiscal policy and the exchange rate is arguably not obvious from the experiences of a number of industrial countries.

Bergsten advocates the idea that fiscal consolidation in Europe would lead to a depreciation of the exchange rate. I would reply that the U.S. "balancing the budget" process will lead to a depreciation of the dollar (prompted by the decline in interest rates). And as fiscal consolidation is also implemented in Japan as well as nearly everywhere else in the world, the argument is invalidated. (If the euro, the dollar, and the yen are simultaneously depreciated, there will be no depreciation at all.)

I totally disagree with the scenario according to which "an 'effective' Stability and Growth Pact could . . . produce much more severe international risks than a more permissive [fiscal policy]" (Bergsten, p. 34). According to the author, the Stability and Growth Pact would suppress any flexibility in the use of macroeconomic policies, so that the two solutions to counter European unemployment problems would be competitive depreciation and/or trade protection. This is obviously very unlikely.

Generally speaking, I do not agree with the idea that fiscal consolidation in Europe will lead to further depreciation of the European currency[1] for three reasons.

First, it is true that fiscal consolidation contributes to lower interest rates and therefore possibly to a lower exchange rate. However, as the European fiscal consolidation has been announced for a long time, this decrease in the interest rate is expected by the markets. Therefore, the current exchange rate already includes the effects of fiscal consolidation. The further evolution of the European exchange rates will not be affected by this expected fiscal policy, for it is already discounted in the present exchange rates. More generally, the exchange rate of a country is driven not only by its interest rates but also by its net external assets. As fiscal consolidation improves domestic savings, the country will accumulate net foreign assets or will reduce its foreign debt.

---

[1]See the IMF's October 1995 *World Economic Outlook*, which concluded that if the short-run effect of fiscal consolidation is to depreciate the real exchange rate, "for the long run, there is a more general presumption that a sustained reduction in the government deficit that raises national saving [. . .] will eventually lead to a real exchange rate appreciation" (p. 80).

Second, fiscal consolidation provides healthier conditions for the whole economy. The decrease in interest rates that it allows does not mean that the monetary policy stance is looser.

Third, Bergsten assumes that European monetary policy may become easier in order to fight unemployment, as fiscal policy will be tighter. That would be totally inefficient since, according to the IMF, 80 percent of European unemployment is structural. European unemployment certainly ought to be solved, but with suitable structural reforms, and not with monetary or fiscal stimuli. It would also be counterproductive for sustainable growth. The main purpose of the ECB will be to design and implement a policy of credibility and to provide the European economies with the best financing conditions, that is, with very low market interest rates. That would not be the case if the market had the feeling that the ECB's objective was not monetary and price stability, but some magic recipe for managing interest rates to improve employment. Any loosening of monetary policy will result in an increase in the expected inflation and in long-term rates, which will affect only economic growth adversely. In the long run, a stable monetary policy will provide better conditions for growth, by lowering the interest rates for all maturities.

A stable monetary policy could be expected for the euro. A stable exchange rate is also likely. There is no benign neglect of the international impact of EMU (even though it is true that the debate has so far been subdued), and there will be no European benign neglect of the future evolution of the euro. As has been frequently stressed (and sometimes criticized) on this side of the Atlantic, exchange rate issues do matter for European decision makers. There is no reason to think that the monetary policy of the ECB will be different from what can be described as an optimization of the yield curve in an orderly exchange rate environment, which is presently the aim of monetary policy in the European countries.

Session II
Exchange Arrangements of Other Countries vis-à-vis the EMU

4

Exchange Rate Arrangements Between the Ins and the Outs

Paul De Grauwe

At the European Council Meeting of Florence in June 1996 the broad outline of a new exchange rate mechanism (ERM II) was agreed upon. This new mechanism will guide the exchange rate relations between the countries inside (the "ins") and the countries outside the euro area (the "outs"). It will be set in place at the start of Stage III of EMU, that is, on January 1, 1999 (assuming that EMU starts on time).

In this paper we analyze several issues. First we describe the main features of ERM II and compare them with those of ERM I as it evolved during the 1980s and the 1990s. Second, we analyze the question whether and under what conditions ERM II will be more successful than its predecessor in avoiding disruptive speculative crises. To do so, we will use both new theoretical insights about the factors that affect the occurrence of speculative crises and an historical analysis of the turbulence within ERM I.

Description of ERM II

The main features of ERM II can be described as follows. First, the agreement is a voluntary one. This principle was introduced at the insistence of the United Kingdom. It is to be understood, however, that those countries who have committed themselves to participating in EMU at some later stage should join ERM II if they want to qualify for entry into EMU. In addition, the agreement is seen as a mechanism that should help countries in converging toward the Maastricht norms.

Second, the new exchange rate mechanism is based on central rates using the euro as the anchor currency. Around these central rates a band of fluctua-

The author is grateful to Filip Abraham, Paul Masson, Jacques Mélitz, Bart Turtelboom, and Horst Ungerer for many useful comments.

tion will be defined. No number on the exact size of that band was decided upon. The agreement only stipulates that this band "is expected to be relatively wide." It is generally understood that this means that the band would be comparable in magnitude to the normal band of 2 × 15 percent in the present ERM I.

Third, the band of fluctuation of a non-euro currency with the euro will be relatively wide, and the fluctuation margin between two non-euro currencies participating in ERM II will be twice that size. Therefore, the agreement foresees that the countries of these non-euro currencies can make ad hoc arrangements to limit the fluctuation margins of their bilateral exchange rates.

Fourth, the commitment by the ECB to intervene in the foreign exchange market to support a particular non-euro currency is limited. The agreement stipulates explicitly that interventions by the ECB should not be undertaken if these would interfere with the main objective of the ECB, that is, the maintenance of price stability. The agreement adds (rather academically) that this constraint also holds for the intervention commitment of the non-euro countries participating in ERM II.

Finally, adjustments in the central rates shall be done in a timely fashion so as to avoid significant misalignments. All parties to the agreement, including the ECB, will have the right to initiate a confidential procedure aimed at reconsidering the central rates.

When comparing these features of ERM II with ERM I as the latter evolved after 1993, the resemblance is striking. First, the band of fluctuation of ERM II is likely to be of the same order of magnitude as the one in the post-1993 ERM I. This should allow for a significant amount of flexibility in exchange rate movements. Second, ERM II will have an anchor currency, the euro, very much like ERM I has an (informal) anchor, the deutsche mark.

In some sense, however, ERM II is quite different from ERM I. First, ERM II will have more flexibility than ERM I in that it is very explicit on allowing speedy realignments of the central rates if the need to do so arises. Second, the formal intervention commitments of the central banks in ERM II appear to be weaker than those in ERM I. In the latter, central banks have an obligation to intervene when an exchange rate reaches the limit of the band. In practice this difference may not be significant, however. As is well known, despite the formal commitment of the Bundesbank to intervene in unlimited amounts to support other ERM currencies, the Bundesbank stopped its interventions when it felt that these were interfering with its domestic monetary policy objectives.[1] Third, ERM II is very much seen as a temporary arrangement for countries that want to join the third stage of EMU. Whether

[1]There is some dispute whether the Bundesbank was bound by a formal commitment to intervene. The so-called Emminger letter seems to indicate that the Bundesbank did perceive itself as being bound by such a commitment.

this rather unique feature will help to stabilize the exchange rates is one of the issues we want to analyze in this paper.

The most important issue confronting the future ERM II is whether and how it can be made robust and resistant to speculative crises. One thing we have learned from history is that almost all fixed exchange rate arrangements ultimately collapse. The question then is whether ERM II will experience the same fate. To shed some light on this question we analyze the collapse of ERM I and relate it to recent theoretical insights about collapsing fixed exchange rate regimes.

Collapse of ERM I

Broadly speaking, two stories have been told about the collapse of ERM I. One is based on the idea that when fundamentals (e.g., price levels) diverge, a fixed exchange rate cannot be sustained and ultimately will come under attack. This view has found a theoretical expression in so-called first-generation models of speculative attacks (Krugman, 1979, and Flood and Garber, 1984). A second story stresses the fragility of fixed exchange rate regimes because of the self-fulfilling nature of speculative attacks. This story has been given a strong theoretical foundation in so-called second-generation models of speculative attacks (Obstfeld, 1986 and 1995).

There appears to be some consensus that the collapse of ERM I can be seen as a combination of these two stories. There is less consensus, however, on the relative importance given to these two explanations.

There is little doubt that the lira and peseta crises of September 1992 should be seen as examples of speculative attacks triggered by increasing divergencies in some important fundamentals. We present evidence in Figures 1 and 2. These show the evolution of the real exchange rate of the lira and the peseta vis-à-vis the deutsche mark (the anchor currency in ERM I). We also show the yearly inflation differentials between Italy and Spain on the one hand and Germany on the other. The remarkable thing is that the inflation differentials steadily declined. However, since the nominal exchange rate was fixed since 1987,[2] the positive, albeit declining, inflation differentials accumulated into increasing price level divergencies when converted into the same currency. Put differently, the lira and the peseta experienced an increasing real appreciation relative to the deutsche mark (and also relative to the other ERM currencies). This also led to increasing current account deficits that became unsustainable and that led to a speculative crisis in September 1992. The lira dropped out of the ERM and depreciated substantially. The peseta, together with the escudo, devalued several times.

[2]In the case of the peseta there was in fact a nominal appreciation during part of the period.

Figure 1. Inflation Differential Between Italy and Germany and the Real Lira–Deutsche Mark Rate (1980 = 100)

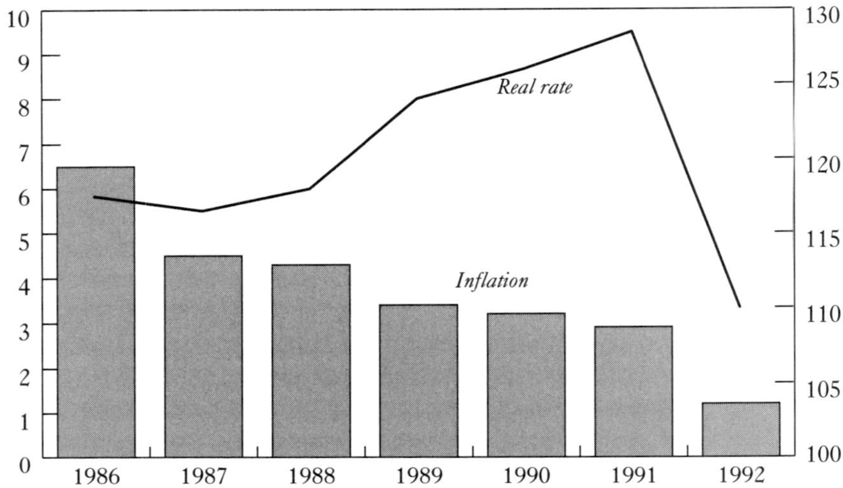

Source: IMF, *International Financial Statistics.*
Note: The real lira–deutsche mark rate is defined as the nominal lira–deutsche mark rate times the ratio of the Italian and the German CPI.

Figure 2. Inflation Differential Between Spain and Germany and the Real Peseta–Deutsche Mark Rate (1980 = 100)

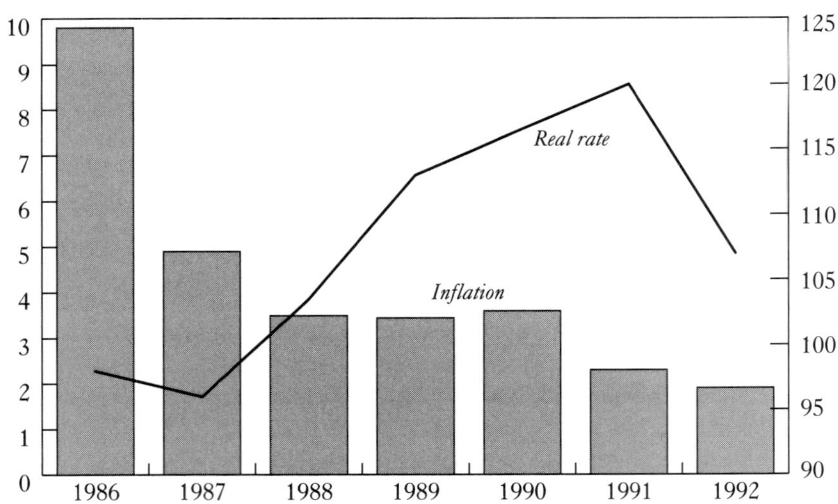

Source: IMF, *International Financial Statistics.*
Note: The real peseta–deutsche mark rate is defined as the nominal peseta–deutsche mark rate times the ratio of the Spanish and the German CPI.

Whereas one can find divergent fundamentals to explain the lira and peseta crises of September 1992, it is much more difficult, if not impossible, to identify fundamental variables responsible for the sterling crisis of September 1992 or the crisis of August 1993 that involved the French franc and other ERM currencies, and which led to the dramatic widening of the band of fluctuation (see Eichengreen and Wyplosz, 1993; Eichengreen, Rose, and Wyplosz, 1996; and Jeanne and Masson, 1996). Thus, the most severe speculative crises during 1992–93 cannot easily be explained in the context of the first-generation models of speculative behavior. Rather, one has to rely on second-generation models stressing the role of self-fulfilling speculative attacks and multiple equilibria. It is clear, however, that these models can easily become black boxes. In these models, trivial events ("sunspots") can trigger a speculative attack. This is not a very interesting explanation because it leads to new unresolved questions, for example, why did it take speculators so long to make their attack, and why have some currencies never been attacked (e.g., the guilder)?

For these second-generation models to be instructive, the process that leads to the speculative trigger must be specified. Recent theoretical progress has been made to do this (see Obstfeld, 1995; Flood and Marion, 1996; and Jeanne and Masson, 1996). These models make clear that the trigger that leads to a speculative attack is most likely related to (observable or not yet observable) fundamental developments. The sterling and French franc crisis can be used to illustrate this point.

The major event that can be invoked as the trigger mechanism is the German unification and the ensuing strongly unsynchronized business cycle in the ERM. Countries like the United Kingdom and France experienced a deep recession during 1991–93.[3] Germany, on the other hand, had just experienced its unification. This had created a booming economy and inflationary pressures. Figures 3 and 4 illustrate this. In Figure 3 we exhibit the growth rates of GDP in France, the United Kingdom, and Germany. In 1991, France and the United Kingdom had already moved into a serious recession, while Germany still experienced a healthy boom. On the inflation front (Figure 4), the reverse was true. Germany saw its inflation rate increase while the other EMS countries experienced a decline in their inflation rates, which in the case of France even dropped below the German level in 1991.

These differences in economic conditions set the stage for the coming conflict. Germany insisted on pursuing an anti-inflationary policy. The other countries, like the United Kingdom and France, were very reluctant to do so. As long as they kept the exchange rate peg with Germany, they were forced to follow Germany in its monetary restriction, despite the fact that their problem was one of too much deflation, not too much inflation. These problems

[3]The recession in the United Kingdom was earlier, about 1990–92, whereas the recession in France occurred mainly during 1991–93 (see Figure 3).

Figure 3. Real GDP Growth in Germany, France, and the United Kingdom

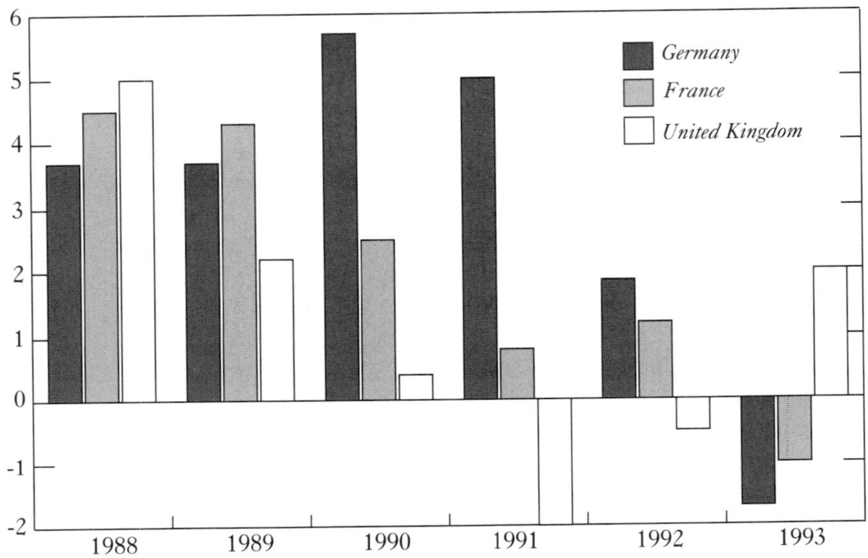

Source: European Commission, *European Economy*.

Figure 4. Inflation Rates in Germany, France, and the United Kingdom

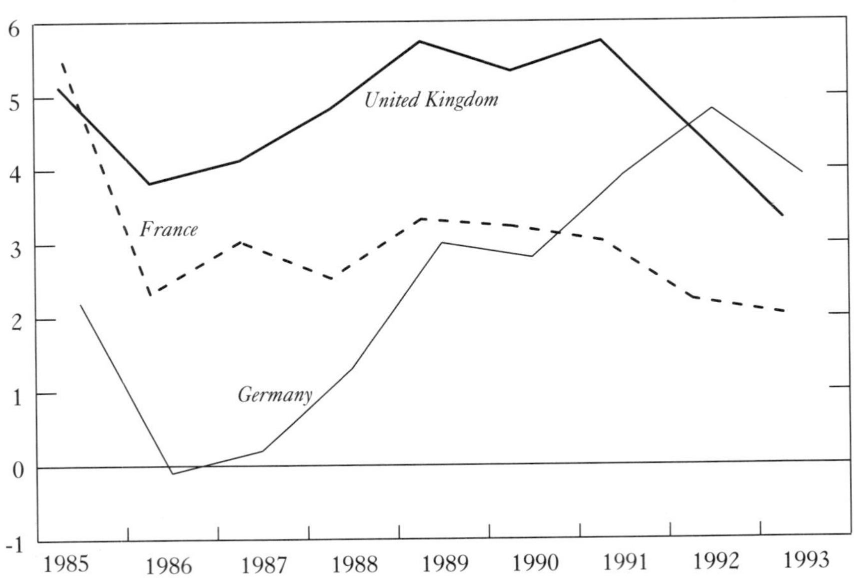

Source: European Commission, *European Economy*.

and the merit of continuing fixing the exchange rate with the deutsche mark were widely discussed in countries like France and the United Kingdom. Well-known academic economists, and also politicians, came out against such a policy. This created doubts in the mind of speculators concerning the resolve of the governments in these countries to maintain a fixed exchange rate with the deutsche mark. More important, speculators realized that a speculative attack would increase the cost of the exchange rate peg because it would force the authorities to raise the domestic interest rate, thereby increasing the intensity of the recession. Speculation acquired a self-fulfilling aspect. In such an environment of weakened credibility of the fixed exchange rate arrangement, trivial events (a pronouncement by ministers or well-known professors) could easily trigger a speculative crisis.

Two additional points should be made here to understand the timing of the collapse of the ERM. First, at the end of the 1980s, ERM I changed in nature in that the authorities of the major ERM countries began aiming at avoiding any realignment. As a result, the ERM evolved into a truly fixed exchange rate system. Up to 1987, realignments were frequent and relatively small in comparison with the size of the band of free fluctuation. As a result, after most realignments the new market rate stayed within the bounds of the previous band, so that few discrete jumps in the exchange rate occurred. This meant that the pre-1987 ERM I did not have the asymmetric "one-way bet" character that is a major attraction for speculators. After 1987, as the parities remained fixed for many years, the probability that the next realignment would be large relative to the size of the band increased over time. This introduced a "one-way bet" situation and attracted large speculative funds. With the substantial widening of the band of fluctuation in August 1993, the "one-way bet" feature of ERM I was eliminated. It is therefore no surprise that major speculative attacks have not occurred in ERM I since August 1993.

A second factor increasing the size of the pool of speculative funds was the liberalization of capital movements, which occurred in 1990 in countries such as Italy and France. This feature has been very much stressed by Eichengreen and Wyplosz (1993), who have argued that in order to stabilize the ERM, capital controls in the form of compulsory deposits of net foreign asset positions of commercial banks may be necessary.

Lessons for ERM II

What can we learn from the experience with ERM I that is relevant for the future stability of ERM II? We concentrate first on the role of fundamentals. Then we ask whether self-fulfilling speculative attacks are likely to occur in the future ERM II.

Role of Fundamentals in the Stability of ERM II

The recent significant convergence of a number of important fundamental variables (inflation, budgetary policies), if maintained, will reduce the scope for classical speculative attacks of the kind stressed in the first-generation models. This increased convergence of important fundamental variables is often stressed by policymakers as a condition for the stability of the future ERM II. The question, however, is whether this increased convergence will be sufficient to stabilize the future ERM II. Two points are important in this context. First, although there is now, in 1997, more convergence than in 1992–93, small changes in the fundamentals are likely to trigger large responses of speculators in the future ERM II. The reason is that small changes in, say, inflation or the government budget deficit can lead a country to be disqualified at the next decision round concerning entry into EMU. Thus, the markets are likely to analyze the evolution of inflation, budget deficits, and debts with a magnifying glass. In this sense, the Maastricht entry conditions are likely to increase the sensitivity of speculative movements with respect to a number of important fundamental variables, especially when moving closer toward the decision about entry into EMU. ERM II may become quite sensitive to speculative attacks.

A second important point to be made here is that it is not clear whether the present structure of real exchange rates corresponds to an equilibrium structure. This can be seen from Figures 5 and 6, which show the cumulative real effective appreciations and depreciations of the currencies of the candidate EMU members from 1991 until the end of 1996 according to two different sources—the European Commission and the IMF. It is striking to find that the structure of real exchange rates has changed considerably since the signing of the Treaty of Maastricht. The "peripheral" countries (with the exception of Portugal) have experienced strong real depreciations of their currencies. Part of these real depreciations should be considered as corrections for the real appreciations that some countries (e.g., Italy and Spain) experienced during the late 1980s. There is, however, reason to believe that the subsequent depreciations of these currencies may have overshot their equilibrium values.

The experience of the "core" countries is quite different. However, here the two sources tell quite a different story. According to the European Commission data, the countries pegging to the deutsche mark have experienced real appreciations of close to 10 percent. The IMF data tell a somewhat different story. According to this source, among the core countries, only Germany (together with Portugal) experienced a strong real appreciation. The other core countries stabilized their real exchange rates during the 1990s.

From the preceding analysis, one may come to the following conclusions. It is quite possible that the currencies of the "peripheral" EU countries (with the exception of the Portuguese escudo) are still somewhat undervalued. This

Figure 5. Real Effective Appreciation (Depreciation) from 1991 to 1996, Based on EU Data

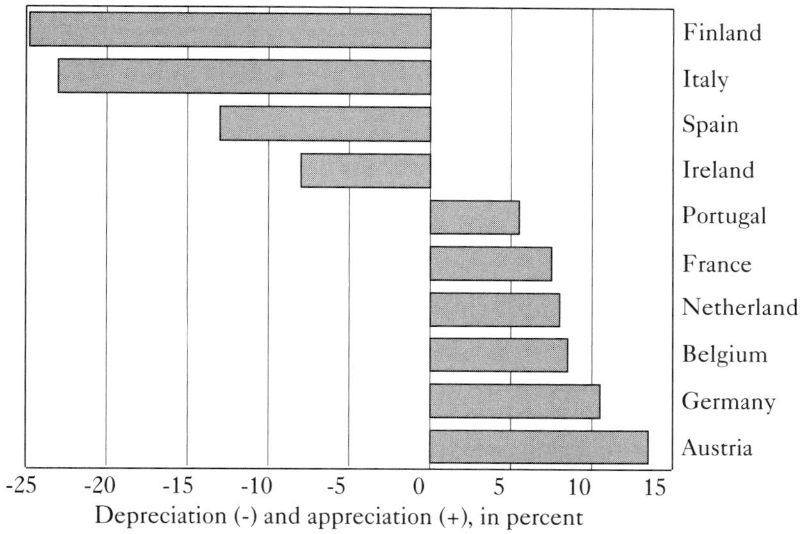

Source: European Commission.

Figure 6. Real Effective Appreciation (Depreciation) from 1991 to 1996, Based on IMF Data

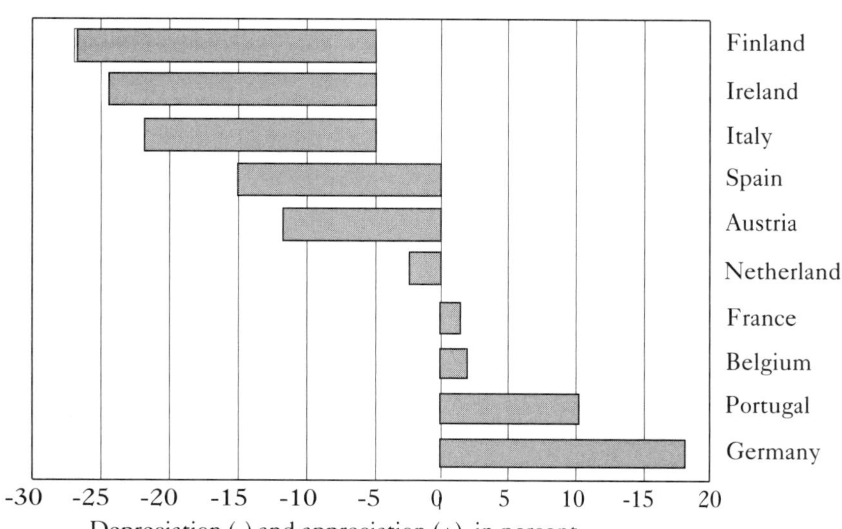

Source: IMF, *International Financial Statistics*

conclusion should be considered tentative, of course, because as mentioned earlier, the depreciations of the Southern European currencies during the 1990s occurred as a correction to the real appreciations experienced during the 1980s. As far as the core currencies are concerned, the situation of the deutsche mark stands out. This currency is most likely to be overvalued by 10 to 20 percent at the end of 1996. The conclusion has been confirmed by a recent study of Sinn (1996), who arrives at the conclusion that the deutsche mark is overvalued by 15 to 20 percent, and that this overvaluation is due mainly to the depreciations of the Southern European currencies and the pound sterling since the early 1990s.

The large real appreciation of the deutsche mark may lead to problems of exchange rate management in the future ERM II. The nature of the problem will depend on who will be in and who will be out. Let us consider two scenarios.

Scenario A: The core EU countries are in EMU whereas the peripheral countries stay out

In this case the problem arises of whether major exchange rate adjustments should be undertaken between Germany and the other EMU participants, leading to a depreciation of the deutsche mark vis-à-vis the other in currencies. Sinn (1996) argues that the present overvaluation of the deutsche mark is mainly due to the overvaluation against the out currencies, and that the exchange rate relationship among the core currencies is more or less in equilibrium. This is also confirmed by the European Commission data. If that is so, EMU can start without a major realignment. A new issue would arise, however. There would still be a need for Germany to correct for the overvaluation against the out currencies. This need to correct for an overvaluation of the German currency may lead to pressures toward depreciation of the euro relative to out currencies. Thus, paradoxically, the euro may become the weak currency until the equilibrium exchange rates are restored. Given the relatively large size of the band of fluctuation, such an appreciation of the out currencies versus the euro could most probably be dealt with relatively easily. However, if the ECB were to resist this (driven by an ambition to establish "credibility"), the disequilibrium structure of the exchange rates may impart a deflationary bias in the euro area, forcing the ECB to reduce inflation relative to the out countries.

Scenario B: The core and the periphery together form EMU

In this scenario the problem of the disequilibrium structure of exchange rates should be tackled as soon as the decision concerning the conversion rates is made. This would imply that the "peripheral" countries (with the exception of Portugal) accept a revaluation of their currencies relative to the deutsche mark as the price to pay to enter EMU. If this appears to be impossible, EMU would start with a structural adjustment problem exerting deflationary pressures in the core countries. This would not be a good way to start monetary union in Europe.

Self-Fulfilling Speculative Attacks in ERM II

In this subsection we analyze whether the speculative attacks of the kind analyzed in second-generation models of speculative crises are likely to occur in the future ERM II. In this connection, there are two opposing features of ERM II. First, ERM II will have relatively large bands of fluctuation. In addition, the ERM II agreement is quite explicit on the need for speedy realignments if the need arises. As argued earlier, the size of the band of fluctuation in combination with the expected rate of devaluation (revaluation) is quite important in limiting the scope for self-fulfilling speculative crises. This is usually not taken into account in the existing theoretical models. With a band of fluctuation of close to 30 percent, expectations of devaluations (revaluations) will typically be below the size of the band. This creates an expectation that after the next realignment, if it occurs, the new exchange rate will fall within the *old* band of fluctuation. Therefore, speculators do not expect a discrete jump in the exchange rate after the realignment. As a result, they expect little profit after the realignment. Large speculative movements of the kind that occurred in 1992–93, therefore, are unlikely. In this connection, ERM II will resemble the post-1993 ERM I. It will also be closer to the pre-1987 version of ERM I, during which frequent realignments occurred that remained relatively small in relation to the band of fluctuation. This was especially the case with the currencies using the wider band of 2 × 6 percent (e.g., Italian lira). We show the evidence in Figure 7. We observe that after each realignment of the lira, the new lira–deutsche mark rate remained within the old bounds of the fluctuation band. The sharp changes in the lira rate always happened prior to the realignment. As a result, speculators made little profits, and large-scale speculative attacks were avoided. In Figure 8 we show the case of the French franc–deutsche mark rate. Here we find that during 1982–83 there were several realignments that were significantly higher than the (smaller) size of the band, producing large jumps after the realignment and large speculative profits. As a result, the speculative crises during this period were intense, leading to a near collapse of ERM I.

There is another feature of ERM II that may increase the probability of self-fulfilling speculative attacks. This can be described as follows. Every two years the out countries' performance toward convergence will be evaluated, based on the Maastricht convergence criteria. Sufficient convergence will lead

Figure 7. Deutsche Mark–Lira Exchange Rate

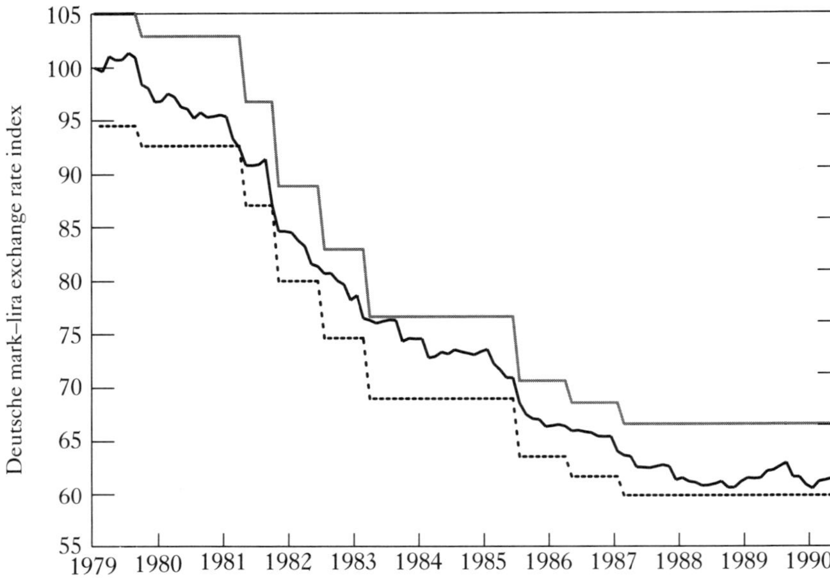

Figure 8. Deutsche Mark–French Franc Exchange Rate

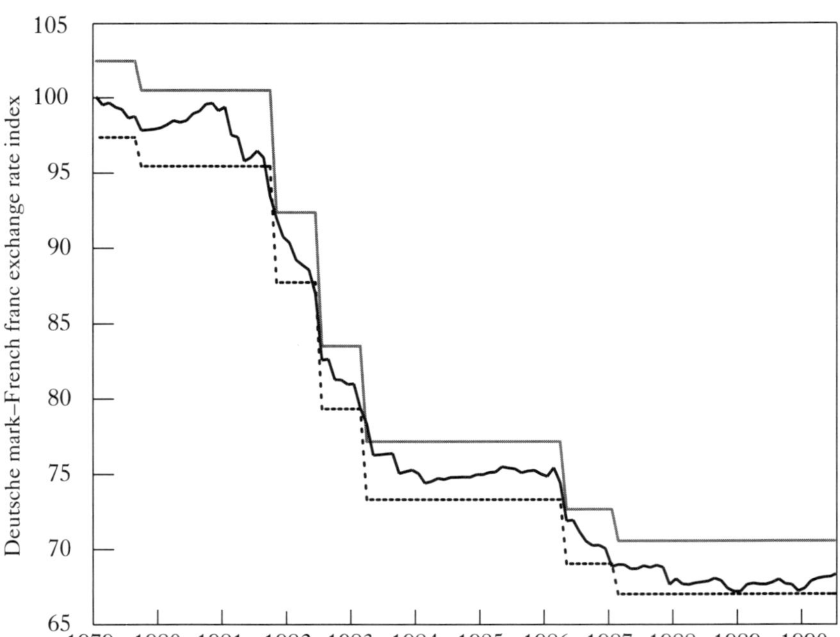

to entry into EMU; insufficient convergence will lead to postponement of entry. In this dynamic of convergence there are several features that may trigger self-fulfilling speculative crises. The first is the interest rate convergence requirement. If the market expects a country to join, this will quickly lead to a reduction of the interest rate margin over the euro interest rate, alleviating the burden of the government debt. In countries with a large government debt, this can lead to a significant decline in the budget deficit, thereby helping to achieve the budgetary convergence requirement. Note that the latter effect occurs because the market is optimistic about the probability of joining EMU. A reverse dynamic can be triggered by bad news about the convergence process. This will lead to higher interest rates in the out country and thus a larger budget deficit, thereby validating the prevailing pessimism about a country's chances of joining EMU.

The interest rate and fiscal dynamics can be reinforced by speculative attacks in the foreign exchange markets. Pessimism about the prospects of entry into EMU may trigger a speculative attack and produce the multiple equilibria that are stressed in the second-generation models. Speculators know that if the attack leads to a realignment, the country cannot enter EMU at the set date. Their pessimism about the prospects for entry then leads them to attack the currency, which, by leading to a realignment, validates that pessimism. The probability that this speculation will be set in motion depends on the perception speculators have about the commitment of the authorities to maintain the existing band of fluctuation. If the authorities are seen to have a weak commitment (because they find the defense of the exchange rate costly), speculation will be forthcoming. Here also the size of the government debt matters. A speculative attack raises the domestic interest rate and increases the debt burden. The higher the debt burden, the greater the cost of the defense of the fixed exchange rate. This leads to the conclusion that the self-fulfilling nature of the speculative attack is a positive function of the debt level. (In the next section we present a model that formalizes this feature.)

The perception speculators will have about the strength of the commitment in the future ERM II also depends on other factors. First, as mentioned earlier, the ECB does not intend to give unlimited support to a currency under attack. This will be perceived as a signal that the commitment toward a fixed exchange rate is weak and may invite speculators to attack the currency. Second, since the "entry exam" will be organized every two years (the country can even take the initiative earlier to "take the exam"), there is always a relatively cheap option to postpone entry. The existence of this option may weaken the resolve to defend the currency at all costs.

In this section we have stressed two opposing forces that may influence the probability of self-fulfilling speculative crises. One, the large band of fluctuations, reduces this likelihood. The other, the self-fulfilling nature of the convergence dynamics, may increase this probability. Which of the two features of ERM II will prevail is difficult to say a priori. The start of a totally different monetary regime is a unique historical experience so we cannot easily learn from other exchange rate arrangements of the past.

A Model of Self-Fulfilling Speculative Attack in ERM II

In this section we present a stylized model of a speculative attack based on Obstfeld (1995) (see also Calvo, 1988, and Obstfeld, 1986). We change the structure of the model, however, to fit the dynamics of convergence by which countries in ERM II are constrained.

We start with the budget constraint of the country taking part in ERM II:

$$\dot{b} = g - t + (i - \pi)b - \pi m, \tag{1}$$

where b is the debt-to-GDP ratio (a dot represents a rate of change); g is the primary government spending as a percent of GDP; t is tax revenues as a percent of GDP; i is the nominal interest rate, π is the inflation rate, and m is the ratio of money to GDP (the inverse of the velocity of money); thus πm is the revenue from monetary financing (seigniorage). For a typical European country, this term is very small (typically about 1 percent of GDP) and of a second-order nature compared to the other terms in the equation. We will therefore disregard seigniorage as a source of financing of the government budget. Note that we assume (without loss in generality) that the real growth of output is zero.

The nominal interest rate can also be written as

$$i = r + \pi^e, \tag{2}$$

where π^e is the expected inflation rate, and r is the real interest rate.

Substituting equation (2) into (1) yields

$$\dot{b} = g - t + (r + \pi^e - \pi)b. \tag{3}$$

We observe that it is only the unanticipated component of inflation ($\pi^e - \pi$) that affects the budget constraint, that is, inflation that is higher than expected lowers the debt burden. Fully anticipated inflation ($\pi = \pi^e$) does not lower the debt burden. The reason is that a fully anticipated inflation reduces the real value of the outstanding debt and increases the nominal interest rate at the same time.

We assume that purchasing power parity holds, so that

$$\varepsilon = \pi, \tag{4}$$

where ε is the rate of depreciation of the domestic currency. For the sake of convenience we set the rate of inflation in the euro area equal to zero.

Setting $\dot{b} = 0$ in equation (3), we obtain the condition necessary to stabilize the debt-to-GDP ratio. It can be interpreted as a necessary condition for solvency of the government. We will also interpret it as a necessary condition for the country to join EMU. (It is clearly not sufficient.) Using equation (4), we can rewrite this condition as follows:

$$t = g + rb + (\varepsilon^e - \varepsilon)b. \tag{5}$$

We observe that, given the level of spending, g, and the real interest rate, r, there is a trade-off between the tax rate and the rate of depreciation (inflation rate), that is, an unexpected depreciation (increase in inflation) allows the government to reduce taxes (as percent of GDP) while keeping the solvency constraint intact. Put differently, an unexpected depreciation reduces the debt burden. This trade-off, however, only holds if the depreciation is unanticipated. In a rational expectations world, there can be no systematic deviation between expected and realized depreciation, so that on average $\varepsilon^e - \varepsilon = 0$ ($\pi^e - \pi = 0$). Thus, from equation (5) we can write the "long-run" trade-off between depreciation (inflation) and taxation that is necessary to maintain solvency as follows:

$$t_N = g + rb, \tag{6}$$

where we interpret t_N as the "natural" rate of taxation given the level of spending, the accumulated debt, and the real interest rate. This natural level of taxation is independent of the depreciation (inflation).

It will be clear that we have formulated the problem in a similar framework as the Phillips curve framework. (The latter is also the framework in which the Obstfeld (1995) model of self-fulfilling speculation is formulated.) Equation (5) is the "short-term" solvency constraint. It has a structure reminiscent of the short-term Phillips curve. Unanticipated depreciations (increases in inflation) reduce the burden of the debt, very much like unanticipated inflation reduces unemployment. Equation (6) is the long-run solvency constraint, which is similar to the long-run (vertical) Phillips curve. The "natural" tax rate is independent of the rate of depreciation (inflation), very much like the natural unemployment is.

One can represent equations (5) and (6) graphically. This is done in Figure 9. The short-term trade-offs are represented by the downward sloping lines.

Figure 9. Trade-Off Between Inflation and Taxation

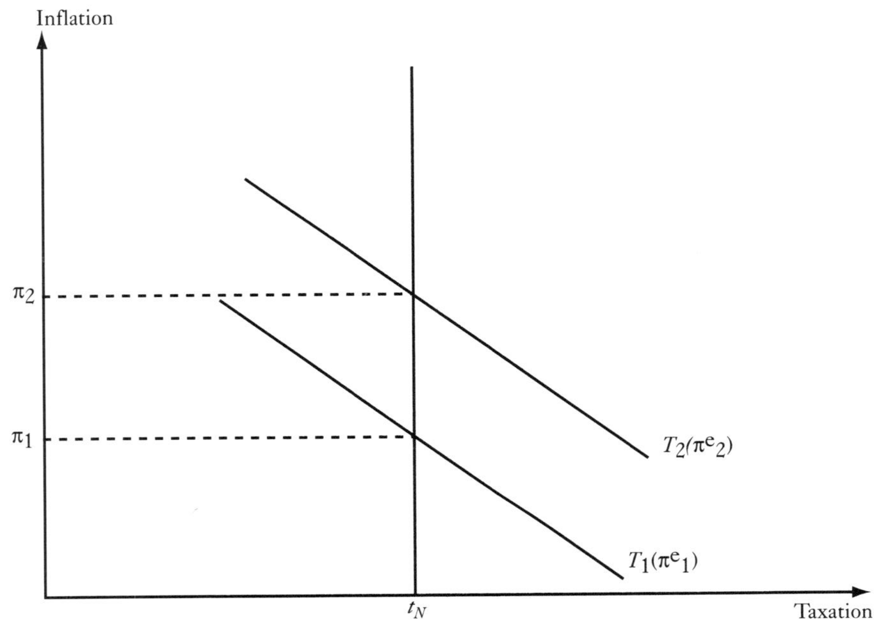

There is one such trade-off for every level of expected inflation. The slope of these short-term trade-offs is given by the parameter b (the debt-to-GDP ratio) in equation (5). It can be seen that as b increases, the short-term trade-off becomes flatter. This means that in a country with a high debt-to-GDP ratio the same inflationary surprise reduces the debt burden more than in a country with a low debt-to-GDP ratio. Note also that a higher b leads to a displacement to the right of the "natural" taxation rate.

Assume now that the authorities aim at minimizing a loss function of the type

$$L = t^2 + a\varepsilon^2 + C(\varepsilon), \tag{7}$$

where a is a parameter expressing the weight given by the monetary authorities to the exchange rate target. Both inflation and taxation are perceived to be costly to the monetary authorities. The authorities therefore set inflation (the exchange rate) so as to minimize the cost of inflation given that they also care about minimizing the tax burden. The latter can also be interpreted as minimizing the debt burden. As in Obstfeld (1995), we have added a second term in the rate of depreciation $C(\varepsilon)$. This term expresses the fixed cost C of devaluing the currency. It takes on two values: c_D when a devaluation occurs, and c_R when a revaluation happens. In the context of our ERM II country, this cost can be interpreted as the cost of having to postpone entry into EMU when the currency is devalued. As will be remembered, a country cannot be accepted into EMU if it has devalued the currency during a period of two years prior to the entry date. This implies that c_R (the cost of a revaluation) is low compared to the cost of a devaluation.

We will assume that stochastic shocks occur in g, the level of government spending, that is,

$$g = g^* + u,$$

where u is a random variable with zero mean.

These shocks in g occur, for example, because of disturbances in output: during a recession the government is forced to increase spending for the unemployed, and during a boom government spending declines. Thus, the stochastic shocks in g can be seen as expressing stochastic shocks in output.

The authorities now select an ε that minimizes the loss function given the shock they observe in g and given the devaluation expectations of private agents. If we initially ignore the fixed-cost term, the government chooses the optimal rate of depreciation

$$\varepsilon = \frac{b(g^* + rb + u) + b^2\varepsilon^e}{a + b^2}. \tag{8}$$

Substituting this solution into equation (5) yields the tax level (the burden of the debt)

$$t = \frac{a(g^* + rb + u) + ab\varepsilon^e}{a + b^2}. \tag{9}$$

Substituting equations (8) and (9) into the loss function (7), we obtain the value of the loss under flexible exchange rates:

$$L_{flex} = \frac{a}{a + b^2}(g^* + rb + u + b\varepsilon^e)^2. \tag{10}$$

Under a rigidly fixed exchange rate, this loss would be

$$L_{fix} = (g^* + rb + u + b\varepsilon^e)^2. \tag{11}$$

It can be seen that $L_{flex} < L_{fix}$.

However, taking into account the fixed cost of devaluing the currency, $C(\varepsilon)$, the authorities will only devalue if u (the shock in g) is large enough to make

$$L_{fix} - L_{flex} > c_D.$$

Similarly, the authorities will only revalue if the negative shock in u is large enough to make

$$L_{fix} - L_{flex} > c_R.$$

We can compute the critical value of u for which a devaluation occurs,

$$u_D = \frac{1}{b}\sqrt{c_D(a + b^2)} + g^* + rb - b\varepsilon^e, \tag{12}$$

and the critical value of u for which a revaluation occurs,

$$u_R = -\frac{1}{b}\sqrt{c_R(a + b^2)} + g^* + rb - b\varepsilon^e. \tag{13}$$

We note the following interesting result:

$$du_D/d\varepsilon^e = -b.$$

This implies that an increase in the expected depreciation lowers the critical value at which the devaluation occurs, the more so as the level of the debt is high. Thus, a country with a high debt level will more likely be forced to devalue when expectations of a depreciation increase than a country with a low debt level.

This result lies at the heart of the self-fulfilling nature of speculation: an expected devaluation increases the cost of the debt service because it raises the domestic nominal interest rate. This expectations-induced increase in the debt service increases with the size of the debt. Thus, with a higher debt, the authorities have a higher incentive to devalue than with a lower debt. Since speculators know this, they also realize that by speculating against the currency they increase the incentive of the authorities to devalue, the more so as the debt is high.

Rational agents take equations (12) and (13) into account and compute the probability of a change in the exchange rate. Assuming that u is uniformly distributed on $[-\mu, \mu]$, we obtain the following rational expectation of the rate of depreciation:

$$E(\varepsilon) = \frac{b}{a + b^2}\left[\left(1 - \frac{u_D - u_R}{2\mu}\right)(g^* + rb + b\varepsilon^e) - \frac{u_D^2 - u_R^2}{4\mu}\right]. \tag{14}$$

This nonlinear expression gives rise to the possibility of multiple equilibria. We represent them graphically in Figures 10a, b, and c. The nonlinear line

Figure 10. Government Debt and Self-Fullfilling Speculative Attacks

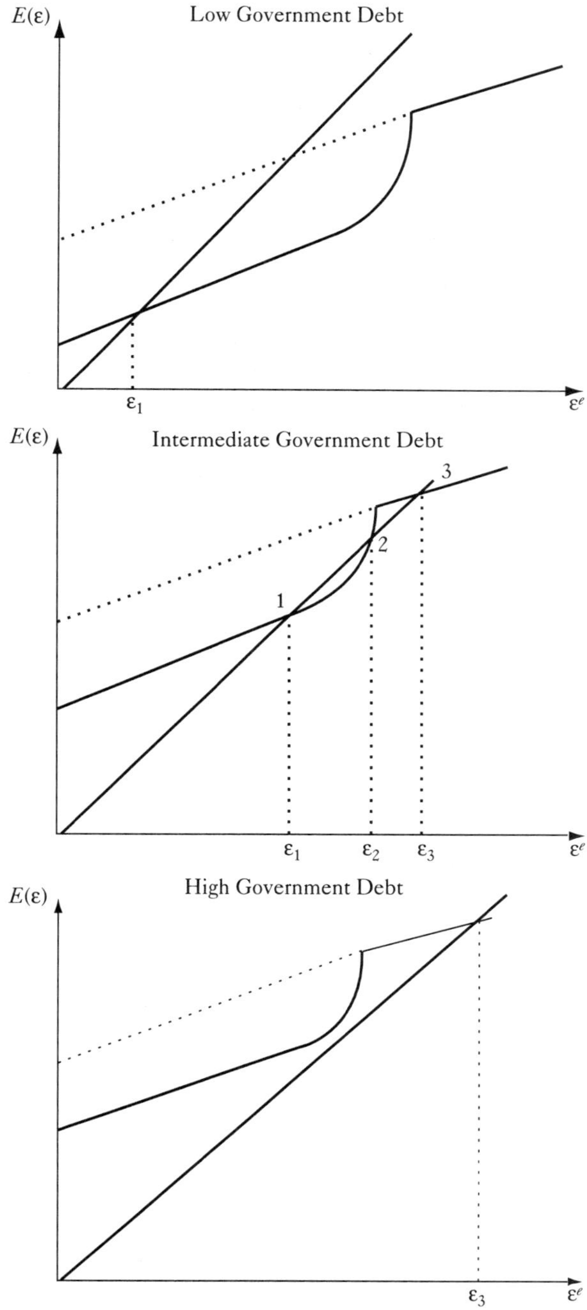

represents equation (14). The dotted line is the expected depreciation under a free float. We show three cases depending on three levels of government debt. In the low government debt case there is only one equilibrium with a low devaluation probability. The size of the realignment conditional on devaluation is ε_1.

The case of the high government debt is represented in Figure 10c. This case also exhibits one equilibrium. In this case, the probability of the devaluation is 1, so that the expected realignment is ε_3. In this case, the authorities are forced to devalue.

The most interesting case is represented by Figure 10b, which shows the case of an intermediately high level of government debt. This case shows three equilibria. It embodies the possibility of self-fulfilling attacks. For example, a country can be moved from the first to the second equilibrium by a change in the perceived probability of a devaluation. In equilibrium 1, relatively large shocks in g are needed to force the country off its fixed exchange rate commitment. In equilibrium 2, however, the country can be forced to abandon the fixed exchange rate by a relatively small increase in g.

This model illustrates the potential problem that outside countries, with a relatively high government debt, participating in ERM II may face. The model also makes clear what the role is of the cost of devaluing the currency. If c_D is high, we are more likely to be in the situation represented by Figure 10a: the probability of a devaluation is low and so is the probability of a speculative crisis. As c_D increases, we are more likely to find ourselves in the case of Figure 10b or even 10c. Thus, if countries are perceived to take the next convergence "exam" very seriously, c_D will be large, so that speculative attacks become less likely. On the other hand, if these countries are perceived to take it less seriously, because they can "take the exam" at a somewhat later date anyway, then the speculative attack becomes more likely.

Conclusion

In this paper we have analyzed the future exchange rate relations between the ins and the outs (assuming that there will be ins and outs). We asked whether ERM II, which will guide these relations, will be stable. We analyzed this question by studying two subsidiary questions.

First, we asked how likely it is that classical ("first-generation model") speculative crises will erupt. At first sight, the risk for these speculative attacks is small since the outs are most likely to have converged significantly in terms of underlying fundamentals (e.g., inflation rates). However, the nature of ERM II as a stepping-stone toward access into EMU may interfere in two ways. First, since countries have to pass a "convergence exam," small changes in some fundamentals can make all the difference. As a result, speculators may become very sensitive to small movements in these fundamentals. Second, the structure of the real exchange rates between the ins and the outs may not correspond to an equilibrium. In particular, there is some evidence that the deutsche mark is overvalued (in 1997), mainly against the "peripheral" countries. This may necessitate exchange rate adjustments. If the "peripheral" countries are the outs, this may generate speculative pressures within ERM II.

A second question we asked is whether ERM II will be subject to self-fulfilling ("second-generation model") speculative crises. We argued that the convergence dynamics may indeed lead to such attacks, especially against currencies of countries with a large government debt. The probability that this happens depends on a number of factors. First, if the authorities are perceived to take the next "entrance exam" very seriously, the probability of such attacks will be low. If, however, the perception is that the authorities take a more relaxed attitude because they can "take the exam" a year or two later anyway, then the probability of a speculative attack may increase significantly. Second, if the commitment to intervene in the foreign exchange market by the ECB is low, the probability of such an attack may be high.

A factor that will reduce the probability of speculative attacks is the large size of the band of fluctuation. This will significantly reduce the "one-way bet" situation, which typically attracts large speculative activity. This feature of ERM II, together with a willingness of having timely realignments, may eliminate the danger of large-scale speculative crises of the type that erupted in 1992–93.

The conclusions arrived at in this paper should be handled with care. The new monetary regime taking shape in Europe is without historical precedence. This makes the analysis difficult, and forecasts of what may happen very hazardous.

It has been assumed in this paper that, from 1999 on, the monetary regime will consist of a core group of countries forming EMU and a second group that has been refused access into EMU. It should be emphasized that it is not clear at all that such a scenario is realistic. Many of the peripheral countries will fight very hard to obtain access right from the start, and as a group they will have the power to force the issue, given that the entry decision will have to be taken by qualified majority (see De Grauwe, 1996, on this). It is more likely, therefore, that EMU will start with all potential candidates or that it will be postponed. If this scenario comes out, there will be no ERM II worth analyzing.

But even if the scenario of a core group of countries forming EMU and another group waiting outside is realized, it will have been preceded by great political conflicts that may destabilize the foreign exchange markets. It would then not be an easy affair to start ERM II smoothly on January 1, 1999.

References

Calvo, Guillermo, 1988, "Servicing the Public Debt: The Role of Expectations," *American Economic Review*, Vol. 78 (September), pp. 647–61.

De Grauwe, Paul, 1996, "The Prospects of a Mini Currency Union in 1999," CEPR Discussion Paper No. 1458 (London: Centre for Economic Policy Research, September).

Eichengreen, Barry, and Charles Wyplosz, 1993, "The Unstable EMS," *Brookings Papers on Economic Activity: 1*, Brookings Institution, pp. 51–143.

Eichengreen, Barry, Andrew K. Rose, and Charles Wyplosz, 1996, "Speculative Attacks on Pegged Exchange Rates: An Empirical Exploration with Special Reference to the European Monetary System," in *The New Transatlantic Economy*, ed. by Matthew B. Canzoneri, Wilfred J. Ethier, and Vittorio Grilli (Cambridge: Cambridge University Press), pp. 191–228.

Flood, Robert, and Peter Garber, 1984, "Collapsing Exchange Rate Regimes: Some Linear Examples," *Journal of International Economics*, Vol. 17 (August), pp. 1–13.

Flood, Robert, and Nancy Marion, 1996, "Speculative Attacks: Fundamentals and Self-Fulfilling Prophesies," NBER Working Paper No. 5789 (Cambridge, Massachusetts: National Bureau for Economic Research, October).

Jeanne, Olivier, and Paul Masson, 1996, "Was the French Franc Crisis a Sunspot Equilibrium?" (unpublished; Washington: International Monetary Fund).

Krugman, Paul, 1979, "A Model of Balance-of-Payments Crises," *Journal of Money, Credit and Banking*, Vol. 11 (August), pp. 311–25.

Obstfeld, Maurice, 1986, "Rational and Self-Fulfilling Balance-of-Payments Crises," *American Economic Review*, Vol. 76 (March), pp. 72–81.

———, 1995, "Models of Currency Crises with Self-Fulfilling Features," NBER Working Paper No. 5285 (Cambridge, Massachusetts: National Bureau for Economic Research, October).

Sinn, Hans-Werner, 1996, "International Implications of German Unification," NBER Working Paper No. 5839 (Cambridge, Massachusetts: National Bureau for Economic Research, November).

Comments on De Grauwe

Jacques Mélitz

Paul De Grauwe reasons that in a future EMU with "ins" and "outs," the "outs" that want "in" will be subject to speculative attacks. According to present rules, these "outs" will need to keep their exchange rate nearly perfectly still for two years, while to all appearance, the burden of doing so will fall to them entirely. Any incident that may temporarily dim their prospects for entry into EMU could be the signal for a speculative attack. Since these countries will also lack capital controls, speculative attacks could be particularly difficult to resist. The argument looks very sensible. De Grauwe also tries to model it in a simple and attractive way. I will merely go over his logic and make a few suggestions and observations.

De Grauwe tries to base a speculative attack entirely on the problem of public debt. Thereby he brings into focus the fiscal criteria for admission into EMU. Automatic stabilizers represent the starting point for De Grauwe's analysis: adverse shocks to output induce budget deficits. Discretionary fiscal policy is entirely absent in his reasoning: the only macroeconomic policy instrument is monetary policy. In his formulation, government spending and taxes are distinct, and the automatic stabilization operates entirely through spending. However, this is inessential, and his argument does not require any separate consideration of spending and taxes.

Debt and inflation enter as the crucial arguments in the official objective function. The essential debt variable is $(b - b^*)^2$, where b is the ratio of debt to output and b^* its optimal level. The condition $b > b^*$, which De Grauwe takes for granted, then spells some fundamental distortion, for example, too much "crowding out" of investment, too little private saving, and too much current consumption relative to future consumption. In fact, De Grauwe does not reason this way but includes t^2 in the objective function, where t is the ratio of taxes to output, and he interprets official concern with t as resting on the problem of maintaining government solvency. But I believe this to be a mistake. As the model stands, sustainability of the debt is not an issue. Any debt/output level could be financed. Introducing an issue of government solvency into the model would also destroy the simplicity that De Grauwe strives to achieve. Quite apart from this, the authorities could not possibly wish to minimize t^2 independently of spending, precisely because of a concern with debt.

Finally, De Grauwe assumes that monetary policy automatically affects *b*. More specifically, depreciation lowers *b*. Some of the government debt is long term. If all debt were short term, a depreciation would raise the current cost of financing the government as much as the price level and keep *b* the same. There must therefore be some percentage of long-term debt in the model, assuring that in case of depreciation of the currency, the cost of financing the debt will rise less than the nominal interest rate.

Under the previous conditions, the rest of De Grauwe's argument goes through—at least in essence. The excess of *b* over b^* guarantees an official incentive to inflate. Consequently, under fully discretionary policy, equilibrium obtains at a positive rate of inflation. This rate is simply the one in which any further lowering of *b* through expansionary monetary policy will bring a benefit that is matched by the marginal disutility of inflation. A credible promise to lower inflation below the fully "discretionary" level, if possible, will then be useful. In the event of such a promise, there will necessarily be "an incentive to cheat," and therefore, there must also be some cost of cheating or the arrangement would fail. Under the old ERM, we had trouble explaining the relevant cost of cheating, or why a surprise devaluation, or surprise movement out of the system, did not occur. In the new ERM (ERM II), the cost of cheating becomes particularly clear. Cheating disqualifies a member of the ERM for entry into EMU. Hence, promises not to inflate acquire more credibility than ever. I would even argue that the wide bands in the ERM since August 1993 do not weaken the argument at all. Bands or no bands, once a country loses eligibility for entry into EMU, the new equilibrium will entail a discrete jump in the exchange rate. Thus, the wide bands do not interfere with the virulence of a possible speculative attack (which hinges on a possible jump).

The early empirical sections of the De Grauwe paper also contain an attractive argument to the effect that any movement in the cost of cheating will have an inverse effect on the incentive to cheat. Specifically, if some event reduces the probability that an "out" will be admitted into EMU, the country will immediately need to pay a higher interest rate on its debt at the existing exchange rate. The collapse of the old equilibrium exchange rate will therefore be that much closer. Unfortunately, this argument is not reflected in the modeling. De Grauwe adopts the usual style of reasoning according to which any change in the costs of breaking the promise not to inflate (or the promise to inflate below the fully "discretionary" level) will only bear any market repercussions if the exchange rate changes. Based on his equations (2) and (4), as long as the exchange rate stays the same, the expected rate of inflation does not move, and therefore no change in the probability of entering into EMU can affect the current nominal interest rate. Yet the early argument to the contrary is convincing, and it could be easily integrated.

De Grauwe closes his reasoning by pointing to the possibility of a speculative attack if an adverse shock raises the government deficit sufficiently. As in Obstfeld,[1] the subsequent speculative attack would then have a self-fulfilling nature. More specifically, the old equilibrium could still subsist after the shock. Each individual would be in a position where he knew that if he took speculative action alone, he would not prevail. However, if enough others behaved like him, a new equilibrium would result and he could make a fortune. The speculation thus depends on a certain element of mental telepathy. That is why, in the case of a successful attack, the event has a self-fulfilling character. Yet it is important to observe that this reasoning simply represents a choice and is not the only possibility by any means.

Quite specifically, Obstfeld's logic relies heavily on risk neutrality. In Obstfeld's theoretical context, there is always some dose of risk aversion that would be sufficient to assure that the old equilibrium would collapse and a speculative attack would follow. The attack would then be inevitable and lose its self-fulfilling character. In order to see the empirical relevance of the point, consider the example of the speculative attack against the French franc just prior to September 20, 1992, the date of the French referendum on the Maastricht Treaty. The risks of a depreciation of the franc were manifest. But the franc hardly budged after the attack, and once the uncertainties receded, French reserves and interest rates went back to their previous levels. Yet any risk-averse speculator who had taken a position against the franc would have had little call for regret—no more than most of us do when we do not have a claim to file after purchasing car insurance. Those speculators bought safety and got it. But the Obstfeld speculators took an uncompensated loss: they simply made a mistake. When evaluating the merits of De Grauwe's argument about the perils of ERM II, we should note that the argument can be brought to a head without multiple equilibria and self-fulfilling prophecies. To my mind, that only makes the argument stronger: in a risk-averse world, the threats are even bigger.

---

[1]Maurice Obstfeld, "Models of Currency Crises with Self-Fulfilling Features," NBER Working Paper No. 5825 (Cambridge, Massachusetts: National Bureau of Economic Research, October 1995).

5

Exchange Arrangements Between the EU and Countries in Eastern Europe, the Mediterranean, and the CFA Zone

John Berrigan and Hervé Carré

The creation of a single currency for the EU will be a major international event. While the introduction of the euro will mainly have an impact on EU countries, there will also be important implications for third countries. The scale of these implications will reflect the EU's substantial presence in world trade and in the international monetary system. Many of the broader external aspects of the euro are considered elsewhere in this volume. This paper, however, has a narrower focus in considering the implications of the euro for present and future exchange rate arrangements between the EU and a specific subset of countries with which it has particularly close economic and financial links. Three groups of countries fall into this category. These are (1) the countries of Central and Eastern Europe (CEECs); (2) the non-EU countries of the Mediterranean; and (3) the countries located in French-speaking sub-Saharan Africa (the CFA zone). For each of these groups of countries, the EU is a principal trading partner, a major donor of development aid, and a counterpart in economic cooperation. Their links with the EU take various forms (e.g., Europe agreements, the Lomé Convention, and free trade agreements), and these links make their economies relatively sensitive to developments in the EU economy. Accordingly, the economies of these countries are likely to experience important indirect effects related to the introduction of the euro.

At present, there is no exchange rate arrangement between any of the countries concerned and the EU per se, although the possibility of such an arrange-

The authors would like to thank O. Bodin, C. Ghymers, B. Kaufmann, J. Kröger, and R. Wissels for helpful comments.

ment is addressed in a Declaration[1] annexed to the Treaty. Some of them have pegged their exchange rates unilaterally to the ECU, but they have never participated in or been formally linked to the ERM of the EMS. This situation is unlikely to change in the short term. The newly agreed exchange rate mechanism (ERM II), which will replace the present ERM at the time of the introduction of the euro, has been devised with a view only to the participation of *existing* EU member states not adopting the single currency from the outset. The objective of this paper is, however, to examine the more medium-term outlook for exchange rate arrangements involving these groups of countries and the EU in the new single currency environment.

As prospective EU member states, an exchange rate relationship involving the euro and the CEECs is likely to be high on the policy agenda in the coming years. The CFA zone already has an exchange rate arrangement with France and, to the extent that France is likely to adopt the euro, the implications for this arrangement will need to be considered. The Mediterranean countries are intensifying their trade links with the EU, which begs the question whether such links could lead in the direction of an exchange rate arrangement involving their currencies and the euro. In the following three sections of this paper, the prospects for an exchange rate arrangement with the euro will be considered separately with respect to the CEECs, the non-EU countries of the Mediterranean, and the CFA zone. A final section will draw some general conclusions.

Exchange Rate Arrangement for the CEECs with the Euro

The countries of Central and Eastern Europe[2] are highly dependent on developments in the EU. This dependency reflects not only their proximity to the EU but also the close political, economic, and financial links developed between the two regions since the collapse of communism in the late 1980s.

More significantly, the EU has concluded wide-ranging Europe Agreements[3] with 10 of the CEECs. These are Bulgaria, the Czech Republic, Estonia, Hungary, Latvia, Lithuania, Poland, Romania, the Slovak Republic, and Slovenia. All of these CEECs aspire not only to membership of the EU

---

[1]Declaration No. 5 on monetary cooperation with non-Community countries, which states that "the Community shall be prepared to cooperate with other European countries and with those non-European countries with which the Community has close economic ties."

[2]For the purposes of this paper, the term CEECs refers only to Bulgaria, the Czech Republic, Estonia, Hungary, Latvia, Lithuania, Poland, Romania, the Slovak Republic, and Slovenia, which have signed formal agreements with the EU.

[3]Europe Agreements provide the framework for membership negotiations with the relevant CEECs and cover a broad spectrum of issues, including those of an economic and financial nature.

Table 1. Exchange Rate Regime of CEECs

Country	Regime
Bulgaria	Managed float
Czech Republic	Exchange rate pegged within fixed band against a basket comprising the deutsche mark (65 percent) and the U.S. dollar (35 percent)
Estonia	Currency board with deutsche mark: 1 Kr = 8 DM
Hungary	Exchange rate pegged within crawling band to basket comprising the ECU (70 percent) and the U.S. dollar (30 percent)
Latvia	Exchange rate pegged to SDR: 0.8 LVL = 1 SDR
Lithuania	Currency board with U.S. dollar: 4 LTL = $1
Poland	Exchange rate pegged within crawling band to basket comprising the U.S. dollar (45 percent), the deutsche mark (35 percent), the pound sterling (10 percent), the French franc (5 percent), and the Swiss franc (5 percent)
Romania	Free float
Slovak Republic	Exchange rate pegged within fixed band to basket comprising the deutsche mark (60 percent) and the U.S. dollar (40 percent)
Slovenia	Managed float

Source: IMF, *Exchange Arrangements and Exchange Restrictions: Annual Report 1995.*
Note: CEECs that have "Europe Agreements" with the EU.

but ultimately to the adoption of the euro as a means to achieve their objective of *full* participation in EMU. The longer-term challenge is, therefore, how to organize the transition from their current exchange rate regimes to the irrevocable fixity of exchange rates against other euro area currencies, which would be implied by the adoption of the euro. While the Europe Agreements recognize the aspirations of the CEECs and provide assistance to these ends, the economic elements of the Agreements do not include an exchange rate arrangement. So, what are the prospects for exchange rate relations between the currencies of these CEECs and the euro?[4]

In their transition from centrally planned economies, the CEECs concerned have opted for different exchange rate regimes, ranging from complete fixity in the form of a currency board to a free float (see Table 1). The range of exchange rate regimes adopted reflects the extent of economic divergence within a relatively heterogeneous group of countries. The choice of regime also reflects differences in opinion among respective national policymakers on the appropriate exchange rate arrangement to ensure a smooth transition to a market-based system. It is beyond the scope of this paper to assess the eco-

[4]The assumption is, of course, that immediate participation in the euro area on entry to the EU will not be an option for the CEECs.

nomic performance of the 10 CEECs under their chosen exchange rate regimes. Suffice it to say, however, that each of them has enjoyed a measure of success, making it difficult to draw definitive conclusions on the optimal exchange rate regime for a transition economy. Consequently, it is unlikely that a standardized exchange rate arrangement with the euro would be appropriate for or acceptable to these CEECs. Instead, a rather diverse set of arrangements may be necessary.

Negotiations with the CEECs on their prospective EU membership have focused on the need for structural improvements in their economies without particular reference to exchange rate arrangements. However, while the ERM II is not seen as the "natural habitat" of exchange rate arrangements involving the CEEC currencies and the euro, participation in such a mechanism as members of the EU could have attractions for the CEECs. The credibility to be gained from a formal link to the euro through ERM II participation could offer significant advantages, for example, in terms of providing an anchor for macroeconomic policies, lowering interest rate premiums, and attracting capital inflows. Many of these CEEC countries already have unilateral exchange rate links with the ECU and the deutsche mark so that a bilateral link to the euro would seem to be a logical course of action. Moreover, the attractiveness of a link to the euro will increase as the new single currency evolves as an important international currency.

Given the diversity in their current regimes, any exchange rate arrangement involving the currencies of the CEECs with the euro must be adapted to the economic conditions of the countries concerned and to the policy commitments of the relevant national authorities. The transition path to the adoption of the euro would likely vary among the CEECs and a series of steps (implying possibly different exchange rate arrangements for each country, which would evolve over time as economic convergence is achieved) toward an increasingly stable exchange rate with the euro can be envisaged. In this context, the flexibility offered by the ERM II (in the form of bilateral parities against the euro with a relatively wide standard fluctuation margin, timely realignments, and the possibility of closer exchange rate links when appropriate) would be an important advantage. This flexibility allows one to conceive of a broad spectrum of exchange rate arrangements within the new mechanism, ranging from very loose pegs to progressively tighter arrangements, even including a currency board.

Support for any exchange rate arrangement involving the euro could be expected on two conditions. First, the arrangement would need to be consistent with the price stability objective of the ECB's monetary policy. Second, the arrangement would need to buttress the CEEC countries' commitment to stability-oriented macroeconomic policies and foster necessary structural adjustment. In sum, it is clear that the relevance and usefulness of exchange rate arrangements between the CEEC currencies and the euro would be assessed on the basis of their contribution to economic convergence as the means to achieve a successful catch-up and ultimately the adoption of the single currency. The flexibility within the ERM II would allow both of these conditions to be fulfilled by minimizing the necessity for large-scale foreign exchange intervention by the ECB and minimizing the risk that ERM II participation on some standardized set of terms might impede structural adjustment and the catching-up process.

Despite the advantages of ERM II participation for the CEECs, a cautious approach to establishing a hard peg with the euro would seen appropriate. The market-based systems in many of the CEECs are still in their infancy and time will be needed before they are fully effective. The structural adjustments required in these economies are daunting and derive not just from the need to adapt to market discipline but also from the need to diversify their production from the specialization characterizing their relations with the former communist bloc. As the transition to the market system is not complete, relative prices have not yet fully adjusted and there is no way of determining (even with the customary degree of uncertainty) the equilibrium level for their exchange rates. Moreover, the absence of relevant data and the dynamic nature of these economies would make any model-based calculations of an equilibrium rate particularly hazardous, as fundamental relationships within their economies remain difficult to determine and would be subject to significant change over relatively short periods of time. Without some understanding of equilibrium conditions, agreeing on a central parity for the CEEC currencies against the euro could in many cases be a rather "hit and miss" affair.

Attention must also be paid to the fact that the CEEC countries are catch-up economies where productivity, particularly in the manufacturing sector, is likely to grow faster than that in the EU countries. While a successful catching up in the context of a hard exchange rate peg is not precluded, the implied productivity differential with other euro area countries would ordinarily be reflected in an exchange rate appreciation in the CEEC currencies and could provoke exchange rate tensions in the context of a hard peg. Similarly, the positive expectations effects linked to EU membership could also create exchange rate tensions, as an expansion in aggregate demand ahead of supply potential in the economy creates a need for a *temporary* real exchange rate appreciation to contain inflationary pressures. In this latter respect, the ERM experience of Spain and Portugal is revealing. Accordingly, while the ability to maintain a hard peg against the euro would differ from one CEEC to another, a strong case can be made for adopting a flexible approach to ERM II participation for the CEECs in general.

Given the specific characteristics of the CEEC economies, exchange rate surveillance will be of particular importance in the context of their participation in the ERM II. EU membership would mean that these CEECs would be subject to the multilateral surveillance procedures provided in the Treaty.[5] These procedures—to be enhanced in the context of new convergence programs required under the Stability and Growth Pact—will help to ensure a macroeconomic framework consistent with whatever exchange rate arrangement the country might have in place. However, the addition of a *regional* dimension to the individual efforts of the CEEC countries would bring important benefits. Given the difference in levels of development between many of the CEECs and the EU in general, there is much to recommend an exchange of information and of best practices between transition economies themselves as a supplement to the standard EU surveillance procedures. A regional surveillance framework might, therefore, be expected to improve the prospects of a successful and rapid transition for the CEECs. In this context, there would be considerable merit in extending the existing dialogue established between the individual CEECs and the EU to a similar dialogue among the applicant CEECs, with a view to developing a flexible framework of regional cooperation and surveillance.

Non-EU Mediterranean Countries In Search of Freer Trade

In 1995, all 15 EU countries and 12 non-EU partner countries from the Mediterranean region (Algeria, Cyprus, Egypt, Israel, Jordan, Lebanon, Malta, Morocco, the Palestinian Authority, Syria, Tunisia, and Turkey) adopted the Barcelona Declaration. The Declaration established a so-called Euro-Mediterranean Partnership comprising three elements: a political and security arrangement, an economic and financial arrangement, and an arrangement in the area of social, cultural, and human affairs. Within the framework of economic and financial cooperation, the EU has entered into bilateral "Euro-Mediterranean" association agreements with Tunisia, Israel, and Morocco, and is about to do so with Jordan. Similar agreements are currently being negotiated with Algeria, Egypt, and Lebanon, and an interim agreement has been concluded with the Palestine Liberation Organization on behalf of the Palestinian Authority. Three other Mediterranean countries have close links to the EU: Cyprus and Malta have association agreements and Turkey a customs union. These latter three countries have applied for mem-

[5]See provisions of Article 103. These provisions have been reinforced in the context of the Stability and Growth Pact, which will enter into effect from January 1, 1999.

Table 2. Weight of EU in Trade of Mediterranean Countries, 1995

Country	Imports from EU (As percent of total)	Exports to EU (As percent of total)
Algeria	56.0	63.5
Cyprus	51.7	34.7
Egypt	38.9	45.8
Israel	52.4	32.3
Jordan	31.1	5.0
Lebanon	43.6	15.8
Malta	72.8	71.4
Morocco	53.1	61.3
Syria	31.7	56.7
Tunisia	69.1	79.0
Turkey	47.2	51.2

Source: Eurostat, *Euro-Mediterranean Bulletin on Short-Term Indicators, 1997.*

bership in the EU[6] and negotiations on Cyprus' accession to the EU are expected to commence soon.

Unlike the case of the CEECs, the intensification of links between the EU and these 12 Mediterranean countries is not in general expected to lead to their membership in the Union. Nevertheless, the Barcelona Declaration aims to establish a Euro-Mediterranean free trade area by the year 2010. Regional integration is an essential element of the Barcelona process, so trade between the two groups of countries would be expected to intensify in the coming years. In this respect, Table 2 indicates the significant trade linkages that already exist, and more particularly the importance of the EU as a major trading partner for these countries. Although these countries presently have a higher share in total extra-EU trade (some 9 percent) than do CEECs, this is likely to change if the rapid expansion of EU trade experienced by those countries over the last couple of years persists. This underlines the importance of the Euro-Mediterranean Partnership, which provides for the gradual dismantling of tariff and nontariff import restrictions over the next 12 years—particularly on the side of the Mediterranean countries—and the expected intensification of Euro-Mediterranean trade. The partnership also provides for a harmonization of statistical standards, customs procedures, market regulations, financial sector development, and investment mechanisms that will stimulate a more efficient allocation of resources, and the transfer of know-how and investment. As a result, the international competitiveness of these Mediterranean countries is expected to improve and the regional cooperation—now quite limited—is expected to be stimulated. With the strengthening of EU-

[6]Although Malta has recently decided to put its application on hold.

Mediterranean trade links, and at a later stage of links between individual Mediterranean partners, the need for economic dialogue as foreseen in the Euro-Mediterranean Agreements will become apparent.

Like the CEECs, the Mediterranean countries operate a wide range of exchange rate regimes (see Table 3). The diversity in arrangements reflects the differences in underlying economic conditions in terms of resource allocation, inflation, trade, and financial integration as well as different priorities among policymakers in the conduct of macroeconomic polices. In addition, a particular feature of Mediterranean partner countries is that their terms of trade are highly volatile. This is because some of them (in particular Algeria, but also to a limited extent Egypt and Syria) are oil exporters and face fluctuating world prices, while others have a relatively high concentration of their trade in a small number of sectors (e.g., over 50 percent of Egyptian, Moroccan, Syrian, and Tunisian manufacturing exports are concentrated in textiles and clothing). The expected strengthening of trade with the EU as well as with other Mediterranean countries is likely to reduce the vulnerability of the Mediterranean countries to external shocks. In the meantime, however, the high volatility of the terms of trade provides a strong argument that an immediate locking of the exchange rates to the euro would probably be premature.

The economies of these Mediterranean countries share many common features with the economies of the CEECs. They are catch-up or emerging economies, they are engaged in a process of liberalization, and they recognize the benefits of open competition and a market-based economy. Moreover, the implementation of the Euro-Mediterranean agreements is likely to require

Table 3. Exchange Rate Regime of Southern Mediterranean Countries

Country	Regime
Algeria	Managed float
Cyprus	Exchange rate pegged to currency basket
Egypt	Managed float
Israel	Managed float
Jordan	Exchange rate pegged to U.S. dollar
Lebanon	Free float
Malta	Exchange rate pegged to currency basket
Morocco	Exchange rate pegged to currency basket
Syria	Exchange rate pegged to U.S. dollar
Tunisia	Managed float
Turkey	Managed float

Source: IMF, *Exchange Arrangements and Exchange Restrictions: Annual Report 1995.*

further structural reform. In such circumstances, the economies of the Mediterranean countries are likely to be relatively dynamic. Similar arguments to those made in the case of the CEECs would recommend that the Mediterranean countries should not be constrained to move toward a hard exchange rate peg to the euro from the outset, in particular to preserve sufficient flexibility to adjust the real exchange rate.

None of the bilateral agreements between the EU and individual Mediterranean countries—neither those concluded nor those under negotiation—include an exchange rate arrangement, and apart from the few countries that might become EU members it is presently not expected that relations will develop in this direction. However, as these countries continue to integrate with the EU, they may find the euro increasingly attractive as a vehicle currency and as a reserve asset. Moreover, the euro might also be attractive to these countries as an anchor for their exchange rate policy.

Change in Peg for the CFA Zone from the French Franc to the Euro

Although the EU per se has no exchange rate arrangement with the CFA zone of sub-Saharan Africa, one member state—France—maintains a special monetary link with these countries. The central element of this special link is a fixed exchange rate against the French franc and, as France is expected to adopt the euro as its new currency, there may be implications for the CFA zone.

The CFA zone comprises two separate monetary unions with their own respective single currencies. These monetary unions are the UMOA (Union Monétaire Ouest Africaine) in the west of the zone and the UDEAC (Union Douanière des Etats de l'Afrique Centrale) in Central Africa. Each of the monetary unions has its own central bank. The BCEAO (Banque Centrale des Etats de l'Afrique de l'Ouest) issues a single currency—the CFA franc—for the seven countries of the UMOA (Benin, Burkina Faso, Côte d'Ivoire, Mali, Nigeria, Senegal, and Togo). As indicated, the CFA franc has a fixed exchange rate with the French franc. Recently, the seven countries in this union added an economic dimension to their monetary links. The BEAC (Banque des Etats de l'Afrique Centrale) issues a separate currency for each of the six countries of the UDEAC (Cameroon, Central African Republic, Chad, Congo, Gabon, and Guinea). These six countries have a monetary agreement among themselves and with the French authorities. Despite having distinct currencies, they also share the same fixed exchange rate with the French franc.

The monetary agreements between the BCEAO and BEAC and the French authorities are identical and are based upon the following general provisions:

- the fixity of exchange rates against the French franc;
- a guarantee from the French treasury of full convertibility of their currencies to French francs;
- the pooling of foreign exchange reserves by all of the CFA countries; at least 65 percent of the reserve assets of the BCEAO and the BEAC are deposited with the French treasury; and
- participation of the French authorities in the formulation of monetary policy in the CFA zone as a counterpart to the guarantee of convertibility.

The agreements themselves must be seen against the background of the substantial economic cooperation aid provided by France to the CFA zone, although there is no formal linkage between the agreements and the aid. The involvement of the French authorities in the agreements is of major significance. The French francs needed for convertibility of CFA francs are provided by the French treasury under a specific budget line and not by the Bank of France. Although the future status of this type of arrangement has yet to be decided in the context of EMU, the essentially budgetary nature of this exchange rate arrangement appears to make it compatible with the requirements of the Treaty. Accordingly, the introduction of the euro will merely entail the replacement of the French franc as the peg and an arithmetical adjustment in the exchange rate of the CFA countries. The new fixed exchange rate against the euro will be derived from the conversion rate of the French franc against the euro. In this way, the current arrangements governing the CFA franc zone will continue largely as they are now. There will be no need for change in the exchange rate regime as long as the French (budgetary) authorities are ready to guarantee the convertibility of the CFA franc by providing the necessary resources and as long as the member countries of the CFA zone are willing to maintain the agreements.

Although the introduction of the euro will not of itself imply a change of exchange rate regime for the CFA countries, they may be affected to the extent that the path of the euro exchange rate may differ from that which would have been followed by the French franc exchange rate. Some have argued that, irrespective of underlying economic conditions in the EU, the euro will appreciate strongly in the early years of EMU as the ECB seeks to reinforce its credibility by adopting a relatively tight monetary policy stance. Of course, a sharp and sustained appreciation of the euro—implying a corresponding appreciation of the franc CFA—could present problems of competitiveness in the CFA zone as a whole, with negative consequences for economic growth and development. Others have argued, however, that high unemployment rates in the EU will require the ECB to adopt a relatively accommodating monetary policy stance, implying a depreciation in the euro in the early years of EMU. A weak euro would probably contribute to higher economic growth in the CFA zone but could have negative consequences for inflation performance. In fact, it is difficult to predict with any certainty the likely path of the euro in the early years of EMU. However, one could equally argue that concerns over the euro exchange rate are exaggerated. Given that the ECB will inherit the credibility of its constituent national central banks and the similarities between the monetary policy regime to apply in the euro area and the regime currently applying in most EU countries—and notably in France—the shift from a peg against the French franc to a peg against the euro may not be particularly dramatic for the CFA zone.

Whatever the implications of the introduction of the euro may be, the CFA zone has been profoundly influenced by the EMU project in general. The protracted economic slowdown and recession in the CFA zone countries from the mid-1980s to the mid-1990s was provoked by a severe overvaluation of currencies. This overvaluation reflected the inconsistency of a fixed exchange rate peg against the relatively stable French franc and imbalances in their domestic macroeconomic policy mix. The impact of their overvalued currencies on economic activity was compounded by persistent protectionism in trade relations within the CFA zone. The scale of the recession forced an economic regime change. Facing a choice between dismantling existing monetary arrangements or building upon them, they opted to maintain the existing arrangements but to intensify their regional integration. The seven countries of the UMOA decided in January 1994 to add an economic element to their monetary union, and so became the Western African EMU (UEMOA). The six members of the UDEAC-BEAC followed this lead and in October 1996 signed conventions making operational a new economic Treaty built upon their existing arrangement. This union was renamed the Central African Economic and Monetary Community (CEMAC). These moves toward greater economic integration acknowledged the inappropriateness of sharing a single currency without a single market and the need to have freer trade within the CFA zone. In addition, the countries recognized the need for greater compatibility between their other economic policies at the national level and the single regional monetary policy. In this latter context, they agreed to establish a cooperative scheme involving regional surveillance of their economic policies.

The new Treaties were clearly inspired by the EMU project. The Maastricht Treaty embodies a new consensus among EU countries on the benefits of stability-oriented macroeconomic policies in terms of economic growth and development. This consensus also underlies Article 3a of the Treaty, which states that

> . . . the activities of the Member States and the Community shall include . . . the adoption of an economic policy which is based on close coordination of Member States' economic policies, on the internal market and on the definition of common objectives, and conducted in accordance with the principle of an open market economy with free competition.

The CFA countries are adopting a similar stability-oriented approach to macroeconomic management. Exchange rate stability and guaranteed convertibility should attract inward investment by reducing uncertainty. In addition, CFA producers will have access to each other's markets without exchange rate risk. There are also advantages of a more systemic nature. The credibility of a monetary union in a single market will require a common approach to budgetary discipline in order to ensure balanced economic growth in the entire zone. The positive implications of such a fundamental regime change should not be underestimated.

There were, however, arguments against the present monetary and exchange rate arrangements. First, it must be acknowledged that nearly 50 years of a fixed exchange rate has not resulted in much-needed economic development in the CFA zone. While the CFA countries have a much better record of price stability than do neighboring countries, they have experienced a similarly mediocre economic growth rate. The unavoidable conclusion to be drawn is that the choice of an appropriate monetary policy/exchange rate regime alone is not the key to successful economic development. Many other factors matter just as much. Indeed, the main benefit of the current exchange rate regime is that it offers a framework for a regional approach to economic development. The economic development of sub-Saharan countries must be based on the principles of a free-market system and a stability-oriented macroeconomic framework. These countries have shown the political will to proceed further with regional integration based on these principles and must be supported in their endeavors by the international community. If successful, this regional approach could be extended to other parts of Africa.

The European Commission recently issued a "green paper" on the relationships between the EU and African countries, with the intention of triggering a public debate on the future of development assistance. Some basic requirements for improving assistance between the EU and these countries—notably through deeper monetary and macroeconomic cooperation—were identified.[7] Among these requirements were the need to:

[7]The green paper also considered the institutional aspects of assistance and possible reform of the conditionality aspects of aid in close coordination with the other donors.

- merge—when feasible from a legal and institutional point of view—different financial assistance instruments into a single regional instrument. When this is not possible, one might improve the visibility and objectivity of coordination among instruments and donors by including agreed criteria for conditionality, especially macroeconomic conditionality. In any case, criteria should be agreed with the recipients. This approach would foster competition among recipients based on "good governance" conditionality.
- set up a regional surveillance framework to assess compliance with the agreed criteria. The CFA Treaties provide for multilateral surveillance of economic policies along the lines currently employed by the EU and the IMF. If, as expected, regional surveillance succeeds in delivering stability-oriented macroeconomic policies and improved prospects for economic growth and development, it should be seen as a possible precedent for other African countries.

Conclusions

The introduction of the euro will have important international implications. Given the likely economic size of the euro area, its stability-oriented macroeconomic policy framework, and the eventual depth of its financial market, the euro can be expected to evolve into a major international currency. As such, the introduction of the new currency will be of particular significance to those countries with which the EU has particularly close economic and financial links. In this paper, the implications for three groups of countries—the CEECs, the Mediterranean countries, and the CFA zone countries—have been reviewed.

The economic conditions and aspirations of each of these groups of countries vary significantly. At one extreme are the CEECs, which aspire to full EU membership—implying ultimately the adoption of the euro. However, the starting points of the CEECs in terms of economic development and macroeconomic policy framework are not the same. In particular, they operate an array of different exchange rate regimes, ranging from managed floating to a currency board. The transition of these economies from their current regime to adoption of the euro could be managed through the new ERM II, which will operate with a high degree of built-in flexibility. However, a pragmatic approach will be needed in deciding on any exchange rate arrangement involving the CEEC currencies and the euro. At the other extreme are the countries of the CFA zone, whose exchange rate relationship with EU comes indirectly via a fixed exchange rate against the French franc. The introduction of the euro will not in itself imply a change in exchange rate regime for these countries. A fixed exchange rate against the euro will be derived from the conversion rate of the French franc against the euro. Between these extremes are the Southern Mediterranean countries, which are unlikely to seek an exchange rate arrangement with the euro in the foreseeable future. However, the euro may become increasingly attractive to these countries as a vehicle currency and/or reserve asset as their integration into the global economy progresses.

Comments on Berrigan and Carré

György Szapáry

I agree with Berrigan and Carré that the creation of EMU is a major international development, which will affect not only the member states of the monetary union but also their trading partners. The Berrigan-Carré paper rightly examines the impact of EMU on those countries that have particularly close economic and financial links with the EU, namely, Central and EU, African sub-Saharan countries, and Mediterranean countries. I will discuss the impact of the establishment of a single European currency only on the first group of countries, since that is the one I am most familiar with.

Preparing for the advent of the euro is important for the CEECs from several points of view. First, those members of the EU that are likely to be the first to participate in the monetary union (the "core" countries) are the major trading partners of the CEECs. For example, the most commonly assumed core countries—Germany, France, Austria and the Benelux countries—account for about 50 percent of the exports and imports of the Czech Republic, Hungary, and Poland. If more countries were to join the EMU in the first wave, that share would of course be even greater. Second, the economies of most CEECs are by now highly integrated into those of the EU: their trade is practically liberalized and the remaining restrictions on capital flows hardly constitute a serious constraint on the flow of capital, legal or otherwise. This means that changes in the monetary and exchange rate policies of EMU will have an immediate impact on their economies. Third, even though the CEECs have made great progress in developing market institutions and policy instruments, in adopting EU-conforming legislation, and in upgrading technologies in the financial sector, there is still much to be done in these areas. Since they are in an earlier stage of development, they have an opportunity to leapfrog. Hence, they have to follow closely the institutional and legal developments leading up to the creation of EMU. Finally, the CEECs have concluded agreements with the EU recognizing the aim of membership in the EU. The establishment of EMU will fundamentally change the "acquis communautaire" to which the acceding CEECs are expected to adapt.

Exchange Rate Policy

The most important question is whether the advent of EMU will mean that the CEECs will face more or less global exchange rate stability. This question can be divided into two subquestions: will the euro be more or less stable than the deutsche mark vis-à-vis the currencies of nonparticipating EU members; and will the euro be more or less stable than the deutsche mark vis-à-vis the dollar and the yen?

To answer the first question, one could argue that there should be more stability since the principle has been laid down that the exchange rates between the euro and the nonparticipating EU countries (the "outs") are of common interest. This will mean in practice that the ECB and the interested national central banks of the outs will coordinate their intervention policies to maintain the currencies of the outs within a certain limit around a central rate within the framework of ERM II. However, it was also made clear that the interventions should not jeopardize the commitment of the ECB to its primary anti-inflationary goal, which has an implication of asymmetry with respect to intervention obligations. An asymmetric system can imply a higher burden for the outs and can be less persuasive for market players. On the other hand, in a more symmetric scenario the credibility of the commitment of the ECB toward price stability could be weakened: although the exchange rates between the euro and the currencies of the outs could be more stable, inflationary pressures could emerge within the euro region itself as a consequence of unlimited support for weaker currencies. It is hard to predict at this early stage what the outcome will be. It would seem to me that the objective of the outs, or at least of most of them, will be to join the EMU, that is, they will want to achieve convergence in fundamentals. This should result in increased exchange rate stability.

There is, however, another argument put forward by Gros,[1] which brings me to the second question. Since the trade of the core countries with the rest of the world is much larger than that with the outs, Gros argues that for the ECB the dollar and yen exchange rates will be more important than the exchange rates of the outs. The ECB will therefore be more inclined to react to developments in the euro-dollar rate then be concerned with the exchange rates of the outs.

It is not my task to second-guess the intentions of the future ECB. From the point of view of the acceding countries, EMU will certainly mean some degree of increased exchange rate stability because the core countries, which, as said, represent a major share in the acceding countries' trade, will have elim-

[1]Daniel Gros, *EMU: The Ins and the Outs* (Brussels: Centre for European Policy Studies, 1996).

inated the exchange rate fluctuations between them, however small these fluctuations have become by now. This will reduce the price level changes transmitted to CEECs due to exchange rate changes beyond their control. More important, it will have eliminated the individual exchange rate risks vis-à-vis this group of countries, replacing them with a single exchange rate risk vis-à-vis the euro. In parallel, transaction costs will be reduced in relation to these countries. Also, as already mentioned, it is reasonable to assume that the euro exchange rate against the currencies of the outs will move toward greater stability as convergence takes place. We can also expect the euro to become more important in currency baskets and the acceding countries increasingly to formulate their external policies by reference to the euro zone.

As to the value of the euro against the dollar and the yen, the big question is to what extent the current strength of the deutsche mark might be diluted by the establishment of the EMU. Strict adherence to the Maastricht criteria will lessen that risk, as will the large size of the euro financial market. Nevertheless, the question is raised of how the establishment of the euro will affect portfolio choices. If the euro is perceived to be stronger than the deutsche mark, a shift into the euro from other currencies will take place. The opposite will happen if the euro is perceived to be weaker than the deutsche mark. Acceding countries that hold most of their reserves in deutsche mark or dollars will be confronted with this problem, as will of course the other countries.

If there is a large portfolio shift out of the dollar and toward the euro, the latter will appreciate, confronting the CEECs with the question of whether they could afford to let their currencies appreciate along with the euro. The Balassa-Samuelson effect means that over time the currencies of catch-up countries such as the CEECs will appreciate. Nevertheless, since these countries need to restructure their output and absorb a large amount of reform-induced unemployment, while some countries, such as Hungary, have also a relatively high level of external debt, great care has to be taken to maintain competitiveness. I therefore agree with Berrigan and Carré that there is a strong economic case against the premature adoption of a fixed exchange rate regime by the CEECs.

A point can be raised here concerning relative risk perceptions. With the establishment of EMU, participating countries and their financial institutions, backed as they will be by a strong central bank, are likely to be judged less risky than others by the markets. As a consequence, the perceived relative riskiness of the outs, including the CEECs, might increase, leading to higher interest rate spreads between the "ins" and the others, even if nothing happened in these other countries to warrant such increase. To some extent this has already taken place, as there is evidence that the most likely first-round participants in the EMU enjoy by now more favorable spreads than the others. This will provide a powerful incentive for the outsiders to join.

Alternative Monetary Policy Strategies

The possible monetary policy strategies of the ECB have been outlined in the EMI's January 1997 report.[2] However, the strategy to be adopted is still debated. One view is that the ECB should operate along the principles of the Bundesbank and adopt an intermediate monetary target. The main merit of such a strategy according to its proponents would be continuity with the German monetary policy, inheriting its reputation as a successful practice. On the other hand, many argue that monetary targets based on Europe-wide demand for money are too unreliable to serve as a rule for monetary policy action. To be useful, monetary targeting needs a predictable and stable relationship between money growth and inflation. Critics of monetary targeting point out that in some countries, notably in the United States and the United Kingdom, such targeting resulted in excessive interest rate volatility because it prevented the flexible adjustment of the money growth target to the changing demand for money. As a result, monetary targeting has been abandoned in these countries.

The other alternative is direct inflation targeting. Those favoring this approach argue that it would be more understandable and would make the ECB more accountable to the general public. Also, inflation targeting would allow for more flexibility when the demand for money changes and could thus lessen the volatility of interest rates. But it could also be harder for market participants to judge how the ECB assesses the inflationary pressures arising from actual monetary developments and how and when it will react to them. While this regime would leave a greater degree of flexibility and discretion to the ECB, it would create greater uncertainty for market participants about the monetary authorities' reactions. This is true in principle, but steps such as the publication of Federal Reserve Bank's Open Market Committee minutes in the United States and of the minutes of the meetings between the Chancellor and the Governor of the Bank of England can reduce that uncertainty.

The EMI's report acknowledges the ongoing debate by stating that it is not necessary to determine the precise details of the ECB's strategy at this stage. However, the different strategies can result in a slightly different monetary and financial environment for the outs and the CEECs, to which they must adapt. Theoretical considerations would suggest that a strict monetary targeting can result in higher volatility of interest rates, whereas inflation targeting could alleviate this problem. But in the real world, the dividing lines are not so clearly drawn. As is pointed out by Lamfalussy,[3] there is room for compro-

[2]European Monetary Institute, *The Single Monetary Policy in Stage Three: Specification of the Operational Framework* (Frankfurt: EMI, January 1997).

[3]Alexandre Lamfalussy, "Monetary and Exchange Rate Policy Co-operation Between the Euro Area and Other EU Countries," oral report to the informal ECOFIN Council in Verona, April 12–13, 1996.

mise between intermediate monetary and direct inflation targeting, and they need not be strictly exclusive strategies. Inflation targeting does not exclude monitoring monetary targets; it simply means that the authorities do not interpret them in a mechanistic way, disregarding other useful indicators of inflation. On the other hand, it is known that intermediate monetary targeting has not prevented the Bundesbank from using this tool flexibly in its pursuit of price stability. Indeed, there no longer seems to be a very predictable demand for money in Germany. This probably reflects both the impact of reunification and the growing use of the deutsche mark in other countries. In fact, some works have suggested that the demand for money in the EMS as a whole has been more stable than the demand for money in Germany. Nevertheless, money targeting might be difficult at the beginning within EMU because there will be no experience how the demand for money behaves in the *new* setting of the euro.

Looking at the transition economies like Hungary, the demand for money is even more unstable and more difficult to predict than in the other, more developed countries. There are several reasons for this. The breakup of large firms as a result of privatization and the emergence of hundreds of thousands of new enterprises have led to an increase in the transaction demand for money of the enterprise sector. The informal economy is relatively large in Hungary—due in part to the high tax burden—which normally increases the demand for cash, but it is unclear how the informal economy will react to the easing of the tax burden now being implemented. Financial innovation, improvements in the payment system, the liberalization of the money and financial markets, and the traditional demand for foreign currency have all affected the demand for money in such ways that it is hard to assess their combined impact. All this means that strict monetary targeting does not seem to be a workable solution in the immediate future in the transforming economies. Over time, however, as the transition is being completed, the behavioral relationships should normalize in the transforming economies and there are no reasons to believe that the demand for money would be more difficult to predict in these countries than in the EMU.

The monetary and exchange rate policy of the ECB will be concerned with the economic performance of the whole EMU rather than with that of the individual member countries. Therefore, monetary and exchange rate policy will not be available to deal with asymmetric shocks, such as a supply or a wage shock, affecting only an individual member or affecting individual members in different ways. This will leave fiscal policy as the only effective tool to respond to such shocks. Since there are limits to the flexibility of fiscal policy to respond to shocks in the short term, there could be greater fluctuations in the output of individual member countries if such shocks were to take place, affecting not only the economy of the monetary union but also the economies of the CEECs. Whether the fluctuations in output caused by asymmetric shocks will be greater in the new setting will depend in part on how the automatic stabilizers can work within the fiscal deficit constraint adopted within the framework of the stability pact. This raises the issue of the differences in the structures of government budgets in the individual member countries. Somewhat surprisingly, this issue has received insufficient attention in the ongoing discussions on convergence as the attention has focused on the permissible size of the overall fiscal deficit. However, the sustainability of this deficit in the long term and the budget's ability to respond to shocks depend on the structure of budget receipts (taxes) and expenditures. Therefore, some degree of harmonization in this area seems to be unavoidable in the long run for the monetary union to work efficiently. An important issue in this respect is the reform of the pension systems, since the unfunded pension obligations faced by the individual countries in the medium term are quite different.

Choice of Monetary Policy Instruments

The EMI Council has defined a set of monetary policy instruments that will be available to the ECB. The principal tool of monetary policy will be repurchase transactions. In addition, there will be two standing facilities: a marginal overnight lending facility and an overnight deposit facility. The interest rates on these facilities will define the corridor within which money market rates will fluctuate.

Repo facilities have been used in Hungary for some time and are the principal monetary policy tool. The National Bank of Hungary uses repos and reverse repos, and the respective interest rates provide a corridor for interbank money market rates as in the proposal described above. Thus, Hungary has already in place the main policy instruments proposed for the ECB. The same is true for several other acceding countries, such as the Czech Republic and Poland. The ECB will also be able to resort to outright transactions, swaps, and the issuance of debt certificates. These instruments are available to the Hungarian National Bank and to the central banks of several CEECs as well.

An infrastructure that will allow the ECB to impose reserve requirements will be established. However, views differ on the role to be played by reserve requirements within the EMU. Current practices still differ considerably within the EU, although there has been some tendency toward harmonization in recent years. Despite considerable reduction in their level, required reserves continue to play an important role in German monetary policy. Compulsory reserves make German banks more dependent on central bank money than banks in countries where there are no reserve requirements. This helps the Bundesbank to stabilize the demand for central bank money and makes it easier to follow intermediate quantitative monetary targets. Since these reserve requirements have to be met on an average basis over a period, they play a buffer role as well, helping to stabilize short-term interest rates. Also, short-term interest rate actions by the Bundesbank do not transmit themselves as rapidly to the longer segments of the yield curve, making longer-term interest-rates less volatile.

By contrast, several countries have abandoned reserve requirements as a monetary policy tool, most notably the United Kingdom. Banks in the United Kingdom are therefore less dependent on central bank money, rendering direct monetary targeting more difficult. Nor do required reserves play a buffer role as in Germany. This is one explanation of why short-term interest rates can be more volatile in the United Kingdom and why changes in short-term rates are transmitted faster to the longer maturities of the capital markets. Required reserves represent an implicit tax on banks. In a world where global competition dictates regulation, the ECB could well be forced to adopt a nonreserves strategy for common monetary policy.

The reserve requirement policy eventually adopted by the ECB will affect the acceding countries in a number of ways. If the above reading of the German and the British practices is correct, adoption of one or another alternative will imply different monetary policy strategies, which might result in money and capital markets with different volatility properties. Even if the ECB generalizes the current German practice, acceding CEECs must prepare themselves to reduce considerably reserve requirements. Currently, the reserve requirement is 12 percent in Hungary and even higher in some of the other CEECs. The announced policy of the Hungarian monetary authorities is to gradually reduce the rate of compulsory reserves to a level in line with EU standards, but this shall be done in a manner that will not jeopardize the anti-inflationary goals of the monetary authorities. In other words, the reduction will have to be gradual.

Payment System

The EMI has made considerable progress in its preparatory work toward establishing a Europe-wide payment system called TARGET (Trans-European automated real-time gross settlement express transfer). The system will be built on the basis of the existing national real time gross settlement (RTGS) systems, with an interlink network connecting the national central banks and using a version of the SWIFT language. Although the outs will not be part of the TARGET, they will be connected to the system. CEECs are in the early stages of developing their national payments system, which provides an opportunity for them to leapfrog, introducing right at the outset the systems that are compatible with and best suited for TARGET.

RTGS systems involve intraday borrowing and lending. A corollary of these transactions is the extensive use of high-quality collateral to cover against the risk of nonpayment. This requirement can pose some difficulties for countries that are at an early stage of securitization and development of their securities markets. It can turn out that these countries do not have enough papers of the necessary quality to meet the needs of the payment system. The development of the securities markets and the building up of confidence in them takes time. This is another good reason why CEECs should make it a top priority to develop their capital markets.

Accession to the EU

Meeting the Maastricht criteria is *not* a condition for joining the EU. However, the establishment of EMU will change the *acquis communautaires* to which the acceding countries are expected to adapt. Of particular importance to the acceding countries is the question of what they will have to do to join the EU, that is, what obligations will they have to undertake during the accession negotiations as a sign that they are willing and able to take on the *acquis communautaires* in the area of the EMU. These obligations will crystallize progressively and will become more precise once EMU has been established and working for some time. This is why representatives of the CEECs have to keep close pace with the proposals, studies, and evolution of thinking about the future of EMU in order to best prepare themselves for the entry into the EU and eventually the EMU as well.

What If . . .

It is my sincere hope that EMU will be established as scheduled on January 1, 1999. This is not only in the interest of the current member states of the EU, but also in the interest of the CEECs. Nevertheless, policymakers in the CEECs must be prepared to deal with the consequences of developments that are beyond their control. Hence, we must ask ourselves the not-to-be-asked question of what would happen if the start of Stage III were postponed. Such postponement could take place if performance deviated significantly from the Maastricht criteria in one or two of the most important core countries. Two scenarios are possible.

If there were an "orderly" decision to postpone, announcing a new date along with strong measures to achieve the Maastricht criteria, markets would be likely to perceive the postponement as credible. In this case, I think that there would be no abrupt changes in the exchange and capital markets. In fact, such credible delay could increase the chances of more countries joining EMU from the start, which could actually stabilize the markets and reduce interest rate spreads. On the other hand, if there were a "disorderly" delay accompanied by rancor and mutual recrimination, the markets could react strongly. In such a case, I am afraid that there would be greater exchange rate volatility with a flight to the deutsche mark, and a widening of spreads would also take place. This would complicate the task of policymakers everywhere, but especially in the CEECs, where the mechanisms of adjustment to sudden shifts in external conditions are less sophisticated and the room for maneuver to adjust is narrower.

Discussion

Mr. Eichengreen enquired about the suggestion in the Berrigan-Carré paper that the relationship between European currencies and the French franc on the one hand and the CFA currencies on the other could remain unchanged after EMU. In particular, who would assume the role played by the Bank of France and the related French government role in Stage III?

Mr. Carré noted that the Bank of France played a very small role in the current arrangement. It was the French treasury that had the major role, and that would continue in the future if the French treasury was still willing and if the African members of the zone agreed. In his opinion, the relationship between the French and the CFA zone was not a monetary arrangement.

Mr. Goos noted that while he largely agreed with Mr. Carré's statement, it was not only up to the French authorities and the CFA countries to decide on the future arrangement, but rather a matter to be decided by the Community. The provisions for exchange rate relationships clearly stipulated that whatever happened vis-à-vis third countries had to be agreed upon by the respective Community institutions. That was not to imply that the Community already had a position on that issue, which had yet to be discussed.

Mr. Dairi recalled that, in his paper, Mr. Carré had indicated that Mediterranean countries did not wish to join the EU. He considered that too hasty an assessment. He understood that Turkey, for one, was very much eager to join, and Morocco had requested full EU membership a few years ago. So the question was really whether the EU was ready to bring those countries into full-fledged membership.

He wondered whether, given that most of the free trade agreements being signed under the European initiative were in fact looking at greater integration of the whole Mediterranean region with Europe and the flow of foreign investment to the Mediterranean countries, it would not make sense for the Mediterranean region to seek stronger ties with Europe, at least in terms of exchange rate arrangements. Would that not move the Mediterranean countries to peg their currencies to, for example, the euro, in order to promote foreign investment from Europe?

6

Implications of EMU for the IMF

Philippe Maystadt

The creation of EMU will make history in the world. It will be a remarkable development in international relations, without precedent in the history of the IMF. It will be—allow me to quote the Managing Director—"the most important and the most promising monetary development in the post–Bretton Woods period."

The challenge today is to fully grasp the external implications of this development for both the international monetary system and the International Monetary Fund. This is a major task and I have no doubt that this conference will provide a good basis for the Fund and its membership to adjust to the introduction of the euro.

In this context, I would like to share with you some thoughts on its implications for Fund/EMU relations. This, of course, will be a preliminary exploration of the many questions related to this issue, on which discussions both within the Community and with the Fund will have to take place in the coming months.

Implications for the Fund Membership

The first question I would like to address, concerns the implications of EMU for the membership of the Fund. Little has yet been said on this question. This is not a reason to avoid addressing the issue. Time is ticking away; there are only 654 days left to January 1, 1999. It is time to draw a number of tentative conclusions.

I believe that EMU members will remain individual members of the Fund, at least during a transition period. In other words, the status quo is likely to be the preferred or compromise solution, at least in the short term, and not the other main alternative, namely, the merger of EMU members into a single member of the Fund with a single quota.

The main reason that will push toward the status quo is the fact that EMU will imply only a limited transfer of areas of decision making at the supranational level. Indeed, the transfer of competence from national to EMU level will mainly concern the monetary policy of the EU, which will be the exclusive responsibility of the ECB, and its exchange rate policy, which will be in the hands of ECOFIN and the ECB. On the other hand, economic policies will remain mainly within national competence. Of course, member states are expected to regard their economic policies as a matter of common concern, to coordinate them closely, and to avoid excessive government deficits. However, the general view in Europe remains that member states retain ultimate responsibility for economic policies. For this reason, a number of member states may wish to maintain a close relationship with the Fund.

Two other factors will need to be taken into account. First, a decision to merge EMU members into a single member of the Fund with a single quota would require unanimity of the member states participating in EMU. As the reshuffling of EMU members' quotas into a single quota would imply a loss of national sovereignty, I doubt that it would be easy to reach a consensus among EMU members on this possibility. Second, the status quo will be in line with the Articles of Agreement of the Fund, which require that membership in the Fund is available to countries individually. Thus, if EMU members would opt for a unique representation of EMU to the Fund, this would require an amendment of the Articles and complicate the matter even further, at least in the short term. Against this background, it is most likely that EMU members will remain individual members of the Fund, at least during a transition period and perhaps forever.

This is not to say that the status quo in the membership of the Fund will be an easy approach to solving all the issues that will arise in Fund/EMU relations with the introduction of the euro. The opposite is probably true. Indeed, the Fund's Articles of Agreement are based on the norm that a member of the Fund is a country with a currency of its own. Thus, the fact that the euro will be the currency of a number of members of the Fund will imply some problems for individual EMU members in performing some of their obligations of Fund membership and for the Fund in ensuring that EMU members will enjoy the same rights as any other member of the Fund.

There are, of course, precedents of monetary and currency unions, and the Fund has always adjusted to changing situations. However, past experience will not provide all the answers, because it will be the first time that the single currency of a group of Fund members will most likely emerge as a major international currency. The result of this is that EMU will have a global impact and raise policy issues of a systemic nature. For this reason I am convinced that a substantial amount of work will be required to adapt Fund/EMU relations to the introduction of the euro. This is what I would like to stress by discussing the potential implications of EMU for (1) the SDR, (2) Fund surveillance over EMU countries and policies, and (3) the potential access of EMU members to Fund resources.

Future of the SDR

My first point is on the principles of the valuation of the SDR. Those principles are provided in a decision that was adopted by the IMF Executive Board in September 1980 and that requires, first, that the SDR basket includes the currencies of the five members with the largest exports of goods and services during a five-year review period and, second, that the weighting system reflects the exports of goods and services of the members and their reserve liabilities.

Following the 1980 decision, the SDR basket includes the U.S. dollar, the deutsche mark, the Japanese yen, the French franc, and the pound sterling. With the creation of EMU, it is very likely that at least two of these currencies will disappear. Therefore, the currency composition of the SDR will need to be reviewed, and I also believe that such a change will call for a review of the method of the SDR's valuation. Indeed, although it is quite clear that the euro will join the SDR, the question arises whether the euro will be considered as the currency of two or three members with the largest exports, in line with the 1980 decision, or as the currency of the EMU as a whole.

To address this question, it will be necessary to review the principles governing the composition of the SDR with a view to deciding whether the SDR should be a "country-based" basket or a "currency-based" basket. Obviously, a "country-based" SDR basket would be in line with a decision to preserve the status quo as regards the representation of EMU members in the IMF. Following this approach would imply determining the weight of the euro on the basis of the value of the exports of goods and services by a small group of EMU members. This would mean that the weight of the euro would not reflect its relative—and potential—importance in international trade and finance. Would this make sense?

On the other hand, if the "currency-based" approach is followed, questions such as the following are likely to arise: Should other currencies join the SDR to keep five currencies in the basket or should the number of currencies concerned be revised downward after the introduction of the euro? How should the weight of the euro be determined, given there will be no data available on international trade and financial activities in euros before January 1, 1999?

As you can see, the introduction of the euro in the SDR basket will raise questions of principle and measurement, which will be indirectly related to a fundamental issue—the place of the euro in the international monetary system and its relative position vis-à-vis the dollar.

Thus, it will be difficult to avoid debating very sensitive issues, and appropriate solutions will have to be adopted, in a spirit of cooperation between the Fund, its membership at large, and EMU countries.

Fund Surveillance of EMU Countries and Policies

The start of the euro is also likely to raise challenging questions about Fund surveillance of EMU countries and policies.

Assuming that EMU participants remain members of the Fund, the Fund will need to maintain its Article IV consultations with each of the countries that will participate in EMU. However, in the context of those consultations, EMU will have to be taken as a fact and advice will center on economic and structural policies. I believe that, in many respects, the existing relations between the Fund and its European members that have pegged their currencies to the deutsche mark for a number of years predetermine the type of bilateral consultations that the Fund will conduct with EMU members.

The pursuit of those bilateral consultations will allow the Fund to remain well informed about the economic situation in EMU members, to give advice in areas such as medium-term fiscal consolidation, restructuring of the tax system, social security reforms, and strengthening of the banking system, and in this way to promote sound economic policies and stronger economic performance. In this respect, I fully agree with Professor Thygesen that "Fund surveillance will be a useful supplement, precisely because it is broader in scope . . . [and] confronts EMU Fund members with a wider and still highly relevant policy experience throughout the world."

This being said, it is clear that, conversely, the country-by-country surveillance will have to be supplemented by consultations between the Fund and the main European institutions or bodies having responsibilities in the field of economic and monetary policymaking. Obviously, this will be required because the definition and conduct of the monetary and exchange rate policy will cease to be a national responsibility after the start of EMU. Furthermore, it is quite clear that the Fund will wish to examine the policy mix of the euro zone and discuss its implications for the world economic outlook.

To this effect, suitable arrangements will need to be established. Without wanting to prejudge the concrete and final form of these arrangements, I would like to put forward a few remarks to contribute to the debate.

First, with respect to *monetary policy*, the Fund will need to engage in a close and fruitful relationship with the ECB. I have no doubt that the long tradition of cooperation between the Fund and central banks, on the one hand, and the centralization of monetary sovereignty in the hands of the Governing Council of the ECB, on the other hand, will help in finding suitable procedures of consultation between the Fund and the ECB. It would appear desirable that these procedures provide for discussions of a staff report in the Executive Board, which could reach conclusions on monetary policy in EMU.

Second, surveillance over the *exchange rate policy* of EMU will also fall within the core mandate of the Fund. This may prove more difficult to organize because exchange rate policy under EMU will be a joint responsibility of the ECOFIN Council and the ECB. Nevertheless, EMU members will have "to collaborate with the Fund and other members to assure orderly exchange arrangements and to promote a stable system of exchange rates," in accordance with their general obligation under Article IV. Accordingly, specific procedures will need to be adopted to help the Fund exercise its surveillance over the exchange rate policy of the EMU region.

Third, EMU members will have to be ready to engage in consultations with the IMF on the *policy mix of the euro zone*. Those consultations will be particularly important in the context of the preparation of the World Economic Outlook by the Fund staff, and the Broad Economic Guidelines by the European Commission. On the latter, which constitute the institutional framework for the coordination of economic policies between the member states of the EU, a strengthening of the relationship between both institutions could be called for to enable the European Commission to benefit from the Fund's advice and to enrich the IMF staff's knowledge with lessons drawn from multilateral surveillance in the EU.

Fourth, the ECOFIN Council and the ECB will have to decide about the *representation of EMU at meetings of the IMF's Executive Board* when the above-mentioned matters will be discussed. This is a matter to be settled, in agreement with the Fund, in accordance with the provisions of Article 109 (section 4) of the Maastricht Treaty. For example, a consensus could be reached that these institutions—ECOFIN Council and ECB—should be represented in the Fund by Alternates in the office of Executive Directors representing EMU members.

Finally, *consultations between the Fund and EMU members and the Community institutions concerned*, could also take place at the level of the Economic and Financial Committee, which will replace the present Monetary Committee after the establishment of EMU. This could be a natural body of dialogue between the Fund staff and EMU members for three reasons. First, this committee will keep under review the financial and economic situation of EMU members and of the Community, and report regularly thereon to the ECOFIN Council; second, the committee will have a key role to play to ensure the coordination of economic policies; and third, EU member states, the European Commission, and the ECB will be represented on the committee.

Access of EMU Members to Fund Resources

A third area of concern is the impact of EMU on the potential access of EMU members to Fund resources. Here, too, a number of questions will need to be examined carefully. The questions are simple: Will EMU members still be entitled to use the resources of the Fund? Will it be possible for the Fund to provide financial assistance to the euro area as a whole?

Although it can be argued that any request by EMU members to use conditional credit from the IMF is very unlikely, I believe that these are valid questions because they relate to the need to preserve the general rights of members of the Fund as well as the capacity of the Fund to provide a safety net for countries and currencies that are in difficulty.

The first question relates to the interpretation of the concept of "balance of payments need" for members of a monetary union. Indeed, it should be recalled that the conditions governing the use of the Fund's general resources (Article XIX, section 3) require that the member concerned "has a need because of its balance of payments or its reserve position or developments in its reserves."

Well, are we sure that after joining EMU, countries will still be open to balance of payments difficulties? Will the participation in EMU not relieve its members from their balance of payments constraint? These are questions on which it would be useful to have the opinion of the Fund.

Indeed, imagine—for a second—that the Fund would be of the opinion that it could not assist EMU members in a manner consistent with the provisions of the Articles of Agreement. This would limit—in an exceptional way—the general rights of EMU members and the fundamental principle of universality of treatment of different members.

On the other hand, not all issues would be settled if a broad interpretation of the concept of the "balance of payments need" is accepted and if the Fund is allowed to provide financial assistance to individual EMU members. Indeed, the question would arise whether it would be possible for the Fund to assist the euro area as a whole if EMU were not a member of the Fund.

One way to solve this issue would be to permit a joint request by the EMU members. However, if it is agreed that a simultaneous purchase from the Fund is possible, it remains to be decided with whom the Fund would negotiate the conditionality attending the use of its resources.

My view is that one should not overlook the validity of this question because it is closely related to the implications of EMU for the architecture of the international monetary system. Indeed, with the advent of the euro, the international monetary system will probably move from a dollar-denominated system to a new system with two or three reserve currencies—the dollar, the euro, and the yen. Obviously, the emergence of this new system will pose challenging questions and the Fund will have the major responsibility of overseeing the orderly transition to this new system. On the part of the Fund, this will require not only reviewing the mechanisms of surveillance of the international monetary system, but also reassessing its financial relations with the three reserve currencies. The point I want to stress in this context today is the following: one will have to ensure that the Fund provides a safety net against the risks of excessive exchange rate fluctuations, not only with regard to the dollar and the yen, as is the case today because the countries that issue those currencies are full members of the Fund, but also with regard to the euro, even if EMU does not become a member of the Fund.

Concluding Suggestions

The creation of EMU will have important implications for the working of the IMF and the international monetary system as a whole. Even though this conference will help to highlight a number of these implications, important questions will remain unsolved tomorrow evening. The reason is simple. Neither the EC Treaty nor the Articles of Agreement of the Fund provide all the answers.

Against this background, by way of conclusion, I would like to make the following two suggestions. First, I would recommend that the Fund take all the necessary steps to be ready to welcome the euro as the new currency of a group of its members. The experience shows that one should not underestimate the time and the energy such a change requires, and therefore it might be useful to set up a special task force within the Fund to prepare the decisions that will be required to adjust the financial organization and operations of the Fund to the advent of the euro.

Second, I see a need to agree on a "working method" to deal with the questions that will require consultation and resolution at the international level between the main actors concerned. The range of questions that should be examined ranges from seemingly technical questions to obviously political ones. That is the reason why not only academics but also politicians should take the necessary time to discuss them seriously.

As regards the calendar, it seems to me that the Interim Committee of the IMF, which—let's not forget—was established to advise and report to the Board of Governors on issues related to the management and the adaptation of the international monetary system, will wish to discuss the implications of EMU for the Fund and the international monetary system, at the latest during the fall of 1998 and perhaps even before, during its spring meeting next year. The time constraint we are facing is therefore quite tight.

One way to make rapid progress could be for the Fund staff to prepare, possibly after consultations with the European Commission and the European

Monetary Institute, a paper accompanied by a questionnaire on the main issues to be addressed in the short, medium, and long term, which could stimulate the discussions within, on the one hand, the Executive Board of the IMF and, on the other hand, the ECOFIN Council and the Monetary Committee of the EU. Assuming that this approach would be followed, it seems to me that it would be useful if this paper could be prepared early enough for the ECOFIN Council to have a first exchange of views at its informal session next September. This would clarify the extent of the challenges facing the IMF and the international monetary system about 15 months before the introduction of the euro, and give the main actors concerned the time needed to prepare the orderly adjustment of the international monetary system to EMU.

The model that the EU has adopted to lay down its monetary union does not fit in perfectly with all the existing arrangements and practices that have been developed over the years to allow the Fund to carry out its mission. A number of adaptations will be necessary to align the Fund's arrangements and practices with the characteristics of EMU. This will require serious discussion within the Community to come forward with practical proposals to be discussed with the Fund. Without denying the potential difficulties, I am confident that the ability the Fund has shown in the past to adapt to changing circumstances and the willingness of the EU to be an effective and responsible actor on the international stage will allow the necessary consensus on suitable arrangements to be reached in due time.

Session III
The Euro as a Reserve Currency and Exchange Rate Volatility

7

The Euro and Exchange Rate Stability

Agnès Bénassy-Quéré, Benoît Mojon, and Jean Pisani-Ferry

This paper deals with a single issue: will EMU increase or reduce exchange rate volatility between European and non-European currencies? As the volatility of exchange rates between the dollar, the yen, and the mark has been the focus of discussions and policy actions within the Group of Seven industrial countries since the early 1980s, this is an issue of some relevance in the discussion on the international implications of EMU.

In addressing this issue, we are concerned with the *permanent* impact of EMU, which should analytically be distinguished from the *transitory* effects that could arise from the introduction of the euro. In other words, we do not discuss here whether EMU could initially lead the euro to depreciate (because of a lack of credibility of the ECB, or a diversification of private portfolios and transaction balances arising from the elimination of exchange rate variability and risk within the euro zone) or to appreciate (because the European currency will become an international one and its unified financial market will attract capital flows). These issues have been investigated in the literature (European Commission, 1990; Gros and Thygesen, 1992; Kenen, 1995; Bénassy-Quéré, Italianer, and Pisani-Ferry, 1994; Aglietta and Thygesen, 1995), but without reaching firm conclusions, and they are the main focus of some of the papers in this volume (Bergsten; Alogoskoufis and Portes). In order to put aside these transitory issues, we shall assume throughout this paper that the ECB has established its credibility and that whatever portfolio rebalancing that could arise from the introduction of the euro has already taken place. This leaves us with an analytically neat question, to which the literature has repeatedly alluded, but has only recently started to address ex-

The authors are grateful to Karim Gebara for efficient research assistance, and to Michel Aglietta, Ralph Bryant, Philippe Martin, Paul Masson, and Bart Turtelboom for discussions on a previous version of this paper. We also wish to thank Marin Bénassy-Quéré for his cooperation.

plicitly (Martin, 1997; and the papers by Cohen and by Ghironi and Giavazzi in this volume).

It was suggested early on by some observers that the creation of EMU could increase exchange rate volatility vis-à-vis the dollar. There are two main grounds for such a claim, which rest respectively on a *stochastic stability* channel and on a *policy preference* channel:

1. By removing exchange rate volatility *within* Europe, monetary union could result in a higher volatility *between* Europe and the rest of the world. The basic reasoning behind this intuition is that the locking of intra-European exchange rates will prevent them from fulfilling their buffer role, thereby leading to a transfer of shocks to the interest rate of the euro zone and ultimately to the euro-dollar exchange rate. A related motive for increased volatility could be that through aggregating several currencies, EMU could decrease the stability of the fundamental equilibrium exchange rate of the euro in comparison to that of constituting currencies (Collignon, 1997). In other words, there could be a transfer of volatility from intra-European exchange rates to exchange rates between the euro and other currencies.
2. As the euro zone will be comparatively larger and less open than individual member countries, it may collectively attach less weight to exchange rate stability as a policy target (Kenen, 1995). A kind of "reciprocal benign neglect" could thus develop between the United States and Europe, resulting in an increase in exchange rate volatility. Additional arguments stem from the provisions of the Maastricht Treaty, which emphasize the priority of controlling domestic inflation rather than external objectives.

These arguments clearly carry some weight. However, they fall short of being fully convincing. The validity of the volatility transfer argument is disputable: in principle, shocks affecting participant countries in an opposite way (e.g., a negative shock to Germany and a positive shock to France) should not trigger policy reactions from the ECB and therefore not have an impact on the exchange rate of the euro, and symmetric shocks should not affect the volatility of the euro exchange rate either, because the ECB would be able to react in order to offset any undesirable consequence they might have, exactly in the same way as national central banks do in a floating exchange rate regime. Furthermore, the volatility transfer argument has been challenged by Flood and Rose (1995), who have shown that fixing exchange rates does not increase the instability of other macroeconomic variables. If fixing intra-European exchange rates basically removes a source of excessive volatility, there is no reason why this volatility should show up elsewhere in the macroeconomic system, and it could well be that the volatility of the dollar exchange rate would in the end be reduced. Stochastic stability considerations therefore do not lead to concluding unambiguously in favor of the increased volatility hypothesis.

The "reciprocal benign neglect" argument can also be challenged. It is certainly true that because of its lesser openness, policymakers in the euro zone should attach less weight to the union's *effective* exchange rate than previously to those of the constituent countries. However, this does not imply that they should pay less attention to the exchange rate vis-à-vis the U.S. dollar or the yen. At least, the argument needs to be refined. One reason for being less concerned with the value of the dollar could be that within the framework of the ERM of the EMS, intra-European exchange rates are sensitive to shocks to the dollar–deutsche mark rate (Henning, 1995).[1] EMU would obviously remove this factor, but the extent to which this should affect the volatility of the dollar exchange rate depends on whether (under present monetary arrangements) the burden of stabilizing intra-European exchange rates falls on the Bundesbank or on the central banks of other European countries. Furthermore, it was argued by the European Commission (1990) that a single European central bank could also find it easier to embark on exchange rate policy coordination with the U.S. Federal Reserve and the Bank of Japan than would several European central banks acting in a loosely coordinated way, if only because the reduction in the number of players would lower the informational cost of coordinating policies. There is therefore a clear case for examining how changes in European policy preferences could affect global exchange rate stability, but the issue has to be looked at in a precise way.

Although it has been the subject of casual remarks, the link between EMU and global exchange rate stability has until recently not been explored in a systematic fashion within the framework of a clearly specified model. Stochastic simulations with empirical macroeconometric models should provide some indications of the impact of EMU on the volatility of the dollar exchange rate, but since this was not the focus of their study, Masson and Symansky (1992) and Minford, Rastogi, and Hughes Hallett (1992) do not give the corresponding results. Only the European Commission (1990) provides an evaluation of the effects of EMU on the bilateral exchange rates vis-à-vis the dollar, which suggest that its volatility should decrease in comparison to the free-float regime. However, the Commission's results have been criticized for relying on the assumption that most of the observed exchange rate volatility results from noise. Available stochastic simulations therefore fail to provide convincing evidence on the issue.

In this paper, we therefore begin by providing an analytical setup for analyzing the repercussions of supply, demand, and speculative shocks in a world consisting of three countries, two of which decide to form a monetary union. We use it to develop a model in order to analyze the volatility of the real

[1]BIS (1996) provides evidence of the effects of fluctuations in the dollar–deutsche mark exchange rate on intra-European exchange rates.

effective exchange rate (REER) of the U.S. dollar under alternative European monetary regimes. We then use a similar setup for dynamic numerical simulations.

European Monetary Regimes and Dollar Exchange Rate Stability: An Analytical Framework

In order to tackle the problem, we need a model that allows us to represent the formation of a monetary union among a subset of countries while remaining sufficiently simple to be solved analytically. This leads us to the realm of three-country models, which are notoriously hard to keep tractable. We shall therefore make a number of simplifying assumptions.

The world economy is made up of three countries called U, G, and F, which represent the United States, Germany, and France. The last two, the union of which forms the euro zone (which will be called Europe for the sake of simplicity), are supposed to be identical in all respects, but can be subject to asymmetric shocks. Furthermore, Europe is supposed to be identical in size and openness to the United States. Initially, France exports a fraction, η, of its GDP to Germany and another, η, share to the United States and Germany does the same vis-à-vis France and the United States. The United States exports a fraction, η, of its GDP to Europe, equally divided between France and Germany. Along the baseline, all bilateral trade flows are therefore balanced, with each European country being twice as open as the United States and (ignoring French-German trade) Europe as a whole being as open as the United States. These assumptions are roughly consistent with empirical evidence. This kind of setup is similar to those used by Cohen and Wyplosz (1989) and Canzoneri and Henderson (1991).

We shall consider three alternative exchange rate regimes between France and Germany: a floating exchange rate regime, in which each country separately sets its monetary policy; a monetary union regime, in which the ECB sets the common monetary policy for the two European countries; and an asymmetric system representing the ERM of the EMS, in which the German central bank sets monetary policy while France keeps a fixed French franc–deutsche mark nominal exchange rate.[2] Europe is always assumed to be in a floating exchange rate regime vis-à-vis the United States. For countries in a floating exchange rate regime, no coordination is envisaged, that is, the only outcome is a Nash equilibrium. In other words, we only envisage coordination within the framework of fixed exchange rate regimes.

The model for each economy is a standard open economy model with short-run nominal rigidity adapted from Blanchard and Fischer (1989, Chap-

[2]Realignments and fluctuation bands are ignored.

ter 10).[3] It has a short run, in which nominal wages are fixed, and a long run, in which they are flexible. Before exogenous shocks occur, full employment is assumed to hold, because wages are set at a level consistent with expected labor market equilibrium. After a shock occurs, there is no immediate wage renegotiation, so the short-run supply curve has a positive slope. Unanticipated shocks may initially give rise to unemployment, but monetary policy is able to react to shocks and attempts to minimize a macroeconomic loss function. In the long run, real wages clear the labor market and the supply curve is vertical. Each country is specialized in the production of one good, which is an imperfect substitute for the production of the other two. Aggregate demand depends on the real exchange rate and the real interest rate, so that goods markets are linked through relative price effects (quantity linkages are ignored for the sake of simplicity). Capital is perfectly mobile between countries, and uncovered interest rate parity holds.

The model is presented in Appendix I. It is made tractable through an Aoki transformation, which consists of defining sum variables that refer to European averages (with E subscripts) and difference variables that capture asymmetries between France and Germany (D subscripts). Finally, U subscripts refer to U.S. variables.

It is assumed that monetary policy aims at minimizing a macroeconomic loss function $L(X)$, where X represents a set of macroeconomic variables. Obviously, the loss function depends in turn on the exchange rate regime. In what follows, we shall alternatively consider separate loss functions for France and Germany, and European loss functions representing the behavior of the ECB. Then, the robustness of the results will be discussed according to the choice of the variables to be included in the loss functions.

Long-Term Equilibrium

Appendix II gives the long-term solution to the model, assuming that shocks may have a permanent component. Except when the nominal exchange rate is fixed (ERM regime), the price flexibility ensures that inflation does not have any real effect. Thus, the only possible aim of monetary policy in the long run is to minimize inflation, and the long-term solution does not depend on the exchange rate regime or on the choice of a particular loss function. It is easily shown that the world real interest rate (which equals the nominal interest rate in this stationary equilibrium) is affected by symmetric worldwide shocks, while shocks affecting Europe and the United States have an asymmetric impact on the real exchange rate of the dollar, and shocks affecting France and

[3]Canzoneri and Henderson (1991) use a similar model to study policy coordination in the world economy.

Germany have an asymmetrical impact on the real French franc–deutsche mark exchange rate.

Short-Term Equilibrium

The short-term equilibrium is determined by setting nominal wages to zero. This nominal rigidity leads to a positively sloped short-run supply curve:

$$y_i = \frac{1-\alpha}{\alpha} p_i - \frac{1}{\alpha} u_i \qquad 0 < \alpha < 1 \qquad i = E, D, U, \tag{1}$$

where y stands for output, p, the price level, and u, a negative productivity shock. Goods market equilibrium implies that supply equals demand, that is,

$$y_i = \theta\omega_i q_i - \delta r_i + v_i \qquad \theta, \delta > 0 \qquad i = E, D, U, \tag{2}$$

with q being the real exchange rate; ω, the openness ratio (identical in France and Germany, $\omega_F = \omega_G = 2\eta$, while in the United States, $\omega_U = \eta$), r the real interest rate; and v a positive demand shock.

Combining equations (1) and (2) gives prices as functions of real exchange rates, real interest rates, and shocks:

$$p_i = \frac{1}{1-\alpha}(\alpha\theta\omega_i q_i - \alpha\delta r_i + \Gamma_i) \qquad i = E, D, U, \tag{3}$$

with $\Gamma_i = u_i + \alpha v_i$.

Consumer prices are easily derived:

$$z_i = p_i + \omega_i q_i \qquad i = E, D, U. \tag{4}$$

Equations (1) to (4) describe the functioning of each economy. Equations (5) and (6) represent the interactions through goods and capital markets. Goods market interaction results from changes in the real effective exchange rates:

$$\begin{aligned} q_E &= \frac{1}{2}(s_E + p_U - p_E) \\ q_D &= \frac{3}{2}(s_D - p_D) \\ q_U &= -s_E - p_U + p_E = -2q_E. \end{aligned} \tag{5}$$

It is important to realize that, owing to the Aoki transformation, q_E is the average real effective exchange rate of France and Germany, which is not identical to the real effective exchange rate of Europe. The latter is simply the opposite of the exchange rate of the dollar ($q_U = -2q_E$). In a similar way, q_D is not the bilateral real exchange rate between France and Germany (which equals $2(s_D - p_D)$), but half the difference of their effective real exchange rates. This is why a 3/2 factor intervenes in the equation for q_D.[4]

The international asset market equilibrium is described by two real interest rate parity conditions that stem from the uncovered interest parity condition:

$$\begin{aligned} r_U &= r_E + (q_U^{LT} - q_U) - \varepsilon_E \\ r_D &= \frac{2}{3}(q_D^{LT} - q_D) + \varepsilon_D. \end{aligned} \tag{6}$$

ε_E and ε_D are transitory speculative shocks to the exchange rate equation, which can be seen as representing time-varying risk premiums. We introduce these shocks because we want to represent the effect of speculative shocks that are correlated across currencies.

The model is closed with the three first-order conditions derived from the minimization of the loss function. We now have to choose a loss function.

Central Bank Behavior

As we intend to determine whether European monetary union is likely to affect the stability of the exchange rate vis-à-vis the dollar, a straightforward approach is to explicitly include the real exchange rate in the central bank's loss function. This kind of representation is able to capture recent (and possibly future) policy dilemmas facing the central bank when significant swings in the external value of the currency occur. Article 109 of the Maastricht Treaty explicitly envisages such dilemmas, as it states that the Council may formulate "general orientations" for the exchange rate policy of the euro zone vis-à-vis other currencies (implicitly, the dollar and the yen), but that these orientations "shall be without prejudice to the primary objective of the ESCB to maintain price stability."

This approach can also be considered a reduced form representation of the traditional trade-off between domestic objectives and the achievement of external equilibrium, under the assumption that the current account essentially depends on the real exchange rate. It was, for example, used by Persson and Tabellini (1996). But we consider it more relevant in the present context to take the real exchange rate as an objective in its own right than to use more tradi-

[4]An example may help to clarify the reason for this factor. Suppose French price rises by 1 percentage point. The French real effective exchange rate appreciates by 1 percent, while the German one depreciates by 0.5 percent. Thus, the half-difference q_D decreases by 0.75 percent, while the half-difference of prices, p_D, increases by 0.5 percent. Hence, the 3/2 factor.

tional ways of including an external variable among the policymakers' main objectives, like including a current account target in the objective function.

Therefore, let the loss function be

$$L_i = \frac{1}{2}(p_i^2 + \beta_i q_i^2) \qquad i = G, F, U, \tag{7}$$

where β is a coefficient that measures the relative weight of the real exchange rate objective as compared to the price objective.[5] We shall consider other loss functions in the section on robustness. What we need to do here is to determine the weight of this objective for the European central bank, that is, calculate β_E from β_F and β_G.

A natural way to proceed is to take as the European loss function a simple average of those of France and Germany:[6]

$$L_E = \frac{L_F + L_G}{2}. \tag{8}$$

French and German prices and real exchange rates can be expressed as functions of the "sum" and "difference" variables, using the property that $x_F = x_E + x_D$ and $x_G = x_E - x_D$. Assuming that $\beta_G = \beta_F = \beta$, and rearranging the expression, we obtain

$$L_E = \frac{1}{2}(p_E^2 + \beta q_E^2) + H(p_D, q_D). \tag{9}$$

The H term can be dropped from the expression since it only depends on difference variables, which cannot be affected by the monetary policy of the European central bank. Furthermore, equation (5) indicates that the average real effective exchange rate of France and Germany, q_E, can be replaced by $-q_U/2$, where $-q_U$ is the effective real exchange rate of the euro zone. This leads to the following expression, which is formally similar to equation (7), except for the division by four of the β coefficient:

$$L_E = \frac{1}{2}(p_E^2 + \frac{\beta}{4} q_U^2). \tag{10}$$

[5]The price variable in the loss function is the producer price. Using the consumer price instead does not qualitatively affect the results. The loss function is normalized so that the targets are set to zero.

[6]Masson and Symansky (1992) challenge this approach. They claim that as monetary policy in the euro zone will be based on aggregate variables, the monetary union's loss function should be directly expressed in terms of aggregate variables. However, this distinction is only relevant if the loss function is used for measuring the welfare effects of alternative exchange rate regimes. It is inconsequential if it is used for deriving policy rules, since the first-order condition remains unchanged.

Moving to monetary union therefore reduces the weight of the effective exchange rate objective. This reduction does not arise from any particular assumption about the behavior of the ECB. Rather, it is the mechanical outcome of the reduction in the openness ratio resulting from the creation of the euro zone, which is half as open as for the two constituent countries individually, and whose central bank is not able to target the real French franc–deutsche mark exchange rate. Note that this result does not mean that the ECB attaches less weight to the exchange rate of the dollar than do the central banks of France and Germany. On the contrary, we explicitly assume here that its preference for keeping the dollar around its equilibrium value does not change.

In minimizing the loss function, we may directly use the real interest rate as the policy instrument when the long-run equilibrium does not require domestic price changes (because as inflation has no real effect in the long run, minimizing the loss function at period $t + 1$ simply leads to equating inflation to zero; thus, $p_i^{LT} = p_i$ and $r_i = i_i - [E(p_i^{LT}) - p_i] = i_i$; see Appendix II). This always applies to floating exchange rate regimes, because any required change in the real exchange rate results from corresponding changes in the nominal exchange rate rather than domestic prices. This also applies to fixed exchange rate equilibria in Europe when shocks are either temporary or symmetric (because the long-run real exchange rate remains constant in both cases). The only case in which shocks imply the long-run value of the domestic price to change is that of fixed exchange rate regimes (EMU or ERM) in the presence of permanent asymmetric shocks. We shall therefore use the real interest rate as the policy instruments in all cases but this last one.

ERM in Europe

Which European exchange rate regime should be taken as a benchmark for assessing the effects of EMU is a matter for discussion. There are two reasons for taking a floating rate regime as a benchmark. First, the current wide-band ERM does not differ much from a floating rate regime, de jure at least. Second, many observers consider that, should the EMU perspective be abandoned, Europe would forsake its attempts at exchange rate stabilization and move to a floating rate regime. However, Europe has been attempting to stabilize exchange rates at least since 1979, and the wide-band ERM has de facto been a fixed rate regime since 1993. There are therefore also grounds for comparing exchange rate volatility between Europe and the rest of the world in EMU and the ERM.

Like any target zone system, the ERM has complex features, but for this comparison it will be considered here as an asymmetric system in which the

Bundesbank freely defines its monetary policy while the Bank of France maintains a fixed exchange rate with the deutsche mark. This kind of representation does not contradict the conclusions of the literature, and it is adopted in most empirical simulations (European Commission, 1990, or Masson and Symansky, 1992). Furthermore, we disregard the possibility of realignments, we ignore the existence of fluctuation bands, and we assume that the system is perfectly credible and there are no speculative shocks to the French franc–deutsche mark exchange rate. These rather crude assumptions are debatable, especially as they prevent us from taking into account a possible correlation between the deutsche mark–dollar and the intra-ERM exchange rates. They should be relaxed for an empirical evaluation with model simulations. Finally, we assume that the Bundesbank behaves as a Stackelberg leader, that is, that it takes into account the behavior of the Bank of France when making its monetary policy choices. But the loss function of the Bank of France is no longer similar to that of the Bundesbank: its only aim is to keep the deutsche mark–French franc nominal exchange rate stable.

As developed above, the real interest rate can be taken as the policy instrument as long as shocks are either symmetric or temporary. Hence, the monetary policy in the ERM regime can be described as follows:

$$\underset{r_G}{\text{Min}}\ L_G = \frac{1}{2}(p_G^2 + \beta q_G^2) \tag{11}$$

$$\text{subject to} \qquad r_F = r_G + \varepsilon_D.$$

In the case of permanent, asymmetric shocks, the implications of exchange rate targeting for nominal interest rates must be explicitly taken into account.

Exchange Rate Stability Under Various European Policy Regimes

U.S. Behavior

As the U.S. policy regime does not depend on exchange rate arrangements in Europe, the behavior of the U.S. economy can be represented by a relation between the real exchange rate and the real interest rate that is invariant with respect to policy changes in Europe. To establish this relation, we combine the U.S. goods market equilibrium condition (3) with the first-order condition from the minimization of the U.S. loss function:

$$\frac{dL_U}{dr_U} = p_U \frac{dp_U}{dr_U} + \beta q_U \frac{dq_U}{dr_U} = p_U\left(\frac{\partial p_U}{\partial r_U} + \frac{\partial p_U}{\partial q_U}\frac{\partial q_U}{\partial r_U}\right) + \beta_U q_U \frac{\partial q_U}{\partial r_U} = 0 \quad (12)$$

with $\frac{\partial q_U}{\partial r_U} = -1,$

$\frac{\partial p_U}{\partial r_U} = -\frac{\alpha\delta}{1-\alpha}$, and

$\frac{\partial p_U}{\partial q_U} = \frac{\alpha\eta\theta}{1-\alpha}.$

The first-order condition for the United States is therefore

$$p_U = -\frac{1-\alpha}{\alpha}\frac{\beta_U}{\delta+\eta\theta}q_U. \quad (13)$$

Combining equations (3) and (13) gives a relation between the real exchange rate and the real interest rate, which can be represented in a (r_U, q_U) diagram as an upward sloping schedule *UU*:

$$q_U = H_U(\delta r_U - \Gamma_U), \quad \text{(UU)}$$

with $H_U = \dfrac{\alpha}{\dfrac{(1-\alpha)^2}{\alpha}\dfrac{\beta_U}{\delta+\eta\theta}+\alpha\eta\theta}$ and $\Gamma_U = u_U + \alpha v_U$.

UU is independent of shocks affecting Europe or the dollar exchange rate, but is not independent of domestic U.S. shocks. It represents the reaction of the U.S. central bank, and is upward sloping because the Federal Reserve reacts by raising interest rates to a depreciation of the currency that affects both p and q.

European Behavior Under Floating Exchange Rates and EMU

Similar relations can be derived for Europe under alternative exchange regime assumptions. We begin by comparing a free-float regime and monetary union. The ERM will be introduced thereafter.

Floating Exchange Rate Regime

Minimizing separately the loss functions for France and Germany yields the first-order conditions, which can be expressed in the sum-difference system as

$$p_F\left(\frac{dp_E}{dr_F} + \frac{dp_D}{dr_F}\right) + \beta q_F\left(\frac{dq_E}{dr_F} + \frac{dq_D}{dr_F}\right) = 0$$

$$p_G\left(\frac{dp_E}{dr_G} - \frac{dp_D}{dr_G}\right) + \beta q_G\left(\frac{dq_E}{dr_G} - \frac{dq_D}{dr_G}\right) = 0, \tag{14}$$

with $\frac{dp_E}{dr_G} = \frac{dp_E}{dr_F} = \frac{1}{2}\frac{dp_E}{dr_G}$ and

$$\frac{dp_D}{dr_G} = -\frac{dp_D}{dr_F} = -\frac{1}{2}\frac{dp_D}{dr_D},$$

and the same for q. Adding the two conditions therefore yields

$$p_E\left(\frac{dp_E}{dr_E} + \frac{dp_D}{dr_D}\right) + \beta q_E\left(\frac{dq_E}{dr_E} + \frac{dq_D}{dr_D}\right) = 0 \tag{15}$$

and a similar condition for variables p_D and q_D.

European aggregate behavior can thus be represented by a relation between variables p_E and q_E, which is similar to equation (13) for the United States and can be calculated using goods market equilibrium conditions (3) and real interest rate parity conditions (6):

$$p_E = -\Phi^{Float} q_E, \tag{16}$$

with

$$\Phi^{Float} = \beta \frac{\frac{dq_E}{dr_E} + \frac{dq_D}{dr_D}}{\frac{dp_E}{dr_E} + \frac{dp_D}{dr_D}} = \frac{\beta}{\frac{\alpha}{1-\alpha}(2\eta\theta + \delta)}.$$

Relation (16) gives the implicit trade-off between aggregate price and real exchange rate stemming from noncooperative policies conducted independently by French and German authorities.

EMU

The equivalent relation under EMU can simply be obtained by minimizing the aggregate loss function $L_E = ½(p_E^2 + \beta q_E^2)$. This leads to changing coefficient Φ in equation (16):

$$p_E = -\Phi^{EMU} q_E, \tag{17}$$

with

$$\Phi^{EMU} = \beta \frac{\frac{dq_E}{dr_E}}{\frac{dp_E}{dr_E}} = \frac{\beta}{\frac{2\alpha}{1-\alpha}(\eta\theta + \delta)}.$$

It is apparent that $\Phi^{EMU} < \Phi^{Float}$, that is, that the slope of the schedule described by equations (16) and (17) is smaller under EMU than in the free-float regime. This means that moving from the floating rate regime to EMU tilts the European trade-off between price and exchange rate stabilization toward price stabilization and away from exchange rate stabilization.[7] The reason for it can be grasped from the expression for Φ in equations (16) and (17): moving from a floating rate regime to monetary union affects the responsiveness to changes in the real interest rate of both exchange rates and prices, that is, it affects the numerator and the denominator of the expression for Φ. Both terms are in fact lowered, since we have both

$$\left|\frac{dp_E}{dr_E}\right| = \frac{\alpha}{1-\alpha}(\eta\theta + \delta) < \left|\frac{dp_D}{dr_D}\right| = \frac{\alpha}{1-\alpha}(3\eta\theta + \delta)$$

and

$$\left|\frac{dq_E}{dr_E}\right| = \frac{1}{2} < \left|\frac{dq_D}{dr_D}\right| = \frac{3}{2},$$

but the reduction in the numerator is proportionally larger because the move to EMU basically affects a country's ability to modify its real exchange rate through monetary policy changes. Since prices are affected by monetary policy both directly and through the exchange rate channel, this effect exceeds the parallel reduction in the control over domestic prices.[8]

Nash Equilibrium Between Europe and the United States

Whatever the European regime, the euro-dollar exchange rate will result from a noncooperative game between Europe and the United States. In order to calculate the corresponding Nash equilibrium, we need to transform equation (16) into a real exchange rate–real U.S. interest rate relation. Substituting

[7]This was already apparent in equation (10). However, the result we have obtained takes into account both changes in the relative weighting of the policy objectives and changes in the transmission channels resulting from the reduced openness of the euro zone.

[8]With $\delta = 0$, that is, no direct domestic demand impact of monetary policy, the two effects would exactly offset.

equation (16) into the goods market equilibrium condition (3) and using the real interest rate parity condition (6) leads to the following expression:

$$q_U = H_E(\Phi)[-\delta r_U + \Delta_E], \tag{EE}$$

where

$$H_E(\Phi) = \frac{1}{\frac{1-\alpha}{2\alpha}\Phi + \eta\theta + \delta}$$

is a decreasing function of Φ, and Δ_E is a combination of shocks:

$$\Delta_E = \frac{1}{\alpha} u_E + v_E - \delta\varepsilon_E + \delta q_U^{LT}.$$

The model can now easily be used to calculate the impact of supply, demand and exchange rate shocks on the euro-dollar exchange rate. Equations (UU) resulting from U.S. behavior and (EE) resulting from European behavior can be represented as upward- and downward-sloping schedules UU and EE in an (r_U, q_U) diagram, whose intersection determines the U.S. real interest rate R_U and the real effective exchange rate of the dollar Q_U (Figure 1). Although not conventional, this representation is equivalent to the familiar determination of the Nash noncooperative equilibrium in a two-country game.

Figure 1. Impact of a U.S. Shock

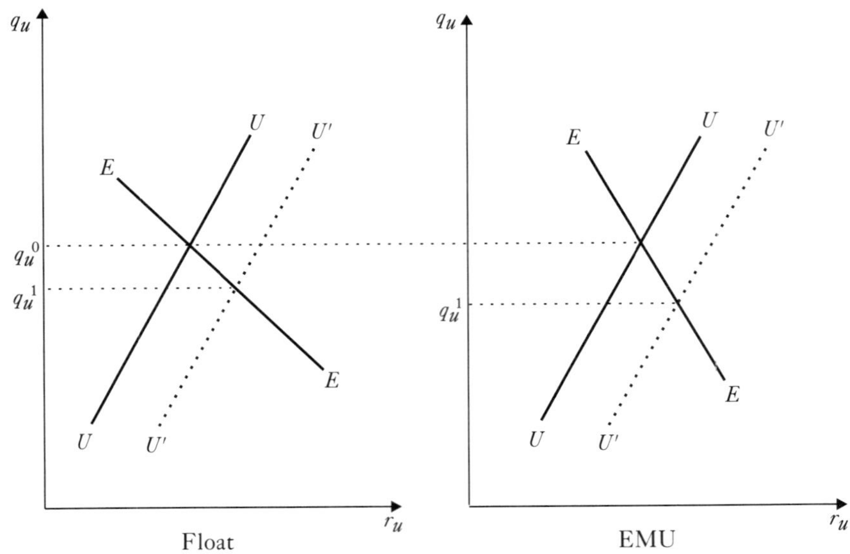

We want to determine whether the responsiveness to shocks of the real exchange rate of the dollar decreases or increases with EMU. To this end, equations (UU) and (EE) can be written as a system of two equations:

$$\begin{aligned} q_U &= H_U(\delta r_U - \Gamma_U) \\ q_U &= H_E(\Phi)(-\delta r_U + \Delta_E), \end{aligned} \tag{18}$$

where Γ_U represents shocks to the United States and Δ_E symmetric shocks to France and Germany (see equations UU and EE).

The solution of the above system is

$$q_U = \frac{H_E(\Phi)}{1 + \dfrac{H_E(\Phi)}{H_U}} \Delta, \qquad \text{where } \Delta = \Delta_E - \Gamma_U. \tag{19}$$

Δ represents shocks affecting Europe and the United States asymmetrically.

It is apparent that $\frac{dq_U}{dH_E} > 0$, and therefore that $\frac{dq}{d\Delta d\Phi} < 0$. Since $\Phi^{EMU} < \Phi^{Float}$, this demonstrates that forming a monetary union in Europe increases the responsiveness of the real effective exchange rate of the dollar to shocks originating in the United States or affecting European countries symmetrically. Figure 1 depicts it graphically in the case of positive U.S. shocks: the resulting appreciation of the dollar is more pronounced under EMU than under floating exchange rates.

The reason for this result is that under a floating exchange rate regime, France and Germany fail to internalize the externality resulting from their macroeconomic interdependence. Assume for example that Europe is hit by a positive demand shock or an adverse supply shock ($\nu_G = \nu_F > 0$ or $u_G = u_F > 0$). In a floating rate regime, both countries raise their interest rate to stem the inflationary consequences of the shock, but as they do not internalize the externality, they tend to overestimate the impact of their policy.[9] In the event, the actual REER appreciation turns out to be lower than expected (because both currencies appreciate vis-à-vis the dollar), and inflation remains higher. Failure to internalize the externality results in a weaker tightening of monetary policy than when countries coordinate. Thus, a side effect of the absence of policy coordination under a floating rate regime is that monetary policy tends to overweight the real exchange rate objective and to stabilize the real effective exchange rate of the dollar.

When the two European countries form a monetary union, they internalize their common externality, and the ECB assesses more accurately the impact

---

[9]This is because $\left|\frac{dp_E}{dr_E}\right| < \left|\frac{dp_D}{dr_D}\right|$.

of its policy. Therefore, it goes for a higher increase in interest rates than under a floating rate regime, and the resulting appreciation vis-à-vis the dollar is more pronounced. By providing automatic coordination in the response to symmetric shocks, monetary union removes a coordination failure and thereby results in increased real volatility of the dollar.[10]

Equation (19) also indicates that *asymmetric* intra-European shocks (u_D, v_D, and ε_D) do not have an impact on the real exchange rate of the dollar, because the effects of the changes in French and German variables automatically offset. This contradicts the naive version of the volatility transfer argument: as long as we compare two symmetric exchange rate regimes in Europe (i.e., float and EMU), suppressing an intra-European adjustment channel can increase the volatility of French and German macroeconomic variables, but does not have an impact at all on U.S. variables, and in particular has no effect on the (nominal or real) effective exchange rate of the U.S. dollar.

An interesting case is that of speculative shocks. A well-known stylized fact is that the French franc tends to depreciate against the deutsche mark when the deutsche mark appreciates against the U.S. dollar. This asymmetry can be represented in our framework as

$$\varepsilon_D = -\rho\varepsilon_G \qquad 0 \leq \rho \leq 1, \tag{20}$$

where ρ measures the correlation between speculative shocks to the deutsche mark-U.S. dollar and the French franc–deutsche mark exchange rates. Equation (20) is equivalent to

$$\varepsilon_D = -\xi\varepsilon_E, \quad \text{with } \xi = \frac{1}{\frac{1}{\rho} - 1}. \tag{21}$$

Such a correlation of shocks does not change the volatility of q_E, which does not depend on ε_D. But it increases the volatility of both q_F and q_G for a given volatility of q_E. As the asymmetry of shocks should disappear in EMU (q_F and q_G by definition will have the same volatility), this removal of intra-European

[10]In the standard, game-theoretical framework, failure to coordinate frequently results in a tighter monetary policy (and thereby a stronger appreciation vis-à-vis third countries) in reaction to positive demand shocks, because each country thinks it can stabilize its economy through appreciating its exchange rate vis-à-vis its partner. This is not the case here because the monetary authorities target both inflation and the real exchange rate. In the absence of coordination, they overestimate the impact of their monetary policy on the real exchange rate. Thus, the monetary policy underreacts to shocks. The robustness of our result is further discussed in the section on robustness.

speculative shocks leads to a lower volatility in the exchange rate of each European country in EMU, while the volatility of the average exchange rate remains unchanged.

More generally, an increase in the real effective volatility of the dollar does not necessarily apply to the deutsche mark–dollar and French franc–dollar real exchange rates. Under a floating rate regime, asymmetric shocks in Europe have an impact on the two bilateral dollar exchange rates without affecting the effective exchange rate of the dollar, but this effect vanishes in a monetary union. Depending on the relative size of symmetric versus antisymmetric shocks in Europe, the bilateral euro-dollar real exchange rate could be either more volatile or less volatile than the deutsche mark–dollar and French franc–dollar real exchange rates under a floating rates regime. This is a matter that could only be decided upon empirically.

Behavior Under Fixed Exchange Rates: The ERM Case

The response of the dollar exchange rate when European monetary policies are coordinated through the operation of an asymmetric fixed exchange rate system can be computed in the same fashion as for EMU or floating exchange rates. The derivation of equation (11) leads to the following trade-off for Germany:

$$p_G = \Phi_G^{ERM} q_G, \qquad \text{with } \Phi_G^{ERM} = \Phi^{EMU}. \tag{22}$$

As the Bundesbank knows that France will follow a fixed exchange rate policy, it internalizes the externality and behaves exactly in the same way as the European central bank as regards the price/exchange rate trade-off. The only difference is that the Bundesbank does not react in the same way to shocks occurring in France and in Germany. This is clear from the modified (EE) relation:

$$q_U = H_E(\Phi_G^{ERM})(-\delta r_U + \Delta_E + \Delta_D), \tag{EE$'$}$$

where $H_E(\Phi)$ and Δ_E are the same as in equation (EE), and Δ_D is a combination of "difference" shocks.

Taking the behavior of the Federal Reserve (UU) into account, the dollar real exchange rate can be expressed as a function of shocks:

$$q_U = \frac{H_E(\Phi)}{1 + \dfrac{H_E(\Phi)}{H_U}} \Delta', \tag{23}$$

where $\Delta' = \Delta_E + \Delta_D + \Gamma_U$.

Equation (23) indicates that the reaction of the dollar REER, q_U, to common shocks ($\Delta_D = 0$) is the same as in the EMU regime. This is a well-known result from the theory of policy coordination: a fixed exchange rate system behaves in the same way as a monetary union as long as shocks are symmetric (Canzoneri and Henderson, 1991).

The difference arises with asymmetric shocks. In a floating exchange rate or EMU regime, asymmetric shocks do not have an impact on the (nominal or real) exchange rate of the U.S. dollar because shocks to French and German variables offset. However, they do have an impact in an ERM regime because the Bundesbank, whose loss function only includes German variables, reacts asymmetrically to shocks affecting the German and the French economy. Hence, under an ERM regime, asymmetric shocks in Europe lead to real exchange rate fluctuations between the United States and Europe that would vanish in either an EMU or a floating rate regime.

How important can this effect be? It should be expected that as asymmetric shocks tend to be rare among core European countries, they do not account for a large part of the volatility of the dollar–deutsche mark exchange rate, and that moving from the ERM to EMU should not reduce it significantly. But here again, the relevance of this effect is a matter for empirical investigation.

The outcome is similar for correlated speculative shocks: in the ERM regime, a speculative shock to the deutsche mark–U.S. dollar exchange rate that makes the deutsche mark appreciate against both the dollar and the French franc leads to less loosening from the Bundesbank than in EMU. In the ERM regime, the Bundesbank knows that the Bank of France will support part of the stabilization through an increase in its interest rate. This again makes the dollar more volatile against European currencies in the ERM than in EMU.

Summing up, the REER of the dollar appears more volatile in EMU than in a floating regime, while the comparison with the ERM depends on the share of symmetric, asymmetric, and correlated shocks (Table 1).

Robustness

To what extent are these results robust? Two obvious limitations are (1) the choice of a specific loss function, on which the results might be dependent, and (2) the way the interactions between countries are described in the model. In this section, we address these limitations. We start by describing more precisely the behavior of European countries in the presence of symmetric shocks.

Table 1. Effect of Shocks on the Real Effective Exchange Rate of the Dollar

Shocks	Float	EMU	ERM
Common shocks			
Positive demand shock $v_F = v_G > 0$	+	++	++
Negative supply shock $u_F = u_G > 0$	+	++	++
Asymmetric shocks			
Demand shock $v_F = -v_G > 0$	0	0	+
Supply shock $u_F = -u_G > 0$	0	0	+
Correlated speculative shock $\varepsilon_D = -\xi\varepsilon_G$	+	+	++

Note: A plus sign indicates dollar depreciation.

Intra-European Policy Game

To clarify the results of the previous section, it may be useful to present them in a traditional game theory framework, which explicitly shows how the interest rate of each country reacts to shocks and to the interest rate of other countries.

The reaction functions of France and Germany in a floating exchange rate environment can be derived from equation (16) and its equivalent in terms of difference variables:[11]

$$\begin{aligned} r_F &= \frac{1}{2}\frac{A_E}{A_E+\delta}(r_U + r_G) + \frac{B_F}{A_E+\delta} \\ r_G &= \frac{1}{2}\frac{A_E}{A_E+\delta}(r_U + r_F) + \frac{B_G}{A_E+\delta}, \end{aligned} \tag{24}$$

with $A_E = \theta\omega_E + \phi\dfrac{1-\alpha}{\alpha}$,

$$B_F = A_E\left(\frac{\varepsilon_E - q_U^{LT}}{2} + \frac{3}{2}\varepsilon_D + q_D^{LT}\right) + \frac{\Gamma_F}{\alpha}$$

$$B_G = A_E\left(\frac{\varepsilon_E - q_U^{LT}}{2} - \frac{3}{2}\varepsilon_D - q_D^{LT}\right) + \frac{\Gamma_G}{\alpha}.$$

Conversely, under EMU, we have

$$r_F = r_G = r_E. \tag{25}$$

[11]With $p_F = p_E + p_D$, $p_G = p_E - p_D$, and the same for q_F and q_G.

Figure 2 depicts, in the case of a shock affecting the United States or the two European countries symmetrically, both the free-float Nash equilibrium N and the cooperative EMU equilibrium E, together with the two countries' reaction functions under flexible exchange rates r_F (r_G) and r_G (r_F), and the $B_F B_G$ locus of cooperative equilibria. Note that E is also the equilibrium under fixed exchange rates, with French behavior being represented by the diagonal DD.

The figure is similar to usual representations of two-country policy games, but with two differences. The first difference is that, although only the German and the French behavior are represented, the U.S. reaction function is explicitly taken into account. The second difference is that, in contrast to usual results, Figure 2 makes clear that when the European countries set monetary policies independently, they tend to underreact to symmetric shocks. As developed above, this behavior results from the inclusion of the real exchange rate among the policy targets. What if we adopt a more standard loss function instead?

Another Loss Function

Let us now replace the loss function $L = p^2 + \beta q^2$ by the more conventional function $\Lambda = z^2 + \beta y^2$ (we drop the country subscripts for the sake of simplification). Using exactly the same method as in the previous section, we derive from the first-order condition a relation between z and y:

Figure 2. Equilibrium with Fixed French Franc–Deutsche Mark Exchange Rate

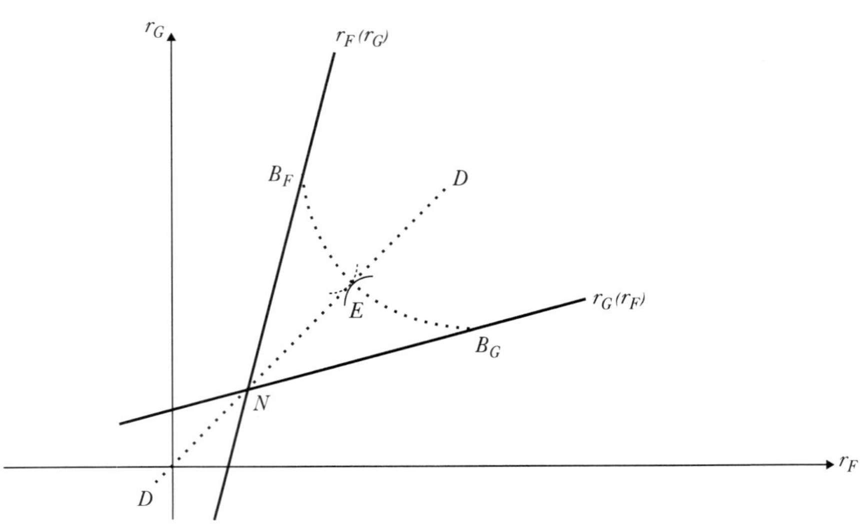

$$z = -\Psi y, \tag{26}$$

where

$$\Psi_U = \beta \frac{\frac{dy_U}{dr_U}}{\frac{dz_U}{dr_U}}, \Psi_E^{EMU} = \beta \frac{\frac{dy_E}{dr_E}}{\frac{dz_E}{dr_E}},$$

and

$$\Psi_E^{Float} = \beta \frac{\frac{dy_E}{dr_E} + \frac{dy_D}{dr_D}}{\frac{dz_E}{dr_E} + \frac{dz_D}{dr_D}}.$$

After some algebra, we get

$$\Psi_E^{FLOAT} = \beta \frac{1}{\frac{\alpha}{1-\alpha} + \frac{2\eta}{2\eta\theta + \delta}}$$

and

$$\Psi_U = \Psi_E^{EMU} = \beta \frac{1}{\frac{\alpha}{1-\alpha} + \frac{\eta}{\eta\theta + \delta}}. \tag{27}$$

We therefore have

$$\Psi_E^{FLOAT} < \Psi_E^{EMU}.$$

Forming a monetary union reduces the percieved effectiveness of momentary policy regarding both consumer prices

$$\left|\frac{dz_E}{dr_E}\right| < \left|\frac{dz_D}{dr_D}\right|$$

and output

$$\left|\frac{dy_E}{dr_E}\right| < \left|\frac{dy_D}{dr_D}\right|$$

because the reduced openness of the euro zone negatively affects the significance of the exchange rate channel for the transmission of monetary policy impulses. But this reduction effect is stronger for consumer prices. This is because consumer prices are affected by the exchange rate both directly (through its effect on the price of imported goods) and indirectly (through its effect on producer prices), while output (and producer prices) are only affected indirectly. This difference, which does not depend on a particular assumption about price elasticities, is crucial to our results.[12]

Combining equation (26) with equations (7) and (12) gives

$$p + \omega q = -\Psi\left(\frac{1-\alpha}{\alpha} p - \frac{1}{\alpha} u\right).$$

Hence,

$$p = \frac{\Psi_U - \alpha\omega q}{\alpha + (1-\alpha)\Psi}.$$

Substituting into equation (3), we get the following relation between q and r:

$$\omega\left(\theta + \frac{1-\alpha}{\alpha + (1-\alpha)\Psi}\right)q = \delta r - \frac{1}{\alpha + (1-\alpha)\Psi} u - \upsilon. \quad (28)$$

For the United States, equation (28) immediately gives a relation between q_U and r_U that is equivalent to equation (UU) and is also upward sloping:

$$q_U = G_U(\delta r_U - \Omega_U) \quad \text{(UU')}$$

with

$$G_U = \frac{1}{\eta\left(\theta + \frac{1-\alpha}{\alpha + (1-\alpha)\Psi_U}\right)}$$

and

$$\Omega_U = \frac{1}{\alpha + (1-\alpha)\Psi_U} u_U - \upsilon_U.$$

Equation (UU′), which represents its reaction, means that the U.S. central bank reacts by raising interest rates to a depreciation of the currency that increases both prices and output.

[12]With output prices instead of consumer prices, the reduction in the exchange rate channel in EMU is the same for prices and for output, and EMU no longer modifies the dollar volatility. Nevertheless, the consumer price index seems more representative of the actual monetary policies in Europe (the Maastricht criterion refers to consumer prices).

To get the equivalent relation for Europe, we have to substitute the real interest rate parity condition (10) into equation (28). After some tedious calculation we obtain

$$q_U = G_E(\Psi_E)(-\delta r_U + \Omega_E), \qquad \text{(EE'')}$$

where

$$G_E(\Psi_E) = \frac{1}{\delta + \theta + \eta \dfrac{1-\alpha}{\alpha + (1-\alpha)\Psi_E}}$$

and

$$\Omega_E = \frac{1}{\alpha + (1-\alpha)\Psi_E} u_E - \upsilon_E - \delta\varepsilon_E + \delta q_U^{LT},$$

which is formally equivalent to equation (EE), and also downward-sloping. For U.S. shocks as well as demand and speculative European shocks, the resolution is formally similar to that of the (UU, EE) system. Since $G_E(\Psi_E)$ is increasing in Ψ_E and

$$\Psi_E^{Float} < \Psi_E^{EMU}, \left.\frac{dq_U}{d\Omega}\right|_{EMU} > \left.\frac{dq_U}{d\Omega}\right|_{Float},$$

shocks have a stronger impact on the real effective exchange rate of the dollar when Europe is in a monetary union. This is the same result as with the previous loss function. For European supply shocks, however, things are different because Ω_E depends on Ψ_E. Considering European supply shocks only, we get the following system:

$$\begin{aligned} q_U &= G_U \delta r_U \\ q_U &= G_E(\Psi_E)(-\delta r_U + B_E(\Psi_E) u_E), \end{aligned} \qquad (29)$$

with

$$B_E(\Psi_E) = \frac{1}{\alpha + (1-\alpha)\Psi_E},$$

the solution of which is

$$q_U = \frac{G_E(\Psi_E) B_E(\Psi_E)}{1 + \delta \dfrac{G_E(\Psi_E)}{G_U}} u_E. \qquad (30)$$

q_U is decreasing in Ψ_E because $G_E(\Psi_E)B_E(\Psi_E)$ is. We therefore find that European supply shocks have a lesser impact on the real exchange rate of the dollar when Europe forms a monetary union, while demand shocks have a larger impact in EMU.

The intuition behind this result comes from the fact that a demand shock hits both output and prices in the same direction, while a supply shock hits output and prices in opposite directions. Take, for example, an adverse supply shock that has both an inflationary and a contractionary impact. The policy reaction tends to be muted, as authorities agree to accommodate part of the inflationary consequences of the shock in order not to add to its contractionary effects. As Europe forms a monetary union, with the effect that monetary policy loses more of its perceived effectiveness as an instrument to control consumer prices than to control output, the central bank tends to react less aggressively to the inflationary effects of the supply shock. This weaker tightening results in a less pronounced appreciation of the currency.

In the case of a positive demand shock, the monetary authorities increase the interest rates in order to stabilize both output and prices. As consumer prices are more sensitive to exchange rate changes than output, minimization of the loss function results in a limited increase in interest rates, because authorities keep a balance between the deviations from their two policy targets. In the absence of cooperation, this factor limits the extent of interest rate increases and of the resulting exchange rate appreciation. Moving to EMU results in an evening-out of the differences between output and prices as regards the effects of monetary policy. Hence, the monetary authorities accept a larger exchange rate appreciation in order to stabilize both prices and output.

Summing up, we find that as long as demand shocks prevail, or in the presence of U.S. supply shocks, the previous results remain when social welfare is measured in terms of consumer price inflation and output rather than in terms of producer price inflation and the real exchange rate: monetary union in Europe will tend to increase the real effective volatility of the dollar (Table 2). The significant exception is European supply shocks, which tend to be less consequential for the dollar REER when Europe is in a monetary union regime. Which of the effects will on average dominate can only be decided

Table 2. Effect of Shocks on the Real Effective Exchange Rate of the Dollar, with the Λ Loss Function

Shocks	Float	EMU	ERM
Common shocks			
Positive demand shock $v_F = v_G > 0$	++	+++	+++
Negative supply shock $u_F = u_G > 0$	++	+	+
Asymmetric shocks			
Demand shock $v_F = -v_G > 0$	0	0	+
Supply shock $u_F = -u_G > 0$	0	0	+
Correlated speculative shock $\varepsilon_D = -\xi\varepsilon_G$	+	+	++

Note: A plus sign indicates dollar depreciation.

upon on the basis of a quantitative assessment of the size and the probability of the various shocks.

Alternative Spillover Effects

Our representation of the three economies is rather standard and fits the usual macroeconometric models used for forecasting. However, a number of assumptions can be disputed.

A first difference from simplified policy coordination models results from the explicit introduction of two spillover effects, through outputs and prices. In the game-theoretical framework, there is frequently only one exchange rate externality, which is removed under EMU. Thus, cooperation unambiguously leads to smaller reactions of monetary policies to shocks, and thus to a smaller exchange rate volatility. In our model, there are two uneven exchange rate externalities, which are both internalized under EMU. This is why we obtain a different result.

The most important simplification in our model is the equal treatment of the three economies except for openness—for instance, the price elasticity of external trade is assumed equal for intra-European trade and for trade with the United States. This simplification is removed in Cohen's paper in this volume, where the European market is assumed to be more closely integrated than the world market, which results in a higher price elasticity for intra-European trade. In the EMU regime, European countries internalize both a price externality and an output externality, with the former being relatively higher. Thus, monetary union leads to reducing the volatility of the real exchange rate in the presence of demand shocks and to increasing it in the presence of supply shocks. This is exactly the opposite of our result with the (price, output) loss function.

The reason for this difference is twofold. First, Cohen takes output prices and output as arguments of the loss function, which would in our model lead EMU to have neutral effects on exchange rate volatility (because output and output prices move in tandem). Second, Cohen's additional assumption as regards intra-European trade results in the elimination of intra-European externality having more impact on output than on prices.

Other models hinge on further simplifications. For instance, Martin (1997) assumes that there are only supply shocks, and that all interactions between countries arise from the supply side only. He also assumes that purchasing power parity holds, so the real exchange rate is constant by definition. In his model, monetary union removes the supply-side externality between European countries, which has the effect that monetary policy becomes less effective for output stabilization. The smaller variance in monetary policy translates into less variance in prices and nominal exchange rates. In our model, the impact of monetary union on nominal exchange rate volatility is ambiguous (whereas the impact on inflation is not, as price volatility is lower in EMU), but we consider that real exchange rate volatility is more consequential.

Finally, all analytical models involve highly simplified dynamic interactions. In our model, the second period is the long run, so no further inflation is expected, and the real interest rate equals the nominal one. This simplification is removed in simulations that are based on a dynamic model.

Quantitative Evaluations

The above developments only provide qualitative results. In this section, we provide a rough evaluation of the associated quantitative effects. We first give a numerical evaluation of the multipliers from the theoretical model and then we present simulations with a simple dynamic model.

The first approach is to start from equation (19), which gives the theoretical short-run impact of shocks on the REER of the dollar when policy preferences are represented by the loss function L, and to evaluate the impact of moving from a floating exchange rate regime to monetary union in Europe. We take the following values for the parameters:

$$\alpha = 0.3; \quad \eta = 0.1; \quad \theta = 1; \quad \delta = 0.2.$$

For α, the elasticity of output to labor input, this corresponds to usual orders of magnitude for a Cobb-Douglas production function. The value for η, the openness ratio, is close to the empirical magnitudes for the United States and Europe. For θ, the output/real exchange rate elasticity, and δ, the sensitivity of demand to the real interest rate, the values are usual orders of magnitude corresponding to a wide range of macroeconometric models (see, e.g., Bryant, Helliwell, and Hooper, 1988; or Mitchell and others, 1995).

We can then compute

$$\left.\frac{dq_U}{d\nu_E}\right|_{Float} \text{ and } \left.\frac{dq_U}{d\nu_E}\right|_{EMU}$$

as a function of β, the coefficient of the real exchange rate objective in the European loss function.[13] It is apparent that the impact of shocks is larger when Europe is in a monetary union, but the difference does not appear to be large. For example, for $\beta = 0.01$ (which means that a 10 percent deviation in

[13]We take $\beta = 0$ for the United States, that is, we assume that the U.S. authorities have no exchange rate objective.

the real exchange rate has an equal weight to a 1 percent increase in prices), we obtain

$$\left.\frac{dq_U}{d\nu_E}\right|_{Float} = 1.53 \text{ and } \left.\frac{dq_U}{d\nu_E}\right|_{EMU} = 1.60.$$

That is, moving to EMU would increase the volatility of the real effective exchange rate of the dollar by less than 3.6 percent.

Figure 3 indicates that the difference is increasing in β, the weight of the exchange rate objective in the loss function, but remains low for values of β that correspond to present behavior in Europe. For example, with $\beta = 0.04$ (which means that a 4 percent REER deviation and a 1 percent increase in prices have an equal impact on social welfare), moving to EMU would increase the REER volatility of the dollar by 7 percent. The intuition behind this result is obvious: EMU will only make a difference if European countries attach some weight to real exchange rate stabilization. If central banks only focus on domestic inflation, there is no reason why moving to a monetary union would have a significant impact on exchange rate stability. Obviously, one could argue that moving to monetary union would lead to a reduced value of β because the provisions of the Maastricht Treaty are conducive to reducing the

Figure 3. Ratio of the U.S. REER Elasticity to Shocks, EMU/Float

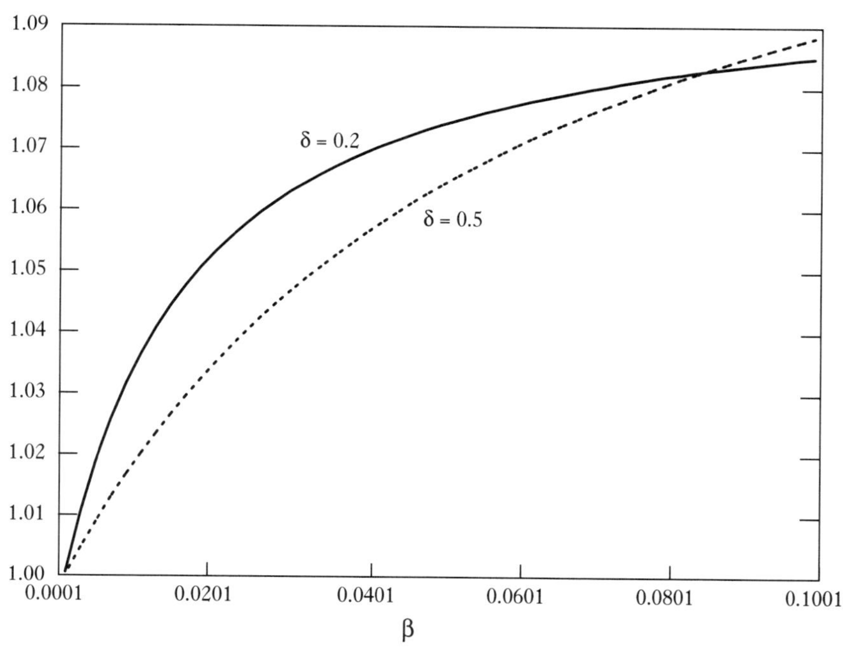

weight of the exchange rate as a policy objective. This would be an additional reason for increased REER volatility.

The increase in REER volatility resulting from EMU also depends on the value of δ, the sensitivity of domestic demand to changes in the real interest rate. For $\delta = 0$, the two regimes would be equivalent. As there is uncertainty regarding the actual value of δ, we plot in Figure 3 the increased volatility of the REER of the dollar as a function of β for two values of δ (0.2 and 0.5). It illustrates that the difference between the two regimes remains low for realistic values of β and δ.

Numerical evaluations can be misleading because of the highly simplified character of the model. We therefore also provide the results of illustrative simulations with a three-country model that resembles the theoretical model but includes dynamic wage and price equations.

The main characteristics of the model are as follows. Wage inflation depends on past wage inflation, consumer price inflation (i.e., a weighted average of GDP deflator and import price inflation), and excess demand, as with a standard augmented Phillips curve. Producer prices are determined by a markup on wages. Excess demand reacts negatively to the ex ante real interest rate (calculated with model-consistent expectations of producer price inflation), and positively to the real effective exchange rate. Identities define the real effective exchange rate as an average of bilateral real exchange rates. Finally, nominal bilateral exchange rates result from uncovered interest rate parity (with one-quarter-ahead model-consistent exchange rate expectations). Although highly simplified, this model captures familiar features of empirical macroeconometric models, from which the values of the parameters are taken. The three countries have similar characteristics except for two well-known stylized facts. First, we introduce a stronger nominal rigidity in the United States, where the average delay for wage inflation adjustments is four quarters instead of two in Europe. Second, the long-term elasticity of final demand to the real interest rate is twice as high in Germany as in France and the United States.

Policy regimes are represented by interest rate reaction functions for the three countries. We consider two regimes in Europe: a floating exchange rate regime and EMU, and two policy rules represented by linear reaction functions (Table 3).

The policy rules correspond to the loss functions used in the analytical model and involve the same target variables, but the weights attached to the objectives are not formally derived from a loss function. In the first column of Table 3 the monetary policy authority sets its instrument in reaction to deviations from consumer price inflation and to output gap targets, as in the loss function Λ.[14] The weights presented are John Taylor's original coefficients,

[14]The European Commission (1990) uses a weight of 0.4 for the excess demand objective of European countries.

Table 3. Policy Rules Used in the Simulations

	Consumer Price Inflation $\hat{z}$ and Excess Demand y	Producer Price Inflation $\hat{p}$ and REER q
United States	$i_U = \frac{3}{2}\hat{z}_U + \frac{1}{2}y_U$	$i_U = \frac{3}{2}\hat{p}_U + \frac{1}{20}q_U$
Germany with float	$i_G = \frac{5}{4}\hat{z}_G + \frac{1}{2}y_G$	$i_G = \frac{3}{2}\hat{p}_G + \frac{1}{10}q_G$
France with float	$i_F = \frac{5}{4}\hat{z}_F + \frac{1}{2}y_F$	$i_F = \frac{3}{2}\hat{p}_F + \frac{1}{10}q_F$
ECB with EMU	$i_E = \frac{3}{2}\hat{z}_E + \frac{1}{2}y_E$	$i_E = \frac{3}{2}\hat{p}_E + \frac{1}{20}q_E$

that is, the real interest rate reacts equally in the United States and in EMU, which have the same openness ratio. When Germany and France are in a floating regime, the weight of consumer price inflation is reduced to account for the higher effectiveness of monetary policy on prices relative to output, consistent with the theoretical model. In the second column, we use the target variables of the loss functions **L**, giving to the REER a weight equal to half the openness ratio.

The results of the simulations are presented in Figure 4 in the case of a temporary symmetric demand shock in Europe (a rise of demand by 1 percent of GDP lasting four quarters). As expected, the response of the U.S. REER is more pronounced with EMU in Europe than with floating exchange rates, and this is true for both policy rules. This also applies to the deutsche mark–dollar nominal exchange rate. These results hold for a wage shock also, and are robust with respect to reasonable changes in the value of the parameters of the equations.[15]

Conclusions

It has been repeatedly suggested by European policymakers and politicians that one of the significant benefits of EMU would be its contribution to greater exchange rate stability between the dollar and European currencies. In this paper, we have investigated whether a simple three-country model could substantiate such a claim.

The short answer is that it does not. On the contrary, there are grounds to consider that in comparison to a floating rate regime in Europe, EMU should

[15]Some changes of the parameters lead to unstable dynamics and divergence. We exclude these. The range of parameters within which we have simulated the dynamic model is available from the authors on request.

Figure 4. Response of U.S. REER and Deutsche Mark–Dollar Exchange Rate to a Symmetric Demand Shock in Europe[1]

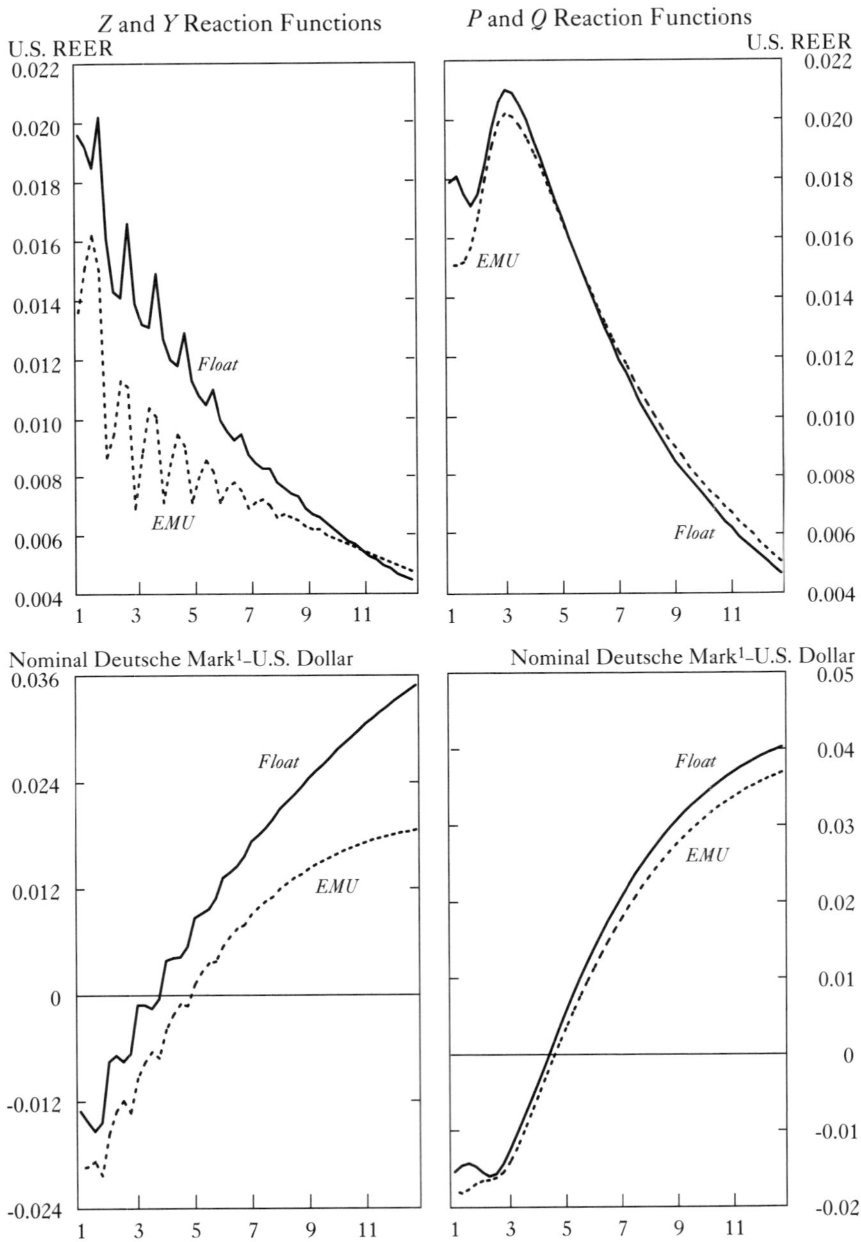

[1]Excess demand is increased by 1 percent over four quarters.

increase real exchange rate instability between Europe and its major trading partners, such as the United States or Japan. This result holds for all categories of shocks if one assumes that in addition to their inflation objective, monetary authorities have an explicit real effective exchange rate target. It holds for all but symmetric European supply shocks if it is assumed, rather, that they have an output target.

Three caveats should be kept in mind. First, these results concern the real effective exchange rate of the dollar (or of the euro zone), and not the bilateral real exchange rates vis-à-vis the dollar of the individual European countries. As asymmetric shocks affecting individual European countries offset at the level of the euro zone, EMU could simultaneously increase the real instability of the euro zone's dollar exchange rate and reduce those of the member countries (however, the results are unambiguous for the dollar's REER). The second caveat relates to the baseline situation to which EMU should be compared. We have taken as a baseline a floating exchange rate regime, because we doubt that the ERM would survive if EMU were forsaken. In comparison to an ERM baseline, the effect of a move to EMU would be more ambiguous. Third, the model we have used for deriving these results is highly simplified as, for example, France and Germany are considered identical countries and the representation of domestic markets and international linkages is skeletal. This especially applies to the exchange rate, which is derived from an uncovered interest rate parity condition.

What degree of confidence can we place in such a highly simplified model? We tend to believe that the result we come up with has some relevance. Furthermore, the institutional set-up of the Maastricht Treaty does not weaken this result, as Article 109 explicitly subordinates the pursuit of exchange rate aims to the overriding objective of price stability.

If this proves to be true, monetary union in Europe would at the same time reduce exchange rate instability within Europe and increase it between Europe and the other major monetary regions. As is already the case for the United States (Bergsten and Henning, 1996), European countries would thus have a high degree of real exchange rate stability within Europe, and real exchange rate instability vis-à-vis the dollar and the yen. This could not be inconsequential for trade and investment relations within Europe and across the Atlantic.

The empirical significance of this effect should, however, not be exaggerated. The numerical evaluations provided in this paper, which at this stage of research should be taken as preliminary, suggest that the increase in real exchange rate instability should remain moderate. This is because, as European central banks tend to give priority to price stability rather than to stabilizing the real exchange rate, moving to EMU will not fundamentally alter Europe's policy objectives.

APPENDIX I

Model Equations

The model is written in log-linear form, except for interest rates, with lowercase variables representing deviations from the zero-disturbance equilibrium, and i standing for the country ($i = F, G, U$).

Goods Market Equilibrium

Demand in each country d increases with the real effective exchange rate q and decreases with the real interest rate r. It is affected by an exogenous demand shock ν, which has zero mean. The impact of the real exchange rate is proportional to the degree of openness ω, which is 2η for France and Germany, and η for the United States.

$$d_i = \theta\omega_i q_i - \delta r_i + \nu_i \qquad \eta, \theta, \delta > 0, \text{ and } \omega < 1/2 \qquad i = F, G, U. \tag{A1}$$

Aggregate supply y is derived from a standard Cobb-Douglas production function under the assumption that the capital stock remains fixed both in the short run and in the long run. Labor, n, is therefore the only production factor. Supply is affected by an adverse exogenous supply disturbance, u, which also has a zero mean.

$$y_i = (1 - \alpha)n_i - u_i \qquad 0 < \alpha < 1 \qquad i = F, G, U \tag{A2}$$

Goods market equilibrium holds in the short run and in the long run, which implies that in the short run output and employment are demand determined, while they are supply determined in the long run:

$$y_i = d_i \qquad i = F, G, U. \tag{A3}$$

Labor Market Equilibrium

As firms maximize profits, the marginal productivity of labor is equal to the product wage $w - p$ (where w is the nominal wage and p is the price of domestic production):

$$w_i - p_i = \alpha n_i - u_i \qquad i = F, G, U. \tag{A4}$$

Labor supply is fixed. In the long run, real wages clear the labor market, but in the short run, nominal wages remain at the level set before shocks are observed. As the expected value of supply and demand shocks is zero, the corresponding conditions are

$$\begin{aligned} &\text{Long run: } n_i^{LT} = 0 \\ &\qquad\qquad\qquad\qquad i = F, G, U. \\ &\text{Short run: } w_i = 0 \end{aligned} \tag{A5}$$

Capital Market

The real interest rate r is defined as the nominal interest rate i less expected inflation:

$$r_i = i_i - [E(p_i^{LT}) - p_i] \qquad i = F, G, U, \tag{A6}$$

where $E(x^{LT})$ represents the expected long run value of variable x. We make the usual rational expectations assumption, that is:

$$\forall x, E(x^{LT}) = x^{LT}.$$

Long-run equilibrium values are supposed to be perfectly anticipated by the agents after the shocks have occurred at the beginning of the short-run period.

Uncovered interest rate parity holds. If s_F is the nominal dollar–franc exchange rate (1 U.S. dollar = s_F French francs) and s_G, the dollar–deutsche mark exchange rate,

$$\begin{aligned} s_F &= E(s_F^{LT}) + i_U - i_F + \varepsilon_F \\ s_G &= E(s_G^{LT}) + i_U - i_G + \varepsilon_G, \end{aligned} \tag{A7}$$

where ε_F and ε_G are speculative shocks to the exchange rate equation, which can be seen as representing time-varying risk premiums. We introduce these shocks because we want to present the frequently held view that floating exchange rates are responsible for unproductive volatility.

Finally, we define the effective real exchange rate q, which depends on trade patterns, and the consumer price index z, which depends on the openness ratio:

$$\begin{aligned} q_F &= \frac{1}{2}(s_F - p_F + p_U) + \frac{1}{2}(s_F - s_G - p_F + p_G) = s_F - p_F + \frac{1}{2}(p_U + p_G - s_G) \\ q_G &= \frac{1}{2}(s_G - p_G + p_U) + \frac{1}{2}(s_G - s_F - p_G + p_F) = s_G - p_G + \frac{1}{2}(p_U + p_F - s_F) \\ q_F &= \frac{1}{2}(s_F - p_F + p_U) + \frac{1}{2}(-s_G - p_G + p_U) = \frac{s_G + s_F}{2} - p_U + \frac{p_G + p_F}{2} \end{aligned} \tag{A8}$$

$$z_i = p_i + \omega_i q_i \qquad i = F, G, U. \tag{A9}$$

There are altogether 29 variables, and 26 equations for either the short-run or the long-run equilibrium. In order to close the model, we have to determine the interest rate, which is done by assuming that monetary policy aims at minimizing a macroeconomic loss function $L(X)$, where X represents a set of macroeconomic variables:

$$\text{Min } L_i(X_i), \qquad i = F, G, U. \tag{A10}$$

List of Variables

d_F, d_G, d_U	Aggregate demand
y_F, y_G, y_U	Aggregate supply
n_F, n_G, n_U	Employment
w_F, w_G, w_U	Wage rate
p_F, p_G, p_U	Producer prices
z_F, z_G, z_U	Consumer prices
i_F, i_G, i_U	Nominal interest rate
r_F, r_G, r_U	Real interest rate
s_F, s_G	Nominal dollar exchange rate
q_F, q_G, q_U	Real effective exchange rate

Transforming the Model

The model can be made much more tractable by exploiting the symmetry between France and Germany through the usual Aoki transformation. For each variable x, we therefore define the "sum" European variable as

$$x_E = \frac{x_F + x_G}{2}$$

and the "difference" variable as

$$x_D = \frac{x_F - x_G}{2}.$$

The model can thus be rewritten with variables x_E and x_D replacing x_F and x_G. Obviously, $x_F = x_E + x_D$ and $x_G = x_E - x_D$, which means that country variables can easily be calculated from aggregate sum and difference variables. This transformation allows equations (A1) to (A6) and equation (A9) to be rewritten with $i = E, D, U$. Only equations (A7) and (A8) are modified:

$$\begin{aligned} s_E &= E(s_E^{LT}) + i_U - i_E + \varepsilon_E \\ s_D &= E(s_D^{LT}) + i_D + \varepsilon_D \end{aligned} \qquad \text{(A7')}$$

$$\begin{aligned} q_E &= \frac{1}{2}(s_E + p_U - p_E) \\ q_D &= \frac{3}{2}(s_D - p_D) \\ q_U &= -s_E - p_U + p_E = -2q_E. \end{aligned} \qquad \text{(A8')}$$

q_E is the average of the effective real exchange rates of France and Germany, which differs from the effective real exchange rate of Europe, $-q_U$.

APPENDIX II

Long-Term Solution of the Model

Goods market equilibrium conditions in the long run are

$$\begin{aligned} y_E^{LT} &= -u_E^{LT} = -\eta\theta q_U^{LT} - \delta r_E^{LT} + \nu_E^{LT} \\ y_D^{LT} &= -u_D^{LT} = 2\eta\theta q_D^{LT} - \delta r_D^{LT} + \nu_D^{LT} \\ y_U^{LT} &= -u_U^{LT} = \eta\theta q_U^{LT} - \delta r_U^{LT} + \nu_U^{LT}, \end{aligned} \tag{A11}$$

where u^{LT}, v^{LT} represent the long-run values of the shocks (we do not necessarily assume that supply and demand shocks are temporary). Real exchange rate stationarity implies that there is only one world real interest rate, which ensures goods market equilibrium:

$$y_E^{LT} + y_U^{LT} = -(u_E^{LT} + u_U^{LT}) = -2\delta r^{LT} + (\nu_E^{LT} + \nu_U^{LT}), \tag{A12}$$

Equations (A13) and (A14) give the long run real interest rate and the long-run real effective exchange rate of the dollar:

$$r^{LT} = \frac{1}{2\eta\theta}(\nu_E + \nu_U + u_E + u_U)^{LT} \tag{A13}$$

$$q_U^{LT} = \frac{1}{2\eta\theta}[(u_E + \nu_E) - (u_U - \nu_U)]^{LT}. \tag{A14}$$

Shocks affecting the United States and Europe symmetrically have an impact on the world real interest rate, while asymmetric shocks have an impact on the real exchange rate of the dollar. Finally, the French franc–deutsche mark real exchange rate depends on asymmetric shocks in Europe:

$$q_D^{LT} = -\frac{1}{2\eta\theta}(u_D + \nu_D)^{LT}. \tag{A15}$$

References

Aglietta, Michel, and Niels Thygesen, 1995, *International Currency Competition and the Future Role of the Single European Currency* (Boston: Kluwer Law International).

Bank for International Settlements, 1996, *Annual Report* (Basle: BIS).

Bénassy-Quéré, Agnès, Alexander Italianer, and Jean Pisani-Ferry, 1994, "The External Implications of the Single Currency," *Économie et Statistique* (special issue), pp. 9–22.

Bénassy-Quéré, Agnes, 1996, " Potentialities and Opportunities of the Euro as an International Currency," CEPII Working Paper No. 96-09 (Paris: Centre d'Etudes Prospectives et d'Informations Internationales, August).

Bergsten, C. Fred, and C. Randall Henning, 1996, *Global Economic Leadership and the Group of Seven* (Washington: Institute for International Economics).

Blanchard, Jean, and Stanley Fischer, 1989, *Lectures on Macroeconomics* (Cambridge: MIT Press).

Bryant, Ralph C., John Helliwell, and Peter Hooper, 1988, "Domestic and Cross-Border Consequences of U.S. Macroeconomic Policies," in *Macroeconomic Policies in an Interdependent World*, ed. by Ralph C. Bryant and others (Washington: IMF and Brookings Institution; London: Centre for Economic Policy Research), pp. 59–115.

Canzoneri, Matthew B., and Dale W. Henderson, 1991, *Macroeconomic Policy in Interdependent Economies: A Game-Theoretic Approach* (Cambridge, Massachusetts: MIT Press).

Cohen, Daniel, and Charles Wyplosz, 1989, "The European Monetary Union: An Agnostic Evaluation," in *Macroeconomic Policies in an Interdependent World*, ed. by Ralph C. Bryant and others (Washington: Brookings Institution and IMF; London: Centre for Economic Policy Research), pp. 311–37.

Collignon, Stefan, 1997, "Bloc-Floating and Exchange Rate Volatility: The Causes and Consequences of Currency Blocs," forthcoming in *Exchange Rate Policies in Emerging Asian Countries*, ed. by Stefan Collignon, Yung Chul Park, and Jean Pisani-Ferry (London: Routledge).

European Commission 1990, "One Market, One Money: An Evaluation of the Potential Benefits and Costs of Forming an Economic and Monetary Union," *European Economy*, No. 44 (October).

Flood, Robert P., and Andrew Rose, 1995, "Fixing Exchange Rates: A Virtual Quest for Fundamentals," *Journal of Monetary Economics*, Vol. 36 (August), pp. 3–37.

Gros, Daniel, and Niels Thygesen, 1992, *European Monetary Integration: From the EMS to EMU* (London: Longman).

Henning, C. Randall, 1995, *The External Impact of EMU* (unpublished; Washington: Institute for International Economics).

Kenen, Peter B., 1995, *Economic and Monetary Union in Europe: Moving Beyond Maastricht* (Cambridge: Cambridge University Press).

Martin, Philippe, 1997, "The Exchange Rate Policy of the Euro: A Matter of Size?" CEPII Working Paper No. 97-06 (Paris: Centre d'Etudes Prospectives et d'Informations Internationales, April).

Masson, Paul, and Steven Symansky, 1992, "Evaluating the EMS and EMU Using Stochastic Simulations: Some Issues," in *Macroeconomic Coordination in Europe: The ERM and Monetary Union*, ed. by Ray Barrell and John Whitley (London: SAGE Publications).

Minford, Patrick, Anupam Rastogi, and Andrew Hughes Hallett, 1992, "The Price of EMU Revisited," CEPR Discussion Paper No. 656 (London: Center for Economic Policy Research, March).

Mitchell, P., J. Sault, P. Smith, and Kenneth Wallis, 1995, "Comparing Global Economic Models," ESRC Macroeconomic Modelling Bureau Discussion Paper No. 40 (Warwick, England: University of Warwick, October).

Persson, Torsten, and Guido Tabellini, 1996, "Monetary Cohabitation in Europe," *American Economic Review, Papers and Proceedings*, Vol. 86 (May), pp. 111–16.

8

Characteristics of the Euro, the Demand for Reserves, and Policy Coordination Under EMU

Paul R. Masson and Bart G. Turtelboom

EMU in Europe will be a major event for the international monetary system. The creation of a new currency, the euro, will provide a potentially serious rival for the U.S. dollar at the center of the international monetary system. The euro will be a currency whose economic base, as measured by the combined GDP of the currency area, will be close to, and perhaps even greater than, that for the dollar, depending on the countries that actually proceed to Stage III of EMU. It will be a currency in its own right, rather than a basket currency like the ECU. Moreover, the statutes of the ECB provide strong guarantees that the new currency will be backed by monetary policies oriented toward price stability. The excessive deficit procedures established by the Maastricht Treaty, reinforced by the recently concluded Stability and Growth Pact, should help to ensure that fiscal policies will not interfere with that monetary policy objective.

However, the euro will face considerable initial uncertainties. First, the set of countries that will proceed to EMU on January 1, 1999, is yet to be determined, and, since not all countries are likely to qualify (or, like Denmark and the United Kingdom, may not choose to join if they do qualify), there will remain uncertainty even after the start of monetary union concerning its ultimate composition. Indeed, the EU may admit further members, in particular from Eastern Europe, which would also increase the dimension of

The authors are grateful to Ralph Bryant, Matt Canzoneri, Morris Goldstein, Randall Henning, Peter Isard, Masahiro Kawai, Thomas Krueger, Flemming Larsen, Doug Laxton, Michael Leahy, Don Mathieson, Bandid Nijathaworn, Roger Nord, Ramana Ramaswamy, Julius Rosenblatt, Steve Symansky, and Günther Wittich for discussions of the issues in the paper and for advice on the stochastic simulations, to Richard Hides for access to reserves data, and to Susanna Mursula and Manzoor Gill for research assistance.

EMU in a more distant future. Second, the precise way in which the ECB will operate will not be clear from the beginning, even though some issues will no doubt be resolved between now and 1999, including its monetary policy operating procedures. One important choice will be that of an intermediate target; the EMI considers that monetary or inflation targeting procedures are potential candidates (EMI, 1997). Third, whatever the announced policy objectives and operating procedures, there will be doubts about how closely the ECB will attempt to achieve those objectives. In other words, the *credibility* of the central bank will depend on establishing a track record. The public (including financial markets) will need to see results before fully believing the new institution's stated policy intentions. Finally, there will be considerable uncertainty about the way the economy works after a major regime change like the introduction of unalterably fixed exchange rates and the replacement of national currencies. This will affect the transmission mechanism for monetary policy as well as the private demand for assets in euros. As a result, traditional indicators of the stance of monetary policy will not give the same signals or be interpretable in the same ways. This will complicate both the ECB's task of implementing monetary policy and the public's monitoring of its success, which is important for establishing credibility.

This paper is an attempt to assess the prospects for the euro from the perspective of the past behavior of European economies, while recognizing that the future will in some respects not look like the past. However, we will not analyze all aspects of this vast, and very speculative, question. Instead, we will focus on a few selected topics. In particular, we first use stochastic simulations of the MULTIMOD[1] model to analyze the effects of replacing European currencies by the euro, and replacing an asymmetric monetary policy (mainly influenced by events in Germany) with a symmetric policy that reflects Europe-wide[2] developments. This will affect the inflation and exchange rate stability properties of the euro (relative to the deutsche mark) in a number of ways that depend on the nature of historical shocks to various economic relationships. For instance, shocks to consumption and investment may average out at the European level, and hence aggregate shocks may be less large and variable (relative to the size of the economy) than those for a single country, like Germany. EMU will also eliminate currency risk among member countries relative to each other, which can be expected to help stability. These channels are discussed in some detail in the next section, and the simulated effects on variability of going to EMU are presented for a range of financial variables. The simulations are performed under the two alterna-

[1] See Masson, Symansky, and Meredith (1990).

[2] That is, for those European countries that are members of EMU.

tive intermediate targets mentioned above, namely, a monetary aggregate or inflation target plus a variant of inflation targeting that includes a weight on output.

The third section proceeds to analyze the potential demand for reserves after EMU in light of the stochastic simulations of the previous section. The attractiveness of the euro will depend on its expected rate of return and its covariances with other reserve assets, though clearly other factors (such as the extent that trade will be denominated in euros, and the depth and liquidity of financial markets) will also be very important. The latter have been discussed by other authors; here, we limit ourselves to considering reserve holdings from an optimal portfolio perspective, where only expected returns and covariances of returns among the major reserve currencies matter. These are calculated on the basis of the stochastic simulations; implications for the attractiveness of the euro relative to the dollar and yen are then derived.

After having considered the international impact of EMU using historical relationships (modified only with respect to the monetary regime), the remaining sections highlight how uncertain a guide those historical relationships may be in the face of a major regime change. Among other effects, this may have important implications for what the ECB chooses to do in the initial years of monetary union. First, it is argued that uncertainty will make both monetary and inflation targeting frameworks problematic, because the transmission mechanism and the demand for money will not conform to historical relationships, and because there will be little quantitative evidence available for updating them. This may induce the ECB initially to give more weight to indicators, like the exchange rate, whose interpretation is less questionable and on which monetary policy may have a more predictable effect. Then, the issue of policy coordination between EU members (and the ECB) and other major countries is considered in light of this increased uncertainty about the effects of monetary policy. Contrary to other authors, we argue that EMU will not necessarily decrease the incentives for international policy coordination, because coordination may help to contain the overall uncertainty facing Europe.

Will the Euro Facilitate Macroeconomic Stability?

We will begin by analyzing whether European monetary policy, when oriented to developments in a wider area than Germany, would be associated with greater or lesser variability of macroeconomic variables, including output, inflation, interest rates, and the exchange rate. A potentially important issue will be the choice of monetary policy framework, an issue discussed in EMI (1997). At present, the Bundesbank puts stress on the value of an intermediate target for the broad money supply (M3) in framing its monetary policy,[3] and one of the tasks of the EMI has been to harmonize monetary aggregates to facilitate the calculation of a European aggregate. How the ECB will frame policy has not been resolved (and may not be decided until it begins its operations), but a target for M3 is one major possibility. The other is inflation targeting, even though it is not practiced by any of the "core-ERM" countries, which are the likeliest ones to proceed to Stage III of monetary union in 1999. Both alternatives are considered in the MULTIMOD simulations discussed below.

It is of interest to analyze the possible channels by which monetary union could make financial variables more or less variable than in the current operation of the ERM. Take the case in which the ECB is assumed to put some weight on hitting money targets, in the same way as the Bundesbank. There are several considerations that would affect the relative stability of interest rates in euro relative to those in deutsche mark. First, if shocks to national money demands in Europe are negatively correlated, for instance because of currency substitution, then going to EMU might lead to lower aggregate variability of money demand and hence of European interest rates. However, it may also be the case that other countries' demands are subject to larger shocks than Germany's, tending to go in the other direction. Second, asymmetry in the behavior of real GDP and prices (the arguments of money demand) across EU countries could also lead to lower variability of European money demand than that of individual countries, leading to the same sorts of effects as under the first point. Alternatively, shocks to Germany could conceivably have amplified effects on other countries, so that EU prices and output could be more variable. Third, our EMU simulations remove the risk premium relative to the deutsche mark affecting other European currencies. This might reduce overall volatility of European variables. Fourth, to the extent that exchange rate movements offset asymmetric aggregate demand or money demand shocks, removing this channel might cause European output to become more variable, other things being equal. Finally, and contrary to the previous point, under a single currency the EU will be less vulnerable to fluctuations of the dollar, which when it is weak has tended to put pressure on the deutsche mark relative to other ERM currencies.

If one compares monetary targeting in Germany with inflation targeting under EMU, then other things enter into the comparison. One could view both policy frameworks as implying feedback rules of real income and prices onto short-term interest rates, the policy instrument. However, the two feedback rules differ in the explicit weight given to output: it is zero for inflation

[3] Though in fact the Bundesbank seems to act in a way that suggests that it responds to inflation and output developments in a similar fashion to the U.S. Federal Reserve. See Clarida and Gertler (1996).

targeting, but typically nonzero for money targeting, since money demand depends positively on output. A second major difference relates to the timing of variables. As discussed in Svensson (1996), implementation of an effective inflation targeting framework involves targeting forecast, not actual, inflation, because the lags involved in influencing inflation using monetary policy are long. This tends to blur the difference concerning the weight given to output, since variations in the latter may influence the forecast for inflation. Indeed, Moutot (1996) argues that differences between the two frameworks should not be exaggerated. In fact, empirical work for several countries, including the United States and Germany, suggests that they follow a Taylor-type rule[4] linking interest rate settings to output gaps and inflation.

Clearly, evaluating the effects of EMU on macroeconomic variability is extremely complicated. The net effect of these and other effects is impossible to gauge without a detailed model, and we therefore use the stochastic simulations of MULTIMOD[5] to examine the implications of EMU for the financial variables of interest. In doing the EMU simulations, we assume that all 15 EU countries go to Stage III, and that the ECB targets a broad money aggregate summed over those 15 countries, a GDP-weighted average 15-country inflation rate, or a combination of the latter with an EU-wide output gap. In our simulations of EMU, we consider both contemporaneous and forward-looking inflation targeting, as well as a (forward-looking) inflation rule with a positive weight on output. We ignore any problems of instability of money demand (beyond the variability captured in the historical residuals), an issue to which we will return in a subsequent section. In addition, we assume that the mean inflation rate, and also the mean rate of return on short-term assets, would be the same as what would have occurred in Germany in the absence of monetary union. Hence we do not address in the simulations whether the ECB's anti-inflationary credibility will be the same as that of the Bundesbank.

Table 1 gives a comparison of simulated standard deviations of the short-term interest rate and other macroeconomic variables, on the assumption that both the Bundesbank and the ECB target M3, but in the latter case, a European instead of a German aggregate.[6] The variability of the short-term euro interest rate is considerably lower in the EMU simulation than is the case for

---

[4] Taylor (1993) and Clarida and Gertler (1996).

[5] Using a version of the model in which all 15 countries are included separately (except for Luxembourg, which is aggregated with Belgium).

[6] The form of the reaction function for the short-term interest rate is assumed to be the same as Germany's (see Masson and Meredith, 1990). Deviations from the center of the range of targeted money growth are resisted, but not eliminated completely, within a year. Also, the parameters of European money demand (income elasticities, lags, etc.) are assumed to be the same as those for Germany.

Table 1. Standard Deviations of Selected Variables Under ERM and EMU (with M3 Target)

(Variables in percent)

	United States		EU		Japan	
	ERM	EMU	ERM	EMU	ERM	EMU
Short-term rate	2.01	2.14	3.27[1]	2.32	2.59	2.64
Real GDP growth	1.65	1.65	3.23	1.97	4.36	4.34
Inflation rate	1.07	1.08	1.51	1.50	2.36	2.34
Exchange rate	4.21[2]	4.46[2]	5.70[3]	5.80[3]	7.17[4]	7.12[4]

[1] German short-term interest rate for EU under ERM.
[2] Nominal effective exchange rate for United States.
[3] Deutsche mark–dollar rate under ERM; bilateral dollar exchange rate of the euro under EMU.
[4] Yen-dollar rate.

the German short-term rate in the ERM simulation, as is the case for European real GDP. Inflation variability is virtually unchanged, but the exchange rate of the euro against the dollar is somewhat more variable than that of the deutsche mark in the ERM. All in all, these simulations, subject to caveats discussed below, suggest that moving to a more symmetric European monetary policy has the result of reducing the variability of European macroeconomic variables, even if the same monetary policy framework is used by the ECB as by the Bundesbank.

Table 2 compares the two major alternative intermediate targets that have been proposed for the ECB, namely, M3 and inflation. In implementing inflation targeting, we have specified a feedback rule for the short-term interest rate that makes changes in the latter respond to deviations between observed or expected inflation and its target value.[7] The form of the rules and the values chosen for the parameters are given in the Appendix. Table 2 suggests that inflation targeting would further improve European macroeconomic stability relative to money targeting. In particular, a contemporaneous inflation targeting procedure (aimed at the current year's outcome) would lower the variability of inflation, short-term interest rates, and the exchange rate of the euro against the dollar, without increasing output variability. Note that the feedback rule does not attempt to hit inflation targets exactly, and there are considerable deviations from target; otherwise, instrument instability would no doubt result, and this is also the reason that inflation targeting frameworks are forward looking. Column 3 gives standard deviations of the same variables when expected inflation next year is targeted. Here, the effects of today's shocks on deviations from next year's target are resisted, not effects on this year's inflation. Not surprisingly,

[7] It is assumed that the target for inflation is the same as that underlying the money target.

Table 2. Standard Deviations of Selected EU Variables Under EMU with M3 or Inflation Target

(Variables in percent)

	Money Target	Inflation Target		
		Contemporaneous	Forward-looking	Clarida-Gertler-Taylor rule
Real GDP growth	1.97	1.94	1.87	1.82
Inflation[1]	1.50	1.27	1.58	1.53
Exchange rate ($-euro)	5.80	4.48	5.02	5.05
Short-term interest rate	2.32	1.78	1.52	1.70

[1] GDP-weighted average for 15 EU countries.

interest rates move somewhat less, but also each year's inflation target is hit less accurately (target inflation is constant in these simulations, so that the standard deviations also measure deviations from target). GDP is also somewhat less variable, though not by much, while the exchange rate is somewhat more variable.

Finally, a forward-looking inflation targeting rule is combined with a weight on the EU output gap, as suggested by Taylor (1993) and Clarida and Gertler (1996). The results here further lower output variability, as well as improving the performance relative to *this year's* inflation target, but increase the variability of the other variables.

On the face of it then, the above results suggest an optimistic conclusion concerning the stability properties of the euro, which should be enhanced relative to those (already excellent) of the deutsche mark. One needs to recognize, however, that the simulations are based on various assumptions, none of which is likely to be strictly correct. First, the characterization of actual German monetary policy as based strictly on money targeting (albeit with an element of interest smoothing) is a simplification. Clearly, other factors are also important, and other indicators influence the Bundesbank's monetary policy settings. Second, the choice of parameter values for the feedback rules is somewhat arbitrary, though influenced by rough conformity with historical experience and by the attempt to find reasonably well-behaved specifications. However, it is possible that other parameter values might give a better performance for one or another of the policy rules. Third, and an issue we will discuss later, the structural relationships (including the demand for money and the transmission mechanisms for monetary policy) are assumed unchanged in the face of the major regime change that EMU would involve. Finally, issues of credibility are ignored; credibility concerns might well induce additional volatility in domestic financial and foreign exchange markets.

Reserve Currency Use After EMU

With the achievement of EMU and the creation of the euro, there will be a potentially attractive international currency that may rival the dollar, for both official and private use. There are a number of dimensions to the use of an international currency.[8] These include its use in official foreign currency reserves, as the currency of denomination of goods, trade and cross-border claims, and as a vehicle currency in markets for foreign exchange. Several authors have dealt with these issues, first giving estimates of the extent to which existing European currencies currently serve these functions, and then speculating on the extent that the euro would either increase or decrease in importance relative to the currencies it replaced. It has been pointed out that the financial role of the dollar exceeds the economic weight of the United States, while the reverse is true for Europe; the discernible trend toward diversification away from the dollar might be expected to be accelerated by EMU. Nevertheless, the scope for major shifts seems limited (European Commission, 1990, pp. 187–8).

As calculated by Bénassy-Quéré, the dollar's share in cross-border banking positions in foreign currencies declined from 75 percent in 1977 to 48 percent in 1995, while the share of the European currencies rose from 16 percent to 30 percent; the dollar's share of international bonds outstanding declined from 62 percent in 1985 to 33 percent in 1995, benefiting mainly the yen. In addition, the share of Latin American countries' external debt denominated in U.S. dollars also declined, by some 15 percentage points from 1983 to 1991 (Bénassy-Quéré, 1996, pp. 13–17). Others have stressed that the development of a deep and liquid government securities market in Europe, with bonds denominated in euros, as well as an efficient payment system, is likely to be an important stimulant for the international use of the currency after EMU (Thygesen, 1995). Prospects for European financial markets are analyzed by Prati and Schinasi and by McCauley and White, both in this volume.

As for the use in foreign exchange markets, a direct implication of EMU, and of course one of its key objectives, is the elimination of the need for foreign currency transactions by the creation of a single currency (Kenen, 1993). Hartmann (1996), on the basis of 1995 data, estimates that the importance of the U.S. dollar in spot foreign exchange trading could increase (from 71 percent to 87 percent[9] for an EMU composed of all EU countries), while at the same time the role of the euro could exceed the current share of the deutsche mark (attaining 61 percent, compared with 54 percent for the latter). Though European currencies would not be traded against each other, the euro would

[8] A good discussion of these various uses is given in Eichengreen and Frankel (1996).

[9] Shares sum to 200 percent, since each transaction includes two currencies.

replace existing European currencies (and the ECU) in transactions against third currencies. Moreover, network externalities could favor an enhanced vehicle currency role for the euro relative to the present role of the deutsche mark. However, the dollar would remain the dominant currency in Hartmann's scenarios. In addition, a key unanswered question that will affect its attractiveness is the relative volatility of the euro when compared with the U.S. dollar and other potential vehicle currencies, since volatility would be associated with higher transactions costs (Hartmann, 1996). In any case, past experience suggests that international currency use changes gradually.

In this paper, we focus on just one of the international uses of the euro, namely, on the official demand for euros in foreign exchange reserves. After surveying the existing literature and examining the overall need for reserves of European countries after EMU, we focus on the currency composition of global reserves. In particular, we examine incentives to hold reserves from the perspective of optimal diversification, to gauge the scope for the use of the euro as a store of value, using the results of the stochastic simulations detailed in the previous section.

Current Holdings of Foreign Exchange Reserves

Table 3 gives the holdings of foreign exchange reserves by industrial and developing countries, the totals for which are roughly equal. Among countries, however, the distribution is very unequal. Aside from EU countries, most reserve holdings are concentrated in Asia. In fact, eight Asian territorial entities—China, Hong Kong, Japan, Korea, Malaysia, Singapore, Taiwan Province of China, and Thailand—held 41.4 percent of world reserves at the end of 1995, and 56.3 percent if the EU is ignored. Moreover, this group (excluding Japan) constitutes 56.2 percent of the total reserves of developing countries, whose currency composition is detailed in the IMF's *Annual Report* (though, in fact, the data given there are based on submissions from only some of the central banks, and exclude five of the seven Asian countries). As pointed out by Ilzkovitz (1996), the potential for reserve currency use of the euro depends importantly on the portfolio decisions of these countries. Though we do not have individual country data for most of them, what data exist[10] suggest that their reserves are primarily held in U.S. dollars. There are also a few large reserve holders in Latin America, notably Brazil.

Table 4 presents data on the currency composition of foreign exchange reserves, again broken down by industrial and developing countries. It is interesting to note the decline in the share of the U.S. dollar, which occurred

[10] See, for instance, Dellas and Yoo (1991, p. 408), for data on Korea, where on average over 1980–87 the proportion of dollar assets in foreign exchange reserves was 86.4 percent.

Table 3. Foreign Exchange Reserves, End-1995
(In billions of U.S. dollars and in percent)

Industrial Economies			Developing Economies		
	(In US$)	(As a % of total)		(In US$)	(As a % of total)
Total	655.65	100.00	Total	671.24	100.00
USA	49.10	7.49	Asia	368.35	54.88
Japan	172.45	26.30	Of which:		
EU	349.80	53.35	China	73.58	10.96
			Hong Kong	54.90	8.18
Other	84.30	12.86	Korea	31.93	4.76
			Malaysia	22.95	3.42
			Singapore	68.35	10.18
			Taiwan, Province of China	90.30	13.45
			Thailand	35.46	5.28
			Latin America	125.29	18.67
			Of which:		
			Argentina	13.75	2.05
			Brazil	49.71	7.41
			Chile	14.14	2.11
			Mexico	15.25	2.27
			Peru	8.22	1.22
			Other	177.60	26.46

Source: IMF, International Financial Statistics.

mainly between the late 1970s and mid-1980s, and a corresponding increase in the share of the yen and European currencies, in particular of the deutsche mark and the ECU. However, it is important to distinguish the reserve holdings of EU countries from those of other central banks, since the former at present have a greater need for holding other ERM currencies for intervention purposes, and because monetary union, by converting EMU member currencies into internal claims, will eliminate them from the reserves of those countries. In addition, the reported rise in the share of the ECU is to some extent spurious, because official ECUs are issued against dollars and gold, and with EMU will be converted back to them.

EU Countries' Reserve Holdings Before and After EMU

A number of authors have noted that as a result of monetary union, both the demand for reserves by EMU countries and their holdings of reserves will

Table 4. Currency Composition of Foreign Exchange Reserves, End of Year 1977–95

(In percent of total)

	1977	1987	1995
All countries			
U.S. dollar	80.3	56.0	56.4
Pound sterling	1.8	2.2	3.4
Deutsche mark	9.3	13.4	13.7
French franc	1.3	0.8	1.8
Swiss franc	2.3	1.8	0.9
Netherlands guilder	0.9	1.2	0.4
Japanese yen	2.5	7.0	7.1
ECU	n.a.	14.2	6.5
Unspecified currencies	1.6	3.4	9.7
Industrial countries			
U.S. dollar	89.4	54.8	52.8
Pound sterling	0.9	1.0	2.1
Deutsche mark	5.5	14.1	15.7
French franc	0.3	0.3	2.1
Swiss franc	0.8	1.5	0.1
Netherlands guilder	0.6	1.1	0.2
Japanese yen	1.8	6.3	6.9
ECU	n.a.	19.9	12.3
Unspecified currencies	0.7	1.0	7.8
Developing countries			
U.S. dollar	70.9	59.1	60.5
Pound sterling	2.8	5.4	4.9
Deutsche mark	13.3	11.5	11.4
French franc	2.3	2.0	1.5
Swiss franc	3.9	2.7	1.8
Netherlands guilder	1.2	1.3	0.8
Japanese yen	3.2	8.6	7.3
ECU	n.a.	n.a.	0.0
Unspecified currencies	2.5	9.5	11.8

Source: IMF *Annual Report*, 1986 and 1996, Table I.2.

change. Of course, the extent of these changes will depend on the countries that actually proceed to Stage III; in what follows, we will suppose that all 15 EU members do so. In these circumstances, present reserve holdings of EU currencies by EU central banks will cease to be reserves, and their holdings of reserves will decline. However, demand for reserves will also decline, since much of what was foreign trade will then be trade between members of the

Table 5. EU Countries' Holdings of Foreign Exchange Reserves[1]
(In billions of U.S. dollars)

	Actual, End-1995	After ECU Conversion[2]	After Elimination of EU Currencies
Total	340.5	295.5	204.7
Of which:			
U.S. dollars	135.9	171.3	171.3
Japanese yen	17.9	17.9	17.9
Swiss francs	0.9	0.9	0.9
ECUs	80.3	n.a.	n.a.
EU currencies	90.7	90.7	n.a.
Deutsche mark	68.8	68.8	n.a.
French franc	11.7	11.7	n.a.
Pound sterling	9.2	9.2	n.a.
Dutch guilder	1.0	1.0	n.a.
Unspecified	14.7	14.7	14.7

[1] Excluding Finland, for which data were not available.
[2] Official ECUs, which are claims against the EMI, would be converted back to the dollars and gold that back those ECU claims when Stage III of EMU starts. The calculation in the table converts ECUs to dollars in the proportion used to calculate the last column of Table I.2, of the IMF's 1996 *Annual Report*, p. 164.

monetary union, and should therefore not be associated with reserve holdings. There have been various calculations of the net effect of those two factors, with all authors agreeing that existing dollar reserves are greater than will be needed after EMU—see European Commission (1990), Kenen (1993), and Leahy (1996), among others. Their calculations have been based only on estimates of current holdings, not actual data, since figures for individual countries are not made public. Table 5 is, however, based on actual data reported on a confidential basis to the IMF; the aggregation preserves the confidentiality but gives a more precise picture of current reserve holdings than other authors' estimates.

With EMU, the holdings of EU currencies will become domestic currencies, though what are labeled ECUs will be swapped back into dollars and gold.[11] Thus, for purely accounting reasons, dollar holdings in reserves would rise. The resulting reserves of EU countries, if they should all proceed to monetary union, would total about $205 billion. However, their *demand* for reserves would likely fall. As other authors have calculated, the proportion of current trade that would be internal to the union would decrease the need for international reserves, by a large proportion. Using IMF data on

[11] The data include a certain amount of private ECUs. However, these could not be identified separately.

the Direction of Trade for 1995, imports from other EU countries constitute about 60 percent of total imports of EU countries. If the demand for reserves is proportional to imports, as is often assumed, then the demand for reserves after EMU would fall by 60 percent, and equal about $100 billion on the basis of Table 5. Thus, about $105 billion (most of it held in U.S. dollars) would be excess, and might lead to some tendency for depreciation of the U.S. dollar over time, as EU countries decreased their reserve holdings. This figure is considerably below the range of $200–230 billion excess reserves provided by the Commission (1990, p. 183), based on what Kenen (1993) characterizes as a "shirt-cuff calculation." The European Commission's calculation makes no allowance for the reduction in the holdings of other EU currencies as reserves, and it also includes gold, which is arguably not held for the same reasons as currencies. In contrast, Leahy (1996) cites a figure of a possible decline in dollar holdings to 65 percent of what they were, which using 1992 reserve levels would translate into a decline in dollar holdings of $55 billion.

There are a number of uncertainties involved in such calculations, as detailed by Leahy (1996). First is the issue of whether there are economies of scale that operate as a result of pooling of reserves, allowing the ECB to economize further on reserve holdings relative to the national central banks at present. Indeed, the statutes of the ECB provide for a transfer of up to only 50 billion ECUs (about $60 billion, at current exchange rates)—though national central banks would also want to keep some reserves as working balances. Leahy surveys the empirical literature and provides new tests of scale effects, finding only inconclusive evidence of such effects, however. Second, and related to the use of historical data to gauge scale effects, the past decade has seen a large measure of exchange stability with respect to a subset of European currencies, as well as increased integration (in part due to the Single Market). Hence, it seems arbitrary to include all intra-EU trade before EMU. Third, and going the other way, the exchange rate commitments within the ERM have themselves generated a demand for holding other EU currencies for intervention purposes, and this need would of course disappear after EMU for those countries proceeding to Stage III. Finally, as mentioned above, the calculations assume all 15 EU countries join EMU, which is unlikely, at least in the next few years.

Whatever the exact magnitude of the desired reduction of dollar reserve holdings by EU countries, the possible resulting pressures on the dollar are not likely to be the dominant force on exchange rates after EMU. Other factors, like the monetary policy stance and credibility of the ECB and the cyclical position of the EU relative to the United States and Japan, will be more important influences on the exchange rate of the euro. First, the amount of excess reserves, though not negligible, is not enormous. The international investment position of the United States involved assets and liabilities of

$3.35 trillion and $4.13 trillion, respectively, dwarfing the reserves figure.[12] Even compared to annual balance of payments flows, the estimation of excess reserves is not too large; for instance, the U.S. current account deficit was on the order of $150 billion in 1995. Second, empirical studies have long failed to isolate a consistent effect of changes in foreign exchange reserves on exchange rates of major currencies.[13] Third, European central banks and the ECB would have no desire to reduce their holdings in a disruptive way, and they would be unlikely to rush to do so, especially in the early years of EMU. Indeed, there might be a desire to hold precautionary reserve levels to smooth out any possible volatility in exchange markets, especially in a period in which the credibility of the euro was yet to be established.

The conclusion that excess reserves in Europe are not likely to lead to significant downward pressure on the dollar after EMU is generally shared by other commentators, but with varying emphasis on the extent that it may be a problem at all. Kenen (1993), for instance, argues that changes in dollar holdings and the use of the euro as reserve currency will both occur gradually, not suddenly as a result of asset switching. He points to the fact that total reserve holdings were not adjusted quickly after the breakdown of Bretton Woods in 1973. Because EU central banks may want to resist a depreciation of the dollar, they may be reluctant to reduce their holdings at all; for this reason, it may be desirable to consider establishing a substitution account (Kenen, 1993, note 13). A report of a working group of the ECU Institute argues that "the European authorities may simply choose to hold longer-term dollar assets rather than shift out of the U.S. currency altogether" (Thygesen, 1995, p. 135). Goldman Sachs (1996) and Salomon Brothers (1996) estimate that shifts in central banks' foreign exchange reserves will not cause exchange market upheavals or have a big impact on the euro's external value.

Scope for Diversification in Reserve Holdings by Non-EU Countries

The use of the euro as a reserve currency depends, of course, on its potential use by non-EU (or at least non-EMU) countries.[14] There is an extensive literature on the demand for reserves in different currencies by central banks and other monetary authorities, focusing on the various uses for international money, paralleling the domestic store of value, medium of exchange, and unit

[12] IMF, *Balance of Payments Yearbook*, 1996.

[13] See Jurgensen (1983). Some recent studies have highlighted effects of intervention when it is coordinated (Catte, Galli, and Rebecchini, 1994) or when it signals future changes in monetary policy (Domínguez and Frankel, 1993). However, neither factor is likely to be relevant here.

[14] EU countries not part of the first group to go to Stage III would likely participate in the ERM II and hold reserves in euros in order to intervene as necessary to prevent their exchange rate from going outside pre-agreed bands.

of account uses. Dooley, Lizondo, and Mathieson (1989) have shown that the currency denomination of reserve holdings is strongly influenced by the country's exchange arrangements, the direction of its trade flows, and the currency denomination of its debt. Official use to a large extent reflects private use, and the latter evolves slowly, as witnessed by the use of sterling to denominate trade long after the economic weight of the United Kingdom had declined.

Several authors in recent articles have turned their attention to the potential of the euro to become an important reserve currency rivaling the dollar, and whether this depends on first developing its *private* international use. The European Commission (1990) argues that private use of the ECU (now euro) as a vehicle currency in trade and for denominating private claims might increase substantially, though the euro would still not rival the dollar. Hartmann (1996) agrees with this assessment, concluding that even with all 15 EU countries participating in EMU, the share of the dollar in trade invoicing would still be over twice that of the euro. Bénassy-Quéré (1996) acknowledges that private use of vehicle currencies might be slow to change, but argues that official use might change more quickly, given the unique nature of the creation of a new international currency. In particular, its greater attractiveness as an anchor currency (for instance, for central and eastern European countries, and those in Africa) than the deutsche mark would lead to an immediate demand for reserve holdings. Kenen (1993) has stressed the potential in the medium to long term of a switch away from dollar reserves toward euros.

Here, the more limited question of the attractiveness of euro reserves held as a store of value by central banks is considered from the perspective of optimal diversification. Though it is not claimed here that central banks are primarily guided by such considerations in their choice of reserve holdings, they cannot be indifferent to them over the longer run. A currency that either does not hold its value in real terms, or fluctuates wildly in real value, will not be as attractive as a stable currency. Thus, it is argued, the risk and return properties of the euro will have some significant impact on whether it eventually becomes as attractive as the dollar as a reserve currency. Using the simulation results discussed above, with alternative assumptions concerning the monetary policy framework of the ECB, the implications for the attractiveness of the euro can be derived from a framework in which central banks are assumed to be influenced by risk and return considerations.

The framework we will use to assess optimal diversification is the standard Capital Asset Pricing Model.[15] In particular, assuming that the objective function takes a simple form,

---

[15] See, for instance, Kouri and Macedo (1978) and Heller and Knight (1978). A recent application to the currency composition of Korea's reserves is given in Dellas and Yoo (1991), who conclude that the model seems to adequately describe the central bank's currency diversification. Bénassy-Quéré, Italianer, and Pisani-Ferry (1994) use such a framework to analyze the effect of EMU on global portfolios through reducing the number of European currencies.

$$U = m(r) - (b/2)\,\mathrm{var}(r), \tag{1}$$

where $m(r)$ is the mean (weighted average) return on the portfolio, $var(r)$ is the variance of the portfolio return, and b is the coefficient of relative risk aversion, portfolio shares can be calculated as a simple function of the expected return and the variance-covariance matrix of returns. In particular, if portfolio shares are given by a vector χ and returns on the various currencies have expected values and covariances given respectively by a vector ρ and a matrix Ω, then

$$m(r) = \chi'\rho \tag{2}$$

and

$$var(r) = \chi'\Omega\chi \tag{3}$$

and optimal shares can be written as a function of these expected returns and covariances:[16]

$$\chi = A(\Omega)\rho. \tag{4}$$

We first examine the historical experience of real returns on the major reserve currencies and what it would imply for optimal reserve shares, and then consider how the characteristics of those returns, and hence optimal shares, might change after EMU. Our initial calculation uses annual ex post returns since 1981 on the U.S. dollar, the Japanese yen, and the deutsche mark. Annual returns on each currency are calculated as the previous year's average short-term rate (on treasury bills or comparable instrument), plus the change in the exchange rate from the end of the previous year to the current year-end. In order to take the point of view of a global investor, these calculations use the SDR as numeraire currency, and returns are calculated using SDR exchange rates for each of the three currencies. Moreover, we calculate a global price index using the same weights on the price indices of the United States, Japan, Germany, plus France and the United Kingdom, as those used in calculating the value of the SDR.[17] The returns are then converted to real terms by subtracting the ex post change in the global price index from the nominal SDR returns. The choice of a starting year is somewhat arbitrary, but the use of ex post returns makes it important that a long enough period is used to avoid having the results dominated by particular episodes of currency movement. For in-

[16] The formula used is the same as in Dooley, Lizondo, and Mathieson (1989), p. 393.

[17] SDR weights are revised every five years. The weights established in 1996 were the following: United States, 0.39; Japan, 0.18; Germany, 0.21; France, 0.11; and United Kingdom, 0.11.

Table 6. Ex Post Returns and Inflation, 1981–95

	Nominal Returns		Inflation		Real SDR Returns[1]	
Country	Mean	Standard deviation	Mean	Standard deviation	Mean	Standard deviation
United States	8.54	4.02	4.20	2.00	3.35	8.75
Japan	5.85	2.20	1.83	1.35	5.21	7.52
Germany	7.08	2.22	2.93	1.81	4.00	7.22

[1] Converted to SDRs and net of the rate of change of an SDR-weighted consumer price index.

stance, the decade of the 1970s was dominated by the decline of the dollar associated with the breakdown of the Bretton Woods system and the 1973–74 oil price shock. Starting in 1980 includes extended periods of dollar strength and weakness.

The dollar has the highest nominal returns over the period 1981–95, but also the highest average inflation (Table 6). Moreover, both are more variable than for the other currencies. As a result, the yen and deutsche mark have somewhat higher mean real returns and lower standard deviations for that variable than the dollar, and hence should dominate it, other things being equal, in a global portfolio. Associated with the lowest rate of inflation, the yen has the highest return when expressed in SDR terms (in part because of yen appreciation against the SDR), but also a higher standard deviation (due mainly to exchange rate fluctuations) than the deutsche mark, whose real SDR return is intermediate, but its standard deviation is the lowest of the three currencies. The correlation structure of returns is also important when considering optimal portfolios. In particular, an asset with a lower return may still be held in positive proportions if it contributes to lowering the portfolio's standard deviation, for instance because it is negatively correlated with the return on other assets in the portfolio. The correlations among ex post real returns in SDRs over the period 1981–95 are set out in Table 7.

Thus, the fact that currency returns are not perfectly correlated implies that there is some scope for diversification even when a currency, like the dollar, is dominated in terms of the mean and standard deviation of returns. In particular, dollar returns are strongly negatively correlated with deutsche mark re-

Table 7. Historical Correlation of Real SDR Returns, 1981–95

	United States	Japan	Germany
United States	1		
Japan	−0.47	1	
Germany	−0.76	0.14	1

Table 8. Currency Shares of Global Holdings of Foreign Exchange Reserves

(In percent)

Currency	Calculated Shares	Actual Shares, 1995[1]
U.S. dollar	38	74
Japanese yen	23	9
Deutsche mark	39	17

[1] The three currencies' shares are rescaled to sum to 1.0.

turns, so that holding both dollars and deutsche mark allows hedging of risks. In contrast, the yen is less negatively correlated with the dollar, and has a weakly positive correlation with the deutsche mark.

Using these mean returns and their covariance structure, we proceed to calculate "optimal" portfolio shares from the perspective of a world investor. Here we need to make some assumption concerning the degree of risk aversion. In the limiting case of $b = 0$, only expected returns matter, so that only the currency with the highest return (in the ex post data, the yen) would be held. We restrict ourselves to a range of 1 to 5 for b;[18] it turns out that in this range, shares do not vary much. Table 8 gives these calculated shares for $b = 3$, and compares them to actual data on currency denomination of global foreign exchange holdings (see Table 4). The three currencies (which accounted for 83 percent of foreign exchange reserves, when ECUs issued against dollars are converted to dollars) are rescaled so that their shares sum to 1.

As can be seen from Table 8, each of the calculated shares is positive, something that was not imposed in the calculation (in principle, optimal shares could have involved borrowing in one currency to invest in another). The calculated shares for the dollar and deutsche mark are almost identical, with the yen's share considerably smaller. However, the calculated shares do not correspond at all closely to actual shares, suggesting that other motives influence reserve holdings, as discussed by Dooley, Lizondo, and Mathieson (1989). The calculated share for the dollar is half of the actual share—the latter no doubt reflecting the other important roles of the dollar, including its use as a vehicle currency and intervention currency.[19] Therefore, one should not give too much weight to these "optimal" shares, since they do not incorporate all the reasons for holding reserves. What they do suggest is that there may already be some forces leading toward diversification away

[18] A frequently mentioned value for relative risk aversion is $b = 2$.

[19] A recent article, Garber (1996), explains the small reserve-currency role of the yen by the lack of liquidity of short-term yen instruments. See also Frenkel and Goldstein (1997) for a discussion of the international role of the deutsche mark, which has been discouraged by the German authorities.

Table 9. Simulated Changes in Returns and Portfolio Shares

Standard Deviation of Returns			Correlation of Returns			Calculated Shares (in percent)		
	M3	Inflation		M3	Inflation		M3	Inflation
$	0.33	−0.01	$/¥	0.08	0.02	$	−1.7	−5.8
¥	−0.08	−0.04	$/euro	−0.06	0.02	¥	−5.0	−5.2
euro	−0.64	−2.17	euro/¥	0.01	0.04	euro	6.7	11.0

from the U.S. dollar, and increases in holdings of the deutsche mark and the yen.

We now turn to the issue of how those incentives toward greater reserve currency diversification might change after EMU, when the deutsche mark has been replaced by the euro. To examine this question, we use the results of stochastic simulations of MULTIMOD pre- and post-EMU to calculate effects on the covariance matrix of returns on reserve currencies. We then calculate new optimal reserve shares. In particular, we calculate the change in the covariance matrix of returns in the pre- and post-EMU simulations, and add it to the historical covariance matrix;[20] the mean returns are virtually unaffected and were kept unchanged. The changes relative to pre-EMU simulations (and the deutsche mark) are set out in Table 9 for the two alternative intermediate targets, money and contemporaneous inflation.[21]

Under M3 targeting the standard deviation of returns on the euro is considerably below that for the deutsche mark, that for the dollar has increased moderately, and that for the yen is slightly lower. Under inflation targeting, the reduction in the standard deviation of returns in euro is considerably larger. There are also changes to the correlation structure; under money targeting, euro returns are even more negatively correlated with dollar returns than were those on the deutsche mark, but the reverse is true for (contemporaneous) inflation targeting. The implications for optimal reserve holdings (with $b = 3$, but as before there is very little difference in the range $b = 1$ to 5) are given in the last two columns of Table 9. Interestingly enough, the incentives for diversification toward the euro seem to be greater than for the deutsche mark. Under money targeting, this comes about not primarily at the expense of the dollar, but rather at the expense of the yen. Under inflation targeting, the in-

[20] Simulated covariances in the pre-EMU case are not identical to historical covariances, principally because the stochastic simulations do not incorporate shocks to all of the exogenous variables.

[21] Forward-looking inflation targeting produced such a large negative correlation between euro and dollar returns that optimal weights could not be calculated since the covariance matrix was not positive definite.

crease in reserve share for the euro is even greater, and results from about equal declines in dollar and yen shares. These results should be taken as illustrative only, as they are sensitive to the assumptions made in doing the simulations, including the rules guiding monetary policy under EMU—as is evidenced by problems doing the calculations for some policy rules. Moreover, small changes in expected return (which are ignored in this calculation) might induce offsetting changes in the calculated shares. In addition, of course, the simulations assume unchanged structure, an issue that is reexamined in the next section.

A tentative conclusion to be drawn from these results is that, absent credibility problems and changes in structure, holdings of euro reserves should be more attractive than the deutsche mark for portfolio reasons, leaving aside the other factors affecting reserve use (see Dooley, Lizondo, and Mathieson, 1989). We have already concluded that there are already some unexploited possibilities of portfolio diversification in favor of the deutsche mark, which our calculations suggest would be amplified under EMU (in favor of the euro). Against this it must be noted, as does Bénassy-Quéré (1996), that the euro is unlikely to serve as exchange rate anchor for the Asian countries that hold the largest reserves (Table 3)—and the anchoring function has been shown to be important in determining the currency composition of reserve holdings.

Uncertainties in the Demand for Euros and the Monetary Transmission Mechanism

The discussion until now has assumed that structural relationships remain unchanged after EMU. In particular, monetary targeting requires for its effectiveness a stable and predictable money demand. For the use of an inflation targeting framework, as it is practiced for instance in Canada, the United Kingdom, and New Zealand, the predictability of the link between monetary policy instruments and inflation 12–18 months in the future is crucial.

There has been some work on the demand for money at the European level (see, for instance, Kremers and Lane, 1990; Artis, Bladen-Hovell, and Zhang, 1993; Monticelli and Strauss-Kahn, 1992 and 1993; and Cassard, Lane, and Masson, 1995 and 1997). These studies have typically found that a cross-border aggregate calculated by adding up national money supplies has better stability properties and more sensible parameter values than the typical national monetary aggregate. It has been pointed out, however, that national monetary aggregates do not capture some of the deposits (deposits of nonresidents with domestic banks, or resident deposits in foreign currency), which could vary substantially in response to currency substitution—something that should have become increasingly important with exchange rate stability and moves to monetary union (Angeloni, Cottarelli, and Levy, 1991). Therefore, one may question whether cross-border aggregates calculated on the basis of national money supplies would provide a good measure of money holdings after EMU. One view is that the existing holdings of other EU national currencies by European residents will simply disappear, because they are the result of transactions demands (holding correspondent balances, etc.) or for taking positions in anticipation of exchange rate changes, neither of which will be present after EMU; hence, the demand for money will decrease (Kenen, 1993). Of course, if those balances were not captured in existing national aggregates, then the simple aggregation of those aggregates might be an adequate measure. But other uncertainties, related to the potential size of the monetary union (if not all countries join at once), and the use of euro currency outside the EMU area (for instance, in other EU countries and in central and eastern Europe) will make estimation of the demand for any euro monetary aggregate particularly imprecise. This would clearly complicate the monetary policy of the ECB if it were to use money as its intermediate target.[22]

As concerns an inflation targeting framework, in which monetary policy instruments are varied in response to expected future inflation, it needs to be recognized that the effects of monetary policy on inflation in the medium run will also be very unpredictable in the early years of monetary union. As Moutot (1996) points out, an inflation targeting strategy depends very much on the ability of the central bank to forecast and control future inflation, so that a detailed knowledge of the transmission mechanism is essential. There have been a number of studies of the transmission process in Europe, and these studies have isolated some differences across countries, for instance, a greater or lesser role for long-term interest rates and differences in the speed with which output is affected (Moutot, 1996). Such differences have led to concerns that monetary policy changes might have damaging effects in some countries; an optimistic view is that structures would adapt to the common monetary policy, with long-term rates becoming more important in the transmission mechanism (as in Germany).

What is certain is that the existing empirical estimates will not be expected to remain valid after EMU, which is a particularly stark example of a regime change subject to the Lucas critique. Evidence of the domestic effects of monetary policy in individual countries will not translate straightforwardly to an estimate of how monetary policy changes will work when exchange rate changes (and currency risk premiums relative to the deutsche mark) have been ruled out and when changes have been made to the implementation of monetary pol-

[22] A dissenting view is, however, that of Ramaswamy (1997), who argues that targeting of an observable and easily monitored variable like the money supply will be important for the ECB to establish credibility, especially if EMU includes a large set of countries and not just a core group.

icy as a result of the creation of the ECB. Moreover, to get the combined effects of a *European* monetary policy, one would need to allow for spillover effects *across countries*, and these will be especially problematic in a currency area with no exchange rate flexibility relative to historical experience.

As a result of these uncertainties affecting intermediate targeting frameworks, it seems likely that the ECB will be forced, at least initially, to practice a reasonably discretionary policy, whether or not it announces an intermediate target, probably even more so than the Bundesbank at present. Such discretionary policy would no doubt rely on various economic indicators of current and future developments with respect to economic activity and inflation. One indicator that might be given prime attention is the exchange market value of the euro. The exchange rate is a particularly visible and publicly recognized indicator. Indeed, since national currencies will remain in circulation during a transition period, EU citizens will be able to compare exchange rates pre- and post-EMU.[23] Unlike newly calculated EMU aggregates (including those for the money supply, output, inflation, and the trade balance), the exchange rate against the dollar or yen will have a clear interpretation for the general public. Indeed, there is much current discussion in Europe of whether the euro will be "as strong as" the deutsche mark. In order to judge this, the public is unlikely to be guided in the first instance by European inflation, which will be an unfamiliar aggregate to them. They will be more sensitive to their own country's inflation figures, but it will not be possible (or desirable) to target any particular country's inflation rate; in a monetary union, only aggregate inflation matters. Of course, if all countries' inflation rates are about the same, this is not an issue, but there is no reason to expect this to be so. Other monetary unions exhibit considerable relative price fluctuations across regions (Poloz, 1990). EMU-wide money growth will also be subject to major problems of measurement and interpretation, and it is a variable that is not likely to be familiar to, or monitored by, the general public, at least initially. Thus the problem of establishing credibility may lead the ECB to pay more attention to the exchange rate than does the Bundesbank at present, not less.

Incentives for International Policy Coordination

There has been considerable discussion of whether international policy coordination between Europe and other major countries, in particular the United States and Japan, would be stimulated or hindered by the creation of EMU. The European Commission took a fairly upbeat view of the issue in *One Market, One Money*, namely that the reduction in the number of players through

[23] We are indebted to Michael Mussa for this point.

consolidating European monetary policy would have beneficial results, as would the creation of a bloc more clearly comparable to the United States, increasing the incentives on the latter to take the spillovers from Europe seriously (European Commission, 1990, Chapter 7). Others have been less convinced. For one thing, a Europe that is relatively closed will have fewer incentives to coordinate with other countries (Kenen, 1993). Also, Goodhart (1993) disputes the implication that the United States has not been seriously engaged in the international coordination process, and points out that fiscal policy coordination will in any case be severely constrained, both by the division of powers within the U.S. system and by the dispersion of fiscal responsibilities across EU national governments, which will not speak with one voice. Alogoskoufis and Portes (1992) and Henning (1996) raise the problem of representation in Europe, since monetary policy is the responsibility of a single ECB, but responsibility for exchange rate policy is shared with the Council, made up of national Ministers of Finance, which will not have an obvious single representative in such meetings as those of the Group of Seven industrial countries (or Group of Three). In these circumstances EMU may increase, not decrease, the number of players.

A factor that has not been sufficiently taken into account is the increase in structural uncertainty facing European monetary policy, as discussed above. As discussed in Ghosh and Masson (1994), uncertainty can provide a powerful inducement to coordination, because it may in some circumstances reduce the risks of particularly bad outcomes. The reasoning is as follows. Coordination makes the transmission of monetary policy across countries (in particular, through exchange rate movements) more certain. Thus, coordination around exchange rates might become more likely than at present, at least in a transition period. And that transition period before the structural uncertainty is resolved may be fairly long, not least because EMU is likely to involve a progressive enlargement of the EMU area, rather than a once-and-for-all change affecting all the (current) EU countries. Neither monetary nor inflation targeting will be free from the types of uncertainty discussed in the previous section—namely, money demand instability and unpredictable changes in the transmission mechanism—so that the exchange rate may be given considerable weight by the ECB in formulating monetary policy. In these circumstances, coordination with the United States and Japan to limit exchange rate fluctuations may naturally emerge.

To illustrate the potential gains in terms of reduced volatility of attempting to lean "against the wind" of exchange rate fluctuations, we present in Table 10 calculated standard deviations (under both the ERM and EMU) of money targeting with a weight placed in the reaction function on deviations of the nominal effective exchange rate from its "equilibrium" level (see Appendix for details). This policy rule is assumed to be followed by the United States

Table 10. Standard Deviations of Selected Variables Under ERM and EMU with International Policy Coordination

(Variables in percent)

	United States		EU		Japan	
	ERM	EMU	ERM	EMU	ERM	EMU
Short-term rate	1.80	2.13	2.60[1]	1.98	2.22	2.42
Real GDP growth	1.62	1.61	2.99	2.05	4.14	4.24
Inflation rate	1.26	1.19	1.26	1.40	2.06	2.14
Exchange rate	2.24[2]	1.90[2]	2.07[3]	1.93[3]	4.30[4]	4.29[4]

[1] German short-term interest rate for EMU under ERM.
[2] Nominal effective exchange rate for United States.
[3] Deutsche mark–dollar rate under ERM; bilateral dollar exchange rate of the euro under EMU.
[4] Yen-dollar rate.

and Japan, as well as the EU. Comparing Table 10 with Table 1, we see that in addition to lower exchange rate variability, short-term interest rates are also less variable in all three regions, while output and inflation variabilities are on balance little changed. If some importance is given to reducing financial market volatility, therefore, there may be benefits from such coordination around exchange rates between the three blocs. Of course, the simulations ignore problems of credibility and uncertainty about actual equilibrium values.

As was already mentioned, there are two counterarguments against the likelihood that such coordination would emerge. First, it is argued that this would be unrealistic for a large economy like the EU, which will be comparable in size to the United States and not very open, so that the exchange rate will not matter much for EU inflation or output. However, when the de facto fixing of the currencies of a core group to the deutsche mark is taken into account, Germany is already not very sensitive to exchange rate movements. Moreover, lack of openness does not necessarily mean that the exchange rate is a matter of indifference; after all, both the United States and Japan have at times been the impetus behind Group of Seven cooperation on exchange rates. Second, it is argued that the ECB will want to establish, and fiercely defend, its independence in the conduct of monetary policy, and hence avoid exchange rate agreements. Exchange rate policy is shared with the Council, which has the possibility of entering into formal agreements as well as suggesting "general orientations" to the ECB. In these circumstances, it could be argued, the ECB would not venture into an exchange rate policy, which might limit its room for maneuver (Henning, 1996). While these considerations may be important, they argue against a formal target, but do not preclude some use of the exchange rate as an indicator of the tightness or ease of policy, and occasional cooperation with other Group of Three central banks to limit movements in the euro's exchange rate against the dollar and yen. Thus, though the problem of representation may remain for fiscal policy, it is not inconceivable that a start at reinforced coordination might be made among central banks. Whether this might continue once the ECB had resolved some of the uncertainty facing intermediate targets of monetary policy would of course remain an open question.

Conclusion

Monetary union will, over time, no doubt bring major changes to the international monetary system that are impossible to envisage with any precision at this time. In this paper, we have tried to analyze some selected topics related to this vast question. Assuming that economic structures are unchanged, results of model simulations suggest that EMU is likely to promote stability of major macroeconomic variables. However, EMU will produce structural changes that are not captured in our models and that are hard to forecast, and there will be considerable uncertainty about the interpretation of economic indicators and about monetary transmission mechanisms. This will considerably complicate the task of the ECB, and may suggest that the traditional intermediate targeting procedures, whether of money or inflation, may not be closely followed. A more discretionary policy, in which the exchange value of the euro (among other indicators) is given a certain amount of attention, may instead emerge.

Turning to prospects for reserve currencies, it seems likely that after monetary union, holdings of dollar reserves by EU central banks would be somewhat too large. However, there is no reason to think that this would be a major influence on the exchange rate between the euro and the dollar, which is more likely to be influenced by the relative stance of monetary policies, relative cyclical positions, and policy credibility. Simulation results for financial variables suggest that the incentives to hold foreign exchange reserves in euros for store of value purposes would be at least as great as for the deutsche mark at present.

Appendix

Methodology

MULTIMOD, the IMF's global macroeconometric model, is used for the simulations in the second section of the paper. For this exercise, we use the MULTEU version of the model, which disaggregates for all EMU countries separately. Except for the alternative monetary policy rules (see below), the original specification and parameter values of the model are maintained. See Masson, Symansky, and Meredith (1990) for a detailed overview of the model.

The methodology of stochastic simulations is well known and is reviewed only briefly here. The interested reader can consult Frenkel, Goldstein, and Masson (1989) and Bryant, Hooper, and Mann (1993) for a detailed discussion. Stochastic simulations are designed to quantify the response of the endogenous variables in the model to a large number of shocks taking into account the historical variance-covariance matrix of the residuals. In principle, shocks are drawn for each residual in the model for a long period consistent with their historical joint probability distribution. This experiment is repeated for the different policy regimes and a set of summary statistics is then presented for the endogenous variables of interest.

Several practical difficulties arise when implementing this methodology. First, since it is beyond the scope of this paper to reestimate the model based on the updated data set, some residuals might not be truly identically and independently distributed. In order to deal with this issue, the residuals were regressed on a constant, a time trend, and an autoregressive term before constructing the historical variance-covariance matrix. These equations were then added to the model.

Second, in order to keep the simulations manageable, only the most relevant residuals of the model were used to construct the variance-covariance matrix. For the 15 EU members, the United States, Japan, Canada, and a group of other industrial countries—Australia, New Zealand, Norway, and Switzerland grouped together—the residuals included were those for the equations on consumption, investment, oil consumption, exports, imports, the long-term interest rate, the exchange rate, the GDP deflator, price of exports, capacity output, money demand, and the tax reaction function. Of these residuals, the residual on the interest rate parity condition is particularly important since it captures the exchange rate risk premium in the model (see below).

Third, the large number of residuals and relatively short time series result in a singular variance-covariance matrix; a small number was added to the diagonal of the matrix to make it non-singular.

The simulations are implemented as follows. Residuals are calculated based on annual data for 1975–95. After making the necessary corrections just mentioned, a 215 $\times$ 215 variance-covariance matrix is constructed and its Cholesky decomposition is calculated. Draws from the standard normal distribution are made and premultiplied by the Cholesky matrix; the resulting residuals are added to the appropriate equations.[24] This was repeated for each of the monetary policy regimes described in the next section.

Monetary Policy Rules

The different monetary policy rules in Tables 1 and 2 were implemented as follows. For the pre-EMU simulations (i.e., ERM regime), the money supply reaction function is the standard MULTIMOD function for targeting a monetary aggregate (M3) for all countries in the model that do not participate in the ERM, and for Germany:

[24] The model was stimulated 35 times with shocks for 10 years each, yielding 350 trials.

$$\Delta i_t = \frac{0.333}{-0.05402} \log\left(\frac{M_t^T}{M_t}\right), \tag{A1}$$

where i_t is the short-term nominal interest rate, M_t^T is the target level for M3, and M_t is the actual money stock given by money demand. The countries participating in the ERM—except for Germany—leave their interest rates unchanged when their exchange rate is within the band but revert to an exchange rate target at either limit of the band:

$$\begin{aligned} \Delta i_t &= 1000\left[\log\left(\frac{E_t}{\alpha * P_t}\right)\right]^3 \quad if\ E_t \leq \alpha * P_t \\ \Delta i_t &= 1000\left[\log\left(\frac{E_t}{P_t / \alpha}\right)\right]^3 \quad if\ E_t \geq \frac{P_t}{\alpha}, \end{aligned} \tag{A2}$$

where E_t is the nominal exchange rate expressed as local currency per deutsche mark, P_t is the central parity, and α is 1 minus the width of the band. Austria, Belgium, France, and the Netherlands are assumed to target small bands ($\alpha = 0.9775$), whereas the other ERM participants—Denmark, Finland, Ireland, Italy, Portugal, and Spain—have wide bands ($\alpha = 0.85$).

For the EMU simulations, four alternative monetary policy rules are implemented. The first assumes that the ECB targets a Europe-wide monetary aggregate and the monetary reaction function is similar to equation (A1). In the second case, the ECB tries to hit a target for contemporaneous inflation:

$$\Delta i_t = \left(\pi_t^{EU} - \pi_t^T\right), \tag{A3}$$

where π_t^{EU} is Europe-wide inflation and π_t^T is its target. A forward-looking rule is implemented in the third case; here the ECB targets inflation one year ahead:

$$\Delta i_t = \left(E_t\left(\pi_{t+1}^{EU}\right) - \pi_{t+1}^T\right), \tag{A4}$$

where $E_t(.)$ is the expectations operator. In the fourth case, we follow Clarida and Gertler (1996) and implement an adaptation of the Taylor rule:

$$\Delta i_t = \left(E_t\left(\pi_{t+1}^{EU}\right) - \pi_{t+1}^T\right) + \frac{1}{3} * \left(\frac{Y_t^{EU} - YC_t^{EU}}{YC^{EU}}\right), \tag{A5}$$

where Y^{EU} denotes real GDP for the EU and YC^{EU} measures European-wide capacity output. The original Taylor specification used quarterly data and lagged inflation, and gave weights of 1.5 and 0.5 to inflation and output. To maintain the comparability with our results for the forward-looking inflation-targeting rule, we maintained a unit weight on inflation and added the output gap with the same *relative* weight as in the original Taylor specification.

The results in Table 10 were obtained using the following rule for monetary policy:

$$\Delta i_t = \frac{0.333}{-0.05402} \log\left(\frac{M_t^T}{M_t}\right) + 100 * \log\left(\frac{NEER_t^T}{NEER_t}\right), \tag{A6}$$

where $NEER_t$ is the nominal effective exchange rate, and $NEER_t^T$ is its target level; the other variables are defined as in equation (A1).[25]

Finally, the exchange rate risk premium—captured by the error term for the open interest rate parity equation in the model—is modeled differently under ERM and EMU. To illustrate this point, consider the following open interest rate parity condition:

$$\left(1 + \frac{i_t^{US}}{100}\right) = \left(1 + \frac{i_t^j}{100}\right) * \left(\frac{E_{t+1}^{\$}}{E_t^{\$}}\right) + \alpha_1 * \left(\varepsilon_t^j - \varepsilon_t^{common}\right) + \varepsilon_t^{common}, \tag{A7}$$

where i_t^j is country j's short-term interest rate, $E_t^{\$}$ is the nominal exchange rate expressed in dollars per local currency, ε_t^j is risk premium against the dollar specific to the exchange rate of country j, and ε_t^{common} is the risk premium common for EMU participants; α_1 is a zero-one parameter. Under ERM, each EU currency faces a different risk premium vis-à-vis the U.S. dollar; hence, the bilateral exchange rates for those countries participating in the ERM are also subject to risk premiums. In this case, α_1 is set to unity in equation (A7). In EMU, the bilateral risk premiums for EMU participants disappear, and only a premium between the euro and the U.S. dollar remains ($\alpha_1 = 0$).

The introduction of the euro is not assumed to affect the risk premium vis-à-vis the U.S. dollar for nonparticipants in EMU. See Masson and Symansky (1992) for a further discussion of this issue.

References

Alogoskoufis, George, and Richard Portes, 1992, "European Monetary Union and International Currencies in a Tripolar World," in *Establishing a Central Bank: Issues in Europe and Lessons from the US*, ed. by Matthew Canzoneri, Vittorio Grilli, and Paul R. Masson (Cambridge: Cambridge University Press), pp. 273–300.

Angeloni, Ignazio, Carlo Cottarelli, and Aviram Levy, 1991, "Cross-Border Deposits and Monetary Aggregates in the Transition to EMU," IMF Working Paper 91/114 (Washington: International Monetary Fund, November).

[25] The nominal effective exchange rate is constructed with average trade weights (imports plus exports) for 1990–95 as percent of total trade with the two other trading partners (i.e., German imports plus exports to Japan as a fraction of total imports and exports of Germany with the United States and Japan). Under ERM, German trade weights are used; under EMU, trade weights for the EU.

Artis, Michael J., Robin C. Bladen-Hovell, and Wenda Zhang, 1995, "A European Money Demand Function," in *Policy Issues in the Operation of Currency Unions*, ed. by Paul R. Masson and Mark P. Taylor (Cambridge: Cambridge University Press), pp. 240–63.

Bénassy-Quéré, Agnès, 1996, "Potentialities and Opportunities of the Euro as an International Currency," CEPII Document de Travail No. 96–09 (Paris: Centre d'Etudes Prospectives et d'Informations Internationales, August).

———, Alexander Italianer, and Jean Pisani-Ferry, 1994, "The External Implications of the Single Currency," *Économie et Statistique* (special issue), pp. 9–22.

Bryant, Ralph C., Peter Hooper, and Catherine L. Mann, eds., 1993, *Evaluating Policy Regimes: New Research in Empirical Macroeconomics* (Washington: Brookings Institution).

Cassard, Marcel, Timothy D. Lane, and Paul R. Masson, 1997, "Core ERM Money Demand and Effects on Inflation," *The Manchester School*, Vol. 65 (January), pp. 1–24.

———, 1995, "ERM Money Supplies and the Transition to EMU," Chapter 4 in *France: Financial and Real Sector Issues*, ed. by Paul R. Masson (Washington: International Monetary Fund), pp. 112–45.

Catte, Pietro, Giampaolo Galli, and Salvatore Rebecchini, 1994, "Concerted Interventions and the Dollar: An Analysis of Daily Data," in *The International Monetary System*, ed. by Peter B. Kenen, Francesco Papadia, and Fabrizio Saccomanni (Cambridge: Cambridge University Press).

Clarida, Richard, and Mark Gertler, 1996, "How the Bundesbank Conducts Monetary Policy," NBER Working Paper 5581 (Cambridge, Massachusetts: National Bureau of Economic Research, May).

Dellas, Harris, and Chin Bang Yoo, 1991, "Reserve Currency Preferences of Central Banks: The Case of Korea," *Journal of International Money and Finance*, Vol. 10 (September), pp. 406–19.

Domínguez, Kathryn, and Jeffrey A. Frankel, 1993, *Does Foreign Exchange Intervention Work?* (Washington: Institute for International Economics).

Dooley, Michael P., J. Saúl Lizondo, and Donald J. Mathieson, 1989, "The Currency Composition of Foreign Exchange Reserves," *Staff Papers*, International Monetary Fund, Vol. 36 (June), pp. 385–434.

Eichengreen, Barry, and Jeffrey Frankel, 1996, "The SDR, Reserve Currencies, and the Future of the International Monetary System," in *The Future of the SDR in Light of Changes in the International Financial System*, ed. by Michael Mussa, James M. Boughton, and Peter Isard (Washington: International Monetary Fund), pp. 337–78.

European Commission, 1990, "One Market, One Money: An Evaluation of the Potential Benefits and Costs of Forming an Economic and Monetary Union," *European Economy*, No. 44 (Brussels: Commission of the European Communities, October).

EMI, 1997, "The Single Monetary Policy in Stage Three: Specification of the Operational Framework" (Frankfurt: European Monetary Institute, January).

Frenkel, Jacob A., and Morris Goldstein, 1997, "The International Role of the Deutsche Mark" (unpublished; Washington: Institute for International Economics, January).

Frenkel, Jacob A., Morris Goldstein, and Paul R. Masson, 1989, "Simulating the Effects of Some Simple Coordinated versus Uncoordinated Policy Rules," in *Macroeconomic Policies in an Interdependent World*, ed. by Ralph C. Bryant and others (Washington: International Monetary Fund), pp. 203–39.

Garber, Peter, 1996, "The Use of the Yen as a Reserve Currency," *Monetary and Economic Studies*, Bank of Japan, Vol. 14 (December), pp. 1–21.

Ghosh, Atish R., and Paul R. Masson, 1994, *Economic Cooperation in an Uncertain World* (Oxford: Basil Blackwell).

Goldman Sachs, 1996, "EMU's Excess Foreign Reserves," *EMU Briefing*, Issue Number 6 (London, September 4).

Goodhart, Charles A.E., 1993, "The External Dimension of EMU," *Recherches Economiques de Louvain*, Vol. 59, No. 1–2, pp. 65–80.

Hartmann, Philipp, 1996, "The Future of the Euro as an International Currency: A Transactions Perspective," LSE Financial Markets Group, Special Paper No. 91 (London: London School of Economics, November).

Heller, H. Robert, and Malcolm Knight, 1978, "Reserve-Currency Preferences of Central Banks," *Princeton Essays in International Finance*, No. 131 (Princeton: Princeton University, Department of Economics International Finance Section, December).

Henning, C. Randall, 1996, "Europe's Monetary Union and the United States," *Foreign Policy*, Vol. 102 (Spring), pp. 83–100.

Ilzkovitz, Fabienne, 1996, "Prospects for the Internationalization of the Euro," DG-II, doc II/362/96-EN (Brussels: European Commission, June).

Jurgensen, Philippe, 1983, *Report of the Working Group on Exchange Market Intervention* (Washington: U.S. Treasury, March).

Kenen, Peter, 1993, "EMU, Exchange Rates, and the International Monetary System," *Recherches Economiques de Louvain*, Vol. 59, No. 1–2, pp. 257–81.

Kouri, Pentti J.K., and Jorge Braga de Macedo, 1978, "Exchange Rates and the International Adjustment Process," *Brookings Papers on Economic Activity: 1*, pp. 111–50.

Kremers, Jeroen J.M., and Timothy D. Lane, 1990, "Economic and Monetary Integration and the Aggregate Demand for Money in the EMS," *Staff Papers*, International Monetary Fund, Vol. 37 (December), pp. 777–805.

Leahy, Michael P., 1996, "The Dollar as an Official Reserve Currency Under EMU," *Open Economies Review*, Vol. 7 (December), pp. 371–90.

Masson, Paul R., and Guy Meredith, 1990, "Domestic and International Macroeconomic Consequences of German Unification," in *German Unification: Economic Issues*, ed. by Leslie Lipschitz and Donogh McDonald, IMF Occasional Paper No. 75 (Washington: International Monetary Fund, December), pp. 93–114.

Masson, Paul R. and Steven Symansky, 1992, "Evaluating the EMS and EMU Using Stochastic Simulations," in *Macroeconomic Policy Coordination in Europe: The ERM and Monetary Union*, ed. by Ray Barrell and John Whitley (London: Sage Publications), pp. 12–34.

Masson, Paul R., Steven Symansky, and Guy Meredith, 1990, *MULTIMOD Mark II: A Revised and Extended Model*, IMF Occasional Paper No. 71 (Washington: International Monetary Fund, July).

Monticelli, Carlo, and Marc-Olivier Strauss-Kahn, 1992, "Broad Money Aggregates and Money Demand in Europe," *Economies et Sociétés*, Vol. 26 (September-October), pp. 147–97.

———, 1993, "European Integration and the Demand for Broad Money," *The Manchester School*, Vol. 61 (December), pp. 345–66.

Moutot, Philippe, 1996, "Monetary Policy in a European Union: Instruments, Strategy and Transmission Mechanism," paper presented at a conference on Monetary Policy in Transition, Vienna, November 17–19.

Poloz, Stephen, 1990, "Real Exchange Rate Adjustment Between Regions in a Common Currency Area" (unpublished; Ottawa: Bank of Canada, February).

Ramaswamy, Ramana, 1997, "Monetary Frameworks: Is There a Preferred Option for the European Central Bank?" (unpublished; Washington: IMF Research Department, January).

Salomon Brothers, 1996, "Managing Convergence: Market Implications for 1997 and Beyond," *Economic and Market Analysis: Prospects for Financial Markets* (New York: Salomon Brothers, December).

Svensson, Lars E.O., 1996, "Inflation Forecast Targeting: Implementing and Monitoring Inflation Targets," NBER Working Paper No. 5797 (Cambridge, Massachusetts: National Bureau of Economic Research, October).

Taylor, John, 1993, "Discretion versus Policy Rules in Practice," *Carnegie Rochester Conference Series on Public Policy* (December), pp. 195–220.

Thygesen, Niels, 1995, *International Currency Competition and the Future Role of the Single European Currency, Final Report of the Working Group: European Monetary Union—International Monetary System* (London: Kluwer Law International).

Comments on Bénassy-Quéré, Mojon, and Pisani-Ferry and on Masson and Turtelboom

Ralph C. Bryant

The title of this session as printed on the program is "The Euro as a Reserve Currency and Exchange Rate Volatility." Yet the two papers begin to ask analytical questions about whether the prospective move to EMU will facilitate macroeconomic stability in a broader sense. This broader perspective is, in my view, more appropriate than a narrow focus on exchange rate volatility.

My main assignment is to discuss the paper by the three authors associated with the Centre d'Études Prospectives et d'Informations Internationales (which for shorthand I will refer to as the CEPII paper). But I would also like to make some comments that apply to the Masson-Turtelboom paper.

The questions asked in the two papers are important and complex. There is no chance of addressing them satisfactorily without using an analytical framework—a model of some sort. The papers are therefore necessarily technical. And a full evaluation of them would have to dwell on their technical features. As in all analysis of this sort, there is a risk that the conclusions reached will be model-contingent—that is, that the results may depend sensitively on the particular models being used.

This conference is not the most appropriate place for an in-depth technical discussion of the strengths and weaknesses of the models used in the papers, important though such a discussion is to a full evaluation of the papers. For the most part, I am thus not going to discuss the technical features of the models used in the papers. Rather, I shall focus on the suitability of the analyses to the questions that are asked, and on the conclusions themselves.

As discussants inevitably do when fulfilling their task, I will concentrate on aspects of the papers where I have questions or doubts. But I emphasize at the outset that the two papers are thoughtful, stimulating, and helpful contributions to the growing literature analyzing the likely consequences of EMU.

How suitable are the models in the two papers for answering the analytical questions we want to ask about the likely effects of EMU on macroeconomic stability? The models are substantially different. It is an advantage of the CEPII model that it is fairly small, and can be solved analytically. But in several respects, I feel somewhat more comfortable with the MULTIMOD model of the staff of the IMF's Research Department. MULTIMOD treats the individual European countries separately. And MULTIMOD explicitly incorporates key intertemporal stock-flow interactions that we believe to be important on both theoretical and empirical grounds. In the MULTIMOD model, the flows of investment add to capital stocks, which feed back into production functions; imbalances in government budgets alter the stocks of government debt, which have to be willingly held in asset holders' portfolios and hence influence interest rates; and imbalances in current accounts lead to increases or decreases in countries' net foreign asset positions, which in turn feed back into wealth and consumption, and indirectly into interest rates and exchange rates. More generally, there is an explicit specification of dynamic adjustments through time in MULTIMOD, which is missing in the simpler versions of the CEPII paper's model.

Here is another pertinent point of comparison: the CEPII paper relies on comparative-statics analysis of its model, or at the end of the paper on an illustrative deterministic simulation. Such results can be interesting and useful. And they are perhaps a necessary prelude for understanding results from stochastic simulation analysis. For the types of questions being asked by both papers, however, I believe that stochastic simulations are a more appealing approach. For my taste, therefore, the methodology used in the Masson-Turtelboom paper has the greater potential for generating robust conclusions about the variability or stability of macroeconomic variables.

The CEPII paper examines EMU only after all the transitional problems are assumed to have receded in the past. To be sure, that focus is interesting and valid. In contrast, however, the Masson-Turtelboom paper acknowledges and raises some of the problems of transition from today's arrangements to the brave new world. My instincts are that the hardest issues are transitional, and that it is those issues that merit our greatest attention in the next several years.

I now turn to some comments on the CEPII paper alone. Its analysis focuses exclusively on the consequences of EMU for the exchange rate of Europe vis-à-vis the rest of the world (in the model described as the United States, since there are only three countries in the analytical model). In a minute, I want to question that emphasis, asking whether that perspective is appropriate. But for a moment, let us accept that emphasis and consider several points about the paper's approach and conclusions.

First, a clarification about the "volatility" of exchange rates. It may be helpful to remind ourselves that the CEPII paper gets at only part of what most observers think of when the words "volatility" or "variability" are used. The CEPII paper is not directly addressing the issue of higher-frequency variations in exchange rates, such as daily or weekly variability. Instead, it is concerned with the changes in the "levels" of exchange rates that would be produced by various types of shocks, persisting or transitory. The paper also does not deal directly with the asset-substitution effects of the sort emphasized by (for example) the Bergsten and the Alogoskoufis-Portes papers for this conference.

My greatest concern about the analytics of the CEPII paper is that it tends to downplay the important differences among alternative monetary policy regimes that the ECB might employ. (And there is no discussion at all of alternative fiscal regimes in European countries.) Even in the text of the paper there are some important clues about how important this issue is. Contrast, for example, the results with the two alternative loss functions they analyze in the comparative-statics model. They report the result that, under the **L** loss function (which has the monetary authority targeting inflation in producer prices and the real exchange rate), the dollar-euro exchange rate will move more under EMU than under a pre-EMU float for all the stylized shocks they consider. But under the alternative **Λ** loss function (which assumes the monetary authority is targeting inflation in consumer prices and an output gap), the results are revealingly different for supply shocks originating in Europe. European supply shocks result in *less*, not more, movement in the dollar-euro exchange rate.

More generally, I would place even greater emphasis than the CEPII paper does on differences among alternative monetary policy regimes that might be adopted by the ECB. (The Masson-Turtelboom paper goes a bit further than the CEPII paper in this regard, recognizing more explicitly that the choice of monetary regime may have very important implications for macroeconomic outcomes.)

A further clue about the importance of this issue: when the CEPII authors present simulations from a dynamic version of the model—see their Figure 4—there are quite significant differences across the ECB monetary policy regimes that they use for their single illustrative simulation. In that figure, the differences across the two alternative monetary policy regimes seem larger and more noteworthy than the differences for any given regime between the EMU and pre-EMU float cases!

I feel fairly sure that the CEPII paper properly solves its model to generate the conclusions it reaches about the movements of the dollar-euro exchange rate. But one can wonder whether other considerations, not treated in the model, might lead to amendments in the conclusions.

For example, suppose one focused more attention on the size and degree of openness of the interacting economies. In raising this question, I am influenced by having seen a recent paper by Philippe Martin, a CEPII colleague of the authors. Martin comes to a conclusion that, after the establishment of EMU, the variability of the EU's exchange rate against the rest of the world might be *lower*, not higher, than the variability of the dollar–deutsche mark exchange rate in today's international monetary system. The line of thought suggesting this outcome emphasizes the relative sizes of economies as a determinant of exchange rate variability, as the literature on optimum currency areas does. A small, open economy tends to be buffeted proportionately more than a large, relatively closed economy by shocks originating outside the economy ("foreign" shocks are more salient than "domestic" shocks). Thus a large, relatively closed economy's output variability and price variability tend to be influenced by exchange rate movements *less* than is the case for a small, open economy. Hence, a large, relatively closed economy's macroeconomic policies can be less concerned with exchange rate volatility. In a model such as Martin's, such considerations appear able to overturn the CEPII paper's main conclusion about the post-EMU variability of Europe's exchange rates.

Martin's analytical model is different from the CEPII model in several important ways. And he focuses on nominal rather than real exchange rates. I have not examined Martin's model carefully, and do not mention it because I regard his model as preferable to the CEPII paper's model. I bring up the two papers' contradictory conclusions only as a reminder that an emphasis on different factors could modify the CEPII paper's main conclusion.

When considering the CEPII paper's results about exchange rate movements, we should also remember that what is called in the CEPII model the "dollar-euro rate" is in concept the exchange rate of the EU against the rest of the world (ROW) as a whole. In actual practice, we have to deal with a ROW that is many dimensional. The dollar-euro exchange rate will not behave the same as the yen-euro exchange rate, for example, and a variety of other countries will be independently floating as well.

To begin to come to grips with these hard analytical issues, we will have to work with an analytical framework that has four or five regions, rather than merely three. For example, for some purposes a model will have to have three European regions—"Germany," the other "ins" that participate in EMU core from the outset, and the European "outs" ("pre-ins") that initially are not in the core. And outside Europe, the model might distinguish between at least two regions, say, the United States (or North America) and a Japan/Asia/developing country region. A model with four or five regions will not be nearly as analytically tractable. It is much easier to define the need for such a model than it is to build it and use it. But such a model may be a minimum configuration for getting at some of the issues.

To illustrate, consider the question of incentives that non-Europeans—either private investors or even official governments—will have to substitute out of dollar-denominated assets into euro-denominated assets, and hence what sort of pressure, if any, these substitutions would bring to bear on exchange rates. Many conference participants appear to believe that the euro would appreciate sharply against the dollar, perhaps even overshooting an equilibrium path, in the years after EMU's inception. My own conjecture is like that in the Masson-Turtelboom paper. Such substitution pressures on dollar and euro exchange rates are not likely to be the dominant forces on exchange rates (as suggested in the Bergsten paper). Other factors, such as the relative cyclical positions of the European, U.S., and Asian economies and the relative monetary policy stances of major central banks (including the ECB), are likely to be more important.

Even so, if we want to get an analytical handle on the substitution pressures, we will have to consider the "relative variability" of the euro and the dollar vis-à-vis third currencies. For example, if the euro were much more variable against the U.S. dollar than against Asian currencies, the incentives of asset holders within Asia and the developing countries to substitute euro assets for dollar assets would be greater than if the dollar and third currencies fluctuated against the euro by relatively similar amounts.

The general thrust of my comments about the CEPII paper's analysis of the relative size of exchange rate movements of the euro vis-à-vis the ROW is cautionary. Conclusions about exchange rate movements could be significantly modified by factors that are not considered, or not considered fully, in the CEPII paper. (Again I cite the example of the initial asset-substitution effects that figure prominently in several of the other papers for this conference.)

I have so far accepted the CEPII paper's emphasis on the consequences of EMU for the stability of exchange rates. But we also should ask whether that emphasis is really appropriate—whether it addresses the questions of greatest interest to us.

My inclination is to believe that the stability of *other* macroeconomic variables is usually much more noteworthy and important. For Europe itself, should we not be much more interested in the variability of inflation, output, and consumption? Analogously, if we want to study the implications of EMU for non-European countries, should we not be focusing on those countries' inflation rates, outputs, and consumption paths?

When one looks at the CEPII paper's results on exchange rate movements, the differential effects on exchange rates of the pre-EMU float and the EMU environments tend to be rather small in magnitude. I believe Jean Pisani-Ferry used the adjective "moderate." At first glance I thought of the word "small."

In a limited way, it is possible to make a direct comparison between the CEPII paper's conclusions about exchange rate variability and the Masson-Turtelboom stochastic simulations. The revised Masson-Turtelboom paper in its Table 1 reports standard deviations for the deutsche mark–dollar exchange rate under the ERM and the euro-dollar exchange rate under EMU. The CEPII model and MULTIMOD stochastic simulations do appear to agree on the point that moving to EMU could augment the variability of the exchange rates of European currencies vis-à-vis the outside world. Interestingly, the MULTIMOD results also show the variability of the weighted average exchange rate of the dollar increasing if Europe moves to implement EMU, whereas variability for the yen decreases slightly. In the MULTIMOD stochastic simulations, however, note that the differences between the ERM and EMU cases also do not appear to be large.

Nevertheless, suppose the differential exchange rate effects reported in the two papers are deemed "large" in some sense. Even then, we should probably not be looking primarily at the exchange rate effects when trying to make welfare judgments. We would be looking, again, at consumption, or at least outputs and inflation rates.

The Masson-Turtelboom paper, in its sections describing the simulations with MULTIMOD, has a broader focus of the sort I have in mind. It reports the consequences for exchange rate variability, but more of its focus is on other macroeconomic variables. Their focus seems to me more interesting and appropriate.

The revised Masson-Turtelboom paper understandably does not highlight how the move to EMU and alternative monetary policy regimes within Europe might affect the stability of macroeconomic variables *outside Europe*. But there are a few results in their Table 1 that bear on the stability of variables outside of Europe. The European move to EMU appears to raise slightly the variability (measured by the standard deviation) of short-term interest rates in the United States and Japan. The reported consequences for real GDP growth and the inflation rate in the United States and Japan, on the other hand, appear quite small. It will be interesting to see whether further research on the effects of EMU on the United States and Japan confirms this finding of minor effects on outputs and inflation rates.

I have another suggestion for the Masson-Turtelboom paper, or more properly for extensions of their research that might be attempted in the future. It could be valuable to do further work on stochastic simulations of the sort they have carried out, but with an "unbundling" of the types of shocks. As implemented so far, the authors formed a variance-covariance matrix of all the key residuals for the 15 EU member countries and other major countries. All the 350 trials in the exercise (35 simulations for each of 10 years) involved random draws from the entire matrix for all the residuals. Hence, no distinctions were made between shocks originating inside Europe and those originating outside. And no distinction was made between demand shocks versus supply shocks versus shocks to the risk premium in the key interest-parity equations determining exchange rates.

In the Brookings-sponsored stochastic-simulation analysis of monetary policy regimes carried out several years ago, resulting in the volume on *Evaluating Policy Regimes* referred to by Masson and Turtelboom, the participating model groups also did not do such an "unbundling" of the shocks. But with the wisdom of hindsight, we very much wished that such an unbundling analysis had been done. Focusing separately and sequentially on a few key types of shocks, one type at a time, but with stochastic simulation techniques, would be a helpful halfway house between the deterministic simulations used at the end of the CEPII paper and the full-blown stochastic simulation analysis in the Masson-Turtelboom paper for this conference.

I would like to make a final point applicable to the analysis in both papers. The specification of monetary policy regimes, which are used in the simulations in both papers, can be very sensitive to the values of the "feedback parameters" that are used. (The feedback parameters are the coefficients in the policy rules that govern how aggressively or how mildly the policymakers move their instrument, the short-term interest rate, in response to deviations of their target variables from desired values.)

The values of the feedback parameters used in both papers are probably still fairly arbitrary, and the authors have probably not been able to subject them to much if any sensitivity testing. Other research on policy rules tends to underscore the importance of such sensitivity testing. Conclusions of simulation analysis can in some instances be changed quite substantially by varying the sizes of feedback parameters.

As an example, consider the inflation-plus-real-output targeting rule (in the last several years referred to as a "Taylor-type rule"). Both the CEPII and Masson-Turtelboom paper report some results with this type of monetary regime. Implicit if not explicit in most macroeconomic models, there is probably a "trade-off frontier" between output variability and price variability. Along this frontier, policy can only reduce price variability further by accepting somewhat greater output variability, and vice versa. But if the analyst implementing an inflation-plus-real-output targeting rule assumes relatively weak values of the feedback parameters for the rule, model simulations will yield fairly high values of both price variability and output variability. Moving to larger values of the feedback parameters can reduce price variability and output variability simultaneously. Misinterpretation of such results could lead to the incorrect impression that a trade-off frontier between price variability and output variability does not exist in the model.

My conjecture is that the conclusions in the two papers about the consequences of EMU for the stability of macroeconomic variables could be significantly influenced by the particular values of the feedback parameters chosen for the simulations. (The authors of both papers are aware of this issue. I emphasize it not as a criticism of the papers, but as a reminder of further research to be done.)

To conclude, I note again that both of the papers in this session are thoughtful and stimulating. They provide much food for thought, and help to carry us forward in our exploration of the possible consequences of European monetary union for macroeconomic stability.

Comments on Masson and Turtelboom

Bandid Nijathaworn

Let me begin first by thanking the Fund for inviting me to be a discussant in this session. Today I have been asked to comment on the paper by Masson and Turtelboom. Also, I have been asked to go beyond the scope of the paper and to speculate on the attractiveness of the euro from the perspectives of Asian countries. Because time is limited, I will focus my comments on these two topics.

First, the paper. I find it to be a major undertaking that tries systematically to come up with initial answers to the two important questions that are now on the mind of most market participants regarding the euro. First, will the euro facilitate greater macroeconomic stability in Europe? And second, what would be the prospect of the euro as a reserve currency?

In spite of the limitations posed by simplified assumptions and model calibration, the paper has come up with two important tentative findings. The first finding is that a more symmetric European monetary policy would have the result of reducing the variability of European macroeconomic indicators, with inflation targeting providing the largest gains in macroeconomic stability, as well as lower variability of short-term interest rates and the exchange rate of the euro against the dollar. The second finding is that, drawing on the above results and assuming away credibility problems, the paper concludes that holding of euro reserves should be about as attractive as the deutsche mark from a portfolio balance perspective.

These findings are very positive for the EMU and they sound very plausible. However, they must be carefully interpreted in light of a number of important limitations and uncertainties that cannot be adequately captured by a modeling exercise, as well as in light of the recent developments in financial markets. It is on this basis that I would like to offer specific comments.

First, if we look at the recent macroeconomic data, say, from 1986–95, it is clear that the EU data aggregates already give the picture of a relatively more stable European economy than do the national numbers. For example, the standard deviations of output, inflation, and short- and long-term rates do exhibit reduced volatility compared to the national variables, and compare quite well with the United States and Japan. There is, however, a trade-off between volatility and level. While the aggregate EU data on GDP growth from 1986 to 1995 has been approximately equal to that of the United States and Japan,

EU inflation and interest rates have been higher than those in either the United States or Japan.

Against this background, the main uncertainty in moving to a single monetary policy is that there is no guarantee that the stability of the money demand function would continue after EMU. If the relationship was more unstable, the gains in macroeconomic stability might not be as large as postulated by the model. The point I would like to stress is that EMU is, by all accounts, an important "institutional" change. And we have seen that for a number of countries over the last decade, institutional change has been an important explanation of at least some changes that have taken place in the demand for money behavior. This is also likely to occur in the case of EMU because the shock of the conversion process will induce the private sector to shift their currency holdings in the early stage of EMU. This effect, therefore, is an important qualification in interpreting the model results, especially on the expectation of reduced volatility in interest rates. My view is that reduced volatility in short- and long-term interest rates might not be as great as those depicted by the model despite lower inflation expectations and the removal of foreign exchange risk. The trade-off on the level could also be slightly higher because of the added uncertainty on the fiscal outlook.

Second, another important qualification that may weigh on the model results is the transmission mechanism of monetary policy itself. Under one monetary policy–one interest rate setting, the effect of an interest rate change on price and output would be even more limited compared with the situations under individual monetary policies. As we know, the effect depends on how efficiently the product and factor markets respond to changes in interest rate. On this very point, many observers have raised the issues of productivity differentials and limited labor market flexibility and mobility as being possible limiting factors that could hinder the effectiveness of a European-wide monetary policy. On this note, interpretation regarding the effectiveness of monetary policy, especially on output, would have to be made very carefully. These points on the structural changes have also been noted in the paper, and they are quite important.

Let me now turn to the second part of my remarks, on the attractiveness of the euro from the perspective of Asian countries. As noted in the paper, Asia's combined holding of global foreign exchange reserves was about 41 percent in 1995. The figure could be slightly higher at end-1996 on account of continued capital flows to Asia. The primary purpose of holding reserves is for foreign exchange intervention. Given that the U.S. dollar is an important anchor currency for a large number of exchange regimes in Asia, a large proportion of reserves tends to be held in U.S. dollars.

With the introduction of the euro, a key question is how the relative proportion of reserve holdings will change. This is a very difficult question to answer because it depends on a number of factors. In my view, the attractiveness of the euro will depend on three important factors.

The first is the confidence in the external value of the euro. This will relate primarily to the economic fundamentals of EMU and the soundness of financial policies. As we all know, market preference is for currencies with relatively low inflation costs.

The second factor is the openness and the degree of financial markets development of the issuing country, in this case the EU-15. Such development will help support the liquidity function of the euro through a large assortment of financial instruments as well as a deep and well-developed secondary market.

The third factor is, of course, trade volume between EMU and Asia. This will be an important demand side factor for enhancing the demand for the euro as reserve asset.

Let me elaborate on each of these three points in turn. The ECB's main mandate is to preserve price stability. I believe there will be a strong showing on the part of the ECB to demonstrate this commitment in its conduct of monetary policy, resulting in a low and stable rate of inflation in Europe. This will definitely provide support for the euro and build credibility for the ECB's monetary policy. The main risk, as I see it, is how far fiscal commitment will go to support the configuration of financial policies that is necessary for sustaining macroeconomic stability within EMU in the medium term.

Although the Stability and Growth Pact has laid down a number of important procedures for fiscal consolidation within EMU, some observers have pointed to the problems of weakening competitiveness and the possible need to stimulate demand to lessen pressure on unemployment at the national level as being possible conditions for the fiscal deficits to remain stubborn. How such pressure will evolve over time remains to be seen. But a loose fiscal policy will not act to consolidate the strength of the euro in the medium term.

On the issue of financial markets development, I am quite positive that a market in euro-dominated financial instruments will be developed quickly to support the role of the euro as an international currency. The market is, and has been, preparing for this change for some time. As a result, the market for euro financial instruments is expected to be large and liquid, supported by the presence of and the competition between European financial institutions in the global market, as well as by the efficient clearing and settlement system. These facilities will increase the liquidity of the euro and hence the attractiveness of the euro as a reserve currency.

A more uncertain issue is the evolution of trade between EMU and Asia. At present roughly 14 percent of trade of the EU-15 is with Asia, while about 61 percent is intra-EU trade. After EMU, the intra-EU component will become domestic, thereby raising Asia's share in EMU international trade to about 35 percent. A first key question is how the structure of European international trade will evolve after EMU. Because of the absence of foreign exchange risk, it is expected that initially intra-EU trade and investment will expand in response to the benefits of increased economies of scale, reduced transaction costs, and the benefits of more direct price comparisons, which tend to induce stronger competition. Thereafter, the scope for a further expansion of trade between Asia and EMU should be strengthened on account of Asia's continued demand for specialized machinery and capital goods from Europe while supplying the lower-cost consumer products and basic commodities to the EMU. Trade relations should also be strengthened through bilateral government arrangements, for example, through the initiatives of the recent Asia-Europe summit. These developments should raise the relative importance of European trade in Asia, and enhance the demand for euros in the Asia-Pacific region.

On the whole, I see good prospects for the euro to emerge as an important reserve currency in Asia. The three factors cited above will be important especially in the medium term. The implications associated with the immediate transition period are, however, more difficult to gauge with a firm degree of confidence. On this note, the prevailing attitude is to wait and see. And in the process, the three developments I cited above will be closely monitored.

9

Roundtable on Lessons of European Monetary Integration for the International Monetary System

Mervyn King

Today is St. Patrick's day. It is also John Major's day. Earlier this morning, he announced that the British general election would be held on May 1. As you will no doubt recall, the significance of that day is that it is the 290th anniversary of the Act of Union between England and Scotland—the Act that created the United Kingdom and led directly to a single currency. The Bank of England became, in effect, the Bank of Britain. One country, one currency.

That link—one country, one currency—reflects monetary history. And only countries, not currencies, can be members of the IMF. EMU challenges that link. EMU aims to replace "one country, one currency" by "one market, one money." In my view, the importance of EMU for the international monetary system stems directly from the attempt to move from a system of "one country, one currency" toward a new system based on the idea of "one market, one money." The immediate implication is that a wide range of decisions that are now taken within a country will instead be taken *jointly* by a group of countries. That is overwhelmingly the most important feature of EMU—both within Europe and between the EU, on the one hand, and the rest of the world, on the other. If successful, it would represent a major change in the way we view the role of nations in the international monetary system. A whole host of questions about the institutions of that system follow—some of which were raised by Philippe Maystadt in his lunchtime speech, and others that I shall mention in a moment.

The timetable for monetary union means that the key decisions on the initial members, and the choice of parities at which currencies will be irrevocably locked, will be taken under the British presidency of the EU in the first half of 1998. Whether the United Kingdom will choose to exercise its opt out by the end of this year remains to be seen. But, even if not a bride on this occasion, the United Kingdom will surely play the role of the best man, organizing the ceremony and ensuring that the principals turn up on time.

For monetary union is a marriage: a commitment to share our economic lives, and face shocks—both symmetric and asymmetric—together. Questions of compatibility can, for the moment, be left to the partners themselves. But monetary union, like marriage, is an institution that affects all of us. It matters that it works because divorce, not mentioned in the Maastricht Treaty, would be costly, not just to the partners directly involved, but also to all of their friends and colleagues.

The key question is how will separate countries take joint decisions on a wide range of economic issues. I shall identify three of these: monetary and exchange rate policy; fiscal policy; and representation of the monetary union and its member countries at the international level.

First, on monetary and exchange rate policy, the Maastricht Treaty is very clear. Article 109 describes the allocation of responsibilities between the ECB and the political authorities. The first paragraph of Article 109 makes clear that as far as *formal* exchange rate arrangements between the euro and non-Community currencies are concerned, the responsibility lies with the political authorities. On less formal arrangements, paragraph two gives the European Council—the politicians—the right to "formulate general orientations for exchange rate policy," providing that these are "without prejudice to the primary objective of the ECB to maintain price stability." So for informal target zone arrangements—Bergstenian orientations—of exchange rates, the ECB would have a veto unless such arrangements were embodied in a formal target. It follows that the governments of the member countries would need to reach agreement on these matters outside of the meetings of the independent ECB. It is hard to see how a stability council, or some other such forum, for those countries in the monetary union can be avoided. Some commentators have been confused by the idea of a stability council. Its role is *not* to provide a political input into monetary policy; it is to provide a forum for the "ins" to reach agreement on all those issues that are not the responsibility of the ECB. For some considerable time it is likely that the monetary union will comprise only a subset of the EU as a whole, and there are many issues, such as those covered by Article 109, where the voting power is restricted to the ins. Discussing such matters in a forum of the full EU (ECOFIN, for example) may not be appropriate.

Second, on fiscal policy, agreement on the Stability and Growth Pact is close. Discussions on the fiscal policy of the ins more generally will also require some sort of stability council. That would affect the monetary and fiscal policy mix of the monetary union, and hence the level of the exchange rate of the euro. That would be of direct interest to other countries, especially the Group of Seven industrial countries. The monetary union will have to express views on both monetary and exchange rate policy to other member countries of the IMF. That brings me directly to the final issue.

Third, how will the monetary union be represented at the international level? There has certainly been some recent excitement about this issue. Undoubtedly, there are many formulas that one could imagine to answer the question of how the monetary union will be represented. There has also been discussion of whether the Group of Seven would contract, at least when discussing macroeconomic issues, to a Group of Three. But the real issue is less the form than the substance of getting agreement among the member countries of a monetary union on a common view across a range of issues. Again, what will matter is that the monetary union will not for some time comprise the full EU. That is why so many of the ins versus outs issues are, at heart, not a question of an exchange rate mechanism for the outs but of the governance of the monetary union area.

What does all this add up to? Well, the engagement party is well under way. The dance floor is full—most look happy, although some have a grim stare. Everyone has a fiancé—indeed, some have several. But the United Kingdom is circling the dance floor with that sobriety that comes from experience and gray hair, knowing only too well that mere infatuations rarely last. The vital thing is to find a partner who will be by your side when that asymmetric shock comes along. That is known, in the technical literature, as sustainable convergence. If we are to meet 50 years from now to celebrate the golden wedding of EMU, it will be because we in Europe will have succeeded in making joint decisions, not just at the central bank level where the mechanism (the ECB) is clearly specified, but also among finance ministries, where it is not. Success would be a powerful example to the international monetary system as a whole, and I have little doubt that a successful EMU would soon lead to similar examples elsewhere in the world.

André Szász

In the spring of 1998, European heads of state or government will have to agree which EU countries qualify for participation when EMU is to start in 1999, as required by the Maastricht Treaty. It is only now being widely realized what a complex and far-reaching operation this will be.

As the implications are sinking in, disagreements are emerging even between the main movers of EMU, France and Germany, and even on issues supposed to have been settled in the Treaty, including that of relations between the ECB and governments.

Whether and how participants are going to solve their differences largely depends on their motives for pursuing EMU. These motives are partly economic, but mainly political.

EU countries, notably the continental ones, are too interdependent to allow free floating of their currencies. In the absence of monetary union, they require exchange rate arrangements with each other. But with increasing capital mobility, an EMS-type arrangement of stable but adjustable central rates does not produce sufficient stability if adjustments are expected. Exchange rate stability is only likely if member states convincingly abandon the use of central rate adjustments. This would in effect imply a deutsche mark bloc, in which the monetary authorities of the other countries follow the policies of the Bundesbank, decided not only on the basis of German priorities but also on the basis of conditions in Germany alone. This would cause resentment and tensions.

A number of EU countries, in particular France, reject a deutsche mark bloc. They want to be in a position to influence monetary decision making, feeling that monetary discipline would be more acceptable in their country if it was not regarded as imposed by Germany but followed from European decision making. Establishing EMU is the way to achieve this. For Germany, this could hardly be a sufficient motive to pursue monetary union. Yet, Germany too is in favor of establishing EMU. With its geographical position in the center of Europe, and with the history of the past century in mind, Germany wants political union. Establishing EMU is the way to achieve this too.

It was German Chancellor Willy Brandt who proposed the establishment of EMU at the summit in The Hague in December 1969. At the time, Germany's growing economic strength, reflected in an increasing dominance of the deutsche mark, was troubling France. In reply to French fears the new German chancellor, who needed French support for his incipient Ostpolitik, offered to merge the deutsche mark into EMU provided certain conditions were met. Similarly, in the beginning of 1988, Chancellor Kohl and Foreign Minister Genscher reacted positively to a proposal by French Finance Minister Balladur to discuss a possible future ECB. In September 1987, Genscher had argued in a speech that the period of stalemate in East-West relations was over and that Germany should be actively involved in establishing new relations; however, this had to be balanced by an active policy of integration in Western Europe. It was mainly owing to this attitude that the Delors Committee was established, whose report—published in April 1989—was to become the core of the Maastricht Treaty. Finally, when the Berlin Wall crumbled toward the end of that year and German unification suddenly became an early prospect, President Mitterrand—after a first erratic reaction—accepted this development provided that preparations for EMU were accelerated. This

Chancellor Kohl accepted, declaring that German unification and European integration were two sides of the same coin. Thus, each time the process toward EMU received a new impulse, this was because EMU was the German answer to French concerns.

But giving up the deutsche mark is only acceptable in Germany if price stability remains safeguarded to a sufficient degree. To this end, Germany posed two conditions to EMU: the future ECB should have price stability as its priority objective and should not be subject to political instructions; and member states should accept the obligation to avoid excessive budget deficits. Otherwise, the result would be an unbalanced policy mix, resulting in rising interest rates. Experience has shown that these are blamed not on public sector deficits but on central bank policies. The ECB would come under political pressure, the more so since, in EMU as a whole, a genuine consensus on the need for price stability has still to be established.

These conditions have been established in the Maastricht Treaty. But as the start of EMU is approaching, there are indications that they are not interpreted everywhere in the same way. French President Chirac stated publicly in December 1996 that the ECB should be faced with what he called a government bearing responsibility—the European Council—entitled to call it to account and to draw the limits of its actions. If anything, this can only mean that in case of differences in view the European Council could insist on lower interest rates, a lower exchange rate of the euro against the dollar, and thus on more expansionary monetary policies, than would be pursued by a genuinely independent central bank with price stability as its primary objective. Should this happen, the core of the Treaty would be called into question, and thus the basis of EMU. Severe tensions would be the inevitable result.

Chances to avoid such tensions are best if convergence precedes participation in EMU. The Treaty stresses the requirement of sustainable convergence, and notably sustainability of the government budgetary position. The date of 1999, when EMU has to start, has been added to the convergence requirements at the last minute, so to say, at the meeting in Maastricht itself. As a result, judgment in 1998 on the question of which countries qualify for participation may tend to focus on a single year, 1997, the last year for which realization figures will be available. Unfortunately, this is an invitation to influence the 1997 figures even by measures without any lasting effect. The differences between countries with a more sustainable budgetary position and those relying heavily on temporary measures might thus be blurred. This increases the risk that EMU will start with a fundamentally heterogeneous composition.

EMU will be a large currency area, bound to affect the international monetary system as a whole. If it functions well, it can contribute to global stability. If, due to internal inconsistencies, it is characterized by internal disagreements and tensions, it will tend to become inward-looking, and have inflexible external positions and an unbalanced policy mix. The international monetary system as a whole therefore has a major interest in an EMU that functions well. That can only be the case if its participants genuinely respect the Treaty. Even those who at present fear the deflationary impact of several countries simultaneously reducing their budget deficits in order to qualify for participation should realize the importance of participants keeping their public finances under control once EMU has been established.

With the establishment of EMU, the international monetary system will tend to develop into a two- or three-polar system. The system's stability will to a large extent be determined by the cooperation between those poles. The institutional framework of this cooperation will raise many questions, due to the hybrid nature of EMU, with monetary competence centralized in the ECB and budgetary competence remaining at the national level.

The emergence of a large currency area will tend to make its participants less vulnerable to exchange rate fluctuations since the area will be a more closed economy than the individual countries at present. At the same time, it might improve conditions for increased global exchange rate stability. Exchange rate stability cannot be attained unilaterally, but only if there is a mutual interest to pursue it. That might be the case with the emergence of several large currency areas of comparable economic openness.

Stability requires both internal and external consistency, and forms of international cooperation that cannot have an ad hoc character. In all this, the IMF has a crucial role to play.

Edwin M. Truman

When Mike Mussa approached me about appearing on this panel, I asked him whether, given our topic, he expected the panelists to engage in a bit of "pre-history," that is, anticipating history before the event. His reply was yes, in part, we are invited to speculate about how the international monetary system will evolve or function in the context of Stage III of EMU. Given in particular that central bankers are rarely comfortable answering hypothetical questions, I hasten to state that my views should not be identified with those of either the Federal Reserve or the U.S. government.

With that qualification, I take our basic question to be whether the process of European monetary integration to date has on balance contributed positively to the constructive evolution of the international monetary system and whether it is likely to continue to do so. To help answer this question, I would like to pose, and attempt to answer, four subsidiary questions.

1. How strong has the connection been between European monetary integration and the evolution of the international monetary system?
2. Will the introduction of the euro on January 1, 1999, be a step toward the restoration of a global system of fixed exchange rates?
3. What are the implications of European monetary integration for the functioning of the international monetary system?
4. Will the dollar's hegemony end on January 1, 1999, to the benefit of Europe and the world economy?

On the first question, there are, I think it is fair to say, two extreme views. One view is that European monetary integration is the extension of a process that began with the founding of the European Coal and Steel Community in 1951, which followed the establishment of the European Payments Union in 1950. While further monetary integration was not embraced by all, many Europeans, at least from time of the Treaty of Rome, saw it as an inevitable and desirable part of the European integration process. Concrete steps were taken in this direction at the Hague Summit in 1969, which led to the production of the Werner Report in 1971. All of this was prior to the breakup of the final Bretton Woods system in 1973.

An alternative view is that European monetary integration is a more recent development and has been a reaction to the breakdown of the Bretton Woods system, the subsequent currency instability, and the nonsystem of international currency arrangements that some argue we have today. Supporters of this view cite the circumstances surrounding the establishment of the EMS in 1979, in particular the weak U.S. dollar at that time.

In my view the "truth" lies somewhat in between these two extreme views, but closer to the former than the latter. Progress on European monetary integration has been driven principally by broad progress on economic and financial integration in Europe over the past half century. If anything, developments affecting the international economy over the past 25 years or so—the collapse of the Bretton Woods system, the oil shocks, and the global acceleration of inflation—probably slowed down and complicated that process. To those who argue, on the other hand, that the EMS to date has lived up to its potential as a zone of monetary stability, meaning exchange rate stability, I would note that the current 15 percent margins in the ERM are hardly convincing evidence of success in this regard. However, Europe *should* take some credit for contributing to the global process of disinflation that began in the late 1970s; at the same time, the success of that process not only within Europe but to a large extent in the rest of the world has contributed to prospects that the third stage of EMU may start before the end of the century.

My second question was whether the introduction of the euro on January 1, 1999, would be a step toward the restoration of a global system of fixed exchange rates. Some believe that once European currencies are locked into the euro on January 1, 1999, the next logical and desirable step would be to return to a global regime of fixed exchange rates or at least to a regime of target zones among the Group of Three currencies. I think they are mistaken in this view, and if this were the goal or consequence of European monetary integration, the Europeans would be doing a disservice to the international monetary system.

As suggested by my answer to the first question, European monetary integration to date has little to do with the evolution of the international monetary system per se. Moreover, those who ask whether exchange rates will be more or less stable once EMU has been fully implemented are asking the wrong question with respect to the successful functioning of the international monetary system. The question that should be asked is whether as a consequence of EMU the global economy will be more or less likely to benefit from global forces of integration and liberalization. From this perspective, the very forces that drove the Europeans to adopt 15 percent bands within the ERM—increased international mobility of capital in a more integrated world economy—are likely to dictate that substantial flexibility be permitted among the exchange rates of the major currencies.

The more interesting issue is not whether EMU will tend to promote greater exchange rate stability either de facto or de jure but whether it is likely to suggest that a widespread movement toward a world currency or several regional currencies would be desirable. If EMU is a success in the sense that as many as 15 countries are judged to be able to enjoy a higher level of prosperity with a single currency and a supranational central bank, why shouldn't a larger portion of the world adopt such arrangements? From this perspective, European monetary integration might ultimately make a positive contribution to the international monetary system, but I suspect that most of us would agree that any payoff is likely to be a long way down the road.

The third question is what are the implications of European monetary integration for the functioning of the international monetary system? In my view, this is a more serious and immediate question than that of the implications of European monetary integration for the structure of the exchange rate regime. What are the practical implications for the smooth functioning of the international monetary system of a situation in which major countries participate without currencies of their own and the system includes an essentially stateless currency? Quite frankly, I do not think we know. We do know that there is some unfinished business in terms of short-run arrangements in Europe and some large questions in terms of longer-run evolution of Europe.

Ever since the establishment of the EMS, one preoccupation of some economists and officials has been whether economic policy in the context of increased European monetary integration will tend to have a deflationary bias. That is an important question for Europe as well as for the rest of the world, but the more important question for the rest of the world is whether the process of cyclical adjustment within Europe generally will have benign or adverse implications for the global economy. After January 1, 1999, Europe will have a supranational monetary authority. Its relationship with both the Brussels process and national governments will be complex; it will be governed by a combination of legal obligations and arrangements, but it will be shaped and tested by experience. The concern is that because Europe will be living in a halfway house where economic decision making is shared in an uncertain manner, the smooth functioning of the international monetary system could be adversely affected.

For example, what will be the process of economic policy coordination *within* Europe? This is a delicate question in any democracy with an independent central bank. From this perspective, what will be the European equivalent of the weekly breakfasts between the U.S. Secretary of the Treasury and the Chairman of the Federal Reserve Board? My sense is that Europe has not yet answered this question, or more precisely, different Europeans have different answers to it. I am skeptical that the proposed Stability and Growth Council will provide an adequate answer. Moreover, I am concerned that too much of the thinking about the coordination of policy within Europe appears to be focused on something called "exchange rate policy" rather than on more serious issues of fundamental economic policies. To the extent that the coordination of monetary and fiscal policy in Europe is not smooth, consistent, and coherent, there will be adverse consequences for the business cycle in Europe as well as for exchange rates and the global economy.

To cite another example, one of many possible examples involving today's global institutions of monetary cooperation, what if we had another Mexican type of financial crisis and this time it was proposed to activate the New Arrangements to Borrow to help to finance drawings on the IMF, including euros. How would Europe go about reaching a decision on this subject? Could one European country effectively veto the participation of its partners? Is there not the possibility that, as in 1995, Europe would be so preoccupied with its own problems at that time that it would fail to appreciate the nature of systemic threat involved? A possible difference this time might be that Europe could do some real damage, not just because it might not reach the right decision but, as was the case with the U.S. Congress in 1995, it might not be able to reach any decision within a realistic time frame.

I assume enlightened cooperation will prevail both within Europe and between Europe and the rest of the world, but I think the rest of us have some reason to be concerned about the effects of creaky decision-making process in Europe that is likely to prevail on some internal and external issues that will be important for the continued stability and prosperity of the global economy.

Finally, the fourth question: Will the dollar's hegemony end on January 1, 1999, to the benefit of Europe and the world economy? This question involves a historical perspective, as did my first. My sense is that the hope of many Europeans is that the answer is yes. A preoccupation with this subject often lies behind calculations about the role of the euro in the world financial system after January 1, 1999. People want to prove that the role of the euro will be equal to the dollar, in what they describe as a bipolar or multipolar global financial system that they believe will be characterized by greater symmetry of obligations and burdens. They want to make sure that Europe captures some of the economic and financial benefits from the international role of the euro that they believe the United States has enjoyed from the international role of the dollar over the past 50 years or so.

This line of thinking is seriously misguided. First, it appears to be founded on a view that the international monetary system will be and should be based on a regime of fixed exchange rates in which center countries can postpone the adjustment of their exchange rates through the accumulation of external liabilities. This always was a debatable advantage for the United States and, as I have argued today, it would be based on an unrealistic presumption about the nature of the exchange rate regime.

Second, I do not believe that the dollar's international role during the post-war period—either during the Bretton Woods period or over the past 25 years—has provided any significant economic or financial advantages to the United States on balance. (The only significant advantage is one that has emerged principally in the past 10 years or so as the result of the dollar's increased use as a currency for physical transactions; this pure seignorage "benefit" was not an element of the debate over most of the postwar period about the supposed advantage to the United States of the international role of the dollar.) This view, I know, is contrary to what one hears in Europe, particularly east of the English Channel and west of the Rhine! Indeed, I was asked by a senior European official last September whether the United States is not concerned about how it will finance its imports once EMU comes fully into effect. My answer was there will be no change: financing for U.S. imports will continue to come from the market, whether in dollars, euros, or yen.

Third, and most important, any change in the dollar's international role, whether as a reserve currency, a transactions currency, or a means of denominating international assets, will come about gradually and more as a consequence of the development of broad, deep, and stable financial markets in Europe rather than as a consequence of governmental actions per se. Most observers tend to agree on this point.

My concern is that those who tend to think that the dollar's role has provided the United States with a special advantage in recent years to the detriment of other participants in the international monetary system also tend to think that this advantage will disappear instantly on January 1, 1999, and immediately accrue in whole or in part to Europe. There is a serious risk that this mistake in analysis will add one more disappointing dimension to the first days of Stage III of EMU.

In summary, my answer to my basic question of whether the process of European monetary integration to date has on balance contributed positively to the constructive evolution of the international monetary system and whether it is likely to continue to do so is that the contribution of European monetary integration to date has been and will continue to be marginal. I am hard pressed to draw any profound lessons. Any positive contributions in the future will depend on how consistently Europeans concentrate on the core issues that are important to their own prosperity and to global growth and on how effective they are in achieving balanced, noninflationary growth at a high level of resource utilization.

Takatoshi Kato

Within the time constraints we have today, let me try to give you some idea of Japan's perspective at this stage on EMU. First of all, I would like to touch upon how we in Japan conceive of EMU. From a macroeconomic point of view, the medium- to long-term effect, in addition to trade expansion, would be to enhance the volume of financial and capital transactions within Europe. This would follow from the unification of European money and capital markets in a single currency, which would increase the depth and stability of the markets. As a result of the development of this wide single market, economic transactions with the outside area would also become more active, attracting foreign financial institutions and foreign investors to the more developed European money and capital markets.

Next, I will consider how Japanese financial institutions and investors see the introduction of the euro from the point of view of portfolio preference. It seems that the current stance of Japanese financial institutions and investors regarding the introduction of the euro is that it will make no fundamental change in the period leading up to 1999 because of various uncertainties involved in EMU. However, some expect an increase in investment in euro-denominated securities if the introduction of the euro increases the liquidity of the euro-related markets, expands the scope of investable financial products, and thus widens and deepens the euro-related markets.

It should be noted, however, that there are uncertainties regarding how the convergence criteria for participation in EMU will be applied, how strictly the Stability and Growth Pact will be applied once EMU is achieved, and how the level of parities will be determined and announced. There are many Japanese financial institutions and institutional investors that claim that their portfolio strategies will be significantly influenced by these factors. They are paying close attention to how the EU countries will move toward the introduction of the single currency.

As is clear from the foregoing observations, in order for the introduction of the European single currency to have a positive effect on the global economy, it is essential that it be introduced in an orderly manner and that potential confusion associated with the transition to EMU be avoided. In this regard, it seems that the following two points, in particular, are important in connection with EMU.

First, the determination of the parity between the euro and the participating currencies should be made in a manner and with timing that would increase its credibility in the market. Second, even after the introduction of the single currency, the countries participating in Stage III of EMU should continue their efforts at economic convergence, thus increasing the credibility that the convergence of economic fundamentals supporting the euro is solidly based.

At the same time, we attach importance, under the single currency, to the overall financial system, including the settlement and payment system, and that these continue to maintain their open character. With the introduction of the single currency, even countries outside the area will incur certain costs associated with the transition, such as the cost of introducing new computer programs and other administrative costs. It is hoped that they will share equally not only the costs but also the benefits of introducing the single currency.

Some of these observations come from the exchange of views within the private study group on EMU at the Japanese Ministry of Finance, established last year. The group includes professors of economics and law, lawyers, bankers, and institutional investors. One of the areas of keen interest to the group is how the continuity of contracts will be secured both inside and outside the single currency area after introduction of the euro.

From a slightly broader perspective, the Japanese government made public last November its objective of undertaking far-reaching financial sector reform to transform the Tokyo markets into markets of comparable stature to those of New York or London by the year 2001. As an important first step, legislation to substantially liberalize and simplify the legal requirements concerning foreign exchange and cross-border financial transactions has already been presented to the Diet. Following this, the current thinking is to make public by the middle of this year a blueprint for reform in other areas, including securities transactions and a holding company framework.

Finally, let me briefly refer to the reaction of some Asian countries on the subject of EMU. A relatively active interest was observed through sketchy and preliminary contacts with some of the Asian authorities. It seems that their interests lie more in the area of the possible impact on Asian countries' portfolio management than in EMU's impact on the international monetary system. Two weeks ago, Japan hosted the first meeting of the so-called Six Markets Meeting, comprising authorities of Australia, China, Hong Kong, Japan, Singapore, and the United States. It is hoped that closer contacts among Asia-Pacific countries will be facilitated in this and other, similar forums.

Jacob Frenkel

As André Szász reminded us, to travel hopefully is better than to arrive. And as Francis Bacon told us, it's much to have hope for breakfast; it's a terrible thing to have for supper. But most importantly, in a different context once somebody told me, "If you want your dreams to come true, you had better wake up first."

As I looked at the title of this roundtable, "Lessons of European Monetary Integration for the International Monetary System," I wondered how there could be lessons from integration if it was still not complete? So I prepared a speech about the transition and then Stan Fischer told me that the transition is not to be discussed until tomorrow. And then I remembered that one does not really need to complete an event in order to draw lessons from it, because as some of you are aware, literally a few weeks after the demise of Bretton Woods, there was a conference in Paris on the top of the Eiffel Tower, at which a panel discussed "Lessons from Floating Rates." Participants in the panel were Jacques Rueff, Milton Friedman, Bob Mundell, Harry Johnson, and Fritz Machlup. I remember that those of us in the crowd were sitting there saying, gee, how can these people tell us about lessons from something that is just being born, but people spoke with great confidence. Jacques Rueff told us that the system had collapsed and, as a matter of fact, the demise of the flexible rates that had been with us for the past few weeks revealed how important it was to return to gold; Harry Johnson told us that we see how great flexible exchange rates can be; and so on. And then, after all, we learned that what you see is what you want to see.

But still, upon further reflection, I think that the lessons from European monetary integration, even though they are not complete, are that how you get there is very important for the questions, will you get there and will the way you get there determine whether you will stay there, whether you will arrive, and so on? I think that, in this regard, European monetary integration and the transition to EMU is a good example of how important it is to prepare an infrastructure of the transition if you really want to make sure that when you get there, you are not surprised.

But then I thought to myself that maybe the coordinators of the conference decided on the title "Lessons from the European Monetary Integration for the International Monetary System" because they assume that in the post-European monetary integration there will need to be a new international monetary system and, as a matter of fact, the old one is passé. Be it as it may, my own belief is that we are going to remain a multipolar world and, as a matter of fact, what European monetary integration reveals to us—and there are good lessons from it—is how to create a pole and how to make sure that the infrastructure within a pole is indeed in place.

Let me make a few remarks about some implications. First, in the old international monetary system, there was initially excessive focus on exchange rates in the debate of international monetary coordination. Only with the passage of time and with the increasing role of the Fund and the like did one realize the need to shift attention toward coordination or discussion of macroeconomic policies and less on the consequent elements of the narrow exchange rate feature. I believe, therefore, that this forced to the fore some issues: how the policymaking process differs among countries, how the legal structures are different, how the jurisdictions of policymakers differ, and the like. In this regard, we also saw in the old policy coordination framework that when there is a conflict of interest that arises from a lack of convergence—whether it is because of the budget, the business cycle, inflation differences, or unemployment differences—then macroeconomic coordination becomes extremely difficult to coordinate. We also saw that when there is unequal political support among the parties for the process, it is very difficult to coordinate.

These are the lessons that have been integrated into the European monetary integration process, and indeed it was political force that moved the process forward. Progress was based on the recognition that you need to have convergence first and a macroeconomic setting in place to give the process a chance. It was understood that if new legislation is necessary, it must be in place first, and if there is to be a central bank, then the laws of the central banks that are composing it should be harmonized or adapted to it. In other words, these were the lessons that came from the difficulties in the old coordination exercises and that I believe are now much better ingrained into the pole called Europe. But then the question is, with the new Europe, what will happen to the old coordination exercises with the other members?

Well, I want to recall that when the Group of Five industrial countries expanded itself into the Group of Seven, many argued, and with some justification, that this gave new life to the Group of Three. In other words, it became very difficult to have a very large group of very unequal countries. In this regard, if the new Europe is indeed represented by one entity that will represent the joint interests of the various countries, then the coordination amongst the various countries might be revived once again.

What is the role of the Fund in this regard? I think that in the new world, when capital markets are the main elements of linkages among countries and among poles, surveillance should indeed be adapting to it. Instead of just focusing on what we call surveillance of exchange rate policies, we will see much more focus on capital markets. Maybe we will see a new Article VIII associated with capital account convertibility and much more interaction with the bodies that link and deal with it, such as the Bank for International Settlements.

But there are some new concepts that are now governing economic policy-setting in general. First, we all recognize today that fiscal policies are inflexible, and therefore not suitable for fine-tuning. We all recognize that monetary policies operate with variable and long lags, and therefore are viewed as a medium-term strategy. We all accept that commercial policies are passé as policy instruments because we have the World Trade Organization and therefore this is a noninstrument. We all recognize that exchange rates cannot be pegged at the wrong levels. As a matter of fact, there are not enough international reserves to peg a wrong exchange rate. And therefore the question is what policy instruments are left? Fiscal policy is medium term. Monetary policy is medium term. Exchange rate policy had better be consistent with the that of other countries, and commercial policy is ruled out by the World Trade Organization.

Well, there is a new world and the new world views policies not as being responsive in a countercyclical way, but rather as providing the structure within which markets operate. And what is this structure telling us? It is telling us that the relationship between the policymaker and the market is not what it used to be. In the old days, policymakers thought that to be effective, they had better surprise the market. Announcements should be made when the markets were closed. Everyone had to be surprised. The markets were adversaries to the policymakers. However, it is a new world now. Now, the role of policies is a dialogue with the markets; but in order to have a dialogue, your actions must be transparent, clear, accountable, and predictable. You must have an open way of policymaking.

Now, this leads toward the strategy, for example, of inflation targets, of explicit objectives, of sharpening the objectives of central banks, and the like. But then the question is, considering the title of the roundtable, what is the lesson from the European monetary integration for the international monetary system? Will the new system become a new fixed exchange rate world, like Europe? I believe not.

I believe that, as I mentioned earlier, we will still have a multipolar world. Europe will have a good system because the infrastructure is in place, and the old debate between fixed and flexible exchange rates will continue many, many years into the future because, after all, we also have learned that the debate is not between fixed and flexible exchange rates, but rather what is the system that generates good economic policies, and this depends on the circumstances.

Let me conclude with a couple of quotes. First, in the nineteenth century John Stuart Mill described the arrangements of currencies over the world as follows: "So much barbarism, however, still remains in the transactions of the most civilized nations that almost all independent countries choose to assert their nationality by having, to their own inconvenience and that of their neighbors, a peculiar currency of their own." Then he goes on to ask how the world will look in the future. In our own world, we will say the world will converge into a single currency, and he describes that situation as the situation that comes from the progress of political improvement. Well, maybe in Europe we see it, but as I mentioned earlier, I don't believe that this is going to be the name of the game for the world at large, where the question is "Are we going to have postponement or not, and what will be the impact of it if it happens?" Well, can you imagine the impact if EMU were to be postponed for the next decade, which might happen? This would be extremely detrimental to the credibility of all involved policymakers, and therefore if something along these lines is going to happen it will be a two-speed implementation rather than full postponement, because the stakes are just too high. You know, you need to have motivation. There is the story of the guy who was condemned to die in the electric chair, but he was too heavy; he did not fit into the chair. So when he came he was told, well, go home and go on a diet and come back next time. When he came back next month, he was five kilos heavier and he was asked, "What happened? we told you to lose some weight." And he said, "Well, I did not have motivation." So the real question is, is there enough motivation, or a penalty for postponement? It would be politically prohibitively expensive, so one needs to proceed in a hurry. But if one does hurry, one needs to remember what Menendes-France said once when he wanted his people to stop drinking alcohol. He put signs in the Paris Metro saying "Be careful, alcohol kills you slowly," and somebody added a note underneath it saying, "That's all right, I'm not in a hurry." But in this case, we are in a hurry. We should not kid ourselves that just having EMU in place is the solution for all problems of the international monetary system. It is just an evolution. The same issues will come up. All difficulties in the past came from an unbalanced stance of economic policies, fiscal policies, typically, and overburdening monetary policies and the like. All of these problems will remain in the new system, so we will have here in the next millennium a conference called "What Were the First 50 Years Like?"

10

An American Perspective on EMU

Paul A. Volcker

When the Managing Director called a few weeks ago to suggest that I might join you for dinner, I accepted much too easily. The simple fact is that, instead of speaking tonight, I should have been with you all day learning. The only claim I can make at this point is that I come with a fresh mind, unencumbered by absorbing the wisdom of the day. I will acknowledge, however, that I am encumbered by a few prejudices and preconceptions.

It has long seemed to me that a common currency is an appropriate and crowning development for the European Community. It is, in fact, a step that would really begin to justify institutionally the new nomenclature of the Community as "the European Union." My conclusion is derived from broadly political considerations as much as, or more than, the economics. But I also happen to believe that the economic benefits will be real, compared to the alternatives.

Given the desire for a close economic union—a true "single market"—the logic of wanting to maintain exchange rate stability seems to me compelling. Whatever we think of floating exchange rates as a practical and desirable regime on a wider world scale, we do know enough to understand that very large, often seemingly capricious, fluctuations can be anticipated even among close trading partners—large defined by experience as 20 or 30 percent or more. Those fluctuations are far larger than consistent with any notion of purchasing power or competitive parity. Faced with the prospect and presence of exchange rate changes of that magnitude, it is hard for me to see (indeed impossible for me to see) that the "common market" can, in fact, become a true "single market." Ultimately, political support for the degree of unity already achieved, much less further consolidation, could erode. To the extent that instability is related to pressures external to the common market—possibly by dollar instability among other things—multilateral liberalization could be jeopardized.

Concerns of that kind have led to repeated efforts to stabilize the intra-European exchange rates within narrow margins. Those efforts have never been easy, for familiar reasons. Nonetheless, the main continental members of the EU have made it a matter of high priority. They have achieved substantial success, arguably at significant cost. Specifically, flexibility in the pursuit of more purely domestic objectives has been forgone. However, one can wonder just how great a sacrifice that has been, assuming as I do that great priority would have been given to the objective of domestic price stability with or without tightly fixed exchange rates. Moreover, at least the smaller members of the EU may, de facto, have found it necessary to coordinate their monetary policies with the German center, whatever the formalities of the exchange rate system.

Be that as it may, once the decision is made to fix exchange rates within a narrow margin, the argument shifts. Then the retention of national currencies may only add to the costs. The market is bound to interpret such retention as a kind of "safety valve" to relieve pressure when strains arise. That possibility will both encourage speculative attacks at times of pressure and undermine the political will to encourage more competitive and flexible labor markets and business practices.

It is obvious that, whatever the longer-run advantages, the EU is now entering into the most sensitive and delicate stage of the transition. The underlying economic circumstances—prolonged sluggish growth and high unemployment—are not ideal, to put it mildly. As a result, the possibilities of meeting the arbitrary Maastricht budget and debt criteria—even in Germany—are problematic. The strong efforts to satisfy those criteria are, in the short run, a dampening influence on expansion. That tension may yet derail the project.

That seems to me doubly unfortunate given the progress that has been made toward convergence on the more critical price stability criteria. The approach of the common currency has also led to another healthy circumstance—greater recognition through Europe about the importance of economic restructuring to achieve greater flexibility and competitiveness.

Many commentators have made the point that, assuming a critical mass of members do decide to proceed, both monetary and fiscal policies will be further constrained for some time ahead: fiscal policy to meet the stability criteria and monetary policy as the new central bank strives to achieve full credibility. But I wonder if there is a practical alternative. If postponement—or even abandonment—were to be decided on, and that became the excuse for looser policies, market reactions could be strong and disturbing. As with fixed but adjustable exchange rates, the implication is that macro policies may need to be at least as constraining as with the common currency.

The construction of the ECB is, of course, a unique enterprise. I know of no precedent for still independent countries in effect ceding monetary sovereignty to a jointly sponsored entity—and without a parallel governmental body with which the central bank can even interact. Set out not by law but by treaty, it is the extreme of formal central bank independence.

I do not happen to believe any central bank can long be comfortable as an island unto itself, operating entirely outside a political context—broadly defined. By one means or another, in democratic society, it must be able to justify its policies to the general public and to political leaders. For that reason, without knowing the details—and the details are important—it is easy for me to be sympathetic to the discussions under way to establish an intergovernmental council as an interlocutor with which the central bank, retaining full power of decision, can communicate, in the process elucidating, explaining, and defending its policy decisions while listening to the concerns and plans of governments.

These are, of course, internal matters more of concern to Europe than to the rest of the world. But the significance of what happens to all of us is clear. The EU, in total economic weight, will about match the United States. Consequently, a strong restraining influence on European economic activity during an extended transitional period will have consequences for the world economy—not, I suspect, overpowering, but something to take into account. On balance, it probably means less risk of inflation. Countries (such as those in Eastern Europe) more dependent on exports to Western Europe may be hurt. In either case, I see no way out of that situation, for Europe or its trading partners.

A failure to move ahead, with the probable consequence of exchange market disturbances and renewed uncertainty about domestic economic policies, could have equally restraining effects. I realize that the United Kingdom, contrary to that kind of concern, appeared to benefit upon leaving the ERM. But the situation would be different in the event of a general breakdown. Members of EMU cannot all devalue against each other, and markets might be more apt to anticipate inflationary repercussions than was the case in the particular situation of the United Kingdom. At any rate, a delayed European expansion and the potential restraining influence on the world economy needs to be kept in perspective: slow growth in Europe need not and should not mean a general recession.

The more interesting question—the question with which this conference is mainly concerned—is the longer range consequences of the single currency. I can summarize my own views in three unhelpful words: it all depends. And it depends upon enough variables, and variables that are themselves uncertain, that I, for one, would not want to place a lot of bets on the direction of the euro exchange rate or the general level of euro interest rates.

Even something so straightforward as the consolidation of Europe's official foreign exchange reserves seems to have ambiguous implications. The mechanical effect will be, as I understand it, to reduce the total. Presumably, the joint need for international reserves will also decline. Most likely, for some substantial transitional period, the inherent uncertainties surrounding the operations of the ECB and the underlying European economic situation will discourage really sizable shifts of either official or private liquid assets into or out of the euro.

In time, a common currency should encourage more competitive, flexible, and liquid financial markets. So, all other things being equal, the euro might indeed come to be considered more on a parity with the dollar as a reserve and trading currency and thereby tend to appreciate. But so much depends upon those "other things." Will internal stresses, sluggish growth, aging populations, and the cost of social programs lead to persistent European fiscal deficits and raise doubts about the priority to be given for price stability? Or will broader markets, needed economic restructuring, and enhanced competitiveness enhance both the stability and attractiveness of the euro?

I don't know the answer to those questions—not at least with any conviction. But we can be pretty sure, judging from the course of human events, that things will not always go smoothly, that doubts (political and economic) will arise not only in Europe but in the United States, in Japan, and elsewhere. We also know for sure that markets will be prone to exaggerating trends and to excesses, moving away from presumed equilibrium for long periods.

It won't surprise you that one issue worth considering is what we should be doing, collectively, to deal with that uncertainty and to enhance stability among currencies and markets. Or, to put the question more broadly, what should we be doing to reinforce the prospect that the creation of the euro, with all its implications, will support rather than undercut international economic cooperation?

The possibility of a regional trading area turning inward at the expense of an open multilateral trading order is an old issue. It was raised with particular force at the beginning of the European Common Market. The potential threat then (and later with NAFTA and other regional arrangements) has happily never really materialized. For the time being, at least, those regional arrangements have not held back the strong tide of worldwide liberalization under the auspices of GATT or otherwise. A persuasive case can be made that on balance they have helped prepare the way for broader liberalization.

In a direct sense, a successful euro will reduce instability of exchange rates and the volatility of international financial markets. It will do so by eliminating a number of important currencies. That is a central purpose.

The question that remains is whether the creation of the euro—successful in its intra-European objective—will also tend to stabilize trans-Atlantic and trans-Pacific exchange rates and capital flows.

One possibility is that with two such large and relatively stable economic masses—the United States and the EU—facing off, their currencies should move in a relatively narrow margin vis-à-vis each other. Presumably relative competitive positions and price levels should change rather slowly and relatively predictably. Similarly, small and gradual changes in equilibrium exchange rate values would be appropriate. With firm expectations about equilibrium exchange rates, cyclical fluctuations in interest rates could be accommodated by relatively small adjustments in spot and forward exchange rates.

That's a nice textbook picture. But I wonder whether it will have much more correspondence with reality than many of the theoretical expositions of how floating exchange rates might work from back in the early 1970s. The closest test case we have had is not reassuring: The exchange rate between the two largest world economies today—the dollar-yen rate—has been notoriously unstable.

Presumably, the new ECB, and the European fiscal authorities, faced with difficult internal challenges and tension, will be at least as insouciant about the euro external exchange rate as has been recurrently the case in the United States. Certainly, trade external to EMU itself will be, if not de minimus, less important.

If markets sensed that governments and central banks were neglectful, benignly or otherwise, of the desirability of exchange rate stability, huge amounts of capital could be easily mobilized to ride a trend. And it may be even more difficult than now to find a forum and a focus for international decision making and to achieve a political consensus.

So far as domestic monetary policy is concerned, the Group of Seven apparatus will effectively be shrunk to three—with authority largely independent of ministries of finance. It is not transparently clear that that will ease coordination in pursuit of international objectives, particularly when these central banks have not been ceded formal authority over exchange rates.

What is clear is that, in Europe at least, there will not be a central fiscal authority to act as a counterpart to the central bank, making coordinated decision making more difficult. Given the size of the major currency zones, I suspect the influence of some authority purporting to represent the wider international community—in a word, the IMF—may be weakened rather than enhanced. The now chronic political difficulty of managing fiscal policy at all flexibly even for evident domestic priorities may well be reinforced.

We can take comfort, I suppose, in the thought that even if concerns about the instability in the dollar-euro-yen exchange rates are borne out, we will be better off than with a multiplicity of European currencies. Perhaps so, if we look at the exchange rate system in isolation. But the situation would hardly be ideal, and looming in the background is the possibility that events will tend to insulate and isolate the three main currency blocs, at the very least dampening enthusiasm for further liberalization or leveling the playing field for trade, investment, and services.

My hope from all this is that those three poles of economic and financial power—Europe, the United States, and Japan—will find it in their mutual interest to work more closely together, and with the IMF, in determining and defending a range of equilibrium exchange rates. That I well know is not—for the time being at least—a popular idea. But I've now lived long enough to have learned one thing: intellectual fashions change, just as they do in other areas of life. I'd like to think that the creation of the euro, with all its profound implications and promise for European political and economic life, could become the impetus for renewed thinking on the international front.

Perhaps that only shows that advancing age is no inhibition on dreams. But after all, the idea of a common European currency germinated almost 20 years ago in dreams of some farsighted leaders that seemed to most unrealistic. I'd rather start the intellectual process now than wait for the crisis and conflict that, if not inevitable, are all too possible.

Session IV
Euro Financial Markets and the International Financial System

11

EMU and International Capital Markets: Structural Implications and Risks

Alessandro Prati and Garry J. Schinasi

If the process of European monetary integration remains on schedule, January 1, 1999 will see the beginning of the union of currencies of economically and financially diverse European countries. Regardless of the precise number of countries that initially join, a European EMU of any size will pose challenges, opportunities, and risks for both private and official participants in European and international financial markets. Although the introduction of the euro is a significant step toward European financial integration, it is by itself only one step in a long process. Previous steps have included, in the area of monetary and exchange rate policy, the creation of the EMS with the ERM, and the Basle/Nyborg agreement; and in the area of financial integration, the adoption and ongoing implementation of the EU Second Banking, Capital Adequacy, Investment Services, and other financial directives.

Even with these important initiatives, European financial markets have tended to remain segmented, with banks retaining their strongholds in providing retail banking services, and with markets for debt and equity securities retaining distinctly national orientations. Hence, the achievement of the full potential financial market benefits of EMU is not assured. Much remains to be accomplished by market participants, by national authorities, and at the EU level to capture the efficiency gains of the envisioned single European financial market. Whether the introduction of the euro becomes a catalyst for change and finally creates the "critical mass" necessary to begin the completion of the financial integration process remains to be seen. What is clear is that

The authors are grateful to David Folkerts-Landau for providing direction. They would like to thank Marcel Cassard, Peter Christoffersen, Flemming Larsen, Paul Masson, Donogh McDonald, Todd Smith, and Charles Thomas for helpful comments on an earlier draft. Subramanian S. Sriram and Scott Anderson provided research assistance.

the establishment of EMU provides the opportunity to dismantle the barriers between the now segmented European markets for bank deposits and loans, securities, and payments and other financial services, and the opportunity for creating capital markets that rival the size, efficiency, and international importance of the U.S. markets.

The purpose of this paper is to survey the potential structural implications of EMU for European and international capital markets and to identify unresolved issues. Much is still unknown about key decisions and how market participants will react to them, and so the paper is necessarily conjectural. However, it attempts to identify outcomes conditional on the changes in incentives brought about by the introduction of the euro and EMU. Because the paper covers many areas, it might be useful to summarize its main themes and observations.

Regarding *financial intermediation*, the introduction of the euro is likely to encourage the further securitization of European finance, and it opens up possibilities for increased market integration, greater uniformity in market practices, and more transparency in pricing. How far these processes will evolve depends on the degree of cross-border competition and, perhaps more important, on EMU financial policies. Particularly important will be the evolving design and implementation of monetary policy operating procedures and whether they will be used to encourage or discourage the development of deep and liquid EMU-wide euro securities markets.

In *European banking systems*, although restructuring through consolidation has occurred at the wholesale level, where global competition reigns, there is room for significant further consolidation at the retail level, where competitive pressures have been resisted. The main problem is that Europe is overbanked, with relatively inefficient local financial intermediaries. The euro is likely to enhance cross-border competition and encourage greater operational efficiency, and thereby provide additional pressures for consolidation. Although there are private mechanisms through which consolidation can occur, important barriers might prevent the necessary adjustments from occurring and create the need for public support of inefficient retail banking systems.

In the *international monetary system*, the euro is likely to surpass existing EU currencies combined as both a reserve currency and a currency of denomination for international financial transactions. As markets sort out this new currency, there is likely to be a rebalancing of official and private portfolios and shifts in the pattern of international capital flows. This rebalancing is likely to have a noticeable impact in global foreign exchange markets and in the major domestic financial markets worldwide. Changes in private portfolios and capital flows will reflect changing assessments by international institutional investors seeking various risk-return profiles in an unfamiliar tripolar global financial market. Whether this implies a weak or a strong euro will depend on perceptions about the European authorities' ability to achieve fiscal consolidation and structural reforms (including in capital markets and retail banking systems), and about the effectiveness and credibility of EMU monetary and exchange rate policies.

The paper is structured as follows. Before analyzing the main issues, we examine the potential size of the domestic euro capital markets and the role of existing European currencies in international capital markets. We then analyze the structural implications for European and international securities markets, including the role of the ECB and its potential impact on securitization, the possible evolution of EMU markets for repurchase agreements (repos), interbank funds, bonds, equities and derivatives, and two aspects of systemic risk management. Next, we look at the implications for wholesale and retail banking markets, and then examine the broader implications of the introduction of the euro for changes in capital flows and international portfolios.

Potential Size of the Euro Markets

In absolute terms, and compared to any reasonable benchmark, the introduction of the euro has the potential for creating the largest domestic financial market in the world. At end-1995, the *market value of bonds, equities, and bank assets* issued in EU countries amounted to more than \$27 trillion (Table 1), roughly the same order of magnitude as world GDP (94 percent of world GDP). By comparison, the market value of assets in North America—with roughly the same population and GDP as the EU—amounted to about \$25 trillion (\$23 trillion in the United States). Were the initial Union to include only Austria, Belgium, France, Germany, Luxembourg, the Netherlands, Ireland, and Finland (the EU-8), the domestic euro market would equal the size of Japan's domestic market (\$16 trillion); and if the Union included Italy, Portugal, and Spain in addition (EU-11), it would roughly equal the size of the U.S. domestic market. An interesting aside is that the value of bonds, equities, and bank assets is roughly three times the respective GDPs in the EU, the United States, and Japan (about 320 percent in the EU and Japan and about 315 percent in the United States).

EU private entities overwhelmingly have tended to finance their activities through bank loans rather than through bond and equity financing, and U.S. entities have relied more heavily on bond and equity financing. In the EU-11, bank loans comprised 54 percent of all outstanding financial assets at end-1995. By contrast, U.S. bank loans accounted for only 22 percent of total assets outstanding.

In contrast to government securities markets, European private debt securities markets are segmented, with all but the largest firms borrowing solely from a domestic investor base. In the EU-11, for each dollar of bank borrowing, private firms borrowed, on average, only 50 cents through private securi-

Table 1. EU, Japan, and North America: Selected Indicators on the Size of the Capital Markets, 1995

	Population (*In millions*)	GDP	Total Reserves Minus Gold	Stock Market Capitalization	Debt Securities[1] Public	Debt Securities[1] Private	Debt Securities[1] Total	Bank Assets[2]	Bonds, Equities, and Bank Assets[3]	Bonds, Equities, and Bank Assets[3] (*In percent of GDP*)
		(In billions of U.S. dollars)								
EU-15[4]	369.0	8,427.0	376.3	3,778.5	4,814.4	3,858.6	8,673.0	14,818.0	27,269.5[5]	323.60
EU-11[6]	286.1	6,803.9	284.5	2,119.4	3,909.7	3,083.5	6,993.2	11,971.6	21,084.2	309.89
EU-8[7]	181.8	5,054.8	199.2	1,693.8	2,330.4	2,611.0	4,941.4	9,456.0	16,091.2	318.34
North America	387.7	8,065.6	106.7	7,314.7	7,332.2	4,411.9	11,744.1	5,652.4	24,711.1	306.38
Canada	29.6	565.6	15.0	366.3	589.1	93.3	682.4	515.8	1,564.5	276.61
Mexico	94.8	246.2	16.8	90.7	30.7	23.5	54.2	136.6	281.5	114.34
United States	263.3	7,253.8	74.8	6,857.6	6,712.4	4,295.1	11,007.5	5,000.0	22,865.1	315.22
Japan	125.2	5,114.0	183.3	3,667.3	3,450.3	1,875.5	5,325.8	7,382.2	16,375.2	320.21
Memorandum items										
EU countries										
Austria	8.1	233.3	18.7	32.5	105.9	105.4	211.3	457.7	701.6	300.66
Belgium	10.0	269.2	16.2	105.0	305.1	165.3	470.4	734.2	1,309.5	486.45
Denmark	5.2	173.3	11.0	56.2	142.1	187.8	329.9	155.5	541.6	312.55
Finland	5.1	125.0	10.0	44.1	94.0	50.2	144.2	143.5	331.9	265.54
France	57.5	1,537.9	26.9	522.1	681.9	803.6	1,485.5	2,923.0	4,930.5	320.61
Germany	81.7	2,412.5	85.0	577.4	893.6	1,286.0	2,179.6	3,752.4	6,509.3	269.82
Greece	10.5	114.3	14.8	17.1	99.7	5.8	105.5	63.9	186.4	163.06
Ireland	3.6	61.9	8.6	25.8	38.5	7.4	45.9	82.3	154.0	248.63
Italy	56.3	1,087.2	34.9	209.5	1,222.0	396.2	1,618.2	1,513.5	3,341.2	307.33

Luxembourg	0.4	19.3	0.1	30.4	1.0	15.8	16.8	555.0	602.2	3,124.56
Netherlands	15.5	395.7	33.7	356.5	210.4	177.3	387.7	808.0	1,552.2	392.28
Portugal	9.3	102.7	15.9	18.4	56.0	15.8	71.8	161.8	252.0	245.25
Spain	38.7	559.2	34.5	197.8	301.3	60.5	361.8	840.2	1,399.8	250.34
Sweden	8.8	229.2	24.1	178.0	233.0	185.7	418.7	202.8	799.5	348.84
United Kingdom	58.5	1,106.3	42.0	1,407.7	429.9	395.8	825.7	2,424.4	4,657.8	421.01

Sources: Bank for International Settlements; Bank of England, *Quarterly Bulletin* (November 1995); Bank of Japan, *Economic Statistics Monthly* (May 1996); Central Bank of Ireland, *Quarterly Bulletin* (Winter 1995); International Finance Corporation, *Emerging Stock Markets Factbook 1996*; OECD, *Bank Profitability: Financial Statements of Banks, 1985–1994*; and IMF, International Financial Statistics and World Economic Outlook databases.

[1]Domestic and international debt securities shown by the nationality of the issuer.

[2]The 1994 data are shown for all banks except for the following: commercial banks plus savings banks for Denmark; commercial banks for Canada (consolidated worldwide), Greece, Luxembourg, and Mexico; domestically licensed banks for Japan (excluding trust accounts); commercial banks plus savings banks plus cooperative banks for Sweden; and commercial banks plus savings banks plus savings and loan associations for the United States.

[3]Sum of the stock market capitalization, debt securities, and bank assets.

[4]Austria, Belgium, Denmark, Finland, France, Germany, Greece, Ireland, Italy, Luxembourg, the Netherlands, Portugal, Spain, Sweden, and the United Kingdom.

[5]This figure is meant to be a measure of the size of net wealth stored in capital market instruments. It should be considered a proxy and may involve some double counting, as in the case of securities issued by banks. Consolidating the balance sheets of the financial institutions of each country would yield a more precise estimate.

[6]Austria, Belgium, Finland, France, Germany, Ireland, Italy, Luxembourg, the Netherlands, Portugal, and Spain.

[7]Austria, Belgium, Finland, France, Germany, Ireland, Luxembourg, and the Netherlands.

ties issues. By contrast, in the United States, for each dollar of borrowing from banks, U.S. firms borrowed slightly more than two dollars through debt securities issues. Japanese private entities were much closer to their EU, than to their U.S., counterparts.

Although the amount of EU private bonds outstanding appears to be sizable enough to suggest a reasonably large market for corporate bonds (roughly three-fourths the size of the U.S. market), the bulk of these bonds were issued by European financial institutions. Looking at this from the side of corporate balance sheets, as of end-1994, bonds accounted for a relatively small share of the total liabilities of nonfinancial firms in France (5.7 percent) and in Germany (less than 1 percent); by contrast, they accounted for 18.8 percent of the total liabilities of U.S. nonfinancial firms.[1] The low share of debt financing by European companies extends to the short end of the maturity spectrum as well, because European companies tend to rely on bank financing for short-term funds. U.S. corporate entities tend to rely more heavily on short-term financing because of their access to the very liquid and highly developed commercial paper market, which accounts for more than half of the world's outstanding commercial paper. These observations about the use of debt securities underscore the greater historical reliance by firms in the United States on direct intermediation through the corporate debt securities markets, the heavy reliance in Europe on bank financing, and the relatively undeveloped European corporate securities markets.

Another way of assessing the potential importance of the euro from a purely quantitative perspective is to examine the use of existing European currencies as currencies of denomination in *international financial transactions*. In international bond markets, 35 percent of the outstanding stock of international debt securities were denominated in EU currencies at end-September 1996 (Table 2). Although this is a substantial share of international issues outstanding, and is a close second to the amount of dollar international issues outstanding, EU countries themselves issued more than 45 percent of all international bonds outstanding. In addition, in the five-year period ending in December 1995, only a minor share of developing country debt was issued internationally in EU currencies.

Still another way to gauge the potential role of the euro is to examine daily turnover in the global *foreign exchange markets*. According to the most recent BIS survey, as of April 1995 the dollar was involved in at least one side of a transaction about 42 percent of the time, the deutsche mark 18.5 percent, the yen 12 percent, and the pound sterling 5 percent. EMS currencies combined were involved in at least one side of a transaction about 35 percent of the time, including European cross-currency trading

[1]OECD and Deutsche Bundesbank.

Table 2. Amounts Outstanding of International Debt Securities by Currency, September 1996[1]

(In billions of U.S. dollars)

	Amounts Outstanding
By currency	
U.S. dollar	1,139.0
Japanese yen	520.8
Currencies of EU countries[2]	1,056.3
Other[3]	346.1
Total	3,062.1
By country of nationality	
EU countries	1,406.1
Austria	66.2
Belgium	44.8
Denmark	33.2
Finland	54.6
France	217.2
Germany	322.8
Greece	21.0
Ireland	16.6
Italy	94.6
Luxembourg	9.7
Netherlands	116.4
Portugal	12.9
Spain	38.4
Sweden	119.3
United Kingdom	238.4
North America	571.2
Canada	178.1
Mexico	44.0
United States	349.1
Japan	360.4
Others	724.4
All countries	3,062.1

Source: BIS (1996b).

[1]Euronotes and international bonds.

[2]Currencies of Austria, Belgium, Denmark, Finland, France, Germany, Ireland, Italy, Luxembourg, the Netherlands, Portugal, Spain, Sweden, and the United Kingdom; plus ECU.

[3]Currencies of Australia, Canada, Hong Kong, New Zealand, Norway, and Switzerland; plus other currencies.

Table 3. Use of Selected Currencies on One Side of the Transaction, April 1989, April 1992, and April 1995[1]

(As percentage of global gross foreign exchange market turnover)

Currency	April 1989	April 1992	April 1995
U.S. dollar	90	82	83
Deutsche mark[2]	27	40	37
Japanese yen	27	23	24
Pound sterling	15	14	10
French franc	2	4	8
Swiss franc	10	9	7
Canadian dollar	1	3	3
Australian dollar	2	2	3
ECU	1	3	2
Other EMS currencies	3	9	13
Currencies of other reporting countries	3	3	2
Other currencies	19	8	8
All currencies	200	200	200
Memorandum item			
EMS currencies including ECU	48	70	70

Source: BIS (1996b).

[1]Number of reporting countries are 21 in 1989 and 26 in 1992 and 1995. Data for 1989 and data for Finland in 1992 include options and futures. Data for 1989 cover local currency trading only, except for the U.S. dollar, deutsche mark, Japanese yen, pound sterling, Swiss franc, and ECU. The figures related to gross turnover because comparable data on a "net-gross" or "net-net" basis are not available for 1989.

[2]Data for April 1989 exclude domestic trading involving the deutsche mark in Germany.

(Table 3). In related derivative markets, the dollar, EU currencies, and the yen accounted for shares of trading that are roughly equivalent to the relative sizes of their economies (in terms of GDP), but most of this activity actually involved U.S. and U.K. financial institutions. Transactions involving currency swaps were clearly tilted toward the dollar, reflecting its now dominant position in international finance and as a reserve currency (Table 4).

In summary, although the EU currencies command a significant share of activity in international financial markets, they do not now command shares in line with either the size of the EU economy or the relative size of their domestic financial markets.

Structural Implications for European and International Capital Markets

Incentives for Further Market Integration and Development

Driven by financial deregulation, changing opportunities for investment, and bank disintermediation, European securities markets have become more

Table 4. Notional Principal Value of Outstanding and New Interest Rate and Currency Swaps, 1995

(In billions of U.S. dollars)

	Amounts	New Swaps
Interest rate swaps	12,810.7	8,698.8
U.S. dollar	4,371.7	2,856.5
Japanese yen	2,895.9	2,259.3
Currencies of EU countries[1]	4,620.9	3,160.9
Of which:		
Deutsche mark	1,438.9	984.5
French franc	1,219.9	1,113.5
Italian lira	405.4	217.3
Netherlands guilder	101.8	62.3
Pound sterling	854.0	433.4
Spanish peseta	163.7	91.9
ECU	223.1	96.4
Other	922.4	422.1
Of which:		
Swiss franc	331.7	159.2
Currency swaps[2]	2,394.8	910.2
U.S. dollar	837.8	307.9
Japanese yen	400.0	164.5
Currencies of EU countries[1]	684.7	248.1
Of which:		
Deutsche mark	238.0	78.1
French franc	81.4	41.6
Italian lira	72.6	18.5
Netherlands guilder	28.1	13.0
Pound sterling	91.5	23.4
Spanish peseta	83.0	28.2
ECU	472.3	189.8
Other		
Of which:		
Swiss franc	150.6	29.7

Source: BIS (1996b).

[1]Includes the currencies of Belgium, Denmark, France, Germany, Italy, the Netherlands, Spain, Sweden, and the United Kingdom; plus ECU.

[2]Not adjusted for reporting on both sides.

highly integrated and liquid. These changes have been associated with the placement of large sovereign debt issues, which provided strong incentives to develop liquid and efficient secondary bond markets, and with the accumulation of large stocks of public debt, which raised yields on government securities, thereby making them an attractive alternative to bank deposits. Facilitated by the recent convergence of macroeconomic policies, greater capital mobility has contributed to market integration by linking national securities markets, reducing bond spreads, and increasing co-movements in bond and equity returns across EU countries.[2]

Against the background of these ongoing structural changes, the introduction of the euro will alter incentives to encourage the further *securitization*[3] of European finance, greater uniformity in market practices, more transparency of pricing, and increased market integration.[4] *First*, by eliminating currencies, the introduction of the euro reduces the direct cost of spot transactions and eliminates a relatively volatile element of market risk—foreign exchange risk—in longer-dated real and financial contracts between entities in EMU member countries. While foreign exchange risk between some ERM currencies may have diminished recently (as measured by implied volatilities, for example), the costs incurred by market participants—including central banks—during the violent disruptions in the ERM crisis in 1992–93 will long be remembered, as will the frequent realignments, often preceded by speculative attacks, in the early years of the EMS and in the less formal exchange rate arrangements before the EMS.

Second, the elimination of currency risk increases the relative importance of other elements of risk, including credit, liquidity, settlement, legal, and event risks. Credit risk is likely to be the most important component of securities pricing within EMU, with the implication being that the "relative value" of underlying credits rather than judgments about the stability and volatility of currency values will drive securities prices.

Increased attention will be paid to other elements of risk. Bond issues of two otherwise identical credit risks—say, a German company and a French one producing the same goods and having similar balance sheets—may be priced differently if issuing techniques, clearing and settlement procedures, and legal procedures are different in the respective countries. The impact of these remaining and less volatile components of risk on the cost of raising

---

[2]See Artis and Taylor (1990), Eijffinger and Lemmen (1995), and Frankel, Phillips, and Chinn (1993).

[3] Securitization refers to the creation of any credit, ownership, or derivative claims that are publicly tradable, either in organized exchanges or over-the-counter, and whose prices are determined at frequent intervals in an open market. The popular press has used this term, almost exclusively, to describe *asset-backed securities* (the creation of high-quality negotiable, liquid securities that are funded by setting aside illiquid claims, such as mortgage obligations, consumer receivables, and other classes of assets).

[4]Even without the euro, full implementation of the EU Investment Services Directive (ISD), which creates a single passport for securities firms (brokers and dealers), portfolio managers, and investment advisories, would provide renewed stimulus for the creation of an EU single market in financial services. The euro is likely to enhance the impact of the ISD.

funds will provide incentives to suppliers of securities to narrow further their interest rate spreads by increasing transparency and by improving issuing techniques and financial infrastructures to attract investors. This competitive process, if allowed to run its course, could lead to sufficient harmonization of market practices within the euro zone to eliminate the advantages a particular geographical market may now have. In this way, the elimination of currency risk could lead to greater uniformity and transparency of market practices, with the benefits of more uniform pricing and a breakdown of market segments within Europe.

The elimination of currency risk, the convergence of credit spreads, and more uniformity in market practices together can be expected to increase the depth and liquidity of European securities markets. In short-term markets (money, swap, and short-term treasury bill markets, for example), contracts denominated in individual currencies will be denominated in euros and could be traded across national markets, even if small credit spreads remain. For securities with multiple exchange listings, competition among exchanges could lead to a consolidation of trading in a single location. Even in markets that remain somewhat segmented (because of higher credit spreads or restrictions), lower transaction costs (elimination of commissions on foreign exchange transactions and of the costs of hedging exchange rate risk) and the elimination of trading restrictions (for example, on institutional investors) will add liquidity. Moreover, competition among issuers—no longer based on the strength of the currency—will encourage sovereign borrowers to introduce market reforms.

Third, the euro will directly reduce the number of existing barriers to cross-border investment and eliminate some restrictions on currency exposures of various pools of capital (pension funds, insurance companies, other asset managers). To begin with, all intra-EMU foreign exchange restrictions on the investments of pension funds will become irrelevant within the EMU area. The EU matching rule (liabilities in a foreign currency must be 80 percent matched by assets in that same currency) for insurance companies—which has been extended to pension funds in some countries—will also cease to be binding within EMU, as insurance companies will be able to invest their assets in any country of the euro area as long as their liabilities are denominated in euros. The size and country diversification of assets managed by institutional investors in the EU, say, mutual funds—still far smaller than in the United States—could rapidly increase together with their share of foreign investments (Table 5). Finally, the "anchoring" principle, restricting lead managers of issues to full subsidiaries domiciled in the issuing country, will become irrelevant and will thereby increase the potential for intra-EMU market penetration.

Fourth, the possibilities for portfolio diversification will change. The advantages of currency diversification will be lost to the extent that business cycles have been asynchronous and shocks asymmetric. This will encourage in-

Table 5. Mutual Funds, June 1996

	Equity	Bond	Money Market	Total
Net assets (in billions of U.S. dollars)				
EU[1,2]	366.74	533.94	496.32	1,396.99
United States	1,532.46	741.78	817.75	3,091.99
Japan	119.12	189.39	102.22	410.73
Number of funds (in numbers)[3]				
EU[1,2]	7,136	4,436	1,912	13,484
United States	2,611	2,390	995	5,996
Japan	4,118	2,060	15	6,193

Source: Investment Company Institute.
[1]Does not include Ireland and the Netherlands for the equity and bond funds.
[2]Does not include Austria, Denmark, Ireland, and the Netherlands for the money market funds.
[3]The equity funds also include balanced funds and "other" funds.

vestors and financial institutions to search for, and find, new opportunities for portfolio diversification within EMU repo, government securities, and corporate securities markets, but it may also encourage them to seek diversification outside the euro area as well.

European securities markets will also be shaped by other important factors. Technological progress will soon make fully integrated EU-wide securities and derivative markets unavoidable, by making the location of trading, clearing, and settlement largely irrelevant. Continued fiscal consolidation—as part of the Stability and Growth Pact—is likely to reduce the volume of new government bond issues, providing room for private entities to issue new equity shares and debt securities. Finally, as the role of the unfunded social security system might diminish, the role of institutional investors, like insurance companies and private pension funds, will increase the demand for public and private paper of various maturities and types, perhaps including corporate bonds.

Overall, the introduction of the euro could become an important catalyst in the development of securities markets because it may enhance the impact of EU financial directives, increase transparency in credit evaluation, accelerate the processes of financial market integration, and further expand Europe's institutional investor base.

EMU-Wide Repo and Interbank Markets

Monetary Policy Operating Procedures and Securitization

Whether or not these incentives lead to the development of deep and liquid short-term securities markets will depend, in part, on demand and supply factors and the extent of cross-border competition between financial intermediaries, both within and outside EMU. Also important are the financial policy choices by EMU member countries, as there are remaining legislative, regulatory, and tax impediments to cross-border investment and, therefore, to the development of EMU-wide markets. Potentially greater in importance are the institutional arrangements for the implementation of monetary policy and, more generally, financial policy.

Historically, the nature and development of private money markets has had an important bearing on the development of domestic securities markets.[5] In the highly liquid and securitized markets in the United States, for example, the central bank traditionally has played an active role in the markets by intervening daily. The objectives of this active participation are to smooth out fluctuations in liquidity during the day and to provide stability to the pattern of interest rates on overnight funds. Financial institutions have come to expect this active participation, and the structure of financial activities and balance sheets reflects this mode of central bank operations. This active participation has fostered the development of efficient money and securities markets in the United States.[6]

The European models for conducting monetary and financial policies, and in particular the German model, rely extensively on minimum reserve requirements, reserve averaging, and infrequent (biweekly) market interventions to smooth liquidity in the banking system and to provide stability to the pattern of interest rates. The reliance on reserve requirements, the preference for infrequent market interventions, and the "narrow" concept[7] of central banking adopted by some European central banks has tended to discourage the development of private securities markets and to foster the predominance of bank-intermediated finance.

---

[5]See Folkerts-Landau and Garber (1992).

[6]There are other reasons for this active participation, including the mandate to ensure the smooth functioning and stability of financial markets. The functions of the U.S. Federal Reserve System were expressed by Chairman Volcker in 1983: "A basic continuing responsibility of any central bank—and the principal reason for the founding of the Federal Reserve—is to assure stable and smoothly functioning financial and payments systems. These are prerequisites for, and complementary to, the central bank's responsibility for conducting monetary policy as it is more narrowly conceived. To these ends, the U.S. Congress has over the last 70 years authorized the Federal Reserve (1) to be a major participant in the nation's payments mechanism; (2) to lend at the discount window as the ultimate source of liquidity for the economy; and (3) to regulate and supervise key sectors of the financial markets, both domestic and international. These functions are in addition to, and largely predate, the more purely "monetary" functions of engaging in open market and foreign exchange operations and setting reserve requirements; historically, in fact, the "monetary" functions were largely grafted onto the "supervisory" functions, not the reverse." See Volcker (1984).

[7]"Narrow" in the sense that price stability is the overriding objective, and that banking supervision, financial market surveillance, and management of systemic risks in the payments system are secondary, or are not, functions of central banking. See Folkerts-Landau and Garber (1992).

At this point in the process of establishing the institutional structure of the ESCB, it is uncertain which paradigm will prevail over the next few years. According to Article 105 (1) of the Maastricht Treaty, "the primary objective of the ESCB shall be to maintain price stability," and the Treaty does not explicitly envisage an active role for the ECB in ensuring the smooth functioning of the financial system.[8] Although final decisions have not been made, the current plan for monetary policy operating procedures is to rely on a system of minimum reserve requirements, with reserve averaging, and to have infrequent (biweekly) and decentralized repo operations, and decentralized fine-tuning operations. The national central banks will collect repo bids from local markets, send them to a central computer in Frankfurt, and allocate the repo transactions according to instructions from the ECB once all the bids are collected and the market price determined.[9] Although the ECB has the authority to intervene more frequently and to issue its own paper, it remains to be seen how it will adapt to market pressure that will require more frequent interventions.

Two related policy uncertainties—involving the TARGET payments system and supervisory and lender-of-last-resort functions—will be discussed in the subsection on systematic risk management, following the discussion of the potential impact of the euro on European repo, money, bond, equity, and derivative markets, to which the paper now turns.

Repurchase Agreements and Money Markets

The decision that the ECB will use repurchase agreements as the main instrument for implementing monetary policy could give an incentive for the development of an EMU-wide market for repurchase agreements (repo markets). Although private repo markets currently exist in some countries, except for a few exceptions they are not highly developed and lack the liquidity and depth of the repo markets in the United States.

In the United States, repo markets are an important alternative money market instrument. By providing ready access to *secured* borrowing, and by enhancing liquidity in the securities markets, repos facilitate portfolio financing and the ability to short the market. Banks also can use repurchase agreements for extending credits to securities dealers collateralized by a zero-risk-weighted central government bond. In Europe, only France has a transparent

[8]The Treaty empowers the ESCB to promote the smooth operation of payment systems, but the treaty only empowers the ECB to "*contribute* to the smooth conduct of policies pursued by the competent authorities relating to the prudential supervision of credit institutions and the stability of the financial system" (emphasis added).

[9]See European Monetary Institute (1997).

and liquid repo market, with 20 primary dealers being required to post prices on Reuters. The United Kingdom recently introduced a gilt repo market, while other countries, notably Germany, have discouraged them until the end of 1996 by subjecting repo transactions with nonbanks to reserve requirements, with the result that a large share of the German repo business migrated to London. In Italy, legal, taxation, and settlement obstacles have prevented the development of a liquid repo market.

An open question is whether the different market structures characterizing the interbank markets in each member country will survive or whether market pressures—acting through price differentials—will lead to a single EMU-wide interbank market. Integration has already increased somewhat, with growing shares of foreign interbank deposits and smaller discrepancies between interest rates on euro and domestic markets (Table 6). On short maturity transactions, especially shorter than one month, interest-rate arbitrage is still imperfect, in part because of differences in taxation and regulation. With the euro, the elimination of European cross-currency risk, the establishment of ECB repo operations, and the provision of intraday liquidity for settlement purposes, there would be few, if any, impediments preventing first-, second-, and third-tier European banks from dealing directly with each other for supplying or accessing overnight funds. This overnight borrowing and lending

Table 6. EU: Cross-Border Interbank Assets, 1992–96

(In percent of GDP)

	1992	1993	1994	1995	1996
EU countries					
Austria	17.71	16.72	17.77	17.89	21.16
Belgium	56.01	60.33	59.20	58.29	58.03
France	17.81	18.22	20.12	18.80	18.51
Germany	8.60	10.21	12.64	13.08	12.67
Ireland	26.26	35.66	38.82	50.80	55.90
Italy	15.81	17.74	18.22	16.71	16.25
Luxembourg	914.54	921.38	937.81	908.43	840.15
Netherlands	26.45	26.54	27.39	27.04	31.24
Portugal	7.63	13.50	20.36	22.17	20.75
Spain	7.38	9.14	10.85	9.61	10.24
United Kingdom	58.14	74.71	74.59	81.59	79.99
Memorandum items					
North America					
Canada	8.27	9.27	10.10	9.92	10.41
Mexico	6.07	5.07	6.57	7.88	6.18
United States	9.36	8.96	9.49	9.65	8.89
Japan	16.97	13.85	13.49	12.78	12.67

Sources: BIS; and IMF, World Economic Outlook.

could quickly lead to the creation of an efficient EMU-wide interbank market with total volumes at least equal to the sum of those of current domestic interbank markets. In this scenario, domestic interbank rates would be harmonized across EMU with residual differences reflecting only different credit standings of second- or third-tier banks.

It is a possible next step, although by no means certain, for a private repo market to develop in all EMU countries, in which a private yield curve will offer instruments ranging in maturity from overnight to long-term contracts. In such a market, financial and nonfinancial entities alike can engage in short-term collateralized refinancing operations for conducting day-to-day treasury operations in supporting their real economic activities. Many European multinationals now conduct such refinancing in New York, London, Tokyo, and other international financial centers.

With the development of an EMU repo market, collateralized borrowing and lending will enable financial institutions to refinance their operations at interest rates below those in the interbank market. The development of this Europe-wide market could help set the tone for the development of other capital markets in Europe. It would also open up opportunities for large global financial institutions to participate more fully and actively in short-term EMU markets for liquidity management, in much the same way as they participate in the markets in New York and London. European capital markets would benefit significantly from the participation of these large global players in terms of added depth, liquidity, and efficiency to European capital markets.

Possible remaining impediments to the establishment of EMU-wide repo markets would be reserve requirements on repo operations (remunerated at below-market interest), other longstanding legal and settlement obstacles, and elements of tax systems. In addition, interest rates in the repo market might not become fully uniform across Europe if different margins ("haircuts") are applied to Tier 1 and Tier 2[10] collateral for repurchase transactions with the ECB. Alternatively, if the ECB does not discriminate between the quality of collateral, the distinction between issuers at the short end of the curve may become blurred and lead to a "race to the bottom" in quality in providing collateral.

New Focus on Credit Risk in EMU Bond Markets

Government Bond Market

By eliminating currency risk on European cross-country transactions, and by directly reducing transactions costs, the introduction of the euro reduces the

[10]Tier 1 includes assets that fulfill eligibility criteria specified by the ECB for the whole euro area; Tier 2 includes other assets that EMU national central banks may consider eligible in accordance with ECB guidelines.

cost of issuing and investing in government securities. The increased transparency of costs and benefits is likely to influence both demand and supply and to provide strong incentives for the harmonization of market practices—auctioning techniques, issue calendars, the maturity spectrum—toward the most transparent and cost-effective practices for both issuers and investors. As investors and issuers become familiar with these transactions and investors search throughout EMU sovereign markets for their preferred risk-return profiles among the sovereign issuers in the union, it is reasonable to expect market segmentation to diminish. EMU member governments can therefore no longer take for granted their "home-currency" market, and will try to appeal to a broader investor base. Whether or not this harmonization of market practices and market desegmentation occurs in full, market participants who in the past focused on the relatively volatile currency risk will now focus attention on the other less volatile risks, including credit (sovereign), liquidity, settlement, legal, and event risks.

The refocus on credit risk by both issuers and investors is likely to increase cross-border competition between financial intermediaries for bringing new issues to market, for "rating" new credits, and for allocating investment funds across the national markets. Competition is likely to involve non-European as well as European financial institutions and asset managers. Financial intermediaries from the United States—where investment houses and institutional investors have, respectively, specialized on the issuer and investor sides of these markets for decades—would appear to have a comparative and competitive advantage in supplying many of these services against all but the largest European financial intermediaries. Thus, the establishment of EMU is likely to contribute to the restructuring of the global business of investment banking and universal banking.

How far market desegmentation will go and how liquid the European sovereign debt market becomes will depend on how credit risks are priced. Several potential EMU member countries enjoy top ratings on debt denominated in domestic currencies and lower ratings on debt denominated in foreign currency (Table 7). There are several reasons for these differences. First, foreign currency debt cannot be repaid by printing domestic money and it has, therefore, higher default probabilities associated with it. Second, debt issued in domestic currency is mostly locally held, so that governments, for political reasons, are more likely to continue to service domestic debt. Third, governments may find it easier to raise taxes or cut expenditures to repay domestic debt than to repay foreign investors. If these considerations are valid for euro-denominated debt issued by future EMU members, then interest rate spreads, and in particular credit spreads, could change to become more in line with those currently observed on the foreign currency–denominated debt of these countries. This could amount to a downgrading of asset quality for those

Table 7. Ratings of Foreign and Local Currency Debt of Sovereign Governments, April 21, 1997

	Foreign Currency						Local Currency		
	IBCA		S & P		Moody's		IBCA	S & P	Moody's
	Long-term	Short-term	Long-term	Short-term	Long-term	Short-term	Long-term	Long-term	Long-term
EU countries									
Austria	AAA	A1+	AAA	A-1+	Aaa	P-1	AAA	AAA	—
Belgium	AA+	A1+	AA+	A-1+	Aa1	P-1	AAA	AAA	—
Denmark	AA+	A1+	AA+	A-1+	Aa1	P-1	AAA	AAA	Aa1
Finland	AA	A1+	AA	A-1+	Aa1	P-1	AAA	AAA	Aaa
France	AAA	A1+	AAA	A-1+	Aaa	P-1	AAA	AAA	Aaa
Germany	AAA	A1+	AAA	A-1+	Aaa	P-1	AAA	AAA	Aaa
Greece	BBB–	A3	BBB–	A-3	Baa1	P-2	—	A–	—
Ireland	AA+	A1+	AA	A-1+	Aa1	P-1	AAA	AAA	Aaa
Italy	AA–	A1+	AA	A-1+	Aa3	P-1	AAA	AAA	Aa3
Luxembourg	AAA	A1+	AAA	A-1+	Aaa	P-1	AAA	AAA	—
Netherlands	AAA	A1+	AAA	A-1+	Aaa	P-1	AAA	AAA	Aaa
Portugal	AA–	A1+	AA–	A-1+	Aa3	P-1	AAA	AAA	Aa2
Spain	AA	A1+	AA	A-1+	Aa2	P-1	AAA	AAA	Aa2
Sweden	AA–	A1+	AA+	A-1+	Aa3	P-1	AAA	AAA	—
United Kingdom	AAA	A1+	AAA	A-1+	Aaa	P-1	AAA	AAA	Aaa
Memorandum items									
North America									
Canada	AA	A1+	AA+	A-1+	Aa2	P-1	AAA	AAA	Aa1
Mexico	BB	B	BB	A-2	Ba2	NP	—	BBB+	—
United States	AAA	A1+	AAA	A-1+	Aaa	P-1	AAA	AAA	Aaa
Japan	AAA	A1+	AAA	A-1+	Aaa	P-1	AAA	AAA	Aaa

Sources: Bloomberg Financial Markets; IBCA Ltd.; Moody's Investors Service; and Standard & Poor's.

Table 8. EU Countries, North America, and Japan: Foreign Currency Debt, 1996

(In percent of total government debt)

Country	Foreign Currency Debt	Year[1]
EU countries		
Austria	21.70	1995
Belgium	11.40	1995
Denmark	15.10	1995
Finland	54.80	1995
France	1.79	1995
Germany	0.01	1995
Greece	39.20	1995[2]
Ireland	35.00	1995
Italy	12.90	1996
Luxembourg	3.50	1995
Netherlands	0.00	1996
Portugal	18.00	1996[3]
Spain	7.30	1996
Sweden	28.60	1996[4]
United Kingdom	5.30	1995
North America		
Canada	4.00	1996[5]
Mexico	89.00	1996
United States	0.00	1996
Japan	0.00	1996

Source: IMF staff, country desks.
[1]The years for which the latest data are available.
[2]Preliminary data.
[3]Data as of October 1996.
[4]Data as of September 30, 1996.
[5]Data as of March 31, 1996.

countries.[11] If EMU members redenominated all outstanding debt into euros, the share of foreign currency debt would increase from current levels to 100 percent (Table 8). In this scenario spreads could increase above those observed on the relatively small stocks of foreign currency debt presently outstanding.[12] Counteracting some of this pressure for spreads to rise would be the improved fiscal positions of several countries to meet the Maastricht criteria and the stability pact.

[11]Standard & Poor's has already indicated that it will initially award each country's euro-denominated debt the rating currently applied to foreign currency–denominated debt and that European companies will be able to obtain ratings higher than those of their own governments. Moody's will adopt a case-by-case approach.

[12]See Drudi and Prati (1997).

There are other factors that would influence credit spreads. Although the "no-bailout" clause in the Maastricht Treaty rules out the possibility of direct EU assistance to individual EMU member countries, it is unlikely that market participants would price sovereign debt as if it were corporate debt.[13] The mere size of public debt outstanding in any potential EMU member country relative to any single corporate issuer would imply significant systemic implications of an involuntary restructuring or an outright default by an EMU member country. This would increase the pressure to find alternative solutions. One possible mechanism for dealing with fis-cal problems when they arise is to provide EU financial assistance conditional on implementation of a macroeconomic stabilization plan. In addition, strict enforcement of the stability pact would reduce the "free-rider" problem of governments running fiscally irresponsible policies from time to time.

Pricing Credit Risk. From a pricing perspective, credit risk will become the most important risk and will make up the largest part of the remaining interest rate spreads among EMU issuers after the introduction of the euro. Unfortunately, there is no unambiguous guide to the likely levels or dispersion of sovereign credit spreads in EMU. One way of estimating credit spreads is to compare interest rates on sovereign debt issues that trade in a common currency. Among the potential EMU member countries that have issued dollar-denominated debt, as of end-1996, spreads between 10-year dollar issues trading in domestic markets and comparable U.S. treasury issues ranged from a low of 24 basis points for Austria to a high of 34 basis points for Italy (Table 9).[14] Spreads on five-year issues ranged between a low of 10 basis points for Austria and a high of 22 basis points for Italy. Although it is difficult to assess whether these spreads are "high" or "low," it would appear that they are probably reflecting a good deal of market optimism about the prospects for a successful EMU and about the adjustments made in some countries.

Another rough benchmark of credit spreads is the pricing of debt issued by the separate legal entities making up the separate states of the United States and of the provinces of Canada. In the case of the United States, a sample of municipal bond traders collected over the period 1973–1990 indicates that the largest spread during the 28-year period was 146 basis points; the mean of the

[13]The "no-bailout" clause—Article 104b of the Maastricht Treaty—states that "the Community shall not be liable for or assume the commitments of central governments, regional, local, or other public authorities, other bodies governed by public law, or public undertakings of any Member State, without prejudice to mutual financial guarantees for the joint execution of a specific project." The same provision applies to individual member states.

[14]One problem with using this method for estimating credit spreads is that the spreads may also reflect the market's assessment of other factors, including liquidity, tax differences, name recognition, and investor preferences.

Table 9. Estimates of Credit Spreads for EU Sovereigns, September 11, 1996

(In basis points)

	2-year	5-year	10-year
Austrian schilling	+1	+10	+24
Belgian franc	+3	+15	+28
Danish krone	+3	+13	+27
Finnish markka	+4	+16	+30
Irish pound	+3	+11	+25
Italian lira	+8	+22	+34
Spanish peseta	+6	+19	+32
Swedish krona	+6	+17	+27

Source: Paribas Capital Markets (1996), Table 5.

spread was 32.4 basis points, with a standard deviation of 24.8 basis points.[15] The sample also reveals that in December 1989, the last date of the sample, the maximum difference in spreads on 20-year general obligation issues of 41 U.S. states was 84 basis points. Regarding the Canadian provinces, a much more limited sample suggests that spreads over Canadian federal U.S. dollar issues in 1997 ranged from 35 basis points for Saskatchewan to 78 basis points for Quebec (Table 10).[16]

Yet a third indication would be the pricing of European corporate debt. If EMU member countries maintain their sovereign ratings of AAA, it is reasonable to expect that credit spreads between EMU member country issuers would be in the range of Standard & Poor's AAA-rated corporate issuers. As of a few weeks ago, spreads for five AAA-rated corporate issues were in the range of between 10 and 45 basis points above their respective domestic benchmarks.[17]

Overall, it should be expected that there would be a convergence of interest rates on sovereign debt issued—and outstanding—by EMU member countries. Whether or not all of these issues trade at identical spreads will be determined by the market. To the extent that spreads remain, market segments will be identifiable. How much of an impact this will have on market liquidity remains to be seen.

Possibilities for Desegmentation: Yield-Curve Benchmarks and Currency Redenomination. The plan to introduce the euro has reopened the competition among

[15]See the analysis in Bayoumi, Goldstein, and Woglom (1995).

[16]See Salomon Brothers (1996).

[17]This range is from a sample of five Standard & Poor's AAA-rated corporate issues with maturities in the 8- to 10-year range: Bayerische Vereinsbank in Germany (14 basis points), Rabobank in the Netherlands (19 basis points), British Telecom in the United Kingdom (42 basis points), Credit Local in France (45 basis points), and Unilever in the Netherlands (11 basis points).

Table 10. Interest Rate Spreads of Canadian Provinces

Province	Rating	Coupon *(percent)*	Maturity	Indicative Bid-Side Spreads *(In basis points)* Dec. 30, 1996	Jan. 28, 1997	Change
U.S. dollar issues						
Ontario	Aa3/AA−	6.000	Feb. 21, 2006	38	38	0
Quebec	A2/A+	6.500	Jan. 17, 2006	58	56	−2
Quebec	A2/A+	7.500	July 15, 2023	83	78	−5
Saskatchewan	A3/A−	6.625	July 15, 2003	37	35	−2
Saskatchewan	A3/A−	8.500	July 15, 2022	59	58	−1
				July 29, 1996		
Canadian dollar issues						
British Columbia	AA+/Aa1		5-year	6		
Newfoundland	Baa1		5-year	27		
Alberta	Aa2/AA		10-year	7		
Nova Scotia	A		10-year	28		

Source: Goldman Sachs (1977); and SBC Warburg (1996).

European sovereign issuers for providing EMU with the *benchmark yield curve* for pricing other sovereign issues and private debt issues. This renewed competition is likely to increase the potential for further desegmentation of national debt markets. From an investor's point of view, the benchmark issue offers the highest return possible on what is deemed to be a "safe" investment. Such issues are usually high in volume, extremely liquid, and associated with various hedging instruments, with the added advantage of low bid-ask spreads. Benchmark issues also are used widely in repo markets, and are typically usable as collateral for a wide range of other financial contracts. From the issuer's point of view, the key advantage is that the yield is the lowest possible for that particular market segment; the added liquidity also provides easy access to a wide investor base for issuance. Thus, the importance of benchmark status is that it provides access to the lowest cost financing in a liquid market.

The main candidates for benchmark status are German and French instruments, and it would appear that France possesses several technical advantages (Table 11).[18] First, the French sovereign market is widely seen to be very

[18]Another possibility is that the euro benchmark yield curve will be based on swap yields. Swap markets in EMU could become extremely liquid as all interest rate swap contracts, which are currently segmented by currency, will become perfectly fungible and will be unaffected by the credit standing of governments. If the ECB issues short-term paper, in the form of ECB "debt certificates," it is likely to become a benchmark for very short-dated paper.

Table 11. The Euro Benchmark—Yield Curve: Germany vs. France

Germany		France	
1. Instruments			
Bu-bills	Six-month maturity only; issue size is up to ECU 3.2 billion	BTFs	Maturities (every Thursday) up to one year; issue size averages ECU 2.8 billion
SCHATZ	Two-year maturity; first issue was ECU 5.2 billion	BTANs	Usually two- and five-year maturities; average size is ECU 8–11 billion
OBLs	Five-year maturity; issue size ECU 4.2–6.8 billion	OATs	Maturity of up to 30 years; average size issue is ECU 15.5–17 billion
Bunds	Ten- and 30-year maturity; issue size ECU 5.2–13 billion	TEC10	Floating rate OAT
Treasury notes	Issuing ceased in mid-1995	Treasury bonds	No longer issued
Treuhand notes	Issued in 1993 and 1994 only; maturity was five years	STRIPs	Available every six months; available from zero to 30 years
2. Issuing Procedure			
The Federal Bond Consortium operates under the lead management of the Bundesbank. It has the characteristics of an underwriting and placing syndicate. Since 1992, membership is open to foreign firms' legally dependent branches in Germany. At end-1995, there were 95 institutions in the consortium, including 48 foreign-owned banks.		Primary dealer system that numbers 20 members (7 foreigners). These are required to stimulate the secondary market; inform the treasury about market developments; and take active part in tenders. Any financial institution may apply and receive primary dealer status after a brief period of observation as a reporting dealer. The advantages of becoming a primary dealer are access to tenders; noncompetitive bids, enabling the purchase of more securities at the marginal price at the tender; the authorization to strip and reconstitute OATs; and the ability to market their trading status to clients.	
Since August 1990 the majority of Federal bonds are issued by a combined method: one part via the syndicate and another by tender. In the case of Bunds and OBLs a portion of the issue amount is set aside for market management operations by the Bundesbank and is subsequently sold in stages through the stock exchange.		The treasury states its issuing plans in BTANs and OATs at the beginning of the year.	
		Almost all national negotiable debt is issued through tenders, Dutch style.	
An auction schedule is published roughly two weeks before the beginning of each quarter. The two-year		The issuing agenda is very regular:	

Table 11. (concluded)

Germany	France
and five-year bonds are now issued on a regular quarterly schedule. However, the issuing calendar 10-year and more so 30-year paper remains the focus for speculation. In addition, while issue size has been increased, liquidity across the yield curve varies considerably.	BTFs on Monday, monthly OAT tenders, on the first Thursday of each month and usually include a 10-year; monthly BTAN tenders, usually on the 2-year and 5-year benchmarks. Issue amounts are set two days before the lender after consultation with the primary dealers.
3. The STRIPs Market On June 13, 1996, the Bundesbank announced plans to introduce the separation and separate trading of principal and interest for particular 10- and 30-year Federal bonds during the course of 1997.	Since 1991, all OATs maturing on April 25 and October 25 (being 13 bonds in total) can be stripped. There is a principal certificate type for each strippable bond, but all coupon certificates with the same maturity are fungible, making it possible to rebuild OATs with coupons from another line. The amount that has been effectively stripped comprises 17 percent of the strippable bond total and 4.75 percent of the total French franc debt (whereas U.S. STRIPs are 25 percent and 4.35 percent respectively).
4. Repurchase Market The deutsche mark repo market is hindered by two key factors: the absence of a government-approved universal repo agreement; and the fact that many domestic institutions do not make their bond holdings available for lending. This has meant that the bulk of repo trading is located offshore, mainly in London.	The French franc repo market is by far the most sophisticated in Europe, whose development has followed the model of the U.S. The French treasury initiated a legally binding repo-agreement that forms the basis of the markets functioning. The market is very transparent and liquid, with 20 primary dealers being required to post prices on Reuters from which any institution can trade.

Source: Paribas (1996).

liquid because relatively larger issues are more evenly distributed across the maturity spectrum to generate a smooth yield curve. Second, French markets are supported by a transparent and liquid market for repurchase agreements; the bulk of deutsche mark repo trading is located offshore, mainly in London, mostly as a result of reserve requirements. These requirements have been lifted and so this French advantage will be eliminated soon. Third, France has already developed a STRIP market—which can be used to recalculate the exact value of each security on issue. Fourth, the French auction schedule has been for some time very regular and predictable, with the treasury announcing its plans at the beginning of the year. Finally, the French government has already announced its intentions to redenominate in euros the outstanding stock of debt on January 1, 1999. Although French paper is well placed to provide the benchmark yield curve for euro markets, all these advantages could be matched by other markets if measures are taken by other countries, and in particular by Germany, before the euro is introduced.

The "critical mass" approach requires that, starting in 1999, all new issues of government bonds and bills (at least those traded on the secondary market and expiring after 2001) will have to be denominated in euros.[19] Countries have the option to redenominate their outstanding stock of debt in euros as of January 1, 1999. The coexistence of new euro-denominated bonds and old national-currency bonds issued by the same government could segment the newly created euro market for government securities and reduce its relative liquidity. In addition to France, Belgium has also announced its intention to redenominate debt on January 1, 1999; Germany is in the process of deciding.[20]

Prospects for a European Corporate Bond Market

EU financial market legislation and the rapid development of the fund management industry have begun to chip away at longstanding regulatory and tax impediments to the development of European corporate debt markets. These markets have remained relatively small, however. Although outstanding debt securities issued by EU private entities totaled about $4 trillion (about 87 percent of the size of the U.S. corporate debt market), about 25 percent of this total was issued in international markets, of which about $268 billion were issued by nonfinancial entities. Domestic issuance in 1995 was also low compared to other more highly developed markets: German firms issued only $0.142 billion and French firms only $6.4 billion, whereas U.K. firms issued $20.7 billion, Japanese firms $77.2 billion, and U.S. firms $154.3 billion (Table 12).[21]

---

[19]See European Commission (1995).

[20]Debt redenomination creates a number of technical problems: not all public debt is dematerialized and there are different numerical trading and clearing conventions. Price display systems will have to adapt to show national currency and euro pricing for the same bonds. See Bank of England (1996) for a discussion of some of these technical problems.

[21]This figure for the United Kingdom refers to international bond issues as well because the domestic corporate bond market in the United Kingdom has become inseparable from the Euromarket.

Table 12. Funds Raised in Capital Markets by Nonfinancial Enterprises in Selected Industrial Countries, 1990–95

(In percent of total)

	Bonds[1]	Shares	Others[2]	Total
EU countries				
Italy	−0.68	25.55	75.13	100.00
Netherlands	1.17	42.19	56.65	100.00
Spain	1.71	29.27	69.02	100.00
Sweden	−0.88	33.73	67.15	100.00
Canada	7.14	27.91	64.95	100.00
United States	50.94	13.22	35.84	100.00
Japan	5.48	11.38	83.14	100.00

Source: OECD, *Financial Statistics*, 1995.
[1]Data for short-term bonds are not available for Italy, the Netherlands, and Japan.
[2]Residual including bank financing.

The introduction of the euro is likely to accelerate the development of corporate bond markets, especially if the increased focus on credit risk in the EMU sovereign markets leads to the development of a credit-risk culture, as now exists in the United States and the United Kingdom. First, as noted earlier, a single currency provides incentives for the creation of a much larger effective European institutional investor base. The increasingly yield-conscious behavior of European investors, and the coincident growth in fund management in Europe, has expanded the investor base for corporate debt securities—EU mutual funds now manage close to $1.4 trillion (see Table 5). Although the credit-risk culture has yet to take off in Europe the way it has in the United States, even a moderate shift will have a significant impact on international capital markets. For example, if the degree of disintermediation in EU countries was to close the securitization gap (adjusted for economic size) with the United States by 25 percent, this would unleash capital flows equal to roughly $2 trillion into international capital markets. This is roughly half the size of the entire market capitalization of EU or Japanese equity markets.

Second, EU firms have begun to show an increased desire to tap debt securities markets. An important factor spurring firms to issue debt securities is that European firms are beginning to adopt the increasingly sophisticated, value-maximizing corporate financial policies. However, the underdevelopment of domestic corporate debt securities markets has presented an obstacle to firms wishing to issue debt securities. Although this obstacle has been circumvented to some degree by tapping the international securities markets, there are significant additional obstacles to accessing the international markets for all but the largest, "brand-name" firms.

While there are reasons for optimism about the development of a Europe-wide corporate debt market, it will most likely not occur quickly. The remaining impediments to the development of these markets fall into two categories: excessive regulation and the narrow institutional investor base. Excessive regulatory burdens have simply prevented these markets from developing in some countries. For example, tax policy and issuance requirements prevented the development of commercial paper and bond markets in Germany until very recently. More generally, regulators in virtually all EU countries have stifled corporate debt securities markets by discouraging issuance of lower-grade corporate debt securities. Regarding institutional investors, corporate debt securities are often highly heterogeneous across issuers as well as across issues (by the same issuer), so the costs involved in evaluating their currency risk, credit risk, and legal risk—contract terms, such as covenants—effectively means that these markets will be successful only if there is a large institutional investor base. Smaller issuers, small issues, and firms in smaller countries—in which currency risk figures more prominently for foreign investors—therefore may face a limited investor base.[22]

Equity Markets

The introduction of the euro is likely to accelerate the processes of competition, consolidation, and technological innovation that has characterized equity markets in recent years. In the second half of the 1980s, the London Stock Exchange attracted an increasing share of turnover in continental equities by creating a screen-based dealer market for non-U.K. stocks called SEAQ International (SEAQ-I), separate from the London dealer market. During this period, competition among the European exchanges was fierce. Since the early 1990s, continental exchanges have recouped a substantial share of trading with new electronic continuous auction markets, particularly CAC in Paris and IBIS in Frankfurt, and SEAQ-I has declined in importance as an organized exchange. Nevertheless, London dealers are still the primary source of liquidity for large block transactions and for "program-trading" in a significant number of continental stocks, even though they engage in considerably less customer *dealing* in continental equities, and considerably more *brokering* through the continental bourses.[23] Thus, since the introduction of continuous

[22]The importance of this heterogeneity of corporate debt securities is illustrated by the dominant role played by institutional investors in the most developed corporate debt securities market, the U.S. market: at end-1995, 72 percent of the stock of corporate bonds were held by domestic institutional investors, 7 percent by foreign investors, and 14 percent by households. Insurance companies were the largest single investor, holding 35 percent; public and private pension funds held 16 percent; and mutual funds, 8 percent. See Smith (1995).

[23]Pagano, 1996.

electronic trading on the continent, London dealers have taken a smaller proportion of orders on their own books and have worked orders mostly through the continental markets. As such, the activity of London dealers is reinforcing the liquidity of auction markets, and the London-based dealer market and the continental-based auction markets are simultaneously competing and interdependent. Currently, London is by far the dominant equity market in Europe in terms of companies listed, market capitalization, and turnover (Table 13). On the continent, Frankfurt and Paris have the largest exchanges, with a similar number of listed companies and capitalization. All other exchanges are significantly smaller.

Together with ongoing pressures from computerization and the implementation of the EU Investment Services Directive (ISD), the introduction of the euro will provide strong incentives for concentration among the European exchanges.[24] The euro will eliminate differences in the continental electronic trading systems and make them virtually identical. The most likely development is that a Europe-wide equity market for blue-chip stocks will emerge into a single electronic exchange with a screen-based automated order-driven trading system, like IBIS. This will be possible only if the trading costs of this system will remain competitive vis-à-vis those of proprietary trading systems. National bourses may survive by specializing in trading low-capitalization companies. While there are incentives for this kind of trading to concentrate in a pan-European electronic trading platform, local custody, settlement, and tax systems may allow for local trading to continue. Overall, EMU is likely to further increase cross-border equity trading and to enhance both the integration of national markets and overall market liquidity.

Also uncertain is EMU's impact on competition between auction and dealer systems. If EMU enhances market efficiency and reduces equilibrium equity prices and spurious price volatility, then execution risk will diminish and immediacy will become less important. This implies that dealer markets, where investors pay a premium for immediacy in terms of higher bid-ask spreads, will experience competitive pressures from auction-agency markets, where increased liquidity will reduce execution risk. In addition, to the extent that EMU will increase cross-border asset holding and trading, counterparty risk could increase or become more difficult to assess. This will also put dealer markets at a disadvantage, because dealers would have to raise bid-ask spreads to compensate for the higher counterparty risk. By contrast, auction-agency markets usually pool this risk.[25]

[24]The ISD may facilitate cross-border branching of trading systems and remote trading. Article 15.4 favors remote membership: exchanges designated as "regulated markets" no longer require approval from EU states in which they want to establish as remote members.

[25]A dealer market might be preferred because some traders may want to remain anonymous, which is usually not possible in the very transparent continental markets.

Table 13. EU Countries, United States, and Japan: Equity Markets, 1996

	Listed Companies		Domestic Market Capitalization		Annual Turnover						
	Domestic	Foreign			Domestic	Foreign	Total	Domestic	Foreign	Total	Domestic
	(In numbers)		*(In millions of ECUs)*	*(In percent of GDP)*	*(In millions of ECUs)*			*(In percent of EU total)*			*(In percent of GDP)*
Markets in EU countries											
Amsterdam	217	216	302,452	96.10	149,587	653	150,241	8.96	0.11	6.58	47.53
Athens	217	0	18,988	19.64	5,695	0	5,695	0.34	0.00	0.25	5.89
Brussels	146	145	95,752	45.40	17,849	2,914	20,763	1.07	0.47	0.91	8.46
Copenhagen	237	12	57,281	41.46	29,111	698	29,810	1.74	0.11	1.31	21.07
Dublin	61	10	27,659	52.29	4,711	3	4,714	0.28	0.00	0.21	8.91
Germany	681	1290	531,553	28.34	621,454	18,778	640,231	37.22	3.06	28.04	33.13
Helsinki	71	0	49,444	50.41	17,538	0	17,538	1.05	0.00	0.77	17.88
Lisbon	158	0	19,706	23.40	5,658	0	5,658	0.34	0.00	0.25	6.72
London	557	833	1,368,000	153.61	335,644	580,777	916,421	20.10	94.59	40.13	37.69
Luxembourg	54	224	25,910	164.53	604	17	620	0.04	0.00	0.03	3.83
Madrid	357	4	194,681	42.25	63,869	18	63,888	3.83	0.00	2.80	13.86
Milan	244	4	206,997	21.79	82,532	18	82,551	4.94	0.00	3.61	8.69
Paris	686	187	472,426	38.48	220,608	4,828	225,436	13.21	0.79	9.87	17.97
Stockholm	217	12	194,045	97.42	106,434	5,021	111,455	6.37	0.82	4.88	53.44
Vienna	94	35	25,719	14.16	8,265	281	8,546	0.50	0.05	0.37	4.55
EU total	3,997	2,972	3,590,614	52.83	1,669,560	614,006	2,283,566	100.00	100.00	100.00	24.56
Memorandum items											
New York	2,617	290	5,395,889	90.23	3,014,383	190,392	3,204,775				50.41
Nasdaq	5,138	418	1,192,290	19.94	2,505,177	98,767	2,603,944				41.89
Tokyo	1,766	67	2,374,733	64.88	738,711	1,214	739,925				20.18

Sources: Federation of European Stock Exchanges; Federation of International Stock Exchanges; Nasdaq; New York Stock Exchange; and Tokyo Stock Exchange.

There are remaining impediments that could slow down consolidation. Some provisions of the ISD—the concentration provision and the concept of "regulated market"—leave scope for "protectionism" on behalf of national stock exchanges. Differences in accounting can also prevent institutional investors from purchasing stocks of certain countries. Finally, clearance and settlement procedures can affect equity trading by increasing transaction costs, which could be reduced through centralization of clearance and settlement services in a single European central securities depository (CSD), the so-called "Euro-hub."[26]

Derivatives Markets

The euro will affect derivatives markets in two ways: several contracts will disappear or consolidate into a single contract; and a smaller number of contracts will increase the competition among European derivatives exchanges. With the establishment of EMU and only euro interest rates, nearly 200 contracts involving 13 different currencies are likely to disappear. How the associated reduction in diversity will affect the 16 European futures and options exchanges is an open question. Initiatives are likely to emerge among the smaller exchanges to establish technical linkages and common settlement procedures. This will confine the race for post-EMU supremacy in derivative contracts to Europe's big three exchanges: the London International Financial Futures Exchange (LIFFE), Europe's biggest derivatives exchange, followed by the Deutsche Terminbörse (DTB) and Marché à Terme International de France (MATIF).[27] In light of their specialization in interest rate contracts, LIFFE and MATIF are likely to be most affected by EMU. Competition among the exchanges will also be affected by the development of electronic trading. DTB will be able to capitalize on its technological prominence with a fully electronic order-driven system with almost one-third of its members trading from workstations outside Germany. Both LIFFE and MATIF have maintained an open outcry structure. While LIFFE already has an electronic capability, MATIF is likely to be seriously handicapped by the failure in the summer of 1996 to finalize a link with DTB.

---

[26]There are five mechanisms for cross-border trades: (1) direct access to the home-country CSD; (2) indirect access through local members; (3) indirect access through global custodians; (4) international CSDs; and (5) local-CSD-to-local-CSD. The second and third methods are most widely used. See Giddy, Saunders, and Walter (1996).

[27]LIFFE derives half of its volume from short-term German Bund and interest rate futures and options, while 90 percent of trading on MATIF is in French national bond and short-term interest rate contracts. Two-thirds of DTB's volumes come from stock index futures and options. Foreign exchange contracts are mainly traded in the highly liquid interbank market.

Other factors could also play a role. LIFFE's leading position may be damaged if the United Kingdom is not included in EMU and if access to TARGET (see discussion below on reaping the rewards of RTGS) and intraday liquidity is limited. DTB might gain a competitive edge from being located in Frankfurt. MATIF could benefit from the fact that the French government has been actively issuing ECU-denominated debt since 1989 and is the leading sovereign borrower in ECU. Experience in the ECU bond market suggests that where the active cash market resides, the futures business is likely to follow. In addition, some consider MATIF the best-placed exchange to trade the future euro benchmarks, since a smooth transition from the French franc to euro could be ensured by enhancing the liquidity of existing contracts. Smaller exchanges in core euro countries (Belgium and the Netherlands) will be the first to see business decline, followed by the exchanges in peripheral countries (Italy and Spain). The likely outcome is that these exchanges will offer a smaller range of equity-based local contracts.

The most direct impact of EMU on the *structure of derivatives contracts* will be the elimination of currency derivatives between the currencies of countries joining EMU. If EMU begins with the core ERM countries, the negative impact on trading volumes will be muted, because trading in intra-core currency derivatives is relatively limited. Higher volume contracts between core and noncore currencies will simply change into contracts between the euro and noncore currencies; for example, deutsche mark–lira contracts will simply become euro-lira contracts. The high volume contracts between dollars, yen, and deutsche mark–bloc currencies will be little affected by the euro substituting for European currencies. If EMU enhances trading within, and capital flows to, the euro area, the demand for currency derivatives could increase. Activity in the European derivative markets may also increase during 1997–98 and 1999–2002 as foreign exchange and interest rate options are used to hedge risk in the transitional periods.

With the creation of EMU, the market for *interest rate swaps* will become larger and more liquid, as contracts of participating currencies become perfectly fungible. Enhanced liquidity is also likely to increase the use of swaps outside the banking sector. EMU will also boost the demand for options contracts on interest rate spreads and allow investors to hedge credit-risk spreads between bonds of high-debt countries and the euro benchmark. Contracts based on interest rate spreads may also develop for private debt securities.

For *bond market futures*, it is difficult to know whether the market will demand a futures contract for each national bond, or whether a generic contract will emerge. This will depend on the volatility of credit spreads between the various national issues. If the spreads are stable, the low basis risk could lead the market to develop a single liquid 10-year futures contract similar to the U.S. treasury bond future. Otherwise, there could be a range of futures contracts, with one for each national benchmark issue. The selection of deliverable bonds will also be crucial. If two or more national bonds are deliverable for a generic bond futures contract, the contract could favor the cheapest bond to deliver and create liquidity of that bond at the expense of higher quality bonds. Basket-type euro futures contracts are unlikely to emerge because derivatives exchanges would like to avoid repeating the experience of LIFFE with 10-year ECU futures contracts between 1990 and 1991. At that time, LIFFE's basket of deliverable bonds included ECU OATS, EIB bonds, U.K. gilts, and Italian government bonds. While all bonds in principle had the same rating, there was in practice always one that was cheaper to deliver. In effect, LIFFE's contract turned out to be an inadequate hedging tool.

Systemic Risk Management in EMU

This subsection examines two remaining institutional challenges. The degree of securitization and the liquidity of financial markets rest on the ability to quickly and efficiently settle payments and to move cash. A wholesale payments system capable of safely processing a large volume of intraday payment orders is necessary to support the large turnover in securities markets needed for liquidity, the rapidly changing dealer positions financed with repurchase agreements, and margin requirements arising from futures and options markets. The first challenge involves reaping the full benefits from the TARGET payments system. Who has access, and on what terms, could have important implications for systemic risk management and for fully capturing the potential risk reductions of real-time gross settlement (RTGS). The second challenge involves linking supervisory and lender-of-last-resort functions to the center of the payments system for effective systemic crisis prevention and management.

Reaping the Rewards of RTGS Across Europe

The main systemic problem in payments systems is the very low probability but very high cost (payments gridlock) of settlement failures. RTGS systems are being implemented in EU countries to improve payments efficiency and to reduce the potential for settlement problems. Because the euro will increase integration across national markets, cross-border transactions are likely to increase significantly, even for European countries not included in EMU. In order to implement an EMU monetary policy, improve payments efficiency, and reduce the potential for payments system problems, the EU will implement a new TARGET payments system that links the separate national RTGS payments systems. To the extent that European (EU and non-EU) countries that have significant volumes of transactions with the euro zone are not part of EMU, the full benefits of RTGS systems will not be internalized within EMU. This is a rationale for making TARGET a pan-European payments system.

By not including all European countries in the TARGET system, alternative settlement systems for euro transactions will be developed, some of them private, and this could reduce the number of transactions across TARGET. Most private systems are end-of-day settlement systems in which participants in the system accumulate large gross exposures, net them at various well-defined times throughout the day, and then finalize payment through a national RTGS system at the end of the day. If the legality of netting arrangements is tested, this could create the potential for serious liquidity problems in the unlikely event that a major institution would fail to settle. The unwinding of positions would have very high-cost consequences for third parties, with ripple effects throughout the netting system. In "out" countries, where netting arrangements are likely to be used to settle a significant share of these daily euro transactions, the systemic risk reductions that can be achieved in RTGS systems will not be realized. To the extent that TARGET participants in EMU have counterparties in non-EMU EU countries that are subject to the risks of netting arrangements, TARGET members will not be fully insulated from the kind of systemic risk that RTGS systems are specifically designed to eliminate.

Another remaining issue in the design of TARGET is access to intraday and overnight borrowing facilities. Some EU countries view access to TARGET intraday credit by non-EMU countries as having monetary policy implications. This view can be perceived as recognition of the importance of measuring the impact of payment-system intraday liquidity on the ability to achieve monetary objectives, and of determining the optimal interval over which to measure this impact—a day, a week, a month, the middle of the trading day, or the end of the trading day. A longstanding working assumption is that intraday liquidity for smoothing payments flows has no impact on the achievement of monetary policy objectives. There is, however, little analytical work that examines the relationship between payments system design and the impact of intraday liquidity on the ability to achieve monetary objectives.

Managing Systemic Risks in TARGET

Another aspect of the TARGET payments system that has not yet been clarified is the allocation of responsibility for safeguarding the Europe-wide payments system during a financial crisis and against liquidity problems that may arise in the course of payments settlement. Safeguards would normally include mechanisms for determining when and if a problem exists, whether or not a particular institution is having difficulties during settlement because it is liquidity constrained or insolvent, and how to resolve the problem—either by providing access to lender-of-last-resort facilities or by denying access to the payments system. The challenge is one of creating clearly understood and easily implemented crisis management mechanisms for very low probability events that impose costs on the payments system and its participants.

A potential risk is the lack of clarity about the mechanism for assessing and resolving a financial crisis involving cross-border payment flows between financial institutions within TARGET. At this stage, lender-of-last-resort responsibility has not yet been assigned. Because the ECB is at the center of the TARGET payments system and has sole responsibility for monetary policy, it would be inappropriate to assign this responsibility to the national central banks even though they are responsible for the smooth functioning of their national RTGS systems. In addition, the Maastricht Treaty neither mandates nor denies ECB authority for supervising European financial intermediaries, whether they are ECB counterparties or not. The national authorities, only in some cases the national central banks, will continue to be responsible for banking supervision, and for enforcing EU directives on capital adequacy, accounting standards, disclosure requirements, and other important aspects of financial supervision and regulation and financial market surveillance.

The history of financial crisis suggests that during a fast-breaking crisis, it is important for central banks to have sufficient information for making decisions about whether to provide support during a temporary liquidity problem. In many situations, problems could be addressed by the relevant national supervisory authorities, but there may arise situations where the ECB will have to act decisively and quickly. For example, the Bank of New York, a major clearing bank in the U.S. payments system, experienced a computer breakdown on November 21, 1985. Because the U.S. Federal Reserve System had recently completed a routine inspection of the bank, it was able to assess quickly the solvency of the Bank of New York and to decide that the bank was experiencing a severe liquidity problem. Because of its roles as supervisor and lender of last resort, the Federal Reserve System was able to avert a major systemic crisis by extending an overnight loan of $22.6 billion from the discount window, collateralized by $36 billion in securities. If European capital markets become more highly securitized, this feature of systemic risk management will need to be addressed.

There is also the potential problem of incompatible incentives: there may arise situations where national supervisory authorities would have information about the solvency of an institution but for practical reasons they are not willing or able to quickly or adequately inform the ECB. It would increase transparency of the supervisory framework and the surveillance over EU payments systems if a mechanism was designed to deal with these and related problems. Even though "constructive ambiguity" about the conditions under which lender-of-last-resort facilities will be available is a necessary element in preventing moral hazard, there should be no ambiguity among policymakers about the mechanisms that will be called upon to manage crisis situations.

Structural Implications for European and International Banking: Further Disintermediation, Competition, and Consolidation

The existence of larger and more liquid capital markets in Europe and the unavoidable reforms of European health, pension, and social security systems will create a large private pool of investable funds and will most likely expand the role of institutional investors and the demand for specialized asset management. This could open up each national market to cross-border competition. Continental banks will respond to this challenge by stepping up their current efforts to acquire, or merge with, specialized firms, and additionally to diversify their businesses against the risk of disintermediation by forming groups with institutional investors.

The creation of more liquid European capital markets—if not a Europe-wide capital market—is likely to encourage small and medium-sized corporations to access securities markets. Direct access to securities markets will in turn affect the competitive position of banks and could accelerate the gradual process of disintermediation that has been taking place in European banking markets. In this scenario, credit evaluation and local market underwriting skills will become extremely valuable. Thus, by creating incentives for the creation of broad, deep, and liquid private securities markets in Europe, the introduction of the euro and the establishment of EMU creates an *environment of competition* for shares of markets traditionally closely held and maintained by domestic universal banking institutions, both at the wholesale and retail level.

Wholesale Banking

At the *wholesale* level, with the removal of currencies and foreign exchange risk for intra-EMU cross-border transactions, there will be few remaining barriers to entry for the large global institutions. The commoditization of wholesale services and the cost of supplying them will determine customer relations. Competition in wholesale banking is driven by price, access to distribution networks, and geographic reach. Only a limited number of large financial institutions have the capital, resources, and geographic reach to compete globally in providing services to the top tier of multinational corporations and large and medium-sized companies with international operations.[28]

[28]There is now a consensus in the international financial markets that there is room for only 10 large global players. The "names" most often mentioned, in industry magazines and by market participants, are ABN Amro, Barclays, Citicorp, Deutsche Bank, Goldman Sachs, J.P. Morgan, Merrill Lynch, Morgan Stanley, S.B.C. Warburg, and Union Bank of Switzerland. Others that are viewed as vying for a slot include Credit Suisse, First Boston, and Lazard Frères. The recent mergers of Chase and Chemical banks and of Morgan Stanley and Dean Witter are examples of what may occur in the coming years.

It is possible to identify several aspects of this competition and consolidation at the wholesale level that are related to the introduction of the euro. As noted earlier, the euro directly eliminates the "anchoring principle," advocated by many European central banks, which requires domestic financial institutions to lead-manage bond issues, creating cross-border competition for providing this investment banking service. This new competition could lead to consolidation and greater concentration through cross-border mergers and acquisitions. The euro also eliminates the 80 percent matching rule on foreign currency exposures of insurance companies and pension funds within Europe. Under the existing rules, an EU insurance company, for example, cannot hold more than 20 percent of its assets in foreign currencies unless they are matched by liabilities denominated in the same currencies. The lifting of this restriction is likely to increase cross-border investment flows, and will open up this pool of investment funds to investment banks in EMU for providing underwriting, trading, brokerage, rating, and merger and acquisition advisory services. Banks strong in the above areas, with good placement power, are likely to see their franchises increase in value, and banks weak in these areas could be in the market for acquisitions of merchant banks and asset managers by continental European banks. Universal banks with strong investment banking franchises are also likely to benefit from EMU.

As a direct effect of a single currency, European banks will experience a substantial drop in banks' foreign exchange trading revenues on intra-EMU transactions. A single currency will eliminate revenues from intra-EMU exchange trading, sale of exchange rate and interest rate hedging instruments, commissions on cross-border money transfers, and government securities underwriting. These revenue losses will be permanent and likely to be concentrated in wholesale banking with an expected reduction in profits between 10 and 15 percent. EMU is likely to affect credit institutions unevenly, reducing mostly revenues of those banks with a competitive edge in certain currencies or in the placing of assets denominated in such currencies. EMU is then expected to cause a sharp reduction in employment of foreign exchange traders and possibly a consolidation of firms specialized in foreign exchange business.

The euro is also likely to have a number of indirect effects, all pointing in the direction of further consolidation in wholesale banking in Europe: lower profit margins through its general impact on competition; rationalization of foreign exchange and corporate and industrial treasury functions, which would reduce the demand for cash-management services provided by wholesale and investment banks; and reduction in the number of providers of regional and global payments processing services. This consolidation can only be hastened by the elimination of European currencies.

Competition is also likely to increase in correspondent banking as non-EMU banks reduce the number of correspondents they need inside the euro bloc. Consortia of banks providing basic electronic banking services, including payments to each others' customers in Europe, are also likely to emerge. The TARGET system will handle only large-value euro payments for central banks, large private banks, and very large companies, and smaller companies will have to go through banks' own payments systems and correspondent networks for low-value payments in euro. Competition in the market for wholesale money transmission services will also increase. As companies increase their cross-border activities, introduce more sophisticated treasury management, and concentrate their euro business with fewer banks, traditional home-currency correspondent banks may be unable to compete with the global banks, which assure cost-effective and efficient payment services around the world through their own networks.

Retail Banking

At the *retail* level, there is a greater need for restructuring and consolidation. The key problem is that Europe is overbanked at the retail and local levels (Tables 14 and 15). The most glaring consequence of this overbanking is that potential EMU countries—France, Italy, Belgium, the Netherlands, Austria—have banking systems that are overstaffed, and staffs that are underemployed, relative to banks operating in more efficient banking systems (the United States, for example) (Figure 1).[29] European banks are also known to provide services at noncompetitive prices. This leaves the least well capitalized and inefficient banking systems, and the banks within them, vulnerable to competitive pressures.

Despite these longstanding problems, consolidation has not occurred in Europe to the extent that it has in the United States. There have been a significantly smaller number of mergers and acquisitions, and they have tended to be smaller in size (Table 16). The absence of significant consolidation is difficult to explain against the background of strong competitive pressures and incentives for change. In recent years, local banking markets in Europe have experienced competitive pressures associated with deregulation, the abolition of capital controls, and single market initiatives. These competitive pressures have lowered net interest margins (Table 17) and reduced bank profits (Table 18).[30] Some banking systems have also had to increase provisions for nonperforming loans as real estate and property-related sectors weakened in the presence of declining or soft real estate prices. In most cases, European banks have been unable to counteract these trends with cost reductions and increased rev-

[29]The United States is a valid benchmark because it has experienced a first wave of bank restructuring and technological innovations.

[30]See OECD (1996a).

Table 14. Banks' Restructuring: Number of Institutions and Size Concentration, 1980, 1990, and 1995[1]

	Number of Institutions						Concentration: Top Five (Ten)[2]		
	1980[3]	1990	1995[4]	Peak (since 1980)			1980[5]	1990	1995[6]
					Year	Percent change[7]	(Percentage share in total assets)		
EU countries									
Belgium	148	129	150	163	1992	−8	64(76)	58(74)	59(73)
Finland	631	498	352	631	1985	−44	63(68)	65(69)	74(83)
France	1,033	786	593	1,033	1984	−43	57(69)	52(66)	47(63)
Germany[8]	5,355	4,180	3,487	5,355	1980	−35			17(28)
Italy	1,071	1,067	941	1,109	1987	−15	26(42)	24(39)	29(45)
Netherlands	200	180	174	200	1980	−13	73(81)	77(86)	81(89)
Spain[9]	357	327	318	378	1982	−16	38(58)	38(58)	49(62)
Sweden	598	498	112	598	1980	−81	64(71)	70(82)	86(93)
United Kingdom	796	665	560	796	1983	−30	63(80)	58(79)	57(78)
United States[10]	35,875	27,864	23,854	35,875	1980	−34	9(14)	9(15)	13(21)
Japan	618	605	571	618	1980	−8	25(40)	30(45)	27(43)

Other countries									
Canada	1,671	1,307	1,030	1,671	1984	−38		55(78)	65(88)
Australia	812	481	370	812	1980	−54	62(80)	65(79)	67(79)
Norway	346	165	148	346	1980	−57	63(74)	68(79)	58(71)
Switzerland	478	499	415	499	1990	−17	45(56)	45(57)	50(62)

Sources: British Bankers' Association; Building Societies Association; national data; and OECD.

[1]Deposit-taking institutions, generally including commercial, savings, and various types of mutual and cooperative banks; for Japan, excluding various types of credit co-operatives; and for Canada, excluding trust and loan companies (in 1994, 83 institutions).

[2]Figures shown in parentheses are the concentration for the top ten institutions.

[3]For Finland, 1985; Canada and France, 1984; Spain, 1981; and the United Kingdom, 1983.

[4]For Finland, Japan, and Sweden, 1994.

[5]For Finland and the Netherlands, 1985; France, 1986; Italy, 1983; and Switzerland, 1987.

[6]For Belgium, Japan, Switzerland, and the United Kingdom, 1994; and Finland, 1993.

[7]From peak to most recent observation where applicable.

[8]For number of institutions, western Germany only. Data for the whole of Germany in 1995 = 3,784; percentage change = −30.

[9]Concentration data for commercial and savings banks only.

[10]Excluding credit unions: 1995 = 12,067; percentage change = −36.

Table 15. EU Countries: Population per Bank Branch, 1985, 1992, and 1994

	1985	1992	1994	Change 1985–92	Change 1992–94
				(In percent)	
EU countries					
Austria	. . .	1,695	1,715	. . .	1.18
Belgium	395	613	. . .	55.19	
Denmark	1,534	2,096	2,316	36.64	10.50
Finland	1,670	2,106	2,784	26.11	32.19
France	. . .	. . .	2,212	. . .	. . .
Germany	1,569	2,050	1,832	30.66	−10.63
Greece	. . .	8,943	8,384	. . .	−6.25
Italy	. . .	3,221	2,862	. . .	−11.15
Luxembourg	1,523	1,287	1,090	−15.50	−15.31
Netherlands	3,025	2,019	2,116	−33.26	4.80
Portugal	6,633	3,431	2,917	−48.27	−14.98
Spain	1,182	1,100	1,101	−6.94	0.09
Sweden	2,794	2,990	3,281	7.02	9.73
United Kingdom	4,163	4,937	5,272	18.59	6.79
Memorandum items					
Mexico	21,814	25,330	21,441	16.12	−15.35
United States	5,596	4,885	4,690	−12.71	−3.99

Source: OECD (1996a).

enues in other areas of financial services. The resistance to consolidation might be attributable to factors such as home currency advantage, legal and regulatory restrictions, ownership structures that inhibit entry and exit, extensive branch networks, and strong traditional and cultural relationships.

An open question is whether EMU will provide the impetus for change necessary for restructuring and consolidation. One possible channel is the introduction of the euro itself. In the past, exchange rate stability has been associated with narrowing net interest margins among the "core" countries. One possible inference is that the euro might provide an added element of competition (see Table 17).[31] Additional pressures on interest rate margins would come from the emergence of EMU-wide securities markets, the harmoniza-

[31]The link between exchange rate stability and net interest margins is supported by the experience with Italian and U.K. spreads, both of which stopped converging during the 1992–93 period of extreme exchange rate turbulence. In addition, the independent role of exchange rate stability is supported by the significant convergence of margins before the introduction of single market initiatives in 1992.

Figure 1. Labor Costs and Productivity in Banking, 1994

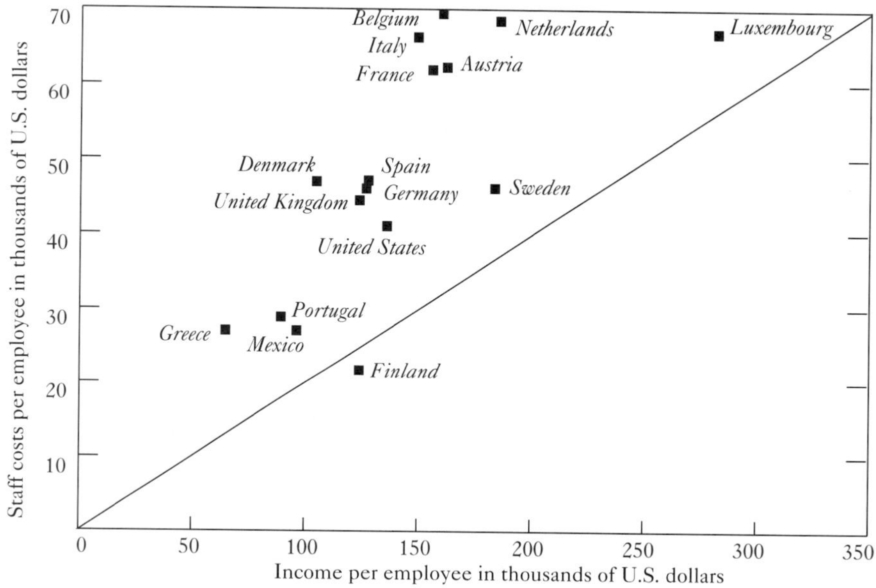

Source: OECD, 1996.

tion of reserve requirements, and the greater transparency of financing terms and conditions associated with a single currency.

EMU could also increase the likelihood of consolidation through cross-border bank mergers and alliances, as the more aggressive institutions position themselves to satisfy the increased demand for EMU-wide banking services that could come from greater cross-border trade and competition in European industry. While large European corporations are already requesting Europe-wide banking services, EMU could extend this demand to small and medium-sized firms that rely on retail banks for many of their needs. Households would also be likely to increase the demand for EMU-wide banking services. Competition in all of these areas is likely to increase between the stronger domestic and European financial institutions looking to increase market shares and to penetrate markets in other EMU countries. Some competition could also come from large and fully vertically integrated financial institutions, including some global banks (Citicorp and Deutsche Bank, for example). In addition, some economic barriers to entry could be eroded by the introduction of the euro, although this is likely to occur indirectly through the euro's impact on securities markets and institutional investors and their impact on bank disintermediation. What all this implies is that EMU could make banking markets in Europe more "contestable" in the sense that the potential for competition

Table 16. Mergers and Acquisition Activity in Banking[1]

					Value							
	1989–90	1991–92	1993–94	1995–96[2]	1989–90	1991–92	1993–94	1995–96[2]	1989–90	1991–92	1993–94	1995–96[2]
	(In numbers)				*(In billions of U.S. dollars)*				*(In percent of mergers and acquisitions in all industries)*			
EU countries												
Belgium	11	22	18	12	0	1.0	0.6	0.4	0.2	14.1	7.0	7.9
Finland	6	51	16	4	0.4	0.9	1.0	0.8	13.9	22.3	21.7	11.3
France	52	133	71	43	2.7	2.4	0.5	3.2	5.1	4.3	1.0	10.4
Germany	19	71	83	27	1.1	3.5	1.9	0.7	4.5	6.5	7.6	3.5
Italy	41	122	105	65	8.2	5.3	6.1	3.0	22.7	15.6	17.7	19.7
Netherlands	12	20	13	7	10.9	0.1	0.1	0.8	56.3	0.2	0.5	9.5
Spain	30	76	44	26	4.0	4.3	4.5	2.1	18.5	13.5	21.5	34.1
Sweden	10	38	23	8	2.0	1.1	0.4	0.1	8.8	3.8	2.0	0.4
United Kingdom	86	71	40	28	6.4	7.5	3.3	21.7	2.6	6.5	3.4	12.4
United States	1,501	1,354	1,477	1,176	37.8	56.8	55.3	82.5	7.3	18.7	9.0	13.5
Japan	8	22	8	17	31.2	0	2.2	33.8	71.8	0.3	18.8	77.0
Other countries												
Canada	13	29	31	14	0.8	0.5	1.8	0.1	1.3	1.9	4.1	0.3
Australia	23	19	20	9	2.3	0.9	1.5	2.5	4.3	3.6	5.7	5.8
Norway	12	23	24	2	0.4	0.1	0.2	0.4	9.2	1.2	5.7	4.4
Switzerland	31	47	59	14	0.5	0.4	3.9	0.7	4.7	9.5	43.4	1.6
Total	1,855	2,098	2,032	1,452	108.6	84.7	83.2	153.0	9.6	11.7	8.5	14.0
Memorandum item												
Total nonbank financial	2,075	2,723	3,267	2,267	99.0	63.7	122.2	90.7	8.8	8.8	12.5	8.3

Source: Securities Data Company.

[1]Classified by the industry of the target; completed or pending deals; announcement date volumes.

[2]As of April 4, 1996.

Table 17. Net Interest Margins[1]

(In percent of average earning assets)

	1989	1990	1991	1992	1993	1994	1995	Change from High to 1995
EU countries								
Austria	1.91	1.95	1.95	2.13	2.01	1.96	2.13	0.00
Belgium	2.07	2.04	1.84	1.85	2.06	1.98	1.76	−0.31
Denmark	2.18	2.47	2.28	2.63	2.40	2.37	2.10	−0.53
Finland	1.96	2.19	1.89	1.34	2.90	2.73	2.12	−0.78
France	3.20	2.89	3.28	3.18	2.49	2.51	2.21	−1.07
Germany	1.72	2.10	2.07	2.43	3.35	2.96	2.60	−0.75
Greece	3.69	2.73	1.26	0.12	−0.65	0.83	1.75	−1.94
Ireland			1.27	0.91	2.92	2.04	1.98	−0.94
Italy	3.62	3.71	3.38	3.41	3.75	2.97	3.06	−0.69
Luxembourg	0.46	0.50	0.46	0.88	1.02	1.01	0.93	−0.09
Netherlands	0.92	0.93	1.03	1.27	2.72	1.66	1.70	−1.02
Portugal		6.32	6.06	5.89	3.45	2.84	2.87	−3.45
Spain	4.93	5.25	4.85	4.18	5.12	3.98	3.23	−2.02
Sweden	2.17	2.72	3.65	2.15	1.62	−0.99	5.52	1.87
United Kingdom	0.35	0.48	0.68	1.67	2.22	1.68	1.66	−0.56
Memorandum items								
North America								
Canada	2.40	2.60	2.43	2.29	2.10	1.81	1.93	−0.67
Mexico	1.21	5.21	6.53	6.73	3.54	2.27	3.10	−3.63
United States	3.25	3.32	3.43	6.47	4.39	3.40	2.77	−3.70
Japan	0.48	1.90	2.07	3.53	2.72	2.22	2.36	−1.17

Source: IBCA Ltd.

[1]Shaded numbers indicate the highest net interest margin for the 1989–95 period for each country.

from new entrants could act as a disciplining mechanism on incumbents, and perhaps lead to more consolidation.

Given these pressures for change, how might restructuring take place within EMU? If the competitive pressures outlined above are allowed to exert their influence unconstrained, it would be reasonable to expect competition to lead to further mergers of small and medium-sized domestic institutions (some defensive, some offensive), cross-border mergers, significantly fewer institutions, more electronic branching, better and more efficiently provided services, and customer access to regional, international, and global markets. The number of institutions and branches would decline gradually, and the average size of institutions would increase as consolida-

Table 18. Banks' Profitability

	Pretax Profits[1]			Return on Assets[2]	
	1980–82[3]	1986–88	1992–94	1994	1995
		(In percent of assets)			
EU countries					
Belgium	0.40	0.40	0.30	. . .	. . .
Denmark[4]	. . .	. . .	. . .	0.29	1.20
Finland[5]	0.50	0.50	−1.60	−0.69	−0.16
France	0.40	0.40	−0.10	0.17	0.27
Germany	0.50	0.70	0.50	0.52	0.56
Italy	0.70	1.00	0.80	. . .	. . .
Netherlands	0.30	0.70	0.60	0.69	0.72
Spain	0.70	1.10	0.60	0.70	0.79
Sweden	0.30	0.80	0.50	0.55	1.23
United Kingdom	1.10	1.00	0.70	1.22	1.27
Memorandum items					
North America					
Canada[6]	0.50	1.00	1.10	1.12	1.16
United States	1.00	0.70	1.60	1.81	1.87
Other countries					
Japan[6,7]	0.50	0.60	0.20	−0.21	−0.75
Australia[8]	0.90	1.20	0.70	1.60	1.82
Norway	0.60	0.00	0.20	1.31	1.81
Switzerland	0.60	0.70	0.60	0.63	0.52

Sources: IBCA Ltd.; and OECD as adapted from BIS (1996c).

[1]All banks for Australia, Belgium, the Netherlands, and Switzerland; and commercial banks only for other countries (OECD data).

[2]Pretax profits of major banks (IBCA data).

[3]For Australia, Belgium, and France, 1981–82; and for Canada, 1982.

[4]The portfolio of securities is marked to market.

[5]The 1994 and 1995 reserves are not fully comparable due to a break in series.

[6]Fiscal years.

[7]The 1994 and 1995 date are combination of half-year results at an annual rate and IBCA estimates.

[8]Fiscal years for 1994 and 1995.

tion takes place. Staff levels would decline slowly through attrition. Much of the adjustment could be internalized within the banking industry itself. In an environment in which regulations, union strength, and extensive public ownership make it difficult to close banks and to reduce costs through downsizing, the stronger institutions may be called upon to merge with poorly capitalized banks. In other instances, mergers will aim to boost profits without incurring the pain of cost cutting. Among the more successful or viable institutions, large banks will continue to purchase smaller banks (savings institutions, community banks), in part to obtain access to relatively high-margin deposit bases and to diversify funding sources by expanding the branch network. Some of the more aggressive smaller banks would engage in defensive mergers or outright takeovers. Larger banks may also try to increase diversification and acquire a hedge against disintermediation, by establishing alliances with mutual funds and insurance companies. Computer technology will aid the consolidation process by allowing banks to concentrate back-office operations away from individual branches and to realize important economies of scale. The acquisition of technology may motivate some mergers, because it may allow some banks to gain access to the financial resources necessary to fund the investments required to acquire and maintain competitive information technology infrastructures.

The euro will provide additional pressure for change but major progress will occur only after some structural issues are addressed. Obstacles have remained in place even after the introduction of the Second Banking Directive,[32] and differences in taxation, regulations, and accounting and business practices, combined with the absence of an EU company law impede cross-border entry. Labor market laws will also continue to place limits on the potential efficiency gains from consolidation. Labor laws in Europe are estimated to limit the potential costs savings from bank mergers to half the savings that would be possible in the United States. Ownership structures in Europe are also likely to continue to prevent market forces from operating. Extensive state ownership delays both entry and exit from the banking system,[33] resulting in a continued buildup of imbalances in troubled public institutions. In addition, institutions may continue to pay little attention to profitability because creditor and shareholder discipline is reduced by the fragmentation of debt and equity claims and by regulatory obstacles to takeovers.[34] Another factor is that European banking is still characterized by institutions with a national and often regional orientation. U.S. experience suggests that the inability to diversify across state boundaries was a major factor in the difficulties faced by several banking institutions. Finally, in the United States, where labor market legislation provides significant scope for downsizing, the most important benefit of mergers was increased profitability

---

[32]For example, a British bank that established operations and began to offer interest-bearing current accounts in France was forced to cease this practice on the grounds that French banks were prohibited from paying interest on such accounts and that the efficacy of monetary policy was threatened.

[33]Even where there is a strong political will to do so, privatization is complicated by public ownership structures. German savings banks (*Sparkassen*) carry as capital a guarantee from local municipalities. Italian public banks are controlled by nonprofit organizations (*Fondazioni*). In addition, exit may also be delayed, as state-owned inefficient banks are usually more difficult to close down than private ones.

[34]See BIS (1996c).

from a better diversification of funding sources and loan portfolios—not cost savings.[35]

The experience of Nordic and English-speaking countries, where banking crises occurred before restructuring took place, and the more recent experience with resolving financial system problems in Japan suggest that it is unlikely that Europe will be able to either grow out of its problems or resolve them entirely through private efforts unless there are further reforms. In addition, restructuring and consolidation in Europe are unlikely to be aided significantly by state interventions on a scale similar to the interventions that accompanied the restructuring of the European industry in the 1980s.[36] The funds available to bail out banks are likely to be limited, in the short run, by the commitments of EMU member countries to uphold the stability pact and to achieve further fiscal consolidation. In addition, any attempt to bail out troubled institutions might be prevented by EU regulations that guarantee fair competition and try to maintain a "level playing field" in the market for banking services.[37]

In summary, the introduction of a single currency is likely to provide additional competitive pressures that could potentially accelerate the desirable processes of restructuring and consolidation in the European banking system. Unless structural reforms are implemented across Europe, there is the risk that rigidities in labor markets, public ownership structures, and other policies affecting the adjustment in banking markets would delay the desirable effects of enhanced competition. This would allow financial problems in troubled institutions to build up to the point where crises might be unavoidable. If this occurs, the inconsistencies between EMU-wide plans for fiscal consolidation and existing financial sector policies will become glaring.

Financial Institutions

Overall, it is an open question which types of financial institutions will be able to take advantage of these opportunities and to deal better with the likely increase in bank disintermediation. Those firms that are better positioned to compensate for the decline in loan demand with noninterest income, for example, from placement services, will have an advantage. If the introduction of the euro leads to the creation of less segmented and more liquid securities markets, then it will encourage the development of financial intermediation

[35]See OECD (1996b).

[36]In that instance, several European governments smoothed the process by directly injecting funds, extending the scope of unemployment and welfare subsidies, and authorizing costly early retirement.

[37]Within the EU, public funds have been injected into financial institutions in recent years in Finland, France, Italy, Norway, and Sweden.

based on direct access to securities markets. The predominance of this model of finance in the United States, the United Kingdom, and international markets reflects the market reality that, in the absence of strong regulations that create and protect a clear niche for banks, the business of taking deposits and providing loans—banking—has a role in finance as long as the cost of borrowing directly (through private placements of the securities markets) exceeds the cost of borrowing indirectly through banks.[38] By making European capital markets more liquid and efficient, the introduction of the euro has the potential of encouraging further direct financing and reducing the role of bank intermediation throughout Europe.

Another factor that could drive European entities toward more direct financing is the cost of acquiring information. It has been argued that financial intermediaries emerged because it is inefficient for many shareholders each to incur the cost of monitoring a firm's management.[39] To some extent, information costs explain the development and growth of universal banks[40] in Europe, as their role as shareholder allows them to have an informational advantage over individual investors. To the extent that EMU will increase the integration of European markets for goods and services, it will be easier for investors to assess the performance of firms as the need for detailed knowledge of each local market diminishes. If this occurs, the comparative advantage of universal banks is likely to diminish. As such, American investment firms would have a significant skill-based advantage, because they specialize in credit evaluation in the context of liquid securities markets.[41] The development of European capital markets could then be seen as a reduction in the barriers to entry for securities firms.

Only the largest of the European universal banks appear to be reasonably well positioned to counteract some of these advantages. First, they should have little problem in using their information-gathering advantage to move into credit valuation and bring an increasing number of firms to the bond and equity markets. In addition, their role as shareholders will be crucial in influencing the financing choices of corporations and preventing too rapid a shift toward equity and bond financing. When banks act as shareholders, they can distort the financing decisions of a firm to the point that the share of debt of the participating firm exceeds the level that maximizes the firm's value.[42] In this respect, a major penetration of American-style investment banks in the

[38]See Gurley and Shaw (1960).

[39]See Diamond (1984).

[40]A key feature of universal banks is that they hold equity shares large enough to monitor corporations. See Steinherr (1996).

[41]See Steinherr (1996).

[42]See Aoki (1984).

banking market of continental Europe would be possible only if a parallel shift in the prevailing form of corporate governance toward the securities model of financial intermediation were to be demanded by customers and take place.[43] These counterbalancing factors suggest that any shift of financial activities away from the large European universal banks will be gradual. However, it is likely that the many small and medium-sized financial institutions within Europe that have tried to emulate the universal banking model will be vulnerable to competition from larger financial institutions and more efficient small and medium-sized intermediaries. One can also expect greater specialization among the middle-tier institutions.

The Euro and International Capital Flows

In 1995, EU entities purchased assets worth about $142 billion from U.S. entities (including foreign direct investment) and sold assets worth about $155 billion to U.S. entities; by year-end, European entities held roughly $650 billion in U.S. financial assets (including bank loans and deposits), while U.S. entities held roughly $638 billion in European paper.[44] The introduction of the euro and the establishment of EMU are likely to alter the size and pattern of capital flows to and from the euro zone and the allocation of international portfolios. These flows will be driven by three main forces: (1) the strength and stability of the euro; (2) the role of the euro in the international monetary system both as a reserve currency and as a vehicle currency for trade invoicing and payments; and (3) the future depth and liquidity of the EU financial markets.

Official Flows

The role of the euro in the international monetary system will ultimately be determined by the future stability and strength of the euro vis-à-vis the dollar and yen and by the share of the euro in international trade and payment flows. Although it is difficult at this stage to speculate on the future monetary policy stance of the ECB, the independent status and strict mandate to pursue price stability that have been entrusted to the institution, and the strict fiscal stability pact agreed by the member countries would be conducive to a strong and stable euro.

[43]The greater the liquidity of the secondary market, the more effective is the securities model of financial intermediation as a form of corporate governance based on the takeover mechanism. See Bolton and von Thadden (1996).

[44]These figures are from various recent issues of the *U.S. Survey of Current Business*.

There has been considerable discussion in the research publications of the large commercial and investment banks about the impact of the euro on central bank reserves.[45] For several reasons, the initial impact of EMU on the level and currency composition of the reserves of EU central banks is likely to be smaller than suggested by many of these analyses. As of October 1996, the foreign currency reserves held by the eight central banks deemed by markets as most likely to join EMU on the first round totaled about $200 billion. About 25 percent of these reserves are in core EU currencies that will probably be converted into euro domestic assets and either kept on central banks' balance sheets or transferred to the treasury. A leading investment house has estimated that monetary union would leave EMU central banks with up to $50 billion in excess reserves that will be sold on foreign exchange markets. Such estimates, which are based on an arbitrary ratio of reserves to imports, overestimate the excess reserves of the ESCB, as trade flows are an inappropriate yardstick for determining the optimal level of reserves of industrial countries' central banks. Indeed, although there is a correlation between trade flows and foreign reserves in most developing countries, such a link is generally weak in industrial countries. In industrial countries, reserves do not finance imports, which are funded by the private sector, but instead are used solely for intervention purposes. In the absence of capital controls, the size and variability of the ESCB foreign reserves would be determined by capital flows and the exchange rate policy of the ECB rather than by trade flows,[46] and by ERM II commitments.

Outside the euro zone, shifts in international official reserves into euros are likely to be influenced by the future role of the euro in foreign exchange markets, the liquidity of the euro treasury bill market, and the stability and diversification benefits of the euro. One of the reasons for the predominant role of the dollar as a reserve currency is the existence of liquid U.S. treasury securities markets. In contrast, German and Japanese short-term treasury markets are relatively illiquid.[47] As EU financial markets become more integrated under a single currency, the euro treasury bill market will gain in size and liquidity and offer an attractive alternative to central banks' holdings of U.S. treasury bills. It may also be the case that a number of Asian and Middle East central banks would welcome increasing the nondollar share of their reserves if vehicles for short-term investments were to be developed. The euro treasury bill market may not attain the liquidity and standardization of the U.S. treasury markets, however, because of the lack of a single European federal issuer.

---

[45]See, for example, J.P. Morgan (1996) and Paribas Capital Markets (1996).

[46]See Masson and Turtelboom's paper in this volume for a detailed discussion of this issue.

[47]German Bu-bills have been limited to DM 20 billion, too small an amount to satisfy central banks holdings of short-term government paper.

The role of the euro as a reserve currency would also grow as a number of countries, especially in Eastern and Central Europe and perhaps in North Africa, anchor their currencies to the euro in their drive to become part of the monetary union at some point in the future. The number of countries pegging their currency to the euro may also increase relative to those that currently peg their currency to a basket of European currencies, as a single currency peg is easier to manage and more stable than a multiple currency peg.

Private Flows

The most significant source of capital inflows to the euro zone is likely to emanate from international private investors rather than from central banks, given the relative size of their assets. In addition to the factors discussed earlier, the direction and size of private capital flows to the euro zone will be determined by the size, depth, and liquidity of the euro capital markets, and the diversification benefits of the euro vis-à-vis the main international currencies.

As discussed above, the introduction of a single currency is expected to increase the degree of homogeneity in European capital markets and the standardization of financial products across Europe, bringing the full fruits of the single market to European financial markets. The extent and speed of integration of the European government bond markets and the emergence of a single euro government bond market would be key factors in attracting international flows to the euro zone. The immediate consequence of a single currency and monetary policy would be the development of a single euro repo market, which would act as a catalyst for the development of a single euro bond market. A single euro bond market would become the main competitor of the U.S. bond market for international capital. It is inevitable that international institutional investors would be attracted by the large pool of funds in a single currency and reallocate a significant portion of their portfolios to the euro capital markets to be exposed to such a market.

Over the medium term, the single currency is also likely to lead to the development of a euro corporate bond market. A corporate bond market would increase the number of European firms with credit ratings, further enhancing their attractiveness to foreign institutional investors constrained by internal regulations to invest only in rated companies. Although a higher issuance in the euro debt market could have some dampening effect on the external value of the euro, it is likely that the demand effects would more than offset the supply effects.

In addition to the expected international flows in bond markets, private flows to euro equity markets are likely to increase. In particular, large institutional investors that have avoided taking an exposure to some of the European equity markets because of their small size would shift a greater share of their international portfolios to those markets as they become more integrated. Similarly, the emergence of index funds across Europe—a prized investment vehicle for international pension fund managers—would expand the vehicles available for institutional investors to invest in EU capital markets. International portfolio flows into euro equity markets are likely to be less marked than portfolio flows into bond markets, however, because segmentation among domestic markets may persist, and the market capitalization of continental Europe remains small relative to that of the United States.

The disappearance of core European currencies may affect the volatilities and cross-country correlations of euro securities prices, and hence the diversification benefits of the euro to international investors. The theoretical literature examining the relationship between exchange rate volatility and asset price volatility, although extensively researched, remains largely inconclusive. Comparisons of the volatility of bond or equity market returns across various exchange rate regimes suggest that there is a positive correlation between exchange rate volatility and securities market volatility. For example, core-EMU countries that credibly pegged their exchange rate to the deutsche mark between January 1989 and December 1994 experienced low volatility in both the foreign exchange and bond markets.[48] The relationship between the exchange rate volatility and equity prices volatility was also positive, albeit weaker. Insofar as the EMU would be a credible and irrevocable fixed exchange rate regime, the volatility of euro bond and equity prices is likely to decline in the euro zone, further enhancing the attractiveness of euro capital markets to foreign investors.

The relationship between exchange rate stability and the cross-country correlation of securities prices is also unresolved theoretically. There is evidence, however, that greater exchange rate stability and market integration tend to increase the cross-country correlation of securities prices.[49] To the extent that EMU would increase the economic integration of its member countries and the integration of their financial markets, cross-country correlation of business cycles in the euro zone should increase. The higher correlation of the fundamentals of the constituent countries, and the elimination of idiosyncratic monetary policy shocks within the euro zone would in turn lead to a higher correlation of euro bond and equity prices. The higher correlation of euro asset prices, however, would lower the diversification benefits of the euro relative to its constituent currencies and may lead to some portfolio shifts toward non-EMU currencies (e.g., Swiss franc, pound sterling) to recapture these diversification benefits. Considering that core EU asset prices have been highly cor-

[48]See Bodart and Reding (1996).

[49]See Bodart and Reding (1996) and Frankel (1996).

related in the past few years, portfolio shifts related to losses of diversification benefits are likely to be small.

The impact of the euro on the capital flows of European pension funds and insurance companies is likely to be negligible initially as most of the regulations limiting the foreign investments of these institutions are based on allocations between bond and equity markets, and domestic and international markets. As pension and insurance funds' international investments are governed by the 80 percent currency matching requirement of the EU Third Life Directive, the introduction of the euro should not affect the noneuro currency allocation of pension funds.[50] The introduction of the euro would only allow greater diversification of European pension funds within the euro zone, as the removal of foreign exchange risk allows pensions to tap into a broad array of assets that have become eligible investments. As such, insofar as the euro zone becomes a domestic market for pension funds and insurance companies, flows into euro bond and equity markets would increase, further deepening euro capital markets.

The introduction of the euro would have marginal implications on EU pension fund investments outside the euro zone, however. The rules that have anchored institutional investors and pension funds to their domestic markets will be broadened to the EU market, but will not necessarily spill over, at least initially, to international capital markets. Over the medium term, however, the move of European pension funds from fixed-benefit schemes to fixed-contribution schemes may have an impact on asset allocation, as fixed-contribution schemes are more return oriented than fixed-benefit schemes, and hence may induce greater investments in international markets.

Investors' shifts of funds into the euro zone are likely to be gradual, as both the euro and the credibility of the ECB would be untested. Some divestment away from the deutsche mark and into the dollar by U.S. and Asian investors has already occurred in view of uncertainty about the composition of the euro and the future monetary stance of the ECB. As the euro reveals its colors and the euro bond markets acquire liquidity and depth, a significant reallocation of portfolios by both institutional investors and central banks toward euro-denominated assets would undoubtedly occur, with a positive impact on the external value of the euro. Shifts of funds would reflect the greater attractiveness of euro bond and equity markets, and the share of EU economies in international trade and payment systems. In the long run, the euro may become a strong competitor to the dollar as a reserve currency. As an international transaction currency, however, the euro may take longer to challenge the dol-

[50]Currently, EU pension funds invest 11 percent of their assets overseas, compared to less than 10 percent for U.S. pension funds.

lar, owing to the predominant role of the dollar in international payments systems, the size and liquidity of the U.S. capital markets, and the low transaction costs of the dollar.

Summary and Conclusions

By directly reducing transactions costs and removing the volatile currency-risk component of intra-EMU cross-border financing costs, the introduction of the euro provides incentives for, and opens up the possibility of, greater reliance on direct financing in European capital markets. These important changes will shift the focus of both borrowers and savers to the remaining, and significantly less volatile, components of risk and asset pricing, including credit, liquidity, settlement, legal, and event risks. In effect, the "currency culture" that now exists in European financial capitals will be transformed into a "credit-risk culture." Borrowers will try to minimize the impact on financing costs of each of the remaining perceived risks under their control by improving their credit ratings and by borrowing in the lowest cost "locations" across a more geographically diverse investor base within Europe. At the same time, lenders will try to accurately assess and monitor underlying relative asset values and credit risk and will focus on pricing-in all the remaining components of risk. Simultaneously, if current fiscal reform plans are implemented, there soon will be a large pool of investable funds flowing out of the public sectors—pensions, social insurance, and health insurance funds—into the European and perhaps international capital markets, all denominated in euro and all seeking various trade-offs of risk and return.

All these structural changes in European finance point in the direction of less-segmented markets for repurchase agreements, short-term interbank funds, sovereign and private bonds, equities, and derivative instruments. From a pure finance-efficiency perspective, a favorable outcome would be the creation of deep, liquid, and efficient *EMU-wide* money, financial, and capital markets. The market pressures for pushing European capital markets in this direction may be strong enough to achieve the efficiency gains promised by the creation of a single European market envisioned in the Maastricht Treaty. But there are remaining barriers and restrictions that may prevent this outcome, and the architecture of the ECB and the way it implements monetary policy could have a constraining influence on how far securitization can go in EMU.

Whether or not the potential improvements in market depth, liquidity, and efficiency are achieved, the greater reliance on direct financing in EMU will have important implications for the shape of European and international capital markets, cross-border competition, and the ongoing global processes of competition, restructuring, and consolidation. The ongoing, and perhaps accelerated, process of disintermediation will deepen and broaden the effect of competition on bank restructuring and consolidation that would have occurred across the banking markets in Europe even without the introduction of the euro. At the wholesale level, competition will be strong for bringing new bond and equity issues to market and for capturing the customer relationships that have been traditionally the domain of European universal banks. Only the largest and strongest of European universal banks will be able to compete in wholesale markets, and there may be a spate of mergers and acquisitions to achieve the scope and scale of bank operations necessary for survival. The greatest competition may well come from U.S. investment banks and U.K. merchant banks.

At the retail level, local banks will most likely maintain their stronghold on local deposit bases, as has occurred in the United States. But local banks will have to become somewhat larger and significantly more efficient in supplying modern financial services at competitive prices to small local businesses and to households. There is significant scope for consolidation and restructuring among local domestic institutions, and also room for cross-border mergers for diversification and for buying into expertise of local investor bases. There is also the possibility for some fully vertically integrated operations to make successful inroads into smaller local markets in small cities and even villages (Citicorp, Deutsche Bank, Societe Generale, and NatWest). If these private market adjustments are to take place, the remaining obstacles will have to be dismantled, and if they do not take place, small and medium-sized inefficient intermediaries will find it difficult to earn sufficient revenues to cover costs.

All of these changes, not just the introduction of the euro, have implications for international portfolio adjustments and for capital flows. To the extent that the euro is perceived as a stable store of value, it will assume an important role as a reserve currency, probably exceeding the aggregate roles of the former currencies of EMU member countries. Arithmetically, this would make the euro the second most important reserve currency next to the dollar. Whether the euro also takes a significant share of international financial transactions and trade invoicing is less certain, though clearly possible. Although it is difficult to say with certainty, it is reasonable to expect that as market segmentation diminishes across the various national capital markets within EMU, more capital will flow to and from the euro zone. Whether this implies a strong or weak euro is difficult to project. This will depend on the now uncertain macroeconomic outcomes, including the monetary and exchange rate policies pursued by the ECB and the ability of EMU members to continue along the path of fiscal consolidation and structural reform.

References

Aoki, Masahiko, ed., 1984, *The Economic Analysis of the Japanese Firm* (Amsterdam; New York: North-Holland).

Artis, Michael, and Mark Taylor, 1990, "Abolishing Exchange Control: The U.K. Experience," Chapter 5 in *Private Behaviour and Government Policy in Interdependent Economies*, ed. by Anthony S. Courakis and Mark P. Taylor (Oxford: Clarendon Press), pp. 129–58.

Bank for International Settlements, 1996a, *Central Bank Survey of Foreign Exchange and Derivatives Market Activity 1995* (Basle: Bank for International Settlements, May).

———, 1996b, *International Banking and Financial Market Developments* (Basle: Bank for International Settlements, November).

———, 1996c, *66th Annual Report* (Basle: Bank for International Settlements).

Bank of England, 1996, *Practical Issues Arising from the Introduction of the Euro*, Vols. 1, 2, and 3 (London: Bank of England).

Bayoumi, Tamim, Morris Goldstein, and Geoffrey Woglom, 1995, "Do Credit Markets Discipline Sovereign Borrowers? Evidence from U.S. States," *Journal of Money, Credit and Banking*, Vol. 27 (November, Part I), pp. 1046–59.

Bodart, Vincent, and Paul Reding, 1996, "Exchange Rate Regime, Volatility, and International Correlations on Bond and Stock Markets" (unpublished; Namur, Belgium: Department of Economics, University of Namur).

Bolton, Patrick, and Ernst-Ludwig von Thadden, 1996, "Blocks, Liquidity and Corporate Control," LSE Financial Markets Group Discussion Paper No. 249 (London: London School of Economics, October).

Deutsche Bundesbank, *Kapital Market Statistik* (Frankfurt: various issues).

Diamond, Douglas W., 1984, "Financial Intermediation and Delegated Monitoring," *Review of Economic Studies*, Vol. 51 (July), pp. 393–414.

Drudi, Francesco, and Alessandro Prati, 1997, "Differences and Analogies Between Index-Linked and Foreign Currency Bonds: A Theoretical and Empirical Analysis," in *Managing Public Debt—Index Linked Bonds in Theory and Practice*, ed. by Marcello De Cecco, Lorenzo Pecchi, and Gustavo Piga (United Kingdom: Edward Elgar), pp. 195–216.

Eijffinger, Sylvester C.W., and Jan J.G. Lemmen, 1995, "Money Market Integration in Europe," *Swiss Journal of Economics and Statistics*, Vol. 131 (March), pp. 3–37.

European Commission, 1995, *Green Paper on the Practical Arrangements for the Introduction of the Single Currency* (Luxembourg: Office for Official Publications of the European Community).

European Monetary Institute, 1997, "The Single Monetary Policy in Stage Three: Specification of the Operational Framework" (Frankfurt: EMI).

Folkerts-Landau, David, and Peter Garber, 1992, "The European Central Bank: A Bank or a Monetary Policy Rule," NBER Working Paper No. 4016 (Cambridge, Massachusetts: National Bureau of Economic Research, March).

Frankel, Jeffrey A., 1996, "Exchange Rates and the Single Currency," Chapter 10 in *The European Equity Markets: The State of the Union and an Agenda for the Millennium*, ed. by Benn Steil (Copenhagen, Denmark: European Capital Markets Institute), pp. 355–93.

Frankel, Jeffrey, Steven Phillips, and Menzie Chinn, 1993, "Financial and Currency Integration in the European Monetary System: The Statistical Record," in *Adjustment and Growth in the European Monetary Union*, ed. by Francisco Torres and Francesco Giavazzi (Cambridge: Cambridge University Press), pp. 270–306.

Giddy, Ian, Anthony Saunders, and Ingo Walter, 1996, "Clearance and Settlement," Chapter 9 in *The European Equity Markets: The State of the Union and an Agenda for the Millennium*, ed. by Benn Steil (Copenhagen, Denmark: European Capital Markets Institute), pp. 321–50.

Goldman Sachs, 1977, Fixed Income Research: Corporate Bond Monthly (February), p. 47.

Goldstein, Morris, and Michael Mussa, 1993, "The Integration of World Capital Markets," IMF Working Paper 93/95 (Washington: International Monetary Fund, December).

Gurley, John G., and Edward S. Shaw, 1960, *Money in a Theory of Finance* (Washington: Brookings Institution).

International Monetary Fund, *International Capital Markets Report: Developments, Prospects, and Policy Issues* (Washington: IMF, various issues).

J.P. Morgan, 1996, "The euro, FX reserves and vehicle currencies: some unusual findings," Morgan Guaranty Trust Company, Foreign Exchange Research, September 13.

Organisation for Economic Cooperation and Development, 1996a, *Bank Profitability: Financial Statements of Banks 1985–1994* (Paris: OECD).

———, 1996b, "United States Banking Consolidation: Current Trends and Issues" (Paris: OECD, November).

———, *OECD Financial Statistics, Part III, Nonfinancial enterprises financial statements* (Paris: OECD, various issues).

Pagano, Marco, 1996, "The Cost of Trading in European Equity Markets," LSE Financial Markets Group Special Paper Series No. 83 (London: London School of Economics, March).

Paribas Capital Markets, 1996, "EMU Countdown," *International Research* (September 9).

Salomon Brothers, 1996, "Managing Convergence," *Prospects for Financial Markets* (December).

SBC Warburg (1996), "EMU: Opportunity or Threat?" (December).

Smith, R. Todd, 1995, "Markets for Corporate Debt Securities," IMF Working Paper No. 95/67 (Washington: International Monetary Fund, July).

Steinherr, Alfred, 1996, "Universal vs. Specialized Banks," Economic Studies Working Paper No. 20 (Washington: American Institute for Contemporary German Studies, December).

Volcker, Paul A., 1984, "The Federal Reserve Position on Restructuring of Financial Regulation Responsibilities," *Federal Reserve Bulletin*, Vol. 70 (July), pp. 547–57.

Comments on Prati and Schinasi

Gert-Jan Hogeweg

Although this is already the second day of this conference, it is not too late to welcome the conference as a sign of the increasing interest in and recognition of the EMU process as it unfolds. We within the EMI are frantically trying to meet the very short deadlines of our extended master plan in which we are trying to develop, as much as possible, a turnkey central bank that will be able to take up its huge responsibilities on January 1, 1999. The intention is not to be just an isolated central bank but very much the central decision-making body of a system of central banks that works together, which in many ways complicates the technical preparation for the transition. While we are embroiled in all this preparation, we are grateful for opportunities to discuss these issues in a much broader context. I also welcome the focus on the IMF's role in this regard.

We do realize that many of the things we are doing at the EMI have implications and ramifications that go far beyond Europe, and that is why I think this conference is a useful initiative. I do hope that this will be a start of a more intensive discussion of this nature, as no doubt will be some of the papers that the IMF staff is preparing for the Executive Board on the basis of a number of visits we have received from the IMF staff, which we have also very much appreciated.

In reading the Prati and Schinasi paper I was struck by two things. One is that the title refers to international capital markets, but that in actual fact the paper also focuses on domestic euro capital markets. At first, I was wondering why that was so and whether it was a "mis-title" or a "mis-content," but then I decided it was neither of the two because it is indeed logical that you would envisage the impact on international capital markets to run via the development of domestic euro financial markets. In that sense, upon reflection, I think the focus of the paper is right, but it does imply, obviously, that the two papers we are discussing (Prati and Schinasi, and McCauley and White), do indeed belong to the same session and that there is a certain degree of overlap in their coverage. But the richness of the material in the paper I am discussing forces me within the short time span allowed to be very selective in the issues I would like to comment on. So this means that when I am silent on something, it does not necessarily mean approval.

My prime focus will be on the part of the paper in which the authors discuss the influence of the monetary policy framework of the ESCB on the development of euro financial markets. These are important issues that are close to heart of the EMI, which has done much preparatory work in this very area and has recently released a report on these issues. In designing the monetary policy framework, we at the EMI have tried to make it fully consistent with the operation of markets. Of course, whatever we do in preparation for the transition should be viewed only as a toolbox to be offered to the ESCB upon its establishment—no firm decisions have been taken on what exactly to apply and how exactly to apply it. In that sense, the paper is right in saying that not all decisions have been taken and that, hence, not all conclusions can be drawn.

The main monetary instrument, as we envisage it, would be a regular weekly tender with a 14-day maturity as the main refinancing instrument, which would regulate short-term interest rates and would serve the signaling function. This would take place within a corridor of two standing facilities, as is well known. We would have various other open-market instruments to react both to structural developments in the money market and, conversely, to fine-tuning operations. We envisage a longer-term refinancing facility that would replace the discount facilities that are still in operation in some countries, with the essential difference being that no subsidization would be involved in this new instrument whatsoever, thus adding to its market orientation.

On reserve requirements, as with all instruments, it will be up to the ECB to decide whether or how to apply them. We have prepared these instruments in a way that leaves open the modalities, so that the ECB has a choice to make on which liabilities it would apply, how high the ratio would be, whether or not there would be remuneration, and other issues of that kind.

Another important characteristic of the ESCB monetary policy framework is the decentralized nature of its implementation, combined with fully centralized decision making. Finally, we characterize our framework with a broad range of counterparties and a broad range of collateral—and the possibility of cross-border use of that collateral, meaning that counterparties are not restricted to mobilizing only that collateral located in their own central banks. It struck me that relatively little analysis is given in the Prati and Schinasi paper to the decentralized character of operations that would take place in every financial center by every participating central bank. Also, comparatively little analysis seems to have been given to the fact that the instruments will be fully harmonized, so that in each and every local money market both the central bank and its counterparties would have to adapt to a new environment.

My most important remark in this respect, though, is that reserve requirements seem to have been overemphasized in the paper. They are mentioned first where the authors describe the ESCB monetary policy framework, and the authors also give quite a bit of importance to the averaging provision, which, together with the planned infrequent interventions of the central bank and the money market, are—certainly by contrast to the U.S. model—seen as not fostering the development of efficient money and securities market. In reaction to that, I would say that the way an averaging facility works—"averaging" meaning that counterparties do not have to conform to the reserve requirement every day, but only on average over a period—in stabilizing interest rates is precisely by fostering markets because it forces the counterparties to take a view on interest rate developments and manage their liquidity accordingly.

Likewise, less frequent intervention of the central bank in the money market forces the counterparts to deal among themselves more. So, I would see this not as an impediment to the functioning of markets but, on the contrary, an opportunity for markets to develop within a given framework. In that sense, I do not quite understand the context of the authors' remark that they wonder how the central bank would react to pressure on the part of its counterparties to intervene in the markets more frequently than it is planning on doing. It may be that the authors have the German model in mind, whereby reserve requirements do indeed coexist with less developed markets. But I believe other institutional constraints are at work in the German case with regard to the existence and use of short-term instruments. And the German model also includes a discount window, which implies a subsidization that does, in a way, discourage markets. But that is an environment that would be completely changed in the ESCB context.

Turning to the TARGET payment system, which links the RTGS payment systems in all European Union countries, this system is specifically designed to allow the integration of the different money markets that are now in existence into a single euro-area-wide money market. The building of TARGET is part and parcel of the impact that the central bank will have on the development of markets. Although the authors characterize the likely working of the ESCB as narrow, focused on price stability only, I think the effort we are putting into the creation of TARGET illustrates that we are not that narrow, although we are of course proud of our narrowness in another sense, namely that we are not catering to other macroeconomic desiderata. I agree with Prati and Schinasi that, in order for the full benefits to be achieved, it is desirable for a large part of high-value payments within the EU to be channeled through national RTGS systems. But we should realize that TARGET does not have a monopoly and that other systems will coexist. For instance, the euro clearing that will be organized by what is now called the ECU Banking Association will no doubt exist regardless of whether TARGET has a pan-European character.

Finally, a technical point: Prati and Schinasi seem to think that the current debate on the intra-day credit access in TARGET for central banks located outside of the euro area has to do with whether intra-day credit is regarded as relevant for monetary policy in itself. In fact, the current debate is not so much about that as about how to limit the risk of spillover of intra-day credit to overnight credit, which is part and parcel of the monetary policy framework.

12

The Euro and European Financial Markets

Robert N. McCauley and William R. White

Many uncertainties as regards timing, scope, and other issues still surround the introduction of a single currency in Europe. Nevertheless, the event seems probable enough, imminent enough, and important enough to warrant some consideration of what the effects might be on the structure of European financial markets and the implications of such changes both within Europe and for the international financial system.

The story line in this paper is dynamic but simple. The starting point is that Europe-based financial firms are already under significant competitive pressure to restructure. Moreover, existing forces of technological change and deregulation affecting cross-border activity (the First and Second Banking Directives) must eventually cause those pressures to intensify, even if the effects to date on international competition in corporate and retail banking have been limited. However, the introduction of the euro seems likely to be a catalyst for change going well beyond the need to absorb the direct costs of transition. It seems probable that it will play an important role in stimulating the growth of a much larger and more liquid securities market in Europe (both private and public). This could be a significant new source of competitive pressure for banking firms providing traditional forms of intermediated credit in Europe. While the bond market in euros is likely to attract both more international investment and more issuance in that currency, implying an enhanced role for the euro in the international financial system, the associated profits may be rather highly concentrated. The direct influence of the euro in stimulating in-

The authors would like to thank, without implicating them and in alphabetical order, Palle Andersen, Stephan Arthur, Jeremy Barson, Florence Béranger, Henri Bernard, Claudio Borio, Dierk Brandenburg, Stephen Collins, Clifford Dammers, Phil Davis, Angelika Donaubauer, Charles Goodhart, Gregor Heinrich, André Icard, Serge Jeanneau, Frederick Marki, Danielle Nouy, Denis Pêtre, Costas Tsatsaronis, and Jürgen von Hagen.

ternational competition among banks for traditional kinds of business will be a second new source of competitive pressure, but in itself likely to be of a lower order of importance. Existing legal, fiscal, regulatory, and cultural factors will continue to divide markets. Nevertheless, it is not difficult to tell a dynamic story in which increased competition among banks, aided by ongoing disintermediation, leads to increased pressure for more harmonization and in turn still more competitive pressure.

Should such a competitive environment emerge, it will be all the more important to have in place adequate incentive structures and supervisory arrangements to promote sound banking practices. Issues having to do with managing banking problems in a single currency area, should they occur, are also important but of course cannot be addressed without recognizing the complications posed by moral hazard problems. Whatever Europeans choose to do in these areas, there will also be international implications. Given the nature of integrated international financial markets, any adjustment problems that might occur could have spillover effects beyond Europe. Globally integrated financial markets also imply that the approach taken to problems of systemic risk within Europe should be coherent, with any approach adopted more globally. While this is in fact already the case, the bargaining dynamics of achieving global agreements could well be different in the future should Europe increasingly speak with a single voice.

The Euro and the Balance of Competitive Pressures in European Financial Markets[1]

If European banks are about to enter a period of enhanced competition, the starting position for many banks is not particularly strong. As indicated in Table 1, the rate of return on the assets of continental European banks rebounded in 1995 and, according to preliminary reports, it rose further in 1996. However, this should not overshadow two other trends. The rate of return continues to be relatively low in some countries (compared with U.S., U.K., and restructured Scandinavian banks)[2] and profits seem to have been trending down since the mid-1980s (see Table 2). Net interest margins have tended to

[1]It is appropriate to begin this paper with a warning. We try to provide a brief summary of some very broad trends in the European financial industry. We recognize that, in the process, assertions will be made that do not apply at all (or only in part) to banks from particular national jurisdictions. For individual banks, broad statements may be even less applicable.

[2]In the late 1980s, a lower cost of equity for German banks allowed them to earn as much as a 20 basis point lower return on their (risk-adjusted) assets than their U.K. or U.S. competitors. See Zimmer and McCauley (1991).

Table 1. Profitability of Major Banks in 1994 and 1995

		Return on Assets[1]		Loan Loss Provisions		Net Interest Margin		Operating Costs	
		1994	1995	1994	1995	1994	1995	1994	1995
Country	Number of Banks	(As a percentage of total assets)							
Denmark[2]	2	0.29	1.20	0.61	0.42	2.85	2.55	2.20	2.07
Finland[3]	2	−0.69	−0.16	1.65	0.60	1.98	1.57	2.30	2.21
France	6	0.17	0.27	0.63	0.39	1.60	1.54	2.04	2.00
Germany	2	0.52	0.56	0.35	0.23	1.82	1.57	2.06	1.98
Netherlands	3	0.69	0.72	. . .	. . .	2.27	2.18	2.17	2.26
Norway	4	1.31	1.81	0.16	−0.38	2.96	2.86	2.82	3.01
Spain	6	0.70	0.79	0.52	0.45	2.47	2.46	2.45	2.62
Sweden	4	0.55	1.23	1.09	0.59	2.34	2.39	1.76	1.81
United Kingdom	4	1.22	1.27	0.31	0.34	2.45	2.44	3.02	2.98
Memorandum items									
Japan[4]	21	−0.21	−0.75	0.88	2.03	0.90	1.01	0.74	0.74
Switzerland	3	0.63	0.52	0.30	0.33	1.17	1.07	2.17	2.18
United States	12	1.81	1.87	0.33	0.31	3.57	3.35	3.80	3.49

Source: IBCA Ltd, as reported in BIS (1996a).

[1]Pretax profit.

[2]The portfolio of securities is marked to market.

[3]1994 and 1995 results are not fully comparable owing to a break in series.

[4]Combination of half-year results at an annual rate and IBCA estimates. Fiscal years.

Table 2. Long-Term Accounting Indicators of Banks' Performance[1]

	Pretax Profits			Noninterest Income		
	1980–82[2]	1986–88	1990–94	1980–82[2]	1986–88	1990–94
Country	(As a percentage of assets)			(As a percentage of gross income)		
Belgium	0.4	0.4	0.3	15	22	26
Finland	0.5	0.5	−1.6	49	58	53
France	0.4	0.4	−0.1	16	17	46
Germany	0.5	0.7	0.5	29	30	29
Italy	0.7	1.0	0.8	26	29	26
Netherlands	0.3	0.7	0.6	25	26	30
Norway	0.6	0.0	0.2	27	30	29
Spain	0.7	1.1	0.6	18	20	27
Sweden	0.3	0.8	0.5	30	31	44
United Kingdom	1.1	1.0	0.7	29	37	43
Memorandum items						
Japan[3]	0.5	0.6	0.2	14	24	1
Switzerland	0.6	0.7	0.6	47	49	51
United States	1.0	0.7	1.6	24	30	35

Source: OECD, as reported in BIS (1996a).
[1]For Belgium, the Netherlands, and Switzerland, all banks; for other countries, commercial banks only.
[2]For Belgium and France, 1981–82.
[3]Fiscal years.

narrow, and loan-loss provisions have been high.[3] Reflecting these realities, the ratio of bank share prices to general stock price indices has been falling in most European countries (see Table 3) and downgradings of continental banks by rating agencies have become more common (see Figure 1), even if credit ratings remain relatively high. In sum, there is at least a prima facie case that a significant degree of restructuring is required, leading to some withdrawal of capital from the industry and some concentration of that capital that remains.

There are also a number of reasons for believing that competitive pressures in the European financial industry are likely to increase significantly. Technological change is affecting the financial services industry everywhere, lowering the costs of both information and transactions. This challenges the basis of traditional relationship banking and encourages securitization as well as competition from nonbanks for corporate and retail banking business. The growing interest in many European countries in private pension schemes and

[3]Much of this can be related to losses on loans collateralized with commercial property. The value of such property fell sharply through the first half of the 1990s in many continental European countries (albeit with wide regional variations), though the implications for the profit and loss account tended to be recognized only with a lag.

Table 3. Long-Term Movements in Bank Share Prices

(Ratio of bank[1] index to overall index, 1980 = 100)

Country	1970	1980–82	1984–86	1990–92	1993–95	1995	1996
Belgium	110	97	93	109	155	166	182
Finland	85	98	84	47	22	15	13
Germany	93	94	83	75	78	72	67
Italy	...	138	96	86	72	67	65
Netherlands	...	92	77	56	61	60	64
Norway	101	103	67	17	9	9	10
Spain	56	112	78	85	76	72	70
Sweden	66	99	84	68	66	61	66
United Kingdom	85	97	90	83	118	127	143
Memorandum items							
Japan	71	103	158[2]	189	196	194	181
Switzerland	64	99	92	59	60	55	49
United States	142	111	120	69	92	96	111

Source: National stock exchanges, as reported in BIS (1996a).

[1]For Japan (prior to 1983), Belgium, and the Netherlands, including other financial institutions.

[2]The rise in this period is largely due to the breakdown of restrictive arrangements aimed at controlling bank share prices.

other means to encourage savings on the part of a rapidly aging population will work in the same direction. Finally, the process of financial deregulation in Europe has been under way for almost 30 years, culminating in the Capital Liberalization Directive of 1988 and the Second Banking Coordination Directive, which came into effect on January 1, 1993. The explicit purpose of these Directives was to encourage a heightened level of international competition in the member countries of the EU.

What is somewhat surprising, in light of all these forces for change, is how little impact they have had to date on the structure of the European financial industry, which continues to be basically "national" in the provision of corporate and retail banking services.[4] Moreover, banking products in many continental European countries are still significantly overpriced relative to those supplied by low-cost providers elsewhere in Europe.[5] The reason for this is that there also exist many forces resisting change. One important consideration is that the industry has not had very many years to react to recent de-

[4]See Economic Research Europe Ltd. (1996). The market for wholesale banking services is intensely competitive and highly international. However, this reflects the influence of offshore markets and euromarkets much more than regulatory change within Europe itself.

[5]Emerson's study (see Emerson, 1988) documented the extent of these price deviations. The more recent study by Economic Research Europe Ltd. (1996) indicated that not a great deal had changed on average, although the prices of some financial services had fallen discernibly in some of the countries that had been most highly regulated to begin with.

Figure 1. Long-Term Credit Rating of Major Banks[1]

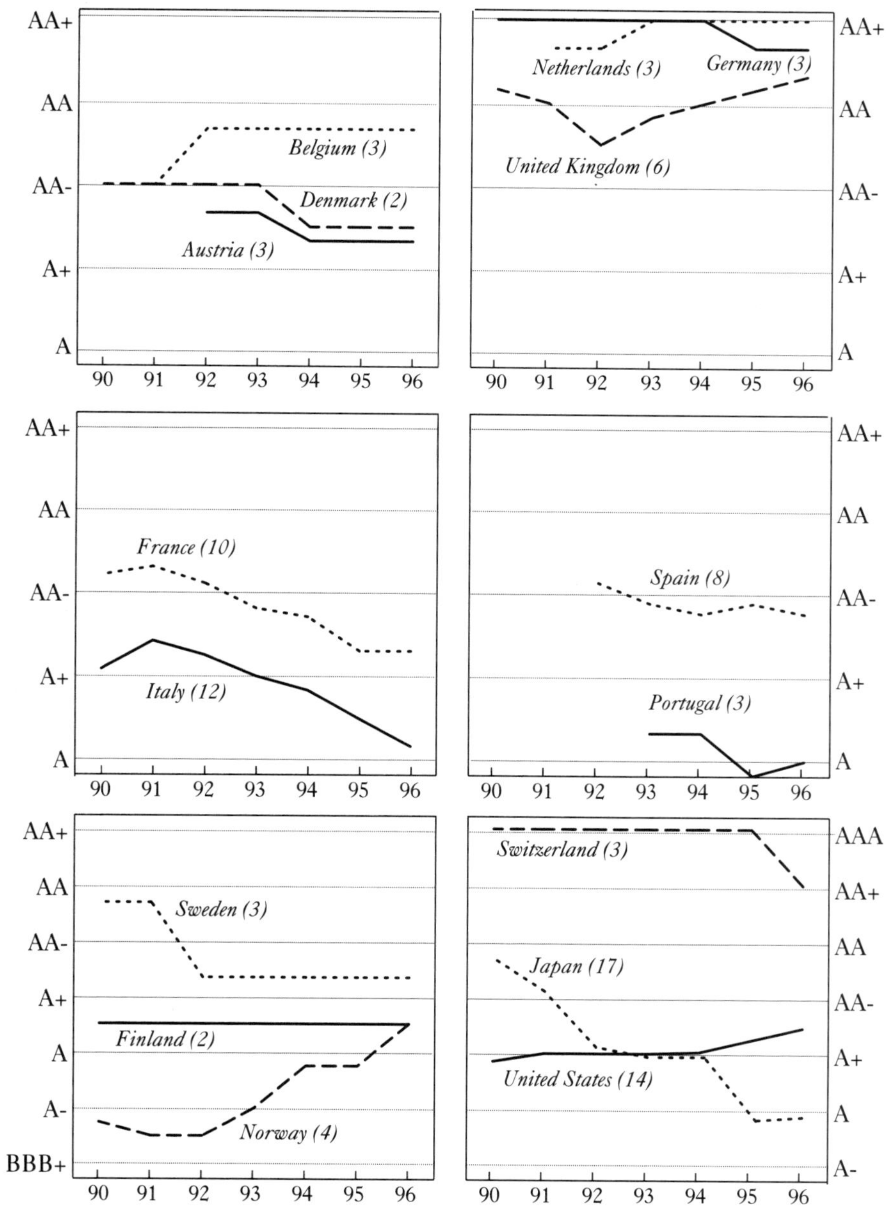

Source: IBCA.

[1]Average of banks' rating at the end of the year. The number of banks included are in parentheses.

regulatory initiatives, and has also had to adjust to a rather sluggish macroeconomic environment. With time, these impediments to change should disappear. However, other impediments to international competition are likely to be longer lasting. There continue to be significant differences across European countries in the legal, tax, regulatory, and supervisory frameworks within which financial firms have to operate. Different accounting and reporting procedures, technical standards, labor practices, and cultural preferences further distinguish national markets. Finally, the continuing and important role of the state in the banking business in many continental European countries (see Table 4) is also a force acting to suppress international competition.

In the rest of this paper, we speculate on how the introduction of a single currency in Europe might tilt the balance of forces described above, potentially acting as a catalyst for pent-up and significant change in the structure of European and indeed global financial markets. We focus on two principal possibilities. First, bond markets may gain in strength, depth, and liquidity from the introduction of the euro and this will be to the disadvantage of those supplying traditional intermediated credit. Second, the euro will lead to transitional costs and an increase in European intrabank competition at a time when

Table 4. Bank Share in Financial Intermediation in 1995

	Assets of Banks as a Percentage of Assets of Banks and Nonbank Financial Institutions			
		Of which		
Country	Total	Savings banks	Mutual and cooperative banks	Share of state-owned banks[1]
Finland[2]	59	...	...	...
France	73	8	15	12
Germany	77	36	14	50
Italy	81	...	16	60
Netherlands[2]	52	...	...	...
Norway	63	19	...	13
Spain	78	26	3	...
United Kingdom	56[3]	...	...	0
Memorandum items				
Japan[2]	79	...	...	0
Switzerland[2]	53	3	5	3[4]
United States	22	4	1	0

Sources: OECD; and national data.
[1]Partly estimated.
[2]1994.
[3]Of which building societies, 8 percent.
[4]Excluding savings and regional banks, which are partly owned by local communities. Their total share of assets is 3 percent.

continental banks are already struggling to cope with global competitive pressures and other EU initiatives directed toward the single market. While, for analytic convenience, we treat separately these two threats to the competitive status quo in European banking, there could be strong interactions between them: lower credit ratings for some banks could encourage direct recourse to financial markets, still stronger competitive pressures, further harmonization, yet more competition, and so on.

The possible implications of these changes for domestic financial stability and European public policy need to be considered. Moreover, given the size of European financial markets, and their close links with the rest of the world, the repercussions elsewhere also need to be considered. The possibility that non-Europeans might also have low-cost access to a large and liquid securities market denominated in euros has international implications. Finally, the need to cope with potentially significant changes in financial structure within the euro area raises supervisory and related issues with broader international dimensions.

The Euro and European Bond Markets

Many analysts of the effect of the euro on European bond markets concede that integration of the private bond market in euros could proceed rapidly. Nevertheless, it is often contended that the government bond market in euros would be likely to remain fragmented, with significant, persistent, and variable credit spreads marking one issuer's bonds off from those of another. What follows partly agrees and partly disagrees with each proposition. The business of pricing private credits in euros should benefit (and almost already does benefit) from a common reference yield curve, and thereby from heightened competition among underwriters of new issues. In the pricing of government debt, prospects for integration in the trading of the bonds of most creditworthy governments look brighter than is generally acknowledged. At the same time, the euro may sharpen credit differences across the full range of governments participating in monetary union.

After discussing the short-term costs of the transition to the euro, we assess the likely effects of the euro on European bond markets, and then we draw some implications. A fully integrated bond market will require a long process of legal, regulatory, and behavioral change that would free institutional investors to invest across the euro area. Given such integration, an implication for the euro area is the probable alteration of the calculus of costs and benefits of bond issuance by European corporations, tilting the balance of corporate credit away from banks and toward the bond market. From an international perspective, a deeper, more liquid bond market can be expected to attract international asset and liability managers to increase the share of euro-denominated securities in their portfolios in relation to the sum of the shares of the euro's constituent currencies.

Transition Costs of Monetary Union

The transition to monetary union confronts the securities industry with direct costs and legal risks that at this stage appear modest. Market makers in European securities have reported that the direct costs of making the transition to the single currency would be quite moderate. A study commissioned by the International Securities Market Association, based on a survey of over 1,000 market participants, put the range at between ECU 110,000 and ECU 8 million per firm.[6] This worked out to an average of 0.058 percent of the total operating costs of financial institutions. This is a tiny fraction compared with some of the estimates from banks (some of which may include these securities firms' conversion costs; see below). In addition, some firms, "such as large brokerage firms," reported anticipated job losses of 15–25 percent, although others, "particularly large investment banking firms," anticipate no reductions in the workforce.

In addition, swap dealers face the risk that counterparties might plead that they cannot fulfill (losing) swap contracts owing to the disappearance of the relevant currency. One estimate is that 14–15 percent of swap contracts extend beyond 1999 and "need to be tightened up with respect to the conversion to the euro."[7] Legal counsels of securities firms in Europe have been working with Brussels to ensure continuity of contracts, but questions remain as to how New York State courts might respond to such cases (see also the next section). In sum, total transition costs in the fixed income markets appear modest.

The Euro and Private Money and Bond Markets

The euro will create a single private yield curve across the euro area. As a result, the field of competition among underwriters will open up and issuers should enjoy better pricing.

Private Yield Curve in Euros

Ranging from an overnight rate, which would be strongly affected by the repo operations of the ECB, to interbank offered rates of maturities from one week to one or two years, a single reference money market yield curve can be

[6]See Scobie (1997, p. 48). No response rate was specified.
[7]Ibid., p. 66.

expected. It is an open question whether the reference yields for the euro money market will be established onshore or offshore. The location of the banks that will be polled for the most widely used reference rates may depend on whether the ECB uses unremunerated reserve requirements as an instrument of monetary policy. At present, French franc futures contracts are based on PIBOR, the Paris rates, while the most heavily traded deutsche mark (and U.S. dollar) contracts are based on London rates, rather than Frankfurt (or New York) rates, owing to the reserve requirements assessed in Frankfurt (and formerly assessed in New York). In the absence of reserve requirements, significant deposit insurance premiums, or the like, the choice of whether to collect rates from banks located in Paris, Frankfurt, Amsterdam, London, or Zurich will in normal circumstances not make any difference in terms of the rates obtained.[8] Rather, the identity of the banks included in the poll would make a difference (as the Japan premium has recently reminded us). That is, a bank might at times or regularly pay a premium over the average interbank rate offered by prime banks, but such risk premiums would depend more on the bank's risk profile than on its location. In sum, a single private money market yield curve seems to be in the offing, and the market's choice of reference rates between onshore and offshore rates will depend on the ECB's reserve requirements.

Whether onshore or offshore, the euro money market is likely to prove a very liquid market from its inception. By liquidity we mean the ability to transact large amounts at short order without moving the market against oneself. Operationalizing this concept presents a real challenge, but transactions measures such as bid-ask spreads and trading volumes probably better indicate liquidity than the size of underlying asset stocks. Table 5 shows derivative transactions in private money market instruments. Focusing on these has the advantage of measuring the transactions with the lowest costs. On this view, even a narrow monetary union would create a money market that would, at current exchange rates, surpass the scale of the yen money market in derivative transactions, and thus probably in liquidity. Admittedly, this comparison may flatter the euro if a substantial fraction of money market

[8]The London International Financial Futures and Options Exchange announced in March 1996 that March 1999 eurocurrency contracts for the deutsche mark, pound sterling, and Italian lira would provide for settlement in euros if these currencies were irrevocably fixed to the euro by three weeks before contract expiry (see *LIFFE*, 1996). Rates on euros would be collected by the British Bankers' Association in London, according to Gregorio (1996, p. 5). Similarly, the MATIF has made provision in Article 12 of the regulations for the three-month PIBOR futures contract for the replacement of the French franc with the euro (see Scobie, 1997, p. 65). Such moves already anticipate a market in which prime names from across the currency area would be able to fund themselves, and manage their interest rate exposure in euros, at rates that would be determined areawide.

Table 5. Derivative Transactions in Private Money Market Instruments in Dollars, Yen, and Euros

(In trillions of dollars a year)

Instruments	1995	1996
U.S. dollar		
Eurodollar futures (CME, SIMEX)	104.125	97.068
Federal funds (CBOT)	3.219	3.042
Forward rate agreements[1]	4.667	. . .
Eurodollar option (CME, SIMEX)	22.369	22.238
Japanese yen		
Euroyen futures (TIFFE, SIMEX)	45.543	34.475
Forward rate agreements[1]	2.518	. . .
Euroyen options (TIFFE, SIMEX)	0.521	0.714
Selected European currencies		
Euro-deutsche mark/franc-lira futures	35.932	42.405
Forward rate agreements	5.244	. . .
Euro-deutsche mark/franc-lira options	7.076	6.907
Deutsche mark		
Euromark futures (LIFFE)	17.960	24.090
Forward rate agreements[1]	2.200	. . .
Euromark options (LIFFE)	2.392	3.251
French franc		
PIBOR contracts (MATIF)	15.513	13.818
Forward rate agreements	2.593[2]	. . .
PIBOR options (MATIF)	4.623	3.038
Italian lira		
Futures (LIFFE)	2.459	4.497
Forward rate agreements	0.451[2]	. . .
Options (LIFFE)	0.061	0.618

Sources: Various futures exchanges; BIS (1996b); and authors' estimates.

Note: Japanese yen, deutsche mark, French franc, and Italian lira amounts converted at year-average exchange rates.

[1]Estimated as average daily turnover in April times 255.

[2]Estimated as deutsche mark forward rate agreements (FRAs) times the ratio of FRA trading in Paris or Milan to FRA trading in Frankfurt.

transactions in the French franc represents one leg of matched transactions in marks. In any case, a considerable gap would remain between the euro and the dollar in this respect, with futures and forward transactions of at least \$40 trillion a year in Europe, compared with eurodollar transactions in excess of \$100 trillion. At such scale it is reasonable to expect that three-month euro futures would offer greater liquidity than do deutsche mark futures, especially in contracts settling four to eight quarters ahead (see Karsenti, 1996).

At longer maturities, the most frequently used private reference rates will be the yields on the fixed rate side of interest rate swaps. These standard and liquid prime-name rates extend from 2 years out to 10 years in maturity and already serve as the most important private reference rates in today's bond markets. The convergence among these swap yields for contracts in Belgian francs, deutsche mark, Dutch guilders, and French francs over the past two years (see Figure 2) carries the strong message that market participants attach a high probability to stable exchange rates among these currencies.[9] This inference is supported by the possibility that, if exchange rates were expected to move, one could contract to pay fixed (and receive floating) payments in the weak currency and to receive fixed (and pay floating) payments in the strong currency. The swap market is precisely where such private arbitrage/speculation takes place at the lowest transaction costs. (In this respect, the swap yield curve represents an extension to longer maturities of the private money rate, LIBOR.) At the inception of monetary union, the currently nearly identical swap curves will collapse into a single swap curve.

The private capital market in euros is also likely to prove to be a very liquid market from its inception. On current evidence, even a narrow monetary union would offer a swap market about as active as those in the U.S. dollar and in the Japanese yen (see Table 6). Even recognizing that convergence trades are providing a temporary boost to the European transactions (see Bradbery, 1996; and Burgess, 1996, p. 4), the euro looks set to offer a private yield curve with world-class depth, breadth, and liquidity.

In view of the uncertain prospects for the integration of government bond markets in the euro area, discussed below, some analysts have suggested that the swap yield curve might perform a benchmark role in Europe (see Adler, 1996; Huteau, 1997; Karsenti, 1996; and Krämer, 1996). Normally, one thinks of the benchmark as the lowest yield, with other yields quoted (and in effect determined) as spreads over the benchmark. However, in principle, the bonds of various governments could be priced as spreads under the swap yield curve. The problem with this suggestion is not a formal but a practical one. Transactions in swaps and swaptions, while very large at trillions of dollars equivalent a year, pale in comparison to the tens of trillions of dollars of transactions in government bonds, government bond futures, and government bond options, as will be demonstrated below. As things stand, it is hard to imagine the private yield curve in euros serving as

[9]See BIS (1996a, pp. 112–113) for the use of swap rates to assess the market outlook for EMU. See also De Grauwe (1996).

Figure 2. Private Interest Rates in Europe
(In percent a year)

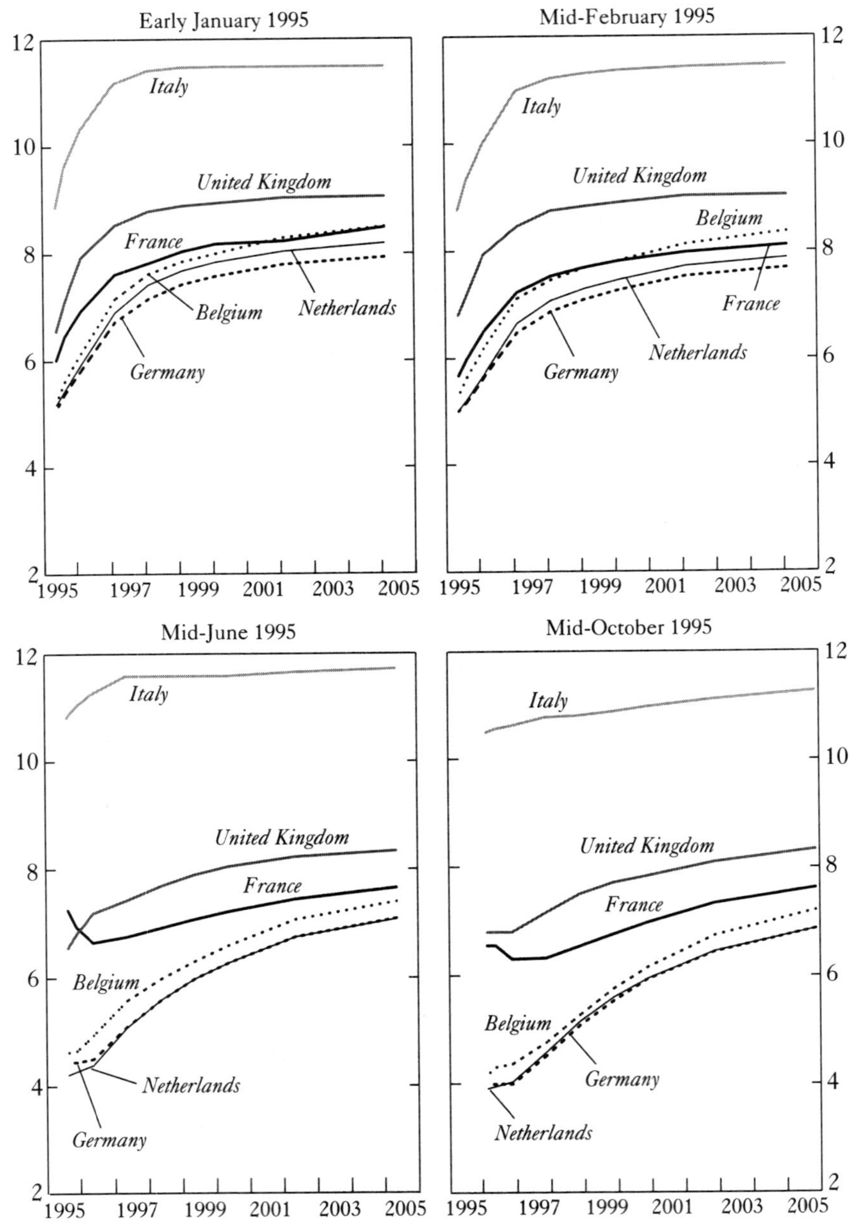

Sources: Datastream; Reuters; and BIS.
Note: The yield curves are based on eurodeposit rates and, for longer horizons, on swap (midpoint) yields.

Figure 2. (Concluded)

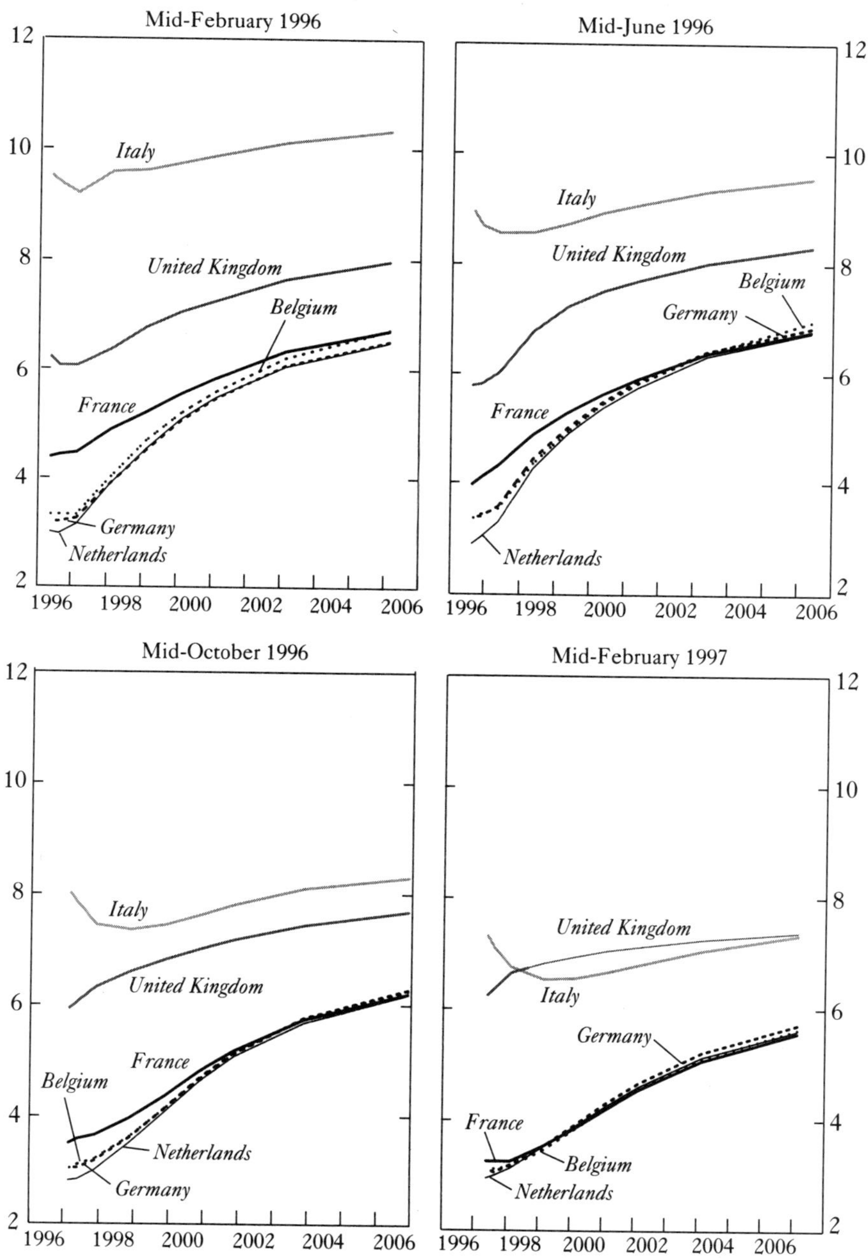

Sources: Datastream; Reuters; and BIS.
Note: The yield curves are based on eurodeposit rates and, for longer horizons, on swap (midpoint) yields.

Table 6. Transactions in Interest Rate Swaps and Swaptions in Dollars, Yen, and Euros

(In trillions of dollars a year)

	Central Bank Survey[1]	ISDA	
	1995	1995	1996[2]
U.S. dollar	5.981		
Swaps	4.283	2.856	3.690
Swaptions	1.698		
Japanese yen	4.904		
Swaps	4.378	2.259	3.128
Swaptions	0.527		
Selected European currencies	4.678		
Swaps	3.907	2.315	3.485
Swaptions	0.771		
Deutsche mark	1.948		
Swaps	1.661	0.985	1.935
Swaptions	0.287		
French franc	2.303		
Swaps	1.879[3]	1.113	1.550
Swaptions	0.424[4]		
Italian lira	0.427		
Swaps	0.367[3]	0.217	...
Swaptions	0.060[4]		

Sources: ISDA; BIS (1996b); and authors' estimates.

[1]Estimated as average daily turnover in April times 255.

[2]First half, at annual rate.

[3]Estimated as deutsche mark swaps times the ratio of ISDA-reported French franc swaps or ISDA-reported Italian lira swaps to ISDA-reported deutsche mark swaps.

[4]Estimated as deutsche mark swaptions times the ratio of swaption transactions in Paris or Milan to such transactions in Frankfurt.

the benchmark for government as well as private risks in the European bond market.[10]

Increased Competition in Underwriting Private and Foreign Bonds

If multiple currencies in Europe tend to segment its bond markets, keener competition in the bond market should result from monetary union. As background, consider the range of factors that bear on competition in a primary

[10]It must be admitted in this connection that transactions in U.S. treasury bills and treasury bill futures also exceeded by a wide margin transactions in bank deposit futures in the early 1980s, only to be left behind by the growth of eurodollar futures.

bond market. One can conceive of bond underwriters drawing their competitive advantage from one of three sources: relations with the issuers, general understanding of the money and bond markets, including the direction of rates and associated movements in spreads, and relations with end-investors. Government bond auctions seek to limit the influence of the first factor, and studies of the U.S. Treasury market have in fact emphasized "a large customer base with heavy order flow" as the principal source of competitive advantage (see Ruocco, LeBlanc, and Dignan, 1991).

The source of competitive advantage bears directly on the question of the effect of monetary union. If relations with issuers are key, then the euro will tend not to disturb competition. But if an underwriter benefits from understanding the direction of national interest rates, or from access to investors, then the euro will sharpen competition. No longer will a French bank have a natural edge in understanding the monetary and fiscal policies that can move the French bond market, and eventually a French bank will not be able to use its French investor base to win deals.

One test for whether the euro will sharpen competition in the bond market, therefore, is to check whether currency makes a difference in the choice of underwriter, controlling for the nationality of the bond issuer. The test can be performed on the international bond market for reasons both of data availability and of relevance. The data are relevant because the international bond market is, to a considerable extent, the euro bond market to be: one-fourth of the outstanding issues feature EU issuers in EU currencies, and a substantial fraction of investors are EU institutional investors. An early study of this question documented a decline of issuer-underwriter relations and a rise in the role of currency in the selection of underwriter (see Courtadon, 1985). A more recent study (Balder, Lopez, and Sweet, 1991) found a strong association between the nationality of the lead underwriter and the currency denomination of the bond for all but eurodollar issues, where customer relations seemed important. Most recently, Dermine (1996) points to the dominance of home-country lead managers in the league tables by currency sector, without distinguishing the influence of customer from that of currency.

An analysis of the effect of customer nationality and the currency denomination of the bond on the choice of lead managers (dubbed bookrunner after a period of title inflation) points to the strong predominance of currency effects over issuer effects in European currency sectors (see Table 7).[11] German,

[11]The association of currency of issue and nationality of underwriter, however, seems weaker in 1996 than it was in 1983 for the mark, pound and guilder sectors (see Courtadon, 1985, pp. 40–41). And even today, some sectors of the international bond market show a stronger influence of customer ties, in contrast to the general finding in the text. For instance, the *Neue Zürcher Zeitung* of February 20, 1997, p. 25, reports that the Japanese big four securities firms plus Tokyo-Mitsubishi and Kankaku captured 46.5 percent of the underwriting mandates of Japanese issuers in the Swiss franc market, more than the 39 percent captured by the Swiss big three plus Gotthard Bank. But this SF 7.4 billion sector features small, often equity-related, issues, and the customer base may include a large proportion of Japanese accounts.

Table 7. Currency and Home-Country Relationship in the Choice of Bond Bookrunner, 1996

(Percentage market share won by bookrunners of indicated nationality)

German Bookrunners				French Bookrunners			
	Currency				Currency		
Borrower	Deutsche mark	Other	All	Borrower	French franc	Other	All
German	44	16	24	French	86	10	25
Other	37	2	5	Other	75	2	5
All	39	4	8	All	77	2	6
U.K. Bookrunners				**Dutch Bookrunners**			
	Currency				Currency		
Borrower	Pound	Other	All	Borrower	Guilder	Other	All
U.K.	40	21	31	Dutch	83	26	48
Other	48	3	5	Other	85	2	3
All	44	4	7	All	84	2	5
U.S. Bookrunners				**Japanese Bookrunners**			
	Currency				Currency		
Borrower	Dollar	Other	All	Borrower	Yen	Other	All
U.S.	86	46	76	Japanese	75	46	59
Other	54	13	28	Other	87	6	14
All	64	16	37	All	84	8	17

Sources: Euromoney Bondware; and BIS.

Note: Each entry shows market share of German, French, U.K., Dutch, U.S., or Japanese bookrunners for issuers of the indicated nationality in the indicated currency. For example, the 44 percent in the upper left-hand corner means that German underwriters ran the books for 44 percent of the bonds of German issuers that were denominated in deutsche mark. Data include all bonds in the Euromoney database, including international bonds issued under medium-term note programs, that are not equity-related. Total amount of bond issuance by currency: deutsche mark: $81 billion; French franc: $37 billion; pound: $54 billion; guilder: $22 billion; dollar: $319 billion; yen: $91 billion; grand total: $725 billion.

French, U.K., and Dutch underwriters capture fairly close to the same share of the business of home-country issuers and foreign issuers, but show huge differences in market shares in their home currencies as against all other currencies. As found previously, the influence of customer and that of currency is much more balanced for U.S. underwriters.

The upshot of this analysis is that separate currencies in Europe have tended to segment the international bond market and that, over time, currency has shown more persistence as a factor bearing on competition than have relations between customers and underwriters. Brown (1996, p. 4) argues that the competitive challenge is not symmetrical: "the advantage German banks have had in the no. 2 international capital market, the euro-DM market, will not carry over into the euro capital market." As underwriter competition becomes sharper under the euro, the cost of corporate issuance of debt should decline. Another factor that could ease the marketing of European corporate bonds would be a more integrated European market for government bonds. To this we turn before discussing the implications of cheaper bond issuance.

The Euro and European Government Bond Markets

The euro is likely to exert both centripetal and centrifugal forces on the European government bond market. The market's demand for liquidity, and its reward for policies that contribute to liquidity, provide powerful integrative forces. At the same time, the unification of monetary policy, and the reevaluation of government risk in terms of fiscal position rather than international asset position, might highlight credit differences that could widen pricing distinctions. Markets might, therefore, simultaneously make little of differences among the most creditworthy of European governments while making much more of a distinction between these and more heavily indebted governments. Thus the centripetal and centrifugal forces need not cancel each other out.

Prospects for an Integrated Government Bond Market in the Core of Europe

The countries judged most likely to enter monetary union in 1999 are among those that tend to enjoy the highest credit ratings (see Table 8). Moreover, bond buyers currently price the bonds of these governments in a very similar manner. To see this similarity, recall the convergence of private yields, as measured by interest rate swaps, in the Belgian, Dutch, French, and German bond markets. Lower than these, more or less AA-rated, private yields are the respective government yields, which are solidly AAA-rated for Dutch, French, and German bonds.

The pricing of generic private risk in relation to government risk bears a great similarity in bond markets along the Rhine (see McCauley, 1996). The spreads between the yield on a 10-year interest rate swap and the yield on a 10-year government bond are unusually close in these three bond markets, where these spreads have converged to a common level of about 20 to 30 basis points (see Figure 3). Never in the history of the swap market has this spread been so similar, for so long, across so many markets.

These measured credit differences are small. In particular, they are small in relation to the potential liquidity benefits of practically fungible trading of European government bonds. To many observers, such trading is inconceivable because it would require accepting "joint and several liability" of the relevant EU governments for each other's debt. Given all the associated moral

Table 8. EMU Membership Poll Results and Sovereign Credit Ratings

	Expected Participation in EMU at Outset (In percent)[1]		Rating[2]		
Country	Poll published in January 1996	Poll published in August 1996	Moody's	S&P's	IBCA
Germany	100	100	Aaa	AAA	AAA
France	97	100	Aaa	AAA	AAA
Netherlands	76	100	Aaa	AAA	AAA
Belgium	79	95	Aa1	AA+	AA+
Austria	79	93	Aaa	AAA	AAA
Ireland	60	82	Aa1	AA	AA+
Finland	36	48	Aa1	AA	AAA
Denmark	50	43	Aa1	AA+	AA+
Sweden	7	13	Aa3	AA+	AA−
United Kingdom	22	8	Aaa	AAA	AAA
Spain	7	7	Aa2	AA	AA
Portugal	0	4	Aa3	AA−	AA−
Italy	2	3	Aa3	AA	AA−
Greece	0	0	Baa1	BBB−	BBB−

Sources: Consensus Economics, January and August 1996, p. 26; Moody's; Standard & Poor's; and IBCA.

[1]The polls of over 200 financial and economic forecasters indicate the percentage of respondents predicting that countries will join EMU at the outset. Respondents' assumptions regarding the likely starting date differed. Luxembourg, rated Aaa and AAA, respectively, was not included in the poll.

[2]Ratings refer to foreign currency issues.

hazard, this is not likely to happen very soon. Such a legal arrangement would indeed be sufficient to unify the bond markets of the participating governments. But is it necessary to render the "sovereign debt of EMU participants largely substitutable products" (Mayer, 1996, p. 10)?

One operational criterion of an integrated bond market is that it be served by a single futures contract (or, more precisely, a single contract at each maturity). One way to achieve such a market is by virtue of a single issuer becoming the benchmark and its obligations serving as the basis for a futures contract. Thus, today, the German government bond contract is used by dealers in Dutch and Belgian government debt for hedging, although changes in the yield spreads render these hedges imperfect (i.e., they introduce "basis risk"). Much market commentary is focused on which government will attain benchmark status. Cited in favor of France's debt assuming such a role is the liquidity and size of individual issues, as well as the French treasury's preannounced issuance calendar. Cited in favor of Germany's debt assuming such a role is its greater size and the greater turnover in the Bund futures. The choice of a single benchmark issuer, however, implies purchasing credit homogene-

Figure 3. Spreads of Ten-Year Government Bond Yields over Interest Rate Swap Yields
(Monthly averages, in basis points)

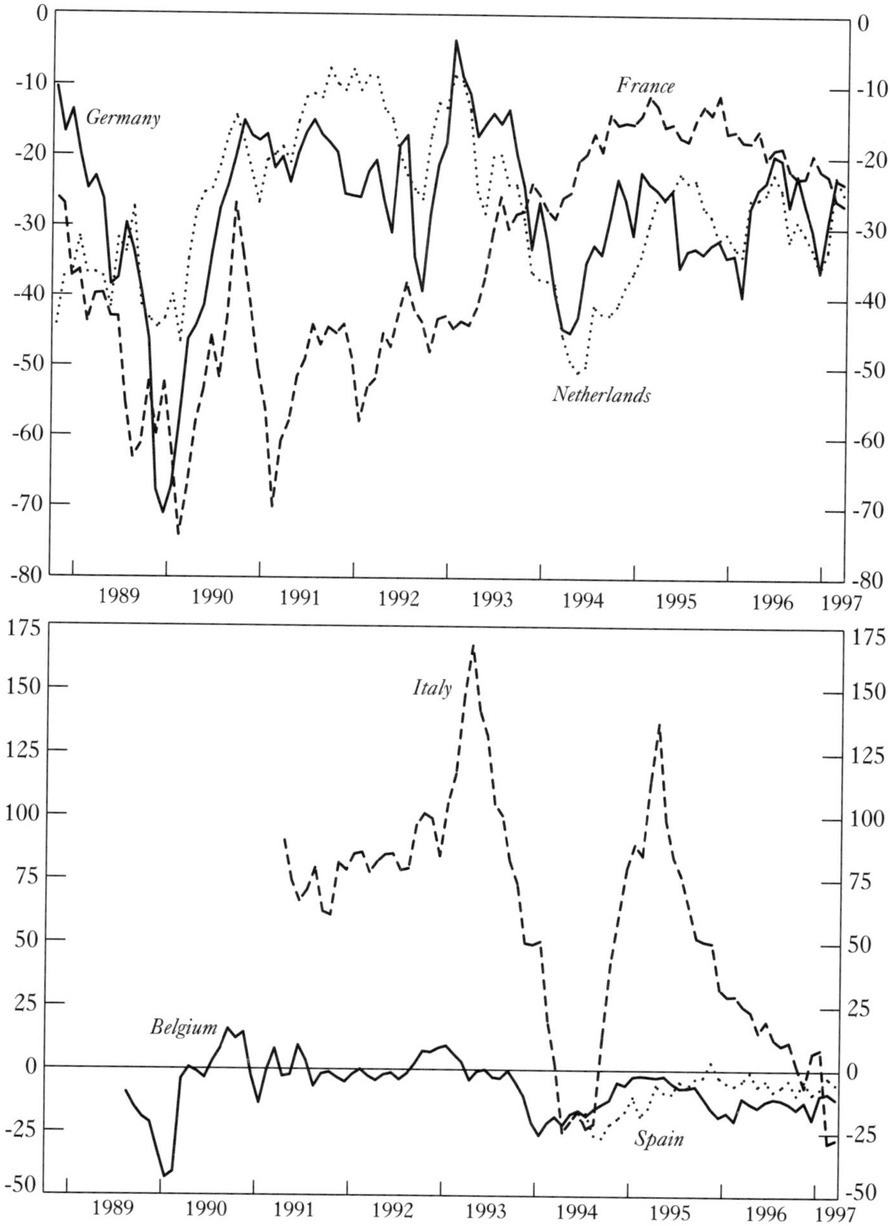

Sources : Datastream; and Reuters.

Box 1. ECU Bond Future: A Cautionary Tale

Mention to London financiers the possibility of a single bond future based on a number of European government bonds, and they often recall the case of the ECU bond contract (see Mazzucchelli, Clarke, and Parry, 1996). Both LIFFE and MATIF inaugurated an ECU bond contract in 1990. LIFFE permitted the bonds of any EU government issuer, as well a number of supranationals, to be delivered into the contract. By contrast, the MATIF limited the deliverable paper to issues of France and the United Kingdom and certain supranationals, and precluded the delivery of Italian ECU bonds.[1]

In the event, given the considerable yield premium of Italian government bonds over French and U.K. government bonds denominated in ECU, the Italian government bonds proved the bonds consistently cheapest to deliver in London. As a result, the LIFFE ECU contract reflected not only the variation of ECU long-term interest rates, but also the volatility of the credit spread between A-rated Italian debt and AAA-rated French government debt. For most portfolios of ECU bonds, or for most underwriters of ECU bonds, the Italian volatility in the LIFFE contract made it an inferior hedge. Partly as a result, the Paris contract stole the march over the London contract. Eventually, LIFFE changed the rules to preclude the delivery of Italian paper, but by then liquidity had tipped to the Paris contract. The lesson drawn in London is that an excessively inclusive collection of credit risk in a futures contract, permitting the delivery of a number of issuers' bonds, can turn that contract into a loser (see Bloem, 1996).

[1]Gerard Pfauwadel, President of MATIF, told Reuters on February 15, 1991, the day that a U.K. ECU bond was admitted into the MATIF ECU bond pool: "The Italian government's signing conditions are such that, looking at the year 2000 time line for Italy, there was a risk that our contract, which after all relates to a basket of underlying securities of three billion in OATs (French treasury bonds), would be transformed into a contract relating only to one billion Italian ECUs, because the construction of the notional bond future is such that the market price is based on the lowest-cost bond to be delivered. These technical conditions at this initial stage of building the market would have made it extremely dangerous to take too small a basket."

ity at the expense of imbuing only a narrow range of bonds with the liquidity benefits of an associated futures contract. Greater liquidity might result from a contract in which a number of issuers' bonds might be delivered into the same futures contract, so-called multiple-issuer deliverability (see Duesing, 1997; Fox, 1996; and Mazzucchelli, Clarke, and Parry, 1996). However, the art of contract design is to avoid permitting such a wide range of signatures as to bring a sort of Gresham's Law into play, according to which the worst signature drives out the other signatures (see Box 1).

Last December the financial futures exchange in Paris published a report on plans to switch its futures contracts to the euro (see MATIF, 1996).[12] The

[12]LIFFE is keeping all options open. See Gregorio (1996, p. 9).

working group entertained two scenarios: one in which the current long-term contract on French government securities in francs becomes a contract on euro-denominated French government securities, and another scenario in which it becomes a contract on euro-denominated bonds of a number of euro-area governments. The report held that a "single yield curve," for at least a small group of European governments, was a necessary condition for a contract into which bonds of more than one issuer could be delivered. On the above evidence, financial markets have come very close to trading the French, Dutch, and German government bonds on a single yield curve.

Somewhere down the road, prospective interest savings through higher liquidity might encourage cooperative debt management by national treasuries. Governments need not hold joint auctions; they could simply match each other's coupons and maturities, in effect "reopening" each other's issues. The potential benefit of such an approach is evident in Table 9, in which the value of transactions in a European government bond market compares favorably with that in Japan and falls not far short of that of the United States.

Liquidity and Cooperative Debt Management: Evidence to Date

The prospect of European treasuries cooperating in debt management may well seem far-fetched. After all, representatives of the German federal government, which has had to bail out ailing Länder (including Bremen and Saarland), worked for the "no-bailout" provision in the Maastricht Treaty to reinforce market discipline on European governments. Any mixing of governmental approaches to the market might seem to raise the (moral hazard) risk that one government would support the other. Cooperation could lead to, or be seen to lead to, coresponsibility. Nevertheless, the brief history of the choice as to whether to redenominate government debt into euros at the first opportunity, now planned for early 1999, points to the power of liquidity to shape a common policy.

EU members agreed in Madrid in December 1995 that, at the margin, new public debt issues should be denominated in euros from the inception of the euro. The intention was to contribute to the euro's reaching a critical mass of transactions, including interbank transactions as well as these public debt transactions, so that private sector parties would opt to use the euro before its use became mandatory (some three years later). Subsequently, the French treasury indicated that it would convert the entire stock of its debt from French francs to euros on day one, creating a whole yield curve in euros. In so doing, the treasury drew attention to its book-entry ("dematerialized") system, which would make such a debt conversion more feasible. The Belgian government has followed suit, announcing that it would con-

Table 9. Derivative Transactions in Long-Term Government Securities in Dollars, Yen, and Euros

(In trillions of dollars a year)

	1995			1996		Memorandum: Cash Market	
		Options					
Bonds and notes	Futures	Exchange traded	OTC[1]	Futures	Exchange-traded options	Trading	Outstanding
U.S. treasury bonds	12.374	3.627	0.435	12.011	3.667	35.843	2.547
Japanese government bonds	15.956	2.163	1.539	12.262	1.824	6.502	1.996
Selected European government bonds	14.067	2.384	0.465	17.848	2.759	18.225	1.608
German bonds	9.090	1.274	0.173	12.388	1.550	16.566	0.727
French bonds	3.367	0.954	0.256[2]	3.452	0.869	1.658	0.490
Italian bonds	1.610	0.156	0.036	2.008	0.340	0.420[3]	0.391[4]

Sources: Salomon Brothers; BIS, 1996b; and various futures exchanges and national sources.

Note: Data on cash market trading and outstandings are for 1995 and end-1995 respectively.

[1]Estimated as average daily turnover in April times 255.

[2]Estimated as OTC trading in interest rate options on traded securities in deutsche marks times the ratio of total OTC trading in interest rate options in Paris or Milan to that in Frankfurt.

[3]Euroclear and Cedel only.

[4]Lira-denominated treasury bonds only; excludes variable rate notes.

vert most of its debt into euros, leaving unconverted only some notes in Belgian francs held mostly by households. The Dutch finance ministry has stated that the prospect for liquidity of the guilder market will figure importantly in its decision whether to redenominate.[13]

Early indications from the German finance ministry suggested that there would be no conversion of existing German debt. Yet strong and apparently successful arguments were subsequently advanced by German banks against such a policy.[14] Essentially, the German banks argued that new issues of German bonds denominated in euros would have to yield 10–15 basis points more if the stock of German government debt were not converted into euros. Such a difference between the deutsche mark stock and the euro debt at the margin would probably be sufficient to interfere with auction strategies, cash/futures arbitrage and cash/cash yield curve positioning. In addition, Frankfurt stood to lose out to Paris as a financial centre were a large mass of French bonds deliverable into a euro contract there while only brand-new issues were deliverable in Frankfurt. Note that the first argument could be made in the absence of any competitive threat. The German government is now expected to redenominate its Bunds (although not the no-longer issued Treuhand bonds that financed reunification with eastern Germany). Without ignoring the competitive tensions—sometimes dubbed the "race to benchmark status"—one should recognize that the liquidity argument has already brought two finance ministries to the same decision on the first important policy question regarding debt management in the single currency area.

Many challenges remain to integrating government bond markets in the euro area. Market conventions (such as interest day counts) and the organization of the primary and secondary markets still vary from one market to another.[15] There may be a prisoners' dilemma here, with major governments tempted by the prospect of achieving benchmark status on their own terms rather than cooperating to maximize liquidity (see Keating, 1996). The liquidity argument could give impetus to the difficult process of harmonizing differences.

---

[13]See Scobie (1997, p. 74).

[14]The Working Group on the Gilt Market after EMU recommended the "complete and simultaneous redenomination of existing gilts from sterling into euro by law . . . early in 1999, if the United Kingdom joins EMU at the outset or as soon as possible after it joins if it participates at a later date" (see Bank of England, 1996, p. 34).

[15]The draft paper of the consultative group on the impact of the introduction of the euro on capital markets (see European Commission, 1997) notes that the French and German governments appear to be considering different modes of redenomination and cites the difficulties and costs resulting from the difference. The draft paper also discusses differences in day counts, coupon frequency, business days, and settlement lags. See also Davies (1996).

Rerating High-Debt European Sovereigns: Lessons from Canada?

How should the bonds of the more indebted European governments trade after the introduction of a single currency? The rating agencies have adopted different approaches to this question, but the remarkable outcome is that ratings judgments are closer together under the scenario of monetary union than they are now (see Box 2). For the most creditworthy governments, no change in their ratings is foreseen; for the rest, their ratings are foreseen at the AA level.

The question may be interpreted as turning on the importance of the "printing press" as the last-ditch mode of debt payment. Governments have been granting rather more independence to central banks, so this option has not been gaining plausibility. A central bank can, however, help its government by increasing the duration of its portfolio of government debt, without running the printing press. Some would say only that with monetary union the probability of one kind of bailout—the central bank buying government debt under duress—would diminish while the probability of another class of bailouts involving European-wide institutions would rise.

It may be informative to consult the experience of Canada, a federation of provinces, for guidance as to how European government debt might be treated under the single currency (see Brookes, 1997; Bulchandani, 1996; Clarke and Parry, 1996; Islam, Eyerman, and Taylor, 1996; Lipsky and others, 1996; SBC Warburg, 1996; and Serfaty, 1996; but also Fox, 1996, and Keating, 1996). In the domestic Canadian bond market, the federal government represents the top-rated benchmark and the cost of provincial debt bears a close relation to provincial credit ratings, with Quebec yielding a premium that may reflect a risk of exit from the federation (see Figure 4). To compare the situation in Canada with that in Europe requires a common measure of spreads across different markets, and the interest rate swap yield in Canadian dollars and in European currencies can be taken as a common (AA-rated) reference point. When the spreads of the Canadian provinces and European governments (see Figure 3) are plotted against their respective ratings, it appears that these various bond markets price lower ratings in a reasonably similar fashion (see Figure 5).[16]

But a juxtaposition of the Canadian and European observations raises a question regarding the consistency of the determinants of the ratings themselves (see Figure 6). When the Canadian ratings are plotted against the debt burdens of the Canadian provinces, the ratings all line up; when the prospec-

[16]While market pricing qualitatively corresponds to the credit rating, the BBB-rated province pays a smaller premium than most similarly rated private borrowers. Some observers interpret the relative flatness of the relationship to suggest that the market attaches more weight to the possibility of a federal bailout than do the rating agencies.

tive ratings of the European governments under the assumption of monetary union are plotted against current debt burdens, the ratings do not line up so well.[17] How good an analogy does the Canadian bond market provide for European debt markets under monetary union?[18] Those who have looked most carefully at such questions have identified three critical dimensions that affect the capacity of a government to carry higher debt burdens: whether household and corporate taxpayers can readily move to avoid tax rises; the degree of federal support in the event of difficulties in debt servicing; and the capacity of the political system to produce coherent governments capable of making difficult choices (see Eichengreen and von Hagen, 1995). On the first dimension, European governments may have scope to carry heavier debt burdens because labor (and capital?) is less mobile than in Canada. On the second dimension, Canada's federal redistribution and constructive ambiguity must be contrasted with the EU's limited budget and Maastricht's clear statement that there would be no Community liability for, or assumption of, the debts of any troubled government. On the third dimension, Canadian parliamentary democracy, like that of the United Kingdom, produces more coherent governments than the electoral systems of some EU countries. The Canadian provinces thus provide a useful if imperfect analogy for European governments under the single market, with two of the three arguments above implying that debt levels should be of more import than in Canada.

Implications for Money and Bond Markets

The greater depth, breadth, and liquidity of the euro bond market carry implications both internal to the euro area and external to it. Internally, one should expect the portfolios of institutional investors gradually to lose their bias toward home-country assets. As this diversification occurs, one should expect that the lower cost and greater benefit of using the bond market should move the boundary between the banking market and the securities market in

[17]It is easy to draw this analogy inappropriately by neglecting differences in fiscal structures. "A 55 percent debt to GDP (gross domestic product) ratio appears to define the limit at which Canadian provinces can maintain investment grade status. What's going to make it possible for European governments to maintain good credit ratings with debt ratios significantly higher?" says Bernard Connolly, addressing a conference in London and quoted in "EMU said to mean higher inflation, weaker bonds," *Reuters*, February 25, 1997. Moody's (1997, p. 5): ". . . a statistical comparison between the debt burdens of EMU entrants and subnational units in federal systems would not be completely appropriate because EMU countries should be able to service higher debt loads than individual American states or Canadian provinces."

[18]The Canadian parallel has the advantage that there is no federal tax exemption for provincial debt interest receipts, as there is in the United States. In the latter case, a combination of federal tax exemption with state tax exemptions for in-state municipal bond interest has produced an extremely segmented and illiquid market. For the comparison between U.S. states and European governments, see Goodhart (1997).

Box 2. Monetary Union and Sovereign Ratings

Over the years, the major rating agencies have approached country (or transfer) risk in a fairly similar fashion. They assign a ceiling to the foreign currency ratings of all the borrowers in a country that reflects the possible unavailability of foreign exchange, even in cases in which the underlying debtor has ample domestic currency to service its debt and the currency is fully convertible. Until Moody's recent rating of Panama, this foreign-currency debt ceiling was also the foreign debt rating of the central government, and was thus often known as the sovereign ceiling. The rating agencies have in addition assigned ratings to the central government's domestic debt. These ratings have tended to be higher than the corresponding foreign currency ratings, particularly for Standard & Poor's and IBCA, on the grounds that the national central bank would help prevent a default in domestic currency or, more generally, that the government's tax base in domestic currency made default less likely.

Generally, the rating agencies are treating EMU as a likely event, and they have already begun to factor the prospect into the sovereign ratings of potential members. Of course, the fiscal discipline of the Maastricht criteria means that a prospective participant in monetary union can hope to see its ratings improve, as with Moody's recent upgrade of Ireland. (Reuss, 1996, shows, however, that of the nine countries with lower than AAA ratings in Table 10, five have seen their Standard & Poor's foreign currency ratings downgraded since their initial ratings, and only two have seen them upgraded.) But the prospect of EMU poses two other questions for the major rating agencies: what should the sovereign ceiling for the euro area be, and how should the foreign currency and domestic currency debt ratings, where they differ, be united?

Moody's (1997) recently agreed with the views of Standard & Poor's (see Beers, 1996, and IBCA, 1996) as outlined last year, that the risk of a transfer problem affecting foreign currency issues by borrowers in the euro area should be negligible. That is, these agencies treat as practically zero the likelihood that a government or other obligor in the euro area would have euros but would be unable to convert these into the dollars or Swiss francs needed to service its debt. This conclusion would apply more or less regardless of the participants in monetary union because the aggregated external creditor status of Europe would be very strong in any case. Moody's and Standard & Poor's, however, approached differently the question of what to do with the split between their foreign currency rating and their domestic currency rating for some European governments.

Moody's argued that the euro would effectively become the domestic currency of any member country, just as the dollar is the domestic currency of Massachusetts.

Therefore, the rating of a government in the euro area should correspond to its (in many cases higher) current domestic currency rating. By contrast, Standard & Poor's argued that under EMU central governments lose their privileged position and that therefore it makes sense to unify the ratings of individual sovereigns on the (in many cases lower) current foreign currency ratings.

The agencies' divergent views seem to be primarily based on a differing weighting of the value of a national central bank to the creditworthiness of the central government. Standard & Poor's believes that the national central bank would help its government to avoid default. Moody's questions this "printing press" view and says that most governments have already abolished this policy option by giving autonomy to their central banks. Thus, market discipline, including the prospect of capital flight, already makes it almost impossible for a central bank to help its government even in extremis. As a result, Moody's has made less of the distinction between foreign currency and domestic currency ratings and has lower domestic debt ratings. The difference between the current domestic currency rating for Italy, rated AAA by Standard & Poor's and Aa3 by Moody's, illustrates this point. It might be noted that the yields on Italian interest rate swaps for prime (AA) names have often been below those for the Italian treasury (see Figure 3), suggesting that financial markets have seen more risk in the treasury's lira debt than has Standard & Poor's (see Banca d'Italia, 1995, pp. 125–26; and Favero, Giavazzi, and Spaventa, 1996).

These differing views of the rating agencies led to speculation that there might be wide disparities (and resulting uncertainty) between sovereign ratings under EMU. In practice, however, Standard & Poor's foreign currency rating for Italy (AA) is just a notch higher than the Aa3 domestic rating of Moody's. Thus, owing to Standard & Poor's more buoyant current ratings of domestic debt, the different approaches to unifying the government ratings will not result in large differences under the euro (see Table 10). Although Standard & Poor's has been described as rating sovereigns marginally higher than Moody's (see Cantor and Packer, 1996, p. 39), at this stage Standard & Poor's indicated EMU ratings are lower than those of Moody's for Finland, Greece, Ireland, and Portugal.

Despite the different starting points of the two ratings agencies, and their different analysis, in the end their ratings would thus not be very different. Moody's could portray its decision to treat the euro as a domestic currency as more logical than Standard & Poor's treatment. In addition, it is easier for the affected governments to accept Moody's planned abolition of their foreign currency ceiling, since only upgrades are implied, than it is for them to accept Standard & Poor's planned downgradings of domestic debt. Standard & Poor's, for its part, could back off somewhat from its domestic currency ratings.

Figure 4. Credit Spreads in the Canadian Bond Market
(At fourth quarter 1996)

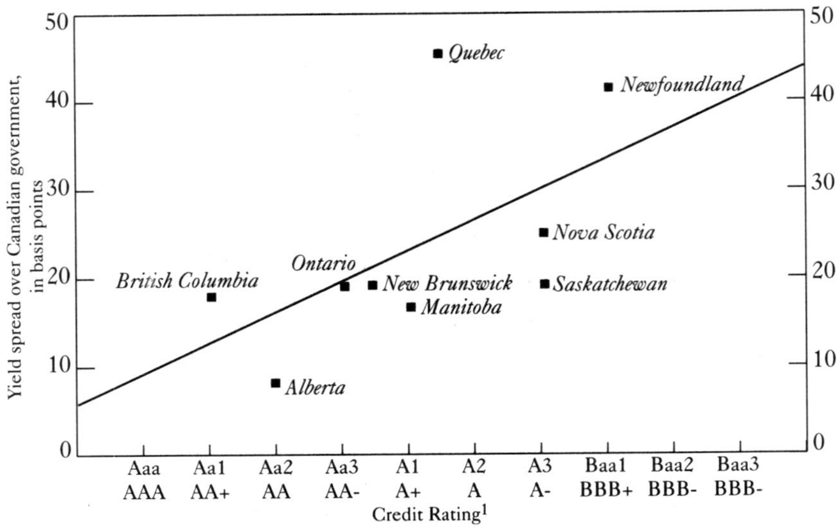

Sources: Moody's; Standard & Poor's; and Morgan Stanley.
[1]Long-term domestic currency rating; for New Brunswick and Quebec, split rating.

Figure 5. Government Bond Yields in the Canadian and European Markets
(Spread over the respective interest-rate swap yields, fourth quarter 1996)

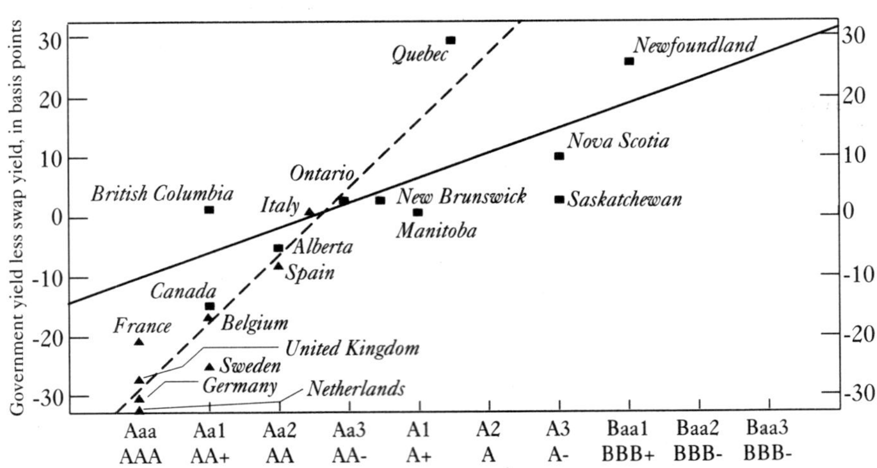

Sources: Moody's, Standard & Poor's; and Morgan Stanley.
[1]For Canadian provincial governments (including the Commonwealth), long-term domestic currency rating; for New Brunswick and Quebec, split rating. For European governments, indicated rating in the event of monetary u for Italy, split rating; for Sweden, no Moody's indication.

Figure 6. Debt Burdens and Credit Ratings in Canada and Europe
(At fourth quarter 1996)

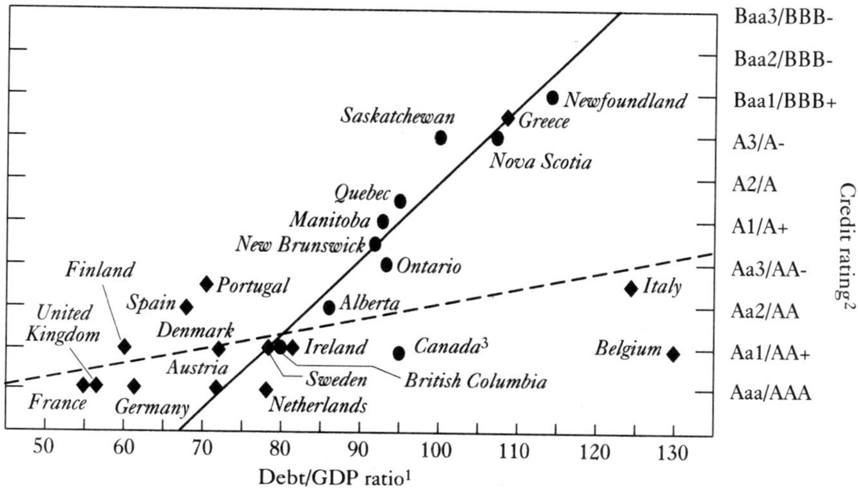

Source: Morgan Stanley; Moody's; Standard & Poor's; and OECD.
[1]As a percentage. Debt data for European countries are the OECD estimates based on the Maastricht definition.
[2]See footnote 1 to Figure 5; in addition, split rating for Finland, Greece, Ireland, and Portugal.
[3]Not included in the provincial regression.

favor of securities away from loans. Thus, the shift by banks from acquiring and holding assets to underwriting and distributing paper should accelerate, with different implications for banks with strengths in these two aspects of the business. Repurchase markets can also be expected to grow, to some extent at the expense of bank deposits.

Internationally, the euro bond market can be expected to be a more attractive place for asset managers, both official and private, in which to invest. Many analysts stop here and draw the conclusion that the euro could be secularly strong, as it benefits from portfolio reallocations at the expense of the dollar. But debtors, both companies and governments, outside the euro area can also be expected to find the euro bond market a more attractive market into which to issue. Thus a larger, broader, deeper, and more liquid bond market in Europe does not necessarily imply that the value of the euro will benefit from net portfolio shifts.

Internal Implications

Gradual process of portfolio diversification. A single reference yield curve for the pricing of private credit risks, in conjunction, perhaps, with a govern-

Table 10. Effect of EMU on Central Government Debt Ratings

	Moody's			Standard & Poor's			IBCA		
Country	FX	Domestic	EMU	FX	Domestic	EMU	FX	Domestic	EMU
Austria	Aaa	nr	Aaa	AAA	AAA	AAA	AAA	AAA	AAA
France	Aaa	Aaa	Aaa	AAA	AAA	AAA	AAA	AAA	AAA
Germany	Aaa	Aaa	Aaa	AAA	AAA	AAA	AAA	AAA	AAA
Luxembourg	Aaa	nr	Aaa	AAA	AAA	AAA	AAA	AAA	AAA
Netherlands	Aaa	Aaa	Aaa	AAA	AAA	AAA	AAA	AAA	AAA
United Kingdom	Aaa	Aaa	Aaa	AAA	AAA	AAA	AAA	AAA	amb
Belgium	Aa1	Aa1	Aa1	AA+	AAA	AA+	AA+	AAA	pos
Denmark	Aa1	Aa1	Aa1	AA+	AAA	AA+	AA+	AAA	pos
Finland	Aa1	Aaa	Aaa	AA	AAA	AA	AAA	AAA	amb
Greece	Baa1	A2	A2	BBB−	nr	BBB−	BBB−	nr	amb
Ireland	Aa1	Aaa	Aaa	AA	AAA	AA	AA+	AAA	amb
Italy	Aa3	Aa3	Aa3	AA	AAA	AA	AA−	AAA	pos
Portugal	Aa3	Aa2	Aa2	AA−	AAA	AA−	AA−	AAA	amb
Spain	Aa2	Aa2	Aa2	AA	AAA	AA	AA	AAA	pos
Sweden	Aa3	Aa1	nr	AA+	AAA	AA+	AA−	AAA	amb

Sources: Moody's (1997); Standard & Poor's; and IBCA (1996).

Note: For each rating agency, FX indicates the current foreign currency rating; Domestic, the current domestic debt rating; and EMU, the prospective unified rating under the hypothesis of participation in the single money. nr denotes no rating. For IBCA, amb denotes ambiguous effects and pos denotes positive effect.

ment benchmark yield curve, is a necessary but not sufficient condition for an integrated bond market. As long as the portfolios of insurance companies, pension funds, and mutual funds show a strong bias toward home-country issuers, then integration will remain partial.[19] Many such portfolios have currency-matching requirements (see OECD, 1996a, pp. 5–17) intended to limit the risk inherent in having obligations to policyholders or fund claimants denominated in one currency and assets in another. Some of these requirements are written in such a fashion that monetary union will automatically permit investment by the affected institutional investors in the euro debt of issuers of a different nationality. Other such requirements confound the nationality of issuer with the currency denomination of the bond and would continue to be binding after EMU. Pressure to remove such portfolio restrictions can be expected, but the European Commission's proposed Pension Funds Directive, which would have limited regulatory restrictions requiring investment in national assets, has not yet been adopted (see OECD, 1996b, p. 19). The process of portfolio diversification within the euro area will not, in these circumstances, be an instantaneous process like the development of a single private yield curve in euros. "Old habits and preference for national debt die hard" (see Bloem, 1996).

Growth of securities markets in the euro area. Bigger and better money and bond markets could lead to a migration of assets from banks' balance sheets through the commercial paper and corporate bond market to the balance sheets of insurance companies, mutual funds, and pension funds. But a widespread misunderstanding of the process of securitization in the United States risks a significant overestimate of its potential in Europe. Much of what goes under the heading of securitization in the United States is the bundling of home mortgages into securities, which has depended on government and quasi-government guarantees to remove the idiosyncratic credit risk from the underlying assets. To be sure, these guarantees have also induced technical developments in the bundling of assets to back bonds and these techniques have also been applied to assets not benefiting from such guarantees, including large mortgages, credit card receivables, automobile loans, and even boat loans and aircraft and equipment leases. But such techniques are only

[19]OECD (1996a, p. 16) shows pension fund holdings of foreign assets in Europe to be bimodal, with funds in Belgium, Ireland, and the United Kingdom having 30 percent or more of their portfolios invested in foreign assets, compared with less than 10 percent for funds in Denmark, France, Germany, Italy, Portugal, Spain, and Sweden. The Netherlands, at 17 percent, is in between. Page 22 shows life insurers in Germany with 1 percent of their assets in foreign securities in 1991 and those in the United Kingdom with 14 percent in 1994.

now finding application in Europe (see Jeanneau, 1996). Here we concentrate on the prospects for the growth of the commercial paper corporate bond markets in Europe.

After the euro arrives, corporate treasurers in the euro area would make a different calculation of costs and benefits in choosing whether to issue commercial paper and bonds or to borrow from a bank. The cost of a new bond issue would be lower because of more competitive underwriting in a market no longer segmented by currency. Moreover, to the extent that the government bond market in Europe becomes more liquid, the cost to underwriters of hedging a new issue, through taking a short position in government bonds in the cash or futures market, would decline and this saving would also be expected to pass through to the borrower. Other costs, such as the cost of obtaining a credit rating and the cost of marketing to a given class of investors, would not rise with the euro. Moreover, with time, the benefits of issuing its own commercial paper or bonds would rise for a corporation in the euro area. That is because the range and size of the investment portfolios to which the securities could be marketed would also rise as asset managers in the euro market looked beyond national boundaries to improve their performance. In these circumstances, a lower yield could be required to place paper and bonds of a given quality.

From the perspective of asset managers in Europe, a greater capacity to analyze credit risk and a greater tolerance for credit risk could be expected to result from the euro's elimination of currency risk. As things stand, the manager of a multicurrency bond portfolio faces a hierarchy of choice, in which the most important choice is across countries, the second-tier choice is duration, and the last choice is credit risk. As matters stand, this last choice is a very safe one: "Almost 50% of nonsovereign issuance is AAA in the European currencies segments" of the eurobond market (see Karsenti, 1996, section 4.4). The elimination of the currency choice within Europe can be expected to result in greater attention to the duration and credit choices and, in the search for higher yields, a greater tolerance of risk in both dimensions.

How far could this improved calculus alter the corporate securities market in Europe? The potential for assets to be stripped out of the banking system is illustrated by the growth of the original-issue junk bond and commercial paper markets in the United States. From a base near zero in the early 1980s, outstanding bonds of non-investment-grade firms rose to over $200 billion in 1996 (see Fridson and Garman, 1996, p. 28), equivalent to about a quarter of outstanding corporate bank loans. In addition, outstanding commercial paper of mostly well-rated nonfinancial firms approached $200 billion in 1996, well beyond the levels reached in the late-blooming European paper markets (see

Alworth and Borio, 1993).[20] Following these precedents, security markets could place at risk one-third of European banks' corporate loans.

If the euro can be expected to accelerate the expansion of securities at the expense of bank loans, it can also be expected to accelerate competition from securities markets on the deposit side. The euro repo market, essentially a money market instrument collateralized against government bonds, would compete with bank deposits for short-term funds. In the United States, mutual funds, state and local governments (and their pension funds), foreign investors, pension funds, and insurance companies are the largest providers of funds under repo arrangements. In contrast, these kinds of investors in Europe would currently hold bank deposits.[21] While banks themselves are the largest takers of funds in the U.S. repo market, followed by securities dealers, these collateralized instruments may compete directly for funds with high-quality European banks that are now able to offer low yields on their low-risk liabilities.

In Europe, repurchase markets are developing rapidly (see BIS, 1996a, p. 74; and BIS, 1996c, pp. 20–24). Once the ECB starts operating in the repo market, with an undifferentiated range of government-paper accepted collateral, then the euro can be expected to accelerate the growth of the repo markets in Europe.

In summary, the stimulus given to the European money and bond markets by the euro can be expected to make commercial papers and bonds more serious competitors for bank loans. More European firms will find it rewarding to issue paper and bonds, and the euro repo market will offer a deep and high-quality alternative to bank deposits.

International Implications: Investment and Borrowing in the Euro

Many analysts foresee that international portfolio shifts into an increasingly broad, deep, and more liquid euro market have the potential to make the euro a strong currency. On the basis of a similar portfolio reasoning, however, we view this presumption as an unsafe one, because the euro would also be a more attractive currency in which to borrow.

---

[20]See Table L.102 in Board of Governors (1996, p. 63). Overall, these accounts place the bond debt of the U.S. nonfarm nonfinancial corporate sector at \$1.4 trillion and commercial paper debt at \$0.2 trillion, against bank debt of \$0.6 trillion. The inclusion of offshore corporate loans brings the corporate loan total closer to \$0.8 trillion (see McCauley and Seth, 1992). The one-third figure following in the text ((junk + commercial paper)/(junk + commercial paper + bank loans)) is apposite under the conservative assumption that all the European firms that could obtain investment grade ratings have already effectively ceased borrowing long-term, fixed rate funds from banks.

[21]See Board of Governors (1996, p. 84).

Greater liquidity and depth could increase the international demand for bonds denominated in euros relative to the total demand for bonds in the constituent currencies. In considering the potential for shifts by private portfolio managers into euro-denominated bonds, a difficult question arises as to whether interest rates in a large euro bond market might show a smaller correlation with U.S. bond yields than current European government bond rates. This is an interesting question because private portfolio managers would find the euro bond market particularly attractive if it offered diversification benefits superior to anything available in the constituent bond markets. Large and diverse investors could provide ballast to a European bond market subject to spillovers from New York. However, it is notable that the trend toward higher correlations across European bond markets in recent years has not to date brought any diminution of the correlation between the German and U.S. markets.

The scope for a potential reallocation of private portfolios from the dollar to the euro is necessarily extremely conjectural. One starting point is the shares across Group of Ten currencies of GDP, trade, and international assets, including both international bank deposits and international bonds. The Group of Ten members of the EU produce about one-third of Group of Ten output and would show a slightly smaller share of international trade (net of their intra-EU trade). After a similar consolidation, however, the share of international assets denominated in euros would be only about one-eighth. For the euro share to match the output and trade share of Group of Ten members of the EU would require a shift of some $0.7 trillion (see McCauley, 1997). This figure should not be taken too seriously. Nevertheless, it serves to make an important point, namely, that private portfolio shifts could prove to be much larger than any possible official reserve shifts.

As well as having strong attractions for asset managers, a more integrated bond market in Europe would also attract debt managers in the steady state. The development of a broad and deep euro bond market could potentially affect debt management more strongly than asset management, and the greater supply of euro-denominated assets could place downward pressure on the euro.

It may seem strange that something as welcome as the development of broad, deep, and liquid markets could weaken the currency concerned, but portfolio theory holds that the shift of funding from one currency to another will result in some combination of a higher interest rate and a lower exchange rate for the currency experiencing the increased supply. For instance, were Thailand to issue new deutsche mark securities and use the proceeds to buy in all its dollar debt, private investors would need to be induced to hold more marks and fewer dollar assets. Depending on the size of the operation, one might expect some combination of higher deutsche mark interest rates and a lower mark in order to make the investors willing to hold the new proportion of assets supplied. The flow conception of exchange rate determination agrees with the result: as the Thais exchanged the marks raised for dollars with which to buy their outstanding debts, demand for the dollar would rise.

The current choice of currency for large issues for global debt managers and the current financing habits of emerging economies make the prospect of heavier use of the euro by debt managers plausible. As things stand, international bond issuers favor the dollar for large deals (see Table 11). A plausible interpretation is that U.S. treasury bond benchmarks in the cash market are larger, the bond futures markets serving the dollar bond markets are more liquid, and the ultimate bond buyers are bigger. If an underwriter of a large bond in euros could more easily hedge against movements in the underlying euro yields, issuing costs might fall, eliminating this bias. The likely result would be more issuance in euros.

Table 11. International Security Issues by Issue Size and Currency
(In billions of U.S. dollars, 1990–95)

	Size of Issue		
Currency by Region	<$1.0 billion	≥$1.0 billion	Total
Developing countries	141.7	10.5	152.2
U.S. dollar	96.8	7.4	104.2
EU currencies	17.6	0.0	17.6
Japanese yen	27.3	3.2	30.5
Developed countries	1,555.7	209.1	1,764.8
U.S. dollar	554.9	119.5	674.4
EU currencies	660.1	58.9	719.0
Japanese yen	340.8	30.6	371.4
International institutions	117.1	39.9	216.9
U.S. dollar	34.1	15.0	49.1
EU currencies	113.9	15.3	129.3
Japanese yen	29.1	9.5	38.6
Total	1,874.5	259.5	2,134.0
U.S. dollar	685.8	141.9	827.7
EU currencies	791.6	74.3	865.9
Japanese yen	397.1	43.3	440.4
Grand total, including offshore centers	2,078.6	276.9	2,355.5

Source: BIS.
Note: Including bonds and medium-term notes.

Table 12. Currency Composition of Developing Country Debt

(In billions of U.S. dollars and percentages at end-1996)

	Currency				
Obligors	U.S. dollar	Japanese yen	EU currencies	Other[1]	Total
Latin America	421.1	66.0	72.0	65.2	624.3
	67.4%	10.6%	11.5%	10.4%	100.0%
Banks[2]	100.3	2.2	7.1	4.2	113.7
World Bank[3]	320.8	63.8	65.0	61.0	510.7
Asia	344.7	243.4	71.7	85.4	745.1
	46.3%	32.7%	9.6%	11.5%	100.0%
Banks[2]	135.7	80.1	10.6	16.9	243.3
World Bank[4]	209.0	163.3	61.1	68.5	501.9
Eastern Europe	138.0	42.6	101.9	90.9	373.4
	37.0%	11.4%	27.3%	24.3%	100.0%
Banks[2,5]	7.3	0.5	14.3	5.3	27.4
World Bank[6]	130.8	42.2	87.5	85.6	346.1
Total	1,044.5	377.1	329.4	331.4	2,082.5
	50.2%	18.1%	15.8%	15.9%	100.0%
Banks[2]	245.0	73.9	32.9	22.3	374.1
World Bank	799.5	303.2	296.6	309.1	1,708.4

Sources: World Bank; and BIS.

Note: Obligor total includes other developing countries. World Bank figures for 1996 are preliminary and refer to debt maturity greater than one year. Multiple-currency debt reported by the World Bank is distributed among underlying currencies according to the composition of the World Bank currency pool. Figures may not add due to rounding.

[1]Including unidentified.

[2]Excludes bank claims of more than one-year maturity; including medium-term debt with remaining maturity of less than one year. Semiannual maturity distribution applied to quarterly currency distribution. Includes own estimates of currency breakdown of debt to banks in offshore centers and other debt to banks for which no official currency breakdown is available.

[3]World Bank subtotal for Latin America and the Caribbean.

[4]Comprises World Bank subtotals for East Asia and Pacific and South Asia.

[5]Includes the former Yugoslavia.

[6]Comprises World Bank subtotals for Europe and Central Asia.

Faced with a broader, deeper, and more liquid bond market in Europe, debt managers outside Europe could be interested in increasing the proportion of their debt denominated in euros. The estimated currency composition of the international debts of countries in Asia and Latin America (see Table 12) shows a very low share of European currencies.[22] Even if the euro does not displace the dollar or, in Asia, the yen as a reserve currency, there is great scope for additional borrowing in euros to cover existing exposures. Currently, the weight placed on European currencies in the reserves of nonindustrial countries is noticeably heavier than that in the debts of those countries.

[22]Contrast Bénassy-Quéré (1996), which takes World Bank–reported debt as representative.

It is possible that the attraction of a larger supply of euro-denominated assets, which in a portfolio balance framework would push down the value of the euro, could outweigh the attraction of a larger demand, which would push it up. Even if the demand shift is foreseen to be larger or faster, it should be recognized that the international bond market regularly shifts the composition of new offerings toward the strengthening currency.[23] At any rate, one should not attempt to calculate the effects of the greater attraction of the euro for official and private asset managers without considering that it might hold a similar attraction for debt managers.

The Euro and the European Banking System

The successful introduction of a single currency will have direct effects on individual financial institutions. In particular, in the transition it seems certain to raise some costs, cut some revenues, and increase uncertainty in some respects. It is also certain to alter the macroeconomic environment in which financial institutions operate. What is much more problematical is whether the introduction of the euro will catalyze a significant increase in international competition between financial institutions. On this issue, views differ widely and predictions are highly uncertain.[24]

Transition Costs of Monetary Union

What is clear is that banks will have to bear increased costs during the transition. Customers will seek advice on EMU matters; computer systems have to be altered; stationery and forms must be reprinted; and personnel need to be trained.[25] Moreover, these costs, especially for computer systems, are liable to increase dramatically for those institutions that choose to delay their preparations in light of perceived uncertainties about the introduction of the single currency. Influenced as well by the need to deal with the "year 2000" problem, the

[23]This shift (which reflects more than valuation effects) is a leitmotif of the *BIS International Banking and Financial Market Developments*. See in particular BIS (1997) and BIS (1996c).

[24]Among those expecting profound changes are Standard & Poor's (see Bugie, 1996). Among those who expect a much smaller impact are Salomon Brothers (see Salomon Brothers, 1996).

[25]The Banking Federation of the EU published the results of a survey of members in March 1995. Assuming a single date of conversion for all forms of business in all EU countries, the costs of conversion were estimated at between ECU 8 and 10 billion. National estimates of conversion costs are broadly consistent. The actual costs of conversion are likely to be significantly higher (the British Bankers' Association estimates up to 50 percent) given the necessity for banks to keep accounts in both national currencies and the euro during the period from January 1999 to 2002. This implies added costs of about 1–1.5 percent of total revenues a year over a three- to four-year period. See Salomon Brothers (1996, p. 5).

salaries of information technology personnel have already begun to rise significantly. Indeed, given shortages in this area and the number of financial firms that have not yet commenced their preparations,[26] some commentators have even started to question whether current deadlines for EMU are technically feasible.[27]

After the introduction of the single currency, banks will have extra note-handling costs and will lose revenues in other ways. An obvious point is that trading revenues from foreign exchange transactions between currencies subsumed into the euro will disappear. On the basis of turnover data collected by 26 central banks for the Central Bank Survey of Foreign Exchange and Derivatives Market Activity 1995,[28] Salomon Brothers (1996, p. 9) estimates that the net revenues derived from foreign exchange trading might fall by up to 10 percent, although this would imply only about a 1 percent decline in total revenues. Receipts from intra-European funds transfers might also be expected to decline, as would fees from the exchange of travelers' checks and banknotes. Revenues from bond trading across European currencies might also be reduced, given that changes in perceptions about credit risk are less volatile than expectations about exchange rate changes. Bond trading is also likely to migrate to larger centers, which could have significant effects on financial institutions based in smaller centers. It is also yet to be determined whether financial institutions within EMU will be subject to reserve requirements. If they are, and these reserves are not interest-bearing, this will be a further charge for banks to bear even if some part of it might well be passed on to their customers.[29] Finally, there may be certain national conventions that are currently profitable for banks but that might disappear under EMU; for example, "sight deposits" in France still do not pay interest even though ECU "sight deposits" do.

The introduction of the euro will also raise other uncertainties for banks. First, the replacement of national currencies with the euro could call into question the legal validity of some outstanding contracts. It cannot be ruled out that (particularly non-European) counterparties on the losing end of a contract will seek to avoid that loss by having recourse to non-European courts.[30] A closely related possibility is that borrowers with high, long-term, fixed-rate obligations in national currencies will litigate for the right to renegotiate at lower euro rates.[31] The final effects of this on banks individually and collec-

[26] A survey reported in the *Financial Times* of February 5, 1997, indicated that 91 percent of European banks polled were confident that they would be ready for the introduction of the euro but only 15 percent of the same banks had allocated a budget for this objective (see Denton 1997).

[27] See Congdon (1996).

[28] See BIS (1996b), p. 96.

[29] For a fuller discussion of this potentially important issue, see Levitt (1995).

[30] See Livingston and Hutchings (1997), p. 63, and International Law Association (1996). See also the subsection above on the transition costs of monetary union.

[31] See Levitt (1995). Levitt notes that litigation in different national jurisdictions might result in different rulings. EU legislation might be called for but, of course, it would have no force outside the EU.

tively are not obvious. Second, during the whole period prior to Stage III of EMU, shocks could occur that might call the commitment of individual countries to participation into question, complicating advance planning by banks.

A last consideration is that many of the sovereign participants in EMU should eventually gain the benefits of faster growth, lower inflation, and lower market volatility that EMU is expected to provide. However, for banks this will be a mixed blessing. Banks will share in the benefits of faster growth, but lower inflation, could well lead to a reduction in interest rate spreads. Lower inflation may also (over the medium term) exacerbate problem loans associated with current low property prices, although (over the longer term) it might make a repetition of such exposures less likely. As for volatility in financial markets, banks will face less market risk themselves but they will also lose the revenues derived from helping their clients cope with market risk. In a more stable environment, credit risk should also be easier to evaluate and should generally be lower. In contrast, under EMU the likelihood of bailouts of national (nonbank) firms by national governments may be significantly reduced, which would imply higher levels of credit risk in some cases.

The Euro and Increased Competition in Banking

Rating agencies do seem to feel that EMU will increase competitive pressures between financial institutions.[32] Indeed, this must happen if the very significant gains for consumers, foretold in the Emerson report of 1988, are to be realized. However, in light of the relatively limited competitive response to date, this conclusion might seem questionable unless one were to ascribe an important catalytic role to the introduction of the euro itself. A number of arguments have been made in this regard, though they vary widely in their persuasiveness and no single argument seems to us to be totally persuasive. The euro is projected variously to cause bank customers, regulators and legislators, and financial institutions themselves to alter their behavior.

Perhaps the loftiest of these arguments has to do with the attitude of bank customers. Recall that the introduction of the euro is intended to serve as a powerful political symbol uniting Europeans and reducing the importance of national differences. Would it not then be expected to play the same role in the financial sector? Indeed, Johnson (1996, pp. 51–52) goes even further to argue that "It is intuitively obvious that the existence of separate currencies must divide the market in money even more than those in other goods and services." However, it remains to be seen how long it might take for a Yorkshire farmer to view German, French, and U.K. banks with equanimity.

[32]EMU "will be negative or neutral for European banks" (see IBCA, 1996); "the profound changes that a successful EMU will bring to the financial services sector will pressure the competitive position and earnings of many banks" (see Bugie, 1996).

Another argument pertaining to customer attitudes has been put forward by the Association Cambiste Internationale (1995, p. 24), which considers that "the single currency, by eliminating foreign exchange rate risk and converging interest rates . . . will result in a greater willingness on the part of customers to look outside national borders for financial services." While more prosaic than the first argument, it is also more compelling. Multinational firms may consolidate their European treasury operations and with them their banking relationships. Increased transparency and increased comparability between fee structures and rates offered by banks in different national jurisdictions should also help to promote convergence. This might apply particularly in border regions, but it could apply much more broadly given the growing influence of electronic banking (often being introduced by firms unencumbered by traditional branches) and the use of credit scoring techniques. The essence of both is that physical proximity to customers is not required. An important counterargument, which may have some force during the transition period at least, is that smaller customers may choose to rely still more heavily on their traditional bankers for advice in a period of change.

It has been further contended that separate currencies also serve to segment the market for bank credit in Europe. However, some limited evidence suggests that separate currencies may not have a great impact on borrowers' preferences. As indicated in Table 13, the effect of currency on the choice of syndicated loan arrangers stands out less than does the home-country relationship. This finding contrasts with that discussed in the section on the euro and European bond markets, where currency plays a more important role in the choice of bond underwriters.

Another argument having to do with transparency notes that regulatory and other such differences that segregate national markets will be put into higher profile in a single currency area; the opt-out clause in the Second Banking Directive (for "the general good") might be particularly vulnerable in this regard. Pressures on regulators and legislators for further change might then be expected to arise from those judging themselves to be disadvantaged. Calls for effective "national treatment" might be expected to lead to pressure for "reciprocal" treatment, which could only be fully satisfied through complete harmonization.

If and when competition does begin to increase significantly, a further and important dynamic process might be generated. With profits under pressure as a result, and some banks' credit ratings potentially declining even below those of some of their customers, the process of disintermediation might be expected to accelerate significantly. In fact, this is broadly what happened in the United States in the early 1980s in the wake of the debt crisis. And as profits decline, there would likely be a further intensification of the attacks on

Table 13. Currency and Home-Country Relationship in the Choice of Syndicated Loan Arranger, 1996

(Percentage market share won by arrangers of indicated nationality)

German Arranger Banks				French Arranger Banks			
	Currency				Currency		
Borrower	Deutsche mark	Other	All	Borrower	French franc	Other	All
German	82	71	80	French	46	10	39
Other	46	3	4	Other	56	2	2
All	62	3	4	All	47	2	3
U.K. Arranger Banks				U.S. Arranger Banks			
	Currency				Currency		
Borrower	Pound	Other	All	Borrower	Dollar	Other	All
U.K.	56	39	53	U.S.	83	28	82
Other	24	2	2	Other	27	13	20
All	53	3	6	All	71	13	61

Sources: Euromoney Bondware; and BIS.

Note: Each entry shows market share of German, French, U.K. or U.S. banks as arrangers of loans for borrowers of the indicated nationality in the indicated currency. For example, the 82 percent in the upper left-hand corner means that German banks arranged 82 percent of the loans for German borrowers that were denominated in deutsche marks. Data include all loans in the Euromoney database that were signed and for which amounts were given, and are therefore more inclusive than the usual data reported by the BIS, which exclude, inter alia, refinancing. Total syndicated loan amounts by currency: deutsche mark: $25 billion; French franc: $31 billion; pound: $102 billion; dollar: $1,254 billion; grand total: $1,514 billion.

those market practices deemed to give some institutions an unfair competitive advantage. In sum, a number of interacting factors could (and this is a possibility rather than a forecast) sweep away remaining barriers to international competition in the banking area while at the same time putting all banks under increasing pressure from securities markets.

A single currency could also change the behavior of financial institutions, inducing them to internationalize both their corporate and retail businesses. The need to change internal computer and information systems could (indeed, should) prompt a strategic rethinking of the business functions those systems are designed to support.[33] Turning first to corporate lending, it must be noted at once that this is not at present a very profitable business in continental Europe.[34] This in itself could inhibit expanded competition, as could

[33]The likelihood of this approach being taken, in contrast to a minimalist solution, will depend on how much advance planning has been possible. Recent surveys assessing the degree of preparedness for EMU indicate that simple "coping" may be the order of the day for many financial institutions. See footnote 26.

[34]See Gemini Consulting and EFMA (1993).

Table 14. Pricing of Cross-Currency LIBOR Basis Swaps[1]

Currencies with Narrower Bid/Ask Spreads[2]			Currencies with Wider Bid/Ask Spreads[3]		
	Receive	Pay		Receive	Pay
Belgian franc	−1	−4	Australian dollar	4	−2
Deutsche mark	4	1	Austrian schilling	9	5
Dutch guilder	4	1	Canadian dollar	7	3
ECU	−1	−4	Danish krone	4	−2
French franc	3	0	Finnish markka	6	0
Italian lira	0	−3	Hong Kong dollar	20	15
Pound sterling	2	−1	Irish pound	5	−5
Swiss franc	3	0	Norwegian krone	4	−2
Yen	−13	−16	Portuguese escudo	−1	−8
			Spanish peseta	7	3
			Swedish krona	1	−3
Average	0	−3	Average	6	0

Source: Intercapital Brokers.

[1]Basis points above or below respective LIBOR that dealers were prepared to receive and pay versus U.S. dollar LIBOR flat on January 8, 1997.

[2]Spread between receive and pay of 3 basis points.

[3]Spread between receive and pay of 4 or more basis points. The correlation between bid/ask spread and the natural log of trading in local currency in April 1995 is −0.69 (see *Central Bank Survey of Foreign Exchange and Derivatives Market Activity*, 1995, Table 1-G).

concerns by lenders that most available foreign clients would be clients that no one else wanted (the adverse selection problem). In contrast, it could also be argued that cross-border "cherry-picking" might become even more attractive given a single currency than it is today.[35]

It has also been contended that making medium-term loans in foreign currencies, using short-term domestic funding sources, exposes banks to special liquidity risks.[36] This discouragement of cross-border lending will certainly disappear with the introduction of the euro, though the magnitude of the resulting effects remains to be determined. However, some guidance on this can be obtained by noting that lenders currently have the possibility, albeit at a cost, of obtaining the required foreign currency for a medium-term period using cross-currency basis swaps; the cost of such swaps (see Table 14) might be seen as a measure of how much different currencies segment the European lending market. In fact, two conclusions arise from Table 14. First, the cost of

[35]Citicorp in Germany has already had a significant degree of success in attracting the business of high-income investors away from German banks.

[36]See McCauley (1984). The bank lending in a foreign currency is likely to have less well-diversified funding sources. In addition, it does not have access to its own central bank for foreign currency.

such swaps is modest, though not trivial. Second, segmentation seems to work to the advantage of banks in some countries more than others. In particular, bank lending in marks, guilders, and French francs seems more protected by borrowing costs than does lending in the lira or Belgian franc.

Whether the introduction of the euro will induce banks to compete more vigorously for retail customers across international borders, ceteris paribus, is even more problematic. Hoschka (1993) and others have argued that foreign banks need some other competitive advantages to stimulate cross-border entry in European retail banking since they face such well-known disadvantages as "reputation" problems, a smaller transaction base, less experience with the local market, and the potential costs of new branches. Could it then be argued in turn that the introduction of the euro might increase the likelihood of such competitive advantage? On the one hand, a consideration of Hoschka's individual arguments gives few grounds for believing that the introduction of the euro would have any more than a marginal influence.[37] On the other hand, a single currency will simplify the accounting of cross-border activities and will allow banks more easily to distinguish those cross-border niche activities that are profitable from those that are not. Moreover, should new competitive opportunities open up in retail banking, because of other changes related to the euro, there is no reason to believe that the banks would be any less inclined to respond than is currently the case.

Need for Adjustment and Potential Difficulties

The direct costs associated with the introduction of a single currency, and the associated increase in competition in the context of EMU, will put further pressure on bank profits and encourage adjustment of various sorts. The severity of that pressure will depend partly on the extent to which the introduction of the euro catalyzes other changes and may well vary in intensity across countries.[38]

[37]Hoschka's first point is that foreign banks may have an advantage from being able to follow domestic clients as their activities become increasingly international. The euro would certainly promote this, though the effects on corporate business would seem greater than the retail effects. A second potential source of firm-level advantage is "know-how" about new products. It is not obvious that the introduction of the euro would have much effect in this regard, and the same might be said about a third possibility mentioned by Hoschka: namely, that cross-border entry might be attracted by ologopolistic profits in domestic retail banking. A fourth possibility, that foreign banks might benefit from diversification of risk through cross-border retail activities, would seem more likely to be reduced than increased by the introduction of the euro.

[38]The banking systems of smaller countries might be thought particularly exposed. They tend to be more reliant on foreign exchange receipts from transactions in their own currencies, and are geographically closer to competing financial systems. In cases where the banking system also relies heavily on "core" deposits paying less than market rates, the implications would be still more serious. See Berlin and Mester (1996).

Whatever one believes in this particular regard, market sentiment is that the European banking industry will be radically transformed over the coming years. A 1993 survey[39] of 65 bankers in 15 different countries foretold a collapse of profits in corporate banking and the survival of only 10 to 20 retail banks across Europe by the year 2005.[40] It is worth considering briefly how banks might react to increased competitive pressures and some of the pitfalls along the way.

Within individual firms, competitive pressures could result in three sorts of efforts to increase profits. In the first place, there could be efforts to increase productivity and to cut costs. Tables 15–17 indicate that this process is not well advanced in Europe. In partial contrast, Gual and Neven (1993, p. 176) note that deregulation in European banking prior to 1990 did lead to some increases in productivity, but that the "rents" earned by workers were nevertheless generally well maintained.[41] One particularly important problem in many European countries is the existence of labor legislation (or the general nature of existing contracts), which not only makes it difficult to lay off staff in general, but also makes it particularly difficult in the financial sector.[42] Indeed, in some cases there are even significant impediments to relocations and other initiatives short of outright loss of employment. The high degree of unionization, allied with strong state involvement in banking, also increases the likelihood of an associated politicization of all measures designed to increase efficiency. All this having been said, the good news is that major efficiency gains are potentially still there to be achieved if these obstacles can be overcome.

A second possibility is that individual firms might be tempted to restore sinking profit margins by taking on more risk. This is not implausible. Indeed, the behavior of U.S. (and many other) banks after the debt crisis of the early 1980s—behavior that led successively to heavy investment in commercial property, leveraged buyouts, market trading, and emerging market debt once again in the early 1990s—may well have been motivated by such considerations. Even if such a possibility were to be discounted, any significant increase in cross-border competition after the introduction of the euro will likely imply that many banks will be making credit evaluations of previously unfamiliar

[39]See Gemini Consulting and EFMA (1993).

[40]It is not clear what the forecast was for retail banking in Germany, where there are currently thousands of mutual and cooperative banks. While independent and actively merging, these banks operate within the framework of national associations offering extremely sophisticated central services. In this respect, they already look much like large retail banks with many branches.

[41]Gual and Neven also note (p. 179) that compensation in European banking continues to be substantially above economy-wide compensation.

[42]For example, in France there are the constraints imposed by the decrees of 1936 and 1937. In Italy, the parliament recently passed a special law regarding the restructuring of the Banco di Napoli. Presumably, this reflected an assessment of the difficulties imposed by existing law.

Table 15. Restructuring: Number of Institutions and Size Concentration[1]

	Number of Institutions						Concentration: Top Five (Top Ten)		
	1980[2]	1990	1995[3]	Peak (since 1980)			1980[4]	1990	1995[5]
Country					Year	Percent change[6]	Percentage share in total assets		
Belgium	148	129	150	163	1992	−8	64(76)	58(74)	59(73)
Finland	631	498	352	631	1985	−44	63(68)	65(69)	74(83)
France	1,033	786	593	1,033	1984	−43	57(69)	52(66)	47(63)
Germany[7]	5,355	4,180	3,487	5,355	1980	−35	. . .	. . .	17(28)
Italy	1,071	1,067	941	1,109	1987	−15	26(42)	24(39)	29(45)
Netherlands	200	180	174	200	1980	−13	73(81)	77(86)	81(89)
Norway	346	165	148	346	1980	−57	63(74)	68(79)	58(71)
Spain[8]	357	327	318	378	1982	−16	38(58)	38(58)	49(62)
Sweden	598	498	112	598	1980	−81	64(71)	70(82)	86(93)
United Kingdom	796	665	560	796	1983	−30	63(80)	58(79)	57(78)
Memorandum items									
Japan	618	605	571	618	1980	−8	25(40)	30(45)	27(43)
Switzerland	478	499	415	499	1990	−17	45(56)	45(57)	50(62)
United States[9]	35,875	27,864	23,854	35,875	1980	−34	9(14)	9(15)	13(21)

Sources: British Bankers' Association; Building Societies' Association; and national data, as reported in BIS (1996a).

[1]Deposit-taking institutions, generally including commercial, savings, and various types of mutual and cooperative banks; for Japan excluding various types of credit cooperative.

[2]For Finland, 1985; for France, 1984; for Spain, 1981; for the United Kingdom, 1983.

[3]For Finland, Sweden, and Japan, 1994.

[4]For Finland and the Netherlands, 1985; for France, 1986; for Italy, 1983; for Switzerland, 1987.

[5]For Belgium, the United Kingdom, Japan, and Switzerland, 1994; for Finland, 1993.

[6]From peak to most recent observation where applicable.

[7]For number of institutions, western Germany only. Data for the whole of Germany: 1995, 3,784; percentage change, −30 percent.

[8]Concentration data for commercial and savings banks only.

[9]Excluding credit unions: 1995, 12,067; percentage change, −36 percent.

Table 16. Banks' Restructuring: Number of Branches[1]

					Peak (since 1980)		Memorandum:
	1980[2]	1990	1995[3]			Percent	Bank
Country	Number (in thousands)				Year	change[4]	density[5]
Belgium	7.8	8.3	7.8	8.5	1989	−8	0.77
Finland	3.4	3.3	2.1	3.5	1988	−39	0.42
France	24.3	25.7	25.5	25.9	1987	−2	0.44
Germany[6]	39.3	39.8	37.9	40.0	1985	−5	0.46
Italy	12.2	17.7	23.9	23.9	1995	0	0.42
Netherlands	5.5	8.0	7.3	8.0	1989	−9	0.47
Norway	1.9	1.8	1.4	2.2	1987	−37	0.36
Spain	25.8	35.2	36.0	36.0	1995	0	0.92
Sweden	3.7	3.3	2.7	3.7	1980	−27	0.31
United Kingdom	20.4	19.0	16.6	21.2	1985	−22	0.28
Memorandum items							
Japan	18.5	24.8	25.7	25.7	1994	0	0.21
Switzerland	3.7	4.2	3.8	4.2	1990	−10	0.53
United States	58.3	67.7	69.6	69.6	1994	0	0.27

Sources: British Bankers' Association; Building Societies' Association; and national data, as reported in BIS (1996a).

[1]Deposit-taking institutions; for Japan and the United States, excluding various types of credit cooperative.

[2]For France and the Netherlands, 1981.

[3]For Belgium, Finland, the Netherlands, Sweden, the United Kingdom, Japan, Switzerland, and the United States, 1994.

[4]From peak to most recent observation where applicable.

[5]Number of branches per 1,000 inhabitants in the latest available year.

[6]Western Germany only, excluding commission agencies of Bausparkassen. Data for the whole of Germany: 1995, 48.2; percentage change, −2 percent.

counterparties. Errors of judgment will be easier to make in such an environment.

A third and more positive possibility is that banks will turn to new products and lines of business to enhance returns. Indeed, this has already begun, with German banks in particular buying up U.K. firms with a view to increasing profits from investment banking. Should there be (as suggested in the second section of this paper) a substantial increase in the issue of euro securities, European banks should be first in line to profit given the revealed preference of issuers to choose underwriters from the same currency area. However, following an investment banking strategy involves enormous infrastructure and staffing costs up front. As for other aspects of the investment banking business, it must be noted that global competition may be more fierce. For example, in 1996 five of the top ten firms doing cross-border merg-

Table 17. Banks' Restructuring: Employment and Staff Costs

	Employment[1]						Staff Costs[2]		
	1980[3]	1990	1994[4]		Peak (since 1980)		1980–82[5]	1986–88	1992–94
Country	Number (in thousands)				Year	Percent change[6]	As a percentage of gross income		
Belgium	68	79	76	79	1990	−5	41	33	39[7]
Finland	42	50	36	53	1989	−32	43	33	24
France	399	399	382	401	1988	−5	47	44	44
Germany[8]	533	621	658	658	1994	0	48	44	39
Italy	277	324	332	333	1993	−0.3	46	48	44
Netherlands	113	118	112	119	1991	−6	42	41	38
Norway	24	31	23	35	1987	−34	42	35	30
Spain	252	252	245	256	1991	−4	47	43	37
Sweden	39	45	42	46	1991	−5	29	23	22
United Kingdom	324	425	368	430	1989	−15	47	38	36
Memorandum items									
Japan	612	597	618	622	1993	−0.6	44	33	39
Switzerland	84	120	112	120	1990	−7	40	37	33
United States[9]	1,900	1,979	1,891	2,136	1987	−12	36	31	27

Sources: For staff costs, OECD; for employment, British Bankers' Association, Building Societies' Association; and national data, as reported in BIS (1996a).

[1]In deposit-taking institutions; for Japan, excluding credit cooperatives.

[2]For Belgium, the Netherlands, and Switzerland, all banks; for other countries, commercial banks (OECD definition).

[3]For France, 1985; for the Netherlands and Sweden, 1984; for Spain, 1981.

[4]For Italy, Norway, and Spain, 1995.

[5]For Belgium and France, 1981–82.

[6]From peak to most recent observation where applicable.

[7]1992.

[8]For employment, western Germany only. Data for the whole of Germany: 1994, 728.

[9]Employment data excluding credit unions: 1994, 1,732; percentage change, −14 percent.

ers and acquisitions in Europe were U.S. firms, and Goldman Sachs for the first time did more business in France than did Lazard Frères. Asset management is another area where fee income seems likely to increase sharply on the basis of changing demographics and a potential substitution of private saving for state-sponsored schemes. Again, however, positioning has already begun and continental banks may expect strong competition from both U.K. and U.S. financial firms.

Other opportunities at the interfirm level will also be exploited to deal with competitive pressures. Mergers and acquisitions are one possibility,[43] though such moves may also run into political resistance and labor legislation, which limits the ability to gain the full benefits of either scope or scale.[44] As indicated in Table 18, not a great deal has happened in this respect in continental Europe to date. Another possible strategy will be the pursuit of cross-border alliances, which will allow firms to supply special services over a much wider area than would have been possible otherwise. In itself, however, such a strategy of alliances among existing market participants does not materially address the underlying problem for the industry as a whole, namely, that the rate of return on capital is likely to remain too low.

The final possibility is that some of the capital currently in the financial services industry in Europe will be withdrawn and/or consolidated in some way. Hopefully, this will happen in an incremental and nondisruptive fashion as smaller firms are closed or taken over. Yet, as the process of consolidation continues, and remaining firms become larger and larger, the likelihood of a disruptive failure could also increase (see Schoenmaker, 1995). This likelihood may also be further increased if two recent trends continue. First, given the high costs of the information technology that will be needed to ensure survival (at least for a time) in such an environment, fixed costs will rise relative to variable costs. This implies that, in the later stages of any restructuring process, it may make sense for some firms to continue to operate at a loss for an extended period of time. Second, if the recent trend toward using "branding" as a competitive tool continues, the purpose of which is to ensure that all parts of a business are associated with the brand name, it may become harder to close down unprofitable parts of a business than in the past. Should the current resistance of national governments to closures also be maintained, ongoing competition from nonviable banks could con-

[43]It is not easy to evaluate the extent to which mergers and acquisitions do add value. Borio and Tsatsaronis (1996) look at movements in relevant share prices (in major industrial countries) just before and after announcements of mergers and acquisitions in the finance area. The evidence for a significant increase in "expected" value is not strong. See also BIS (1996a).

[44]In the United States, the biggest gains have generally come from consolidating back- and middle-office functions. A new development in Canada has been the spinning-off of such functions and their merger into a single and more efficient company owned by a number of banks.

tinue to threaten the prospects of other banks and the health of the financial system more broadly.

Implications for Banking Systems

The possibility of intensified competition and the need for restructuring within European financial markets highlight a number of issues for public policy. Prudence of course demands that these be addressed in the spirit of "planning for the worst," even while anticipating the best. Within Europe itself, the first issue has to do with the incentive structure for sound banking provided by the authorities. Closely related is the issue of preventing problems from occurring and managing them when they do. A third issue is the implications of a single currency for the transmission mechanism of monetary policy and related implications for financial stability. Given the importance of Europe in integrated global markets, all of these issues are of interest to non-Europeans. Finally, the European experience of cooperation might well provide lessons for others as to how to improve global financial cooperation.

Internal Implications

Incentive structures for sound banking. Sound banking practices tend to be discouraged by the likelihood of state bailouts, particularly if the shareholders and management are left intact. Competition policy at the EU level strongly discourages such interference, yet, given the current degree of state involvement in the national banking systems of many countries, it may be politically hard to avoid for some years to come (see Table 19). The continuing important role of mutual and cooperative banks in some European countries is a further complication. However, with time, a different set of problems could emerge. A successful process of consolidation could result in a smaller number of international financial institutions (with no truly national affiliation other than legal incorporation), which might begin to consider themselves either too big or too complex to fail. In such a multinational context, and one without a central fiscal authority, the difficulties of organizing a bailout even for an individual bank could be considerable. Perhaps the good news is that knowledge of this fact would be a welcome incentive for more prudent private sector behavior.

Deposit insurance has obvious merits but there can be associated incentive problems as well. In Europe, the Directive on Deposit Guarantee Schemes (adopted on May 30, 1994) ensures that all EU countries offer a minimum level of deposit insurance, though there continue to be significant differences

Table 18. Merger and Acquisition Activity in Banking[1]

	Number			Value					
				(In billions of U.S. dollars)			(As a percentage)[2]		
Country	1991–92	1993–94	1995–96[3]	1991–92	1993–94	1995–96[3]	1991–92	1993–94	1995–96[3]
Belgium	22	18	12	1.0	0.6	0.4	14.1	7.0	7.9
Finland	51	16	4	0.9	1.0	0.8	22.3	21.7	11.3
France	133	71	43	2.4	0.5	3.2	4.3	1.0	10.4
Germany	71	83	27	3.5	1.9	0.7	6.5	7.6	3.5
Italy	122	105	65	5.3	6.1	3.0	15.6	17.7	19.7
Netherlands	20	13	7	0.1	0.1	0.8	0.2	0.5	9.5
Norway	23	24	2	0.1	0.2	0.4	1.2	5.7	4.4
Spain	76	44	26	4.3	4.5	2.1	13.5	21.5	34.1
Sweden	38	23	8	1.1	0.4	0.1	3.8	2.0	0.4
United Kingdom	71	40	28	7.5	3.3	21.7	6.5	3.4	12.4
Total	627	437	222	26.1	18.5	33.3	7.3	6.7	11.0
Total nonbank financial	1,383	1,361	834	28.0	38.8	27.2	7.8	14.0	9.0

Memorandum items[4]									
Japan	22	8	17	0.0	2.2	33.8	0.3	18.8	77.0
	(22)	(14)	(17)	(0.3)	(1.5)	(0.2)	(3.6)	(12.8)	(0.4)
Switzerland	47	59	14	0.4	3.9	0.7	9.5	43.4	1.6
	(30)	(30)	(28)	(0.4)	(2.0)	(1.3)	(9.7)	(21.9)	(3.1)
United States	1,354	1,477	1,176	56.8	55.3	82.5	18.7	9.0	13.5
	(984)	(1,426)	(1,125)	(30.4)	(72.8)	(56.9)	(10.0)	(11.9)	(9.3)

Source: Securities Data Company, as reported in BIS (1996a).
[1]Classified by the industry of the target; only completed or pending deals; announcement date volumes.
[2]Of mergers and acquisitions in all industries.
[3]As at April 4, 1996.
[4]Numbers in parentheses: nonbank financial.

Table 19. Intrinsic Strength and Ordinary Ratings of European Banks

Country	Number of Rated Banks	Range of BFSRs	Average BFSR	Average Long-Term Deposit Rating
Austria	7	B to D+	C	Aa3
Belgium	7	B+ to C	B	Aa3
Denmark	3	B to C	C+	A1
Finland	4	D+ to E	D	A2
France	27	A to D	C+	A1
Germany	21	A to D+	C+	Aa1
Ireland	4	B to C+	B/C+	A1/A2
Italy	16	B to E	C	A2
Luxembourg	3	B	B	Aa2
Netherlands	5	A to C+	B+	Aa1
Portugal	3	C+ to C	C	A3
Spain	11	A to C	B	Aa3
Sweden	4	C+ to C	C	A2
United Kingdom	24	A to C+	B	A1

Source: Moody's (1997).

Note: Bank financial strength ratings (BFSRs) measure intrinsic safety and soundness on a legal stand-alone basis. Ordinary long-term deposit ratings factor in external credit support from owners, industry group and/or official institutions.

in these schemes across countries.[45] While deposit insurance may make depositors less careful in their choice of bank, this may not be of major concern given that the insurance limit is explicit (barring expectations of a bailout), that it is has often been set at a relatively low level, and that higher insurance levels may be matched (as in Germany) by commensurately strict supervision. However, another problem is that deposit insurance schemes differ across European countries and are essentially "home"-determined. With a single currency, this could lead to an increased flow of deposits to banks domiciled in the most heavily insured jurisdiction, assuming their deposit insurance covers nonresidents.[46] In recognition of this problem, it has recently been agreed that (until December 31, 1999) home-country protection schemes offered by branches abroad cannot provide better depositor protection than the host-country scheme. The European Commission is currently preparing a report on the rationale and consequences of the present situation and will report by the end of the decade.

[45]See Barth, Nolle, and Rice (1997). The minimum amount insured is ECU 20,000. Up to this limit, only 90 percent of losses will be reimbursed.

[46]As is commonly the case. See Barth, Nolle, and Rice (1997, Table 9).

Table 20. Claims on Central Government[1]

(Percentage of Total Bank Assets)

Country	1975	1980	1985	1990	1995
Belgium	17.5	15.3	19.2	18.6	28.9
France	3.9	9.7	11.5	7.2	11.2
Germany	9.9	12.8	14.0	12.4	15.1
Italy	10.1	18.3	21.9	15.3	. . .
Spain	. . .	. . .	22.9	20.4	19.0
United Kingdom[2]	5.5	3.1	1.3	0.9	1.3
Memorandum item					
United States	10.0	7.6	8.6	5.8	7.5

Source: IMF, International Financial Statistics.
[1]Excluding reserves.
[2]Net claims.

A final issue having to do with incentives is related to the fact that all European sovereign debt is zero weighted under the Basle Capital Accord and the Capital Adequacy Directive. Since the introduction of the single currency will heighten the credit risk in sovereign debt, these capital provisions may provide an inappropriate incentive for financial institutions to hold sovereign debt. Moreover, most banking systems in Europe (and also pensions funds) tend to hold only debt of their national sovereign, which means a significant degree of exposure should the credit risk of that particular country be revised upward (see Table 20).[47] The implication seems to be that any remaining national restrictions on outward portfolio flows should be abolished, and that international diversification of bank assets with respect to sovereign risk should be actively encouraged. As discussed earlier, this would also encourage further the development of a single European bond market denominated in euros.

Preventing and managing banking problems. A number of supervisory issues arise in the context of the single currency. The first and most important, at least in principle, is whether supervisory authority should rest with the ECB or the national supervisors. At the moment, it is clearly intended that the national supervisory authorities should continue to carry out their current responsibilities. This will have the effect of helping to separate the monetary policy

[47]Consider the case of Italian or Belgian banks in a situation where very high interest rates were imposed (for whatever reason) in a single currency area. Given high debt ratios in those countries, debt-servicing capacity might be called into question and credit premiums could rise. Recall as well the arguments put forward in the subsection on lessons from Canada. Any such revision of credit ratings would have a direct effect on the value of bank holdings of those securities (see Bruni, 1990, p. 250).

function from the supervisory function,[48] and of ensuring that supervisors are physically close to those being regulated. Moreover, it would seem broadly consistent with a system of national deposit insurance. However, such a diffuse system will also make it harder to monitor exposure to single creditors borrowing in different parts of the integrated market, and will put a large premium on the efficient exchange of information. It also seems likely to encourage the maintenance of existing differences in both supervisory practices and capital standards among member nations, which, as noted above, continue to impede formation of the single market.

It will be important to maintain an efficient information flow under the currently envisaged supervisory arrangements. About half of the national supervisory authorities are central banks, whereas other agencies are involved in other countries (some attached to treasuries and some not). Domestic relations between these generic groups of institutions have not always been easy, though to date it appears that the different kinds of national supervisors interact in an admirable way at the international level (see Kapstein, 1994). A second problem may be differences of philosophy about the extent to which privileged supervisory information should be shared, not only between institutions, but also between supervisors and those responsible for monetary policy.[49] A third issue has to do with the prospective role of the Banking Supervisory Sub-Committee, which meets at the EMI. On the one hand, playing up its role implies that non-central-bank officials have an important role within the framework of the ECB. On the other hand, to the extent that its influence is downplayed, that influence might migrate to the Banking Advisory Committee of the European Commission. Since this committee also includes treasury representatives, the number of parties requiring to be fully informed about banking sector difficulties rises even further, as does the scope for misunderstanding in times of difficulty.

A number of commentators (e.g., Levitt, 1995) have suggested that these problems could prove insurmountable and that authority in the supervisory

[48]The Bundesbank has traditionally argued that a supervisory role for the central bank may cause it wrongly to subordinate its price stability objective (in setting monetary policy) to the financial stability objective associated with its supervisory function. Concerns have also been expressed that the supervisory function is more easily politicized and that this interference could easily slide over into the monetary area. It should be noted for completeness, however, that the Bundesbank does collect supervisory information for the Federal Banking Supervisory Office.

[49]Some would argue that supervisors should not even tell the operational arm of a central bank that an institution was about to fail. Should the central bank close out its position with that institution, it would be accused of "bringing it down." If it did nothing with the information, it would be accused of "wasting the taxpayers' money." On the one hand, this logic ignores the fact that insider information might also help the central bank to better prepare itself to deal with any of the fallout (contagion, etc.) arising from the failure itself. On the other hand, some fear that systemic concerns raised by the disclosure of such information might also lead to an overly expansionary monetary policy.

area would tend to migrate to the ECB.[50] While at present the ECB has only advisory powers in this area,[51] Article 105.6 of the Maastricht Treaty states that it could be given "specific tasks concerning policies" conditional on a unanimous decision of the Council on a proposal by the Commission. Whether this is a likely development remains to be seen but, barring a major crisis that might call into question existing arrangements, it could well take a very long time. Another development supporting such an outcome would be the creation of big European banks whose "home" supervisor was not obvious. It is also worth noting that, were there to be such a major change in approach, the issue of a pan-European supervisor outside the ECB might also be raised again. Whatever the affiliation of the European supervisor, the character of its mandate (in particular, which institutions to oversee), the legal basis of its powers (powers that are currently based in national legislation), and the methods through which it would be made accountable would all still have to be decided upon.

Some similar issues arise in the context of potential official lending facilities under EMU. Rightly respecting the principle of "constructive ambiguity," the Treaty is unclear whether such a facility should exist, and thus provides no guidance as to whether those potentially involved should be national central banks, the ECB, or both. Nor does it assign responsibility for banks whose business is predominantly international. With supervision being conducted by the national authorities, presumably they (if anyone) would be in the best position to advise the national central bank whether an individual bank was solvent and whether liquidity support for the bank was warranted. Moreover, should a bank initially deemed solvent ultimately prove insolvent, it would seem more appropriate that the associated fiscal charge be borne at the national rather than the European level.[52] Such an approach might also be thought attractive in that it would contribute to a separation between the official lending function and the monetary policy function. Yet it also seems clear that, in some circumstances, the ECB might also wish to play a lending role. Within the single market created by EMU, there would be a greater chance of contagion across institutions and borders and this could imply the need for a system-wide response. Indeed, responding to a market-wide shortage of liquidity might be thought the natural function of the ECB. However, while the ECB would presumably be monitoring markets in the course of its everyday

---

[50]Schoenmaker (1995) presents the pros and cons of an intermediate outcome in which a pan-European supervisor might supervise only those large institutions whose failure was thought likely to have systemic implications. National supervisors would concern themselves with all the rest.

[51]This contrasts with the U.S. system, where the Federal Reserve Board of Governors has authority over the regional Federal Reserve Banks, and exercises that authority.

[52]If this were not so, there would be a clear incentive for national supervisors to deem insolvent banks "solvent" such that the fiscal charge would be borne by others.

operations,[53] it might still be uncomfortably dependent on national supervisors for information that might be crucial in a crisis.

Interest rate effects and financial stability. During the ERM crisis of 1992, it became clear that the relatively greater reliance on variable rate mortgages in the United Kingdom meant that the effects of monetary tightening on spending propensities were both faster and greater than in France. Given these different circumstances, the French authorities felt able to effect a more successful defence of their currency within the ERM than did the U.K. authorities. More recently, the BIS (1995) has documented more fully the extent to which the transmission mechanisms of monetary policy seem to differ across the major countries, and the extent to which these differences have their roots in differences in financial structure.[54] The reaction of loan rates charged by banks (at the margin) is much slower in some European countries than in others. Moreover, in some countries, fixed rate loans and longer-term loans are much more common than in others. Some countries also rely less on credit rationing devices (relatively high down payments for houses, cars, etc.), implying that much larger swings in interest rates are required to have the same effects on spending.[55]

Differences of this sort within a single currency area imply that common short-term interest rate changes will have different effects in different national jurisdictions.[56] This is obviously of interest for those who will be concerned about the transmission mechanism of monetary policy within EMU. However, these differences in financial structure could potentially have implications for financial stability as well. Suppose interest rates did have to rise significantly to ensure price stability in the EU as a whole. Those countries in which the impact of this was particularly great, because of their national financial structure, would presumably suffer a commensurate reduction in the quality of both public and private credits.[57] Moreover, if the national banking system was

[53]This would also depend on the extent to which the ECB relied on the national banks to implement monetary policy. If that reliance were as great as the reliance put by the Federal Reserve Board on the Federal Reserve Bank of New York, the ECB might have little hands-on contact.

[54]Another useful reference is provided by Barran, Coundert, and Mojon (1996).

[55]An interesting but often unremarked variation on this theme is the way in which German savings banks and cooperatives try to shelter their business clients from interest rate swings. Such behavior is consistent with the model assumed by Berlin and Mester (1996), but conflicts with most of the recent literature on "credit rationing," which assumes that a separate credit channel makes interest rate swings even more effective. In reality, both hypotheses may be true depending on which set of banks (perhaps differing across countries or by size) one is talking about.

[56]In general it would be simpler and therefore preferable to have a common set of transmission processes. Moreover, it would be particularly unfortunate if a country having a relatively fast-acting and powerful response to higher interest rates were to begin from a starting point of relatively subdued activity due to some asymmetric shock. Conversely, it would be rather fortunate if the starting point were a relatively higher level of economic activity.

[57]The effect on sovereign credit rankings would be particularly severe in cases where the initial level of debt was high and/or its term was relatively short.

heavily invested in national government debt (see point on incentive structures for sound banking, above) and/or was initially weak for other reasons, the direct impact on bank profits could be quite significant. By the same token, any country with a particular tradition of longer-term lending at fixed rates, financed to whatever degree with shorter-term deposits, could find its profits under pressure from this source.

The upshot of this line of thought is that concerns about financial fragility in particular countries could act as a potential constraint on the conduct of monetary policy for the EU as a whole. It is, of course, likely that the single currency will lead to these structural differences disappearing over time. Indeed, it is evident that, once there is a single money market and bond market, all market interest rates (reflecting shifts in implicit forward yields) should move uniformly in different national jurisdictions, barring shifts in risk premiums. Yet other national differences may be longer lasting, implying that transitional difficulties cannot be wholly ignored. This point is further reinforced if the need for fiscal restraint under the Maastricht Treaty, and potentially further agreements still to be reached, call into question the fiscal capacity of national governments to deal with systemic problems in their national banking system.[58] The fundamental point is that both a sound financial system and a sound fiscal position will be required to ensure macroeconomic stability after the introduction of the single currency. It is obvious that not having the former threatens the latter,[59] but the converse may be true as well.

International Implications

To prognosticate about the possible implications for public policy within Europe resulting from the possible effects on financial structure of the possible introduction of the euro involves at least three levels of speculation. To introduce a fourth level, the possible international implications of all the above, is even more fanciful. Yet some broad lines of thought do seem to be suggested, having to do with the harmonization of domestic financial and regulatory structures, the process of international regulation and supervision, and the specific issue of "host-versus-home" supervision.

A process of enhanced competition within Europe will leave a smaller number of large banks, many of which will have a presence outside Europe. With

---

[58]A rough measure of how the market might react to this change in perception is the difference in the credit ratings given to banks (by Moody's) on an "ordinary" as opposed to an "intrinsic strength" basis. See Table 19.

[59]Caprio and Klingebiel (1996) provide estimates of the direct costs to governments (relative to GDP) of resolving banking crises in Spain (1977 to 1985, 17 percent), Finland (1991 to 1993, 8 percent), Sweden (1991, 6 percent) and Norway (1987 to 1989, 4 percent). Honohan (1997) estimates that emerging countries have spent $250 billion for the same purpose since 1980.

a view to possible bankruptcy or other difficulties, it would seem all the more desirable to harmonize bankruptcy laws for financial institutions as well as other aspects of the legal and regulatory framework within which such institutions operate. Indeed, it is possible that under the pressure of intensified international competition and concern about regulatory arbitrage a dynamic might arise in the direction of such harmonization. For example, Barth, Nolle, and Rice (1997, pp. 31–32) make a strong case that, compared with emerging standards in Europe, the regulatory burden for financial institutions in the United States is both too heavy and too diffuse. Such pressures for harmonization are also likely to increase as it becomes clearer that the industrial world's three major financial groupings (North America, Europe, Japan) are all moving toward free trade in financial services, at least within their own geographical area, and that all are now on the road to some version of universal banking as well.

The process of international cooperation in the area of regulation and supervision may also change in light of European developments. Regardless of the degree of harmonization of domestic rules, supervisors will have to cooperate more closely to ensure proper oversight of larger banks with an international presence. Since supervision of financial conglomerates in Europe is already carried out, as much as possible, on a consolidated basis, there may also be increased pressure for a similar approach in other jurisdictions (especially the United States) where this is not currently the case. On the one hand, this would facilitate the pursuit of the "lead regulator" strategy to deal with the problem of international conglomerates. On the other hand, it might increase pressure for a migration of supervisory authority to bodies outside central banks, which some central banks might welcome but others would certainly not. The evolution of supervisory practices in Europe (who, where, what) may also raise further questions. For example, will European banking supervisors increasingly come to the Basle Committee on Banking Supervision with a single voice and, if so, how will that affect the dynamics of achieving consensus: will it be easier or more difficult? If responsibility for supervisory practice migrates to the ECB, what might be the implications for membership of the Basle Committee? In particular, will the current need for international agreements to be ratified by national legislation demand the presence of national supervisors, or not?

A related issue has to do with the question of "home-versus-host" responsibility for supervision. Within Europe, supervisory responsibility is now clearly allocated to home supervisors, and host supervisors (especially in London) are increasingly inclined to remind home supervisors of their responsibilities. It is also the case under the NAFTA that, as Glass-Steagall disappears, foreign branches will replace subsidiaries and home-country supervision may play a greater role in that region too (see White, 1994, p. 18). This raises the possibility of a worldwide agreement to accept home-country supervision, presumably also based on consolidated reporting. Such an agreement would have some obvious advantages. For example, it might eventually allow both internationally active firms and their supervisors to take due account of the global risks being assumed by individual firms as well as the interrelationships between separate categories of risk. This would certainly be the hope of financial institutions themselves. In contrast, the practical difficulties involved in potentially entrusting small countries (with commensurate supervisory capacities) with much larger responsibilities than hitherto should not be underestimated.

References

Adler, Oliver, 1996, "EMU and Banking," paper presented at the 1996 ICMB conference on Forces of Change in International Banking, International Center for Monetary and Banking Studies, Geneva, November 7–8.

Alworth, Julian, and C.E.V. Borio, 1993, "Commercial Paper Markets: A Survey," BIS Economic Papers No. 37 (Basle: Bank for International Settlements, April).

Association Cambiste Internationale, 1995, The Single Currency in Europe: A Working Paper (Paris: ACI).

Balder, John, José A. López, and Lawrence M. Sweet, 1991, "Competitiveness in the Eurocredit Market," in *International Competitiveness of U.S. Financial Firms: Products, Markets, and Conventional Performance Measures*, Federal Reserve Bank of New York Staff Study (New York: Federal Reserve Bank of New York, May), pp. 26–41.

Banca d'Italia, 1995, Ordinary General Meeting of Shareholders, *Abridged Report for the Year 1994*, May 31.

Bank of England, 1996, *Practical Issues Arising from the Introduction of the Euro*, Vol. 3 (London: Bank of England).

Bank for International Settlements, 1997, *International Banking and Financial Market Developments* (February).

———, 1996a, *66th Annual Report* (Basle: BIS, June).

———, 1996b, *Central Bank Survey of Foreign Exchange and Derivatives Market Activity 1995* (Basle: BIS, May).

———, 1996c, *International Banking and Financial Market Developments* (Basle: BIS, November).

———, 1995, *Financial Structure and the Monetary Policy Transmission Mechanism* (Basle: BIS, March).

Barran, Fernando, Virginie Coundert, and Benoît Mojon, 1996, "The Transmission of Monetary Policy in the European Countries," LSE Financial Markets Group Special Paper No. 86 (London: London School of Economics, June).

Barth, James R., Daniel E. Nolle, and Tara N. Rice, 1997, "Commercial Banking Structure, Regulation, and Performance: an International Comparison," OCC

Working Paper 97-6 (Washington: Office of the Comptroller of the Currency, March).

Beers, David T., 1996, "Stronger-Rated Sovereigns Will Lead Way into EMU," *Standard & Poor's CreditWeek* (November 13), pp. 13–18.

Bénassy-Quéré, Agnès, 1996, "Potentialities and Opportunities of the Euro as an International Currency," CEPII Document de Travail, No. 96-09 (Paris: Centre d'Etudes Prospectives et d'Informations Internationales, August).

Berlin, Mitchell, and Loretta J. Mester, 1996, "Why is the Banking Sector Shrinking?" Federal Reserve Bank of Philadelphia Working Paper No. 96-18 (Philadelphia, Pennsylvania: Federal Reserve Bank of Philadelphia, August).

Bloem, Mary, 1996, "The Effect of the Euro on European Bond Markets," paper presented at a *Euromoney* seminar on Implications of EMU for the International Debt Markets, London, October 17–18.

Board of Governors of the Federal Reserve System, 1996, *Flow of Funds Accounts of the United States* (December 11).

Borio, Claudio E.V., and Kostas Tsatsaronis, 1996, "Restructuring in Banking: The Role of Mergers and Acquisitions," paper presented at the conference Toward a Common European Banking Market: National Strategies and Policy Issues, Paolo Baffi Centre for Financial and Monetary Economics, Bocconi University, Milan, May 10.

Bradbery, Adam, 1996, "Swap Traders Say 'Sure Bet' Is Uncertain," *Wall Street Journal* (Europe edition), May 8.

Brookes, Martin, 1997, "Credit Risk and Bond Yield Spreads Within EMU," *European Economics Analyst*, Goldman Sachs, No. 97/07 (March 26).

Brown, Brendon, 1996, "EMU: Implications for the International Debt Markets," paper presented at a Euromoney seminar on Implications of EMU for the International Debt Markets, London, October 17–18.

Bruni, Franco, 1990, "Banking and Financial Regulation: The Italian Case," in *European Banking in the Nineteen Nineties*, ed. by Jean Dermine (Oxford: Blackwell).

Bugie, Scott, 1996, "EMU and the Banks: Costs vs. Opportunities," *Standard & Poor's CreditWeek* (November 13).

Bulchandani, Ravi, 1996, "Spread Economics: Interest Rates After EMU," *Investment Research Europe*, Morgan Stanley (November 8).

Burgess, Arthur, 1996, "An Issuer's Perspective on the European Markets Pre- and Post-Euro," paper presented at the IBC UK conference on Evaluating the Impact of the Euro on the European Securities Market, London, November 5–6.

Cantor, Richard, and Frank Packer, 1996, "Determinants and Impacts of Sovereign Credit Ratings," *Economic Policy Review*, Federal Reserve Bank of New York, Vol. 2 (October), pp. 37–53.

Caprio, Gerard, and Daniela Klingebiel, 1996, "Bank Insolvency: Bad Luck, Bad Policy, or Bad Banking?" paper presented to the Annual World Bank Conference on Development Economics, Washington, April 25–26.

Clarke, Ian, and Clive Parry, 1996, "Government Credit Spreads Too Narrow for the Post-EMU World?" Morgan Stanley, *Fixed Income Portfolio Strategy* (October 8).

Congdon, Tim 1996, "EMU? Not a Chance," *The Banker*, Vol. 46 (October), pp. 14–16.

Courtadon, Carol L., 1985, *The Competitive Structure of the Eurobond Underwriting Industry* (New York: New York University, Center for the Study of Financial Institutions).

Davies, Jonathan, 1996, "Assessing the New Post-EMU-Framework of the Fixed Income Markets," paper presented at the IIR conference on Assessing the Practical Implications and Impact of EMU on the Financial Markets, London, November 18–19.

De Grauwe, Paul, 1996, "Forward Interest Rates as Predictors of EMU," CEPR Discussion Paper No. 1395 (London: Centre for Economic Performance Research, May).

Denton, Nicholas, "European Monetary Union: Impact on IT Systems," *Financial Times*, February 5, 1997.

Dermine, Jean, 1996, "European Banking with a Single Currency," *Financial Markets, Institutions and Instruments* (December), pp. 62–102.

Duesing, Jan, 1997, "European Futures Union: What Benchmark Long Futures Contract after EMU?" *Global Strategy and Relative Value* (London: CS First Boston, February 19).

Economic Research Europe Ltd., 1996, *A Study of the Effectiveness and Impact of Internal Market Integration on the Banking and Credit Sector* (London: Economic Research Ltd., September).

Eichengreen, Barry, and Jürgen von Hagen, 1995, "Fiscal Policy and Monetary Union: Federalism, Fiscal Restrictions and the No-Bailout Rule," CEPR Discussion Paper No. 1247 (London: Centre for Economic Policy Research, September).

Emerson, Michael, and others, 1988, "The Economics of 1992," *European Economy*, Vol. 35 (March).

European Commission, 1997, "Draft paper on the technical preparations of the bond markets by the consultative group on the impact of the introduction of the euro on capital markets" (March).

Favero, Carlo, Francesco Giavazzi, and Luigi Spaventa, 1996, "High Yields: The Spread on German Interest Rates," CEPR Discussion Paper No. 1330 (London: Centre for Economic Policy Research, January).

Fox, Mark, 1996, "The Shape of the Future Euro Market," *Strategic Investor*, Lehman Brothers (August 15).

Fridson, Martin S., and M. Christopher Garman, 1996, "This Year in High-Yield 1995," *Extra Credit*, Merrill Lynch (January/February), pp. 4–33.

Gemini Consulting and EFMA, 1993, *European Banking: A View to 2005* (London: Gemini Consulting).

Goodhart, Charles, 1997, "The Two Concepts of Money, and the Future of Europe," paper presented at a conference on Optimum Currency Areas: The Current Agenda for International Monetary and Fiscal Integration, organized by the Bank of Israel and the International Monetary Fund in Jerusalem and Tel Aviv, December 4–6, 1996.

Gregorio, Giuliano, 1996, "Weighing up the Consequences of EMU on Exchange Traded Derivatives When Formally Converted into Euros," paper presented at the IIR conference on Assessing the Practical Implications and Impact of EMU on the Financial Markets, London, November 18–19.

Gual, Jordi, and Damien Neven, 1993, "Deregulation of the European Banking Industry (1980–1991)," *European Economy/Social Europe*, No. 3, pp. 151–83. (Also published as CEPR Discussion Paper No. 703, August 1992.)

Honohan, Patrick, 1997, "Financial System Failures in Developing and Transition Countries: Diagnosis and Prediction," BIS Working Paper No. 39 (Basle: Bank for International Settlements).

Hoschka, Tobias C., 1993, *Cross-Border Entry in European Retail Financial Services* (New York: St. Martin's Press).

Huteau, Guillaume, 1997, "A Benchmark Swap Curve: The Full Convergence of Post-EMU Swap Curves," *Global Strategy and Relative Value* (London: CS First Boston, London, February 19).

IBCA, 1996, *The Rating Impact of EMU* (November 28).

International Law Association, 1996, Report by the Committee on International Monetary Law, presented at a meeting of the International Law Association, Helsinki, May 31.

Islam, Ifty, Edward Eyerman, and Joseph Taylor, 1996, "The Outlook for Intra-European Spreads after EMU: Assessing Sovereign Credit Risk Within a Monetary Union," *Global Fixed Income Research*, Merrill Lynch (November 1).

Jeanneau, Serge, 1996, "The Market for International Asset-Backed Securities," *International Banking and Financial Market Developments*, BIS (November), pp. 36–46.

Johnson, Christopher, 1996, *In with the Euro, Out with the Pound: The Single Currency for Britain* (London: Penguin).

Kapstein, Ethan B., 1994, *Governing the Global Economy: International Finance and the State* (Cambridge: Harvard University Press).

Karsenti, René, 1996, "EMU: Impact on Financial Markets and Practical Implications for a Large Issuer," paper presented at a *Euromoney* seminar on Implications of EMU for the International Debt Markets, London, October 17–18.

Keating, Giles, 1996, "The Politics of Sovereign Default: An Essay on Credit Spreads after EMU," *Economics Research—Europe*, CS First Boston (October 30).

Krämer, Werner, 1996, "Impact of the Euro for European Bond Markets," Paper presented at the IBC UK conference on Evaluating the Impact of the Euro on the European Securities Market, London, November 5–6.

Levitt, Malcolm, 1995, "Economic and Monetary Union Stage III: The Issues for Banks" (London: Centre for the Study of Financial Innovation).

LIFFE, 1996, "EMU: LIFFE's Response," *LIFFE Market Monitor*, No. 7 (April 3).

Lipsky, John, and others, 1996, "Managing Convergence: Market Implications for 1997 and Beyond," *Economic & Market Analysis*, Salomon Brothers (December).

Livingston, Dorothy, and Bill Hutchings, 1997, "Legal Issues Arising from the Introduction of the Euro," *Journal of International Banking Law*, Vol. 12 (February), pp. 63–6.

MATIF Working Committee on the Changeover to the Euro, 1996, *Report* (December).

Mayer, Thomas, 1996, "Volatility, Liquidity, and Demand: Preparing for the Euro-Market," paper presented at a *Euromoney* seminar on Implications of EMU for the International Debt Markets, London, October 17–18.

Mazzucchelli, Marco G., Ian Clarke, and Clive Parry, 1996, "European Government Bond Markets After EMU," Morgan Stanley presentation to the European Commission Consultative Group, Brussels, October 25.

McCauley, Robert N., 1997, "The Euro and the Dollar," BIS Working Paper (Basle: Bank for International Settlements, forthcoming).

———, 1996, "Prospects for an Integrated European Government Bond Market," *International Banking and Financial Market Developments*, BIS (August), pp. 28–31.

———, 1984, "Maturity Matching in the Euromarkets," *Quarterly Review*, Federal Reserve Bank of New York, Vol. 9 (Spring), pp. 32–33.

———, and Rama Seth, 1992, "Foreign Bank Credit to US Corporations: The Implications of Offshore Loans," *Quarterly Review*, Federal Reserve Bank of New York, Vol. 17 (Spring), pp. 52–65.

Moody's Investors Service, 1997, "Credit Risk Implications of EMU for European Sovereign Credits" (February).

Organization for Economic Cooperation and Development, 1996a, "Institutional Investors and Financial Markets in OECD Countries," DAFFE/CMF(96)18/ANN1 (Paris: OECD).

———, 1996b, "Public Policy and Financial Market Access in the Global Economy," DAFFE/CMF(96)19/REV1 (Paris: OECD).

Reuss, Konrad, 1996, "Standard & Poor's Presentation," paper presented at a *Euromoney* seminar on Implications of EMU for the International Debt Markets, London, October 17–18.

Ruocco, John J., Maureen LeBlanc, and Patrick Dignan, 1991, "Competitiveness in Government Bond Markets," in *International Competitiveness of U.S. Financial Firms: Products, Markets, and Conventional Performance Measures*, Staff Study by the Federal Reserve Bank of New York (New York: Federal Reserve Bank of New York, May), pp. 130–155.

Salomon Brothers, 1996, "What EMU Might Mean for European Banks," *European Equity Research* (October 29).

SBC Warburg, 1996, *EMU: Opportunity or Threat?* (London: SBC Warburg, December).

Schoenmaker, Dirk, 1995, "Banking Supervision in Stage Three of EMU," LSE Financial Markets Group Special Paper No. 72 (London: London School of Economics, June).

Scobie, Hannah M., 1997, *The Cost and Timescale for the Switchover to the European Single Currency for the International Securities Market* (Zurich: European Economics and Financial Centre for the International Securities Market Association).

Serfaty, Bruno, 1996, "Risks and Opportunities Created by EMU in a Bond Environment," paper presented at a *Euromoney* seminar on Implications of EMU for the International Debt Markets, London, October 17–18.

White, William R., 1994, "The Implications of the FTA and NAFTA for Canada and Mexico," Bank of Canada Technical Report No. 70 (Ottawa: Bank of Canada, August).

Zimmer, Steven A., and Robert N. McCauley, 1991, "Bank Cost of Capital and International Competition," *Quarterly Review*, Federal Reserve Bank of New York, Vol. 15 (Winter), pp. 33–59.

Comments on McCauley and White

Age Bakker

It is a great pleasure to commend Bob McCauley and Bill White on a fine and excellently written paper. It is comprehensive and thought-provoking in its coverage of the possible changes for financial markets emanating from the arrival of EMU. I agree with the main line of thought that the switchover to the euro will not drastically change the financial landscape overnight, but rather will reinforce already existing tendencies in financial markets of concentration, disintermediation, and the like. Because many currencies of the future euro area, by stabilizing their bilateral exchange rates, have formed an informal currency union vis-à-vis the U.S. dollar for a decade, EMU provides for a financial quality jump rather than for a structural break.

The paper adds valuable theoretical insights that, I believe, correctly challenge conventional wisdom on EMU and provide a significant contribution to the literature. In this regard, it is rightly argued that a deeper and broader capital market holds benefits not only for investors, but also for debtors. Thus the often heard assumption, forwarded again yesterday by Fred Bergsten, that a stronger euro will emerge due to international portfolio reallocations, may be incorrect. Companies and governments outside the euro area can be expected to find the euro bond market a more attractive market in which to issue. Thus, as the paper states, the value of the euro, or interest rates for that matter, will not necessarily benefit from net portfolio shifts. And if the markets would want to shift their portfolios, they do not have to wait until January 1, 1999, as Mr. Kawai yesterday rightly explained.

The paper also clearly sets out the relative importance of issuer-related factors affecting competition in the bond market, and those factors related to currency segmentation. One thus obtains a better idea of the relative weight to be attributed to the arrival of EMU in the different segments of the financial markets. As a discussant, I would like to provide you with some reflections on what a central banker could or even should infer from all this.

Specifically, I would like to ponder on two issues in the paper that I believe may be of central importance to the development of the bond market and the banking industry. First, as a central banker of one of the countries that will participate in EMU from the outset, I will argue that perhaps the most important determinant of the international attractiveness of euro financial markets will be the internal stability of the currency itself. As a second issue I would like to consider for a moment the implicit assumption in the paper that an international role for the euro is a good thing in itself.

To start with internal stability, it struck me that the authors only deal with a single aspect of this matter. The paper raises the possibility that monetary policy under EMU might be restricted by differential transmission mechanisms and resulting concerns about financial fragility in particular countries. Earlier studies, for example those conducted by the EMI, have acknowledged that differences in monetary transmission processes across EU member states may complicate the conduct of the single monetary policy in EMU. Cross-country differences are and will be mainly notable with respect to the degree of financial intermediation and the relative importance of short-term and variable lending. However, while it is relatively easy to detect differences in structure at the microeconomic level, it is much less straightforward to assess the extent to which these differences have a significant impact on the overall macroeconomic transmission process. Empirical models thus far have suggested that the pass-through of changes in official interest rates to nominal GDP is indeed faster and stronger in the United Kingdom, but sufficiently similar in Continental Europe. Moreover, the financial structures of participating member states will in all likelihood converge over time. All in all, I do not believe that differences in transmission mechanisms will stand in the way of the effective conduct of monetary policy.

This brings me to stability in a broader sense. If anything, the deliberations about monetary transmission underscore once more the necessity of durable convergence within the Union. Monetary unification of an area of low inflation will provide additional impetus to the development of stable financial markets. In this respect, the convergence criteria as laid down in the Maastricht Treaty are among the solid pillars that will have to safeguard monetary and financial stability within EMU. Together with the stability and growth pact, the monetary framework as laid out in the recent EMI report, and the independent status of the ECB, this will have to bring about a euro that will be as strong as the deutsche mark or the French franc. After all, in the longer run the internal stability of the euro itself will turn out to be the most important determinant of its potential role on financial markets. This makes me quite reluctant to take Paul Masson's suggestion on board to focus monetary policy, at least in the early stages, on the behavior of the exchange rate of the euro vis-à-vis third currencies. Of course, if he implied that the exchange rate should be one among many variables to be taken into account, I would have no objection. But the exchange rate cannot be a substitute for internal monetary policy targets.

As the authors note, the euro's importance in the international financial system will gradually increase, and the euro will become an important international reserve currency alongside the dollar. Some of the advantages of a reserve status for financial markets, such as competition, securitization, and deeper markets, are somewhat implicitly covered in the paper. Another argument that has been advanced by some is that the euro would retain some of the seigniorage advantages that are normally associated with a reserve currency role. Those who have advocated this in the past frequently at the same time have been concerned about the relative strength of the European currencies vis-à-vis the U.S. dollar and have wished to preserve the competitive position of Europe. However, one cannot have the two at the same time: a reserve currency must be a hard currency.

What are we to think of the evolution of the euro into a key currency, both from a monetary and an exchange rate viewpoint? One potential drawback is that it may diminish the scope for controlling money supply domestically. The U.S. experience, where traditional relationships between money, economic activity, and prices broke down, presumably partly on account of the development of eurodollar markets, has led some analysts to conclude that it is not possible to conduct a monetary policy focused on monetary aggregates while at the same time fulfilling the role of international reserve currency. In a similar vein, the experiences of Japan and Germany come to mind, where, throughout the 1970s and early 1980s, the monetary authorities imposed controls on capital flows, to prevent their currency from becoming an international currency, in order to increase their influence over the money supply.

However, this problem may not be as great as it would seem at first sight. As regards the U.S. experience, with the benefit of hindsight other factors may have been much more important than instability arising from the international role of the dollar. In particular, a combination of "interest rate deregulation" and technological developments made the predictability of money demand much more difficult. As far as Germany is concerned, capital movements have been liberalized in the course of the 1980s, with negligible effect on the long-run stability of German money demand, a major factor being that the Bundesbank has continued to focus on domestic monetary targets. The ECB, which by virtue of its statutes has to gear its policies to internal price stability, will be able to reap the benefits from this experience. From a monetary standpoint, the euro's position as an international reserve currency should be manageable.

As far as exchange rate implications are concerned, the switching in and out of a key currency may have potentially destabilizing effects. However, in the longer run the fundamentals determine the exchange rate. Here I am quite confident because of the policy consensus that has grown over the past years among the main advanced economies. Inflation rates have converged in Europe and the United States, albeit that inflation tolerance seems to be slightly higher in the United States. Fiscal policies both in the United States and in Europe, in the framework of the Stability and Growth Pact, aim at a balanced budget. This in principle augurs well for relatively stable relationships among the U.S. dollar and the euro as alignment of the fundamentals is a necessary albeit not sufficient condition for international exchange rate stability.

Discussion

Mr. Folkerts-Landau of the IMF noted that in the U.S. money and capital markets there was a full array of instruments and institutions, including repos, derivatives, commercial paper, broker dealers, investment houses, and inter-dealer brokers. Those markets were highly liquid and were supported by a wholesale payment system that imparted liquidity through intra-day credit. In that system, the New York Federal Reserve managed liquidity on a day-to-day basis, intervening fairly regularly. The market was aware of this intervention, which was undertaken partly for the refinancing referred to by Mr. Hogeweg but also to smooth out disturbances to the monetary base coming from a variety of sources.

If he understood Mr. Hogeweg correctly, Mr. Folkerts-Landau continued, within the European system of central banks the emphasis would be on a weekly tender operations supported by fairly minor fine-tuning operations, if necessary. If the New York Federal Reserve were to go to a system whereby it intervened only once every week for refinancing purposes only, on a pre-announced basis, he asked what such a move would do to the array of institutional factors in the U.S. markets, to the markets themselves and to the volatility of overnight rates.

Mr. Truman, in response to Mr. Folkerts-Landau's question, said that the answer one would probably get from U.S. analysts and economists would be that if the Federal Reserve Bank of New York intervened in the market once a week, given the existing structure, the result would be more short-term/overnight interest rate volatility. It was unclear whether that would transmit itself to longer-term interest rate volatility. On the other hand, he certainly agreed that the potential of the central bank being in the market providing liquidity every day, on the margin, increased the liquidity of the market every day. The European view that one was teaching the market to be self-reliant was a nice theory, much along the lines that if one gave children their allowance once a month rather than once a week that would teach them how to budget: it sounded like a good idea, but it was not clear that it would maintain an even flow of the cash to the candy market.

He suspected the reason for the European approach was, first, that it was the way Germany was currently doing it, and second, if one was going to decentralize a system, it was very difficult to run it on a day-to-day basis.

* * *

Mr. Giavazzi noted that both the paper by Prati and Schinasi and that by McCauley and White made the important point that EMU would transform the European banking industry and possibly bring an end to the European universal bank model. He agreed with that, but observed that both papers only mentioned in passing one issue that could cause much of what the authors described unlikely to happen, namely the corporate governance structure of much of the banking system throughout Europe.

Two-thirds of banks in Spain and Italy, accounting for 60 percent of the deposits, were owned either directly by the government or by foundations whose boards were handpicked by political bodies or self-appointed, Mr. Giavazzi said. The entire German savings bank system worked under similar rules and relied on guarantees from local municipalities. Unlike telecommunications or even electricity, banking was a sector in which privatization was happening very slowly. Instead, what was observed were government bailouts of failing banks widening the scope of the state. Unless the issue of privatization of the banking system was addressed, much of what the two papers described on the future of European banks was unlikely to happen.

Mr. Truman said that, in his view, both the paper as well as the discussants stopped short of answering the question that both Garry Schinasi and Bob McCauley put forward: What is the outlook for near-term financial stability in Europe and what are the mechanisms within the new Europe to deal with financial stability? Those were legitimate questions given the current condition of financial systems—and the banking systems in particular—in Europe. If one believed that financial stability was the other side of the coin from macroeconomic stability, then it seemed the lesson of monetary history of the last 10 years was that there would be more problems down the road than some people were willing to admit.

Session V
The External Dimension of the European Policy Mix

13

How Will the Euro Behave?

Daniel Cohen

There is little doubt that the making of monetary integration in Europe will have major effects on the exchange markets. Quoting one European currency rather than six or twelve should matter. But how? In which direction should we expect the euro to go? The conventional wisdom is that the euro will be a "strong currency." For one thing, it should mimic the deutsche mark, typically a strong currency in its own right; second, it should attract new portfolio investors, bidding up its demand and raising its price; and third, it might have to go through a period during which the new monetary authorities will have to demonstrate their willingness to be "tough," hence appreciating the currency at least for a while.

All these points are well known, and fairly extensively discussed in daily appraisals of the euro. The feature that I want to stress here is of a different nature: I want to emphasize the effect of the new conduct of monetary and fiscal policy upon the euro. Not only will monetary policy behave differently, by definition, but fiscal policy itself will change its course, and the new design of economic policy will have major influences on the value of the euro.

Building upon previous work with Charles Wyplosz (Cohen and Wyplosz, 1995), I will attempt to understand the likely implications of these policy regime shifts upon the value of the euro. As I will show, there are few reasons to believe that the euro will be less volatile than European currencies today. This will first be demonstrated theoretically. The core of the argument is as follows: since Europe as a whole is less open than the representative European country, monetary policy will be less constrained than it is now by trade disequilibria. This will make it less accommodative, hence making the euro potentially more volatile. The argument is sometimes known as the effect of a new "benign neglect" of Europe toward the euro, as it will become a "closer" economy (see Bergsten's paper in this volume). The paper will qualify this view. First, openness needs to be defined by the degree of substitutability of

The author thanks Hélène Poirson and Delfim Neto for their brilliant research assistance.

European goods with the "rest of the world" products rather than through the mere average of imports or exports to GDP. Second, I will also show that being less open will imply a more volatile exchange rate in response to one kind of shock—those regarding price determinations (Phillips curve shocks), rather than those affecting aggregate demand. In the last part of the paper I will offer some empirical simulations regarding the value of the euro. I will first demonstrate that its current value is fairly well explained by the macroeconomic "fundamentals" of Europe, and I will then move to simulate the effects of a less accommodative monetary policy toward these shocks. Although these simulations are simply illustrative, they are suggestive of the fact that the euro might become more volatile than are European currencies today.

Theoretical Framework

I elaborate here upon a model of exchange rate behavior and policy design that is developed in Cohen and Wyplosz (1995).

Assume that the world is composed of three countries: Germany and France, which are assumed to be two identical countries, and the rest of the world (ROW), whose currency is called the "dollar." Let e be the (log) of the nominal exchange rate of the franc with respect to the deutsche mark, and let e_1 (e_2) be the (log) of the nominal exchange rate of the franc (deutsche mark) with the dollar. We then have

$$e = e_1 - e_2.$$

We assume that each country produces a representative product whose price is p_1 in France, p_2 in Germany, and p_0 in the ROW. Competitiveness is defined as

$$z(t) = p_2(t) + e(t) - p_1(t)$$
$$z_1(t) = p_0(t) + e_1(t) - p_1(t)$$
$$z_2(t) = p_0(t) + e_2(t) - p_2(t).$$

$z(t)$ is the competitiveness of France with respect to Germany, $z_1(t)$ is that of France with respect to the ROW, and $z_2(t)$ is that of Germany with respect to the ROW. We clearly have

$$z(t) = z_1(t) - z_2(t).$$

I shall describe the economy through two equations, which I will refer to as a price and a demand curve. The price curve is a Phillips curve that is written in each of the two countries as

$$\pi_1(t) = \pi_1^e + a_1 z_1 + az + bQ_1(t) + \varepsilon_1(t)$$
$$\pi_2(t) = \pi_2^e + a_1 z_2 - az + bQ_2(t) + \varepsilon_2(t),$$

in which π_i is inflation in country i and Q_i is the log of the level of output in that country. $\varepsilon_i(t)(i = 1, 2)$ are two white noise disturbances.

As a simple way to understand this equation, assume that output is produced by mixing foreign and domestic (intermediate) goods. Call x_1 the (log of the) nominal price of the intermediate good in France and $e_1 + p_0$ and $e + p_2$ the (log of the) price of the two imported goods. If domestic prices are written as a flexible markup above cost and a random disturbance, one can then write

$$p_1 = \alpha x_1 + \beta(e_1 + p_0) + \gamma(e + p_2) + \delta Q_1 + \nu,$$

in which $\alpha + \beta + \gamma = 1$. One can then write

$$(1 - \beta - \gamma)p_1 = \alpha x_1 + \beta(e_1 + p_0 - p_1) + \gamma(e + p_2 - p_1) + \delta Q_1 + \nu,$$

that is,

$$p_1 = x_1 + \frac{\beta}{\alpha} z_1 + \frac{\gamma}{\alpha} z + \frac{\delta}{\alpha} Q + \frac{1}{\alpha} \nu.$$

Now assume that the price of the intermediate good is contracted at the beginning of the period and set by producers so as to guess the coming period's price. One can then write

$$x_1(t) = p_1(t - 1) + \pi_1^e(t).$$

One then obtains, with obvious changes of notations, the Phillips curve equation that we postulated above.

In the sequel, we shall make the assumption that $\pi^e = 0$. We shall justify this assumption in the next section. Otherwise the model can be taken as a model in which inflation is simply "surprise" inflation.

The second equation that we are dealing with is a demand curve that writes output as a function of competitiveness and fiscal stimuli:

$$Q_1(t) = h_1 z_1(t) + hz(t) + gA_1(t) + \eta_1(t)$$
$$Q_2(t) = h_1 z_2(t) - hz(t) + gA_2(t) + \eta_2(t),$$

in which $A_i(t)$ measures the fiscal stimulus that country i implements.

I will stick here to a static version of the model, and all disturbances are assumed to be white noise disturbances. The full-fledged dynamic model presented in Cohen and Wyplosz (1995) would have the same implications. For simplicity, I will assume that the authorities can act directly upon two instruments: inflation (π) and fiscal stimulus (A).

As a simple way to see how the model is solved, let us take for the time being the case of Europe as a whole, in those circumstances where the economies are perfectly symmetric, leading to an equilibrium value $z = 0$. With zero expected inflation, the European economy boils down to

$$\pi_1 = a_1 z_1 + bQ_1 + \varepsilon_1$$
$$Q_1 = h_1 z_1 + gA_1 + \eta_1.$$

For a given value of π and A, output and competitiveness are determined simultaneously. Diagrammatically this can be solved as shown in Figure 1.

Any positive price shock $\varepsilon > 0$, if unaccommodated, brings the economy from a point A to a point B: output shrinks and competitiveness is reduced. Any negative demand shock $\eta < 0$, instead, if unaccommodated, brings the economy from a point A to a point C: output shrinks, but competitiveness rises. The economics of these shifts are fairly straightforward. A negative domestic demand shock is partially accommodated by a reallocation of domestic output

Figure 1. Output and Competitiveness

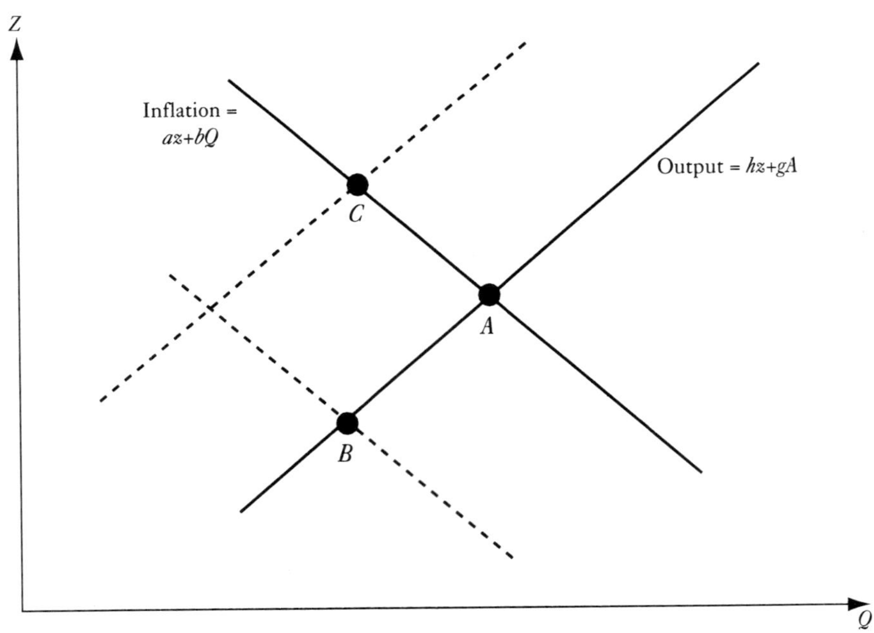

toward foreign markets, and hence by increased competitiveness. By contrast, a negative price shock brings in foreign products and hence tends to lower competitiveness.

One can immediately see the impact of accommodating the shocks through monetary and fiscal policy. First, consider a price shock $\varepsilon > 0$. If it is accommodated by monetary policy, the economy might be brought back to its initial level. So, in response to a price shock, an accommodating monetary policy reduces the volatility of the exchange rate and of output. If instead the price shock is accommodated by fiscal policy (in order to limit the output decline), then clearly this will *raise* the volatility of the exchange rate: the initial decline in competitiveness brought about by the price shock will be exacerbated by an expansionary fiscal policy. Clearly, the opposite will happen when dealing with a demand shock: if accommodated by fiscal policy, one will reduce the volatility of the economy (output and exchange rate), while the volatility of the exchange rate will be raised if the demand shock is accommodated by monetary policy.

Let us now analyze in detail what are the optimal responses of monetary and fiscal policies to these shocks, and how monetary integration will change them.

Exchange Rate Volatility and Design of Economic Policy

Let us focus for the time being on the response of French and German policies to a symmetric shock: $\varepsilon_1 = \varepsilon_2 = \varepsilon$; $\eta_1 = \eta_2 = \eta$. I assume that the ROW is purely passive.

Let us assume that monetary and fiscal policies are designed in such a way as to

$$\text{minimize}\ \frac{1}{2}\left(Q^2 + \phi_0 A^2 + \phi_1 \pi^2\right),$$

subject to the price and demand equations.

Let us briefly explain such an optimization problem. In the standard monetary policy game, such as developed in Barro and Gordon (1983), the monetary authorities would typically solve

$$\text{minimize}\ \frac{1}{2}\left[(Q - Q^*)^2 + \phi_1 \pi^2\right],$$

in which Q^* is (the log of) a full-employment (full-capacity) target level of output. Such objective would typically imply a systematic inflation bias that is expected by the private agents and has no effect on the equilibrium level of output. From an ex ante point of view, the optimum way to achieve the objective that is stated above is to scale down the target level Q^* to a lower level Q_0 that is consistent ex ante with zero inflation. The value Q_0 is simply the output equivalent of the "natural rate of unemployment." From the policymaker perspective, this implies an *expansionary* policy when output is below Q_0 and a *restrictive* policy when output is above Q_0. Such will then be our hypothesis: that policymakers are committed to implement their ex ante best policy response to unexpected shocks. We shall then simply normalize Q_0 to be zero (all values are in logarithm) and therefore interpret Q as the deviation (in log terms) from the "natural rate of output." Correspondingly, we assume that the Phillips curve that we deal with is associated with zero expected inflation. Our analysis consequently does not tackle the role of "credibility" that the implementation of the new ECB would have to tackle. Clearly, within our formulation, such an issue would involve analyzing the credibility issue through the additive term encompassed in the *expected* rate of inflation, but would not change the implication that we are dealing with so far as the response to *unexpected* shocks is concerned.

Another difference between the standard Barro-Gordon model and our analysis involves the role of the fiscal stimulus A. The weight ϕ_0 that is attached to its implementation may be interpreted as the effect of distortionary taxation on the welfare of the economy. In the full-fledged dynamic model analyzed in Cohen and Wyplosz (1995), it also embodies the weight of the intertemporal budget constraint.

As a start to the analysis, let us first compute the outcome of fully cooperative policymaking. Recognizing their symmetry, French and German policymakers adopt the same decisions $\pi_1 = \pi_2 = \pi$ and $A_1 = A_2 = A$ and internalize the fact that their equilibrium real exchange rate will not vary, that is, they design their policy under the assumption that $z = 0$.

The problem can then be written as[1]

$$\text{minimize}\ \frac{1}{2}\left(Q_1^2 + \phi_0 A_1^2 + \phi_1 \pi_1^2\right) + \lambda(-\pi_1 + a_1 z_1 + bQ_1 + \varepsilon_1)$$
$$-\mu(-Q_1 + h_1 z_1 + gA_1 + \eta_1).$$

[1]Here, the first-order optimality condition is set simultaneously by "the" policymaker. But it would not change the analysis to assume that each instrument is determined by two independent branches of the government, provided that each of these branches (determining respectively monetary and fiscal policy) has full information on the other one's decision.

The first-order conditions are then written:

$$\begin{aligned} \phi_0 A &= g\mu \\ \phi_1 \pi &= \lambda \\ Q + \lambda b + \mu &= 0 \\ \lambda a_1 - \mu h_1 &= 0. \end{aligned} \tag{1}$$

For convenience, we drop the country-identifying subscripts on Q and A. Eliminating λ and μ, thus yields two equations:

$$\begin{aligned} & Q + b\phi_1 \pi + \frac{1}{g}\phi_0 A = 0 \\ & A = \frac{a_1}{h_1} \cdot \frac{\phi_1}{\phi_0} g \cdot \pi. \end{aligned} \tag{2}$$

Equation (1) simply reflects the set of preferences of the policymakers. In response to any shock (ε, η), monetary and fiscal policy will partially absorb the shock to the best of their willingness to do so, which is measured by (ϕ_1, ϕ_0), and to the best of the efficiency of their instrument, measured by (b, g).

Equation (2) specifies how monetary and fiscal policy share the burden of the adjustment. Putting these two equations together, we can simply write:

$$\begin{aligned} \pi &= -\frac{1}{\phi_1} \frac{1}{b + a_1/h_1} Q \\ A &= -\frac{1}{\phi_0} g \frac{a_1/h_1}{b + a_1/h_1} Q. \end{aligned} \tag{3}$$

Clearly, when either $1/\phi_1$ or $1/\phi_0$ is zero, the policymaker will not respond through the corresponding instrument: it is simply too costly in terms of welfare. Similarly, the bigger g is, the more efficient is fiscal policy and the larger will be the fiscal policy response.

The interesting parameter that will be key to the forthcoming analysis is the ratio a_1/h_1. When a_1/h_1 is big, fiscal policy will be highly responsive and monetary policy will be kept low. The intuition behind this result can be traced back to the first-order conditions derived from the optimal exchange rate response to a shock. Ceteris paribus, accommodating a shock through monetary policy will involve a depreciation of the currency that will have spillover effects on demand. Raising inflation by 1 percentage point will depreciate the currency by $1/a$ and raise demand by h/a. If h/a is high, or $1/a$ low, monetary policy can achieve two goals at the same time: stabilizing the Phillips curve and accommodating demand. It will be a perfect instrument that dominates fiscal policy.

The other (symmetrical) way of looking at the question is to analyze the consequences of raising the fiscal stimulus: it appreciates the currency by $1/h$ and offsets inflation by a/h. If the number is high, then fiscal expansion achieves two goals—stabilizing supply and demand—and it will be the perfect instrument to stabilize output.

Solving the model altogether, one can then substitute π and A for their equilibrium value and solve the two-equation system.

If we call

$$\Delta = \frac{a_1}{h_1}\left(1 + \frac{1}{\phi_0} g^2 \frac{a_1/h_1}{b + a_1/h_1}\right) + \left(b + \frac{1}{\phi_1}\frac{1}{b + a_1/h_1}\right), \tag{4}$$

we obtain the following equilibrium:

$$\begin{aligned} Q &= \frac{1}{\Delta}\left(-\varepsilon + \frac{a_1}{h_1}\eta\right) \\ z_1 &= -\frac{1}{h_1\Delta}\left[\left(1 + \frac{1}{\phi_0} g^2 \frac{a_1/h_1}{b + a_1/h_1}\right)\varepsilon + \left(b + \frac{1}{\phi_1}\frac{1}{b + a_1/h_1}\right)\eta\right]. \end{aligned} \tag{5}$$

The solution fits the intuition that we obtained from Figure 1. In response to a positive price shock (i.e., one that reduces output, $\varepsilon > 0$), output contracts and the real exchange rate appreciates (competitiveness is reduced). In response to a negative demand shock ($\eta < 0$), output shrinks but the exchange rate is depreciated. The more responsive monetary and fiscal policy are (low ϕ_0 and ϕ_1), the more output will be stabilized. Let us see the implications for exchange rate volatility.

First, consider a price shock ($\varepsilon > 0$). Tough fiscal policy ($1/\phi_0$ is low) *lowers* the volatility of exchange rate, while tough monetary policy ($1/\phi_1$ is low) raises the volatility of the exchange rate. The intuition follows from what was said. By accommodating a price shock through monetary policy, a central bank would dampen the effect of the shock on the exchange rate. This fits the conventional wisdom (à la Volcker or Tietmeyer): tough central banks increase exchange rate fluctuations.

Instead, tough fiscal policies would *lower* the volatility of exchange rates originating from price shocks: if they were to intervene, they would add, as we have seen, another wave of disturbances to the original one. This was the Reagan approach that accompanied the Volcker shock: loose fiscal policy boosted output but increased the volatility of the exchange rate.

Exchange Rate Volatility and (Lack of) Coordination

Let us now investigate in detail how EMU will affect the strategic interactions between European policymakers. In this section we shall deal with a symmetric shock ($\varepsilon = \varepsilon_1 = \varepsilon_2$; $\eta = \eta_1 = \eta_2$) affecting Europe. We deal with asymmetric shocks in the Appendix.

Let us first analyze the noncooperative outcome of a game in which each country picks a strategy π_i^*, A_i^* that is the best response to the other country's choice.

When determining its own choice, a country, say country 1, is subject to the following model originating from country 2:

$$\pi_2^*(\varepsilon,\eta) = a_1 z_2 - az + bQ_2 + \varepsilon$$
$$Q_2^*(\varepsilon,\eta) = h_1 z_2 - hz + gA_2(\varepsilon,\eta) + \eta.$$

When account is taken of the identity $z_2 = z_1 - z$, country 1 calculates the intra-European exchange rate as:

$$z(t) = \theta z_1(t) + f(\varepsilon,\eta),$$

in which $f(\varepsilon,\eta)$ depends upon the response given by country 2 to the shocks (ε,η) while θ is a constant:

$$\theta = \frac{a_1 + bh_1}{a + a_1 + b(h + h_1)}.$$

This implies that the model under which country 1 operates is written:

$$\pi_1 = (a_1 + \theta a)z_1 + bQ_1 + \varepsilon + af(\varepsilon,\eta)$$
$$Q_1 = (h_1 + \theta h)z_1 + gA_1 + \eta + hf(\varepsilon,\eta).$$

Clearly, under this model, the same first-order conditions will apply as those we obtained in the one-country framework set up in the previous section.

Call

$$\hat{a} = a_1 + \theta a$$
$$\hat{h} = h_1 + \theta h.$$

One obtains the following monetary and fiscal policy response:

$$\pi_1 = -\frac{1}{\phi_1}\frac{1}{b + (\hat{a}/\hat{h})}Q_1 \qquad (6a)$$

$$A_1 = -\frac{1}{\phi_0} g \frac{(\hat{a}/\hat{h})}{b + (\hat{a}/\hat{h})} Q_1. \tag{6b}$$

In order to obtain the equilibrium itself, one will recognize that the equilibrium value of intra-European competitiveness, z, is nil by symmetry of the responses.

Call

$$\tilde{\Delta} = \frac{a_1}{h_1}\left[1 + \frac{1}{\phi_0} g^2 \frac{\hat{a}/\hat{h}}{b + \hat{a}/\hat{h}}\right] + \left[b + \frac{1}{\phi_1} \frac{1}{b + \hat{a}/\hat{h}}\right].$$

One can then write the outcome of the Nash game among European policymakers as

$$Q_1^* = \frac{1}{\hat{\Delta}}[-\varepsilon + a_1/h_1\eta] \tag{7a}$$

$$z_1^* = \frac{1}{h_1\hat{\Delta}}\left[\left(1 + \frac{1}{\phi_0} g^2 \frac{\hat{a}/\hat{h}}{b + \hat{a}/\hat{h}}\right)\varepsilon + \left(b + \frac{1}{\phi_1} \frac{1}{b + \hat{a}/\hat{h}}\right)\eta\right]. \tag{7b}$$

The comparison of this equilibrium to the one-country model set up above will then simply depend upon the comparison between a_1/h_1 and $a_1 + \theta a/h_1 + \theta h$, which itself will simply depend upon the comparison between a_1/h_1 and a/h. We then have two cases.

1. $a_1/h_1 < a/h$ is a case in which the goods purchased abroad are relatively more substitutable to the domestic goods than the goods purchased in Europe.
2. $a_1/h_1 > a/h$ is the opposite case. It is reasonable to assume that such is indeed the relevant case. Intuitively, Europe is a market in which "trade effects" matter relatively more than "price effects" because the substitutability between European products is higher than that between goods from a particular European country and goods from the rest of the world. This is demonstrated empirically in Cohen and Wyplosz, 1991, and I will return to it in the section on empirical implications. In the sequel we shall then assume that

$$a_1/h_1 > a/h \tag{8}$$

holds.

To see the implications of such an inequality, let us first compare the policy outcome that is reached under the Nash equilibrium to the one-European country model. Inequality (8) implies that $g(\theta) = a_1 + \theta a/h_1 + \theta h$ is a decreasing function of θ. We then have it that

$$\frac{\hat{a}}{\hat{h}} \equiv \frac{a_1 + \theta a}{h_1 + \theta h} < \frac{a_1}{h_1}.$$

$\hat{\Delta}$ is then higher or lower than Δ depending upon the relative weight of $1/\phi_0$ and $1/\phi_1$, and this will be reflected in the volatility of output. When fiscal policy is more active than monetary policy (g^2/ϕ_0 is high), then $\hat{\Delta}$ will be lower than Δ and output will be *more* volatile in a noncoordinated Europe than in a one-government Europe. In order to understand the intuition behind such a result, let us investigate the effects of a lack of coordination upon the exchange rate. The result is nonambiguous: in response to a price shock, the lack of coordination will *lower* the volatility of the exchange rate, while in response to a demand shock, the lack of coordination will *raise* the volatility of the exchange rate.

The intuition behind this result goes to the root of the problem of designing an optimal policy response in Europe. *The lack of policy coordination leads each European policymaker to overstate the trade effects of exchange rate volatility relative to their price effects.*

When acting on their own, European policymakers fear the intra-European trade disequilibria that an independent economic policy could trigger: they fail to acknowledge the fact that a *symmetric* shock makes such fears irrelevant at the aggregate level. As a result, as evident from equations (6), monetary policy will be overly active, while fiscal policy will be underresponsive. This is why, when fiscal policy is the dominant feature of economic stabilization (g^2/ϕ_0 is high), economic stabilization will be reduced and output will be more volatile. More specifically, consider the implications of a positive price shock ($\varepsilon > 0$). Because monetary policy is *too* responsive, the shock will be more dampened than it needs to be. By exaggerating the trade effect, uncoordinated policymakers will fail to appreciate the European currency against the rest of the world.

Consider now the effect of a demand shock. Here the opposite happens. In their attempt to stabilize the shock, each European policymaker fears trade disequilibria and underreacts to the shock, hence underadjusting the exchange rate response.

We can summarize these results as follows. Lack of coordination leads European policymakers to underadjust to demand shocks and to overadjust to price shocks. At the root of this mismanagement stands an overly responsive monetary policy and an unduly inactive fiscal policy. As a result, exchange rate volatility will be too low in response to price shocks and too large in response to a demand shock.

Since we want to focus on the euro question, only symmetric shocks are relevant for our analysis here. Indeed, asymmetric shocks, defined as $\varepsilon_1 = -\varepsilon_2$ and $\eta_1 = -\eta_2$, would cancel out for Europe as a whole so that the net effect of such shocks on the competitiveness of Europe with the rest of the world is necessarily zero. At this stage, however, it might be important to stress that opposite results would apply in the case of asymmetric shocks so far as the response of each instrument is concerned. In such cases (which we analyze in the Appendix), policymakers fail to internalize the fact that their European counterparts move in a direction that is exactly opposite to theirs. In that case, monetary policy is too tight and should be loosened, while fiscal policy needs to be tightened. This might sound like the Stability and Growth Pact, whose validity, it then seems, would only be relevant for the kind of shocks that were experienced in the 1990s.

Implications of Monetary Integration

We are now in a position to understand the effect of monetary integration on the design of economic policy. In our framework, when dealing with symmetric shocks, monetary union is simply interpreted as the design of a joint monetary policy that sets $\pi_1 = \pi_2 = \pi^*$ for the zone as a whole, while we keep fiscal policy uncoordinated.

Building upon the distinction between a_1/h_1 and $\hat{a}/\hat{h}$ that was spelled out earlier, it is straightforward to see that monetary policy will be designed so as to accommodate output shocks along the following lines:

$$\pi = -\frac{1}{\phi_1}\frac{Q}{b + a_1/h_1},$$

while fiscal policymakers, instead, failing to fully internalize the symmetry of the shocks, will design the following response:

$$A = -\frac{1}{\phi_0} g \frac{\hat{a}/\hat{h}}{b + \hat{a}/\hat{h}} \text{Q}.$$

While the fiscal response is therefore unchanged, monetary policy will be less accommodative under a monetary union than it is currently in response to a symmetric shock. This is not the effect of a change in policy preferences. Indeed, in our framework, we assume that policy preferences are unchanged. Rather, it is the outcome of a change in incentives. When policymaking is designed cooperatively, as will automatically be the case so far as monetary policy is concerned, policymakers can internalize the fact that a symmetric shock will have no effect on *intra-European* competitiveness. They are therefore less worried about letting competitiveness fluctuate: this will "only" trigger trade disequilibria with the rest of the world (which is less responsive to shifts in competitiveness).

As a result, one gets an equilibrium that will be intermediate, between the one-European country outcome and the Nash equilibrium across the two countries. If we call

$$\tilde{\Delta} = \frac{a_1}{h_1}\left(1 + \frac{1}{\phi_0} g^2 \frac{\hat{a}/\hat{h}}{b + (\hat{a}/\hat{h})}\right) + \left(b + \frac{1}{\phi_1}\frac{1}{(b + a_1/h_1)}\right),$$

the new equilibrium will be characterized as

$$Q_1^* = \frac{1}{\tilde{\Delta}}\left(-\varepsilon + \frac{a_1}{h_1}\eta\right)$$

$$z_1^* = -\frac{1}{h_1\tilde{\Delta}}\left[\left(1 + \frac{1}{\phi_0}g^2\frac{\hat{a}/\hat{h}}{b + \hat{a}/\hat{h}}\right)\varepsilon + \left(b + \frac{1}{\phi_1}\frac{1}{b + a_1/h_1}\right)\eta\right].$$

The comparison between monetary union and the Nash equilibrium is now unambiguous, both with respect to output and with respect to exchange rates. One can indeed observe, first, that

$$\hat{\Delta} > \tilde{\Delta},$$

so that output is always *more* volatile under a monetary union. The reason is straightforward, and the intuition should be clear by now. Monetary union leaves the fiscal policy response unchanged, while it tightens monetary policy: output will then be more volatile, but this will nevertheless raise the welfare of Europe.

If we turn to exchange rate volatility, the outcome will clearly depend upon the nature of the shock. In response to a price shock, the lack of a strong monetary response will raise exchange rate volatility, while in response to a demand shock, EMU will dampen exchange rate volatility.

There is then no a priori reason to believe that the euro will be a more "stable" currency than its European predecessors. Only if we trust that we are entering into a world where price shocks (such as those encountered in the 1970s) are a thing of the past while key fluctuations would now originate from demand shocks will such expectations materialize.

Empirical Implications

Let us now try to put some empirical flesh upon the previous reasoning. Our goal here is not to give precise results on the likely behavior of the euro, but rather to give some order of magnitude of the effects that we have been discussing. We first tried to get estimates of what we called price and output shocks and measure their influences on exchange rates. Previous estimates of so-called output and demand shocks have already been offered by Bayoumi and Eichengreen (1993). The question of the relationship between exchange rate and macroeconomic imbalances is also addressed in Canzoneri, Vallés, and Viñals (1996). Our strategy here is to try to estimate as closely as possible the model that is represented in the text. As we shall now see, it works fairly well empirically.

Let us first deal with price shocks. Assume that $\pi^e = \rho\pi_{-1} + (1 - \rho)\pi^*$. Our model can then be estimated as

$$\pi_t = \rho\pi_{t-1} + az_t + bQ_t + \textit{Time dummies} + \varepsilon_t, \tag{9}$$

in which z is taken to be the deviation of the current exchange rate with respect to purchasing power parities (Summers-Heston data) and Q_t represents the deviation of output from potential output (such as measured by the OECD).

We then run the following output regression:

$$Q_t = \lambda Q_{t-1} + hz_t + gA_t + \textit{Time dummies} + \eta_t, \tag{10}$$

in which Q_t and z_t are defined as before and A_t is the structural fiscal deficit (such as measured by the OECD).

We use a panel model with fixed effects. All such regressions are obtained through instrumental variables in which the instruments are the lagged values. The sample of countries includes the following European countries: Denmark, Finland, France, Germany, Italy, Portugal, Spain, Sweden, and the United Kingdom. We obtain the following results (with t-statistics in parentheses):

for Equation (9):

$$\rho = 0.264\ (1.6);\ a = 0.147\ (3.4);\ b = 0.356\ (2.70);\ \text{and } R^2 = 0.81,$$

and for Equation (10):

$$\lambda = 0.384\ (3.36);\ h = 3.9\ 10^{-2}\ (1.51);\ g = 0.397\ (2.54);\ \text{and } R^2 = 0.54.$$

Except for h, which is only significant at the 10 percent confidence level, one sees that all coefficients are significant and fit the intuition spelled out in the text.

The regressions were run for European countries only. When we include all OECD countries, the most significant change is in h, which becomes wrongly signed (but is insignificant). We interpret this as a confirmation of the view that European countries are *relatively* more dependent upon trade effects than other countries.

From Equations (9) and (10) we can reconstruct the price and output shocks. If we call T_Π the time dummies of the price equation and T_Q the time dummies of the output equation, the price and output shocks are (for each individual country) $T_\pi + \varepsilon_i(t)$, and $T_Q + \eta_i(t)$, respectively. For Europe as a whole they simply boil down to T_π and T_Q. We represent these in Figures 2 and 3. As we see, and as should be expected, price shocks were more pro-

Figure 2. European Price Shocks

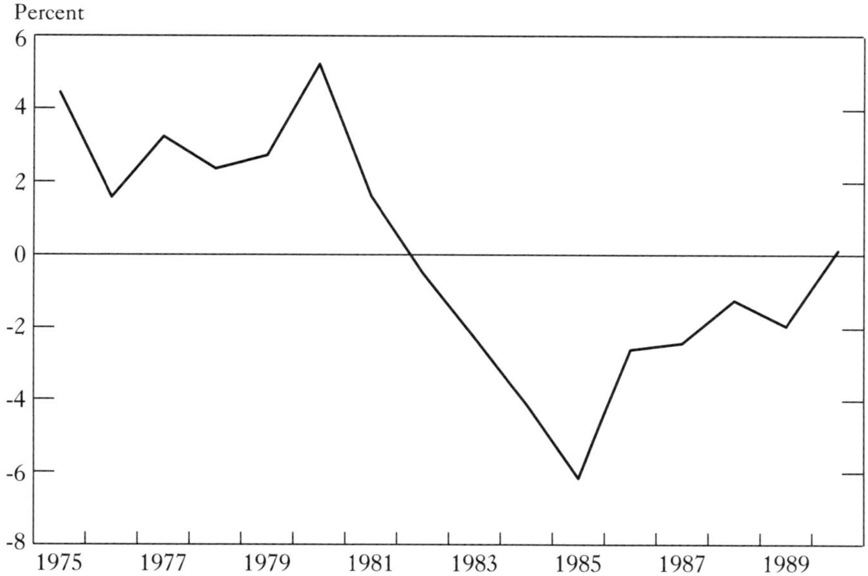

Figure 3. European Demand Shocks

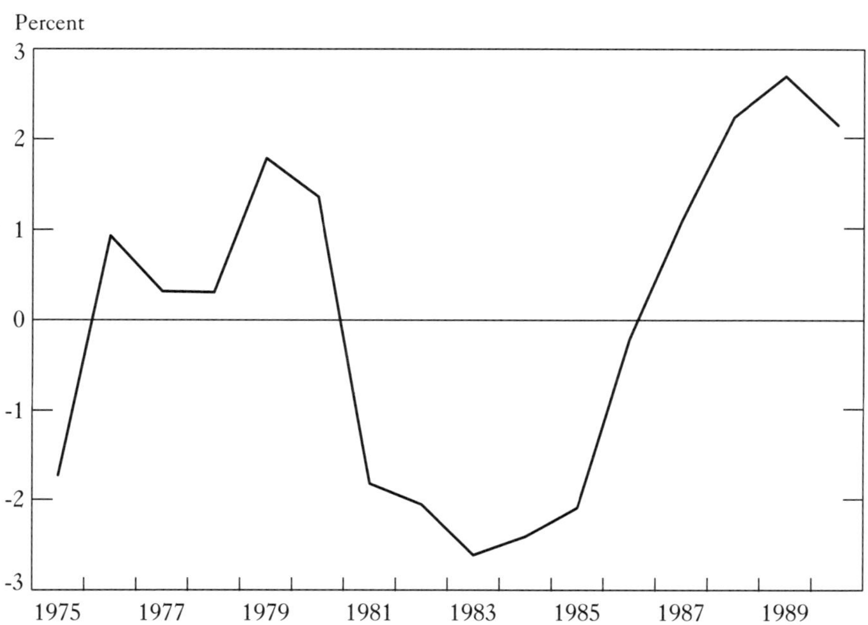

nounced in the 1970s, while output shocks were more pronounced in the 1980s. More specifically, we can decompose the period into three subperiods. During the second half of the 1970s, price and demand shocks were both positive; according to the theory, this leads unambiguously toward a loss of competitiveness and this is indeed what we observe. During the first half of the 1980s, the shocks were both in the opposite direction, leading unambiguously to a rise of competitiveness. This is again what we observe: in the second half of the 1980s, the shocks were in opposite directions: price shocks remained negative, raising competitiveness, while demand shocks were positive, reducing competitiveness. The outcome is theoretically ambiguous, but the observed pattern is in favor of demand shock effects.

To investigate empirically whether exchange rates can be tracked as the outcome of these shocks, we ran a regression in which the average value of European competitiveness is regressed upon the average value of the price and demand shocks: in brief, we simply estimated an equation such as (7b). The result is as follows (with t-statistics in parentheses and N denoting the number of observations):

$$\begin{aligned} z &= 0.11 - \underset{(-5.3)}{1.50\varepsilon} - \underset{(-7.1)}{5.7\eta} \\ R^2 &= 0.87;\ \mathrm{DW} = 1.6;\ N = 16. \end{aligned}$$

As expected, a price shock $\varepsilon > 0$ lowers competitiveness, as does a demand shock where $\eta > 0$. Both coefficients are highly significant and the quality of the fit is excellent (see Figure 4). It is interesting that including a lagged value of competitiveness in the regression (to account for a mean reverting process as in Rogoff, 1996) does not raise the quality of the fit and makes the lagged value of z insignificant. We find these results encouraging: they seem to imply that exchange rates are driven by the macroeconomic fundamentals that our model suggest.

As a simple way to assess the implication of these results for the euro, we have plotted, in Figure 5, the net effects of price and output shocks on the exchange rate such as are captured by the above equation. We see that each shock appears to carry the same weight in the final outcome, and follows the loose characterization that we sketched out above regarding the effects of price and output shocks on exchange rates.

As an illustration of the impact of a "tough" monetary policy, we have simulated the optimal policy response for the case when the preferences of the government are characterized by $1/\phi_1 = 0$. This means that, under our simulation, fiscal stabilization is as important as output stabilization, while monetary policy is assumed to be absolutely passive. Using the value of the parameters a, h, and g that we estimated, we find feedback values of 6.3 and 1.95, for price

Figure 4. Actual and Estimated Values of the Euro

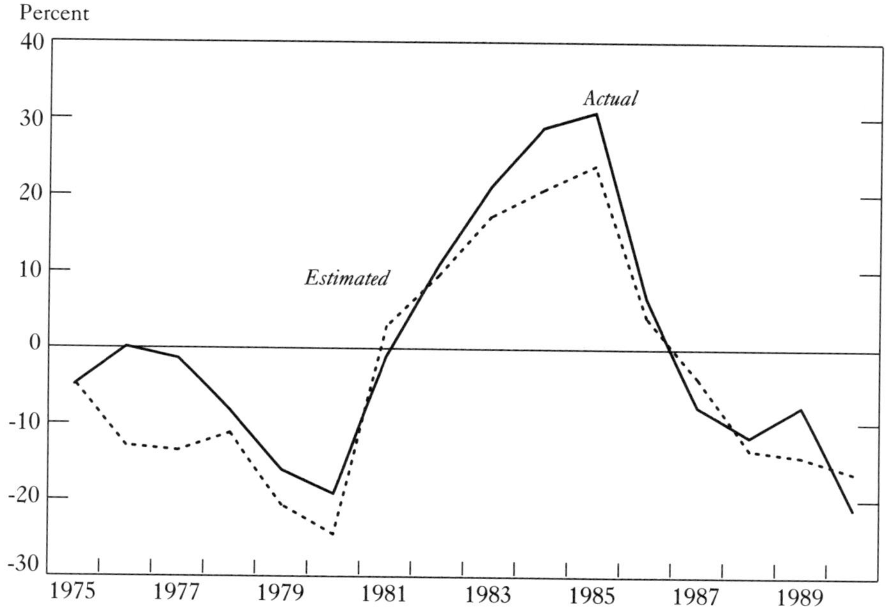

Figure 5. Contribution of Price and Demand Shocks to the Value of the Euro

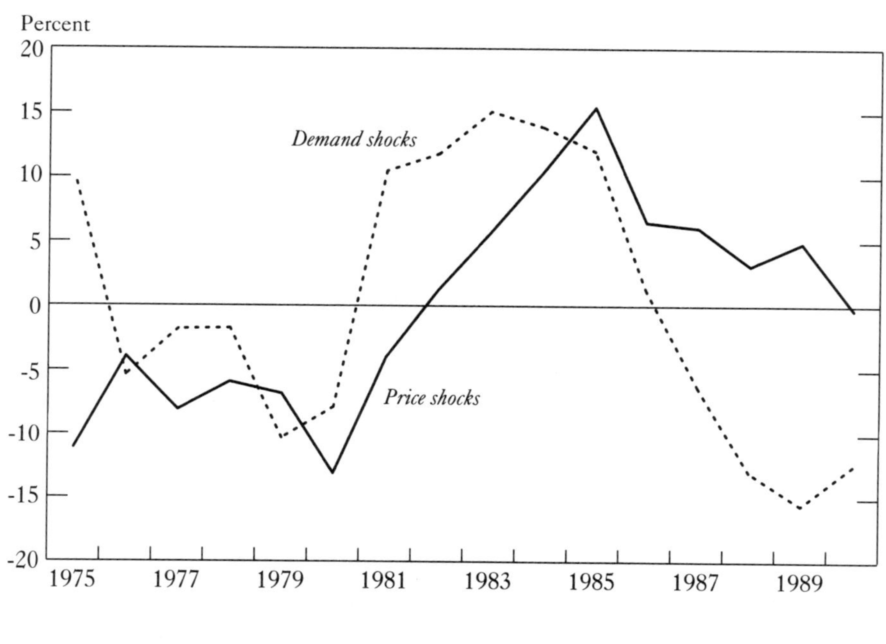

and demand shocks, respectively. The results are shown in Figure 6, in which we also plot the response obtained from our econometric equation. In such a simulation, competitiveness may fluctuate by as much 40 percent instead of the 20–25 percent fluctuation that was obtained in the past. Although clearly only a very ad hoc estimate, this sheds some light on the potential effect of a nonaccommodating monetary policy upon the volatility of exchange rates.

Conclusion

Although our results are still preliminary, they point to a simple conclusion. Price and demand shock management stands at the core of the determination of the real exchange rate. Any tightening of monetary policy carries the risk of raising the volatility of the real exchange rate if price uncertainties are dominant, while it would reduce the volatility if demand volatility is dominant. The conclusions fit what a naive observation of the dollar would imply. Economic policies become bolder in their management of the exchange rate when trade disequilibria are feared less. To summarize this result, we may say that the "benign neglect" of U.S. economic policy toward the dollar may also become, for the same reasons, the attitude of European policymakers toward the euro (see the papers in this volume by Bergsten, and by Bénassy-Quéré, Mojon,

Figure 6. Value of the Euro With and Without Monetary Accommodation

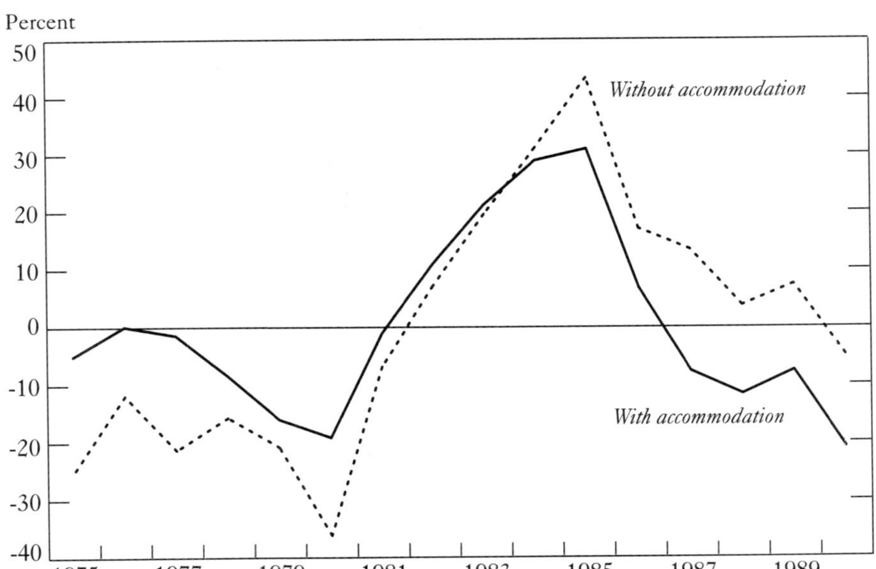

and Pisani-Ferry in this volume, for a similar interpretation). In some circumstances (European domestic price volatility), this is likely to create more exchange rate volatility.

APPENDIX

Asymmetric Shocks

We have dealt in the text with the response of European policymakers to European-wide shocks. Let us now investigate the outcome of an asymmetric shock. (This distinction is also critical in the pioneering work of Canzoneri and Gray, 1985). More specifically, consider one of the following shocks:

$$\varepsilon_1 = -\varepsilon_2$$
$$\eta_1 = -\eta_2,$$

which neutralize each other at the European level. Here, because of the symmetry of the economies, whatever the response of the European policymakers,

$$z_1 = -z_2, z = 2z_1,$$

or in other words, whatever one country gains in terms of competitiveness will be lost by the other.

Consider the outcome of the noncooperative game in which each country retains its sovereignty over both instruments. The same reasoning as before applies so far as the perception of each policymaker is concerned. The response of each policymaker to the shock is still characterized by equations (6). The difference is that the equilibrium is now a solution to

$$\pi_1 = (a_1 + 2a)z_1 + bQ_1(t) + \varepsilon_1$$
$$Q_1 = (h_1 + 2h)z_1 + gA_1(t) + \eta_1.$$

If

$$\Delta_a = \frac{a_1 + 2a}{h_1 + 2h}\left[1 + \frac{1}{\phi_0} g^2 \frac{\hat{a}/\hat{h}}{b + \hat{a}/\hat{h}}\right] + \left[b + \frac{1}{\phi_1}\frac{1}{b + \hat{a}/\hat{h}}\right],$$

then the outcome of the noncooperative game among European policymakers should be written as

$$Q_1^* = \frac{1}{\Delta_a}\left[-\varepsilon + \frac{a_1 + 2a}{h_1 + 2h}\eta\right]$$

$$z_1^* = -\frac{1}{(h_1 + 2h)\Delta_a}\left[\left(1 + \frac{1}{\phi_0} g^2 \frac{\hat{a}/\hat{h}}{b + \hat{a}/\hat{h}}\right)\varepsilon + \left(b + \frac{1}{\phi_1}\frac{1}{b + \hat{a}/\hat{h}}\right)\eta\right].$$

It is straightforward to compare this noncooperative equilibrium to the outcome of the cooperative equilibrium if $\theta = 2$ in the definition of

$$\frac{\hat{a}}{\hat{h}} = \frac{a_1 + \theta a}{h_1 + \theta h}.$$

Under these assumptions the first-best outcome is characterized by

$$\pi_1 = -\frac{1}{\phi_1} \frac{1}{b + \dfrac{a_1 + 2a}{h_1 + 2h}} Q_1$$

$$A_1 = -\frac{1}{\phi_0} \frac{(a_1 + 2a)/(h_1 + 2h)}{b + \dfrac{a_1 + 2a}{h_1 + 2h}} Q_1.$$

Under our (maintained) hypothesis that $a/h < a_1/h_1$, one obtains

$$\frac{a_1 + 2a}{h_1 + 2h} \frac{a_1 + \theta a}{h_1 + \theta h} < \frac{a_1}{h_1}.$$

This shows that, contrary to the outcome of a symmetric shock, fiscal policy is too expansionary in the noncooperative case, while monetary policy is too cautious when coordination is lacking. As we have already stressed, this will imply that exchange rates will be too volatile in response to a price shock and too stable in response to a demand shock.

The intuition is clear. When they act noncooperatively, European policymakers fail to internalize the fact that their European counterparts move in a direction that is opposite to theirs. In other words, more weight than what they perceive should actually be given to intra-European disequilibria (which is clearly the opposite of the case of a symmetric shock). If trade effects are relatively more important *within* Europe than are price effects, this implies that monetary policy should be loosened, while fiscal policy should be tightened. This sounds like a "fiscal stability pact" cum a laxer monetary policy, which is perhaps what the stability pact is about. It would then be only valid in cases of asymmetric shocks, which were indeed dominant in the 1990s, but need not be so in the future.

References

Barro, Robert J., and David B. Gordon, 1983, "Rules, Discretion and Reputation in a Model of Monetary Policy," *Journal of Monetary Economics*, Vol. 12 (July), pp. 101–121.

Bayoumi, Tamim, and Barry Eichengreen, 1993, "Shocking Aspects of European Monetary Integration," in *Adjustment and Growth in the European Monetary Union*, ed. by Francisco Torres and Francesco Giavazzi (Oxford: Cambridge University Press), pp. 193–229.

Canzoneri, Matthew B., and Jo Anna Gray, 1985, "Monetary Policy Games and the Consequences of Non-Cooperative Behavior," *International Economic Review*, Vol. 26 (October), pp. 547–64.

Canzoneri, Matthew B., Javier Vallés, and José Viñals, 1996, "Do Exchange Rates Move to Address International Macroeconomic Imbalances?" CEPR Discussion Paper No. 1498 (London: Center for Economic Policy Research, October).

Cohen, Daniel, and Charles Wyplosz, 1995, "Price and Trade Effects of Exchange Rate Fluctuations and the Design of Policy Coordination," *Journal of International Money and Finance*, Vol. 14 (June), pp. 331–47.

———, 1991, "France and Germany in the EMS: The Exchange Rate Constraint," in *The Exchange Rate Constraint*, ed. by George Alogoskoufis, Richard Portes, and Lucas Papademos (Cambridge: Cambridge University Press), pp. 167–89.

Rogoff, Kenneth, 1996, "The Purchasing Power Parity Puzzle," *Journal of Economic Literature*, Vol. 34 (June), pp. 647–68.

Comments on Cohen

Joly Dixon

This is an ambitious paper dealing with an interesting and relevant question. It develops a model of the relationship between the real exchange rate and monetary and fiscal policy instruments, uses this to investigate the change brought about by EMU, and then provides some empirical results. It gives a provocative answer to one of the key issues by claiming that the euro under certain conditions will be more volatile than the weighted average of the existing currencies.

It should first be noted that volatility in this paper has a very special meaning. It is defined as the failure to restore output and competitiveness or real exchange rates to previous levels after a price or demand shock. This is not what is generally meant by exchange rate volatility, and Bryant made a similar point about the paper by Bénassy-Quéré, Mojon, and Pisani-Ferry in this volume.

Second, it should be noted that even on its own terms the paper's conclusion only holds in a limited set of cases. It holds only with respect to "symmetric" shocks and only in the case in which price shocks are involved. In cases in which demand shocks are involved, the author's arguments conclude that EMU will dampen the volatility of the exchange rate.

I want to discuss two main issues: (1) the nature of the experiment; and (2) the applicability of the model. I will then add a short comment on the empirical results.

The experiment starts by looking at how France and Germany react to a symmetric price shock, that is, a shock that affects them each equally, but which has no effect on the rest of the world. It is assumed in that baseline case that there is no cooperation between the policymakers in each of the countries. From the perspective of each policymaker, competitiveness will be threatened (through higher prices for the representative good) and output could be reduced. Given the absence of coordination, each country will overstate the negative trade impact of the shock and monetary policy will be overly active. Because the overall trade impact is overstated, the policy reaction is overstated and the correction on the exchange rate with the rest of the world is higher than optimal—hence, lower volatility. As I mentioned before, volatility is defined in this specific way: real exchange rate volatility is low if the situation after policy measures have been implemented is close to the situation before the price shock occurred. The dynamics of exchange rate swings in between are not taken into account. That is the baseline against which EMU is compared.

In EMU the single monetary policymaker will in contrast correctly assess the trade impact and apply policy in line with the objective (or loss) function. The erroneous component due to lack of coordination will be absent—hence, in the language of the paper, a less accommodating monetary policy and a higher exchange rate volatility.

The high volatility argument thus boils down to a comparison between two situations in which policymakers have exactly the same set of objectives with respect to output effects of trade distortions and inflation, but in the baseline scenario the result is less optimal than anticipated because of the lack of coordination.

It thus seems erroneous to claim that in EMU volatility will be higher because policymakers care less about trade; they care the same, but now act on the basis of a correct assessment of the situation. Furthermore, I doubt that the baseline as specified in the paper is a good point of comparison. The existing situation in the EU should not be characterized as one of a total lack of cooperation between policymakers in the various countries. In fact, on the fiscal side there are many provisions for Community-level surveillance; and on the monetary side actions are clearly not independent. Some have indeed suggested that a more adequate representation of reality is that German monetary policy is made on the basis of German conditions, and then this policy is applied to the whole area. If this were indeed the case, the model here would give exactly the same results before and after EMU because we are only considering symmetric shocks.

Now I would like to turn to the model itself. As usual, a lot of assumptions have to be made when formalizing economic behavior; some are explicit, some are well hidden in the model. I want to discuss just three of these assumptions. First, the importance, or unimportance, of inflation. It seems that in this model inflation is a nonissue. In the model, real wages are simply assumed to be constant, and inflation has no real impact on the economy. Also, because the model is a static one-period model (which reduces in my view its usefulness as a tool for the analysis of exchange rate volatility, which is essentially a time-dependent concept), any dynamic relationship between an increase in the present price level (caused by the initial price shock) and expected inflation is explicitly assumed to be nonexistent. This is a strong assumption for a model that discusses monetary policy and exchange rate responses to price shocks.

Second, the objective or loss function. The paper constructs a composite loss function. Fiscal and monetary policymakers together aim at minimizing the weighted average of deviations of output from its trend, the fiscal stimulus parameter, and the inflation rate. I will come back to the arguments in this function, but a more fundamental issue is the composite nature of the function. I very much doubt that it can do justice to reality, especially when the main issue being investigated is exchange rate stability, which is often highly influenced by tensions between policymakers. The Maastricht Treaty is clear on the primary responsibility of the ECB toward price stability. Article 109 also lays out the framework within which exchange rate policy will be conducted, and recently a great deal of progress has been made on fiscal policymaking in EMU, with the agreement on the details of the Stability and Growth Pact. But the arrangements for the interactions between policymakers remain to be fully determined and tested. It seems to me that a loss function that treats them all together may well be insufficient. I also doubt that the weights attached to various arguments will be stable over time.

On the issue of the arguments in the loss function, we saw yesterday from the paper by Bénassy-Quéré, Mojon, and Pisani-Ferry that even if only the monetary authority's loss function is considered, results change depending on whether the relevant variable is the real exchange rate or the current account. I imagine that this model is equally sensitive to the specification of the arguments chosen.

Third, the paper assumes that the rest of the world is totally passive. In reality, the stability or instability of the euro will, I think, depend not so much on the European policy mix as on the relative policy mix. As Mr. Szász said yesterday in the roundtable discussion, "exchange rate stability cannot be attained unilaterally." Nor can instability. One of the key issues for the stability of the euro/dollar exchange rate is the effect that EMU may eventually have on international monetary arrangements generally. My own opinion is that it has great potential.

Let me conclude by adding just one comment on the empirical results. A number of regressions have been run, using what is called a sample of European currencies. It is not at all clear why or how those currencies were chosen. It is, however, rather noticeable that a number of currencies that have been stable vis-à-vis the deutsche mark, for example, the Dutch guilder, are not included, and I suspect that this might well have a substantial impact on some of the empirical results obtained.

14

Policy Implications of the Size of EMU for Europe and the United States

Fabio Ghironi and Francesco Giavazzi

As the date approaches when a decision will have to be made on which European states will join the monetary union from the start, two separate camps are emerging in the countries that are likely candidates to be admitted to the currency union. On the one side lie the central bankers, the Bundesbank in particular, mainly concerned about the credibility and the reputation of the new ECB, and about the extent to which the countries that will adopt the euro will come close to forming an optimum currency area. On the other side lie industry and the trade unions, mainly worried about competitiveness, that is, about the effects that splitting Europe in two separate groups of countries, the "ins" and the "outs," may have on relative prices inside the EU. The sophisticated argument is that the single market could not survive if exchange rate volatility between the ins and the outs were high. The unsophisticated argument is that both—industry and the unions—are frightened by the prospect of the outs using the exchange rate strategically.

The argument of the central bankers runs as follows. The ECB will not inherit overnight the reputation of the Bundesbank. For some time it will be carefully watched and tested by the markets—until it builds its own credibility and reputation. How long will it take for the ECB to achieve this? It depends, say the central bankers, on the type of countries that will join the currency union from the start. If the first group of ins consists of those countries that already belong to the "greater deutsche mark area," building a reputation will not take long—as the ECB will look very similar to the Bundesbank from the start. However, as the number of the first group of ins increases, and the

The authors thank Matthew Canzoneri, Tom Krueger, Paul Masson, Lodovico Pizzati, André Sapir, and Bart Turtelboom for their comments. Alberto Monti provided valuable assistance.

Board of the ECB starts speaking more and more languages (and languages that are increasingly distant from German), building a reputation will take longer and longer. Not only because the European Council will appoint to the Board of the ECB individuals from states whose anti-inflationary reputation is doubtful, but also, and perhaps more important, because the monetary union will include regions that less and less resemble an optimum currency area—thus increasing the pressures likely to be exerted on the central bank. Hence, conclude the central bankers, let us start with a small union; this will make it easier for the ECB to build a reputation and once this is achieved, more countries can be allowed in without prejudice to the new monetary institution, which by then will have a strong anti-inflationary reputation of its own.

While the reputation argument is certainly relevant (see De Grauwe, 1996, for an analysis), there are other dimensions to the choice of the optimal size of the currency union. An important one is the interactions that will take place among the various actors in the EMU game: between the ECB and the central banks of the outs; between the ECB and the fiscal authorities of the currency union, that is, the ECOFIN Council; between the central banks of the outs and their own fiscal authorities; and between these institutions and the rest of the world. (In this paper we think of the rest of the world as simply the United States, but further work should allow for the growing impact on Europe of other areas of the world, the Far East in particular.) For example, following a negative supply shock, if the outs were able to engineer a real appreciation, thus successfully shifting some of their inflation upon the ins, the ECB would have a greater incentive to contract its monetary policy and to export inflation to the United States, thus appreciating the euro against the dollar—the more so the larger the size of the outs relative to the EMU. If the Federal Reserve reacts by tightening as well, overall these monetary interactions would have negative consequences for employment both in Europe and in the United States, possibly against the governments' preferences.[1]

In Europe different policymakers are concerned about different aspects of these strategic interactions. Those based in the individual states are above all concerned with the consequences of a division of the EU between ins and outs: thus, the strategic interactions they are interested in are those that may occur between the authorities of one group of countries and those of the other. The European Commission, instead, works under the assumption that the

[1]This is the case studied in this paper, but one could think of different situations, such as, for example, the incentive that the ins may have, if faced with a loss of competitiveness relative to the outs, to weaken the euro relative to the dollar in an attempt to increase their competitiveness vis-à-vis the United States. In the situation we analyze, it is likely that ECOFIN would put pressure on the ECB to loosen the monetary contraction by removing the contractionary bias of noncoordinated policies with the U.S. Federal Reserve Board. See Eichengreen and Ghironi (1997a) on this point.

transition will be short, and that the EMU will soon include all EU states. What worries the officials in Brussels are the effects on the international monetary system of the introduction of a new currency. This paper makes the point that *these two aspects cannot be separated.* The interactions between ins and outs cannot be studied in isolation, since they will be affected by the presence of the rest of the world—as hinted at in the example of the previous paragraph. The interactions between EMU and the rest of the world depend, in turn, on the size of the EMU and on the exchange rate regime between insiders and outsiders, and cannot be studied independently of the ins vs. outs question.

After a long period during which few in the United States believed that EMU would really happen, U.S. policymakers are now becoming increasingly concerned about developments in Europe. Changes in the size of EMU are likely to affect the way the authorities of the currency union will relate to the U.S. authorities. Also, if the outsiders are a very small entity, it seems intuitive that U.S. policymakers will be indifferent as to the nature of the intra-EU exchange rate regime. Things may be different if the outs are a significant fraction of the EU.

This paper discusses the effects of different sizes of EMU and of different exchange rate regimes between the ins and the outs in a framework that explicitly accounts for the interactions between Europe and the United States. We study the incentives that various European policymakers face in determining the optimal size of the currency union and the choice of the intra-EU exchange rate regime, explicitly accounting for the effects of the interactions inside Europe and between Europe and the rest of the world. We overlook the ECB credibility problem—which is well understood—and ask if there are *other* reasons why the central bankers of the likely ins may want to keep the currency union relatively small. At the same time we ask if the optimal dimension of the union, as seen from the viewpoint of the fiscal authorities, is different, thus giving rise to a potential conflict between ECOFIN and the central bankers at the time of deciding who should join the union. Throughout the paper we discuss how the choices faced by European policymakers are affected by the presence of the United States (the rest of the world) and, in turn, how the United States will be affected by the birth of the euro and by the size of EMU.

The tool we use to address these questions is a three-country model designed to describe the interactions among monetary and fiscal authorities within each country and internationally. The model is in the tradition of Mundell and Fleming, as applied to the analysis of international policy interactions by Canzoneri and Henderson (1991). Among its attractive features is the fact that it allows us to study the effects of different dimensions of the European currency union—in a continuum that encompasses a union that extends to the entire EU (except perhaps for a few states of negligible magnitude) as well as one that does not extend beyond Germany and Austria.[2] The model is described in detail in Ghironi and Giavazzi (1997a and 1997c), where we also discuss how the output-inflation trade-off facing the monetary authority of a region changes when its relative size and the monetary regime that links it to the rest of the world change. In the next section of this paper we provide an intuitive description of the most important features of this model.

As is common with three-country models—and we have argued above that three is the minimum number of countries that we can consider—some of the reduced-form coefficients of the model cannot be signed unambiguously. We must thus analyze the effects of the interactions among policymakers computing numerical solutions of the policy game among the various authorities using reasonable values of the parameters. Interestingly, our three-country model vindicates some of the facts described at the beginning of this introduction. For example, in a situation where fiscal authorities are prevented from using the tax instruments (and thus in a situation that closely resembles what could be the consequences of a strict "fiscal stability pact"), strategic interactions are limited to those occurring among central banks, and the intra-EU exchange rate regime is asymmetric (as in ERM II), the ECB would prefer the currency union to be rather small if the outs were nonnegligible. ECOFIN, instead, prefers a situation in which relatively more states join the currency union (see section on monetary policy interactions). In the same section, we compare these results with those obtained assuming monetary cooperation between the ins and the outs. The subsequent section is devoted to the analysis of what happens when fiscal activism is allowed. We then start exploring the importance of the United States by studying what would happen were the United States and Europe completely closed with respect to one another, that is, if there were no transatlantic policy spillovers. We find that the conflict of interests between the ECB and ECOFIN would disappear in this situation. Next, we reintroduce transatlantic policy spillovers and compare the results obtained under an asymmetric intra-EU regime with those obtained assuming a symmetric flexible exchange rate regime between the ins and the outs. The comparison, which is based on the results about the trade-offs summarized in the next section, sheds more light on the policymakers' incentives and on the role of the United States in our analysis.

Analytical Framework

As is common in the literature on international spillovers of fiscal and monetary policies, the model we use for our analysis is essentially a three-country version of the Mundell-Fleming model, in which the authorities of

[2]Using a similar framework, von Hagen and Fratianni (1991) study a different type of asymmetry—the effects of asymmetric demand and supply shocks on otherwise symmetric economies.

each region minimize quadratic loss functions whose parameters differ across different authorities. This particular model was first studied in Ghironi (1993), and used to address different questions in Eichengreen and Ghironi (1997a and 1997b). The model is described in detail in Appendix I.[3]

Inside each region the central bank controls a nominal variable (the money supply or the level of the exchange rate), while the fiscal authority controls taxes or public spending. The interactions among different regions occur via trade flows in the goods market and via capital flows in the assets markets; we assume that assets are perfect substitutes, so that interest rates and nominal exchange rates in the three regions are linked through arbitrage conditions. We use the model to study the response to a common supply shock that hits the three regions simultaneously.[4] The model has two periods: nominal wages are predetermined and set based on the expectation of future variables; the ex ante return on financial assets also depends on expected exchange rate changes. However, because the only stochastic factors are exogenous shocks, whose expectation one period ahead is equal to zero, the rational expectations solution of the model (in the absence of time-consistency problems, which we overlook) is straightforward, since all expectations are equal to zero; thus the model reduces to a static structure. (See also Giavazzi and Giovannini, 1989, for a similar solution.)

A distinct feature of the model is the assumption about fiscal policy. We rule out debt accumulation by imposing that tax revenue equals spending in each period. Government spending falls on home and foreign goods, according to the same pattern as for private consumption (to be described later). We follow Alesina and Tabellini (1987) in assuming that government revenue accrues exclusively from a tax on firms' total revenues, which provides a simple way to capture the distortionary effects of taxation. Firms' demand for labor is a decreasing function of the tax rate: for a given level of demand, a tax cut raises employment. This effect, however, is accompanied by the contemporaneous fall in demand produced by the cut in government spending that must accompany the tax cut. Hence, the net effect on equilibrium employ-

---

[3]A more complete description of the model, together with the solution procedure, is in Ghironi and Giavazzi (1997c).

[4]Although the model would allow us to analyze policy interactions following different types of shocks, we focus on the case of a symmetric negative supply shock for two reasons. On the one hand, this shock causes inflation and unemployment, and thus forces monetary policymakers to deal with a trade-off between the usual macroeconomic targets: monetary contraction will stabilize inflation at the cost of a deeper recession. On the other hand, after the collapse of the Bretton Woods system, large-scale supply shocks—the oil shocks of 1973, 1979, and the 1991 Gulf War episode—have been among the most relevant disturbances to the world economy. It is not surprising that the debate over the advantages or disadvantages of alternative policymaking regimes has been particularly heated in the wake of such shocks.

Figure 1. The Pattern of Trade

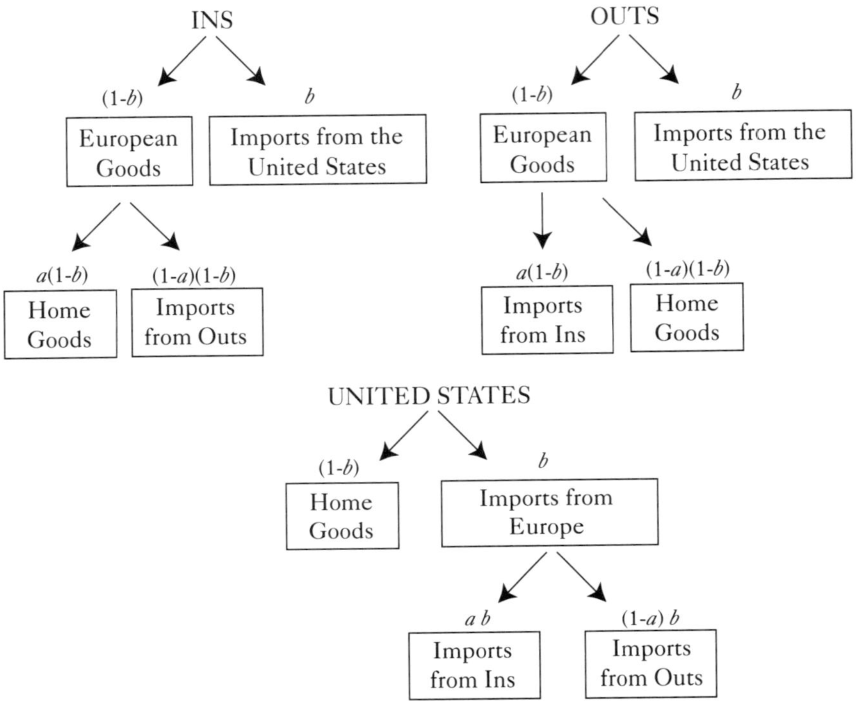

ment remains ambiguous, although for plausible parameter values the supply effect dominates—that is, a tax cut unambiguously raises employment.[5] The fiscal authority responds to a negative supply shock (which raises prices and lowers output) by cutting taxes, thus helping to raise employment and to stabilize the price level because the tax cut creates excess supply in the goods market.

The trade pattern across the three regions (shown in Figure 1) is the novel feature of our model, which allows us to compare different sizes of the currency union. We start from the pattern of transatlantic trade: U.S. consumers spend a fraction $(1 - b)$ of total consumption on home goods, and a fraction b on goods imported from Europe; this in turn is allocated in a fraction a, which falls on goods produced by the ins, and a fraction $(1 - a)$, which falls on goods

[5]See Giavazzi and Pagano (1996) for empirical evidence on episodes of expansionary spending cuts. Eichengreen and Ghironi (1997a) address different issues and discuss also the standard Keynesian case in which increases in government spending have expansionary effects. Eichengreen and Ghironi (1997b) analyze how changes in the extent to which fiscal policy has non-Keynesian effects affect governments' trade-offs and allow the nature of fiscal policy to be asymmetric across countries.

produced by the outs. European consumers in both regions spend a fraction b on goods imported from the United States, and a fraction $(1 - b)$ on European goods; the latter fraction is distributed in a fraction a that falls on goods produced by the ins, and a fraction $(1 - a)$ that falls on goods produced by the outs.[6] The parameter a characterizes the size of the currency union. As a increases, the share of U.S. imports from Europe that comes from the ins increases, while the import share from the outs falls, thus describing a situation in which the size of the ins relative to the outs increases. As a approaches 1, the EU and the ins tend to overlap: the currency union includes all EU states except for a small "residual" economy whose actions do not affect the ins and the United States. When a falls, the number of countries in the currency union becomes smaller and smaller.

As mentioned above, there are two authorities in each region: a fiscal authority and a central bank.[7] Each policymaker minimizes a loss function, which includes, as arguments, the fluctuations of employment and the consumer price index (CPI) around their equilibrium values. In addition, the fiscal authorities also care about the volatility of taxation. There are various reasons for the inclusion of the latter in the governments' loss functions. Governments are likely to care about the distortions they impose on the economy when using their instrument. In addition, penalizing fiscal authorities for an active use of their instrument is a simple way of capturing the relative rigidity that characterizes fiscal policymaking relative to the management of monetary policy. In the world economy we are considering, fiscal flexibility for stabilization purposes is likely to be limited for reasons that we elaborate on below. Our specification of the governments' loss function allows us to capture

---

[6]Our assumptions on the trade pattern are consistent with the implicit assumption that consumers on the two sides of the Atlantic have asymmetric Cobb-Douglas preferences, which lead to constant shares of income being spent on the various goods according to the assumed pattern.

[7]By doing this we assume that inside the currency union there is a single fiscal authority, represented by the ECOFIN Council. This implies two strong assumptions. First, officially, all the members of the EU are currently represented in the ECOFIN Council: assuming that ECOFIN is the fiscal authority of the insiders alone may appear inconsistent with the current institutional framework of the Union. However, officials in Europe have agreed on a two-level structure for the ECOFIN Council, with the representatives of the insiders constituting the first layer of the structure. Given that the Maastricht Treaty does not require EU fiscal policymakers to jointly manage their policies, it is not unrealistic to treat the two levels of ECOFIN as separate authorities, with the first layer, to which we simply refer as ECOFIN, being the fiscal authority of the ins, separated from the fiscal authority of the outs. Second, the first layer itself will include a number of independent fiscal authorities, one for each member of the currency union: we thus overlook the strategic interactions among them. (These are studied in Ghironi, 1993, and Eichengreen and Ghironi, 1997a and 1997b.) Finally, we also assume that the outs can be aggregated into a single entity, with a single central bank and a single fiscal authority. We therefore overlook the consequences of noncooperation among the authorities of the outs, studied in Buiter, Corsetti, and Pesenti (1995).

in a simple way these constraints on the active use of fiscal policy to react to the consequences of disturbances.[8]

We shall first consider the case when no authority cooperates—neither internationally nor within each region. The monetary policy regime between the ins and the United States is symmetric, and, in the absence of international monetary cooperation, it is subject to the well-known inefficiency associated with flexible exchange rates. Each central bank controls its own money stock and believes that by changing it it can affect the bilateral exchange rate. Since exchange rates feed back into the domestic CPI, each central bank believes that monetary policy can affect prices at a relatively smaller cost in terms of output. In the noncooperative equilibrium, monetary policy turns out to be overly contractionary.

Within Europe, instead, we study two different monetary regimes. The first is asymmetric: the central bank of the ins (the ECB) controls its own money stock, but—contrary to the situation relative to the dollar—it is unable to affect the intra-European exchange rate because its partner (the outs) accommodates any change in the money stock of the ins. Therefore, the ECB minimizes its loss function subject to the Europe-wide trade-off between output and the price level. The central bank of the outs, instead, controls the bilateral exchange rate. The alternative regime is symmetric, exactly as we have assumed for the ECB and the Federal Reserve.

Which regime will characterize Europe after EMU is born is still undecided. Policymakers (the Commission and the ECOFIN Council) are oriented toward a new ERM, linking the single currency with the currencies of the outs: as argued in Giavazzi and Giovannini (1989), we believe that our asymmetric regime is a good characterization of an ERM-type arrangement

[8]It could also be argued that the volatility of taxation may be a source of losses for politically motivated governments, although this effect is not captured in our model.

It is interesting to ask how the policy interactions we analyze would change if the governments were not penalized for actively using their instrument. It turns out that there is an interesting special case, at least when $a = 0.5$. If governments are free to change taxes without suffering any direct loss from the volatility of their instrument and if their loss function is a "mirror image" of the central banks' one—that is, it is such that if the central bank attaches weight f to the volatility of inflation and $(1 - f)$ to that of employment, the government does the opposite—the policy choices made by the central bank and the government within each country do not change with changes in the international policymaking regime. In other words, in this special case, the equilibrium of the game between central bank and government inside each country is not sensitive to the nature of the exchange rate regime or to policymaking being cooperative or not. The intuition is that, even if taxation is distortionary, when national policymakers' preferences are symmetric as described, the map of their indifference curves allows them to achieve a two-targets, two-instruments equilibrium for the game between them. Under this "Tinbergenian" situation, changes in the nature of policymaking at the international level have no impact on the policy choices of each country's authorities. Although this special case is interesting—since it suggests that there may be circumstances under which the international policymaking regime is irrelevant—we believe that the case we analyze in the paper is more realistic.

whereby realignments are noncooperative. The alternative view—held by the U.K. authorities and by a number of academic economists; see in particular Persson and Tabellini (1996)—is that a new ERM (ERM II) would not survive speculative attacks, especially since the ECB would be unwilling to provide unlimited intervention. Instead the outs should concentrate on a domestic monetary rule (inflation targeting is the common proposal) and let the bilateral exchange rate vis-à-vis the euro fluctuate.[9]

Within this framework we ask whether different authorities (in particular ECOFIN and the ECB), concerned about the consequences of supply-side disturbances, would agree on the desirable size of the currency union and we analyze the policy implications of changes in the size of EMU for Europe and the United States.

Ghironi and Giavazzi (1997a and 1997b) use the model to derive a set of theoretical results on how the employment-inflation trade-off facing the monetary authority in an open economy is affected by the relative size of the economy and by the exchange rate regime. These results are important to understand the intuition behind the numerical solutions that we shall describe later, and they lend some robustness to the conclusions. The intuition runs as follows.[10]

The main point is that the trade-off a country faces depends on the size of the economy for which the monetary authority sets its instrument. Under a noncooperative flexible exchange rate regime, each central bank sets the money supply for its own economy, taking the money supply of the other country as given; thus, in such a regime, the relevant size for each central bank is that of its own country. Things are different, however, in an asymmetric regime, where one central bank (that of the core country) sets the money supply for the entire region, while the other central bank controls the bilateral exchange rate. In such a regime the relevant size for the central bank of the core country is the entire region, while the size that is relevant for the peripheral central bank remains that of its own country.

It can be shown that, in general, the trade-off a country faces becomes steeper—that is, it improves—the smaller the size of the "relevant" economy. A steeper trade-off allows the central bank to trade a larger inflation gain for a

---

[9]Kenen (1995), Spaventa (1996), and Wyplosz (1996), among others, provide a thorough analysis of the arguments in favor of and against a new EMS regime between the ins and the outs. Persson and Tabellini (1996) argue that a regime that combines inflation targeting with flexible exchange rates is strictly superior to an EMS-type regime. They suggest that this regime would approximate the first-best cooperative outcome of their model quite closely, removing existing incentives to run competitive devaluations, and would outperform an exchange rate–based regime.

[10]Throughout, we refer to the trade-off facing a country's central bank as the country's trade-off. This trade-off is defined by $\partial q/\partial n \equiv (\partial q/\partial k)/(\partial n/\partial k)$, where q is the CPI, n is employment, and k is the instrument controlled by the central bank. Fiscal authorities in all countries face employment-inflation trade-offs defined by $\partial q/\partial n \equiv (\partial q/\partial \tau)/(\partial n/\partial \tau)$, where τ is the rate of taxation of firms' revenues. In what follows, we focus on the trade-offs facing the central banks.

smaller employment loss. This is intuitively more favorable for sufficiently inflation-averse central bankers. Thus, when we argue that a steeper trade-off is better, we are implicitly assuming that central banks care more about inflation than about employment in their loss functions.[11] The intuition is straightforward. Consider for instance the peripheral country in an asymmetric regime. The smaller the economy, the larger the share of imports in the domestic CPI. Thus, the impact of a given change in the exchange rate on the CPI increases as the size of the economy gets smaller—and thus it becomes more open. Therefore, a small open economy in principle needs to engineer a relatively milder recession to stabilize prices, compared with a large country where the exchange rate has only a small impact on the domestic CPI.

This result has two corollaries. Consider, first, the following comparison: the central bank of a peripheral country in an asymmetric regime, and the same central bank in a symmetric flexible exchange rate regime. The size of the relevant economy is the same in the two situations—and thus the trade-off the central bank faces is also identical in the two regimes. This is not true, however, for the central bank of the core country in an asymmetric regime, compared with the situation under flexible exchange rates. The trade-off this central bank faces is always less favorable in the asymmetric regime, when the relevant economy encompasses the entire region, and the two trade-offs coincide when the size of the peripheral country becomes negligible—the Federal Reserve is indifferent between a regime of pegged-but-adjustable or flexible exchange rates vis-à-vis Grenada, but it clearly cares about the exchange rate regime vis-à-vis Germany or Japan.

These results are summarized in Figures 2, 3, and 4. Figure 2 shows the employment-inflation trade-off facing the peripheral country (the outs in our discussion of the European monetary union) in an asymmetric regime. (These figures are drawn assuming that the countries are hit by a supply shock that causes inflation and unemployment.) The steeper line—the one along which the trade-off is more favorable—corresponds to the case in which the size of the currency union is relatively large and, as a consequence, the outs are relatively small. Figure 3 illustrates the trade-offs when the exchange rate regime inside Europe is symmetric (flexible exchange rates) and thus coincides with the exchange rate regime between Europe and the United States. The size of the United States coincides with that of Europe: thus, the trade-off the United States faces is always worse than the trade-off facing the European countries and it coincides with the trade-off facing the ins when $a = 1$, that is, when the size of the outs is negligible. Inside Europe the smaller country faces the best trade-off, and the trade-offs coincide for $a = 0.5$. If, instead, the exchange rate regime inside Europe is asymmetric (see Figure 4), the central bank of the

[11]We believe this is a realistic assumption. If the central banks attached a larger weight to employment than to inflation, a flatter trade-off would be more favorable, as it would allow the trading of larger employment gains for smaller inflation losses.

Figure 2. The Outsiders Employment–Inflation Trade-Off

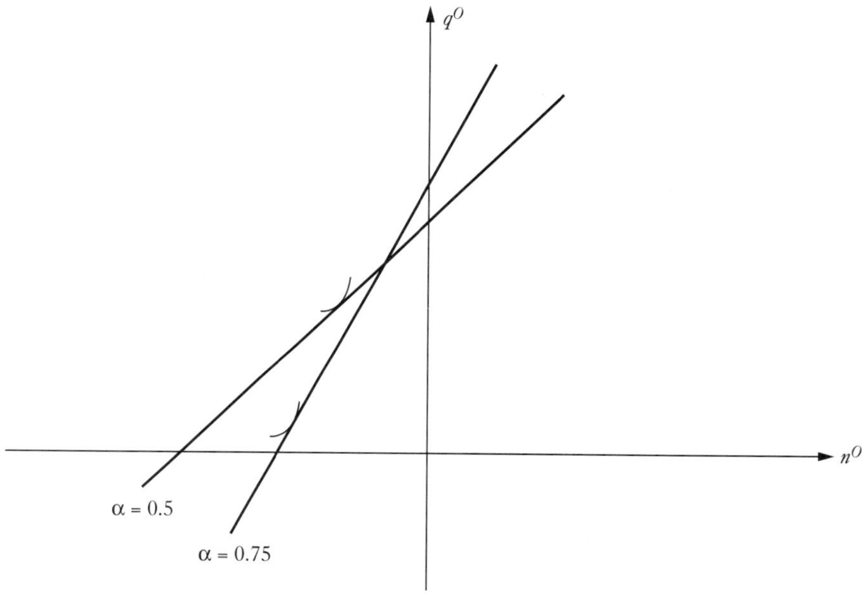

Figure 3. Employment–Inflation Trade-Offs Under a Symmetric Regime in Europe

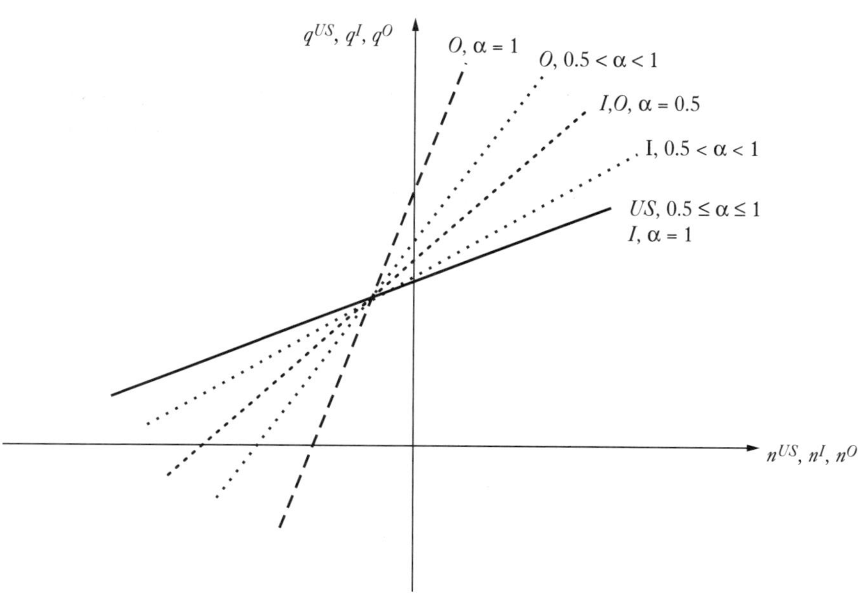

Figure 4. Employment–Inflation Trade-Offs Under an Asymmetric Regime in Europe

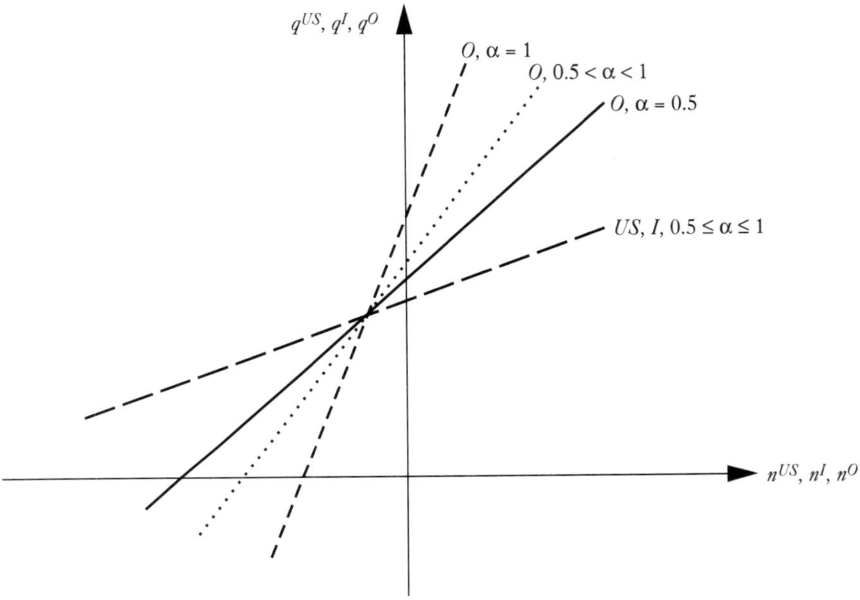

core country, the ins, always faces the same trade-off as the Federal Reserve, irrespective of the actual size of the ins' economy, whereas the outs face the same trade-off they would face under the symmetric regime, which is always better than that faced by the ins.

Monetary Policy Interactions Between the Ins, the Outs, and the United States

The general results stop with those discussed in the previous section—and this is not surprising. Remember that what we are looking for are situations in which some policymakers prefer a relatively larger currency union, while others prefer a relatively smaller one, but all policymakers minimize employment and price-level fluctuations, albeit with different weights. If it turned out that a given size of the currency union was best independent of parameter values, then policymakers would never disagree. Therefore, what we are going to show are situations in which, for instance, the policymakers that attach a larger weight to price level relative to employment fluctuations prefer, say, a relatively smaller union, while the opposite holds for policymakers with different relative weights.

Our first exercise considers only monetary policy interactions; we thus assume that the tax rate is held exogenously constant—for instance, because of an institutional constraint on the active use of fiscal policy. The three fiscal authorities passively watch the interactions among central banks, and their loss functions include only the employment and CPI terms. The three central banks do not cooperate, and the intra-EU exchange rate system is asymmetric.

We believe that this is a good characterization of the way EMU might work, at least for some time. The Stability and Growth Pact will tie the hands of the fiscal authorities of the ins, while the efforts to meet the Maastricht deficit criteria will in turn prevent the outs from actively using fiscal policy to respond to shocks. The constraints imposed by the Stability and Growth Pact are likely to be binding for a significant period—and the flexibility of fiscal policy for stabilization purposes correspondingly limited—also because of the problems European governments are experiencing in the presence of slow (or even negative) population growth and, in particular, costly social security systems.[12] The assumption that monetary authorities do not cooperate is also a serious possibility. The ECB was designed to be independent; even if a new EMS-type arrangement is introduced, linking the currencies of the ins and the outs, it is likely that—at least in its first years—the ECB will not be inclined to compromise its objectives in order to cooperate with other central banks, in particular with those of the outs.[13] As a result, the latter central banks could use the exchange rate strategically in the attempt to shift upon the ins some of the cost of adjusting to exogenous shocks—precisely as in the managed exchange rate regime described in the last section.

Within this institutional framework we investigate how purely strategic incentives will drive European policymakers at the time of deciding how many states should be admitted into the currency union. Although formally this decision is the responsibility of the European Council on a recommendation by ECOFIN, central bankers (the EMI at that stage, since the ECB will not yet be born) will be very influential. (The European Council will decide based on a recommendation by ECOFIN, which in turn will receive two reports, one from the EMI, and one from the European Commission.) We would like to know if the two bodies, ECOFIN and the EMI, will have different views, and what determines such differences.[14] More precisely, we ask the following question: for a given policy regime—no cooperation among central banks,

[12]Although social security is currently a source of net revenues for the U.S. government, slow population growth may also make the problem relevant for the United States in the future. Besides, a balanced budget amendment, if it were introduced, would do away with fiscal flexibility.

[13]For example, Eichengreen and Ghironi (1997a) show that, under reasonable circumstances, the ECB may not be interested in cooperating with the Federal Reserve.

[14]This discussion of the role of ECOFIN is implicitly consistent with all members of the EU being represented in that institution. Recall footnote 7.

monetary policy asymmetry inside Europe, and frozen fiscal policy—following an exogenous supply shock, how large a currency union would each authority prefer, that is, how does the loss function of each authority change as the parameter a changes?

Solving the central banks' minimization problem leads to the first-order conditions displayed in Appendix II. These define each central bank's Nash reaction function to the other monetary authorities' policy actions. The solution of the system, using our assumptions about the parameter values, together with the implied values of endogenous variables and loss functions, are summarized in Table 1.[15]

For both the ins and the outs we report the values of the main variables (CPI, employment, and the real exchange rate) and the value of the policymakers' loss function in equilibrium. We compare two situations: $a = 0.5$ and $a = 0.75$. How closely do these numbers reflect the possible situation in Europe? In an EMU that included only Germany, Austria, France, and the Benelux countries, a would be approximately equal to 0.5. A value of 0.75 would characterize an EMU that also included Italy and Spain, but left out the United Kingdom and the Nordic countries. Finally, we report the results for $a = 1$, that is, for the case where the dimension of the outs is negligible. This reference case is of interest because it describes a situation where the outs' policy choices no longer affect the other economies and the European currency union and the United States face one another as two large symmetric entities.

When the outsiders are relatively small, and the trade-off is relatively more favorable, their central bank "rides" it more aggressively. In the equilibrium, prices are lower than in the case $a = 0.5$, but output is also lower, notwithstanding the relatively favorable trade-off (see Figure 2). Given our assumptions about the preferences of central banks and fiscal authorities, the outsiders' central bank prefers a relatively large union ($a = 0.75$), while the opposite is true for the outsiders' fiscal authority, which suffers because of the larger employment loss when $a = 0.75$.

[15]Because several reduced-form parameters have ambiguous signs, in order to draw clear-cut conclusions, we perform a numerical simulation of the policy game, based on assigning "consensus" values to the structural parameters of the model. Our assumptions about the latter, as well as the implied numerical values of reduced forms and trade-offs, are described in Appendix I. As we shall see below, results of the simulations turn out to be consistent with the general results about the trade-offs described in the previous section, which lends some robustness to our conclusions. Note that in Table 1 and in the following ones, the values of the policy instruments and of the endogenous variables should be multiplied by x (the supply shock), while the values of the loss functions should be multiplied by x^2. A positive value of x is a negative supply side shock, which lowers employment and raises the CPI. Given that all variables in our model are in logs, the numbers we report in the tables are the elasticities of policy instruments and endogenous variables with respect to the supply shock implied by the relevant policymaking regime and EMU size. We then calculate the losses implied by those elasticities.

Table 1. Effects of a Noncooperative ERM II with Fixed Taxes

	Outs' Size Negligible ($a = 1$)	Outs' Size Small ($a = 0.75$)	Outs' Size Equal to Ins' ($a = 0.5$)
Ins' money (m^I)	−1.8423	−1.8843	−1.9060
U.S. money (m^{US})	−1.8423	−1.8506	−1.8550
Nominal outs/euro (e^3)	−0.2130	−0.1815	−0.1376
Real outs/euro (z^3)	−0.1168	−0.0995	−0.0754
Real dollar/euro (z^1)	0.0000	−0.0127	−0.0193
Real dollar/outs (z^2)	0.1168	0.0868	0.0561
Ins' CPI (q^I)	0.4805	0.5127	0.4977
Outs' CPI (q^O)	0.2674	0.3312	0.3601
U.S. CPI (q^{US})	0.4805	0.4843	0.4813
Ins' employment (n^I)	−1.5281	−1.5680	−1.5829
Outs' employment (n^O)	−1.8111	−1.8093	−1.7658
U.S. employment (n^{US})	−1.5281	−1.5282	−1.5308
Loss ECB	0.2206	0.2412	0.2367
Loss ins' government	1.0622	1.1196	1.1399
Loss outs' central bank	0.1962	0.2130	0.2142
Loss outs' government	1.4797	1.4786	1.4095
Loss Federal Reserve	0.2206	0.2223	0.2214
Loss U.S. government	1.0622	1.0626	1.0661

Note: In this table, and in the following ones, the values of the policy instruments and of the endogenous variables should be multiplied by x, while the values of the loss functions should be multiplied by x^2.

We now turn to the insiders. Given the real appreciation engineered by the outsiders, the ECB responds with a tougher monetary contraction compared with what it would have done had it not imported additional inflation from the outs.[16] Symmetrically to what happens in the outs, the ECB prefers a relatively small currency union, while ECOFIN would rather have a larger number of states in the union. Let us first try to understand why the ECB prefers a relatively small union.

As we have argued in the previous section, contrary to the outsiders, insiders face the same output-inflation trade-off, independent of the size of the currency union. Thus, in the ERM II regime, the insiders' central bank does not have the option of choosing a more favorable trade-off when expressing a preference over the size of the European currency union. For any value of a, the trade-off is always the same, and given that trade-off, the ECB can only respond to the other players' policies by varying the degree of mon-

[16]In Table 1 this can be seen comparing the outcome for $a < 1$ with the case $a = 1$, and remembering that with $a = 1$ the impact of the outs on the ins and on the United States is negligible ($m^I|_{a=0.5} < m^I|_{a=0.75} < m^I|_{a=1} < 0$). m^I denotes money in the monetary union.

etary contraction. When the outsiders are relatively small, even if they aggressively shift inflation abroad, the insiders' effective real exchange rate does not depreciate very much, precisely because the outsiders are small.[17] Faced with lower imported inflation, the insiders' central bank contracts less than for $a = 0.5$, and thus domestic producer prices remain relatively high.[18] As a consequence, the insiders' CPI also remains higher, and the central bank ends up being worse off. However, the insiders' fiscal authority benefits from the milder contraction, and thus prefers a relatively larger currency union.

Finally we look at the situation in the United States. For $a < 1$, the strategic interaction between ins and outs inside Europe also affects the United States, whose effective real exchange rate depreciates.[19] The Federal Reserve suffers from the strategic interaction inside Europe, the more so the larger is the currency union, for the same reason that induces the ECB to prefer a smaller union. When $a = 0.75$, the outs' central bank is more aggressive not only toward the ECB, but also toward the Federal Reserve.[20] Nonetheless, the Federal Reserve, analogously to the ECB, chooses a milder monetary contraction in that situation, and ends up suffering because of higher inflation. Hence, when the outs are nonnegligible, the Federal Reserve prefers to face a small currency union in Europe rather than a large one, even though $a = 1$ would be the best situation for both the ECB and the Federal Reserve. Analogously to ECOFIN, the U.S. government prefers a large rather than a small union, since the Federal Reserve's monetary contraction is milder in the former case and the employment loss is smaller. Note that both the ins and the United States face the same employment-inflation trade-off as a consequence of the exchange rate regime in Europe, which presents the ins' authorities with the European-wide trade-off, independent of the size of the currency union. Consequently, the presence of nonnegligible outsiders—and the absence of intra-European monetary cooperation, as we shall see below—is crucial to have movements in the dollar/euro exchange rate in the framework we are examining. In fact, if the outsiders were negligible—or if they were nonnegligible but cross-country externalities in Europe were internalized—equal trade-offs would lead to equal equilibrium policies in the United States and

[17]The effective real exchange rate of the insiders is: $z^I \equiv bz^I + (1 - a)(1 - b)z^3$, where z^1 and z^3 are the dollar-euro and outs-euro real exchange rates, respectively.

[18]When $a = 0.75$, producers' prices (p^I) are equal to $0.4681x$; when instead $a = 0.5$, they are equal to $0.4618x$.

[19]The effective real exchange rate of the United States is defined as: $z^{US} \equiv ab\, z^1 + (1 - a)b\, z^2$, where z^2 is the dollar-outs real exchange rate.

[20]Remember that the outs' trade-off improves with respect to both the ins' and the U.S. trade-off as a increases from 0.5 to 0.75.

in the currency union and there would be no changes in the dollar/euro exchange rate.[21]

The results presented in Table 1 allow us to make an interesting comparison with the analysis of Alesina and Grilli (1994). There the authors show that if EMU does not include all EU central banks from the start and monetary authorities in Europe have different degrees of inflation aversion, the initial insiders may not want the number of the ins to increase, even if a currency union encompassing all EU members would be the best option.

Something analogous happens in our model. If we think of the three values of a that we have considered as steps toward global monetary unification of Europe, if initially $a = 0.5$, subsequently, the ECB will not want to take the intermediate step toward $a = 0.75$, even if $a = 1$ would be the best solution. Interestingly, the Federal Reserve would share the ECB's preferences and—in a sense—shortsightedness, contrary to the respective governments, which would always prefer a large currency union in Europe. We obtain the Alesina-Grilli result in a framework in which all central bankers have the same inflation aversion throughout the world. In our view, this shows that strategic interactions per se may matter at least as much as different degrees of inflation aversion in shaping policymakers' incentives and behavior.

How do these results compare with the case of cooperation among central banks in Europe? We study this case because, according to some officials (but also according to Spaventa, 1996), the exchange rate arrangement (ERM II) that should link the ins and the outs after January 1, 1999, will entail—contrary to our assumption so far—some form of cooperation between the ECB and the central banks of the countries that will not join the currency union from the start. Their interpretation of how the new system could work is that of a cooperatively managed exchange rate system. The response of EU central banks to exogenous shocks would entail an EU-wide change in the money supply and, possibly, a cooperative realignment of intra-EU exchange rates.

We have computed the equilibrium of our model following an exogenous supply shock assuming that the ECB and the outsiders' central bank cooperate with one another—though neither of them cooperates with the Federal Reserve. This is the only behavioral assumption that is changed with respect

[21]This observation shows that facing a more favorable trade-off is not *necessary* to successfully run beggar-thy-neighbor policies: the Federal Reserve faces the same trade-off as the ECB, but still manages to appreciate the dollar in real terms against the euro, thus exporting some inflation to the currency union. The absence of intra-EU cooperation and the presence of nonnegligible outsiders that successfully export inflation to both the ins and the United States shifts the balance between the Federal Reserve and the ECB in a direction that is favorable to the U.S. authorities. Ghironi (1993) and Eichengreen and Ghironi (1997a) show that the dollar-euro exchange rate would also move in a situation in which there are no outsiders—so that the currency union has the same size as the United States—but fiscal authorities inside the currency union do not cooperate.

to the situation analyzed above. The first-order condition for the Federal Reserve choice is unchanged. Instead, the ECB and the outsiders' central bank jointly minimize a weighted sum of their loss functions, with weights equal to a and $(1 - a)$, respectively. This implies that the weight attached to each central bank's loss function in the cooperative agreement is determined by the relative dimensions of the European economies. Although more complicated bargaining mechanisms could be envisaged, we believe that our simple assumption is not unrealistic. The first-order conditions to the central banks' problem are shown in Appendix II. The relevant results are summarized in Table 2. We limit ourselves to values of a strictly smaller than 1 because the ECB will have no incentives to cooperate with a region of negligible outsiders.

The first, unsurprising, observation is that the cooperative response of central banks does not entail a change in the intra-EU exchange rate: the result is unsurprising because, as we have seen above, realignments are the result of the successful attempt by the outsiders to shift some of their inflation on the insiders—a behavior that is ruled out in a cooperative solution. Following the shock, the intra-EU exchange rate remains fixed, independent of the relative size of the ins and the outs.

The equilibrium values of the loss functions (of both fiscal and monetary authorities) are now independent of relative sizes—because size only mat-

Table 2. Effects of a Cooperative ERM II with Fixed Taxes

	Outs' Size Small ($a = 0.75$)	Outs' Size Equal to Ins' ($a = 0.5$)
Ins' money (m^I)	−1.8423	−1.8423
U.S. money (m^{US})	−1.8423	−1.8423
Nominal outs/euro (e^3)	0.0000	0.0000
Real outs/euro (z^3)	0.0000	0.0000
Real dollar/euro (z^1)	0.0000	0.0000
Real dollar/outs (z^2)	0.0000	0.0000
Ins' CPI (q^I)	0.4805	0.4805
Outs' CPI (q^O)	0.4805	0.4805
U.S. CPI (q^{US})	0.4805	0.4805
Ins' employment (n^I)	−1.5281	−1.5281
Outs' employment (n^O)	−1.5281	−1.5281
U.S. employment (n^{US})	−1.5281	−1.5281
Loss ECB	0.2206	0.2206
Loss ins' government	1.0622	1.0622
Loss outs' central bank	0.2206	0.2206
Loss outs' government	1.0622	1.0622
Loss Federal Reserve	0.2206	0.2206
Loss U.S. government	1.0622	1.0622

ters when central banks play beggar-thy-neighbor policies. The loss of ECOFIN and the ECB is unambiguously lower than in the case of noncooperation. Note that, not surprisingly, in the case of monetary cooperation in Europe, all variables for the insiders and for the United States have the same values they had in the case of no cooperation when $a = 1$, so that monetary cooperation between ins and outs is equivalent to no cooperation when $a = 1$ from the perspective of the United States and the ins. The ECB's gain from cooperation increases as the size of the union increases, where the gain is defined as the difference between the loss in the absence of cooperation and the loss under the cooperative ERM II regime. This result can be explained as follows. Smaller outs are more aggressive—which increases the ECB's incentive to cooperate—but their impact on the ins' economy is smaller—and this decreases the ECB's interest in cooperation. However, in the absence of cooperation, it is precisely the smaller impact of the outs that induces the ECB to adopt a counterproductively looser policy when $a = .75$. Cooperation removes both the outs' stronger aggressiveness as a increases, and the consequences of the ECB's behavior. Hence, the potential gains for the ECB from cooperating with the outs' central bank are larger in the large union case.

The situation, however, is different for the outsiders. The outs' central bank is better off in the absence of cooperation—the more so the larger the currency union—because it is then allowed to appreciate vis-à-vis the insiders. (This is also true when the size of the outsiders is negligible ($a = 1$).[22]) The outsiders' government, instead, always prefers monetary cooperation in Europe because it benefits from less contractionary monetary policies. Finally, monetary cooperation inside Europe benefits the Federal Reserve and the U.S. government—because intra-European cooperation removes the more aggressive behavior by the outs' central bank, which induces a real depreciation of the dollar against the outsiders' currency, and alleviates the deflationary bias associated with the lack of monetary cooperation in Europe.

[22]When it plays cooperatively, the central bank of nonnegligible outs is driven to the same situation as that of the ECB and the Federal Reserve with $a = 1$ and no cooperation, and is even worse off than the central bank of negligible outs when there is no cooperation. The result that international monetary cooperation may be counterproductive from the perspective of some or all of the players is not new in the literature on international interactions. In Rogoff (1985), cooperation can be counterproductive when it exacerbates time inconsistency problems in the conduct of monetary policy. In Eichengreen and Ghironi (1997a), ECB-Federal Reserve cooperation can be counterproductive from the central banks' perspective owing to the induced adjustments in fiscal policies. Here, cooperation is counterproductive from a player's perspective essentially because it prevents the player from "riding a favorable trade-off" as much as it would without cooperation.

Monetary and Fiscal Policy Interactions

As we have argued, the results obtained assuming that the fiscal authorities passively watch the interactions among central bankers characterize a currency union accompanied by a very tight Stability and Growth Pact that de facto prevents governments from using their fiscal instruments. In such a situation we have shown that a disagreement between the ECOFIN Council and the central bankers on the optimal size of the union may arise simply as a result of the lack of cooperation among EU monetary authorities, and thus quite independently of the consideration that—at least for some time—the ECB could be more credible in a relatively smaller and more homogeneous union.

Would such a disagreement disappear if governments were allowed to use fiscal policy to respond to exogenous shocks? The answer would almost certainly be positive if the two instruments (money and taxes) were set cooperatively. The ECB, however, will be independent, and throughout the EU member states are changing the statutes of their central banks so as to grant them more independence. The appropriate framework thus appears to be one where both inside and outside the currency union central banks and fiscal authorities do not cooperate. We have considered two situations: first, the case in which the ECB and the central banks of the outs cooperate among themselves but do not cooperate with the two European fiscal authorities—and neither with fiscal nor with monetary authorities in the United States, which also are assumed not to cooperate among themselves. We shall then consider the case where all six institutions act noncooperatively.

When fiscal authorities are active players in the game and the same behavioral assumptions of the previous case are maintained, the first-order conditions for the central banks' problem remain unchanged. When these are combined with the conditions for the optimal choice of the fiscal instruments—see Appendix II—we have a system of six equations in six unknowns, whose solution is summarized in Table 3, together with the implied values of endogenous variables and loss functions. Now governments are no longer forced to "stay out of the game," but are still worried about the costs that distortionary taxes impose on the economy.

We present results for two different degrees of fiscal activism, the latter being lower the higher the weight governments attach to the volatility of distortionary taxes in their loss functions. In what follows, we focus on the case of limited fiscal activism, which is closer to the case of rigid fiscal policy studied above, and seems to be more realistic if we want to capture the relative rigidity of fiscal policy.[23]

[23]The reader can interpret the results for the case of more active fiscal policies on the basis of the intuitions provided below.

Table 3. Effects of a Cooperative ERM II with Active Fiscal Policies

	Rigid Fiscal Policies ($\vartheta = 0.2$)		Flexible Fiscal Policies ($\vartheta = 0.8$)	
	Outs' size small ($a = 0.75$)	Outs' size equal to ins' ($a = 0.5$)	Outs' size small ($a = 0.75$)	Outs' size equal to ins' ($a = 0.5$)
Ins' money (m^I)	−1.4353	−1.4034	−0.2204	−0.1907
U.S. money (m^{US})	−1.4557	−1.4340	−0.2418	−0.2221
Nominal outs/euro (e^3)	−0.0171	−0.0084	−0.0156	−0.0074
Ins' taxes (τ^I)	−0.1956	−0.2227	−0.7937	−0.8203
U.S. taxes (τ^{US})	−0.1670	−0.1668	−0.7605	−0.7592
Outs' taxes (τ^O)	−0.3000	−0.2737	−0.8888	−0.8654
Real outs/euro (z^3)	0.0479	0.0234	0.0435	0.0206
Real dollar/euro (z^1)	−0.0209	−0.0374	−0.0235	−0.0401
Real dollar/outs (z^2)	−0.0688	−0.0608	−0.0670	−0.0607
Ins' CPI (q^I)	0.3798	0.3677	0.0932	0.0816
Outs' CPI (q^O)	0.3627	0.3594	0.0776	0.0742
U.S. CPI (q^{US})	0.3986	0.3979	0.1134	0.1132
Ins' employment (n^I)	−1.2233	−1.1845	−0.3106	−0.2728
Outs' employment (n^O)	−1.1070	−1.1270	−0.2049	−0.2227
U.S. employment (n^{US})	−1.2678	−1.2657	−0.3607	−0.3601
Loss ECB	0.1397	0.1310	0.0087	0.0067
Loss ins' government	0.1514	0.1474	0.0980	0.0943
Loss outs' central bank	0.1205	0.1217	0.0048	0.0049
Loss outs' government	0.1476	0.1458	0.0943	0.0930
Loss Federal Reserve	0.1519	0.1514	0.01229	0.01225
Loss U.S. government	0.1574	0.1569	0.1052	0.1048

Following a negative supply shock, all fiscal authorities cut taxes. This happens because, for the parameter values that we have chosen, a tax cut raises employment and output and contributes to stabilize prices.[24] Note that the strategic interaction among European fiscal authorities induces the intra-European exchange rate to be adjusted even if the ECB and the outs' central bank are cooperating with one another—thus deviating from the case in which fiscal policy did not operate (Table 2), which implied a constant intra-European real exchange rate. In all cases optimal policies produce a real depreciation of the outs' currency against the euro (z^3 positive); the magnitude of the real depreciation increases as the relative size of the currency union be-

[24]Remember that a tax cut raises firms' labor demand, while at the same time reducing government spending because of our assumption that the government budget is always balanced. Thus the net effect on output is ambiguous. However, if the interest rate semielasticity of money demand is sufficiently small, a tax cut unambiguously raises output and employment.

comes larger. The point is that, like monetary policymakers have an incentive to export inflation abroad, fiscal authorities have an incentive to export unemployment. Central banks can achieve their goal by appreciating their currencies in real terms. Governments, instead, will export unemployment by trying to engineer a real depreciation. When the central banks are cooperating, only the second type of behavior is at work. Under the assumptions of our exercise, one can show that the outs' government faces a more favorable employment-inflation trade-off than the ins' government, and that the advantage of the outsiders increases as the size of the currency union becomes larger.[25] Hence, consistent with the intuition that policymakers manage to engineer beggar-thy-neighbor policies when they face more favorable trade-offs than their neighbors, the outs' government manages to export unemployment to the ins via real depreciation, the more so the larger the currency union, as it is confirmed by the results on employment. This explains why the equilibrium value of the loss function of ECOFIN increases when the size of the currency union becomes larger.

What seems counterintuitive is that the ECB's loss also increases with the size of the currency union, even if the real appreciation of the euro against the outs' currency becomes larger. Looking at fiscal authorities' behavior is helpful, though. When a increases from 0.5 to 0.75, the outs' government becomes more aggressive. But, like what happened in the case of only monetary interactions in the interplay between the ECB and the outs' central bank, the ins' government reacts by reducing the degree of its fiscal expansion. Because a tax cut stabilizes inflation in our exercises, this ends up inducing higher inflation in the ins' economy even if the ECB goes for a sharper contraction when $a = 0.75$. As a consequence, in this case there is no disagreement between the ECB and ECOFIN on the desired size of the currency union, and *both* EMU authorities prefer the small union outcome.

The outs' government is more aggressive when $a = 0.75$ and achieves a better stabilization of employment than when $a = 0.5$. Nonetheless, in order to do so, it pays the price that a more active fiscal policy implies in terms of higher loss.[26] The employment gain is more than offset by the loss due to more volatile taxes, and the outs' government is better off when the currency union is small. Instead, the outsiders' central bank still prefers the large union outcome, even though inflation is higher in that situation. Even though central banks mainly care about inflation, the gain from a better stabilization of employment when $a = 0.75$ more than offsets the higher inflation loss. Note that the outs' central bank and the ECB cooperatively realign the nominal

[25] Governments' trade-offs were defined in footnote 10.

[26] Remember that the governments' loss function depends also on the volatility of taxation when governments play actively.

exchange rate between the outs' currency and the euro and let the former appreciate against the latter, the more so the larger the currency union. This is entirely consistent with the observed behavior of the real exchange rate: when the outs' currency depreciates in real terms against the euro due to the fiscal authorities' behavior, inflation in the outs' economy tends to rise. This phenomenon is more relevant when the currency union is large, as the outs' government is more aggressive in that case. The ECB and the outs' central bank are now jointly minimizing the respective loss functions, that is, they are jointly stabilizing the respective inflation rates. Thus, the optimal cooperative reaction to the inflationary effect on the outs' economy of the real depreciation of their currency is given by a nominal appreciation intended to stabilize the outs' CPI. The nominal appreciation of the outs' currency against the euro is no longer a successful beggar-thy-neighbor policy allowed by the outs' central bank's more favorable trade-off. Rather, it is the optimal cooperative reaction of the two European central banks to the fiscal policymakers' actions.

What is the role of the United States in this picture?

While intra-EU monetary interactions are cooperative, both monetary and fiscal interactions are noncooperative across the Atlantic. Even if we do not do it here, one can show that under the assumptions of this exercise, both European governments face more favorable trade-offs than the U.S. government, which always faces the same trade-off irrespective of the size of the currency union. Besides, the ins' government's trade-off approaches the U.S. government's as a approaches 1, while the outs' government's trade-off becomes more and more favorable. The consequences of this can be seen in the pattern of transatlantic real exchange rates. The dollar appreciates against both European currencies, so that both European governments manage to export some unemployment to the United States. The real depreciation of the outs' currency against the dollar increases with the size of the currency union, while the real depreciation of the euro decreases, consistent with what the changes in the trade-offs would suggest. In fact, we know that the outs' government becomes more aggressive as a increases, while the ins' government becomes less aggressive. The real appreciation of the dollar is harmful for the U.S. government, but helpful for the Federal Reserve, as it helps stabilize the U.S. CPI at the expense of the European ones. However, it is easy to check that the effective real appreciation of the dollar is larger when $a = 0.5$ than when $a = 0.75$. Thus, in an attempt at reducing the U.S. inflation, the Federal Reserve adopts a sharper contraction in the latter case. This contraction proves itself harmful for U.S. employment and contributes to make the U.S. government worse off when the currency union is large. Notwithstanding a tougher monetary policy, the U.S. CPI is higher when $a = 0.75$ and the Federal Reserve is worse off in that situation, as well.

Finally, we consider the case where none of the authorities cooperate. To compute the solution we go back to the situation in which there is no monetary cooperation, but we maintain an active role for fiscal policies. All players are active in the game and no distortion due to the externalities that they impose on one another is removed. Results are summarized in Table 4. All loss functions are uniformly lower than when fiscal policy cannot be used, even when we compare them with the case of cooperation among European central banks (Table 2), and even in the case where fiscal authorities can only move taxes by a little. The benefits stemming from the ability to use two instruments exceed the inefficiencies introduced by the absence of cooperation. As in the case of no fiscal policy response, the outsiders' central bank is better off in the absence of cooperation than when European central banks coordinate their policies, as the noncooperative regime allows the outsiders' monetary authority to strategically ride its more favorable trade-off. The ECB is correspondingly worse off. Both EMU authorities prefer the small union situation. Observe also that, when fiscal policy is used together with monetary policy, the Federal Reserve and the U.S. government are basically indifferent with respect to the presence or absence of intra-European monetary cooperation (see Tables 3 and 4). This result suggests that, when both policy instruments are available, flexible exchange rates between the United States and Europe provide a good degree of insulation to the U.S. economy with respect to changes in the way European monetary policies are conducted.[27]

Table 5 allows a comparison of the losses of ECOFIN and the ECB across the different policymaking regimes and summarizes some of the main results obtained thus far. When two instruments are available (money and taxes), both ECOFIN and the ECB are better off—even in the case where fiscal authorities move taxes by very little. More important, the conflict between the ECB and ECOFIN over the optimal size of the currency union disappears: for the reason suggested above both prefer a relatively smaller currency union.

Closing Europe with Respect to the United States

In this section we ask to what extent our results on the choices of European policymakers depend on the presence of the United States—that is, were the two Western blocs completely isolated with respect to one another, would European policymakers' preferences over the size of EMU differ? We study this possibility by closing the European economy with respect to the

[27]Ghironi and Giavazzi (1997c) provide a more detailed discussion of this case.

Table 4. Effects of a Noncooperative ERM II with Active Fiscal Policies

	Rigid Fiscal Policies ($\vartheta_1 = 0.2$)			Flexible Fiscal Policies ($\vartheta_1 = 0.8$)		
	Outs' size negligible ($a = 1$)	Outs' size small ($a = 0.75$)	Outs' size equal to ins' ($a = 0.5$)	Outs' size negligible ($a = 1$)	Outs' size small ($a = 0.75$)	Outs' size equal to ins' ($a = 0.5$)
Ins' money (m^I)	−1.5000	−1.4408	−1.4174	−0.2838	−0.2088	−0.1771
U.S. money (m^{US})	−1.5000	−1.4513	−1.4280	−0.2838	−0.2371	−0.2150
Nominal outs/euro (e^3)	−0.2122	−0.1705	−0.1217	−0.0840	−0.0605	−0.0387
Ins' taxes (τ^I)	−0.1676	−0.1976	−0.2269	−0.7631	−0.7914	−0.8187
U.S. taxes (τ^{US})	−0.1676	−0.1671	−0.1668	−0.7631	−0.7603	−0.7589
Outs' taxes (τ^O)	−0.3802	−0.3431	−0.3055	−0.9673	−0.9239	−0.8892
Real outs/euro (z^3)	0.0002	−0.0137	−0.0236	0.0659	0.0394	0.0174
Real dollar/euro (z^1)	0.0000	−0.0352	−0.0586	0.0000	−0.0275	−0.0462
Real dollar/outs (z^2)	−0.0002	−0.0215	−0.0350	−0.0659	−0.0669	−0.0636
Ins' CPI (q^I)	0.3999	0.3886	0.3793	0.1138	0.0972	0.0855
Outs' CPI (q^O)	0.1877	0.2181	0.2577	0.0298	0.0367	0.0470
U.S. CPI (q^{US})	0.3999	0.3986	0.3981	0.1138	0.1133	0.1132
Ins' employment (n^I)	−1.2719	−1.2361	−1.2065	−0.3620	−0.3093	−0.2720
Outs' employment (n^O)	−1.2714	−1.2694	−1.2637	−0.2022	−0.2137	−0.2290
U.S. employment (n^{US})	−1.2719	−1.2679	−1.2660	−0.3620	−0.3606	−0.35997
Loss ECB	0.1529	0.1444	0.1375	0.0124	0.0090	0.0070
Loss ins' government	0.1584	0.1547	0.1530	0.1059	0.0975	0.0939
Loss outs' central bank	0.0967	0.1020	0.1097	0.0024	0.0029	0.0036
Loss outs' government	0.2036	0.1926	0.1817	0.1083	0.1018	0.0980
Loss Federal Reserve	0.1529	0.1519	0.1514	0.0124	0.0123	0.0122
Loss U.S. government	0.1584	0.1574	0.1569	0.1059	0.1051	0.1048

Table 5. Comparison of Losses Under Alternative Policy Regimes

	Loss to ECB		Loss to Ins' Government	
	Outs' size small ($a = 0.75$)	Outs' size equal to ins' ($a = 0.5$)	Outs' size small ($a = 0.75$)	Outs' size equal to ins' ($a = 0.5$)
Noncooperative ERM II, fixed taxes	0.2412	0.2367	1.1196	1.1399
Cooperative ERM II, fixed taxes	0.2206	0.2206	1.0622	1.0622
Cooperative ERM II, active fiscal policies, rigid taxes	0.1397	0.131	0.1514	0.1474
Cooperative ERM II, active fiscal policies, flexible taxes	0.0087	0.0067	0.098	0.0943
Noncooperative ERM II, active fiscal policies, rigid taxes	0.1444	0.1375	0.1547	0.1530
Noncooperative ERM II, active fiscal policies, flexible taxes	0.0090	0.0070	0.0975	0.0939

United States, so that no transatlantic policy spillovers exist and the only strategic interactions are those between the two groups of European countries.

Two assumptions are necessary in order to close the European economy with respect to the United States. The first one is that no transatlantic trade in goods happens, that is, that $b = 0$ in our model.[28] However, the assumption of no trade in goods between Europe and the United States does not prevent U.S. (European) policies from having effects on the European (U.S.) economy. Trade in assets provides a second channel of transmission, which works through the uncovered interest parity conditions and the impact of nominal interest rate changes on the equilibrium in the money markets. A simple way to remove this channel of transmission is to assume that the demand for real money balances in each country is completely inelastic to the nominal interest rate. In this case, although capital mobility remains perfect, economic policy choices have no external effects across the Atlantic. The United States becomes a large economy totally unaffected by European

[28]Although such an extreme value for b is obviously unrealistic, trade flows across the Atlantic are of much less relevance than those occurring inside Europe, and the extreme case we want to study may still be of interest, as we shall see below.

policies, and insiders' and outsiders' choices affect only the two European economies.[29]

Computing the equilibrium for the noncooperative ERM II regime with fixed taxes leads to the results summarized in Table 6.[30] The first thing to be observed is that the conflict of interest between ECOFIN and the ECB over the dimension of the currency union vanishes: both authorities are monotonically better off when the size of the union increases. In the case of the ECB, this is a consequence of the CPI being a decreasing function of a. As the currency union gets larger, the outsiders' central bank becomes more aggressive—consistent with the results obtained above; however, imported inflation from the outs is less relevant for the ins than when the size of the union is relatively small, since imports from the outs decrease with their size.[31] Consequently, the degree of monetary contraction by the ECB decreases as the union becomes larger, being equal to the Federal Reserve's contraction when $a = 1$. However, in contrast to what happened in Table 1, the ins' CPI decreases monotonically as the union gets larger, indicating that even if the monetary contraction becomes milder, the effect of lower imported inflation from the outs dominates that of less producer-price-index stabilization, thus allowing the ECB to achieve a better outcome in terms of the CPI.[32] ECOFIN benefits from the milder monetary contraction when the union gets larger, as this directly implies a smaller employment loss.

[29]A zero value for the interest rate semielasticity of money demand—λ—is the standard assumption of many models of international policy interactions. (See Canzoneri and Henderson, 1991, for an example.) It implies, however, that economic policies have no effect on output and employment abroad if exchange rates are flexible, and it prevents a negative supply side shock from causing unemployment. Moreover, setting $\lambda = 0$ not only insulates the European and U.S. blocs, when the assumption is combined with $b = 0$, but also removes a channel of transmission of *intra*-European policy spillovers. Thus, the situation that we are going to consider for the two European regions differs from that of a two-country model in which both channels of transmission matter. Nonetheless, the results that follow about the two European regions—which correspond to those that would be obtained in a simple two-country model in which externalities only originated from trade in goods—allow us to make explicit comparisons between the situation in which there are transatlantic policy spillovers and that in which the two Western blocs are completely closed with respect to each other.

[30]The reduced forms for this case are presented in Appendix III. See Table 1 for the corresponding results in the presence of transatlantic spillovers.

[31]The effective real exchange rate of the insiders is now given by $z^I = (1 - a)z^3$. When $a = 1$, this is obviously zero. When a increases from 0.5 to 0.75, the effective depreciation of the euro with respect to the outs' currency diminishes from $-0.0415x$ to $-0.0268x$.

[32]Under the assumptions of this exercise, the reduced form for the insiders' PPI—see Appendix II—reduces to $p^I = \alpha n^I + \tau^I + x = \alpha m^I + (1 - \alpha)\tau^I + x$. Since an analogous expression holds for the United States, one immediately finds the expressions for the reduced form parameters A $(= \alpha)$ and E $(= 1 - \alpha)$. When a increases from 0.5 to 0.75 and 1, p^I increases from $0.4689x$ to $0.4764x$ and $0.4901x$.

Table 6. Effects of a Noncooperative ERM II with Fixed Taxes and a Closed Europe (b = 0, λ = 0)

	Outs' Size Negligible ($a = 1$)	Outs' Size Small ($a = 0.75$)	Outs' Size Equal to Ins' ($a = 0.5$)
Ins' money (m^I)	−1.4997	−1.5398	−1.5621
U.S. money (m^{US})	−1.4997	−1.4997	−1.4997
Nominal outs/euro (e^3)	−0.2246	−0.1953	−0.1517
Real outs/euro (z^3)	−0.1231	−0.1071	−0.0831
Real dollar/euro (z^1)	0.0000	−0.0199	−0.0308
Real dollar/outs (z^2)	0.1231	0.0872	0.0523
Ins' CPI (q^I)	0.4901	0.5032	0.5105
Outs' CPI (q^O)	0.2655	0.3079	0.3587
U.S. CPI (q^{US})	0.4901	0.4901	0.4901
Ins' employment (n^I)	−1.4997	−1.5398	−1.5621
Outs' employment (n^O)	−1.7981	−1.7994	−1.7637
U.S. employment (n^{US})	−1.4997	−1.4997	−1.4997
Loss ECB	0.2205	0.2325	0.2393
Loss ins' government	1.0241	1.0797	1.1111
Loss outs' central bank	0.1933	0.2045	0.2134
Loss outs' government	1.4585	1.4618	1.4062
Loss Federal Reserve	0.2205	0.2205	0.2205
Loss U.S. government	1.0241	1.0241	1.0241

We have observed above that our exercise does not exactly reproduce what would happen in a two-country model in which both channels of international transmission (goods and assets markets) matter. However, the results in Table 6 show that, in the framework of our three-country model, allowing for the presence of transatlantic monetary spillovers is crucial to obtain a conflict of interests between the ECB and the ECOFIN Council.[33] In the following section we reintroduce transatlantic spillovers and we compare the results under the asymmetric intra-EU exchange rate regime analyzed thus far with those obtained under a symmetric regime. The discussion is based on the theoretical results summarized in the analytical framework and clarifies how the presence of the United States is important in determining the results presented in the section on monetary policy interactions.

As in Table 1, the outs' central bank is always better off when a increases, thanks to its more aggressive behavior and the consequently lower CPI.[34] In

[33]Ghironi and Giavazzi (1997b) show that indeed the result also holds in a two-country model in which both channels of transmission are at work.

[34]The intuition for why the central bank of the outsiders is more aggressive when $b = \lambda = 0$ than in Table 1 is explained in Ghironi and Giavazzi (1997c).

Table 1, however, the outs' government monotonically preferred a small currency union in Europe rather than a large one. This was intuitively explained by the lower employment loss induced by less aggressive exchange rate policies. Here, instead, even though $a = 0.5$ remains the best outcome for the outs' government, the situation in which the outsiders are only a small open economy ($a = 1$) is preferred to that of large union coupled with still significant outs ($a = 0.75$). Even though the outsiders' central bank's policy is more aggressive when $a = 1$, the milder monetary contraction by the ECB in that situation ends up inducing a smaller employment loss for the outs than when $a = 0.75$. On the contrary, when $a = 0.5$, the reduced aggressiveness of the outs' central bank prevails on the more contractionary stance of the ECB in affecting the outsiders' employment. Hence, under the assumptions of this exercise, one would expect the government of the outsiders to oppose the choice of a large rather than a small currency union, but to be in favor of a union encompassing all EU countries except a very small country rather than a large union with still significant outs.

The U.S. economy is obviously indifferent with respect to what happens in Europe. Note that both U.S. authorities are better off under the assumptions of this exercise than when transatlantic policy spillovers are present. If anything, this suggests that the U.S. government and the Federal Reserve may be increasingly in favor of a closure of the U.S. economy with respect to Europe, with this conclusion being stronger the smaller the size of the currency union. In the case in which $a = 1$, CPI inflation in the United States and in the currency union is higher than in the presence of transatlantic spillovers, but, even if the weight attached to employment in the central banks' loss functions is much smaller than that attached to inflation, the employment gain from the closure more than offsets the increased inflation loss, making closure attractive not only for the United States but also for European authorities. The lower unemployment more than offsets the higher inflation loss for the Federal Reserve also when the outs are nonnegligible. The only case in which a policymaker prefers the situation in which transatlantic spillovers exist is given by the ECB when the currency union is small. In that case a higher inflation loss, when cross-Atlantic spillovers do not exist, more than offsets the employment gain and induces the ECB to prefer the situation in which policies have effects on both sides of the Atlantic.

Our results suggest a reason why policymakers in Europe and in the United States may find it attractive to adopt unmodeled policies aimed at removing transatlantic monetary spillovers. By closing the U.S. and the European economies with respect to one another, policymakers remove the source of the contractionary bias that affects noncooperative transatlantic monetary interactions when policies have effects on the other side of the ocean. The outcome—in terms of less contractionary policies—is similar to the one that would be achieved in the presence of transatlantic monetary cooperation.[35] However, the implicit "desirability of two isolated Western blocs" that we find for most players must not be overstated. On the one hand, it may be easier for the involved authorities to improve their welfare by explicitly coordinating their policies rather than by working to close the respective economies. On the other hand, our model is an extremely simplified description of reality: even though under the assumptions of this section policies aimed at closing the two blocs with respect to one another would be mutually beneficial in most cases, in a more realistic setting, in which, for example, trade policy is explicitly considered, policies to close the U.S. and European blocs may well have welfare-decreasing effects also, due to the retaliations that aggressive trade policies are likely to cause.[36] Besides, even without considering trade policy, it may be possible that, if fiscal policymakers are active players in the game, conflicts of interests among the players over the benefits from "closure" of the two Western blocs or transatlantic monetary cooperation become relevant.[37]

[35]Although different from that and also from the outcome achievable under a scheme of global monetary cooperation. The intuition for the difference between "closure" as we have modeled it and transatlantic monetary cooperation runs as follows. Each country's policy affects the other countries' endogenous variables through two channels of international transmission when transatlantic spillovers are allowed: trade in goods and trade in assets. Transatlantic monetary cooperation without intra-European cooperation would internalize transatlantic externalities, leaving *both* intra-European externalities at work. Setting $b = \lambda = 0$ removes both channels of international transmission across the Atlantic, but also eliminates the intra-European externality going through the financial markets, thus removing one of the sources of inefficiency in noncooperative intra-EU policymaking as well. Besides, there would be the problem of how to solve for the equilibrium with transatlantic cooperation but without intra-EU cooperation in our model. Conceptually, we would have two coalitions of players that play Nash against each other. But there would be one player—the Federal Reserve—which is a member of both coalitions. Thus, in a sense, there would be a player that is playing Nash *against* itself, and this causes the nonexistence of an equilibrium. It can also be shown that "closure" is different from global monetary cooperation. The difference is again given by the role of intra-European externalities: removing transatlantic externalities eliminates the source of the contractionary bias in *transatlantic* monetary interactions—which is already welfare improving for all players in most cases—but does not remove *completely* the inefficiency of noncooperative policymaking between the two European monetary authorities, as it is done by global monetary cooperation. Note that, from the outs' central bank's perspective, this inefficiency is a source of gains, because it allows the achievement of a lower inflation through aggressive exchange rate policies. (Ghironi and Giavazzi, 1997c, provide more details on this point.)

[36]Basevi, Delbono, and Denicolò (1990) analyze a formal model of monetary and trade interactions. For some contributions to the debate on trade and currency areas, see Federal Reserve Bank of Kansas City (1991).

[37]See Eichengreen and Ghironi (1997a) for a discussion of disagreements between central banks and governments on the desirability of transatlantic monetary cooperation.

As the results of Table 6 are sufficient to make the point that "the presence of the United States does make a difference" in our model, we do not discuss here the results of the simulated game when intra-EU monetary cooperation and fiscal activism are considered. It is possible to show that, when monetary cooperation is coupled with (limited) fiscal activism, all players agree on the desirability of a small currency union under the assumptions of this section. The results of the simulations are available from the authors upon request.

Symmetric Exchange Rate Regime in Europe

We now reintroduce transatlantic policy spillovers and compare the results obtained so far, under the assumption of an asymmetric monetary regime in Europe, with the case of flexible exchange rates: both the ECB and the central bank of the outsiders control the respective money supplies, and the intra-EU exchange rate is determined endogenously and left free to float. As mentioned in the introduction, such a regime is the relevant alternative to the policymakers' plan to set up a new EMS linking insiders and outsiders.[38]

Results for the noncooperative monetary game when fiscal policies are fixed are summarized in Table 7. When we compare them with those reported in Table 1, for the corresponding case of an asymmetric monetary regime, we immediately see that once again—like when we had assumed away all transatlantic policy spillovers—the conflict of interests between the ECB and the ECOFIN Council disappears. Both authorities monotonically prefer a large union to a small one. ECOFIN's preference for the large union is intuitively justified by the behavior of employment as a varies. Instead, the ECB turns out to be better off when inflation is relatively high than when it is lowest ($a = 0.5$).

In order to interpret the results for the alternative intra-EU regimes and to stress the role of the United States in our model, it is important to refer to the results summarized in the theoretical framework about the trade-offs facing the various policymakers. We know from the discussion in that section that, under the symmetric intra-EU exchange rate regime, when the outs' size is nonnegligible ($a < 1$), the insiders face a more favorable trade-off than the United States. Nonetheless, the ECB ends up being worse off than the Federal Reserve, and this happens notwithstanding the fact that consumer price inflation is smaller in the monetary union than in the United States ($q^I < q^{US}$). The crucial point is that the ECB, which has to cope with the impact of the outs' central bank aggressive policy when $a < 1$, "rides" its more favorable trade-off with respect to the Federal Reserve's much more aggressively, the more so the smaller a, in a successful attempt at exporting inflation to the United States via real appreciation of the euro against the dollar. However, in doing so, the ECB imposes an employment loss to the ins' economy, which

[38]The debate mainly focuses on an EMS-style arrangement versus a flexible exchange rate regime coupled with inflation targeting. Here, in order to focus on the role of the exchange rate regime in affecting the results, rather than assuming rigid inflation targeting rules, we maintain the assumption that central banks choose their instruments to minimize loss functions in which a much larger weight is attached to inflation than to unemployment. The implications of rigid inflation targeting are discussed by Persson and Tabellini (1996). Frankel (1989) analyzes alternative rules for the conduct of monetary policy.

Table 7. Effects of a Noncooperative Monetary Game with Fixed Taxes and a Symmetric Intra-EU Regime

	Outs' Size Negligible ($a = 1$)	Outs' Size Small ($a = 0.75$)	Outs' Size Equal to Ins' ($a = 0.5$)
Ins' money (m^I)	−1.8423	−2.0955	−2.2497
Outs' money (m^O)	−2.2532	−2.3023	−2.2497
U.S. money (m^{US})	−1.8423	−1.8619	−1.8685
Real outs/euro (z^3)	−0.1168	−0.0588	0.0000
Real dollar/euro (z^1)	0.0000	−0.0138	0.3810
Real dollar/outs (z^2)	0.1168	0.0726	0.3810
Ins' CPI (q^I)	0.4804	0.4272	0.3735
Outs' CPI (q^O)	0.2674	0.3200	0.3735
U.S. CPI (q^{US})	0.4804	0.4818	0.4823
Ins' employment (n^I)	−1.5281	−1.7195	−1.8315
Outs' employment (n^O)	−1.8111	−1.8620	−1.8315
U.S. employment (n^{US})	−1.5281	−1.5324	−1.5339
Loss ECB	0.2206	0.2230	0.2305
Loss ins' government	1.0623	1.3397	1.5164
Loss outs' central bank	0.1962	0.2194	0.2305
Loss outs' government	1.4797	1.5653	1.5164
Loss Federal Reserve	0.2206	0.2219	0.2223
Loss U.S. government	1.0623	1.0683	1.0704

more than offsets the inflation gain, even if the weight attached to employment in the central banks' loss functions is much smaller than that attached to inflation. As we move from the small currency union toward the situation in which the outs are negligible, the ins' trade-off approaches that of the United States, and the incentive for the ECB to "ride" aggressively a more favorable trade-off with respect to the Federal Reserve's is removed. Even if q^I rises, the ECB is made better off by the relevant employment gain.

When the intra-EU exchange rate regime was asymmetric and significant outs existed (Table 1), the ECB preferred a small union because, facing the same trade-off as the United States irrespective of the union's size, the ins' central bank had a smaller incentive to dump the outs' aggressive behavior to the U.S. economy. As a consequence of this, the ECB's monetary stance was always less contractionary than in Table 7 and, as we saw, when the union was large, the milder monetary contraction ended up destabilizing the PPI. With a symmetric exchange rate regime in Europe, the ECB prefers the large union for exactly the opposite reason: facing a more favorable trade-off than the United States, the ins' monetary authority has a much stronger incentive to "ride" it aggressively in order to export to the United States the inflation it imports from the outs—the more so the smaller the currency union—but this has destabilizing consequences on employment that outweigh the inflation gain.[39] Note that, as it should have been expected, the intra-European exchange rate regime is irrelevant when $a = 1$—in that case, the results in Tables 1 and 7 are identical. When the outsiders are negligible, the monetary arrangement governing intra-EU interactions is irrelevant also from the outs' perspective because in that case the trade-offs faced by *all* authorities do not change across exchange rate regimes in Europe.

If the outs' are nonnegligible and the intra-EU regime is symmetric, their central bank prefers a large rather than a small union—as shown in Table 1 —because in that situation it achieves a better stabilization of the CPI, which offsets the employment loss due to a more contractionary stance. The central bank of the outsiders is more aggressive when $a = 0.75$ than when $a = 1$, even though its trade-off is better in the latter case. Still, the outs' central bank achieves a better outcome in terms of the CPI when $a = 1$, and suffers a smaller employment loss than when the outs are nonnegligible. This is an example of a situation in which, faced with a more favorable trade-off, the policymaker refrains from "riding it" very aggressively, optimally trading control of inflation for employment stabilization. When the intra-EU exchange rate regime is symmetric and the outs' size is negligible, the outs can thus achieve the same outcome as under the ERM II regime without having to increase the contractionary character of their policy with respect to the case $a = 0.75$.[40] Note that when $a = 0.75$, the outs' CPI is lower under the symmetric regime than under the asymmetric one, but this reduction in the CPI is achieved at the cost of a relevant employment loss, which ends up making the outs' central bank worse off under the symmetric regime.

---

[39]This argument is consistent with the pattern of the dollar-euro real exchange rate that we observe in our simulations: the dollar appreciates in real terms against the euro under the ERM II regime, but it depreciates under the symmetric regime, when the ECB implements a much more aggressive monetary policy vis-à-vis the Federal Reserve. Besides, the results of this exercise seem to suggest that the potential gains from "approximating transatlantic cooperation via isolation of the two Western blocs" could be bigger when both European central banks control the respective money supplies, as this induces more contractionary transatlantic interactions than those in Table 1.

[40]The intuition for this result lies in the different characteristics of the alternative exchange rate regimes in Europe. As the reader can check by comparing the reduced-form equations under the two regimes, when the managed exchange rate regime is implemented in Europe, owing to the endogeneity constraint on m^O, the reduction in the ins' monetary contraction going from $a = 0.75$ to $a = 1$ has a *harmful* impact on the outs' CPI. As a consequence, the outs' central bank optimally reacts by strengthening its contractionary stance. When the endogeneity constraint on m^O is removed and the intra-European monetary arrangement is symmetric, going from $a = 0.75$ to $a = 1$, the less contractionary policy by the ECB is *beneficial* in terms of stabilizing q^O—and m^I has a larger impact on it. Consequently, the central bank of the outsiders reacts optimally by loosening its stance.

The previous observations make it clear why the government of the outsiders considers being a "small open economy" the best situation under a symmetric regime, but would choose the small union outcome rather than the large union. In Tables 1 and 6, $a = 0.5$ was the best possible outcome for the outs' government, as explained above. As we go through our exercises, $a = 1$ rises from the bottom to the top position in the ranking of the outs' government's preferences.[41] The change between the ERM II regime with and without transatlantic externalities has been motivated in the previous section, whereas the difference between the asymmetric and the symmetric regimes with transatlantic spillovers is intuitively explained by the outs' central bank behavior. With $a = 0.5$ there is no way for the central bank of the outsiders to actually export inflation to the ins, given the completely symmetric positions of the two European central banks. Thus, although the contractionary bias of noncooperative policies still exists, the monetary stance of the outs' central bank is less contractionary than when $a = 0.75$, when the central bank can actually take advantage of a more favorable trade-off than the ins' and does it aggressively. When a rises from 0.75 to 1, the outsiders' employment-inflation trade-off improves further, as it happened under the asymmetric regime, but the central bank manages to achieve the same outcome as under that regime by means of a less contractionary policy than when $a = 0.75$ and only slightly more contractionary than when $a = 0.5$. Combined with the ECB's and the Federal Reserve's less contractionary policies—motivated by the fact that their trade-offs are now equal—this contributes to give the best employment outcome for the outs' economy when $a = 1$, contrary to what happened under the asymmetric regime.

Finally some remarks on the U.S. authorities. In contrast to the ECB, the Federal Reserve's ranking of preferences when the intra-EU regime is symmetric is driven by the inflation outcome. The U.S. central bank considers $a = 1$ the best possible situation, but would prefer a large union over a small one when the outs are a significant entity. Hence, when $a < 1$, there is a preference reversal with respect to what happened when the ERM II regime was implemented in Europe. Again, the results summarized in the analytical framework help us understand what happens. Under the ERM II regime, both the ECB and the Federal Reserve always face identical trade-offs, and both suffer from the outs' aggressive behavior when $a = 0.75$. When the intra-EU regime is asymmetric, the ECB does not have the possibility of exploiting a more favorable trade-off when the ins' size is smaller than that of the United States. Instead, if the exchange rate regime in Europe is symmetric and the

[41]Letting $>$ denote "preferred to" and omitting the *a*s, under the ERM II regime, the ranking of the outs' government preferences was $0.5 > 0.75 > 1$; under "closure" of the two Western blocs, it was $0.5 > 1 > 0.75$; and under the symmetric regime we have $1 > 0.5 > 0.75$.

outs are nonnegligible, the ECB faces a more favorable trade-off than the Federal Reserve, the more so the smaller the currency union. As we have noted above, a consequence of this is that the ECB's attitude toward the U.S. monetary authority in dumping on it the consequences of noncooperative policies within Europe is much more aggressive when $a = 0.5$ than when $a = 0.75$. Besides, as it happened under the ERM II regime, the outs' central bank always faces a better trade-off than the Federal Reserve, and it faces the same trade-off as the ECB's when $a = 0.5$. Even though the trade-off faced by the outs' worsens as a changes from 0.75 to 0.5, when the intra-EU exchange rate regime is symmetric, the overall monetary stance of Europe toward the United States—measured by $[am^I + (1 - a)m^O]$, where $m^I(m^O)$ denotes money in the monetary union (outs)—is more aggressive when the currency union is small. When $a = 0.75$, the ECB's policy is less contractionary, while the outs' central bank is more aggressive. Combining these observations with the fact that, as the reader can check, the effect of m^I on q^{US} is larger when $a = 0.75$ and the impact of m^O is larger when $a = 0.5$ explains why the U.S. central bank suffers a bigger loss in the latter situation.[42]

Thanks to the change in the Federal Reserve's ranking of preferences, both the monetary authority and the U.S. government share the same ranking of preferences when the intra-European monetary arrangement is symmetric—and no cross-regime preference-reversal happens for the U.S. government. The monetary contraction implemented by the Federal Reserve is tougher the smaller the currency union, reacting to the policies implemented by the two European central banks. As a consequence, even though the Federal Reserve does not achieve the goal of having lowest inflation when the union is smallest, the employment loss increases as the size of the currency union decreases, and the U.S. government monotonically prefers a large union outcome rather than the small union case.

What would happen if the two European central banks cooperated with one another in the game in which only monetary policies are used actively? The answer is straightforward, as we know from the section on monetary policy interactions. Results for the U.S. and insiders' authorities would coincide with those obtained in the absence of cooperation with $a = 1$, while the outs' variables and losses would be "driven" to the same values as for the United States and the ins' ones in the $a = 1$ with no cooperation case. No exchange rate change would be observed. Consequently, policymakers in the United States and in the insider countries would favor monetary cooperation inside Europe, analogously to what happened under the asymmetric exchange rate regime of

[42]We remark that the key in driving the result is the change in the position of the ins' employment-inflation trade-off with respect to the U.S. one, the outs' trade-off being unchanged across intra-EU regimes.

the monetary policy interaction discussion. Instead, a conflict of interests would arise between the outsiders' government and central bank if $a = 0.75$. The former would like European central banks to cooperate, as this would greatly reduce its unemployment loss. But the latter would be prevented from using the exchange rate as a strategic device to stabilize inflation, and would suffer from a larger loss.

Tables 8 and 9 describe the outcome when (limited) fiscal activism is introduced, in the case of a symmetric monetary regime with and without cooperation, respectively.

As in the section on monetary and fiscal policy interactions, adding active fiscal policies as stabilizing devices against the impact of the shock has a welfare improving effect for all players. In the case of monetary cooperation, since the intra-EU exchange rate regime is symmetric, if $a = 0.5$, even if fiscal externalities are not internalized, the euro-outs exchange rate does not move because optimal policies are identical for both the ins' and the outs' policymakers. The exchange rate between insiders and outsiders does move when

Table 8. Cooperative Monetary Game in EU, Limited Fiscal Activism, Symmetric Intra-EU Regime

	Outs' Size Small ($a = 0.75$)	Outs' Size Equal to Ins' ($a = 0.5$)
Ins' money (m^I)	−1.4471	−1.4294
Outs' money (m^O)	−1.4463	−1.4294
U.S. money (m^{US})	−1.4638	−1.4519
Ins' taxes (τ^I)	−0.1973	−0.2263
Outs' taxes (τ^O)	−0.2553	−0.2263
U.S. taxes (τ^{US})	−0.1671	−0.1670
Real outs/euro (z^3)	0.0265	0.0000
Real dollar/euro (z^1)	−0.0203	−0.0358
Real dollar/outs (z^2)	−0.0468	−0.0358
Ins' CPI (q^I)	0.3824	0.3734
Outs' CPI (q^O)	0.3728	0.3734
U.S. CPI (q^{US})	0.3988	0.3985
Ins' employment (n^I)	−1.2246	−1.1877
Outs' employment (n^O)	−1.1602	−1.1877
U.S. employment (n^{US})	−1.2685	−1.2674
Loss ECB	0.1408	0.1333
Loss ins' government	0.1520	0.1488
Loss outs' central bank	0.1299	0.1333
Loss outs' government	0.1486	0.1488
Loss Federal Reserve	0.1520	0.1518
Loss U.S. government	0.1576	0.1573

Table 9. Noncooperative Monetary Game, Limited Fiscal Activism, Symmetric Intra-EU Regime

	Outs' Size Negligible ($a = 1$)	Outs' Size Small ($a = 0.75$)	Outs' Size Equal to Ins' ($a = 0.5$)
Ins' money (m^I)	−1.5000	−1.6083	−1.6941
Outs' money (m^O)	−1.8401	−1.7721	−1.6941
U.S. money (m^{US})	−1.5000	−1.4587	−1.4443
Ins' taxes (τ^I)	−0.1676	−0.2148	−0.2588
Outs' taxes (τ^O)	−0.3300	−0.2981	−0.2588
U.S. taxes (τ^{US})	−0.1676	−0.1673	−0.1671
Real outs/euro (z^3)	−0.0228	−0.0087	0.0000
Real dollar/euro (z^1)	0.0000	−0.0218	−0.0268
Real dollar/outs (z^2)	0.0228	−0.0131	−0.0268
Ins' CPI (q^I)	0.3999	0.3332	0.2789
Outs' CPI (q^O)	0.1960	0.2341	0.2789
U.S. CPI (q^{US})	0.3999	0.3991	0.3988
Ins' employment (n^I)	−1.2719	−1.3413	−1.3675
Outs' employment (n^O)	−1.3272	−1.3623	−1.3675
U.S. employment (n^{US})	−1.2719	−1.2695	−1.2685
Loss ECB	0.1529	0.1399	0.1285
Loss ins' government	0.1584	0.1815	0.1959
Loss outs' central bank	0.1053	0.1175	0.1285
Loss outs' government	0.2025	0.2031	0.1959
Loss Federal Reserve	0.1529	0.1523	0.1520
Loss U.S. government	0.1584	0.1578	0.1576

$a = 0.75$, in which case optimal policies differ. Insiders' authorities prefer a small rather than a large union and the same is true for U.S. policymakers. Instead, the outsiders' central bank and government both prefer a large rather than a small union. These results are analogous to those presented in Table 3 for the case of an asymmetric regime in Europe. We leave it to the reader to interpret them on the basis of the intuitions provided throughout the paper.

All policymakers are better off when governments can use fiscal policy to react to exogenous shocks, even in the absence of monetary cooperation (Table 9). In this case we observe again a conflict of interests between ECOFIN and the ECB on the desired size of the European currency union: the ECB prefers a small union, while ECOFIN prefers a large one. This is different from what happened under the ERM II regime in Europe (Table 4), in which case both the insiders' authorities preferred the small union outcome. The difference in the ranking of ECOFIN's preferences with respect to Table 4 is due to the fact that, under the symmetric regime, the employment loss increases as the size of the union decreases, while the opposite happened under the ERM II regime. When $a = 0.5$ and the exchange rate regime is symmetric, the European authorities face identical employment-inflation trade-offs. As the size of the outs increases from $a = 1$ to $a = 0.5$, the trade-off facing the ECB becomes steeper. The symmetry between ins and outs that is achieved when $a = 0.5$ induces the ECB to behave more aggressively, in contrast to what happened in the ERM II case of Table 4, with contractionary consequences on the ins' economy. The small union case represents the best case for the outs' government, whereas the central bank monotonically prefers a large union. Both U.S. policymakers favor the small union case over the large one. Again, we leave it to the reader to go deeper into the interpretation of the results presented above.[43]

Conclusions

In this paper we have addressed the issue of the optimal size of the European currency union, concentrating our attention on the effects of changes in the size of EMU on the interactions among fiscal and monetary authorities in Europe, and between Europe and the rest of the world. We have argued that explicitly considering the presence of the rest of the world—which we have called "the United States"—is important in understanding policymakers' incentives and behavior. In our analysis, we have always maintained the same assumptions about the way European and U.S. authorities interact with each other, namely, noncooperatively and under a flexible exchange rate regime.[44]

Consider the institutional setup that, we believe, will most likely characterize the future working of EMU, at least initially: frozen fiscal policies and noncooperative monetary policies under an ERM II regime in Europe. In this setup, the view that central bankers would prefer the currency union to be relatively small, while ECOFIN would prefer it to be relatively larger, is confirmed by our analysis—provided the size of the outsiders is nonnegligible. The only way to obtain an agreement between ECOFIN and the ECB on the desired size of the currency union is either by convincing the central banks of the ins and outs to cooperate (in which case the size of the currency union becomes irrelevant), or by allowing governments to actively use fiscal policy in response to exogenous shocks. But the outsider central bank stands to lose

[43]A thorough discussion of the results obtained when fiscal authorities are active players in the game would require references to the trade-offs facing the governments under the symmetric intra-EU regime. We refrain from exploring the issue here for reasons of brevity.

[44]Alternative transatlantic arrangements are studied in Ghironi (1993) and Eichengreen and Ghironi (1997a and 1997b). In both those analyses, EMU is assumed to encompass the whole EU, so that there are no outs. Those models, however, allow for the absence of fiscal cooperation within the currency union.

from cooperating with the ECB—independent of the degree of fiscal policy activism and of the size of the outsiders relative to the insiders. Moreover, it always prefers the currency union to be relatively large because this is the situation in which it can best exploit its ability to export inflation to the insiders by aggressively "riding" the more favorable output-inflation trade-off it faces. This suggests a potentially important reason (which may run against different arguments in favor of joining the single currency) why some states may be unwilling to join the currency union and why, once they are out, their central banks may be unwilling to enter a cooperative agreement with the ECB.

Table 10 shows the preference rankings of the various players over the size of the European currency union for the case of noncooperative monetary interactions with fixed taxes in the three different environments that we have analyzed: ERM II, closed Western blocs, and flexible exchange rates in Europe. In the table, a is omitted to save on notation, and $>$ denotes "preferred to," whereas $\approx$ denotes "indifferent to."

For almost all players and in all the three different settings that we have analyzed, the situation in which the currency union in Europe encompasses the whole EU except for a small entity is the best outcome. This result parallels that obtained by Alesina and Grilli (1994), though in a different model and under different assumptions. The one authority that does not always prefer that outcome is the outs' government, which ranks $a = 1$ first only when the exchange rate regime in Europe is symmetric for the reasons discussed above. Note, however, that preference rankings between $a = 0.5$ and $a = 0.75$ vary across authorities.

Potential conflicts of interests can arise within one country over the optimal size of the currency union. Not only do we find a conflict between

Table 10. Summary of Preference Rankings

	ECB	Ins' Government
Noncooperative ERM II	$1 > 0.5 > 0.75$	$1 > 0.75 > 0.5$
Closed Western blocs	$1 > 0.75 > 0.5$	$1 > 0.75 > 0.5$
Symmetric regime in Europe	$1 > 0.75 > 0.5$	$1 > 0.75 > 0.5$
	Outs' Central Bank	Outs' Government
Noncooperative ERM II	$1 > 0.75 > 0.5$	$0.5 > 0.75 > 1$
Closed Western blocs	$1 > 0.75 > 0.5$	$0.5 > 1 > 0.75$
Symmetric regime in Europe	$1 > 0.75 > 0.5$	$1 > 0.5 > 0.75$
	Federal Reserve	U.S. Government
Noncooperative ERM II	$1 > 0.5 > 0.75$	$1 > 0.75 > 0.5$
Closed Western blocs	$1 \approx 0.75 \approx 0.5$	$1 \approx 0.75 \approx 0.5$
Symmetric regime in Europe	$1 > 0.75 > 0.5$	$1 > 0.75 > 0.5$

Note: In this table, a is omitted, and $>$ denotes "preferred to," whereas $\approx$ denotes "indifferent to."

ECOFIN and the ECB under the ERM II regime in Europe, but also, while the central bank of the outsiders always prefers $a = 0.75$ to $a = 0.5$, the opposite holds for the outs' government. Given a significant size for the outs, the latter would always choose a small rather than a large currency union. Also, the Federal Reserve and the U.S. government may disagree over the optimal size of the European currency union if an EMS-style regime were to be implemented in Europe, with the Federal Reserve preferring a small union and the United States a large one if $a < 1$. Nonetheless, even if U.S. policymakers will be interested spectators of what happens in Europe and transatlantic interactions do affect all policymakers' welfare, it does not seem likely that European policymakers will condition their choices about the size of the currency union in 1998 and in the following years on U.S. authorities' preferences.

As our model suggests, in 1998, when the initial size of the currency union is to be decided, strategic interactions among players could justify considerable strain in the choice process. This may be true irrespective of monetary and fiscal policymakers having different preferences across countries. The outcome will depend on the relative bargaining power of the various involved policymakers as well as on other political considerations that our model does not capture. The institutional framework within which the policymakers interact will play a crucial role in this process.

Note that the outs' government always prefers a small rather than a large union, when a is not 1. This observation suggests that, if we explicitly allow for a multiplicity of outsiders' governments, rather than a single one that has "preferences over the size of its country," in our framework, all of them would want to stay out of the union when it comes to life, because the small union outcome is more attractive to them. As a consequence, in the situation we have analyzed, it would be hard to find outs' governments actually willing to join the union either from its beginning or after that time. Resistance by outsiders' governments to join could lead to an initially relatively small currency union, thus meeting the preferences of the ECB under an ERM II regime.[45] The intuition cannot be overstated, however. The conclusion of our model is based on the assumption that the outs act as a unified bloc, which is analogous to assuming that all outs' central banks cooperate with each other and all outs' governments do the same. Explicitly considering the possibility of noncoopera-

[45]Similarly, the model provides some intuition about what could happen if a multiplicity of outsiders' central banks were considered. For example, one could argue that, in the framework of our model, even if the outs' central bank always prefers the union to be large, the small union outcome may obtain also as a "perverse" result of each of the individual outs' central banks' incentive to be the lucky small outsider reaping the benefits of a relatively more favorable trade-off. The same incentive may have destabilizing implications for cooperative arrangements among outs' central banks.

tive strategic interactions within the group of the outsiders may significantly affect the results, and would allow a better analysis of the problem.[46] We leave these issues for further research on the topic.

The previous observations lead us naturally to a second set of remarks. After the initial size of the currency union has been chosen, the natural evolution of the union itself as dictated by the Maastricht Treaty would be its enlargement over time to cover the whole EU. Our result that $a = 1$ is the best outcome for most players—including the United States!—lends support to the advocates of the desirability of such outcome. Suppose that potential conflicts between the ECB and the ECOFIN Council either are not an issue or are resolved in favor of the enlargement option.[47] Still, the results of our simulations suggest that the remaining outs' governments may not find joining the union attractive.

The analysis of our paper assumes that all players approach 1998 and the subsequent period starting from equal initial conditions, their economies being in equilibrium, and addresses the topic from the limited perspective of the optimal reactions to a supply side disturbance. Reality is much more complicated, though. In 1998 European countries will be characterized by different economic situations. Outs may be outs either because they are not attracted by the perspective of joining the union or because they are not accepted in it, or for both reasons. It is plausible that most outsiders' economies will be classified as relatively weak or plagued by significant disequilibria. If their governments (or their central banks) do not have strong incentives to join the European currency union—and our model suggests potential reasons why this could happen—the process of enlargement of the union envisioned in the Maastricht Treaty could prove itself slower and more conflictive than optimists normally argue.

One of the interpretations of how the process of European integration in different fields has evolved over time has to do with the idea of positive

[46]Recall that we have also implicitly assumed that all ins' governments cooperate within the ECOFIN Council, but this need not be the case.

[47]At least in the first few years after the beginning of Stage III, it is likely that also the European Council will indeed attach a great value to monetary stability and to the establishment of the anti-inflationary reputation of the ECB. Nonetheless, it is not unrealistic to think about conflictive situations of the type that we are analyzing being resolved in favor of the ECOFIN Council. Our model is not suited to analyze whether this could have negative consequences on the ECB's reputation. If the ECB were *forced* to accept the Council's decisions, it is unclear whether its reputation would suffer or not. For example, the Bundesbank's reputation did not suffer when the German central bank was forced to accept one-to-one conversion of ostmark into deutsche mark by the German government, but it will take time before the ECB's reputation is as strong as the Bundesbank's. Note that the model suggests that, if the conflict over intermediate values of a is resolved in favor of ECOFIN's preferences, both ins' authorities may want the transition to a currency union encompassing the whole EU except a small open economy to be relatively fast, because $a = 1$ is preferred to $a = 0.75$ by both players.

spillovers from the economic to the social and political arena, with integration starting in the economic field, deepening, and then being extended to the other areas. The facts of the past lend support to this idea. But if the preferences of the outs' governments were to become an obstacle, this could break down the whole process when the biggest obstacle of the past—German resistance and fear—seems to be overcome. The obvious objection is that the analysis of this paper overlooks important political economy arguments that would explain why the outsiders are indeed likely to eventually join the union.[48] The process of integration in Europe is indeed driven mainly by political reasons, which have their roots in historical events. A failure in the process of Western European integration *before* enlargement to the Eastern European countries, would probably lead to Germany—and *not* the EU—deepening its integration with the latter countries, facilitated by historical linkages and economic interdependencies. As a consequence of the potential economic strength of this bloc, Mediterranean countries, but also the United Kingdom, would bear the risk of living in a continent that "will dance to the tune of Germany, and where other countries will find their views much more difficult to be heard." Our model cannot capture these aspects of the whole process, but it suggests reasons, other than cross-country differences in preferences, why different policymakers may have different incentives in approaching EMU. Combining these economic incentives with political considerations in a unified framework would provide a comprehensive analysis of the problem—but this is well beyond the aim of this paper and it is also left for future work.

Finally, there is another dimension of the choices that the various policymakers will face by 1998 that deserves attention in this conclusion: for a given initial size of the currency union, what will be the optimal intra-European monetary arrangement? Our analysis has been mainly focused on the choice of the optimal size of the European currency union, but the results that we have obtained allow tentative answers to this other question. In order to give an example, we focus our attention on the case of fixed fiscal policies and no cooperation, which, as we have repeatedly argued, seems to be the most likely one. Table 11 summarizes the authorities' preference rankings in the choice between a noncooperative ERM II regime (denoted by A) and the noncooperative flexible exchange rate regime (denoted by B). The rankings are based on the results reported in Table 1 and in Table 7.

When the European currency union includes all countries except for a small open economy, all players are indifferent as to the exchange rate regime that prevails in Europe, which is intuitively justified by the absence of any impact of the outs' policy choices on the rest of the world. But when the outsiders are nonnegligible, in most cases the ERM II regime turns out to be preferred

[48]See Eichengreen and Ghironi (1995) for a discussion of these arguments.

Table 11. Preference Rankings over Exchange Rate Regimes in Europe with No Cooperation

	Outs' Size Negligible ($a = 1$)	Outs' Size Small ($a = 0.75$)	Outs' Size Equal to Ins' ($a = 0.5$)
ECB	$A \approx B$	$B > A$	$B > A$
Ins' government	$A \approx B$	$A > B$	$A > B$
Outs' central bank	$A \approx B$	$A > B$	$A > B$
Outs' government	$A \approx B$	$A > B$	$A > B$
Federal Reserve	$A \approx B$	$B > A$	$A > B$
U.S. government	$A \approx B$	$A > B$	$A > B$

Note: *A* stands for ERM II regime, whereas *B* denotes the symmetric flexible exchange rate regime.

to the flexible exchange rate regime. This is justified by the results that we have discussed in the previous sections. Controlling the exchange rate allows the outsiders' central bank to achieve a better outcome than would be achieved by controlling the money supply. Under the asymmetric regime, the employment loss is smaller, and the outs' government is consequently better off. Therefore, at least if fixed fiscal policies and no cooperation represent a likely scenario, the results of our exercise suggest that the outs' authorities will favor the adoption of an EMS-style regime over that of a flexible rate arrangement. Instead, we observe a conflict of interests between the ECB and ECOFIN over what regime should be implemented. As could have been expected on the basis of the results and intuitions discussed above, the ECB would like a flexible exchange rate regime to be adopted since this would allow it to achieve a significantly better inflation outcome by depriving the outs' central bank of control over the exchange rate. Nonetheless, this would come at the cost of higher employment losses, which induce ECOFIN to prefer the managed exchange rate regime.

Although the ERM II alternative has prevailed as the future intra-EU regime, this further source of conflict among different policymakers over the optimal features of the European currency union is not unlikely.[49] Reasons of brevity prevent us from presenting analogous tables for the other policymaking regimes we have considered. The interested reader can easily reconstruct them from the material presented above and interpret the results using the tools and intuitions discussed in the paper. Nonetheless, Tables 10 and 11 are enough to drive home an important point of this paper: as 1998 approaches, conflicts of interests between policymakers are likely to arise on the different issues they face. We have discussed above the problems that may be caused by disagreements over the optimal size of the union. But also, analyses of al-

[49]Indeed, the proper functioning of an EMS-style arrangement could well be undermined by the ECB's negative attitude toward such a regime.

ternative monetary arrangements between the ins and the outs in the post-EMU era should take into account the possibility of conflicts of interests among policymakers within one group or the other as well as across countries. This would increase the realism of the discussions and could improve the reliability of any normative suggestion based on them. Some ways to deal with the conflicts to which we have referred—and with the many others that we have probably overlooked—will have to be found to ensure a proper functioning to the European integration process. The way institutions are designed and political developments will play a crucial role with respect to these problems.

One more observation is in order before closing this paper. In all our simulations we have seen that some degree of fiscal activism makes all authorities better off with respect to the situation in which only monetary policy is used to react against the consequences of the supply side shock. This result may be interpreted as an argument against the rigid application of a Stability and Growth Pact in Europe. However, the way fiscal policy is modeled in our paper is extremely simplified. Indeed, if fiscal stability is interpreted as referring to the behavior of deficits and debts, active budget-balancing fiscal policies as those considered in the paper are not inconsistent with a "fiscal stability pact" and some flexibility of fiscal policy would be welfare improving, as the results of our simulations suggest. To provide a more thorough analysis of the role of fiscal policy as an active instrument available to policymakers and of the issue of fiscal discipline, extending the model to a multiperiod framework in which deficits and debt accumulation are allowed would be necessary. This is another line along which we believe it is worth extending our research in the future.

APPENDIX I

A Three-Country Model of Strategic Policy Interactions

The world is divided into three countries: the United States, the ins, and the outs. The two European goods are imperfect substitutes for the U.S. good and for one another. In the absence of disturbances, Europe and the United States are symmetric to one another.[50]

[50]All variables represent deviations of actual values from zero-shock equilibrium values. All variables except interest rates, public expenditures, and tax rates are expressed in logarithms, and time subscripts are dropped whenever possible.

Output in each country ($y^j, j = US, I, O$) is an increasing function of employment (n^j) and a decreasing function of a world productivity disturbance (x):

$$y^j = (1 - \alpha)n^j - x, \tag{A1}$$

where $(1 - \alpha)$, with $0 < \alpha < 1$, is the same in all countries. The productivity disturbance is identically and independently distributed with zero mean.

The labor demand of firms is implicit in the following profit maximization condition, where τ indicates the rate of taxation of total revenues:[51]

$$w^j - p^j = -\alpha n^j - \tau^j - x. \tag{A2}$$

Real wages are nominal wages (w^j) minus product prices (p^j).

Consumer price indexes (q^j) are weighted averages of the prices of U.S., ins', and outs' goods. As shown in Figure 1, American consumers allocate a fraction b of their spending to European goods (a to the good produced by the ins, and $(1 - a)$ to that produced by the outs) so the U.S. CPI is

$$\begin{aligned} q^{US} &= (1 - b)p^{US} + ab(p^I + e^1) + (1 - a)b(p^O + e^2) \\ &= p^{US} + abz^1 + (1 - a)bz^2, \end{aligned} \tag{A3}$$

where exchange rates e^1 and e^2 are the dollar prices of the euro and of the currency of the outs, respectively, and z^1 and z^2 are the dollar-euro and dollar-outs real exchange rates:

$$\begin{aligned} z^1 &= e^1 + p^I - p^{US}, \\ z^2 &= e^2 + p^O - p^{US}. \end{aligned} \tag{A4}$$

European consumers allocate a fraction b of their spending to the U.S. good, and divide the rest of their spending between the two European goods, a to the ins' good and $(1 - a)$ to the outs'. The European CPIs are

$$\begin{aligned} q^I &= a(1 - b)p^I + (1 - a)(1 - b)(p^O + e^2 - e^1) + b(p^{US} - e^1) \\ &= p^I - bz^1 - (1 - a)(1 - b)z^3, \\ q^O &= (1 - a)(1 - b)p^O + a(1 - b)(p^I + e^1 - e^2) + b(p^{US} - e^2) \\ &= p^O - bz^2 + a(1 - b)z^3. \end{aligned} \tag{A5}$$

The outs-euro real exchange rate is $z^3 = z^1 - z^2$.

Demand for all goods increases with output. Residents of each country increase their spending by the same fraction $(0 < \varepsilon < 1)$ of an increase in output. The marginal

[51]Using uppercase letters to denote anti-logs, domestic firms maximize Profit $= (1 - \tau)PY - WN$, subject to $Y = N^{1-\alpha}/X$. Each firm is a price taker in the output and in the labor market and is taxed on its total revenues. The first-order condition for maximization with respect to N is $(1 - \tau)P(1 - \alpha)N^{-\alpha}/X = W$. Taking logs, approximating $\ln(1 - \tau)$ with $-\tau$, and omitting unimportant constants, we obtain equation (A2). (See Alesina and Tabellini, 1987.)

propensity to spend is equal to the average propensity to spend for all goods for residents of all countries.[52]

An increase in ex ante real interest rates (r^j) reduces the demand for all goods: residents of each country decrease spending by the same amount ($0 < \nu < 1$) for each percentage point increase in the ex ante real interest rate facing them.

Equilibrium conditions for the three goods are

$$\begin{aligned} y^{US} &= \delta[az^1 + (1-a)z^2] + \varepsilon[(1-b)y^{US} + aby^I + (1-a)by^O] \\ &\quad - \nu[(1-b)r^{US} + br] + (1-\eta)g^{US} + a\eta g^I + (1-a)\eta g^O + u, \\ y^I &= \delta[-z^1 - (1-a)z^3] + \varepsilon[by^{US} + a(1-b)y^I + (1-a)(1-b)y^O] \\ &\quad - \nu[br^{US} + (1-b)r] + \eta g^{US} + a(1-\eta)g^I + (1-a)(1-\eta)g^O - u, \\ y^O &= \delta[-z^2 + az^3] + \varepsilon[by^{US} + a(1-b)y^I + (1-a)(1-b)y^O] \\ &\quad - \nu[br^{US} + (1-b)r] + \eta g^{US} + a(1-\eta)g^I + (1-a)(1-\eta)g^O - u. \end{aligned} \tag{A6}$$

Ex ante real interest rates are[53]

$$r^j = i^j - E(q^j_{+1}) + q^j, \tag{A7}$$

where i^{US}, i^I, and i^O are nominal interest rates on bonds denominated in dollars, euros, and the outs' currency, respectively, and $E(\bullet_{+1})$ indicates the expected value of a variable tomorrow on the basis of information available today. Real depreciation of a currency shifts world demand toward that country's good.[54] We also assume that a random

---

[52]The ins' propensity to import from the outs is $(1-a)$ times one minus the ins' propensity to import from the United States. Thus, if the ins' propensity to import from the United States is b, the ins' propensity to import from the outs is $(1-a)(1-b)$, and the total propensity to import of the ins is $b + (1-a)(1-b)$.

[53]It is $r = ar^I + (1-a)r^O$ because agents can freely borrow in all countries. However, it can be easily shown that identical consumption patterns in the ins and outs economies coupled with perfect capital mobility imply $r^I = r^O = r$.

[54]The increase in demand due to a real depreciation of the domestic currency depends on two factors: the common elasticity parameter δ and the size of the country with respect to whose currency the domestic currency is depreciating. Thus, for example, in the case $a = 0.5$, if the euro depreciates against the dollar, the increase in demand for ins' goods is twice as much as it would be were the euro depreciating against the outs' currency, reflecting the fact that the U.S. economy is twice the outs' one and that, with perfect mobility of goods, "depreciation against a larger market is more profitable." The larger a is, the smaller the impact of a real depreciation against the outs, for a given impact of an analogous depreciation against the dollar. If the outs are a small economy, their impact on the demand for the ins' goods is correspondingly small. This intuition is consistent with our assumptions about the pattern of trade: as a approaches 1, the outs spend a larger share of their income on the ins' goods, but their size is small. Also, the ins spend a smaller share of their income on the outs' goods. Thus, a real depreciation of the euro against the outs' currency has a smaller impact on the demand for the ins' goods as a increases. An alternative explanation for a higher elasticity of demand for European goods to the transatlantic real exchange rates than to the intra-European exchange rate could be based on the characteristics of the goods that are traded and on the presence of impediments to perfect mobility of goods across the Atlantic. In this sense, if the euro depreciates against the dollar, this may have a larger impact on demand for the ins' goods than a depreciation against the outs' currency, because, goods being imperfect substitutes, the characteristics of international trade may make it easier and more convenient for ins consumers to shift from U.S. goods to insiders' than from outsiders' goods to insiders'.

disturbance (u), identically and independently distributed with zero mean, can shift the world demand from European goods to U.S. goods.

The government budget constraints are given by

$$g^j = \tau^j. \tag{A8}$$

Government spending falls entirely on goods (transfers are considered negative taxes and are included in τ); g^j defines the ratio G^j/P^jY^j and government j's budget constraint is $G^j = \tau^j P^j Y^j$. In equations (A6) we have implicitly assumed that the international allocation of governments' consumption resembles that of private consumption, with the parameter η replacing b, and η presumably not greater than b.

There are three stocks of bonds, each denominated in one of the three currencies. Residents of each country, who regard bonds denominated in all three currencies as perfect substitutes, hold positive amounts of all kinds of bonds only when their expected returns, measured in a common currency, are equal:

$$\begin{aligned} i^{US} &= i^{I} + E(e^1_{+1}) - e^1, \\ i^{US} &= i^{O} + E(e^2_{+1}) - e^2. \end{aligned} \tag{A9}$$

In contrast, each country's currency is held only by its residents. Demands for real money balances are given by

$$m^j - p^j = y^j - \lambda i^j. \tag{A10}$$

Making use of the production functions, firms' labor demands, and the demands for real money balances, we obtain

$$n^j = m^j - w^j - \tau^j + \lambda i^j. \tag{A11}$$

At the end of the previous period, competitive unions and firms sign contracts specifying nominal wages for the current period. Unions choose nominal wages to minimize expected deviations of employment and the real wage from zero disturbance equilibrium values.[55] To focus on international interactions, we assume that no time inconsistency problem exists and that all random disturbances are unexpected. The endogenous variables are shown in Ghironi and Giavazzi (1997c) to be linear functions of the policy instruments and of the shocks. Hence, expected values of both authorities' instruments and endogenous variables coincide with their no-disturbance equilibrium values, that is, zero. It will become apparent that zero values for the authorities' instruments are optimal in the absence of disturbances. Thus the rational wage-setting rule turns out to be

$$w^j = 0. \tag{A12}$$

[55]See Ghironi and Giavazzi (1997a and 1997c) for a more detailed discussion of the wage-setting process.

Using this rule and equations (A1), (A10), and (A11), we obtain

$$n^j = m^j - \tau^j + \lambda i^j, \tag{A13}$$

$$p^j = \alpha n^j + \tau^j + x. \tag{A14}$$

Equations (A1)–(A14) comprise the structural model. Next, we present the policy-makers' preferences and the main reduced-form equations.

Each central bank chooses its instrument to minimize:

$$L^{cb^j} = \frac{1}{2}[\gamma_1(q^j)^2 + (1-\gamma_1)(n^j)^2], \qquad 0 < \gamma_1 < 1, \tag{A15}$$

where γ_1 measures the weight attached to inflation relative to employment by central banks. The ECB and the Federal Reserve control the respective money supplies, and the exchange rate between the euro and the dollar is flexible. Within Europe we consider two different monetary regimes: an asymmetric regime, in which the ECB sets the money supply, while the outsiders' central bank sets the value of $e^3 = e^1 - e^2$, the nominal exchange rate between the outsiders' currency and the euro; and a symmetric regime, in which both the ECB and the outsiders' central bank set the money supply, and the intra-European exchange rate is floating.

When it plays actively, the government in each country chooses taxes to minimize a quadratic loss function that depends on the deviations of inflation, employment, and taxation from their equilibrium values. We assume that the volatility of taxation represents a cost for fiscal authorities. As explained in the text, this could be motivated by the presence of convex distortions, but it could also capture the idea that fiscal policy is difficult to fine-tune relative to monetary policy. Thus, country j's government minimizes

$$L^{fa^j} = \frac{1}{2}\{\vartheta_1[\vartheta_2(q^j)^2 + (1-\vartheta_2)(n^j)^2] + (1-\vartheta_1)(\tau^j)^2\}, \qquad 0 < \vartheta_1 < \vartheta_2 < 1. \tag{A16}$$

When ϑ_1 is low, the degree of fiscal activism is reduced and the government is forced (e.g., by unmodeled institutional and political constraints) not to use its instrument aggressively in order to act on inflation and employment. The parameter ϑ_2 measures the weight attached to inflation relative to employment by the fiscal authorities. We assume that, in the limiting case $\vartheta_1 = 0$, in which governments do not play actively and taxes are zero, governments still care about inflation and employment: their welfare is thus evaluated according to the criterion

$$\tilde{L}^{fa^j} = \frac{1}{2}[\vartheta_2(q^j)^2 + (1-\vartheta_2)(n^j)^2]. \tag{A17}$$

Endogenous variables in each country are linear functions of the policy instruments and of the disturbances.[56] This implies that when $x = u = 0$, zero values of the instru-

[56]See Ghironi and Giavazzi (1997c) for the solution of the model.

ments ensure zero losses for all authorities, and proves the rationality of static expectations under the assumption that disturbances have zero mean.

We next show the reduced-form equations for employment and the CPI in each country, in the two European monetary regimes. In the equations that follow, all parameters indexed by a number are functions of a, the parameter that defines the size of the currency union. When $a < 1$, the following are the reduced forms for employment in the three countries.

1. Managed exchange rates inside Europe:

$$\begin{aligned} n^{US} &= \Lambda m^{US} - \Omega\tau^{US} - \Theta m^{I} + \Psi_1\tau^{I} + \Psi_2\tau^{O} - \Delta_1 e^3 + Ku - Hx, \\ n^{I} &= \Lambda m^{I} - \Omega_1\tau^{I} + \Omega_2\tau^{O} - \Theta m^{US} + \Psi\tau^{US} + \Delta_2 e^3 - Ku - Hx, \\ n^{O} &= \Lambda m^{I} - \Omega_3\tau^{O} + \Omega_4\tau^{I} - \Theta m^{US} + \Psi\tau^{US} + \Delta_3 e^3 - Ku - Hx; \end{aligned} \tag{A18}$$

and the following relations hold among the reduced-form parameters:

$$\Psi_1 + \Psi_2 = \Psi,\ -\Omega_1 + \Omega_2 = -\Omega_3 + \Omega_4 = -\Omega.$$

2. Flexible exchange rates inside Europe:

$$\begin{aligned} n^{US} &= \Lambda m^{US} - \Omega\tau^{US} - \Theta_1 m^{I} - \Theta_2 m^{O} + \Psi_1\tau^{I} + \Psi_2\tau^{O} + Ku - Hx, \\ n^{I} &= \Lambda_1 m^{I} + \Lambda_2 m^{O} - \Omega_1\tau^{I} + \Omega_2\tau^{O} - \Theta m^{US} + \Psi\tau^{US} - Ku - Hx, \\ n^{O} &= \Lambda_3 m^{O} + \Lambda_4 m^{I} - \Omega_3\tau^{O} + \Omega_4\tau^{I} - \Theta m^{US} + \Psi\tau^{US} - Ku - Hx; \end{aligned} \tag{A18$'$}$$

and the following relations hold among the reduced-form parameters:

$$\begin{aligned} &\Theta_1 + \Theta_2 = \Theta,\ \Psi_1 + \Psi_2 = \Psi,\ \Lambda_1 + \Lambda_2 \\ &= \Lambda_3 + \Lambda_4 = \Lambda,\ -\Omega_1 + \Omega_2 = -\Omega_3 + \Omega_4 = -\Omega. \end{aligned}$$ [57]

When $a = 1$, the outsiders are a "small open economy" that is affected by the United States' and the insiders' policies but whose choices have no effect abroad; equations (A18) and (A18′) reduce to the following.

1. Managed exchange rates inside Europe:

$$\begin{aligned} n^{US} &= \Lambda m^{US} - \Omega\tau^{US} - \Theta m^{I} + \Psi\tau^{I} + Ku - Hx, \\ n^{I} &= \Lambda m^{I} - \Omega\tau^{I} - \Theta m^{US} + \Psi\tau^{US} - Ku - Hx, \\ n^{O} &= \Lambda m^{I} - \Omega_3\tau^{O} + \Omega_4\tau^{I} - \Theta m^{US} + \Psi\tau^{US} + \Delta_3 e^3 - Ku - Hx. \end{aligned} \tag{A19}$$

[57]The expression is further simplified when $a = 0.5$, in which case the two European countries are symmetric in *each* respect. In this case we have $\Theta_1 = \Theta_2 = \Theta/2$, $\Psi_1 = \Psi_2 = \Psi/2$. United States variables depend on United States policy instruments and on the arithmetic average of the European ones—and also: $\Lambda_1 = \Lambda_3$, $\Lambda_2 = \Lambda_4$, $\Omega_1 = \Omega_3$, $\Omega_2 = \Omega_4$.

2. Flexible exchange rates inside Europe:

$$\begin{aligned} n^{US} &= \Lambda m^{US} - \Omega\tau^{US} - \Theta m^{I} + \Psi\tau^{I} + Ku - Hx, \\ n^{I} &= \Lambda m^{I} - \Omega\tau^{I} - \Theta m^{US} + \Psi\tau^{US} - Ku - Hx, \\ n^{O} &= \Lambda_3 m^{O} + \Lambda_4 m^{I} - \Omega_3\tau^{O} + \Omega_4\tau^{I} - \Theta m^{US} + \Psi\tau^{US} - Ku - Hx. \end{aligned} \tag{A19'}$$

Similarly, when $a < 1$, reduced forms for the CPIs are the following.

1. Managed exchange rates inside Europe:

$$\begin{aligned} q^{US} &= Am^{US} - Bm^{I} + E\tau^{US} + \Gamma_1\tau^{I} + \Gamma_2\tau^{O} - M_1e^3 + \Phi u + \Sigma x, \\ q^{I} &= Am^{I} - Bm^{US} + E_1\tau^{I} + E_2\tau^{O} + \Gamma\tau^{US} - M_2e^3 - \Phi u + \Sigma x, \\ q^{O} &= Am^{I} - Bm^{US} + E_2\tau^{O} + E_1\tau^{I} + \Gamma\tau^{US} + M_3e^3 - \Phi u + \Sigma x, \end{aligned} \tag{A20}$$

and $\Gamma_1 + \Gamma_2 = \Gamma$, $E_1 + E_2 = E$. Note that the insiders' fiscal policy has the same impact on both the insiders' and the outsiders' CPIs, and the same is true for the outsiders' fiscal policy. This can be seen observing that, subtracting q^O from q^I, one obtains $q^I - q^O = -(M_2 + M_3)e^3$, independent of τ. Recalling the expressions for q^O and q^I in terms of PPIs and real exchange rates (equations (A5)) and using the definitions of z^1 and z^2, it is possible to show that it actually has to be the case that $q^I - q^O = -e^3$, that is, that it has to be $M_2 + M_3 = 1$.[58]

2. Flexible exchange rates inside Europe:

$$\begin{aligned} q^{US} &= Am^{US} - B_1m^{I} - B_2m^{O} + E\tau^{US} + \Gamma_1\tau^{I} + \Gamma_2\tau^{O} + \Phi u + \Sigma x, \\ q^{I} &= A_1m^{I} - A_2m^{O} - Bm^{US} + E_1\tau^{I} + E_2\tau^{O} + \Gamma\tau^{US} - \Phi u + \Sigma x, \\ q^{O} &= A_3m^{O} - A_4m^{O} - Bm^{US} + E_3\tau^{O} + E_4\tau^{I} + \Gamma\tau^{US} - \Phi u + \Sigma x; \end{aligned} \tag{A20'}$$

and $B_1 + B_2 = B$, $\Gamma_1 + \Gamma_2 = \Gamma$, $A_1 - A_2 = A_3 - A_4 = A$, $E_1 + E_2 = E_3 + E_4 = E$.[59]

As a consequence of the change in the intra-European exchange rate regime, it is no longer the case that the insiders' fiscal policy has the same impact on both the insiders' and the outsiders' CPIs, and that the same holds for the outsiders' fiscal policy.

[58]This is because the two European countries have identical consumption bundles (see the pattern of trade), and therefore Purchasing Power Parity (PPP) holds in terms of CPIs. The same is not true for the United States versus European economies, because the consumption baskets are asymmetric across the Atlantic. This is due to our implicit assumption that consumers on the two sides of the Atlantic have asymmetric Cobb-Douglas preferences (recall footnote 6). As a consequence, real interest rates are not equalized in Europe and the United States, the differential depending on movements in the real exchange rates.

[59]Again, matters are simpler when a=0.5, in which case we have: $B_1 = B_2 = B/2$, $\Gamma_1 = \Gamma_2 = \Gamma/2$, $A_1 = A_3$, $A_2 = A_4$, $E_1 = E_2$, $E_3 = E_4$.

If the outsiders are very small ($a = 1$), the previous reduced-form equations become

1. Managed exchange rates inside Europe:

$$\begin{aligned} q^{US} &= Am^{US} - Bm^{I} + E\tau^{US} + \Gamma\tau^{I} + \Phi u + \Sigma x, \\ q^{I} &= Am^{I} - Bm^{US} + E\tau^{I} + \Gamma\tau^{US} - \Phi u + \Sigma x, \\ q^{O} &= Am^{I} - Bm^{US} + E\tau^{I} + \Gamma\tau^{US} + e^{3} - \Phi u + \Sigma x. \end{aligned} \tag{A21}$$

Note that, while the outsiders' fiscal policy still affects n^{O} when $a = 1$, it no longer affects q^{O}. Also, in this situation, movements of e^{3} have a one-to-one impact on the insiders' CPI.[60]

2. Flexible exchange rates inside Europe:

$$\begin{aligned} q^{US} &= Am^{US} - Bm^{I} + E\tau^{US} + \Gamma\tau^{I} + \Phi u + \Sigma x, \\ q^{I} &= Am^{I} - Bm^{US} + E\tau^{I} + \Gamma\tau^{US} - \Phi u + \Sigma x, \\ q^{O} &= A_3m^{O} - A_4m^{I} - Bm^{US} + E_3\tau^{O} + E_4\tau^{I} + \Gamma\tau^{US} - \Phi u + \Sigma x. \end{aligned} \tag{A21$'$}$$

When the European exchange rate regime is symmetric, it is no longer the case that the outsiders' fiscal policy has no impact on q^{O} when the outsiders are very small.

The reduced-form parameters in the preceding equations are functions of the structural parameters. Their signs are often ambiguous, since they depend on the interaction of several channels of transmission. In equations (A18, A18$'$)–(A21, A21$'$), all the coefficients are assumed to be positive; the signs are those implied by our assumptions on the value of the structural parameters, which are chosen to provide clear-cut conclusions in the response to a supply shock. Recall also that the values of the reduced-form parameters that are not indexed by a number do not change for given values of the other structural parameters of the model as a does.[61]

The values we assign to the structural parameters are $\alpha = 0.34$, $\delta = 0.8$, $\varepsilon = 0.8$, $\nu = 0.4$, $\lambda = 0.6$, $b = \eta = 0.1$. Though arbitrary, these values can be defended based on the empirical evidence. $(1 - \alpha)$, for instance, corresponds to the share of labor in a Cobb-Douglas production function—and a share of capital equal to one-third is not unrealistic. ε is the marginal propensity to consume out of disposable income—a value of 0.8 does not seem far from reality. b measures the extent of transatlantic trade, which

[60]Recall that it is $q^{I} - q^{O} = -e^{3}$. When $a = 1$, changes in e^{3} have no impact abroad, and the same is true of changes in the outsiders' fiscal policy. Hence, e^{3} has a one-to-one impact on q^{O}, and the latter is not affected by changes in τ^{O}.

[61]Moreover, the parameters whose value does not depend on a are identical across intra-European exchange rate regimes, as our choice of notation indicates. The intuition for this result is apparent if one observes the reduced-form equations for the case $a = 1$. The parameters we are referring to are indeed those that would characterize the interaction between the United States and a European currency union whose size were identical to that of the United States. These two entities are unaffected by the outsiders' policy choices, the outs being a negligible entity. For the same reason, the intra-European exchange rate regime does not affect the values of the parameters in the reduced-form equations for the ins' and U.S. variables when $a = 1$.

Table A1. Reduced-Form Parameters Independent of *a*

Α = 0.26	Β = 0.02	Ε = 0.75	Γ = 0.22	Σ = 0.93
Λ = 0.75	Ω = 0.56	Θ = 0.03	Ψ = 0.49	Η = 0.21

is fairly small if compared to intra-European trade. Similar justifications can be given for the other parameter values. It could be argued that the value of λ is relatively high for a short-run oriented model, although 0.5 would be the value suggested by a standard Baumol-Tobin model of money demand determination. It turns out that choosing a lower value for λ would not change the nature of fiscal policy in the model, budget-balancing tax cuts being still expansionary for smaller λs.[62] Our parameter choice has the advantage of allowing a significant impact of the supply shock on employment and a nonnegligible external effect of domestic economic policies on foreign employment under flexible exchange rates.[63]

We consider three alternative values for a: 0.5, 0.75, and 1. Approximate values of the reduced-form parameters, which are invariant with respect to a, are given in Table A1. We assume that there is no demand disturbance ($u = 0$) and therefore we omit the values of K and Φ. Table A2 shows approximate values of the reduced-form parameters that change with the size of the currency union. As noted above, these parameters differ across exchange rate regimes. Numerical values of the employment-inflation trade-offs facing insiders and outsiders under alternative exchange-rate regimes in Europe are displayed in Table A3. Finally, we make the following assumptions about policymakers' preferences. Three alternative values of ϑ_1 are considered (0, 0.2, 0.8), the degree of fiscal activism being an increasing function of that parameter. For given flexibility of fiscal policy, we make the realistic assumption that central banks care much more about CPI inflation than about employment ($\gamma_1 = 0.9$), while the opposite is true for fiscal authorities ($\vartheta_2 = 0.1$).

APPENDIX II

First-Order Conditions for the Stabilization Game

1. Noncooperative ERM II, fixed taxes.

$$0.9q^j \frac{\partial q^j}{\partial m^j} + 0.1n^j \frac{\partial n^j}{\partial m^j} = 0, \qquad j = US, I; \tag{A23}$$

$$0.9q^O \frac{\partial q^O}{\partial e^3} + 0.1n^O \frac{\partial n^O}{\partial e^3} = 0. \tag{A24}$$

[62]Recall footnote 24.

[63]See footnote 29 and Appendix III.

Table A2. Reduced-Form Parameters Whose Value Depends on a

	Managed Exchange Rates Inside Europe								
$a = 0.5$	$E_1 = 0.42$	$E_2 = 0.33$	$\Gamma_1 = 0.11$	$\Gamma_2 = 0.11$	$M_1 = 0.02$	$M_2 = 0.25$	$M_3 = 0.75$		
	$\Omega_1 = 0.82$	$\Omega_2 = 0.26$	$\Omega_3 = 1.07$	$\Omega_4 = 0.51$	$\Psi_1 = 0.24$	$\Psi_2 = 0.25$	$\Delta_1 = 0.03$	$\Delta_2 = 0.06$	$\Delta_3 = 1.38$
$a = 0.75$	$E_1 = 0.59$	$E_2 = 0.16$	$\Gamma_1 = 0.16$	$\Gamma_2 = 0.06$	$M_1 = 0.01$	$M_2 = 0.12$	$M_3 = 0.88$		
	$\Omega_1 = 0.69$	$\Omega_2 = 0.13$	$\Omega_3 = 1.20$	$\Omega_4 = 0.64$	$\Psi_1 = 0.36$	$\Psi_2 = 0.13$	$\Delta_1 = 0.02$	$\Delta_1 = 0.03$	$\Delta_1 = 1.36$
$a = 1$	$\Omega_3 = 1.33$	$\Omega_4 = 0.77$	$\Delta_3 = 1.33$						
	Flexible Exchange Rates Inside Europe[1]								
$a = 0.5$	$A_1 = 0.39$	$A_2 = 0.13$	$A_3 = 0.39$	$A_4 = 0.13$	$B_1 = 0.01$	$B_2 = 0.01$			
	$E_1 = 0.46$	$E_2 = 0.29$	$E_3 = 0.46$	$E_4 = 0.29$	$\Gamma_1 = 0.11$	$\Gamma_2 = 0.11$			
	$\Lambda_1 = 0.72$	$\Lambda_2 = 0.03$	$\Lambda_3 = 0.72$	$\Lambda_4 = 0.03$	$\Theta_1 = 0.02$	$\Theta_2 = 0.02$			
	$\Omega_1 = 0.83$	$\Omega_2 = 0.27$	$\Omega_3 = 0.83$	$\Omega_4 = 0.27$	$\Psi_1 = 0.25$	$\Psi_2 = 0.25$			
$a = 0.75$	$A_1 = 0.33$	$A_2 = 0.07$	$A_3 = 0.45$	$A_4 = 0.19$	$B_1 = 0.02$	$B_2 = 0.01$			
	$E_1 = 0.61$	$E_2 = 0.14$	$E_3 = 0.32$	$E_4 = 0.43$	$\Gamma_1 = 0.16$	$\Gamma_2 = 0.06$			
	$\Lambda_1 = 0.74$	$\Lambda_2 = 0.015$	$\Lambda_3 = 0.71$	$\Lambda_4 = 0.05$	$\Theta_1 = 0.02$	$\Theta_2 = 0.01$			
	$\Omega_1 = 0.69$	$\Omega_2 = 0.13$	$\Omega_3 = 0.97$	$\Omega_4 = 0.41$	$\Psi_1 = 0.36$	$\Psi_2 = 0.13$			
$a = 1$	$A_3 = 0.52$	$A_4 = 0.26$	$E_3 = 0.17$	$E_4 = 0.58$					
	$\Lambda_3 = 0.69$	$\Lambda_4 = 0.06$	$\Omega_3 = 1.1$	$\Omega_4 = 0.54$					

[1]The values of Γ_1, Γ_2, Ω_1, Ω_2, Ψ_1, and Ψ_2 that appear in this part of the table can induce the reader to believe that these parameters are also identical across intra-EU exchange rate regimes. Indeed, this is not the case, and the similarity is only due to approximation. If the first value is that under flexible exchange rates and that in parentheses refers to the ERM II regime, we have: if $a = 0.5$, $\Gamma_1 = 0.1112(.1077)$, $\Gamma_2 = 0.1112(.1147)$, $\Omega_1 = 0.83081$ (0.82126), $\Omega_2 = 0.2715$ (0.2619), $\Psi_1 = 0.24399$ (0.23844), and $\Psi_2 = 0.24399$ (0.24954); if $a = 0.75$, $\Gamma_1 = 0.1668$ (0.16505), $\Gamma_2 = 0.05561$ (0.05737), $\Omega_1 = 0.69505$ (0.69028), $\Omega_2 = 0.13575$ (0.13097), $\Psi_1 = 0.36599$ (0.36321), and $\Psi_2 = 0.12199$ (0.12477).

Table A3. Employment-Inflation Tradeoffs Facing Outsiders and Insiders

	Outs	Ins
	$a = 0.5$	
Flexible exchange rates	0.54486	0.54486
ERM II	0.54486	0.35337
	$a = 0.75$	
Flexible exchange rates	0.64654	0.44722
ERM II	0.64654	0.35337
	$a = 1$	
Flexible exchange rates	0.7525	0.35337
ERM II	0.7525	0.35337

2. Cooperative ERM II, fixed taxes.
   m^I and e^3 are chosen so that

$$a\left(0.9q^I \frac{\partial q^I}{\partial m^I} + 0.1n^j \frac{\partial n^I}{\partial m^I}\right) + (1-a)\left(0.9q^O \frac{\partial q^O}{\partial m^I} + 0.1n^O \frac{\partial n^O}{\partial m^I}\right) = 0, \tag{A25}$$

$$a\left(0.9q^I \frac{\partial q^I}{\partial e^3} + 0.1n^I \frac{\partial n^I}{\partial e^3}\right) + (1-a)\left(0.9q^O \frac{\partial q^O}{\partial e^3} + 0.1n^O \frac{\partial n^O}{\partial e^3}\right) = 0. \tag{A26}$$

The condition for the optimal choice of m^{US} is unchanged.

3. Cooperative ERM II, active fiscal policies.
   First-order conditions for the central banks' problem are as in case 2. Optimal choice of τ by the governments is such that

$$\vartheta_1\left(0.1q^j \frac{\partial q^j}{\partial \tau^j} + 0.9n^j \frac{\partial n^j}{\partial \tau^j}\right) + (1-\vartheta_1)\tau^j = 0, \qquad j = US, I, O. \tag{A27}$$

4. Noncooperative ERM II, active fiscal policies.
   First-order conditions for the central banks' problem are as in case 1. Conditions for the governments' problem are as in case 3.

APPENDIX III

Closed Blocs

When the assumptions $b = \lambda = 0$ are made, and the monetary regime inside Europe is asymmetric, the reduced-form equations for employment in the three countries (equations (A18)) are simply given by

$$n^j = m^j - \tau^j, \qquad j = US, I, \tag{A28}$$

$$n^O = m^I + \chi(\tau^I - \tau^O) + \phi e^3 - \tau^O, \tag{A29}$$

where our assumptions about structural parameter values imply $\chi = 0.33$ and $\phi = 1.33$. Note that, if the exchange rate regime in Europe were symmetric and both European central banks controlled the respective money supplies—as in equations (A18′)—setting $\lambda = 0$ would imply that domestic policies have no effects on employment abroad. Endogeneity of the outsiders' money supply due to the managed exchange rate regime in Europe allows insiders' policies to have an impact on employment in the outsider countries.

Reduced-form equations for the CPIs when $a < 1$ are as follows:

$$\begin{aligned} q^{US} &= Am^{US} + E\tau^{US} + x, \\ q^I &= Am^I + E_1\tau^I + E_2\tau^O - M_2e^3 + x, \\ q^O &= Am^I + E_2\tau^O + E_1\tau^I + M_3e^3 + x, \end{aligned} \tag{A30}$$

where we have maintained the convention that parameters that are not indexed by a number do not depend on a and $E_1 + E_2 = E$, as before, $M_2 = E_2$ and $M_2 + M_3 = 1$.

In the case in which the outs are a small open economy ($a = 1$), the United States and the ins face each other as two large closed blocs, and CPIs are given by

$$q^j = Am^j + E\tau^j + x, \qquad j = US, I, \tag{A31}$$

$$q^O = Am^I + E\tau^I + e^3 + x. \tag{A32}$$

Our assumptions about structural parameters imply the values for the reduced-form parameters displayed in Table A4.

Table A4. Reduced-Form Parameters When No Transatlantic Spillovers Exist

$A = 0.34$	$E = 0.66$		
$a = 0.5$			
$E_1 = 0.39$	$E_2 = 0.27$	$M_2 = 0.27$	$M_3 = 0.73$
$a = 0.75$			
$E_1 = 0.52$	$E_2 = 0.14$	$M_2 = 0.14$	$M_3 = 0.86$

References

Alesina, Alberto, and Vittorio Grilli, 1994, "On the Feasibility of a One-Speed or Multispeed European Monetary Union," Chapter 6 in *The Political Economy of European Monetary Unification*, ed. by Barry Eichengreen and Jeffry Frieden (Boulder, Colorado: Westview Press), pp. 107–27.

Alesina, Alberto, and Guido Tabellini, 1987, "Rules and Discretion with Noncoordinated Monetary and Fiscal Policies," *Economic Inquiry*, Vol. 25 (October), pp. 619–30.

Basevi, Giorgio, Flavio Delbono, and Vincenzo Denicolò, 1990, "International Monetary Cooperation Under Tariff Threats," *Journal of International Economics*, Vol. 28 (February), pp. 1–23.

Buiter, Willem H., Giancarlo Corsetti, and Paolo A. Pesenti, 1995, "A Centre-Periphery Model of Monetary Coordination and Exchange Rate Crises," CEPR Discussion Paper No. 1201 (London: Centre for Economic Policy Research, July).

Canzoneri, Matthew B., and Dale W. Henderson, 1991, *Monetary Policy in Interdependent Economies: A Game-Theoretic Approach* (Cambridge, Massachusetts: MIT Press).

Council of European Communities, 1992, *Treaty on European Union* (Luxembourg: Office for Official Publications of the European Communities).

De Grauwe, Paul, 1996, "The Pros and Cons of a Mini Currency Union" (unpublished; Leuven: University of Leuven).

Eichengreen, Barry, and Fabio Ghironi, 1995, "European Monetary Unification: The Challenges Ahead," CEPR Discussion Paper No. 1217 (London: Centre for Economic Policy Research, July).

———, 1997a, "How Will Transatlantic Policy Interactions Change with the Advent of EMU?" (unpublished; Berkeley, California: University of California).

———, 1997b, "Fiscal Asymmetries and U.S.-Europe Interactions in the EMU Era" (unpublished; Berkeley, California: University of California).

Federal Reserve Bank of Kansas City, 1991, *Policy Implications of Trade and Currency Zones*, proceedings of a symposium sponsored by the Federal Reserve Bank of Kansas City, Jackson Hole, Wyoming, August 22–24.

Frankel, Jeffrey A., 1989, "International Nominal Targeting (INT): A Proposal for Overcoming Obstacles to Policy Coordination," in *Global Disequilibrium in the World Economy*, ed. by Mario Baldassari, John McCallum, and Robert Mundell (New York: St. Martin's Press), pp. 257–94.

Ghironi, Fabio, 1993, "Regimi di tasso di cambio e coordinamento internazionale delle politiche economiche: Che cosa abbiamo imparato in dieci anni di letteratura?" Tesi di Laurea (unpublished; Milan: Bocconi University).

———, and Francesco Giavazzi, 1997a, "Currency Unions, International Monetary Regimes and the Employment-Inflation Trade-Off" (unpublished; Berkeley, California: University of California; Milan: Bocconi University).

———, 1997b, "Is Small Beautiful? Currency Unions and the Employment-Inflation Trade-Off" (unpublished; Berkeley, California: University of California; Milan: Bocconi University).

———, 1997c, "Out in the Sunshine? Outsiders, Insiders, and the United States in 1998," CEPR Discussion Paper No. 1547 (London: Centre for Economic Policy Research, January).

Giavazzi, Francesco, and Alberto Giovannini, 1989, "Monetary Policy Interactions Under Managed Exchange Rates," *Economica,* Vol. 56 (May), pp. 199–213.

———, and Marco Pagano, 1996, "Non-Keynesian Effects of Fiscal Policy Changes: International Evidence and the Swedish Experience," *Swedish Economic Policy Review*, Vol. 3 (Spring), pp. 67–103.

Kenen, Peter B., 1995, *Economic and Monetary Union in Europe: Moving Beyond Maastricht* (Cambridge: Cambridge University Press).

Persson, Torsten, and Guido Tabellini, 1996, "Monetary Cohabitation in Europe," CEPR Discussion Paper No. 1380 (London: Centre for Economic Policy Research, May).

Rogoff, Kenneth, 1985, "Can International Monetary Cooperation Be Counterproductive?" *Journal of International Economics,* Vol. 18 (May), pp. 199–217.

Spaventa, Luigi, 1996, "Out in the Cold? Outsiders and Insiders in 1999: Feasible and Unfeasible Options," CEPR Discussion Paper No. 1379 (London: Centre for Economic Policy Research, April).

von Hagen, Jürgen, and Michele Fratianni, 1991, "Policy Coordination in the EMS with Stochastic Asymmetries," in *Financial Regulation and Monetary Arrangements After 1992*, ed. by Clas Wihlborg, Michele Fratianni, and Thomas D. Willett (Amsterdam: Elsevier Science Publishers), pp. 255–75.

Wyplosz, Charles, 1996, "An EMS for Both "*Ins*" and "*Outs*": The Contractual and Conditional Approach," *Swiss Political Science Review*, Vol. 2 (Spring), pp. 178–83.

Comments on Ghironi and Giavazzi

André Sapir

One of the most crucial issues facing European policymakers concerns the composition of the group of countries that will enter the third phase of EMU in January 1999, and the process whereby those lagging behind will be able to join the monetary union as swiftly as possible. Luckily, economic analysis provides some guidance for solving this problem. The arguments in the literature can be divided into demand and supply factors.

On the demand side, the optimum currency area (OCA) theory offers reasons why countries may wish to join a monetary union, or stay outside. According to this theory, the demand for membership hinges on the economic structure of a particular country, and on the potential cost associated with the loss of the exchange rate instrument in the face of country-specific shocks. Based on this view, Barry Eichengreen and others have suggested that the EU is divided into two groups of countries: a hard core made up of countries whose disturbances are highly correlated with those of Germany, namely Austria, France, Germany, Denmark, Belgium, Luxembourg, and the Netherlands; and a periphery comprising countries with significantly more idiosyncratic shocks, namely, Finland, Greece, Ireland, Italy, Portugal, Spain, Sweden, and the United Kingdom. But studies based on past behavior may be of little value for predicting the future when it comes to a regime change such as EMU. Thus, countries may meet the OCA criterion ex ante, but not ex post. This is essentially the view held by Krugman,[1] who believes that EMU is bound to foster specialization in Europe and, hence, increase the probability of idiosyncratic shocks. Conversely, countries may meet the OCA criterion ex post, even though they fail to do so ex ante, if EMU reinforces intra-industry rather than interindustry trade, as suggested by Bini-Smaghi and Vori.[2]

On the other hand, the Maastricht criteria may be interpreted as rules for supplying membership to countries able and willing to adhere to a particular brand of monetary union, one characterized by low inflation. Until recently,

[1]Paul Krugman, "Lessons of Massachusetts for EMU," in *Adjustment and Growth in the European Monetary Union*, ed. by Francisco Torres and Francesco Giavazzi (Oxford: Cambridge University Press, 1993), pp. 241–61.

[2]Lorenzo Bini-Smaghi and Silvia Vori, "Rating the EC as an Optimal Currency Area," *Banca d'Italia, Temi di Discussione* (Rome: Bank of Italy, January 1993).

these criteria also suggested that the EU is divided into two groups of countries, roughly equivalent to the two groups identified by the OCA criterion. But the latest evidence shows a great deal of macroeconomic convergence among countries that are nearly EU members, which suggests that the Maastricht criteria may be losing some of their discriminating qualities.

The very interesting paper by Fabio Ghironi and Francesco Giavazzi attempts to provide yet another approach to the insiders-outsiders problem, which differs from the previous two approaches in two fundamental ways. First, Ghironi and Giavazzi are not concerned so much with which countries should be inside or outside the monetary union as with the desirable size of the two groups. In fact, in their paper, there are no differences between the countries that make up the two groupings: no difference in economic structure like in the OCA theory, nor any difference in macroeconomic conditions like in the Maastricht approach. Second, the authors rightly postulate that the relationship between insiders and outsiders needs to be analyzed within a framework that explicitly recognizes the existence of third countries not belonging to the EU.

The goal of Ghironi and Giavazzi is to highlight conflicts that may potentially arise at three separate levels: between different economic authorities within each country; between EU countries inside and outside EMU; and between the EU and the United States, the latter representing all countries outside the EU. To do so, they construct a very elegant three-country model, with two economic authorities in each country: a central bank in charge of monetary policy, and a government controlling fiscal policy. The three economies undergo a common, symmetric shock to which the authorities respond so as to minimize a loss function that depends on inflation and employment. Each of the two authorities has its own loss function, featuring specific relative weights for inflation and employment: the central bank is assumed to care more about inflation, while the government attaches more weight to employment.

The authors analyze different fiscal and monetary policy regimes, but emphasize in the conclusion the setup that, they believe, is most likely to characterize the working of EMU, at least initially: frozen fiscal policies in Europe and in the United States, noncooperative monetary policies under an ERM II regime in Europe, and noncooperative monetary policies under a flexible exchange rate regime between Europe and the United States. Given these assumptions, a number of conflicts emerge: (1) three of the four European authorities favor the largest possible monetary union, but the government of the outs prefers a small union; (2) if a full union is not possible initially, the ECB and the government of the ins are bound to disagree on the merits of enlarging progressively the union; and (3) a similar conflict holds for the central bank and the government of the outs.

I see two problems with the preferred results of Ghironi and Giavazzi. First, they are predicated on the assumption that the monetary authorities of the ins and the outs play a noncooperative game. Essentially, the paper postulates noncooperation and concludes, unsurprisingly, that it implies conflicts of interest. This assumption I find highly unrealistic not only because of existing institutional arrangements in Europe, but also because of the desire of (most of) the outs to join the monetary union. As a matter of fact, the results presented in the paper clearly indicate that cooperation is more desirable than noncooperation, since the values of the loss functions are lower in the former than in the latter case for three of the four European authorities (only the central bank of the outs prefers a noncooperative arrangement). Second, given its extreme complexity, the model cannot be solved analytically. The results, therefore, amount to simulations based on specific numerical assumptions for the key parameters of the model. Hence, in the absence of sensitivity analysis, it is impossible to judge the robustness of these results.

But my main criticism of the paper lies with its basic approach. In particular, I do not share the view of the authors that the most important characterization of the relationship between the ins and the outs is the relative size of the two groupings. To my mind, the crucial differences between the two groupings are in terms of economic structure and macroeconomic conditions. By sweeping these differences under the rug, the authors abstract from the key issue of membership of the ins and the outs. Besides, by focusing on size rather than composition, Ghironi and Giavazzi make the strong assumption of a uniform behavior within the ins and within the outs. While this may be realistic for the presumed ins, it seems a poor assumption for the presumed outs.

Finally, I wish the authors had not treated Europe and the United States symmetrically. What comes to mind, in particular, is the difference in the functioning of labor markets. The paper assumes that, at the start of monetary union, the three countries of the model share equal initial conditions, their economies being in equilibrium. Unfortunately, the reality is far from such ideal. Whereas it can reasonably be argued that the United States is close to full employment, the situation in Europe is one of high unemployment, much of it of a structural nature. This, I believe, is an important potential source of conflict not only between the United States and Europe, but also between central banks and governments in Europe.

Discussion

Mr. Szapáry said he would like to take up two broader issues that had not yet been discussed at the conference but which were worthwhile to consider. First, how would fiscal policy fit into the monetary union? As far as he knew, EMU would be the first large monetary union without a federal budget. There had been earlier examples of similar situations, but not good ones. The Austro-Hungarian monarchy had a monetary union with two separate budgets but the monetary arrangement worked as a quasi-gold standard. So that monetary union was not a good example to illustrate the problems that could result from divergent fiscal policies under EMU.

Having given up monetary and exchange rate policies to treat asymmetric shocks, there remained only fiscal policy for EMU, Mr. Szapáry continued. But depending on the structure of the fiscal policy, asymmetric shocks would affect fiscal policies differently. How could that be dealt with? Should one have a federal budget of some sort? He was not suggesting that one should put on top of the existing budget a federal structure that would actually increase the size of the government, but perhaps some of the responsibilities could be transferred to the federal budget. Otherwise, what kind of coordination in the structure or convergence in the structure of taxes and expenditures would be needed?

Mr. Mussa, in response to a comment by Mr. Alogoskoufis that the potential negative shock to money demand as a result of EMU should be addressed, indicated that there would probably be some effect. The sensible thing to do would be to accommodate the change in the demand for money, and there was no way to do that except by facing up to the difficulty of diagnosing whether and to what extent such a change in the demand for money had taken place.

However, Mr. Mussa continued, there might also be an effect in the other direction. If people had a particular preference to hold on to the old form of bank notes because of a mistrust of the new currency, they might not want to transact them quite as actively. The demand for the old currencies might therefore go up in the short term, and the monetary authorities will need to be alert to whether the demand for high-powered money at given prices, interest rates, and output had changed so that their policy would not become either unduly expansionary or contractionary. The Swiss had faced precisely that type of problem when they changed their reserve requirement procedures for banks and misjudged for a while the impact on the demand for high-powered money.

15

EMU and the Euro: Ensuring a Successful Launch

Michel Camdessus

I hope you have found your discussions at this conference interesting and thought-provoking. Certainly, we at the Fund value this exchange of views and the opportunity it provides to enrich our thinking about the external implications of Europe's forthcoming EMU.

EMU, and the economic convergence it has inspired, is certainly one of the most important and promising developments in the international monetary system in recent decades. For prospective members, the drive toward EMU has provided strong incentives to strengthen domestic economic policies and to begin addressing deep-rooted structural problems. For the EU as a whole, EMU will help reinforce monetary stability and cement economic integration. And for the world, EMU holds out the promise of a strong new pillar for the international monetary system.

For all of these reasons, EMU is a momentous and, indeed, historic enterprise. It is hardly surprising, then, that EMU is also the object of intense public scrutiny and that, as the date for starting Stage III approaches, the inevitable questions concerning the final transition are attracting greater attention. Will Stage III begin on time? How many countries will ride the first wave of monetary union? And what about the other countries that aspire to join EMU but are not among the initial participants? As interest in these and other questions mounts, each new statistic, government action, and barometric reading of market sentiment is scrutinized all the more closely for what it may portend for EMU.

This conference provides a welcome occasion to step back and take a longer view, and in my remarks to you today, I would like to do just that. Let me begin by recalling why Europe has embarked on such an ambitious project and how far EMS members have come toward its achievement. Then, I would like to discuss what remains to be done to ensure EMU's successful commencement in January 1999 and development thereafter.

Why is EMU so important? Certainly, Europe will reap a number of economic benefits from the introduction of a sound common currency. A common currency will lower transaction costs, reduce exchange risk, stimulate competition, and facilitate the broadening and deepening of European financial markets. It will also cement a larger economic space, which will then be better able to face external challenges and more impervious to adverse external shocks. All of these factors should contribute to sustained, noninflationary growth and more rapid job creation, once structural impediments are removed.

But clearly, there is more to EMU than this. Indeed, EMU is the crowning achievement of four decades of European economic integration, a process that, let us not forget, sprang from the ashes of a devastating war among European countries. I would venture to say that, seen from this perspective, EMU is, above all, an essential building block in Europe's growing political unity.

Let us also not forget just how far this process has come. Remember the beginning of the 1950s: European currencies were not convertible, domestic markets were highly protected, and intra-European trade took place on the basis of bilateral clearing arrangements. Today, the situation could hardly be more different: European currencies are freely convertible, and all capital controls have been eliminated. Intra-European tariffs and quotas have long since been removed, and the single market program has further strengthened market integration and the role of market forces.

Meanwhile, during the nearly 20-year existence of the EMS, monetary cooperation among central banks has steadily strengthened. The repeated realignments that marked the early years of the EMS have given way to economic convergence to support exchange rate stability and to limited, and coordinated, central bank action to smooth market fluctuations. In the meantime, intra-European exchange rates have achieved a high degree of stability—at times, even when dollar rates have fluctuated sharply. Indeed, for all intents and purposes, a number of EMS members have already been part of a de facto monetary union for many years.

Certainly, important work still lies ahead, and I will come to that in a moment. Nevertheless, contrary to a widespread popular misperception, the conditions for EMU's successful start are already largely in place.

First, across Europe there is a remarkable consensus on the approach to macroeconomic management—namely, that monetary policy should be directed to price stability; that budgetary policy should aim toward medium- and long-term fiscal sustainability; and that structural reform, especially labor market reform, has an essential role to play in achieving sustained, noninflationary growth and promoting job creation.

Second, most EU members have achieved a high degree of macroeconomic convergence. Inflation in the 15 members of the EU—now projected at

2¼ percent in 1997—is lower than at any point in the last 35 years. Equally striking is the unprecedented narrowing in the dispersion of inflation. All EU members except Greece are expected to have inflation below 3 percent this year and to be in compliance with the reference value in the Maastricht Treaty.

Important progress has also been made in the fiscal area. EU-wide, the general government deficit is projected to be 3¼ percent of GDP in 1997—that is, 3¼ percentage points of GDP below its 1993 peak. Over 2 percentage points of this adjustment is expected to occur in 1996–97, with almost three-quarters of it representing a strengthening of the underlying fiscal position. Among the countries aiming to participate in Stage III from the beginning, all except Italy are projected to satisfy, or come close to satisfying, the Treaty's 3 percent reference value for the fiscal deficit on the basis of measures already announced. In the case of Italy, after the large package adopted last year, the authorities intend to introduce additional measures shortly, with a view to satisfying the reference value. I should add that, when adjusted for the current weakness in economic activity, 1997 deficits are projected to be significantly below 3 percent of GDP in all countries except Greece—although in most cases still short of the close-to-balanced underlying position agreed in the Stability and Growth Pact.

With significant convergence in inflation and public finances, and with progress toward EMU gathering momentum, long-term interest rate differentials vis-à-vis Germany have fallen substantially over the past two years—especially for countries that have had relatively high differentials in the past. The differential for about half of the EU countries is about ½ of 1 percent or less, and all countries aiming to participate in Stage III from the outset would satisfy the Treaty on the basis of the current pattern of interest rates.

But more important, it seems to me, is the fact that this major progress in the macroeconomic and financial areas reflects a significant change in attitudes. Many in Germany, but also in other countries, have rightly sought to make the establishment of a culture of stability a precondition for achieving EMU—and they have prevailed.

Third, solid institutional arrangements are being put in place to ensure the euro's credibility. The Statute of the ECB guarantees the Bank's independence and gives clear priority to low inflation in the conduct of monetary policy. Moreover, the Stability and Growth Pact, with its early warning system and various procedures for enforcing appropriate fiscal adjustment, lays out a strong framework for maintaining budgetary discipline after January 1999. At the same time, the Pact appears to leave sufficient room to tailor policy prescriptions to fit individual country circumstances. All of this augurs well for EMU and the euro.

Finally, I would note that the technical preparations for EMU are well advanced. In particular, the EMI's recently published blueprint of the monetary policy framework in Stage III shows the detailed work that has gone into preparing the full range of monetary policy instruments that the ECB will need to have at its disposal and into readying the cross-border payments system (TARGET) that will help integrate national financial markets. Important agreements have also been reached on the so-called ERM II, which will provide a framework for maintaining stable exchange rates between the euro and EU currencies that do not participate initially in the euro area.

I would observe, however, that the vast amount of internal preparation for EMU stands in sharp contrast to the attention devoted so far to EMU's external dimension. Indeed, the Maastricht Treaty is largely silent on external issues, and little technical work has been done on them so far. Thus, it was high time to hold this conference, which I hope will lead to much more intensive work in this area.

So what does all of this suggest about EMU? In my view, it suggests that this enterprise has been too long in the making, its foundation too solidly laid, and its achievement too important to European integration to court the uncertainties that would stem from its delay. In short, it is time to put to rest, once and for all, any lingering doubts about the future of EMU and to finish the job that is, in any case, so close to completion. So, leaving aside all possible doubts and remaining hesitations, let's concentrate on what "finishing the job" means.

For 1997, finishing the job means that countries must concentrate on fulfilling their Maastricht commitments, especially those concerning deficit reduction. This is the only way to dispel concerns that the desire to begin EMU on time could take precedence over economic fundamentals. Laying these concerns to rest is essential, both to safeguard the credibility of the euro in the financial markets and to ensure public support for EMU. Let me salute countries' courageous efforts to this end.

Will meeting the 3 percent of GDP reference value be an easy task? No, but in most cases, it is feasible. Certainly, this year's budgetary outturn will be influenced by the pace of economic activity in Europe, which has not been as strong as desired. However, there are good grounds for believing that growth will be stronger this year than last and that countries' budgetary positions will improve.

But what if growth turns out to be weaker in 1997 than currently projected? In more normal circumstances—especially where countries were already making a substantial fiscal effort—there would be good reason to allow automatic stabilizers to work. However, the preparations for EMU make the issue more complex. In fact, if slippage in meeting fiscal goals increased market concerns that Stage III were postponed, the consequences could well be more damaging for economic growth than would additional fiscal restraint. In these circumstances, if there were a need to support economic activity—while inflation remained subdued and fiscal consolidation was proceeding—an easing of monetary conditions might be considered. Certainly, the more credible countries' fiscal efforts were, the more scope there would be to pursue such a course.

In the final analysis, however, the most important thing is to ensure that the underlying pace of fiscal consolidation is adequate, and above all, that countries' commitments beyond 1997 are consistent with the Maastricht Treaty. It is on this basis that decisions on which countries will join at the beginning of Stage III will need to be made. Indeed, the Treaty offers some scope for interpretation along these lines. In the meantime, markets need reassurance that the process will be managed in a steady and harmonious way. In this regard, it will be important to avoid taking positions that might unduly narrow the options when the time comes to make decisions on the initial participants in Stage III.

But, let me insist on this: Europe's adjustment task will not be confined to 1997; it also has an important medium-term dimension. First, on the fiscal side, the need to meet the longer-term challenges arising from aging populations and to provide a reasonable amount of scope to accommodate periods of sluggish growth calls for gradually reducing cyclically adjusted budget deficits to near zero, and perhaps, in some cases, turning deficits to surpluses. From this perspective, I would note that the pace of fiscal adjustment required under the Stability and Growth Pact is consistent with the adjustment EU members need to undertake for their own economic well-being, especially given the large uncovered liabilities of their pension systems.

Likewise, both EMU and the need to accelerate growth in Europe call for much more vigorous structural reform, particularly in labor markets and related social policies. In contrast to the record on inflation, fiscal consolidation, and long-term interest rates, progress in addressing labor market rigidities has been painfully slow in most EU countries. Much more determined action is needed, especially in the area of social benefits and the regulations affecting wage structure and severance procedures. As regards EMU, it is widely recognized that greater labor market flexibility is needed to allow economies to adjust to asymmetric shocks. On the other hand, persistently high unemployment associated with labor market rigidities could undermine the credibility of the euro as a stable currency, if markets believe that such rigidities will make it difficult to pursue prudent macroeconomic policies. Beyond these considerations, European economies need to increase labor market flexibility so that they can react more quickly to changing conditions in global markets and raise their potential rates of output growth.

In this connection, EMU must not be saddled with the political blame for necessary, but unpopular, measures to rein in government spending, reform social welfare programs, and remove other structural impediments to growth.

Certainly, the drive to create and participate in EMU has provided some useful political leverage to improve policies and promote convergence. But national authorities need to make it clear to the public that the policy reforms they are undertaking are, above all, good for their own countries—not simply good for EMU.

Let me also say a few words about the countries that plan to join EMU but may not be among its initial members. All countries have a strong interest in seeing that EMU gets off to a good start, even those—or perhaps I should say, *particularly* those—that are not among the first participants. Indeed, those initially outside EMU may benefit most from a solid euro zone, since it is they who would have the most to gain from increased market confidence as their performance converges with that of EMU members. Thus, later entrants must also help ensure that EMU begins on time, and with an appropriate initial size—but most important, that it begins on a sound economic footing. The essential thing is that a clear road map be established for them to join as soon as possible thereafter, so that there are no adverse market reactions and the political will to persevere in the adjustment process is sustained.

Finally, let me say a few words about EMU's implications for the rest of the world—even if more is said on this subject during the regular conference sessions. It is clear that the euro will become a major pillar in the international monetary system. Naturally, this will be an important innovation in the system; hence, it is essential for the rest of the world, as well as for Europe, that the transition be managed well.

At this point, it is very difficult to predict just how the euro will fit into the constellation of other reserve currencies. However, we can safely assume that its position will depend in large part on the strength of its domestic foundations—that is, on the continued macroeconomic convergence of its member countries, the pace of structural reform, the depth and breadth of euro-denominated financial markets, and the degree of political cohesion among EMU members on key policy issues. It is on these grounds that the euro will most likely be judged; and it is in these areas that prospective members must work to ensure EMU's success.

Whatever the uncertainties, we do know that EMU is an ambitious project, but one whose time has come. We know also that the euro's impact on the rest of the world will be large, and that it is our task to make sure that its introduction and development become a positive-sum game for the entire world. Here we must face squarely the risk of higher instability in major currencies' exchange rates in a bi- or tripolar world.

As a matter of fact, the Fund has learned a lot since 1978; each episode of major misalignment—and they were not infrequent—has left us with its lessons. I can tell you that we have learned well a few apparently obvious things:

- how to recognize misalignments;
- how to correct them; and
- what this implies in terms of international dialogue and cooperation.

Thus, we are equipping ourselves to play, in such instances, the role we could be called upon to carry out.

We are mindful of the hesitations of key players today to ask us for assistance in this area. But key players are mindful also of the systemic consequences of their actions, and they are certainly as concerned as we are by the fact that many speakers have reminded us of—namely, that incidences of misalignments could become more frequent and more damaging in a bi- or tripolar world.

If such misalignments do occur, let us hope that the call of Paul Volcker for the expertise of the Fund to be properly used will be heeded and that the Fund will be called upon to do its job, that is—and here I quote Article I of our Articles of Agreement—to "provide the machinery for consultation and collaboration on international monetary problems." The IMF has a major responsibility in this regard. I have no doubt that we will enjoy the full cooperation of the present and future European authorities in developing a constructive dialogue on the potentially difficult issues we may face. Concentrating early enough—and openly enough—on these issues, with the technical support of the professional staff of this institution and the contribution of its entire membership, will be essential in ensuring that EMU and the euro achieve their full potential.

Session VI
Relations Among the IMF, the ECB, and Fund/EMU Members

16

The IMF and Its EMU Members

Jacques J. Polak

The start of EMU in Europe will have a profound effect on the functioning of the international monetary system in general and on the International Monetary Fund in particular. The currencies of a number of major and medium-sized countries will cease to exist and their functions will be taken over by a new, supranational money—the euro. At the same time, these countries will set collectively, rather than on a national basis, some of the most important policy variables of their economies. This paper analyzes the extent to which, in response to these changes in the system, the Fund will need to introduce new approaches and new procedures to ensure that it can continue to discharge effectively the tasks with which it is charged under its Articles of Agreement.

Participation by a country in EMU implies a radical change in that country's ability to control a number of economic and financial variables that have, up to now, been considered essential elements in the management of its economy; that have, accordingly, been the subject of close consultation with the Fund; and that are indeed, to varying degrees, subject to Fund jurisdiction. Specifically, a member of the EMU will differ from most other members of the Fund in these five respects:

1. It will no longer have a currency of its own, but will share a common currency, the euro, which is not the currency of any individual country, with the other members of EMU.
2. It will no longer be able to conduct a monetary policy of its own; instead, the members of EMU will collectively, acting through the ECB, determine a monetary policy for EMU as a whole.
3. Not having a currency of its own, a member will also cease to have an exchange rate of its own as an instrument to influence the operation of its economy.

The author has had the benefit of discussions with a number of IMF staff members, as well as some other experts.

4. It will no longer be able to exercise its own choice in the investment of its holdings of foreign reserve assets. Part of these foreign reserve assets, initially set at 50 billion euros, but subject to subsequent further calls, will have to be transferred to the ECB, which "shall have the full right to hold and manage" these reserves. Nor is a national central bank free in the management of that part of its foreign reserves that is not pooled in the ECB. While it is allowed to perform transactions in fulfillment of its obligations toward international organizations, any other operations in reserves above a certain minimum will be subject to approval by the ECB "in order to ensure consistency with the exchange rate and monetary policies of the [Union]."

5. Finally, a quantitative rather than a qualitative change but nevertheless a change of considerable weight: a member country of EMU will be restrained in the exercise of its fiscal policy in an expansionary direction by its commitment under the Union Treaty to avoid an "excessive deficit" and by the further understandings reached among the EU membership under the Stability and Growth Pact.

The five variables referred to—a member's currency, its monetary policy, its exchange rate policy, its fiscal policy, and, to a lesser degree, the management of its reserves—are all essential elements, in part legal, in part economic and financial, of its relationship to the Fund. A member's exchange rate and its monetary and fiscal policies figure prominently in the consultations with the Fund under Article IV. The Fund's holdings of its currency and the member's holdings of reserves govern many of a member's rights and obligations to the Fund, both in the General Department and in the SDR Department. This paper will highlight the major implications (economic, financial, and to some extent procedural) for a country's membership in the Fund that follow from its membership in EMU. The paper does not enter into legal issues that may arise from the fact that countries that are members of both the IMF and EMU will have to fulfill certain, potentially conflicting, obligations to two international institutions. The discussion of provisions of the Maastricht Treaty will be limited to those of direct relevance to the Fund; for a broader discussion, the reader is referred to Kenen (1995) and Ungerer (forthcoming).[1]

It seems likely at the time of writing that EMU will start with fewer members than the 15 countries that now make up the EU, and that EMU membership will over the years expand as additional countries join the EU and more EU countries qualify for participation in EMU. Ultimately, moreover, further political and policy integration among the membership of the EU may

[1]But neither of these two books contains a reference to the changes that the Treaty brought about in the EU's financial assistance mechanism—a subject that will occupy us in the second part of this paper.

be in the cards. As these developments take place, the relationship between the Fund and EMU will no doubt have to develop. The focus in this paper will be on a situation that lies somewhere between January 1, 1999, when it is expected that a first group of countries will form EMU, and a date well in the next century when "Europe" may have reached a state of not only financial, but also economic and perhaps political, integration. In accordance with this medium-term focus, I shall, on the one hand, ignore the very real problems (not only for EMU but also for the Fund) that may arise in the near term as a result of fact that not all members of the EU will participate in EMU from the start—what has been referred to as the problems of the "ins" and the "outs." I shall also, on the other hand, refrain from any discussion of the (in many respects much simpler) situation that could emerge in a farther distant future if a single "Europe" with a single Fund quota and a single government were to take the place of half-a-dozen, or later perhaps as many as two dozen, countries that were members of both the Fund and EMU.

With respect to the euro, I will assume that it functions as the money of the countries in EMU in much the same way as the dollar functions as the money of the United States. That would imply not only full market convertibility, so that anyone holding euros would be able to acquire in the market any desired foreign currency, but also wide usability for payments outside of its own currency area, so that many payments to countries outside EMU, and indeed outside Europe, could be made in euros. For residents of an EMU country, this would mean that their choice between holding euros and holding dollars or yen would essentially be determined by stock considerations of yield and expected exchange rate movement rather than by the flows of payments to be made.

A further assumption made with respect to the euro is that it will float with respect to the major non-EU currencies. It is true that Article 109 of the Union Treaty starts the provisions on exchange rates for the euro by a discussion of an exchange rate system based on central rates for the euro in relation to those currencies. For the foreseeable future, however, that discussion would appear to have about as much relevance as Article IV, Section 4, of the Fund, which authorizes the Fund to determine that the time is ripe for the reintroduction of a par value regime. That latter provision requires an 85 percent majority of the total voting power in the Fund; a similar system under Article 109 requires unanimity, and there is no indication that the members of EMU would unanimously favor a system of par values or its weaker version, a system of target zones—or that, even if they did favor it, they would find willing partners among the issuers of other major currencies. If, then, it is fair to assume that the euro will float, it is also clear that the ESCB may well adopt monetary and/or intervention policies designed to affect the rate; moreover, as discussed below, the Council of Ministers is authorized to "formulate general orientations for exchange rate policy" in relation to other major currencies. One important effect of the floating character of the euro is that the monetary aggregates for the EMU are not subject to an automatic impact from the side of the balance of payments.

When an important group of members of the Fund joins to form EMU, both the Fund's policy relations and its financial relations with the members of this group will be profoundly affected. The issues arising in these two areas are discussed in this paper.

That discussion can draw to some extent on the Fund's experience with a group of other members that are associated in a monetary union. About a dozen of the Fund's francophone African members have, from before their membership in the IMF, been organized into two currency unions, both of which use the CFA franc as their common currency, and the Fund's relations with these members has always reflected this common feature, as well as their special relationship to France. But the large weight in the world economy of even the initial group of EMU countries, in contrast to the small weight of the CFA countries, transposes the issues posed by a currency union among certain members from marginal to central importance to the Fund.

Fund's Policy Relations with EMU Members

The centralization in EMU of a number of crucial policy areas of its members in no way diminishes the need for the Fund to remain appropriately informed about conditions and policy attitudes in EMU member countries and in the EU generally; to judge the policies followed by the EMU and its members against the requirements of the world financial and economic system; and to exercise such influence on the substance and the execution of these policies as it considers necessary from the point of view of the Fund's membership as a whole. This part of the paper will argue that the achievement of these objectives will require a three-pronged approach by the Fund. (1) The Fund will need to maintain the present arrangements for bilateral consultations with individual EMU countries; (2) it will need to establish relationships with certain organs of the EU that will cover, at a minimum as effectively as at present, the areas of decision making that have moved from the individual countries to EMU;[2] and (3) some further steps will be needed

[2]The Fund's experience in dealing with the CFA franc countries and the two regional central banks is of some relevance in this context. In addition to its annual consultations with CFA franc countries, the Fund holds semiannual discussions with each regional bank, covering monetary policy, the financial situation of commercial banks, bank supervision and restructuring, and regional cooperation issues. But the staff does not report on these discussions to the Executive Board, and the Board does not normally discuss monetary and exchange rate policies of the zone as a whole, with its discussion in the aftermath of the 1994 devaluation of the CFA franc being a welcome exception.

to deal specifically with exchange rate questions among the three reserve currencies of the system.

Continued Need for Bilateral Consultations

The centralization in EMU of such important policy areas as the exchange rate, money, and, to some extent, fiscal matters, might suggest that there would be less need, or perhaps no need at all, for the broad types of consultation that the Fund now conducts with each of the countries that will join in EMU. That would be a mistaken inference, on both legal and economic grounds. Like any other members of the Fund, members of EMU must comply with the general obligations regarding exchange arrangements of Article IV, Section 1, and be guided by the specific principles with respect to exchange rate policies adopted by the Fund (Article IV, Sections 3(a) and (b)). On the economic front, members of EMU are likely to continue to have problems in many areas of concern to the Fund that will require consideration on a country-by-country basis rather than through some overall approach. The countries that will make up EMU account for a large part of the world economy and the Fund will need to continue to understand, for example, for its work on the World Economic Outlook (WEO), the economic and financial forces at work in each of these countries. It will also need to learn how the centralized policies affect the very different parts of the EU and the implications of these effects for the centralized decision making by EMU and the Council of Ministers, where the experience of the individual participants feeds back into the collective action of the group as a whole. For these reasons, consultations between the Fund and its EMU members, under Article IV and in conjunction with the WEO, will need to continue, in most respects pretty much as at present, even though the members concerned would be constrained in terms of exchange rate or monetary policies.

Even though the third phase of EMU is still nearly two years away, this conclusion is more than the result of a speculation on a future set of conditions. For a number of years, Austria, Belgium, and the Netherlands have conducted their affairs as if they no longer had control over either their exchange rate or their monetary policy. More recently, France has moved to the same position. All four countries now treat the benefits of their policy of anchoring on the deutsche mark as paramount and rule out conceivable alternatives, such as a unilateral reduction of short-term interest rates to promote employment. But these attitudes, which are well known from public statements by the authorities, in no way diminish the importance of Fund consultations with these four countries. In all of them, such areas of concern as medium-term fiscal consolidation, labor market policies to attack unemployment, pension reform, restructuring of the tax system, privatization, and strengthening of the banking system received extensive attention in recent years in the discussions of the staff and the subsequent discussion by the Executive Board of the staff's report. On many of these matters, moreover, the consultation process was, it is believed, helpful to the member countries concerned in their own search for policy improvements that are recognized as clearly needed.

These comments on the continued value of consultations with four countries on their way toward monetary union are reinforced by the Fund's experience with Luxembourg, which has been a member of a monetary association for over 70 years. Until the mid-1980s, the Fund acted indeed as if there was no real need for consultations with this junior member of the Belgo-Luxembourg Economic Union. It treated the consultations with Luxembourg (which were required by the Articles of Agreement) as a perfunctory adjunct to those with Belgium. Since 1983, however, the Fund has held full-scale consultations with Luxembourg (every other year, as is done with other small countries with few immediate problems) and has found that country's policies to be distinctly different from (and in many respects more successful than) those of other countries in the region, including Belgium. Luxembourg has a high rate of growth, low unemployment (in spite of nearly all the labor market rigidities that are common in Europe), a budget in surplus in most years, and practically no government debt—just to mention a few features. The absence of independent exchange rate and monetary policies are so much a fact of life that they require no discussion in the consultations. But Luxembourg does have some serious medium-term problems related to its pension system and the high variability of its tax receipts; the extensive discussion of these matters in the consultations was recognized as valuable by the Luxembourg authorities.

Need for Systemic Relationship Between the Fund and EU Central Authorities

While the consultations under Article IV will continue as a useful and necessary procedure for the policy dialogue between an EMU member and the Fund, they will obviously fall short of what that member's relationship with the Fund requires on those policies that under EMU are no longer under the member's control but are exercised centrally by the relevant organs of the EU, in particular the ECB and the Council of Ministers. Since the member has no power by itself to change any policy in the areas of communal management, any view that the Fund might have on the desirability of a particular policy stance for the EU as a whole will need to be pursued in consultations with the appropriate central organs of the EU.

The Fund has for many years been faced with a somewhat similar situation with respect to the discussion of trade policies with members of the EU. Consultation on this subject with individual EU members proved to be somewhat frustrating because control over members' policies on trade is vested in the EU. If the Fund favored a change in the trade policies of an individual member, it was often advised in bilateral consultations that it was not up to the member (whether it agreed with the Fund's view or not) to deviate from a policy decided in Brussels; and the Fund had no recognized standing to argue its case before the EU. However, given the fact that trade matters did not constitute a central component of Article IV consultations with EU countries, the Fund could allow this rather untidy situation to persist.

But for the Fund to take a comparably relaxed attitude toward the surveillance of the exchange rate for the euro, and the monetary policy of EMU underlying this rate, would be irreconcilable with its Articles of Agreement—its Purposes as well as Article IV. The Fund can and should accept the proposition that a group of its members joined in a monetary union have a single currency with, of course, a single exchange rate. It has never questioned that proposition with respect to its CFA members, even when it became convinced, in the late 1980s, that the exchange rate for the CFA franc had become economically unsuitable for many, though not necessarily for all, of the countries in the CFA franc area. At the same time, however, each member, whatever its exchange rate regime, must obey the exchange rate obligations of the Articles; floating exchange rates are not exempt from scrutiny under Article IV.[3] In the EMU setting, however, it would hardly be practical for the Fund to enforce this obligation by means of its Article IV consultations with individual members.

The fact that the exchange rate of the euro against the other major currencies will be one of the most important determinants of competitive conditions in world markets makes it essential that the Fund and its EMU members devise suitable alternative techniques for surveillance over the exchange rate of the euro and the underlying monetary policy of EMU. The objectives of the Fund in this context should be, as a minimum, (1) that it receive a full explanation of the views and objectives of the EMU authorities with respect to the rate for the euro and of the policies pursued by the ECB to influence that rate, and (2) that it be expected to express its view on both this rate and the underlying policies. In view of the prominence of the euro, it would probably be understood that the Fund could, as it does for the dollar and the yen, make public any well-considered expression of view with respect to the euro, for example in the *Annual Report*.[4] Note that the two objectives specified define approxi-

[3]In the 1977 Decision on Surveillance over Exchange Rate Policies, the last item in the list of "developments . . . which might indicate the need for a discussion with a member" specifies "(v) behavior of the exchange rate that appears to be unrelated to underlying economic conditions including factors affecting competitiveness and long-term capital movements" (IMF, 1992, p. 11).

[4]In its *Annual Report* for 1996, the Fund noted that as of July 1995 the yen "had become clearly overvalued in terms of fundamentals" (p. 56) and that "economic policies [in the United States] should not be aimed at specific targets for the dollar's exchange rate" (p. 54).

mately what the Fund achieves from its bilateral consultations with major member countries. But this still leaves a serious gap in the management of the international exchange rate system: the absence of a mechanism to resolve conflicts on the pattern of exchange rates for the three reserve currencies. I shall return to this issue later in this section.

Consultations with the Central Authorities of the EU

If the Fund is to consult with the central authorities of the EU, the question arises what the appropriate authorities of the EU are in this context. No doubt, this matter will require discussions between the Fund and the EU to find a solution acceptable to both. Normally, in its relations with individual members, the Fund conducts its consultations with the ministry of finance and the central bank. In the case of EU members joined in EMU, three rather than two *loci consultandi* would appear indicated: the ECB, the Council of Ministers (ECOFIN), and the Commission. The Treaty lodges with the ESCB the responsibility "to define and implement the monetary policy of the Community" (Article 105.2), but it divides responsibility for exchange rate policy between the Council of Ministers and the ESCB (Kenen, 1995, p. 31). Both organs must under the Treaty pursue price stability as the primary, but not the sole, objective of policy. The "primary objective" laid down for the ESCB "shall be to maintain price stability," but if it can do so without prejudice to this objective, "the ESCB shall support the general economic policies in the Community with a view to contributing to the achievement of the objectives of the Community as laid down in Article 2" (Article 105.1).[5] And the Council may "formulate general orientations for exchange-rate policy," but under the proviso that these "orientations" be "without prejudice to the primary objective of the ESCB to maintain price stability" (Article 109.2). It appears to be understood that such orientations would not be binding on the ESCB (Kenen, 1995, p. 32; Ungerer, forthcoming, p. 232), although the effort that has obviously gone into the drafting of Article 109.2 suggests that the ESCB should give them due attention.

The arrangements (imprecise as they may be) for shared responsibility between the Council and the ECB for exchange rate policy and thus, at one remove, for monetary policy make it clear that the Fund would need to pursue a strong consultative relationship with both ECOFIN and the ECB, in addition to developing further its already existing relationship to the Commission (see below).

[5]These objectives include ". . . balanced development of economic activities, sustainable and non-inflationary growth respecting the environment, a high degree of convergence of economic performance, a high level of employment and of social protection, the raising of the standard of living and quality of life, and economic and social cohesion. . . ."

There would appear to be no technical difficulties in designing a consultation process with the ECB that would replicate the Fund's existing procedures for consultations with individual member countries. These procedures consist of (1) well-prepared discussions with the authorities by a staff mission; (2) a report on these discussions to the Executive Board with a summarizing staff appraisal; (3) a discussion of this report in the Board, with the participation of a representative of the authorities; and (4) a summing-up of the discussion by the Managing Director that is conveyed to the authorities.

Consultation with the Council of Ministers is not so simple a matter. ECOFIN meets normally about once a month, under a presidency that rotates every six months with that of the EU. Unlike the EMI at present and, one may expect, the ECB in future, the Council does not have an economic staff. Perhaps the most promising approach for the Fund might lie in close contact with the EU Economic and Financial Committee (EFC, the successor to the Monetary Committee), which is a committee of high officials from finance ministries and central banks (with two representatives each from the Commission and the ECB) that prepares the work of the Council. The possibility of a Fund observer at the meetings of the Monetary Committee has on a number of occasions been raised between the Fund and the Community. That issue deserves reconsideration in the present context.

The Fund has made a promising start toward "consultations" with the EU by organizing, on an annual schedule since 1994, a kind of proto-consultation with the Commission and the EMI. So far, the subject of these consultations has mostly been limited to the progress toward EMU. These activities have been organized around the four procedural steps listed above, that is, a staff report, discussions in Brussels and Frankfurt, a discussion of the report by the Executive Directors (in a "seminar" rather than in a formal meeting of the Board), and a summing-up by the Managing Director. While no representative of the Commission or the EMI participated in the discussions among the Directors, the views of the Commission on the staff report were (for the first time in 1996) conveyed to Directors by means of a letter from its Director General for Economic and Financial Affairs.

Need for a Strengthened International Mechanism to Deal with Exchange Rate Questions of the System's Reserve Currencies

A review of the Fund's experience with surveillance since the Second Amendment of the IMF's Articles of Agreement (1978) would probably conclude that the organization has been able to exercise a satisfactory degree of surveillance with respect to most currencies by means of its consultation approach and the conditionality it requires in the context of the use of its resources. But with respect to the currencies of the major industrial countries, the Fund has never achieved the "firm surveillance of the exchange rate policies of members" that it has since 1978 been charged to exercise under Article IV, Section 3(b), of the Articles of Agreement. While the consultation mechanism has proved adequate as a source of information to the Fund and to its member countries as well, and has given the Fund the needed opportunities to make its views known in member countries at the highest policy levels, it has failed to provide a mechanism or a forum for conflict resolution in the event of exchange rate conflicts among major countries. The reasons for this failure are well known. The IMF's Executive Board, where any such conflicts would find a hearing, is unsuitable as a forum for conflict resolution, both because it is too large and because Executive Directors lack the authority to negotiate on issues of this weight in national policy. The Interim Committee, even though it operates at the level of ministers, has not shown itself to be any more suitable for this function, if only because it equals the Executive Board in size.

Yet the creation of the euro, which will be the second most important currency in the system, enhances the need for an orderly mechanism of conflict resolution for the major currencies. For the near future, the euro will represent a new and unpredictable element in the world's exchange markets. Unlike its predecessor the ECU, the euro will not be a basket of currencies but, as the Treaty puts it, "a currency in its own right." It will be open to the full forces of the market, being tethered only weakly by effects exercised by purchasing power parity in the long run.

It is important in this connection to recall the meaning in the Maastricht Treaty of the concept of "stability," which, as we noted, both the ECB and the finance ministers must recognize as their primary objective. As in the hierarchy of objectives of the Bundesbank, "stability" means *domestic* or *price* stability and not *external* or *exchange rate* stability. For a small or even a medium-sized country, this may often not be an important distinction: if the external value of its currency declines, domestic inflation is normally either the cause or the effect, and sometimes both. But for very large countries, or a large grouping of countries such as EMU, the distinction is crucial; indeed, such countries may sometimes rely on exchange rate fluctuations to contribute to stabilization of the domestic price level.

In connection with the stability issue it is instructive to consider the experience of the yen over the past 1½ years. In mid-1995 the yen had, by common consent, risen well above its long-run equilibrium value,[6] thus threatening to undermine an already weak recovery. In response to this situation, the Group of Seven industrial countries took collective action with the double aim of bringing the yen to a more appropriate level and putting the re-

[6]See the comment in the Fund's 1996 *Annual Report*, cited in footnote 5.

covery on a more solid footing, an objective that Japan appeared to be unable to achieve by adopting a more expansionary fiscal policy (Polak, 1995, p. 748). The set of policies adopted by Japan, which included an extremely low level of interest rates and, at times but by no means consistently, massive intervention in the exchange market, reduced the value of the yen by one-third (from 80 to over 120 yen/dollar) in a period of about 18 months. The inflationary impact of this depreciation proved to be minuscule: the consumer price index, which had risen by about ½ percent per year from mid-1993 to mid-1995, continued to rise at about the same rate over the next 18 months and for 1997 the underlying rate of inflation (excluding the effect of an increase in consumption taxes) is expected to be less than 1 percent. Thus, Japan succeeded in greatly improving its competitive position by means of depreciation of the yen, without undermining in any significant way its long-standing near-perfect anti-inflationary reputation.

A number of factors contributed to this result, and not all of them would apply to a future EMU. Japan has a very large economy in which the weight of foreign trade in GNP is relatively small; the same will apply to the EMU region. Japan kept down the impact of the depreciating yen on the final costs of imports by market-opening measures; in Europe, imports, at least nonfood imports, from outside the region are already mostly under a liberal regime. Japan also kept the cost of living down by major moves in the direction of deregulation; in Europe, too, there is still considerable scope for action on this front. Finally, Japan's exchange rate action did not succeed fully in dispelling the deflationary cloud hanging over the economy; how would the European economy respond to a falling euro? In any event, such direct evidence as is available from Europe on the inflationary effect of a depreciation seems to point in the same direction as the data for Japan. Over the past year, the deutsche mark and the European currencies linked to it have depreciated against the dollar by about 15 percent; but, to take the example of Germany, its inflation rate over the same period has been lower than in any year since the second half of the 1980s, about 1½ percent.[7]

All this suggests that the pursuit by the EMU participants of "stability" as defined in the Treaty does not ensure the fulfillment by these countries of their exchange rate obligation under Article IV. It would indeed not be difficult to envisage circumstances in which market forces could push the value of the euro to an unduly low level, or different circumstances that would lead to an unduly high level. If the U.S. economy remains strong and the European

[7]It may be observed that the deutsche mark depreciated much less in effective terms, but this misses the point as far as the implications for EMU are concerned. *Because* many European currencies are already linked together almost as closely as in a currency union, their joint depreciation has only a modest effect on the effective exchange rate, and hence on the price level, of any one of these countries.

economy weak, the value of the euro might well follow further on the recent downward path of the ECU, just as the yen has declined in similar circumstances during the last 18 months. If, by contrast, the creation of the euro sets off, perhaps after some years, a widespread reshuffling from dollars to euros in the foreign exchange portfolios of both central banks and corporations around the world, the euro could rise sharply against the dollar. Initial movements in either direction might induce large bandwagon effects, leading to serious misalignments.

Considerations of this nature suggest that the new challenges to the system posed by the euro require of the Fund something more than the mere adaptation of the existing bilateral surveillance mechanism to the special features of a currency union, or the presentation of the issues of the world economy in the WEO. There will be a need for a mechanism that addresses directly potential conflicts of interest arising from the movements of the exchange rates among the reserve currencies.

Some ten years ago there was a rather widespread belief that reliance could be placed on the Group of Seven industrial countries to resolve any such conflicts that might arise. The Group of Seven has indeed booked a few notable successes with respect to the major currencies in the Plaza Agreement and the Louvre Accord (in 1985 and 1987, respectively) and it has on a number of subsequent occasions exercised beneficial effects on exchange markets. But according to Bergsten, perhaps the strongest advocate of the "assigned role" of the Group of Seven in the international monetary system, the Group of Seven has in recent years "consistently failed to exercise its responsibility for currency management" (Bergsten and Henning, 1996, p. 34) and "every G-7 currency has experienced a major realignment during the last decade and none of them have been handled effectively" (p. 30). The Group of Seven members are said to have, as it were, adopted a "nonaggression pact," retreating into a "consensus of inaction" by which each of them manages to avoid commenting on the policies of any of the others (Chapter 5). Bergsten and Henning advocate an action program to shake the Group of Seven out of its lethargy so that it can resume what they consider its assigned role, that of a de facto steering committee for the world economic system (Chapter 7). It seems much more likely, however, that the Group's attitude of "live and let live" that they deplore is not a passing weakness but a natural reaction to the many other problems of the world for which the Group of Seven is a relatively suitable forum,[8] plus the natural desire of ministers not to antagonize their colleagues unless forced to do so by

---

[8]In recent years, these have included conclusion of the GATT negotiations, aid to Russia and Ukraine, solutions to the debt problem, Fund quotas, SDR allocations, the prevention of future "Mexicos," enlargement of the GAB, and other matters of common concern to the Group.

a clear national interest. In addition, the Group of Seven is probably also too large to deal effectively with problems that concern primarily the United States, Japan, and EMU.[9]

The above analysis may perhaps be summarized in four propositions concerning the international monetary system.

1. Once the euro is in place, there will be a clear hierarchy of currencies, with a sharp distinction between, on the one hand, the three reserve currencies of the system (dollar, euro, and yen) and, on the other hand, all other currencies. As far as one can see, the three reserve currencies will continue to float against each other; for all other currencies, each issuer will have to weigh the relative benefits of some degree of fixity versus those of a float, presumably in almost all cases a managed float.

2. Because of the large economic size of the issuers of the reserve currencies, the responses of their economies to exchange rate changes (in terms of both inflation rates and changes in trade flows) are likely to be both small and slow. This enhances the risk of major misalignments developing among these currencies. Against this risk, neither standard Fund surveillance nor the intermittent attention that the Group of Seven gives to exchange rate problems provides adequate protection.

3. The consequences of any such misalignments would be most severely felt by the issuers of the reserve currencies themselves. By contrast, if the rates among these currencies remain within tolerable ranges, other countries will be able to conduct their trade in an acceptable framework, if necessary by making adjustments to the values of their own currencies against one or more of the reserve currencies.

4. The chances of resolving exchange rate conflicts are greatest when these problems are dealt with in a forum of the smallest possible number of participants. In this case, as we have noted, that number would be three—two countries and EMU. In addition, as a practical matter it is desirable, if at all possible, to deal with problems of the system in existing forums to avoid overloading even further the schedules of busy ministers.

These four propositions suggest that the needed strengthening of the international monetary system be directly associated with the periodic meetings of the Interim Committee and of the finance ministers of the Group of Seven. On the occasion of each such meeting—that is, about two or three times a

[9]Political pressures tend, moreover, to increase the size of the Group of Seven, and there is no reason to expect the merger into EMU of the *financial* affairs of certain European countries to provide a counterweight to this tendency. Contrary to the hope expressed by the authors, there seems to be little likelihood that in the foreseeable future the "G-7 could streamline its own membership by becoming a G-3" (Bergsten and Henning, 1996, p. 139).

year—the Managing Director of the IMF could, together with the issuers of the three reserve currencies of the system, conduct a review of the current and prospective functioning of the reserve currency system. If this review brought out unsatisfactory features, such as the presence or the likely development of significant misalignments of the exchange rates among the three currencies, the participants would be expected to seek agreement on measures that would bring about the necessary corrections.

Fund's Financial Relations with EMU Members

The Fund frequently sells, and receives in repurchase, the currencies of countries that are likely to become EMU members. It also arranges many transactions in which members sell or buy the currencies of prospective EMU members for SDRs. By contrast, European members of the Fund have almost never in recent years bought other currencies from the Fund for their own currencies. This second part of the paper discusses how the various types of Fund transactions and operations in currencies and SDRs would be affected by the entry into force of EMU for a group of Fund members. We begin with the use by the Fund of the currencies of EMU members.

Fund Use of the Resources Provided by EMU Members

At the beginning of Stage III, the countries joining EMU will presumably replace the Fund's holdings of their respective national currencies by balances in euros—a bookkeeping operation that will not change the value of the Fund's holdings expressed in SDRs. The balances in euros will not be merged into a single euro account of the Fund. The national positions vis-à-vis the Fund of individual EMU members will be recorded in separate euro accounts for each EMU member. That member will continue to have all the benefits from the position of its account (remuneration, reserve tranche drawing rights) as well as all obligations (burden sharing, maintenance of SDR value). The Fund will be able to sell euros from these accounts in its transactions and receive euros for these accounts in repurchases. Under designation (or the consensual procedures that the Fund uses as a substitute for designation), individual EMU members will buy and sell euros for SDRs. Euros sold by the Fund in drawings or made available against SDRs by an EMU member will be convertible into other currencies in the market or, if the ECB so decides, at the ECB.

Under one of the Protocols of the Maastricht Treaty, the "ECB may hold and manage IMF reserve positions and SDRs and provide for the pooling of such assets" (Article 30.5 of the Statute of the ESCB and the ECB). As far as SDRs are concerned, this seems to raise no problem provided the ECB, as an "other holder" of SDRs, pays interest on the pooled SDRs or the euro balances members acquired from the sale of SDRs to it. Reserve positions in the Fund cannot be treated in the same way, however. They are classified as reserves because they entitle the country "holding" them to an automatic reserve tranche purchase, but they are not an asset that can be transferred to the ECB (or to anyone else) to be used at its discretion.

For the rest, the ECB and the Fund will need to review jointly their treatment of Fund positions, including the criteria that the Fund applies for the selection of countries to be drawn upon (the expression "currencies to be drawn" will no longer serve) and for designation. Questions such as the following are likely to arise. Will the ECB allow EMU countries to freely use their reserve tranche positions in the Fund? Will the ECB stand ready to buy for euros any SDRs that an EMU/Fund member has bought for euros under designation—in which case designation ceases to have any effect on the financial position of the individual EMU member selected for this operation? If the EMU pools all SDR holdings, should the Fund persist in filling up the members' apparent net use of SDRs by designation?

EMU Members as Potential Users of Fund Resources

While the transition from holding the national currencies of EMU members to holding the same amount of assets in the form of euros raises certain technical problems for the Fund, the question whether and in what circumstances EMU members may themselves make use of the Fund's resources has far more important ramifications.

None of the 15 countries that are now members of the EU has used the resources of the Fund in the credit tranches in the last 20 years and none of them has even made a reserve tranche drawing in the last decade or so. It might seem natural to assume that this situation would likely continue and hence to disregard, as a practical matter, any possibility of future use of the Fund's resources by those members of the EU that had joined EMU.

That assumption seems less plausible, however, if it is recalled that one reason why none of these countries found it necessary to draw on the Fund was that in the past the EU itself offered balance of payments assistance to "a Member State [that] is in difficulties or is seriously threatened with difficulties as regards its balance of payments, . . . where such difficulties are liable in particular to jeopardize the functioning of the common market or the progressive implementation of the common commercial policy . . ." (Article 109h). Since 1974, Greece (twice), France, Ireland, and Italy (four times) have received assistance from the EU, in amounts that were on some occasions large in terms of the countries' IMF quotas at the time (Table 1). But the provision in the Treaty under which such assistance could be granted lapses for

Table 1. European Community: Medium-Term Financial Assistance

Year	Beneficiary	Amount (in millions)	Percent of IMF Quota[1]
1974	Italy	$1,391	115
1976	Italy	$1,100	95
1976	Ireland	DM 500	160
1977	Italy	$500	45
1983	France	ECU 4,000	115
1985	Greece	ECU 1,750	330
1991	Greece	ECU 2,200[2]	500
1993	Italy	ECU 8,000[3]	145

Sources: Commission of the European Communities (1990); and IMF, *IFS Yearbook*.

[1]Approximate calculation on the basis of average exchange rates for the year of the currency lent and the SDR; IMF quotas in the year of the loan.

[2]In three installments, of which only the first (ECU 1,000 million) was disbursed.

[3]In four installments, of which only the first two (ECU 2,000 million each) were disbursed.

any country that joins EMU. EMU members will only be able to fall back on an emergency provision that was grudgingly introduced at a rather late stage in the Maastricht negotiations. This provision allows the Council, acting unanimously, to grant conditional EU financial assistance to a member state that is "in difficulties or is seriously threatened with severe difficulties caused by exceptional occurrences beyond its control" (Article 103a.2).[10]

Two sets of considerations seem to underlie the decision to cut sharply the EU's traditional, but by no means automatic, financial support for those of its members that enter upon the new, and in some respects riskier, participation in EMU while leaving it in place for the countries that have not taken this step.

One of these was the overriding concern in the drafting of the financial provisions of the Treaty to establish beyond any room for doubt, either by the markets or within member countries, that a member of EMU will not be rescued from the consequences of its own profligate financial policies. This concern is embodied expressly in the so-called "no-bailout clause" of the Treaty (Article 104) that prohibits the ECB or its constituent national central banks from establishing any type of credit facility in favor of members' central governments or the governments of any lower public bodies, but the same concern also permeates other provisions of the Treaty, such as those on "excessive deficits."

The other consideration appears to have been the view that once countries are joined in a currency union, they no longer have a balance of payments of

[10]It is noteworthy that while the original assistance clause speaks of *balance of payments* difficulties, the new facility introduced by Articles 103a omits any reference to the balance of payments.

their own and are thus no longer open to balance of payments difficulties. Thus, in its "Remarks" accompanying its proposal for a draft Treaty for Economic and Monetary Union, the Commission observed that "[i]n an economic and monetary union, it is the general economic problems of the Member States and economic convergence which concern the Community rather than the balance of payments difficulties of a particular Member State. Present Articles 104 and 109 thus become superfluous."[11] In the same vein: "In EMU, the disappearance of the balance of payments constraint for the individual Member States obviously renders meaningless a facility for balance of payments difficulties" (Papaspyrou, 1993, p. 486—but he follows this by noting that "this does not make the financial constraint less real."). And: "How could a member country [of the Fund] that participated in EMU prove a balance of payments need, indispensable for the use of SDRs, while problems of balance of payments disequilibrium become, once EMU is a reality, interregional problems as is the case within a state?" (Louis, 1997, p. 204, current author's translation).

The views here cited reflect an unduly narrow concept of the balance of payments and one not found in the seminal EC report on the role of public finance in European integration (MacDougall, 1977). That narrow concept, moreover, does not agree with the law and practices of the Fund.

A deficit in the balance of payments, that is, an excess of outpayments over inpayments, is not an experience that is limited to a nation state. Even though balance of payments statistics are more frequently compiled for sovereign states than for smaller political or geographic entities, it is conceptually just as possible for a region, a province, or a county as for a national state to suffer from payments difficulties. Scitovsky (1969, pp. 94–98) deals extensively with interregional payments adjustment in the United States, in particular the financial flows from "East" to "West" that would cover a current account surplus of "West" against "East."[12] The MacDougall Report shows how in each of four European countries (France, Germany, Italy, and the United Kingdom) there was a clear correlation between two items in the balances of payments of the country's relatively poor versus its relatively rich regions: public finance *inflows* are associated with current account *deficits*, *outflows* with *surpluses* (Table 4 on p. 23).

The consequences of a payments deficit are in many respects the same for any area, whether it constitutes a national state or not: a loss of money and other assets to the rest of the world and concurrently (if the deficit is in the current account) a loss of income and the threat of a deflationary spiral. It is of no con-

---

[11]Commission of the European Communities (1990). Unlike the German and French proposals, the Commission's proposed Treaty text introduced a substitute provision, which after considerable hardening became Article 103a referred to above. I am grateful to Horst Ungerer for providing me with the relevant documentation.

[12]For more recent literature dealing with subnational balance of payments questions see, for example, Atkeson and Bayoumi (1993) and literature cited therein.

sequence for the deficit area whether the loss is one of foreign exchange or of the "domestic" money of the country to which it belongs. In the context of EMU, in any event, with the euro a fully convertible and also a reserve currency, the distinction between foreign and domestic money is irrelevant as far as the payments situation of any member is concerned. The same is of course true in the United States: if, for example, the oil industry of Texas becomes depressed, that state is likely to move into both a payments deficit and a recession, even though the drain on its money supply is in dollars, not in foreign exchange.

Within countries a large proportion of a regional trade deficit is likely to be compensated through the public finance system. Because of the small size of the Community budget compared to its aggregate GNP, such automatic compensation is largely absent within the EU. "[A] member of the Community suffering a proportionally much smaller initial disturbance might, because of absence of any substantial compensation through the Community finances, find its balance of payments so seriously in deficit that the difficulty of meeting the situation by borrowing could force upon it a reduction of income larger, perhaps much larger, than the initial fall in its export earnings." (MacDougall, 1977, p. 35).

The Maastricht Treaty has constructed formidable defenses against one source of payments difficulties of any member of EMU, namely, lax fiscal policies (and of course no EMU member can any longer engage in a monetary policy of its own). The members of the EU that are allowed to pass into Stage III will have given evidence of having straightened out their fiscal positions. After joining EMU they will remain subject to surveillance from the Union in order to forestall, it is hoped, or otherwise to correct quickly, any "excessive deficits." And they will have agreed to observe, under penalty of heavy fines, the Stability and Growth Pact. All these are important safeguards against any one of these countries spending itself into balance of payments difficulties. But while balance of payments difficulties are often due to government overspending, this is not the only possible reason for such difficulties.

Countries can price themselves out of world markets by wage or social policies that are more generous than those of their competitors. They can fail to adjust with sufficient speed to changes in the international demand for their products. They can become accustomed to a steady inflow of capital from abroad and may find it difficult to reverse course when that inflow subsides, or turns into an outflow, for reasons that may or may not be related to their economies. To mention only one example from the recent past: Mexico's payment difficulties arose *after* it had achieved a fundamental strengthening of its public finances, with a nonfinancial public sector close to balance in both 1993 and 1994 (Buira, 1996, p. 314), but in the latter year, the quasi-fiscal deficit of the state-owned banks had run up to some 4 percent of GDP.

Members of the EMU, even if they scrupulously avoid the pitfalls of "excessive deficits," thus remain exposed to a variety of asymmetric economic shocks that can lead to balance of payments problems. Yet they have neither the same support from automatic transfer mechanisms—through taxes and welfare payments—nor the labor mobility that characterize a more closely integrated economic union such as the United States (Goodhart and Smith, 1993, analyzing a number of earlier papers on the subject).

Within the EU, the problem of uncompensated asymmetric shocks has long been recognized as one that needed to be addressed, in particular in the context of EMU, with the focus typically on "stabilization" rather than on the compensation of balance of payments problems (Goodhart and Smith, 1993, and many earlier studies cited there). One interesting recent paper (Italianer and Vanheukelen, 1993) proposes a stabilization fund for the Community that would make financial resources available to EMU members on an automatic basis when their monthly unemployment rate had increased by more than the average increase in the EMU, and presents various possibilities for the financing of such a fund. But the lack of action on the many proposals for "stabilization" made over the last 20 years would seem to justify the conclusion, drawn by Papaspyrou, who echoes in this respect the Delors Report that 'genuine' stabilization mechanisms at the Community level are not on the agenda regardless of their merits (p. 483); he therefore advocates, as a second-best arrangement, to build on the new facility created in Article 103a, with support under this facility to be provided partly in the form of credits financed by Community borrowing in the market and partly in the form of grants financed from the Community budget.

The question arises whether the members of the Union—having scrapped the traditional assistance mechanism and then, reluctantly at least on the part of some members, replaced it by a more restrictive new mechanism—would be willing to envisage the almost routine application of that new mechanism on the basis of "a system of suitable economic and financial indicators" as proposed by Papaspyrou (p. 488). In any event, if the alternative to a true stabilization mechanism in the EU is to be the extension of balance of payments credit in particular circumstances, it may be worth bearing in mind that as long as EMU members remain individual members of the IMF, they retain access to the resources of the IMF when they encounter payments difficulties that destabilize their economies.[13]

[13]For a member to be able to draw on the Fund's resources, it must represent that it has a need to draw "because of its balance of payments or its reserve position or developments in its reserves" (Article V, Section 3(b)(ii)). The last two arguments would not be applicable to a country that had pooled its reserves in a common EMU pool, leaving only the balance of payments test. There is no reason to assume that the introduction of the euro would make it impossible to draw up balance of payments statements for individual EMU countries (such statements exist for individual CFA franc countries). Even if EMU countries were at some time to cease preparing such statements, it would surely not prove difficult (as discussed in the text above) to demonstrate on the basis of other economic statistics that an EMU country applying for a credit from the Fund was indeed in serious balance of payments difficulties.

It would probably be unlikely that an EMU member would seek access to conditional credit from either the IMF or (if it meets the restrictive scope of it) the EU's new facility, unless it found it impossible to borrow in the market on reasonable terms. As mentioned, members can find themselves in such a position even though they do not run a large deficit: faced with a decline in confidence, a member may have difficulties merely rolling over maturing obligations. In other instances, however, the member's difficulties may indeed be accompanied by a sharp rise in its fiscal deficit, caused for example by the working of automatic fiscal stabilizers in the face of a large negative shock, and that deficit (including any part financed by borrowing from the Fund or under the restrictive EU facility) may or may not bring the borrowing country into the position of having an "excessive deficit." If the Council decides that such a deficit indeed exists, it "shall make recommendations to the Member State concerned with a view to bringing that situation to an end within a given period" (Article 104c.7). What this would amount to in practice would be that in the event the country planned to draw on the Fund, the fiscal conditionality of the Fund program and the EU's prescription under the Article just cited would have to mesh. Once there was an agreed basis for conditional international financial support, and provided the member stuck to the agreed program, the EU would presumably refrain from pushing the country affected further into the red by the imposition of a financial penalty under paragraph 11 of Article 104c.

Under the approach described, the conditionality attending any use of the Fund's resources by an EMU member would ensure that such use would not serve as a loophole to the no-bailout principle of the Maastricht Treaty, and the recognition of the potential access of EMU members to the resources of the Fund could form part of a sensible safety net to the system, even though actual use of this safety net by EMU countries would most probably remain rare.

References

Atkeson, Andrew, and Tamim Bayoumi, 1993, "Do Private Capital Markets Insure Regional Risk? Evidence from the United States and Europe," in *Open Economies Review*, Vol. 4, No. 3, pp. 303–24.

Bergsten, C. Fred, and C. Randall Henning, 1996, *Global Economic Leadership and the Group of Seven* (Washington: Institute for International Economics).

Buira, Ariel, 1996, "Reflections on the Mexican Crisis of 1994," Chapter 11 in *Private Capital Flows to Emerging Markets After the Mexican Crisis*, ed. by Guillermo A. Calvo, Morris Goldstein, and Eduard Hochreiter (Washington: Institute for International Economics), pp. 307–20.

Commission of the European Communities, 1990, *Draft Treaty Amending the Treaty Establishing the European Economic Union with a View to Achieving Economic and*

Monetary Union, Working Document No. SEC(90)2500 (Brussels: Commission of the European Communities, December 10).

______, 1996, *Review of the Facility Providing Medium-Term Financial Assistance for Member States' Balances of Payments*, Document No. EC COM(96) 545 final (Brussels: Commission of the European Communities, April 11).

______, 1993, *The Economics of Community Public Finance, European Economy*, Reports and Studies, No. 5 (Brussels: EC Directorate-General for Economic and Public Affairs).

Goodhart, Charles A.E., and Stephen Smith, 1993, "Stabilization," in *The Economics of Community Public Finance, European Economy*, Reports and Studies, No. 5 by the European Commission (Brussels: EC Directorate-General for Economic and Public Affairs), pp. 417–55.

International Monetary Fund, 1958, "National Currency Counterpart of Drawings on the Fund," *Staff Papers*, International Monetary Fund, Vol. 6 (April), pp. 171–79.

______, 1992, *Selected Decisions*, 17th Issue (Washington: IMF).

Italianer, Alexander, and Marc Vanheukelen, 1993, "Proposal for Community Stabilization Mechanisms: Some Historical Applications" in *The Economics of Community Public Finance*, Reports and Studies, No. 5, by the European Commission (Brussels: EC Directorate-General for Economic and Public Affairs, 1993), pp. 493–510.

Kenen, Peter B., 1995, *Economic and Monetary Union in Europe: Moving Beyond Maastricht* (Cambridge: Cambridge University Press).

Louis, Jean-Victor, 1997, "Union monétaire européenne et Fonds monétaire international," in *Währung und Wirtschaft - Das Geld im Recht*, ed. by Albrecht Weber (Baden-Baden: Nomos Verlagsgesellschaft), pp. 201–13.

MacDougall, Sir Donald, 1977, *Report of the Study Group on the Role of Public Finance in European Integration*, Commission of the European Communities, Economic and Financial Series, Studies No. 13A-B (Brussels: Office for Official Publications of the European Communities).

Papaspyrou, Theodoros, 1993, "Stabilization Policy in Economic and Monetary Union in the Light of the Maastricht Treaty Provisions Concerning Financial Assistance," in *The Economics of Community Public Finance*, Reports and Studies, No. 5, by the European Commission (Brussels: EC Directorate-General for Economic and Public Affairs, 1993), pp. 481–91.

Polak, Jacques J., 1995, "Fifty Years of Exchange Rate Research and Policy at the International Monetary Fund," *Staff Papers*, International Monetary Fund, Vol. 42 (December), pp. 734–61.

Scitovsky, Tibor, 1969, *Money and the Balance of Payments* (Chicago: Rand McNally).

Ungerer, Horst, forthcoming, *A Concise History of European Monetary Integration: From EPU to EMU* (Westport, Connecticut: Quorum Books).

17

Relations Among the IMF, the ECB, and the IMF's EMU Members

Niels Thygesen

What will be the role of the IMF vis-à-vis the countries that join the third stage of EMU in 1999 or later? This is the important and challenging question that the organizers have put to Jacques Polak and me.

There is currently a very limited basis in official documents for answering the question. The likely candidates for participation in the initial group in EMU have been preoccupied with the internal workings of monetary union, and the January 1997 report by the EMI on monetary strategies and instruments in Stage III, EMI (1997a), does not discuss external relations of the euro area in any detail. The Articles in the Maastricht Treaty—notably Article 109—that refer to the external relations of EMU are somewhat ambiguous. The combination of centralized decision making on—and to some as yet unknown extent, implementation of—monetary policy with decentralized national budgetary policies, though subject to constraints on deviant behavior through the Stability and Growth Pact, makes the relationship between international institutions such as the IMF and the OECD and the participants particularly complex. On the side of the IMF there is apparently and understandably some caution in developing guidelines for the future relationships. Discussions in the Executive Board of developments in the EMU process appear so far to have been largely confined to informal seminars for the members of the Board. One has to agree with Bergsten's paper in this volume that the subject has been neglected to a surprising degree.

Discussions are now picking up on the European side, however. The EU Monetary Committee, consisting of representatives of central banks and treasuries of EU member states, has recently begun to address the external aspects of EMU, albeit tentatively.[1] Preliminary thoughts have so far taken the

[1]Some officials have recently been more explicit; see in particular Maystadt's speech in this volume for a number of operational proposals.

form of an annotated agenda, but it is far too early to say which views will in the end prevail. An agenda would comprise at least the following:

- the exchange rate regime and policy for the euro;
- decision-making arrangements at the European level on matters relating to EMU;
- questions of external representation;
- the international dialogue on the policy mix; and
- the relationship between the euro area exchange rate policy and ERM II.

The list may be useful as a checklist and will be used in the following discussion. However, given the likely divergence of views inside Europe on some of the issues, it is hardly productive to try to guess what will actually happen. The task for an outside observer, justifying the failure by the organizers to find an official to address the topic, might rather be to discuss what ought to happen, that is, to move from the positive to the normative level. I shall try to do so, obviously speaking in a strictly personal capacity.

The organization of the rest of the paper is as follows. The next section discusses the transition to EMU and the potentially constructive role the IMF could play prior to the start of Stage III. The following section, based on a perceptive 1980 paper by Jacques Polak, looks at earlier IMF concerns about European monetary integration as a regional "competitor" to the IMF. These concerns may today appear outdated, but recalling them is useful as a reminder of the major changes in the way European monetary integration is envisaged today relative to the early days of the EMS. The paper then discusses how multilateral surveillance of policies within EMU could be organized and the related issue of representation of the EMU countries in the IMF. Next is a look at the "fringe" arrangements surrounding EMU—ERM II and relations with present and prospective EU member states without any fixed exchange rate regime with the euro—and how the IMF could monitor them. Finally, conclusions are drawn.

IMF Role in the Transition to EMU

The preparations for EMU are now at a critical stage. The EMI has, as required by the Maastricht Treaty (Article 4.2 of the EMI Statute) by the end of 1996 ". . . [specified] the regulatory, organisational and logistical framework necessary for the ESCB to perform its tasks in the third stage, . . ."[2] This review was completed in time despite the postponement of the selection of the initial participants in EMU from late 1996 to the early months of 1998. But the

[2]EMI (1997a), p. 2.

effort was so demanding that it has crowded out any intensification of the coordination of current monetary policies (see Thygesen, 1997).

Like other forms of economic policies, monetary policy will remain a national responsibility for EU member states until the start of Stage III. However, the early vision of the EMU process was that Stage II would begin the transition from the coordination of independent national policies to the formulation and implementation of a common monetary policy in Stage III.[3] In fact, not only has there been no experimentation with joint policy formulation or any delegation of operational tasks to the EMI, but the rule book for monetary coordination that existed when the Treaty was drafted (in 1991) in the form of the narrow-margins ERM was abandoned in August 1993, five months before the start of Stage II and the setup of the EMI. It has not been replaced.

European officials will argue that efforts toward formal coordination would have been superfluous in the recent period, since the continuing acceptance of the primacy of the price stability objective and improvements in most dimensions of economic convergence have brought about a broadly similar monetary stance, not only in the countries that have for some time been considered the most likely candidates for monetary union in 1999, but throughout most of the EU. In particular, all member states with the exception of Greece currently appear ready to meet in 1997 the nominal convergence criteria of having recent (CPI) inflation rates and 10-year government bond rates within the required distance from the three best performers (in terms of inflation). Nominal exchange rates have also, since the spring of 1995—the most recent period of turbulence and realignment—approached the low degree of short-run volatility observed in the most stable ERM period, 1987–91. The EU currencies that had overshot any equilibrium level outside the ERM in 1992–93, and in some cases moved even farther in early 1995, appreciated back to what are considered broadly sustainable positions in the course of 1996. The Finnish markka and Italian lira reentered the ERM with agreed central rates in the autumn of 1996. Although the volatility of the pound sterling—and the Irish pound drawn along with it—has recently become a source of concern, a surprisingly high degree of exchange rate stability has been achieved without explicit coordination efforts. So what is the problem, and what might the IMF say about it?

The problem is that the present relative calm seems unlikely to last until January 1, 1999, which remains the most likely starting date for Stage III. In the months preceding the selection of the first group of participants in March or April 1998, currency markets could become much more turbulent, as financial markets reinterpret the likelihood of various countries actually being ready.

[3]See, among others, Delors Report (1989), para. 57. It was recognized all along that ultimate monetary authority would remain in national hands right up to the start of Stage III.

In 1996–97 a "convergence play," reminiscent of what happened in 1991–92 around the time of the Maastricht Treaty signing, has been in operation, favoring a very significant narrowing of interest rate differentials, particularly for the Southern European countries whose entry has become more likely. But the convergence of long-term interest rates is fragile and could quickly be reversed if the projected activity levels and hence budgetary figures look disappointing for these countries and—even more important—if Germany and/or France are viewed as likely to miss the Maastricht budgetary criteria, rekindling doubts about a delay of the start to Stage III. It is doubtful whether renewed divergence and the currency unrest that it would imply could then be contained simply by tight monetary coordination and a revival of large-scale interventions, which have not been observed since the widening of the ERM margins in 1993. But good working habits to contain turbulences must be discussed in advance of their arrival.

There is a further argument in favor of developing a sense of collective responsibility for monetary policy among the prospective EMU participants now. Policies in 1997 will be one of the factors determining the degree of price stability with which monetary union will start less than two years hence. That justifies considerable attention by the EMI to joint inflation forecasts by the EMU participants, so that they can be subjected to public discussion. The fact that it remains uncertain which countries will participate initially is not a valid counterargument; any forecast would be conditional and more than one may have to be made, notably to allow for possible participation from Southern Europe. That would in itself be a useful service, given the way in which the size of the union is seen in the public debate, probably excessively, as a determinant of the internal and external strength of the euro.

What could the IMF say on these problems in the context of its multilateral surveillance efforts? My own view is that the IMF could play a constructive role by stressing on the one hand its recognition of the economic and political factors that drive the EMU process, while encouraging the Europeans to implement the process in a way that minimizes the risks of backfiring, which would have negative implications from a global perspective.

The first part of this recommendation is essential. For a while after the widening of the ERM margins, the IMF staff appeared to applaud the added freedom of maneuver that this step was seen to imply for differentiated national monetary policies. IMF documents encouraged Germany's partners to cut interest rates at the end of the 1991–93 recession and accept the likely exchange rate consequences of such steps. This advice overlooked the political momentum toward EMU, which made France and other countries anxious not to use their freedom but to preserve the option of keeping EMU as much on track as possible. It also overlooked Germany's interest in not seeing an already excessively strong deutsche mark pushed further into appreciation.

Though the IMF staff and publications have subsequently become more positive in tone about the realization of EMU, the earlier experience combined with the perception that the IMF remains basically sympathetic to some exchange rate flexibility even inside the EU did tend to diminish the readiness to listen to IMF advice, even among officials who have had a long-standing association with the Fund.

This problem should disappear once Stage III begins as far as the initial participants are concerned. Then monetary union will have to be taken as a fact and advice will center on how to make it function as well as possible—from the global perspective, which is that of the IMF. But problems might persist regarding those countries entering later or not at all and the operations of the successor to the present exchange rate mechanism, now known as ERM II. The EMU participants will regard ERM II as a transitional arrangement, while international institutions such as the IMF could well see it as more permanent. There may also be disagreement between those in the EU—the large majority—who regard participation in an exchange rate arrangement as an essential preparation and apprenticeship for joining EMU and those, notably the United Kingdom, who are not convinced of this and would rather continue the present practice of national inflation targeting. The Fund staff, given the environment in which it operates, may have more sympathy for the latter view than for the former, but any advice will have to be carefully balanced by also taking into account the motivation of monetary union. These issues will be taken up again from a longer-run perspective in this paper's penultimate section.

Despite these sensibilities on the European side, the transition poses no new problems. The Fund will (and should) continue to express some concern over the way in which budgetary consolidation is proceeding in Europe in an attempt to roughly meet the deficit criterion in 1997. As explained in Masson (1996), there is a tendency, given the pressure of time, to rely on tax increases and expenditure cuts of a one-off nature, including the postponement of public investment, rather than long-run reforms of major categories of expenditures such as pension and health care systems. With the adoption of the Stability and Growth Pact, the pressure to move in this direction will, of course, be kept up after 1997, but critical advice from the IMF and other outsiders will be helpful in this area.

This is also the case for structural reforms in the participating countries (notably in the labor markets, since goods markets should in principle have become more competitive as a result of the EU's Internal Market) to improve adjustment inside the euro area. The IMF has, like the OECD, put much analytical effort into the monitoring of structural reforms, stressing the virtues of labor market flexibility designed to ". . . reduce the gaps between wage costs and productivity for the most vulnerable groups, including measures that better achieve social objectives without impeding job creation and job search."[4]

Since policies in the areas of public finance and structural reforms continue to be a national responsibility after the start of EMU, these are clearly also issues that the IMF can address without raising questions about the legitimacy of its concerns. But it will be constructive to voice these concerns also during the transition, when they have tended to be pushed temporarily aside.

In the short term, the IMF and many of its non-European members may be tempted to criticize the process of short-term budgetary consolidation because it imposes deflationary pressures on the participants and on their trading partners. In some EU countries, major budgetary corrections have brought such dramatic benefits in the form of lower interest rates—Italy and Sweden are prime examples—that the offsetting stimulus may have been more important than the contractionary effects of tighter budgetary policies. In most countries where interest rate differentials vis-à-vis Germany had already largely disappeared, these contractionary effects cannot be fully offset through slowly declining interest rates and some joint depreciation vis-à-vis the rest of the world. But real interest rates have edged down and competitive positions have improved to an extent that seems to make the effort worthwhile. Fortunately the IMF has not repeated its negative assessment of joint budgetary consolidation in Europe, which was voiced in leaked confidential documents in 1992 shortly after the Maastricht Treaty was negotiated. The increasing attention to longer-run problems is constructive and should not be swamped by the unfortunate short-run impact of the budgetary consolidation process on European unemployment.

Earlier IMF Concerns About European Monetary Integration

At a conference in Geneva in December 1979, external relations of the then-planned European Monetary Fund (EMF), the intended successor to the EMS after a two-year period, were discussed. Jacques Polak (1980) raised a number of pertinent criticisms of the plans—from a personal perspective, but with his authority from long experience with the Fund. The EMF never materialized, in part because the plans in the end seemed to imply institutional changes that required prior Treaty changes, and in part because the first years of the EMS after 1979 were so turbulent that it became impossible to contemplate additional steps in 1981, as had originally been envisaged. Nevertheless, a review of the problems then foreseen with the EMF is instructive.

[4]IMF (1996), p. 43.

The EMF fell far short of the EMU project when a single currency developed a decade later, though it did represent a transfer of authority from the national to the European level. Its main aim was to consolidate the whole range of financing external imbalances—from central bank interventions at the short end to conditional balance of payments assistance at the long end—into a single institutional framework. The mixture of central banking and political functions was no doubt the main reason why Germany and some other European authorities objected strongly. The EMF looked like a powerful regional IMF.[5]

Polak (1980) lists a number of specific issues on which the IMF had concerns about competition from the new regional institutional framework that was developing: the creation of international liquidity, the granting of conditional credit, and the establishment of a regional rival to the SDR in the form of the ECU. It is understandable that these new European initiatives were seen as threatening the commitment that the European countries had made to a global perspective through their membership in the Fund. It is therefore relevant to ask whether these concerns also apply to the EMU process. On the whole, this appears to me not to be the case.

International liquidity has become a less important problem for the industrial countries, not least for the European countries. At the time when Polak wrote his article (in 1979), attention was already focused on the composition of international reserves rather than on their overall adequacy. In view of the weak dollar, plans had developed for a Substitution Account in the Fund, into which members could deposit a substantial part of dollars and receive SDRs. With the subsequent strengthening of the dollar, interest in the scheme faded and the perceptive idea of Polak that the EMF might itself deposit some of the excess dollars that were to be pooled with it into the IMF Substitution Account never reached the official agenda.

Since then the international monetary system has seen a near-quadrupling of reserves (excluding gold). While the dollar share of currency reserves has fallen somewhat and those of EU currencies, mainly the deutsche mark, have risen, the dollar share has remained well above 50 percent,[6] and it is hard to foresee any resurrection of the Triffin dilemma that the size of official holdings might suddenly trigger anxiety, causing major holders to try to shift into other assets. Reserve creation by EU countries through current account deficits has been modest indeed, and that from EU institutions zero or negligible, depending on whether one regards the swap arrangements between individual central banks as a way of mobilizing gold reserves that would not otherwise have been readily usable or just as a substitution. As Polak noted,

[5]For an evaluation of why the EMF project failed to take off, see Gros and Thygesen (1997), Chapter 2.

[6]Eichengreen and Frankel (1996) present a thorough survey of the evolution of reserves.

the most accurate way to describe the three-month swap arrangements between the EU national central banks on the one hand and the EMI[7] on the other would be to see them as an allocation of ECUs, matched by immobilization of a corresponding amount—20 percent of gold and non-EU currency reserves—of existing reserve assets. There has been no net extension of short-term credit, though that possibility was foreseen in the original EMS documents.

However, there may be an indirect effect on the attitude of the EU member states to the evaluation of the adequacy of international reserves. The development over time of a relatively successful regional scheme of monetary coordination, building in part on commitments to intervention at the EMS margins that are in principle unconditional may have made Europeans less sensitive to reserve shortages perceived elsewhere in the international monetary system. Although the shortness of the intervention credits—initially 2½ months, extended in 1987 to 3½ months—has inspired caution in relying primarily on those credits to sustain exchange rates, the relatively reassuring framework may have prompted the Europeans to take a more restrictive attitude in discussions of SDR allocations and the size of IMF-led rescue operations, notably when the Mexican crisis arose. If so, such attitudes might harden further once monetary union has started.

There was an understandable concern in the 1979 Polak paper that the EMF might engage in significant extensions of conditional credit to member states on terms more favorable to borrowers than IMF conditionality. The member states of the EU could well be regarded as too narrow a club to insist on tough terms when extending loans for balance of payments adjustment. In particular, the EU is less independent of influence from EU member states than is the Fund staff when it comes to assessing the need for financial support for a country. Polak therefore argues in favor of recognizing the principle—as outlined in the stillborn safety net facility negotiated in the OECD in 1975—that a borrower should first make use of the IMF multilateral facilities in order to assure that supplementary facilities elsewhere are offered on the same terms.

There have been few instances of longer-term credits extended by the ECOFIN Council (notably, to Greece and Italy). Although these experiences have tended to confirm the relative softness of EU procedures (disbursements continued despite some transgressions of stated objectives), the amounts involved were relatively modest. They have since largely been repaid; the EMI (1997b) reports that at the end of 1996 the amounts outstanding were

[7]Prior to January 1, 1994, the European Monetary Cooperation Fund, better known by its French acronym FECOM.

ECU 500 million in the case of Greece and nearly 3,500 million in the case of Italy (see also Polak's paper in this volume). More important, the Maastricht Treaty (Article 103a) stipulates tough conditions for the granting of longer-term financial support to a member state. The ECOFIN Council has to reach a decision unanimously (except in the case of a natural disaster). The agreement on a Stability and Growth Pact will ensure a far more stringent monitoring of economic policies, as will be discussed further later in this paper. On the whole, therefore, the risks of regional generosity inside Europe that could be seen as a threat to IMF conditionality have proved to be limited and they should be largely eliminated after 1999, consistent with the so-called "no-bailout" provision in Article 104 of the Treaty.

Finally, Polak raised the question whether the ECU was likely to become a global competitor to the SDR. The comprehensive survey by Eichengreen and Frankel (1996) confirms that the SDR's prospects as the principal international asset remain unpromising, but that the main reasons for this are to be found in the rapid growth of currency assets and increasing capital mobility (though the net impact of this factor was found to be ambiguous) rather than in the emergence of the ECU as a competitor to the SDR. The ECU has not in itself been very successful in private financial markets or as an international reserve asset for non-EU-holders. There has certainly been little promotion of the ECU in these roles by European governments. Indeed, the word "promotion" was carefully shunned in the Maastricht Treaty in describing the role of the EMI in the relation to the unit—it was confined to simple "monitoring" and the original ambition of actively fostering the ECU as a reserve asset, very evident in the 1978–79 documents establishing the EMS, was watered down.

In summary, the concerns that appeared legitimate from an IMF perspective in the early stages of the EMS have not materialized in the way foreseen by Polak. There was simply not the will in Europe to engage in substantial regional competition with key activities of the IMF; the European efforts took a different direction, with the main feature being convergence based on rules. Despite this verdict, the global institutions and, in particular, the Fund would be justified in looking back at the long period since the start of the EMS with some disappointment. The preoccupation by the Europeans with their internal unification process has absorbed European official attention to a degree that has not facilitated participation in global forums and initiatives. Advice from the Fund and other outsiders has not been encouraged or well received, given the sensitive nature of Europe's regional integration. And, finally, the Europeans have not yet succeeded in making their external representation more efficient, though this has been one of the aims of the process. The next section of this paper turns to this issue.

Multilateral Surveillance and EMU Representation in the Fund

Turning to the future organization of multilateral surveillance of EMU countries after Stage III has started, and to the closely related issue of the representation of EMU participants in the Fund, it is useful to start from past trends in surveillance within the EU and in the Fund.

Two such trends stand out as both important and likely to continue into Stage III in accentuated form: (1) the highly asymmetric nature of the pooling of authority with full centralization of monetary policy and continuing decentralized national budgetary policies; and (2) the deepening nature of what may most appropriately be labeled country-specific surveillance in the EU. Both trends already complicate the participation of EU countries in Fund multilateral surveillance, and the potential conflicts may sharpen after 1999. On the other hand it could also be argued that Fund surveillance of EMU members could be regarded as a useful complement to internal EMU procedures.

Multilateral surveillance in the sense that it has developed in the Fund over the past two decades hardly existed in the EU some years ago (see Andersen and Thomsen, 1996). Monetary policy was guided by the rule book of the narrow-margins EMS, and other policies were rarely subjected to explicit monitoring by the ECOFIN Council. There were two exceptions to the latter: (1) countries that had borrowed for medium-term external adjustment (Greece and Italy) were subjected to more intensive monitoring, but such cases were rare; and (2) realignments prompted more intensive discussion about the appropriate balance between devaluation and domestic adjustment. But realignments did become rarer and smaller after 1983, and when they resurfaced in 1992 there was no time to design balanced policy packages. Nor was the simple linkage made that countries that had devalued very substantially should be expected to be able to make more rapid budgetary consolidation.

All of this underpins the general impression that macroeconomic policymaking in the EU has not lent itself to multilateral surveillance of the type favored by the Fund—and that future developments in the transition to EMU could make the difficulties worse. The essence of multilateral surveillance is to exchange views on the appropriateness of the policy mix in individual countries in the hope of modifying it in a direction helpful to international adjustment. Sometimes that effort is difficult for large members, in which both monetary and budgetary policies are centralized, but the policy mix appears locked into an undesirable combination for a long period. U.S. policies in the first half of the 1980s and German policies following unification are recent important examples. The fact that the national authorities have policy instruments available in both the monetary and the budgetary area offers no assurance of a productive dialogue between the authorities or with outsiders.

Despite these caveats about international discussions of the policy mix in the past, it must be admitted that the design of EMU will give rise to additional complications. With monetary authority centralized in the ECB and the aggregate fiscal stance emerging primarily from the decisions of national governments and parliaments (in relation to which the—restricted—ECOFIN Council will only have the authority to monitor and sanction "excessive deficits"), discussions focusing on the policy mix will be as handicapped internally as they are in global forums such as the IMF or the Group of Seven industrial countries. It may of course be hoped that the constraints on deviant national behavior imposed by the Stability and Growth Pact will contribute to an acceptable policy mix and avoid the type of imbalances familiar in the United States and Germany (among other examples) in the past, but for the EU to attain a policy mix that will be regarded as satisfactory and beyond discussion by outsiders is only likely to happen by accident. The criticism could go in either direction: either that the sum of cautious national fiscal policies in combination with the expected tough monetary policy of the ECB will produce effects that are considered deflationary in the aggregate by outsiders—this is the current U.S. attitude to policies in the run-up to EMU—or that the sum of national fiscal policies, all or most hovering just below the reference value of 3 percent and hence difficult to correct for the EU, could be regarded as distorting the policy mix and inflicting high interest rates on the outside world.

Whatever the outcome is, it will be difficult to modify through a process of multilateral surveillance in the Fund or any non-EU body. The ECB will be very defensive, at least initially, of its own evaluation of what is required to best meet its mandate of pursuing medium-term price stability as a primary objective, though the ECB may be open to the kind of technical advice on how to implement chosen targets that the Fund staff is particularly well equipped to give. As to national governments, they will want to use as fully as possible the room for maneuver available under the guidelines set by the Stability and Growth Pact. They should welcome any advice on how to operate inside these constraints. And the more national governments insist—correctly—on the fact that they have retained their budgetary powers even in EMU, the stronger are the formal grounds for continuing to subject them to multilateral surveillance in the Fund.

Macroeconomic policy formulation in EMU can only be called indirectly cooperative. In both the monetary and the budgetary areas, the framers of the Treaty and of the supplementary steps taken since Maastricht have adopted a view of policymaking inspired by public choice. Policies will to a large extent be rule bound, with limited room for discretion and justification for deviations due to national circumstances. The monitoring of policies will then center on how well the ECB or national budgetary authorities perform relative to the targets preset for them and will depend hardly at all on whether the targets remain appropriate at all times. In particular, the Stability and Growth Pact, with its elaborate procedures and ultimate threats of sanctions, constrains potentially deviant national behavior by committing participants to guidelines for public debt dynamics designed to assure financial markets that public finances will remain sustainable. Just as the selection of participants for Stage III is in part a process of persuading financial markets that this or that country is becoming ready to participate, so the rule book for subsequent behavior is designed to provide markets with easy references so that they can impose their disciplinary measures in the form of higher credit spreads on a government early in a deviant path. In either case, it is an exercise in which outside advice in a multilateral surveillance process will not necessarily be welcome, even if it is discreet—that is, if it remains unpublished, as is currently the practice with Fund advice.

One further observation again underlines the difference between the ways in which policies will have to be monitored for a large Fund member on the one hand, say, the United States or Japan, and for the group of EMU participants on the other hand. The latter will have no well-developed position on what its aggregate stance should be. The aim of an appropriate aggregate performance in EMU may become lost during the process of detailed country-by-country monitoring. Imbalances on the collective current account balance of the EMU participants may turn out to be a factor that triggers policy adjustment in the ECB's stance, in the modification of long-drawn-up convergence programs of individual participants, or in both. But this is far from certain—indeed, it looks unlikely. The rest of the Fund constituency will, however, be keenly interested in finding out what the scope is for modifying any "benign neglect" on the part of EMU toward its external position.

Other Fund members will be particularly anxious through multilateral surveillance and Article IV consultations to discover the attitude of the ECB to ad hoc efforts of coordinated intervention of the type seen in the 1980s in the Plaza Accord and Louvre Agreement, as well as in more recent periods. But they are unlikely to discover more than can be extracted by careful reading of the verbose Article 109 on exchange rate policy in EMU, namely, that the ECB will be in charge of the external value of the euro, except in the highly unlikely circumstances of a "formal agreement" within the IMF, adopted unanimously by EMU governments, to reconstitute a fixed-but-adjustable exchange rate system. Multilateral surveillance of EMU would have to be two dimensional, exploring both the congenital reluctance of the ECB to undertake commitments in the exchange markets and the likely aim of the finance ministers to minimize misalignments. This has implications for the representation of the EMU countries, to which we return below.

Some years ago, prior to the entry into force of the Maastricht Treaty, it could safely be said that the Fund had developed the procedure for multilateral surveillance further than had the EU countries. Indeed, it was often said during and after the Maastricht negotiations that the EU countries needed to catch up with practices with which they were supposedly familiar at the global level. They may now appear to have done so, according to the experience over the past three years of applying the provisions of Articles 103 on surveillance and 104c on excessive deficits. Some remarks on this experience, comparing it to Fund practice, may now be appropriate.

Surveillance is conducted by the ECOFIN Council, following preparatory work in the Monetary Committee (after January 1, 1999, the Monetary and Finance Committee), the Economic Policy Committee, and—whenever it becomes fully functional—the Labor and Employment Committee.[8] The EC prepares the material and the draft of the broad policy guidelines, which form the basis for surveillance in Article 103. These guidelines refer to both macroeconomic and structural issues, but the balance is different from that of the Fund, with more emphasis so far on budgetary policy, and less on structural problems in the labor market. It must be admitted that the EU is still somewhat behind what has been done by the Fund and, in particular, by the OECD through its massive Jobs Study, to analyze structural impediments to higher employment. This imbalance may be partly rectified before Stage III starts, given the alarming present level of unemployment, but the emphasis will remain different. While the Europeans will continue focusing on what might be done by cutting indirect wage costs, for example, shifting taxation to forms less unfriendly to employment, and by improving training, the focus in Fund surveillance will no doubt remain on more general measures to improve labor market flexibility. This difference in emphasis is explained by the (Continental) European preference for a high level of social protection, but it is healthy to challenge this preference with a more global perspective. It should be recalled that the EMU participants have retained full authority over their labor market and other structural policies, so there is no question as to the recipient of any recommendation arising from Fund surveillance.

Article 104c is specifically tailored to monitoring compliance first with the convergence criteria and after January 1, 1999, with the Stability and Growth Pact. Since inflation and long-term interest rates will then have converged and internal exchange rates will have been frozen, this special type of surveillance will be oriented specifically toward the monitoring of the deficit and debt ratios of participants in Stage III. The legal text on which this second type of

[8]This Committee, composed of representatives of treasuries and ministries of labor, is an outgrowth of the growing concern about employment in the EU, more specifically of the so-called Essen Initiative of December 1994.

surveillance is to be based will be put on the agenda of the European Council meeting in Amsterdam in June 1997, but the principles are already clear. The ECOFIN Council will follow, over the period after a transgression of the reference value of a 3 percent public sector deficit, a policy of graduated sanctions: confidential recommendation, public recommendation, warnings attached to new bond issues by the country concerned, restrictions on lending by the European Investment Bank, and, ultimately, the imposition of deposits into an interest-free account, which after two years without any correction of the policy would be converted into a fine. A schedule for the latter two sanctions has been agreed, which should constitute a powerful deterrent to transgressions of the ceiling for the deficit ratio. But graduated sanctions should begin to bite well before these ultimate steps are taken, not least because of the publicity that will be given to some of the early steps.

There is nothing comparable in the Fund surveillance procedures to the excessive deficit procedure in EMU. National budgetary policies will be monitored more regularly, at a higher political level—ECOFIN Council versus the IMF Executive Board—and the whole process is to be carried out under the scrutiny of the general public and, in particular, financial markets, which have been assigned some of the unpleasant work for the governments. This contrasts strongly with Fund practice, which is to address confidential recommendations to a member government. These recommendations may well be more detailed, even with respect to budgetary policy, than those of the ECOFIN Council and they will cover a wider range of structural issues. They are still likely to carry less weight than the highly focused excessive deficit procedure.

Does the impression that EU surveillance, despite its narrow focus, appears to have finally overtaken Fund surveillance in importance imply that the latter is losing its usefulness and relevance and that it should be organized differently once Stage III of EMU starts? That does not follow. Fund surveillance will be a useful supplement, precisely because it is broader in scope, confronts EMU Fund members with a wider and still highly relevant policy experience throughout the world, and is not tied to the very special features of the Maastricht Treaty with its convergence criteria and Stability and Growth Pact. Although the Fund staff may still need to be cautious about any outright element of criticism of these European features, once EMU has started the whole construction will become more robust and less sensitive to outsider criticism than has been the case during the transition. Finally, there are no formal grounds for keeping surveillance of national budgetary policies strictly within the EMU family. EMU countries cannot expect or claim, while retaining their authority over national budgets, to have different status in this area from other Fund members.

Nor is there any obvious need for involving EMU institutions or bodies other than the national governments and—for some purposes—the ECB. The

Commission has no particular authority in either the monetary or other economic policy areas that requires it to be formally involved in consultations, but its important role in organizing surveillance in EMU would make regular contacts between the two staffs desirable. The ECOFIN Council has neither a president nor a secretariat that could add to the information provided by national governments, except possibly on the formulation of the "general orientations for exchange rate policy" on occasions when the Council has used its capacity to formulate such orientations in Article 109.2.[9]

The only difficult issue seems to be how to involve the ECB, without which an important voice would be missing in most discussions on multilateral surveillance. Since the ECB cannot become a member of the Fund, some ad hoc solution will have to be found to allow the ECB to be present at discussions in the IMF Executive Board—obviously, as an observer—when exchange rate issues and other major policy questions arising from EMU are on the agenda. Much of the IMF's agenda is clearly of limited interest to the ECB, but both sides would lose if it were left to EMU member governments assisted by representatives of their central banks, which would by then be organic parts of the ESCB, to be the sole EMU representatives in Fund discussions of surveillance. The ECB might be encouraged to establish an office at the Fund for smooth coordination when a presence in the Executive Board is warranted.

As long as the EMU countries show no indication of giving up their national budgetary authority, the only realistic solution is to let the Fund member states that are also in EMU continue to be represented by their national governments directly or through the shared constituencies in which they currently operate, while admitting the ECB on an ad hoc basis and conducting Article IV consultations with the ECB.

"Fringe" Arrangements Surrounding EMU

If it is reasonably clear that EMU participants should continue to be subject to Fund multilateral surveillance in areas for which they remain individually responsible in Stage III, it follows that this would also apply to EU countries that have not joined Stage III because they have failed to meet the convergence criteria with a sufficient degree of approximation or have been granted the right to opt out, as is the case for Denmark and the United Kingdom. These countries will obviously have retained authority in both the mon-

[9]For a fuller discussion with a different conclusion, foreseeing in particular Fund contact with the Economic and Financial Committee, see the paper by Polak and speech by Maystadt, both in this volume.

etary and the budgetary areas, even though some of them will feel severely constrained in their policy choices, particularly if they have narrowly missed entry into Stage III and aim to make the additional transition as short as possible.

The IMF, in view of its wide experience in monitoring exchange rate policies throughout the world, will have something to say on the exchange rate relationships between the euro area and nonparticipating European currencies. The experience in 1992–93 underlined the vulnerability of a narrow-margins arrangement comprising currencies for which convergence was still suspect. On the other hand, the experience of Austria over two decades and of the Netherlands over one shows that narrow margins are perfectly feasible once convergence is advanced and the smaller country is seen to mimic the monetary policy of the anchor country. Despite the long record of successful achievements of the EMS prior to 1992, EU official opinion has now moved against the resurrection of a tight arrangement with the euro for those who do not make it into EMU. The earlier vision, when EMU was conceived in the late 1980s, of monetary unification proceeding through a funnel-like process of narrowing margins today has few, if any, advocates. Wide margins have worked rather well for those who remained in any system and the inclination is currently to rely on them in ERM II in Stage III. This is also seen to have the virtue of placing the overwhelming part of the responsibility for stabilizing a currency on the issuer rather than on its partners; wide-ranging intervention commitments are seen as dangerous by some and as unreliable by others—not surprisingly, following the collapse of commitments in 1992.

The question is whether the pendulum has swung too far. Must the transition from a system with some flexibility to full EMU be quite as dramatic as it now appears? If a group of countries that obviously places a high value on exchange rate stability is not prepared to assist those who aspire to join by offering them potentially considerable intervention support, future entry into EMU may become even more difficult than it will have been for the first group. This question is relevant for 1999 if some candidates fail entry with a small margin, because the ERM II that is on offer sounds as if it is devised more for countries far from converging to EMU standards than for countries that have been engaged in convergence efforts over a number of years.

The way in which the ERM II is finally set up is watched with particular attention by the Central and East European countries most likely to join the EU sometime over the next five to eight years. It is improbable that any of them would be in a position to also join EMU right away; their inflation performance, in particular, seems bound to fall short of the requirements for some time. But in each of the prospective member states, the issue of when it would be most appropriate to supplement the domestic efforts to get closer to price stability by firming up any anchoring to the euro will arise as soon as membership is on the horizon. For this group at least, a graduated phasing into EMU will remain on the agenda and the Fund's surveillance of their efforts will be of great importance.

For a couple of EU countries—the United Kingdom and Sweden—which had unhappy and brief links to other European currencies, the preference today is to stay outside EMU for the time being and to reject participation in ERM II as well. These two countries both opted for inflation targets as the basic framework for their monetary policy just after the dramatic foreign exchange crises of 1992, and this has served them well. But the question remains whether purely domestic targets—and one has seen in the recent movements of sterling that they are purely domestic—can deliver anything close to the degree of nominal exchange rate stability that the single market requires for its smooth functioning. This, too, is an area in which Fund surveillance will be valuable.

Finally, there is the interesting aspect that the nonparticipants will not be subject to the same discipline as those already in the euro area. When the Maastricht Treaty was drafted, the main temptation of a relapse into laxer policies was seen to present itself to countries that had joined and were then free of the constraints arising from foreign exchange crises and higher domestic interest rates. Those outside were expected to aspire to early entry and hence to be on their best behavior; they were accordingly not to have sanctions imposed on them. Even though the role of sanctions should not be exaggerated, the absence of both sanctions and any short-term need to perform according to the convergence criteria may create incentives for competitive and divergent behavior, which should be closely watched by the EMU participants and in the Fund's multilateral surveillance.

In short, the "fringe" arrangements surrounding EMU—how best to prepare additional countries for participation, the adequacy of national inflation targeting, and the monitoring without sanctions of the nonparticipants—offer a wide and fertile ground for IMF surveillance. Monitoring of nonparticipants will clearly be more sought after than that of the EMU participants themselves, because there will be less self-assurance among the nonparticipants and they will welcome a second opinion on their options rather than relying solely on the views of the EMU participants.

Conclusions

The subject of the conference is speculative, because there is as yet no certainty as to how EMU will operate, or as to who will initially participate. To try to analyze the future relations between the Fund and the EMU participants is therefore doubly hazardous. This paper therefore starts from the present situation and addresses some IMF concerns that have been expressed in the past as to the potential fragmentation of the global monetary system implied by the emergence of a greatly reinforced regional integration in the EU.

The tasks of the Fund in the transition to EMU have required tact because of the great sensitivity of the Europeans vis-à-vis criticism of their de facto increasingly joint monetary policy, which did not fully incorporate both the economic and the political momentum behind integration. However, Fund surveillance of budgetary and structural policies in the EU member states has been thoroughly welcome.

Early IMF concerns about fragmentation of the global system if European integration proceeded to a more institutional stage do not on the whole appear to have been borne out. European monetary integration has not boosted international liquidity or introduced significant elements of soft lending inside the region. The ECU did prove to be a competitor to the SDR, but the SDR's relative stagnation primarily reflects factors other than European integration.

Turning to the core of the paper, some comparisons are made between the surveillance practiced in the Fund and the monitoring of policies in the EU, which has only been intensified relatively recently. The main weakness of EU monitoring is that it is ill equipped to address issues of improper policy mix, because the arrangements to keep centralized monetary policy with budgetary policies as a national responsibility hamper any dialogue on this subject. Furthermore, EU monitoring takes place on the basis of an elaborate rule book that focuses on how countries perform relative to the rules, be they of monetary coordination or of constraints on national budgetary policies. Precisely for this reason, Fund surveillance should be welcome, because of its likely attention to aggregate performance in the euro area.

On the institutional side, the only truly new development is the emergence of the ECB, whose presence in the IMF Executive Board when multilateral surveillance of macroeconomic policies in the EU is discussed seems very useful. Some ad hoc arrangement is clearly called for.

As long as national EU governments insist that all nonmonetary policies remain a national responsibility even in EMU, they can hardly object to continued Fund surveillance of their policies individually. This also applies to nonparticipants in EMU, for whom also monetary policy will remain to some extent national. The "fringe" arrangements surrounding EM—ERM II and the monitoring of exchange rates of EU countries not in ERM II and of macroeconomic policies of the outsiders more generally—should remain fertile ground for IMF surveillance.

References

Andersen, Bodil Nyboe, and Jens Thomsen, 1996, "International Coordination and Surveillance" (in Danish), *Nationaløkonomisk Tidsskrift* (Danish Economic Journal) (September), pp. 389–400.

Eichengreen, Barry, and Jeffrey A. Frankel, 1996, "The SDR, Reserve Currencies, and the Future of the International Monetary System," in *The Future of the SDR in Light of Changes in the International Financial System*, ed. by Michael Mussa, James M. Boughton, and Peter Isard (Washington: International Monetary Fund), pp. 337–99 (with comments by Tommaso Padoa-Schioppa, Fabrizio Saccomani, H. Onno Ruding, and Wendy Dobson).

European Economic Community, European Council, Committee for the Study of Economic and Monetary Union, 1989, *Report on Economic and Monetary Union in the European Community (The Delors Report)* (Luxembourg: Office for Official Publications of the European Communities).

European Monetary Institute, 1997a, *The Single Monetary Policy in Stage Three: Specification of the Operational Framework* (Frankfurt: EMI).

———, 1997b, *Annual Report* (Frankfurt: EMI).

Gros, Daniel, and Niels Thygesen, 1997, *European Monetary Integration: From the EMS to EMU* (London: Longman).

International Monetary Fund, 1996, *World Economic Outlook* (Washington: IMF, May).

Masson, Paul, 1996, "Fiscal Dimensions of EMU," IMF Paper on Policy Analysis and Assessment 96/7 (Washington: International Monetary Fund, June). Also published in *Economic Journal*, Vol. 106 (September 1996), pp. 996–1004.

Polak, Jacques J., 1980, "The EMF: External Relations," *Banca Nazionale del Lavoro Quarterly Review*, Vol. 134 (September), pp. 359–81 (with comments by Pierre Languetin and Robert Mundell).

Thygesen, Niels, 1997, "Visions on the EMU Process," paper prepared for seminar at the European Monetary Institute, Frankfurt, February 12.

Comments on Polak and on Thygesen

Bernd Goos

It was a great pleasure for me to discuss the two papers before us, which I found most interesting and thought provoking. I really regret that I only have 10 minutes to comment on such papers and that I therefore have to be selective in my comments. I would therefore propose to address first some macroeconomic aspects of EMU that arise from the papers but that have also been addressed in previous presentations, with which I have some difficulties.

What I have in mind here in the first place is the notion that EMU would change the situation in Europe in a rather dramatic way; that this would have profound effects on the functioning of the international monetary system; and that all of this together would necessitate some fundamental rethinking of the relationship between the Fund and EMU member states, including its approach to surveillance.

Now, it is true, of course, that EMU will bring a major change in the policy regime in Europe, inasmuch as responsibility for monetary and exchange rate policy will be transferred to community institutions. But I submit that this regime change will be largely of a formal rather than a substantive nature. After all, EMU candidates will have participated already for a minimum of two years in the ERM, and that means, of course, that with the exception of the anchor country, EMU participants will already have given up the exchange rate and monetary policy as independent policy tools for quite some time. In fact, one could even include the last 10 years in the period during which they have given up those monetary policy tools. In other words, we have already been living, in Europe, in a de facto monetary union for quite some time, at least with the so-called core countries.

Against this background, I fail to see, at least for the foreseeable future, any big bang or dramatic changes arising from EMU, be it for the economic environment in Europe or for the world economy at large, all the more so considering that the ECB is most likely to continue the Bundesbank's anti-inflationary policy stance, and I am pretty sure that exchange rate policy vis-à-vis third currencies will remain unchanged.

In this latter regard, I believe that any significant reorientation of exchange rate policies by the ECB, including, for example, explicit targeting for the euro, would be a risky undertaking, at least in the early years of EMU. I would expect the markets to test very early on the seriousness of any such exchange rate commitment. As a result, the credibility of the ECB could be seriously damaged before it even got a chance to be established.

I do not belittle the difficulties and problems that could arise in the course of EMU in the implementation of exchange rate policy and financial policies in general, but I feel that the international role of the euro will evolve in a gradual manner and will depend very much on the domestic stability outlook for the EMU economies and the euro.

On another score, I was quite surprised at the view expressed in the Thygesen paper that in the EMU setting, a balanced policy mix could be expected to emerge only by accident and not by design. This view seems to rest on the perception that policies in EMU would be excessively rule-bound, leaving too limited discretion to policymakers for responding to national circumstances. Let me offer two brief reactions to this concern.

First, to the extent that Mr. Thygesen has the Stability and Growth Pact in mind as an unduly constraining device, I feel that his concern is not borne out by the facts. As a matter of fact, if you look at the Pact, it provides a considerable degree of flexibility. If you start from the baseline of a balanced, if not surplus, budget and consider the possibility to move to a budget deficit of up to 3 percent of GDP in response to cyclical swings, that is quite a lot of room for maneuver. On top of that, as you know, there are exceptional circumstances clauses that allow even this deficit ceiling to be exceeded in specific circumstances. So I fail to see how the Stability and Growth Pact would put the European economies in a straitjacket.

My second observation is that this concern about an unduly rule-bound approach appears to rest on an economic philosophy that I thought had long been discredited by actual experience—the philosophy of economic fine-tuning. I therefore continue to feel that the main preoccupation of monetary policy and, to a large extent, also fiscal policy should be the creation of a predictable, noninflationary environment. I know, of course, that I am in disagreement with Mr. Polak and others on this, but I think experience shows that such an environment would not only be most conducive to investment growth but would also contribute to a stable exchange rate and financial market development. So, we in Europe believe that if we implement the stability pact properly and heed the mandate of the ECB as defined in the Maastricht Treaty, EMU will make a contribution to a stable international monetary system.

Incidentally, this philosophy is also being shared among the Group of Seven industrial countries, but its implementation, which requires the steady and firm pursuit of medium-term-oriented policies is, of course, much less spectacular than the Louvre Agreement and Plaza Accord that are very often quoted as an example for effective Group of Seven management. But I think one should not mix up the qualities of being spectacular and being effective.

I therefore remain to be convinced that Mr. Polak's proposal for reorganizing the Group of Seven process by including it in the Interim Committee and so on would provide increased protection against currency misalignments.

I will comment very briefly on how to organize Fund surveillance and the financial relations of the EMU countries with the Fund. On the first issue, since responsibility for monetary and exchange rate policy will be transferred to Community institutions, it is clear that ways will have to be found for these institutions to make their views known to the Fund in the context of Fund surveillance.

Obviously, Fund missions will have to continue to meet with national authorities of EMU members. I can assure Mr. Thygesen that there is no concern whatsoever in Europe—at least not in Germany—about future Article IV consultations with the Fund. Quite to the contrary, I think the Fund's views have always been very welcome and appreciated. But at the same time, the Fund missions should also meet the ECB and interlocutors who can speak with authority for the Council, inasmuch as foreign exchange regime issues or matters of foreign exchange policy orientation are concerned. For such foreign exchange policy issues, I do not believe that the Commission or the future Economic and Financial Committee would be the right contacts for the Fund, because they carry no direct responsibility in these policy areas. Therefore, it might be more appropriate for Fund missions to consult with the Presidency of ECOFIN direct—that is, with the finance minister (and his staff) of the euro member in charge of the presidency. I do not know whether this would work in practice but am just introducing it as a personal suggestion.

The situation is, of course, more complex when it comes to the organization of Article IV consultations in the Fund Executive Board, which raises the well-known issue of EMU representation in the Fund. I think it is obvious that merging the European chairs and assigning the remaining single chair to the Community can be ruled out. But I must admit that this idea has some attractive features, inasmuch as it could help restore a clearer distinction in the Fund Executive Board between the interests of traditional Fund creditor and debtor countries. I, for one, feel that the blurring of those interests within mixed constituencies is one of the most unfortunate developments of the Fund of the recent past.

A final observation: even if one has to rule out direct representation of Community institutions in the IMF Executive Board, there are, of course, several ways to introduce the views of the institutions into the Article IV consultation process here in the Fund. For example, decisions to be taken on relevant issues could be formulated by the ECB and the Council and presented to the Board by the Executive Directors of EMU. One can certainly also envisage written statements by the institutions being presented at Board discussions. And last but not least, there is the idea of granting observer status to the ECB at the Fund.

All of these ideas merit further consideration. However, when it comes to the idea of Board representation, one should avoid creating undue precedents for other institutions, which could undermine the effectiveness of the Fund's work.

Concerning financial relations between EMU and the Fund, given the late hour, let me just endorse the proposals made by Mr. Polak, including—I stress that I am speaking on a personal basis here—in particular his proposals with regard to access to the Fund. I found these ideas quite provocative but very interesting, and they should be explored further. There is no ready-made solution, but I am confident that we will find a way that is acceptable to both the European members and the Fund.

Jean-Victor Louis

To start a reflection on the future institutional relations between the EU and the IMF after Stage III of EMU, one has to answer two questions: what does Community law require and what are the ways to meet these requirements?[1]

EMU as a Loss of Sovereignty for the Member States in Favor of the EU

With the transition to Stage III of the EMU, (participating) member states will have a single currency and a single monetary and exchange rate policy (Maastricht Treaty, Article 3a, paragraph 2). The ECB, at the top of the ESCB, will be in charge of monetary policy (Articles 4a and 105). A leading role will be conferred on the Council of the European Union for the conclusion of agreements on and the definition of exchange rates and general orientations related to exchange rate policy (Article 109, paragraphs 1 and 2). This implies that member states will not be in a position individually to assume the obligations deriving, for example, from the code of conduct of the IMF Articles of Agreement.

In the field of economic policy, member states, which have to consider their policies as a common interest, have an obligation of close coordination within the European and ECOFIN Councils (Articles 3a, paragraph 1; 102a; and 103). This situation creates an asymmetry between economic union on the one hand and monetary union on the other. This asymmetry has to be taken into

[1]On these questions, see Martha (1993); Louis (1997); and Smits (1997), especially p. 420 on.

account in the shaping of the relations between the IMF and the EC in Stage-III of EMU, but its importance, as far as the IMF is concerned, should not be overestimated.

The loss of competences of the member states in favor of the EU has important consequences in the international sphere under the Maastricht Treaty. The first consequence of the transfer of competences consists of the necessary substitution of the EC for its member states in the field covered by the allocation of competences to the EU. This rule has been very clearly expressed in an old decision of the Court related to the EurAtom Treaty. In paragraph 32 of Ruling 1/78, the Court underlined that "[t]o the extent to which jurisdiction and powers have been conferred on the Community under the EAEC Treaty the Member States, whether acting individually or collectively, are no longer able to impose on the Community obligations which impose conditions on the exercise of prerogatives which thenceforth belong to the Community and which therefore no longer fall within the field of national sovereignty."[2]

It is not through the substitution of the EU for the member states that these states will surrender their (formal) sovereignty in monetary affairs. They have lost that sovereignty by participating in the euro area. For this reason it is contrary to EC law to create or to maintain a situation in which individual political authorities or national central banks of participating member states should be able to intervene individually within the IMF framework. A possible result of this could be that their individual view could prevail on the common standpoint adopted within the EU Council or the ECB, as the case may be.

So I totally agree with Thygesen's view when he says in his paper that "the IMF . . . will have something to say on the exchange rate relationships between the euro area and nonparticipating European currencies" but this intervention of the IMF cannot allow the views of individual European member states to prevail over the EU's policy in the matter.

But substitution is not an easy undertaking. The distinct position of member states of the EU toward monetary union—as well as the problems of inserting the EU into the IMF framework—could impede the achievement of a clear-cut institutional solution. The case law of the Court regarding the possible accession of the EU to international conventions concluded within the International Labour Organisation requires solitary action by the EU member states acting in the interest of the EU in the Organisation, when the participation of the EU is temporarily or definitively impossible.[3]

In the absence of substitution of the EU for its member states, there are indeed minimal obligations to be respected such as the adoption of a common position and the necessity to speak with one voice, taking into account the dif-

[2](1978) ECR 2151, quoted by Smits (1997), p. 451.
[3]See Court of the European Communities (1993).

ferences in the allocation of competences depending on the matter concerned. Under Article 109, paragraph 4, a position at an international level has to be defined for the EU (the participating member states) by a qualified majority of the Council as regards issues of particular relevance to EMU. Most of the subjects treated at the IMF level are of such relevance. An inventory of such subjects should be done. One should also add that under Article C of the Treaty there is an obligation of coherence that extends to all EU members whatever their situation concerning EMU. This coherence is the specific responsibility of the EU Council.

The representation of the EU (participating member states) in international entities has to be unanimously decided by the Council (with the vote of the participating member states) (Article 109, paragraph 4). Due regard has to be given to the allocation of competences respectively in the economic (Article 103) and in the monetary fields (Article 105). How do these principles apply taking into account the specificities of the role and structure of the IMF? I will discuss this question later.

The IMF Perspective

I would like to stress that the creation of EMU in the EU is a completely new experiment, not only for the Europeans but also for the Fund. Quoting Managing Director Camdessus in some recent remarks, the creation of EMU will be "the most important and the most promising monetary development in the post–Bretton Woods period." Why? Because of the role of the EC in world trade, the importance of the quotas of its member states, the participation of two or three currencies of the future participating member states in the SDR basket, the designed irreversibility of the transfer of sovereignty, and, last but not least, the insertion of EMU in a political project. To quote once again the Managing Director, in his speech at this seminar (Chapter 15) conference: "EMU is, above all, an essential building block in Europe's growing political unity."

There is indeed no precedent for EMU. The Belgian-Luxembourg Monetary Association is not to be considered as such a precedent: it includes no surrender of sovereignty by Luxembourg, which has unilaterally decided to peg its currency to the Belgian one and for reasons of the respective sizes of both countries has agreed with Belgium that the Belgian franc would be legal tender on its territory, without reciprocity for the (small) Luxembourg circulation. It is a pragmatic arrangement consolidated by economic and political interests of both partners.

The CFA franc zone arrangements cannot serve as a model either. Not only is the importance of the respective economies in world trade and of the quotas in the IMF not at all comparable, but the legal and institutional structures are also very different.

The CFA franc zone constitutes an (hegemonic) arrangement whereby the former Metropole decides on the parity of the currency (the CFA franc) with the external world. There is no legal transfer of sovereignty in favor of a monetary institution. The functioning of both regional banks is dominated by the unanimity rule applicable in their respective councils. There is no prospect of political union and the economic union is still to be built.

The EMU has to be looked on by the IMF with new eyes. The problem of asymmetry between economic union and monetary union is a real one but it must not be overestimated in the relations between the EC and the IMF. To quote Wim Duisenberg and André Szász (1991): "The primary functions of the IMF are clearly monetary."

The economic competences of the Fund have been always exercised as an auxiliary to its monetary or lending competences, either as part of the surveillance procedure or in the conditionality imposed while granting a loan. To quote Mr. Camdessus again, the job of the Fund is especially to "provide the machinery for consultation and collaboration on international monetary problems" (IMF Articles of Agreement, Article I).

I would like to submit that in the field of consultations on economic policies in the Community, the Community authorities should take the lead. The process should permit the examination of national economic policies as chapters of a global exercise, with the intervention of national authorities.[4]

It is indeed within the EU Council that coordination of economic policies of the member states has to take place under Articles 3, 102a, and 103 of the Maastricht Treaty. This process cannot be diluted by an examination proceeding country by country without due regard to the participation of that member state in EMU, to the general orientations adopted at the EU level, and to the multilateral surveillance that will be exercised. Although this process has not seemed very impressive up to now, it will no doubt be strengthened with the enactment of the Stability and Growth Pact. Minister Maystadt has mentioned in his speech the need for a structured contact between the Fund and EU authorities.

I do not think I have to elaborate on the question raised by Mr. Polak concerning balance of payments difficulties, after the discussion by Minister Maystadt of that topic. It is indeed true that such difficulties can exist within a state and not only between states. The right orientation is not to refuse the assistance of the Fund but to recognize the necessity of a global EMU view

[4]See also René Smits, op. cit., p. 448.

on the solution of these difficulties. The conditionality imposed for an IMF loan can have repercussions on the EMU as a whole. IMF assistance should also serve as a safety net for EMU as a whole.

The institutional setup of the Fund was not conceived to cope with a new reality such as EMU. A thorough reflection is needed concerning the composition and working of the Board, the composition of the constituencies, and quotas. A revision of the Articles of Agreement appears inevitable.

I would like to say that the fact that Executive Directors of the Fund are not representatives of their state or their constituency should not be a reason to deny the euro area the possibility of having an input within the Fund equal to—and as efficient as—that of its partners in the future (bi- or multi-polar) international monetary system.

The problems are not only raised by the Fund's structure. There are also objective constraints within the EU itself on the establishment of correct relations with the IMF. The EU is an evolving nonstate political entity. Which institution or person will be the interlocutor of and the representative in the IMF for the EU? To be sure, the ECB will have a role and it has the means to decide on that topic under Article 6 of the Statute of the ESCB. But the question is more difficult for the contacts at the political level. Mr. Truman, of the Federal Reserve, raised the question in a practical way during this conference by referring to the weekly breakfast of the Secretary of the Treasury with the Chairman of the Board of Governors of the Federal Reserve System. No institution qualifies at this moment as the (economic) government of the EU. Nobody could be presented as its finance minister. This problem is a big challenge for the member states participating in EMU.

The second difficulty comes from the distinction between participating and nonparticipating member states. The perspective of a more or less permanent splitting in two of the Union will surely make it more difficult for the EU to find its right place within the Fund's structure and will also inevitably lead to the adoption of pragmatic solutions, which, for many, should remain permanent solutions. It raises in my mind many fundamental questions related to the perspectives of the EU in the twenty-first century and connected with the role of monetary union as a catalyst for political union. I can only raise this problem, which is crucial for the Union.

In conclusion, I would like to insist on the necessity (and unescapable obligation) of the participating member states speaking with a single voice in the IMF, on all issues related to EMU. I would also call, as Minister Maystadt has done, for an in-depth and priority reflection on the interests of both the IMF and the EU. In my view, this reflection must be conducted on both sides of the Atlantic.

References

Court of the European Communities, 1993, Opinion 2-91 of March 19, 1993, *Official Journal of the European Communities*, No. C 109, April 19, 1993, p. 37, No. 4.

Duisenberg, W.F., and A. Szász, 1991, "The Monetary Character of the IMF," Chapter 10 in *International Financial Policy: Essays in Honor of Jacques J. Polak*, ed. by Jacob A. Frenkel and Morris Goldstein (Washington: International Monetary Fund), pp. 254–66.

Louis, Jean-Victor, 1997, "Union Monétaire Européene et Fonds Monétaire International," in *Währung und Wirtschaft: Festschrift für Professor Hugo J. Hahu* (Baden: Nomos Verlag), pp. 201–13.

Martha, Rutsel Silvestre J., 1993, "The Fund Agreement and the Surrender of Monetary Sovereignty to the European Community," *Common Market Law Review*, Vol. 30 (August), pp. 749–86.

Smits, René, 1997, *The European Central Bank: Institutional Aspects* (The Hague: Kluwer Law).

François Gianviti

The purpose of this conference is not to discuss all the legal issues that will have to be addressed by the Fund as a consequence of the establishment of EMU. However, a few general remarks may be made, first on the principles that will guide the Fund, and second on the issues that may be raised by their implementation.

Principles

Three principles may be mentioned. The first is that the Fund is not a currency-based but a country-based institution. Membership is only open to countries. Only countries participate in the capital of the Fund (through their quota subscriptions), have access to Fund resources (on the basis of their individual quotas), receive SDR allocations, and select the Governors and Executive Directors of the Fund.

Speaking of Governors and Executive Directors, I have noticed the references in a number of papers for this conference to "representation" in the Fund. The term "representation" when used in this context is even more inaccurate than the term "loans" to describe the use of the Fund's general resources. Governors and Executive Directors of the Fund are not ambassadors to the Fund. Of course, they may represent and defend the views of their constituents, but, when they participate in the decision-making process of the Fund, they are as much officials of the Fund as the Managing Director and the staff. In particular, unlike ambassadors to nonfinancial organizations (e.g., the United Nations), their immunities can be waived not by their constituents—the countries that appointed or elected them—but by the Fund alone. The underlying idea is that they are personally responsible for the sound management of the Fund and may not justify their actions by invoking instructions received from their authorities.

Since the Fund is not currency based but country based, there is no obligation for a Fund member to issue its own currency. Several members may share the same currency. For instance, in each of the two CFA franc areas, there is a central bank, which is an international institution issuing a common currency. It is also possible for a Fund member to use another member's currency in its relations with the Fund. This is in practice the case mostly for countries that do not issue their own currencies. For instance, after the dissolution of the Soviet Union, the Russian ruble has been used as the currency of other countries that were formerly within the Soviet Union. Today the deutsche mark is the currency of Bosnia-Herzegovina in its relations with the Fund (although there is also a Bosnian dinar).

The second principle is that the arrangements entered into by members for the management of their currencies or the conduct of their policies do not exempt them from their obligations under the Fund's Articles. For instance, if a common central bank is established by a group of countries, those countries are collectively responsible to the Fund for the compliance by that central bank with their obligations under the Articles. For example, a manipulation of the exchange rate or a multiple currency practice attribute to the common central bank would be a breach of the member's obligations under the Articles. Even if the charter of that central bank guarantees its independence, the members on behalf of which it is acting remain responsible to the Fund for the central bank's observance of the Fund's Articles.

The third principle is that participation in a common currency, with a common central bank, does not prevent the participants from exercising their membership rights under the Articles. A participant in a monetary union may still request the Fund's financial assistance for a balance of payments problem. The request is made individually by the member, not jointly by all the participants in the union, because the member is exercising an individual right under the Articles, and its balance of payments problem must be assessed on the basis of the member's own situation, and not the situation of the union as a whole.

Implementation

Although these principles are clear, their implementation may raise some questions. For instance, a participant in a monetary union may agree with the other participants not to request the Fund's financial assistance without prior consultation with them or without their prior agreement. The question for the Fund would be whether, in that case, the Fund should deny the request until these procedures have been completed. As far as the Fund is concerned, the fact that the agreed procedures have not been completed may render the country liable to its partners for a breach of its commitments but does not render the request invalid under the Articles because the member's relationship with the Fund is only governed by the Fund's Articles.

A more serious difficulty would arise if a participant in a monetary union decided not to keep accounts of its balance of payments. This would affect its quota calculation, its access to Fund resources, and so on. However, this would also constitute a breach of obligation under the Fund's Articles (Article VIII, Section 5), because the Fund has an interest in these calculations, for instance, for the purposes of its operational budget and the discharge of repurchase expectations or obligations.

Perhaps the greatest difficulty is whether the concept of the individual balance of payments problem is really meaningful in a monetary union where the country's own reserves may be supplemented by those of other members and a common central bank. In that case, the so-called balance of payments problem could be regarded as a shortage of local currency, that is, the common currency, with which foreign exchange can be bought within the union. It could even be a fiscal problem if the government does not have enough resources to service its debt. Clearly, and contrary to what may have been said in some instances, it is not for the Fund to remedy a fiscal problem as such. However, there are precedents of such situations in the CFA franc area, where the Fund had found that a fiscal problem could be the result of a balance of payments deficit and could be remedied as a balance of payments problem. It may be noted in passing that another possibility for the deficit country, before turning to the Fund, would be to borrow the necessary resources within or outside the union and most countries that have access to capital markets would probably choose that course of action before subjecting themselves to Fund conditionality. On the other hand, Fund conditionality does not apply to the reserve tranche, which is available upon representation of a balance of payments need. Moreover, access to Fund resources does not require a demonstration by the country that it has no access to capital markets. Therefore, the issue is not moot.

One last remark, not on balance of payments need, but on reserves—an essential concept for quota calculations, the operational budget, and use of Fund resources. The transfer of part of each central bank's reserves in the EMU to the ECB will raise the question of whether the resulting claim on the ECB can be included in the country's reserves. The transfer of ownership is not by itself determinative. Reserves are not only defined as owned assets. They also include "functional reserves," those that are readily available to the country to make international payments or support its currency. However, statisticians are somewhat schizophrenic in their classifications of reserves: reserve positions in the Fund, including GAB loans, are called reserves, but undrawn swaps are not. This is an area strongly lacking in precise criteria. Perhaps a sui generis concept of reserves in a monetary union should be developed. Alternatively, assuming that existing accounting conventions are maintained, a closer examination of the availability of claims on the ECB to support the euro will be necessary to determine whether and how they can be included in the Fund's calculations of national reserves.

All these remarks are based on the existing law and practice of the Fund. If the present legal structure of the Fund needs to be revised to accommodate the needs of the EMU and perhaps other monetary unions, a whole new set of issues would have to be considered. But that is a different story.

Discussion

Mr. King asked Mr. Goos, who had floated the interesting idea that the IMF might consult with the finance minister of the country holding the EU presidency, what would happen if the presidency were held by a country not in the monetary union?

Mr. Goos acknowledged this difficulty but mentioned that a solution could be worked out.

Mr. Thygesen, in response to a question posed by Mr. Goos, commented that he was not very critical of the Stability and Growth Pact. As far as rules went, it was a very sensible enlargement of the functioning of EMU, but no one should be under any illusions that it was more than it was. It was not policy coordination; it was not multilateral surveillance. It was a mechanism to constrain deviant behavior, which might make it more likely that the policy mix would be appropriate, but that was not its specific aim.

18

Roundtable on the Transition to EMU

Xavier Larnaudie-Eiffel

In a big project, one is usually not supposed to put the cart before the horse. Indeed, the member states, the EMI and the European Commission have been trying to follow this guideline in their ongoing preparations for the transition to EMU. But for once, and given the time constraints, I will put the cart first, if you don't mind. If I would like you to come away with one impression of our day-to-day life in Brussels these days, it is the following: the transition to the euro will not begin with the countdown to January 1, 1999. It has been—and indeed still is—a long process. This transition requests care, transparency, and serious planning to give operators the necessary certainty.

But now I will return to the horses and try to elaborate a bit. Let us look at the transition to the euro more in detail. Many speakers before me in this conference have already stressed that the euro area will be a pole of stability in the international economy because it will abolish all exchange rate fluctuations between the former national currencies of participating countries. The independent and federal ECB will follow a stability-oriented monetary policy. We also discussed the fact that fiscal policies will be aimed at budgetary balance, while providing necessary flexibility to accommodate cycles.

I am, however, not at all convinced that the euro will strongly appreciate vis-à-vis certain currencies, as has been suggested on several occasions by other participants. The euro's exchange rate vis-à-vis certain currencies will be determined by the relative policy mix in Europe and in those countries and, while the demand for euros may be important, one should also consider supply factors as earlier speakers have done. These elements, taken together, do not suggest at all that the euro exchange rate will be too strong or too weak.

Regarding the ongoing preparations for the transition, I will arrange my remarks around two questions: First, what are the next steps in the timetable? And second, how to place it in the broader preparation of the transition?

First, the next steps of the timetable. Well, we expect that at its next informal meeting on April 4 and 5 the ECOFIN Council will try to lay down a precise timetable for the decision-making process in early 1998 to determine the first participating group of member states. The elements we already have are the following: at the end of February 1998 we will have the definite data for the year 1997, which, and for credibility reasons as was agreed at Madrid, will be the basis for decisions on participation. Then, probably during the second half of March 1998, the European Commission and the EMI will issue their reports and make them public. In these reports, the Commission and the EMI will have the interesting but challenging task of trying to assess which member states have reached a "high degree of sustainable convergence." These words are extremely important. They mean that when the EMI or the Commission assesses a situation, it will not only see if the figures are correct for the year 1997 on the basis of definite data, but it will also look at the past trends and, as set out in the Maastricht Treaty, use the planned data for the year 1998, for instance. This ensures that the assessment we make of convergence is an assessment of the sustainability of that convergence, so there is no question of fudging the figures.

Then, it will take about six weeks—the precise length of time has to be discussed with the member states—to consult the European and national parliaments. This is to preserve accountability and democracy, which have been features of the whole process from the start. Immediately after the consultation of the parliaments, the ministers of finance gathered in the ECOFIN Council will make their recommendations. They will recommend the first list of participants to use the euro from the January 1, 1999, onward, and then the European Council, the heads of state and government, will take the final decision, which should be at the end of April or the beginning of May. This schedule will be made public in advance. It is one more piece of evidence that we are looking at all of the steps of this process for certainty, transparency, and accountability.

That was the precise timetable of the months to come. Now, where do we stand in the whole process of the preparation of the transition? One must first recall what was achieved in Dublin. I will skip over the Stability and Growth Pact and the ERM II, which have been discussed already, and focus on one topic that was not addressed much—namely, the legal certainty of the whole operation, which is, of course, of utmost importance to all operators.

In Dublin, the heads of state and government and the ministers of finance agreed that the fundamental text defining in law the status of the euro would have to be made public and decided upon well in advance of the changeover. This objective was reached in Dublin, and in the following form. We have one European regulation based on Article 109 (l) (4) of the Treaty that will enter into force on January 1, 1999, which clearly defines the euro as the currency of the participating member states and states that from January 1, 1999, onward, there will be only one currency in the euro zone, even if it is temporarily expressed in two ways—the main expression being the euro and its cents and the other being a nondecimal expression, the former national currencies that will, at that stage, be irrevocably locked in terms of the euro. However, this regulation was not completely sufficient. Consultations with currency user representatives showed that, because of some legal provisions, there was an urgent need for legal certainty that demanded not only timely preparation but also early formal adoption and an immediate entry into force. The banking industry in particular argued that the formal adoption of provisions relating to the one-for-one conversion rate of the ECU, to rounding rules, and to the continuity of contracts should take place as soon as possible.

That is why a second regulation has established these principles and has already ensured that there will absolutely be no discontinuity in contracts because of the changeover to the euro. On the contrary, it states that the common introduction of the euro does not in any sense alter the terms of the contract. This regulation is drafted and will be formally adopted by the ECOFIN Council pending parliamentary reserve of one member state, which should be lifted in the spring. At that time, the text will come into force.

The European regulations will be directly applicable in the national law of all European participants, which in turn means that the principles cannot be ignored by judges in New York, or in Singapore or any other country. We recently had the occasion to discuss with some New York State authorities the advisability of introducing such a regulation under New York State law. All this is obviously good news for market participants.

A second aspect of preparation is markets and the financial or banking sector. Agreements are under way in the financial centers of the various member states to ensure the consistency of the technical approach of the different partners involved, including the various types of financial sector operators and public administrations. National working groups have been set up to coordinate preparatory activities such as those of the various professional associations. But given the differences that still exist across the EU in both market practices and conventions, it was necessary to determine the specific actions required in each member state. Moreover, it will be essential to determine to what extent increased organization of market mechanics and conventions will be necessary to create, from the start, wide, efficient, and liquid euro markets.

Such work is necessary regardless of whether or not a member state is an initial member of the euro area, since the introduction of the euro will have a significant impact not only on the financial markets of the euro zone but on all financial markets. I participated recently in a debate with some people in the City and was questioned what a U.K. opt-out would mean for British banks.

I replied that, irrespective of whether the United Kingdom was out or in, there is absolutely no doubt that the City of London will be in!

Early preparation is also essential for enterprises in order to achieve the changeover in an orderly and cost-effective manner. Many companies have come to realize that using the euro immediately on its introduction would enable them fully to exploit potential opportunities, such as access to financial services in euros, which would reduce their financing costs; simplified trade and investment throughout the euro area; simplified internal accounting and reporting; competition and early-mover benefits; and avoidance of logistical and personnel bottlenecks, in particular software problems.

When exactly the changeover will be made between 1999 and 2002, the year of the completion of the process, is left open for every firm or corporation to decide, and the timing will vary from one company to another, depending upon such factors as sectoral activity and the degree of international exposure. Now, there are already in Europe a large number of companies that are actively preparing and actually investing in the changeover—for example, Siemens in Germany, Fiat in Italy, Philips in the Netherlands, and Marks and Spencer's in the United Kingdom.

Of course, preparations are also of the utmost importance in the public sector itself. The member states are free to define their changeover plan as far as their public sectors are concerned. In most of our member states, task forces have been set up to coordinate the actions taken by the various ministries and departments. These preparations include, for instance, making the legislation euro-compatible and preparing the progressive changeover of the administrations—tax and social security, for instance—for such operations. Two member states, including Belgium, have already published a full changeover plan, and similar plans are now in preparation in the other member states.

A last point on preparations: we still are left with some very practical issues that we have to deal with before the year 2002. Their early resolution is essential to facilitate preparations and to overcome the uncertainties of currency users, thus gaining public support for the operation. With a view to addressing those practical concerns, we will convene a round table in Brussels on May 15, 1997, on questions like the following: How to get customers used to the new scale of prices before the final completion of the changeover—a big problem in Europe. At which precise date should the new notes and coins be introduced? Should it be January 1, 2002? Should it be two days before? Eight days after? All this is to be reviewed, even if we are not in 2002 yet. While there is time for this, it is essential to have enough time to prepare the population and to make the transition calmly in order to avoid any upheaval. There must be absolute transparency on all of those matters since citizens may be suspicious about things like hidden price increases, extra tax control, and other possible drawbacks. So, it is better to prepare for a smooth transition.

Finally, I would like to refer to a recent speech by Managing Director Camdessus, who said that the arrival of the euro would be one of the great opportunities for the universe but that the creation of EMU should also be seen in the perspective of another ongoing process of European integration. Not only did he refer to the political aspects of European integration, but he also indicated that we should not forget that EMU is nothing more than the logical monetary complement of the European single market. It is no coincidence that, historically, a single market and a single currency have been observed together. What would the American single market be if there were 14 different dollars?

The efficiency gains from market integration are amplified by monetary integration through various effects. First, it is broadly agreed that the introduction of the euro would eliminate the cost of converting one EC currency to another, and a recent study in the Commission shows that these costs amount to not less than roughly 1 percent of GDP per year over the period 1986 to 1995. This is certainly not negligible.

A second effect of monetary integration is a reduction of uncertainty, which will lead to increased intra-EC trade and direct investment and will also lower the risk premium firms have to pay on equity. I have already mentioned that the emergence of a large euro market will reduce financing costs for enterprises.

I know that it is probably superfluous to mention all these benefits of the creation of the EMU to this audience, so I will not talk about the many other reasons why we are so strongly convinced that the introduction of the euro on time and with strong conditions is such a good thing for Europe, but I thought it was nevertheless useful to put the transition to the euro in the perspective of a single and open market.

Klaus Regling

I will try to explain how the German government views the transition process to EMU, particularly over the next 12 to 14 months. To answer this, I should first answer two basic questions: why does Germany want monetary union, and why do we want to give up the successful Bundesbank? It is not only because we see monetary union as a stepping stone to political union, but also because we are convinced that it makes sense economically. On top of that, Germany has realized that the burden of having a reserve currency can sometimes be too great for a medium-sized economy, and we want to share this burden with other countries. And finally, I don't believe that the present system, whereby European monetary policy is decided by one national central bank, could be maintained indefinitely. Our European partners would probably not accept this. So, to summarize, Germany wants EMU for political and economic reasons. We believe it is the logical next step in the more than four decades of European integration, and it will make this process irreversible.

But EMU should start on time only if we are convinced that it will become a success. The political and economic advantages of EMU that I mentioned will only materialize if EMU is successful. Otherwise, it could be counterproductive for European integration in general. For EMU to become a success, certain macroeconomic, institutional, and structural conditions have to be in place, and this is what we have to concentrate on in Europe during this transition period up to the end of 1998.

Let me run quickly through these conditions. I will start with macroeconomic conditions, what is normally called the convergence situation as measured by the convergence criteria. Today, nine countries meet the three monetary criteria—that is, inflation, long-term interest rates, and participation in the exchange rate mechanism—and three more countries are very close. This should be seen as a great achievement, given where Europe was a few years ago.

Fiscal convergence, on the other hand, remains unsatisfactory so far. In 1996, only four countries had a debt of 3 percent of GDP or less. Only three countries had a debt stock of less than 60 percent. All member countries of the EU are concentrating at the moment on meeting these fiscal criteria. All but Greece plan to achieve 3 percent or better in their budget plans this year, but most forecasters do not project that all 14 countries will get there.

Why does the German government place so much emphasis on the convergence criteria in general and on the deficit criterion in particular? There are economic, political, and legal reasons for this. Most Germans do not want EMU. They want to keep the deutsche mark, mainly because they are worried that the stability of the euro will not be as good as the stability of the deutsche mark, and meeting the criteria has become a symbol for stability-oriented policies. There is an instinctive feeling among the German public that large fiscal deficits are not compatible with stability. Also, the German public does not want to pay for unsound fiscal policies in other countries. Most Germans, obviously, do not know about the no-bailout rule that is in the Maastricht Treaty, but they know that the risk of a bailout actually happening is much smaller when fiscal deficits are small.

These concerns of the population cannot be taken lightly in an election year. In addition, the German parliament—the upper and the lower house—will discuss before the European Council meets and decides about the participants in EMU whether individual countries meet the criteria and should join EMU. When the German parliament ratified the Maastricht Treaty, it instructed the government to insist on a strict and narrow interpretation of the convergence criteria, and I have no doubt that the parliament will stick to this approach. Although the vote of the parliament is legally not binding because the Maastricht Treaty has been ratified already, the government would not be able to deviate from a negative vote if there were one. Also, one has to assume that the German constitutional court would be asked for a ruling if the convergence criteria were applied loosely.

Finally, we know that a number of European countries have resorted to so-called creative accounting measures to reach the 3 percent target in 1997. This implies that some countries, if they really reach the 3 percent in 1997, have an underlying fiscal deficit of 3.5 or even 4 percent. In that sense, the limited flexibility that the Treaty allows has been used beforehand. Additional flexibility would not be warranted.

For all these economic, political, and legal reasons, Germany will insist on a strict and narrow interpretation of the convergence criteria. So, you might ask, with all of this typical German inflexibility and stubbornness, how is Germany itself doing in meeting the criteria, in particular, the 3 percent deficit criterion?

Taking into account all of the information available at the moment, including monthly indicators on production, business expectations, revenue, and the situation in the social security system and the states, which in Germany account for half of the public sector, we believe that our official forecast is a realistic one: 2.4 percent growth in 1997 and an overall fiscal deficit of 2.9 percent. Obviously, there is no room for slippage, but as of today, the German government sees no need to change that forecast. If, later in the year, the data looked different, the government would be prepared to adopt additional measures.

I have to admit that Germany will miss the 60 percent debt criterion. It already reached 60.7 percent at the end of last year and will probably increase a bit further this year, and there is not much we can do about that. The fact that German unification has added about 13 percentage points of GDP to our overall debt over the last few years is only small consolation.

So much for the monetary and fiscal preconditions for the start of monetary union from the German perspective. There are a large number of institutional, legal, and technical issues that have to be addressed during this transition period. These include many aspects that have been discussed earlier today and by the previous speaker, so I will not repeat them, but I should point out that these issues have taken up a lot of the time of the central bank and finance ministry officials, as well as EC officials. I am convinced that these problems will be solved in time. They will not prevent EMU from starting on time and from becoming a success.

Instead, I want to touch briefly on another range of issues that is quite important for the proper functioning of EMU—structural reforms. In many

European countries, the flexibility on the structural side is insufficient. In Germany, this is particularly true for the labor market. We believe that by far the largest share of unemployment in Germany is caused by structural problems. All EU member states have to decide for themselves whether the structural responsiveness of their labor and product markets is really sufficient for them to be able to give up the exchange rate instrument and the monetary policy instrument. We have to understand: EMU will not solve structural problems. Instead, EMU could very well make structural problems worse if nothing happens. Therefore, even if a country meets all the convergence criteria, it could still be premature to join EMU if the flexibility on the structural side is insufficient.

A last important transition issue: in the context of deciding on the Stability and Growth Pact, EMU governments have agreed to aim for fiscal positions that are close to balance or even at a surplus in the medium term. This implies that fiscal consolidation must continue in Europe. Most founding members of EMU will have a fiscal deficit of 3 percent or just below. For the Stability and Growth Pact to work properly and in accordance with the treaty, a stable fiscal position is required and these deficits therefore have to be reduced significantly further over the next two to three years at a minimum by, say, ½ of 1 percent of GDP a year.

In Europe, we are not worried that this will restrict growth. Our experience tells us otherwise. And I was glad to hear at lunch that Mr. Camdessus shares this view. I am sure European governments will nevertheless be criticized by some for being too restrictive. But I think the rest of the world has to understand that Europe, by moving to EMU, is giving up the idea of discretionary, anticyclical monetary and fiscal policies, except in very unusual, exceptional circumstances.

Governor Frenkel yesterday explained very well why that is, in general, the appropriate response to today's world of increasing interdependence, open markets, large capital flows, and instantaneous information. He said there has to be a new relationship between policymakers and markets. Policies have to be medium-term oriented, predictable, and transparent. European countries are trying to meet these new requirements. A lot still needs to be done, and that is why this transition period is so important and has to be used well.

Lars Heikensten

Yesterday, in his panel contribution, Mervyn King made an analogy between EMU and a marriage. I was struck by the analogy. After discussing marriage for a while he ended up on the dancing floor (although judging from my experience it is usually the other way around).

Sweden may be one of the few alone on the floor when the music is becoming softer, the room darker, and the last dance is being played. In that situation it is questionable if we can get much comfort from the fact that there is the old, gray-haired gentleman (Great Britain) that Mervyn talked about alone on the other side of the dancing floor.

It is from this perspective—the risk of being left almost alone—that I will deal with three subjects. First, I will say a few things about the labor markets. High unemployment has been put forward as a major reason why Sweden ought to stay outside the EMU. Second, I will deal with a question we have talked a lot about during these two days; exchange rate consequences of EMU, focusing on implications for a small potential out (or pre-in) country. Third, I will discuss in specific and concrete terms some consequences of the changeover for the financial sector and from that to the stability of exchange rates and the changeover process in general.

I should, perhaps, before beginning, underline that the problems I intend to bring up are important for Sweden and have played a role in our discussion. However, I would not have dealt with them here had I not believed that they were of relevance for the EMU project as a whole and in particular for other potential outs.

Let me now turn to the *labor market issues*. We all know that European labor markets are not flexible. This has been put forward as, if not an argument against EMU as such, at least one against starting now, before having pursued reforms. The argument runs in at least two versions. One argument is that the EU countries are vulnerable to asymmetric shocks. Given this, the very rapid increase in unemployment in the 1990s, and the lack of flexibility in the labor market, it is advocated that it would be dangerous to lock monetary policy in. We need monetary policy as insurance for the unlikely—but still possible—event of a real fire. There is also another argument. If you are to pursue labor market deregulation you are better off having your own monetary policy. You can then support the process with lower interest rates. Or to put it another way, measures lowering NAIRU create room for more expansive monetary policy.

I do not have the time in this introduction to dwell very much on these issues. However, given that they have not been discussed earlier at the conference I think that they ought to be mentioned. There are risks for the EMU project as a whole—not least in the transition phase—emanating from the labor markets. The need for the ECB to create credibility in the "start-up period," discussed yesterday, combined with a need for further fiscal consolidation (institutionalized in the Stability and Growth Pact), puts great pressure on the labor markets. Will they be able to adapt? Could reforms be more successful with the support of national monetary policy?

However, in my opinion, the asymmetric shock argument is overstated. The shocks that have hit the Swedish economy have on the whole been created by our own policies (and the same is true for most other European countries during the last two decades). Talking about insurance, although striking in the political debate, is thus misleading. We have in effect a moral hazard problem. The risk of a fire—created by the behavior of labor unions, for example—will be higher if we have the insurance.

Let me now turn to my second subject area—*exchange rate developments*. From the discussion yesterday and today about the potential strength of the euro, one thing has been obvious: we don't know.

For a small open economy, likely to have perhaps 50 percent of its trade within the euro area, this is of course a problem. And our position is not made easier by our recent history, coming from a deep recession, with skyrocketing deficits and volatile markets.

At an early stage of the discussions about monetary cooperation between "ins" and "outs," we drew the conclusion that participation in a system such as the ERM II could be risky, although the system is more flexible than the previous ERM; I agree with Jean-Jacques Rey on that. Even for countries meeting the economic convergence criteria—which we have a good chance to do—the system is vulnerable to speculation.

Paul De Grauwe described some of the risks involved in a pedagogic way, in particular the risks of self-fulfilling prophecies. During the last years several of the potential "outs" have in fact moved from what looked like vicious circles to virtuous ones and then back again. Given this, Sweden would have preferred coordination of monetary policy with common inflation targets.

A difficult institutional aspect of volatility in the exchange markets that we have not touched on in this seminar, but we will have to deal with in the EU, has to do with what happens after EMU has started. Everybody agrees that the principle of equal treatment shall be used when deciding if a latecomer is to be accepted as an EMU member; the same rules should apply to countries in the first group as to possible latecomers. And we are now in a practical way discussing schemes for latecomers. But in reality there might not exist such a thing as equal treatment—the world after EMU might have changed too much.

Finally, a few words on more microeconomic aspects of the changeover. In preparing for EMU the Riksbank has a dialogue with the financial sector. From that dialogue we have learned in a practical way that the move toward EMU is likely to be a gradual one regardless of what position the Swedish parliament will take this fall on EMU membership.

Some of you may know that Sweden changed from left- to right-hand traffic in the 1960s. Preparing for that had some resemblance to what we are doing now. However, there is a difference. That change was not gradual; one could not start with trucks and take cars later, but this is precisely what will happen in the transition to EMU.

- Payments in euros between Swedish companies can become so extensive that the banks will be obliged to introduce a system for handling two currencies. The euro and the krona would then perhaps be placed on an equal footing as regards speed of payments and low transaction costs.
- Equity trading, at least in the 30 or so companies whose shares have the highest turnover, would switch rapidly from kronor to euros according to the Stockholm Stock Exchange. The costs of handling both currencies side-by-side would be high.
- The money and bond markets are affected somewhat less as long as the treasury continues to borrow in kronor and thereby supplies the domestic market with papers denominated in that national currency.
- Many households will see the euro as an alternative to the krona for the investment of savings. If Swedish shares and bonds are quoted in euros, there will be a natural choice. The expected stability of the euro may then prove decisive for the investment or borrowing decisions by households, particularly in the event of a "soft no" that implies Sweden will be joining the euro area at a later date.
- The public sector, on the other hand, will probably stick to the national currency for as long as possible. In most European countries, public expenditures amount to about 50 percent.

This process could divide an "out" country into two parts, one using euros and the other one using kronor. If that happens it would do away with a considerable part of the national control of the "out" economy.

Decisive in the end will be the stability of the euro relative to the currency of an "out." It will be a complicated interplay between political, macroeconomic, and microeconomic factors. If membership is assumed by everyone to take place within a few years the process might accelerate, with more and more business moving into euro. Personally, I believe this is not only a strong reason for early membership in EMU, but also a reason why it will actually happen.

W. Paul Jenkins

I appreciate the opportunity to participate in this conference. While considerable time and energy have been spent examining the implications of

The author thanks his colleagues in the International Department of the Bank of Canada, particularly John Murray, for their assistance in preparing these remarks.

EMU for European countries, it has been only in the past 12 months or so that attention has turned to the implications for non-European countries and for the international scene more generally. This conference has contributed importantly to that assessment.

If there is an overriding theme to my remarks today, it is the need to place more confidence in financial markets to help bring about a successful transition to EMU.

I have organized my remarks around seven questions:

- What would be the implications for financial markets of a delay in EMU?
- How important is strict adherence to the convergence criteria?
- How important are optimum currency area considerations in choosing ins and outs?
- How much exchange rate flexibility should the outs be given?
- What role will the euro play in macroeconomic adjustment?
- Are binding rules needed for fiscal policy implementation?
- What are some of the considerations in establishing the ECB's credibility?

I don't propose to answer all of these questions in detail, but rather will give my perspective on some of the broad issues that they raise and that have a bearing on the transition to EMU both prior to January 1, 1999, and beyond.

Implications for Financial Markets of a Delay in EMU

In the past 6 to 12 months, financial markets have come to accept a start date for EMU of January 1, 1999. Direct market surveys, for example, suggest that EMU is expected to start on time and include at least six to eight "core" countries (Germany, France, Netherlands, Belgium, Luxembourg, and Austria, and possibly Ireland and Finland—the so-called BAFFLING countries).[1] Key financial indicators, particularly the sharp convergence in long-term interest rates, have also been interpreted as a vote of confidence. These same indicators would also suggest that Italy, Spain, and Portugal could be included in the first round, notwithstanding the fact that they are likely to miss the strict fiscal policy criteria of the Maastricht Treaty by a wide margin.

Given the progress that has been made on EMU, many observers have argued that any delay in implementation would result in significant uncertainty and turbulence in financial markets. However, there is reason to believe that the response might not be so negative.

[1]The latest Reuters survey, released March 13, shows a 73 percent probability for a successful EMU launch (down from 83 percent in the previous month).

A case can be made that much of the interest rate convergence and exchange rate stability that we have witnessed in recent months reflects the improved inflation performance of the European countries and the structural adjustments that they have undertaken. As Drazen and Masson (1994) have shown, there is an important distinction between commitment and credibility. Financial markets reward good economic performance and credible policies. Strong commitment to policies that generate unacceptable outcomes is not rewarded. Accordingly, if a delay in the start of EMU were seen as supporting Europe's long-run economic fundamentals, it would not necessarily lead to financial instability, provided of course that countries continue to credibly commit to sustainable policy adjustments.

How Important Is Strict Adherence to the Convergence Criteria?

Similarly, if it were evident that strict adherence to the Maastricht criteria was undermining the short- to medium-term macroeconomic performance of Europe, a case could be made for relaxing the criteria. This could be accomplished by stretching out the time period for meeting the criteria (even in the absence of any delay in the start of EMU), allowing countries to take a more flexible approach to fiscal consolidation.

Some have even suggested that consideration might be given to abandoning the criteria altogether. Economists, such as Paul De Grauwe (1996), have noted that "the criteria have nothing to do with the conditions necessary to make a workable monetary union in Europe." I would not go that far. But as of yesterday's roundtable reminded us, good economic performance is a key element of what this endeavor is all about.

How Important Are Optimum Currency Area Considerations in Choosing "Ins" and "Outs"?

Optimum currency area considerations suggest that not all countries are equally suited to a fixed exchange rate arrangement, and that the problems associated with macroeconomic policy adjustment post-EMU will be much greater if all 15 potential participants were to join. Based on this, a narrower approach to initial EMU participation would be preferred.[2]

[2]The provinces of Canada operate within an economically diverse federal system, but they have the benefit of an extensive system of fiscal transfers and a high degree of interregional labor mobility. For this reason, they might not serve as a reliable guide to how far the optimum currency area criteria can be pushed.

However, as several speakers have pointed out, it is important to remember that empirical analysis of the optimum currency area criteria is necessarily based on past data that may not reflect current or future economic conditions in the various countries. Frankel and Rose (1996) have shown, in a recent paper, that the optimum currency area criteria may themselves be endogenous, in the sense that countries might begin to satisfy the requirements for a currency union after the union has been created. Bayoumi and Eichengreen (1996) have also reported results supporting the notion that monetary and economic integration can "constitute a virtuous, self-reinforcing circle."

How Much Exchange Rate Flexibility Should the Outs Be Given?

Once EMU has started, the adjustment costs that will be incurred by the European community will depend, among other things, on how those who are out of the system are expected to behave. If the outs tie their exchange rates firmly to the euro, the macroeconomic consequences for these countries will be virtually identical to those that they would have obtained under a more inclusive EMU membership. However, they would not have the microeconomic benefits of a common currency or the potential for enhanced credibility from being part of a larger group.

This line of reasoning would lead one to argue for a wider choice of countries for initial EMU participation. But where exchange rate flexibility is needed, the room to maneuver that is offered within ERM II should be used. Indeed, by choosing to exploit the policy independence associated with exchange rate flexibility, those outs needing flexibility could significantly improve economic performance both within their countries and elsewhere.

What Role Will the Euro Play in Macroeconomic Adjustment?

Monetary policy post-EMU will be transmitted through both the exchange rate and interest rates. Movements in the euro will therefore play an important role in establishing the overall ease or tightness of monetary conditions. A rise in the value of the trade-weighted exchange rate, all else being equal, would represent a tightening of monetary conditions, and vice versa.

Based on back-of-the-envelope calculations, we estimate that, for the core European countries, a movement of 5 to 6 percentage points in the trade-weighted value of the euro would be equivalent to a 100-basis-point movement in short-term interest rates, in terms of its impact on aggregate demand in the EMU.[3] This ratio is significantly higher than that which would be calculated for individual European countries (owing to the much smaller trade exposure of Europe considered as a single economic entity). If one were to go to a wider grouping of countries, the ratio would rise to between 7:1 and 9:1, or possibly higher.

On this basis, some might conclude that most of the work in terms of achieving a desired tightening or easing in monetary conditions would have to come about through movements in interest rates (i.e., EMU would be considered a large, relatively closed economy). In fact, the opposite could be the case, depending on the type of shock that monetary authorities had to respond to.

Indeed, in certain circumstances the small weight of the euro in determining the overall stance of monetary conditions may require large movements in the exchange rate to effect the necessary changes in output and inflation. In other words, exchange rate movements will still play an important role in the macro reequilibration process, and the necessary movements could be significant. Such movements should not be viewed as a sign of a "weak" euro, but rather as evidence that the exchange rate is playing its appropriate role.

Are Binding Rules Needed for Fiscal Policy Implementation?

Another issue that has been raised concerns the effect that one fiscally lax country might have on the creditworthiness and risk premiums of other EMU participants. This view largely discounts the ability of financial markets to differentiate between credit risks based on criteria such as deficit and debt levels.

Not only does this view downplay the importance of market discipline as a means of reinforcing sound fiscal policies, but it also runs counter to experience elsewhere, such as in Canada. While issues such as the shift from sovereign to nonsovereign status and the absence of a central government against which to benchmark credit risk need to be addressed by markets, the example of Canadian provinces clearly demonstrates the capacity of markets to differentiate among member states on the basis of credit risk.

As long as individual states do not have access to the printing press or a financial guarantee from their EMU partners, market-based solutions offer both greater flexibility and potentially greater discipline than a rules-based approach to fiscal policy implementation post-EMU.

[3]These calculations were made using the relative importance of trade for each country together with Bank of Canada and IMF estimates of a Monetary Conditions Index for each country.

Another potentially important by-product of placing greater reliance on market discipline is the likelihood that the need for fiscal prudence would increasingly be viewed as an internal (i.e., country-specific) requirement, rather than something forced upon a country as a condition for EMU entry.

Considerations in Establishing the ECB's Credibility

While the draft statutes for the ECB are clear about its policy mandate, delivering on that objective is what will ultimately establish the central bank's credibility. Therefore, it is important that the ECB clarify its overall monetary policy framework as soon as possible. This includes (1) clear identification of the intermediate target that it regards as consistent with achieving its mandate of price stability; (2) clear identification of the mechanism(s) by which monetary policy will be transmitted to the economy; and (3) clear identification of the operating framework that will be used to take policy actions.

Let me stress this point. An important way in which the ECB can enhance its credibility is by being transparent about its objectives and actions. I firmly believe that monetary policy functions better when the goals and methods of operation of a central bank are well understood by the public and the markets.

One issue in this regard is whether the ECB will choose a monetary aggregate or an inflation objective as its intermediate target. While there may be ideological differences in this choice, in practice the differences are not that great and come down to which empirical relationship the ECB can place the most reliance on to deliver price stability. Paul Masson raised concerns about whether either of these relationships would be reliable enough for use in an intermediate targeting framework. Instead, the ECB might, initially at least, have to rely on other indicators, with the exchange value of the euro becoming the indicator that would be given prime attention.

There is a risk, however, that this could result in too much emphasis being placed on the stability of the euro. Indeed, over the next several years, Europe could well experience below-potential economic growth because of additional fiscal restraint (to meet the Maastricht criteria), restructuring, and the effects of uncertainty on consumer confidence. Thus, the euro could come under downward pressure for cyclical reasons. Moreover, resistance to such movements would only exacerbate the below-potential growth scenario.

I would also stress that there are significant benefits associated with giving financial markets a clear understanding of the monetary authorities' interpretation of developments affecting the economy and the rate of inflation. If the views of the ECB are clear and understood, it will frequently lead markets to anticipate central bank actions, or at least not to react in a counterproductive manner because of confusion about the ECB's intentions.

Finally, let me quickly add that I have some doubts about how effective the decentralized approach to the implementation of monetary policy will be. In particular, it seems to me that this is not the right way to go about developing a deep and liquid financial market in Europe.

Conclusions

In conclusion, there remains a high degree of uncertainty regarding the transition to, and functioning of, EMU. The thrust of my remarks is that more emphasis could, and should, be placed on financial markets as a source of information and of discipline. Good economic performance depends on clear, credible policy directions, and in such an environment markets can typically be counted on to do the right thing.

References

Bayoumi, Tamim, and Barry Eichengreen, 1996, "Even Closer to Heaven? An Optimum-Currency-Area Index for European Countries," Center For International and Development Economics Research, Working Paper No. C96-078 (Berkeley, California: University of California, December).

De Grauwe, Paul, 1996, "Reforming the Transition to EMU," in *Making EMU Happen: Problems and Proposals: A Symposium*," Princeton Essays in International Finance No. 199 (Princeton, New Jersey: Princeton University, Department of Economics, International Finance Section, August), pp. 16–29.

Drazen, Allan, and Paul R. Masson, 1994, "Credibility of Policies Versus Credibility of Policy Makers," *Quarterly Journal of Economics*, Vol. 109 (August), pp. 735–54.

Frankel, Jeffrey, and Andrew Rose, 1996, "The Endogeneity of the Optimum Currency Area Criteria," NBER Working Paper No. 5700 (Cambridge, Massachusetts: National Bureau of Economic Research, August).

List of Contributors

Muhammad Al-Jasser
Deputy Governor
Saudi Arabian Monetary Agency

George Alogoskoufis
Professor of Economics
Athens University of Economics and Business

Age Bakker
Deputy Director
Netherlands Bank

Agnès Bénassy-Quéré
Scientific Advisor
Centre d'Etudes Prospectives et d'Informations Internationales

C. Fred Bergsten
Director
Institute for International Economics

John Berrigan
Economist
Monetary Matters Directorate
European Commission

Ralph C. Bryant
Senior Fellow
Economic Studies
The Brookings Institution

Michel Camdessus
Managing Director
International Monetary Fund

Hervé Carré
Director for Monetary Matters
European Commission

Daniel Cohen
Professor of Economics
École Normale Supérieure

Paul De Grauwe
Professor of Economics
Katholieke Universiteit Leuven

Joly Dixon
Director of International Economic and Financial Matters
European Commission

Barry Eichengreen
John L. Simpson Professor of Economics and Political Science
University of California at Berkeley

Stanley Fischer
First Deputy Managing Director
International Monetary Fund

Jacob Frenkel
Governor
Bank of Israel

Fabio Ghironi
University of California at Berkeley

François Gianviti
Director of the Legal Department
International Monetary Fund

Francesco Giavazzi
Professor of Political Economy
Università Commerciale Luigi Bocconi

Jean Godeaux
Chairman
Fondation Camille Gutt

Bernd Goos
Head of the International Relations Department
Deutsche Bundesbank

Hanna Gronkiewicz-Waltz
President
National Bank of Poland

Lars Heikensten
Deputy Governor
Sveriges Riksbank

Gert-Jan Hogeweg
Head of the Monetary, Economic and Statistics Department
European Monetary Institute

W. Paul Jenkins
Deputy Governor
Bank of Canada

Daniel Kaeser
Executive Director
International Monetary Fund

Takatoshi Kato
Vice-Minister of Finance for International Affairs
Ministry of Finance of Japan

Masahiro Kawai
Professor of Economics
University of Tokyo

Mervyn King
Chief Economist and Executive Director
Bank of England

Thomas H. Krueger
Deputy Division Chief
Research Department
International Monetary Fund

Xavier Larnaudie-Eiffel
Chief of Staff
Office of Commissioner de Silguy
European Commission

Jean-Victor Louis
Advisor
Legal Department
National Bank of Belgium

Paul R. Masson
Senior Advisor
Research Department
International Monetary Fund

Philippe Maystadt
Deputy Prime Minister and Minister of Finance and External Trade of Belgium

Robert N. McCauley
Economist
Monetary and Economic Department
Bank for International Settlements

Jacques Mélitz
Professor of Economics
Institut d'Etudes Politiques

Benoît Mojon
Economist
Centre d'Etudes Prospectives et d'Informations Internationales

Michael Mussa
Economic Counsellor and Director of the Research Department
International Monetary Fund

Bandid Nijathaworn
Director of the Banking Department
Bank of Thailand

Alassane Ouattara
Deputy Managing Director
International Monetary Fund

Jean-Pierre Patat
Director-General of Foreign Affairs
Bank of France

Jean Pisani-Ferry
Director
Centre d'Etudes Prospectives et d'Informations Internationales

Jacques J. Polak
President
Per Jacobsson Foundation

Richard Portes
Director
Centre for Economic Policy Research

Alessandro Prati
Economist
Research Department
International Monetary Fund

Klaus Regling
Director
Ministry of Finance of Germany

Jean-Jacques Rey
Director
National Bank of Belgium

Massimo Russo
Special Advisor to the Managing Director
International Monetary Fund

André Sapir
Professor of Economics
Free University of Brussels

Garry J. Schinasi
Division Chief
Research Department
International Monetary Fund

György Szapáry
Deputy Governor
National Bank of Hungary

André Szász
Professor of European Studies
University of Amsterdam

Niels Thygesen
Professor of Economics
University of Copenhagen

Edwin M. Truman
Staff Director of the International Finance Division
Board of Governors of the Federal Reserve System

Bart G. Turtelboom
Economist
Research Department
International Monetary Fund

Michel Vanden Abeele
Executive Director
Fondation Camille Gutt

Paul A. Volcker
Director
Bankers Trust Company

William R. White
Economic Adviser and Head of the Monetary and Economic Department
Bank for International Settlements